The Standard Guide *to* Collecting Autographs

A Reference & Value Guide

Mark Allen Baker

© 1999 by Mark Allen Baker

The author and publishers of this book have made every effort to ensure
the authenticity and accuracy of all information provided. The information is, however,
sold without warranty, either expressed or implied. Neither the author nor
Krause Publications will be held liable or responsible for any damages,
direct or indirect, resulting from the use of any information provided in this work.

Published by

**krause
publications**

700 E. State Street • Iola, WI 54990-0001
Telephone: 715/445-2214

www.krause.com

Library of Congress Catalog Number: 98-87291

ISBN: 0-87341-613-9

Printed in the United States of America

Dedication

To the Richard & Gloria Long Family

Alison, Cyndie, Richard, Laurel & Deborah

In memory of Gordon F. Muck

TRULY UNIQUE COLLECTIBLES

MOVIES • TV • MUSIC • SCI-FI • SPORTS • MODELS

ENTERTAINMENT & SPORTS MEMORABILIA

Celebrity Autographs • Movie Posters • Photos • Music Posters • Toys & Novelties

Limited Edition Collectibles • Cards, Comics & Magazines • Americana & More !!

Visit Our Retail Gallery at 85 Main Street, Nyack, NY 10960

See our web site at www.uniquecollectibles.com

or For a Free Catalog Call 1-888-725-7614

RICH ALTMAN'S
HOLLYWOOD COLLECTIBLES
Picked one of the top 10 Autograph Dealers in the Country

Rich Altman's Hollywood Collectibles is one of the finest sports memorabilia and collectible stores in Florida, carrying autographed items from Babe Ruth, Joe DiMaggio, Mickey Mantle, to Mark McGwire and Sammy Sosa. This is the perfect place for any kind of gift buying and a safe guide to purchasing authentic autographs.

Rich has been interviewed on 60 Minutes and HBO as an autograph expert and prides himself in being able to provide a **Lifetime Guarantee of Authenticity** to every autograph he sells. To quote from a few sports magazines ... He was selected as one of the top 20 Hobby Dealers in the country ... *Trading Cards - December 1984* ... He is reliable, honest, and speaks with experience, as someone who has dealt in autographs since 1983 ... *The Encyclopedia of Sports Memorabilia - July 1995* ... One of the most respected autograph dealers in the USA ... *American Sportscard Monthly - April 1995.*

He recently signed an exclusive partnership with Bill Russell, the famous Boston Celtics superstar center, to represent him exclusively to the hobby. As quoted by Bill, "Rich's reputation as one of the leaders in the sports memorabilia industry is consistent with the qualities and principles that I tried to maintain during my career and life. Rich has earned the trust and respect of not only his thousands of customers, but everyone in the industry. That's why I chose him to exclusively be the guardian of my autograph and autographed products." Bill recently appeared at Rich's grand opening of his second location in Weston, Florida, where Bill met the public and signed limited edition items that were offered to the public through Sports Collectors Digest weekly publication.

These items are 8x10's, 16x20's, basketballs and jerseys specifically produced for this special signing. There are a limited amount of these items still available, along with a great assortment of autographed memorabilia. Please call the numbers below for information to order or any questions you may have.

Hollywood Store:		Weston Store:
3942 N. 46th Avenue,		1948 Weston Road
Hollywood, FL 33021		Weston, FL 33326
954-986-0707		954-384-0846

Index of Advertisements & Sources

Acknowledgments

I would like to thank everyone at Krause Publications for their continued faith and commitment to my work, especially Pat Klug, Don Gulbrandsen, Seiche Sanders and Randy Thern. I would also like to thank some extraordinary gentlemen: John Reznikoff at University Archives, Max Rambod, Steven Raab, Robert Batchelder, and Nate Sanders, all of whom are outstanding autograph dealers and individuals whose contributions to the field have been nothing short of outstanding. To all of you who have placed ads in the many industry periodicals for decades, to every dealer who has placed me on their mailing list for catalogs, thank you for your love of a terrific hobby. I would also like to acknowledge my family for their continued support, Mr. and Mrs. Ford W. Baker, Jeff Baker, Matthew Baker and Tracey Baker Rachid.

A special thanks to Erminio C. Bugliani who gave me chance to peek into the world of Andrew Wyeth.

To Cyndie Long for the years worth of dedicated database compilation: Thank you very, very much. This book is for you.

To Aaron A. Baker, my son, who helped for hours on the entertainment section — thank you!

To Elizabeth M. Baker, my oldest daughter who also helped for hours on the entertainment section — thank you "Sweetness"!

To Rebecca J. Baker, whose wonderful smile and charm provide me the endless inspiration for my work — thank you!

To Alison M. Long, with love!

Contents

Introduction

Not far from where the Brandywine river empties into the Delaware sits the small village of Chadds Ford, Pennsylvania. Similar to the hillsides that guard the serenity of this unique little town in Chester County, it has been an environment respectful of the past, but, like the river that runs through it, resentful to change.

The Swedes and Finns were the first to sail their vessels up the river in 1638. They brought with them the knowledge of how to build shelter and tame the often harsh winters along the river's banks. Flour and gun powder eventually became synonymous with the Brandywine, which is actually several valleys joined together. From the first rise of the Appalachians to the so-called Welsh Hills, soft crests join perfectly to outline Chester County in a simplistic, yet artistic form.

When a historical reference is made to the area it is often applied to the Battle of the Brandywine and the fierce fighting during the American Revolutionary War. While accounts of the battle differ to this day, why it was fought, why it was lost by the Americans and precisely what happened in the defeat will remain hidden among the fields and forests in which it was fought. It is said that if you position yourself correctly on a clear night — just below the hills that guard Route One where it intersects Ring Road —you can hear the ghosts of the redcoats marching their way into position. Perhaps this is why the great illustrator Howard Pyle chose this spot to combine both his boundless imagination with his technical expertise — characteristics he shared with his pupils, one of whom was N.C. Wyeth.

Generations of Americans grew up with the images born in the Brandywine Valley at the studio of Howard Pyle. Pyle conducted a summer school at Chadds Ford for many years in conjunction with his other teaching responsibilities. It was there that N.C. Wyeth settled, after spending a few years in Needham, Massachusetts, and even romping, for awhile, through the still-wild West. The Wyeth pilgrimage between New England and Pennsylvania would remain intact for the decades that would follow. Boundless energy seemed to permeate from Pyle's pupils, in particular Newell Convers Wyeth, who would eventually pass on his zest for life and artistic ability to his daughters, Henriette and Carolyn, and his son, Andrew.

N.C. Wyeth was an incredible visionary, with the unique ability to see between the lines in both a letter and the strokes on a canvas. His intense preoccupation with the past, be it intact or cultivated by Pyle, was positively unparalleled. Wyeth's association with his work was not only deep but incredibly personal. Using familiar sights and models, he painted his own life's history in each of his works. A characteristic that would be inherited by his talented son, Andrew.

Andrew Wyeth, born on Henry David Thoreau's birthday, was predestined to be a great artist and was cultivated as such by his father. Unlike his father, he made the choice of watercolor his own. He followed in the footsteps of Winslow Homer, John Marin and Charles Burchfield, and transformed it into a major medium. Later, through Peter Hurd — both a friend and student of N.C. Wyeth — he would welcome another medium, tempera. When the time came for Andy to step into his father's studio, it was basic training and fundamentals first, imagination and creativity later. Under the watchful eye of his father, N.C. Wyeth passed on the virtues of his artistry to his son. This transformation took place right up until his father's untimely death at a railroad crossing just a few miles from the Wyeth home in Chadds Ford. It was from this point onward that Andrew would draw deep inside both his soul and subject and begin the lifetime task of painting his own biography, his own world.

Although I have always loved painting and drawing, it took a very special art teacher in high school by the name of Gordon Muck to bring out the ability he sensed was there. It would be Muck who came over to my desk one day and handed me a book that would radically change my life, "Andrew Wyeth," published in 1970 by the Museum of Fine Arts in Boston. He said if I ever wanted to earn a scholarship out of high school, this would be my vehicle. Study everything about Wyeth, and learn to paint and draw just like him and when you're done, do it again. To make a long story short, fourteen college scholarships later I learned my teacher knew exactly what he was talking about.

While the years that followed saw me abandon my artwork, I nevertheless drew incredible strength from Wyeth's work every time I viewed it. While I knew everything about the man, I also felt I understood his message. Like a good book, I found myself going back to his material, especially when I found myself complacent and accepting of mediocrity. Sometimes the simplest path can be the hardest to find.

As chance, or perhaps fate, would have it, I found myself living and going through my mid-life crisis one county over from Chadds Ford. One day, following my routine pilgrimage to the Baldwin Book Barn, I was introduced indirectly to Erminio Cosmo Bugliani, an acting agent for Andrew Wyeth. Prior to meeting Bugliani in person, I had conveyed to him through correspondence just how significant a role Andrew Wyeth had played in my life. Bugliani, himself a gifted artist and an incredibly charming individual, understood my feelings. Friends with the Wyeths since 1982, he has also drawn tremendous inspiration from Andrew Wyeth, but unlike myself, had given much in return.

On a chilling November (1997) morning, while in Chadds Ford to pick up a print from Erminio, he asked me if I'd like to meet "Andy." I had told Bugliani that I had a wonderful letter written by N.C. Wyeth to Marjorie Rawlings. In the letter, which is exemplary of the vision and charm of Newell Convers Wyeth, he encourages Rawlings to stay the course with her work, as it will stand the test of time. N.C. Wyeth, who illustrated "The Yearling," pens a wonderful heartfelt four-page letter that I consider one of his finest masterpieces. As we pulled into the driveway of "The Mill," Andrew Wyeth's home, we met the artist halfway. It was there that I finally had the chance to personally thank the man who had contributed so much to my life. He was thrilled when I gave him a copy of his father's letter, as he had never seen it.

Wyeth draws tremendous inspiration from the past, and even the smallest reminders can influence his work. When I told him how his father boastfully mentions him at the end of the letter, a wonderful smile filled his face. I have met the artist numerous times since and even have had the luxury to take a small glimpse into his world. Underneath his complexity is simplicity, complemented by an intensity and vision I have seen in no man.

While I had been an autograph collector since 1965, by the mid-seventies, it gave way to my pure passion for history. I no longer collect autographs, I preserve relics from the past, moments in time — captured, lost, then rediscovered. To think that the simplicity of a letter can elicit so much emotion, or perhaps even inspire the creative process, is a testament to the hobby.

1
The Autograph Market

A Very, Very Brief History of Autograph Collecting

Autograph collecting has had a glorious past that can be traced as far back as ancient Egypt, as well as to both the Greeks and the Romans. In fact the word "autograph" first appears in the writings of Suetonius. It wasn't until the latter part of the 16th century and the preliminary decades of the 17th century that the basis of the hobby formed to become what we know today. In it's infancy, autograph collecting was simply having friends and acquaintances sign a simple vellum album, many of which would eventually be displayed in major museums. While handwriting, or the modest preservation of a memory were the initial attraction to these volumes, it later became the historical significance they possessed. For between the lines, or, in the simple formations of characters, there were stories — delightful tales of numerous individuals who in their own special way were significant. While many names faded from memory, others lived on, eventually leaving a legacy for all of mankind to witness in one form or another.

The persistent seeker of album signatures was soon labeled an "autograph fiend" or "autograph hunter" and it wasn't long before they attracted the attention of many prominent individuals—people such as the poet Henry Wadsworth Longfellow, who stated back in 1857 in his daily diary that he answered 70 autograph requests on a particular day. Similar to today, prominent individuals varied in their compliance and the significance, or lack thereof, they placed on this somewhat effortless, yet often bothersome, task. As with any hobby we had both cynics and supporters; I guess some things never change.

What is often forgotten by the casual observer or non-participant is the incredible value the hobby has brought to mankind. While events and individuals shaped the course of history, the autograph and memorabilia collector preserved the artifacts. We have simple pieces of history that will last long after both the individual and event begin to fade. We saved Shockley's notes on the transistor, Babe Ruth's 60th home run ball, the check used as Ernest Hemingway's down payment for his boat "The Pilar," a copy of "The Evening Dispatch" of St. Louis, Missouri, with its headline: "LEE'S SURRENDER," and even the FBI Wanted posters for the capture of Bonnie and Clyde. For every person who has laughed, mocked or criticized our hobby, there have been two of us to quietly smile back at them.

For those of you knowledgeable about Abraham Lincoln, just think about what price our history would have paid had it not been for the collecting efforts of one individual, Oliver R. Barrett. For those of you unfamiliar with this individual, find a copy of Carl Sandburg's 1960 book "Lincoln Collector: The Story of Oliver R. Barrett's Great Private Collection" and read it! The list of great collectors and contributors to the field of autographs is simply enormous and eventually a book should be done about them. Pioneers such as Daniel M. Tredwell, Adrian H. Joline, Lyman C.

Draper, Chas, De F. Burns, Telamon Cuyler, Pierpont Morgan, Dr. Thomas Addis Emmet, W.J. De Renne, W.H. Bexby, Israel K. Tefft, developers such as Gordon T. Banks, Clifton W. Barrett, Mary A. Benjamin, Walter R. Benjamin, Edmund Berkeley, Jr., Thomas B. Brumbaugh, Michel Castaing, David H. Coblentz, Charles F. Cooney, John C. Dann, Roy L. Davids, C.A.K. Fletcher, Gerhard A. Geselli, Walter Goldwater, Christopher C. Jaeckel, Rudolf F. Kallir, Herbert E. Klingelhofer, James Kritzeck, Walter Langlois, Franklin Lenthall, Irving Lowens, Richard Maass, Michael Papantonio, John Parker, John F. Reed, Diana J. Rendell, Kenneth W. Rendell, Leslie J. Schreyer, Henry Strutz, Carolyn H. Sung, H. Keith Thompson, Robert L. Volz, Robert C. Wiest, John Wilson, Charles Hamilton, Paul C. Richards and George and Helen Sanders, to name only a few, all have contributed immensely to the hobby. There are also many current contributors to major industry periodicals such as "Autograph Collector," "Autograph Times," "Pen & Quill," "Sports Collectors Digest," "Collecting," and "BIBLIO," plus major dealers and auction houses. Lastly there are the principle collectors, often silent, yet many with collections that rival the finest universities. We owe a debt of gratitude to all these wonderful individuals who beat the path on which we choose to travel. It will now be up to us to carry their torch. Hopefully we will do so with equal dignity and honor.

As Our Century Passes

Those of you holding this book have witnessed part of one of the most amazing centuries of man's existence. Hopefully you were smart enough to pick up a few signatures along the way! We witnessed phenomenal advances in technology — from splitting the atom to landing on the moon. We concocted a few new theories and even proved a few old ones along the way. We made new things, evaluated them and then made them better, smaller and easier to use. We built new forms of communication and discarded older forms. We fought for our ideals, lost precious lives and saved many others. If we wanted to go somewhere different, we did, and often even built a highway there, or some form of improved transportation, to get to our destination more quickly and easily. We changed our mind, our clothes, our thinking, our speech and even our morals, and, when one or all got us in trouble, we found a solution or perhaps a vaccine. While our life expectancy got longer, our attention span did not. So we built new forms of entertainment to occupy our time. We had both an acronym and answer for everything, even if it wasn't right.

All of this produced heroes and villains, you know: good guys, not-so-good guys, bad guys and really, really bad guys. The memorable players we sought autographs from, and in many cases access to these individuals has never been better. They can run, push us out of the way, and even say "NO," but they can never hide. Names such as Roosevelt, Lenin, Hitler, Churchill, Gandhi, Ben-Gurion, King, Kennedy, Walesa, and Mandela became so familiar that we, our parents and our children could all spell their names correctly. We put faces to the voices we heard on the radio, heard stories of wars past, saw films of the wars our fathers fought, then watched a new generation, our own, go overseas in pursuit of democracy. When and if our neighbors returned, they had the same name as their predecessors: heroes. Speaking of heroes, we had more than our fair share, it seems. Just when you thought people were getting more selfish, self-centered and self-fulfilling, along came a Mother Teresa, Helen Keller or Princess Diana. We witnessed Woodstock, although we all kind of lived through our own, watched Dylan plug in and Janis and Jimi check out. We had tragedies and triumphs, famine and despair, parodies, symphonies, feats and repairs.

As a witness to this century, we collected what we could, when we could. We became more than just autograph collectors — we became historians. For example, using a database I developed for this book I thought it might be interesting to compare how autograph collectors (based on purchases/appreciation over the past two decades) compared to a group of historians who ranked the top seventeen presidents of the 20th century. Although the first two choices were in reverse order, they were identical — both Roosevelts.

As the decade/century closes, our hobby finds itself in a state of maturity and transformation. While we have never been more creative in seeking a particular type or form of signature, we have also never been as deceptive. This applies to both seeker and subject. Nevertheless, our pursuit and knowledge has never been greater and therefore we believe things will only get better. For those of us who have spent decades with autograph collecting as a hobby, and not a business, we have never been happier. Many private collections now rival major institutions, and we have even had two presidents during this decade who have collected autographs.

This guide is actually more of a research study than a price guide, for many autographed items you will find on the market can't be easily valued. Many of the important issues facing the hobby are not in the book, but will be presented to the market in "Advanced Autograph Collecting," a volume that will be published in 2000.

2
Understanding the Value of an Autograph

Finding out how much your autographed Dwight Eisenhower or Arnold Schwarzenegger photograph is worth usually means turning to a certain page in a price guide, but understanding just how that value was determined requires a greater understanding of the hobby.

The most common misconception in the hobby is that age determines value. In fact, only documents dated before the year 1400 are valued because of age. The key factors that influence the value of autographed celebrity memorabilia are condition, supply/scarcity, demand, form/content, source and subject. The source of an item, although paramount for authenticity purposes, is considered a secondary factor. In recent years, many dealers have put a premium on "in-person" signatures. To what extent this will affect the market still remains to be seen. For those individuals who are in the business of buying and selling autographed celebrity memorabilia, understanding these factors is essential to their success. To a novice or casual collector they are important, but far less significant than the pure enjoyment of the hobby.

There is a demand for celebrity autographs, and individuals willing to sell them. Therefore a market exists. Where there is a market, there is a need to understand value by both the buyer and seller. Most of us started collecting because of an interest in a particular area, occupation or individual. The value of an autograph wasn't even a consideration. Collecting autographs gave us an opportunity to share in the achievements of the celebrities we cherished. To preserve those moments we often wrote a celebrity and asked for their autograph, or tried to acquire a signature in person. It was our assurance that the memory wouldn't fade, and of course our proof that we really did have contact with the person or persons we admired.

As a market, the pricing of autographs can be traced back hundreds of years, which is probably a surprise to many of you participating in the hobby today. Unfortunately, or fortunately, depending upon your perspective, it took the explosion in the sports autograph market to really bring the hobby of autograph collecting to the forefront. With this growth in the hobby came greater needs for communication, even dedicated magazines and, of course, more sophisticated price guides. Those of us who had participated for decades prior to this phenomenon were satisfied to pull out old auction catalog results, or our copy of "The Book of Autographs" by Charles Hamilton to update ourselves on autograph prices.

The Introduction of Television

During the 1950's, most casual autograph collectors weren't interested in values, because many of their autographs were obtained in person, and the value was in the moment — not on the paper. There was radio and cinema, but it took television to really bring many of our heroes to life. Now collectors could finally see for themselves, from a different perspective, the faces of Joe DiMaggio, Bob Hope, Judy Garland, and Groucho Marx. As television evolved, we were treated to an increased number of shows on a variety of subjects. Television became a maternity ward for Hollywood's next biggest and brightest stars.

The mark of a great television show is its profound impact on our culture and its uncanny ability to mimic an era. Characters like Archie Bunker and "Hawkeye" Pierce take on bigger-than-life roles, catapulting the actors who play them into almost instant celebrity-status, and therefore their autographs become valuable.

Fifty Unforgettable Television Shows	
Show	**Autograph Comments**
The Adventures of Superman	A George Reeves signature can command over a thousand dollars.
All in The Family	All cast members good signers, however O'Conner can vary in responses to mail requests.
All My Children	Limited market.
The Andy Griffith Show	Griffith, Knotts are not great signers and Howard now refuses autograph requests via mail.
The Beverly Hillbillies	Donna Douglas is the best signer, while Irene Ryan material will be the most difficult to find.
Bonanza	Authentic Green, Blocker and Landon material is getting tougher to find and will cost you some significant cash.
Burns & Allen	Burns was always a great signer, Gracie will run around $100.
Candid Camera	Funt doesn't sign much anymore.
Carol Burnett Show	All cast members are easy additions.
Charlie's Angels	Kate Jackson is the best signer on Charlie's team, but all have been responsive signers.
Cheers	Danson is a notorious non-signer, good luck!
The Cosby Show	Good shot at an entire cast photo here, all are good.
Dallas	Some evasive signers here, Hagman is the key.
The Dick Van Dyke Show	An entire cast photo still possible, Moore is the key.
Dragnet	Webb is the key! He was never real responsive.
Dynasty	Some evasive signers here, but possible!
The Ed Sullivan Show	Sullivan was always good for an autographed photo and his signed material is becoming easier to find.
Gunsmoke	Arness has always been a great signer.
Hill Street Blues	Some elusive signers here.
The Honeymooners	A classic cast photo can command over $300 with demand out-stripping supply.
Jeopardy	Make your request in the form of an answer.
Leave It To Beaver	The Beaver still signs, over $60 for The Cleavers.
Mary Hartman, Mary Hartman	Louise Lasser is excellent.
The Mary Tyler Moore Show	MTM has never been an easy signature, while Asner has always been excellent
M*A*S*H	Stiers is a notorious non-signer, all others good for one signature apiece.
Miami Vice	Both Johnson & Thomas are often unresponsive.

Fifty Unforgettable Television Shows	
Show	**Autograph Comments**
Mission:Impossible	Graves signs in-person only! Rest of cast, good.
The Monkees	Nesmith is the key signature here, can buy others.
Nightline	Koppel is the man, often unresponsive by mail.
N.Y.P.D. Blue	A good chance at getting everyone here.
The Odd Couple	Klugman is key. Randall is great.
The Rockford Files	Garner is an excellent signer.
Roseanne	Not a chance here, save your stamps by mail and anticipate paying for a photo or trying in person.
Rowan & Martin's Laugh-In	Authentic signature on photo by both over $80.
St. Elsewhere	Some elusive signers here.
Saturday Night Live	Belushi & Radner deceased, Aykroyd can be tough.
Seinfeld	Seinfeld responds with facsimile signed photos. Other cast members can vary significantly to requests.
Sesame Street	We all miss Jim Henson. Anticipate paying big $.
77 Sunset Strip	Edd Byrnes requests $19.95 per photo.
The Simpsons	Groenig tough, responds with information only.
60 minutes	Original cast autographed photo tough. Diane Sawyer is by far the best signer.
Star Trek	Shatner & Nimoy good for facsimiles only. Catch the rest of the cast members signing at toy shows.
Thirtysomething	Some elusive signers here.
TODAY	Current cast is excellent, an easy acquisition.
The Tonight Show	Leno is almost as bad as Carson was at responding to autograph requests.
The Twilight Zone	Rod Serling will cost you more than $100 for just a signature.
Walt Disney Presents	One of the most sought-after signatures — over $1,000!
The X-Files	Anderson & Duchovny, facsimiles & ghosts only.
You Bet Your Life	Groucho on a photo over $300.
Your Show of Shows	Sid Caesar often unresponsive.

The Boom in Sports Autographs

Although the attendance of some sports waned during the 1960's, it began to flourish again in the 1970's. The word "athlete" was slowly replaced by the term "sports personality" or "sports celebrity." The growing interest in professional athletics prompted an increase and often renewed interest in collectibles, especially sports trading cards and autographs. Companies began not only to wonder about what new products they could sell into this market, they became more interested in the appeal of the sports celebrity to sell those products. We knew "Broadway Joe" Namath could throw a football, but could he convince the men watching television to buy a certain brand of shaving cream?

The competitive cable market, new and affordable satellite equipment, and what seemed to be a never-ending appetite for this visual medium was the enticement needed for the birth of many new networks including FOX, ESPN and numerous others. Increased competition meant higher fees for the right to broadcast certain events, especially professional sports. And, of course, there was the celebrity, who felt that he, too, was entitled to his share of the revenues. Lucrative multi-million dollar contracts soon became necessary to assure that a team's "sports celebrities" would remain in town for another season, or that a particular character wouldn't disappear from an actor's repertoire.

Professional athletes turned celebrities were even turning up in magazine advertisements, syndicated television shows, commercials, shopping networks and movies. The growth in sports trading cards, specifically baseball, led to the increased number of sports trading card shows. These shows soon found themselves expanding to include autograph guests to boost revenues and further attendance. The additive cost of a sports celebrity attending a show meant that a promoter was often forced to charge a fee for an autograph. With greater exposure came an increase in autograph requests and the need to find out where and how to contact the person. The growth in sports autographs soon found many collectors branching out into other fields such as entertainment, politics and music.

Major League Baseball was the first of the four major sports that combined all the necessary ingredients to entice autograph collectors. For a market to be viable collectors need:

> access to their subjects at the ballpark or at home
> (Baseball Address List, No.1)
> - a cost-effective acquisition method, through dealers, in person or mail
> - a price guide to validate an autograph's value (numerous)
> - a way to confirm a signature's authenticity (The Baseball Autograph Handbook, No.2)
> - a vehicle for monitoring the market (Sports Collectors Digest)

As the market matured, in-person access to many major players has been reduced, while indirect sources such as satellite shopping networks and product catalogs have expanded. You may not be able to obtain a free Cal Ripken signature at the ballpark, but at least you still have the opportunity to obtain an autograph, despite the purchase price. Recently there have been signs that the market for autographed sports memorabilia is beginning to lose some steam. Over the past twenty years, autographed photos in this niche have shown the greatest increase in value (see chart).

The Dichotomy in the Autograph Market

The boom in signed sports memorabilia created a second tier to the already-established autograph market. This traditional market, made up of hundreds of dealers, has catered to the needs of those participants in the Manuscript Society, Universal Autograph Collectors Club and Antiquarian Booksellers Association of America. While there are parallels to both market segments, there are also significant differences. The traditional market offers material in a wide variety of fields, from signed opera photos to land grants signed by presidents of the United States. Naturally, as an established market segment, their business practices, ethics and organizations are held to higher level of standards than those of newer segments. Their views on autograph values are also much different, with many of the major dealers choosing to sell only a handful of sports autographs, if any at all. A traditional autograph dealer walking around a sports collectibles show would find only a few signed items of interest and would certainly disagree with the majority of prices. This dichotomy is being addressed here because as an autograph collector, there are going to be some instances where the values of certain pieces conflict between the two segments.

The Definition of Value?

The definition of value itself has two different meanings to collectors. Many collectors perceive the word value to mean, "that quality of a thing that makes it more or less desirable; having an intrinsic or inherent worth." These celebrity autograph collectors can't put a value on their collection because there is no monetary equivalent to the satisfaction they have derived from building it. It is this definition that is most referred to by satisfied collectors and hobbyists who still have fun.

The other definition some collectors use is "estimated worth." Dealers participating in this market often find themselves trying to accurately price a wide variety of autographed items. Since pricing autographed items is far from an exact science, dealers will often refer to a number of sources for pricing assistance. These sources can be other dealers, experienced collectors, auction houses, advertisements and a variety of price guides. The buyer, who wishes to pay a fair and not an inflated price, will also find many of these resources useful. Whether you like it or not, your definition of value is going to affect how you collect celebrity autographs.

The Factors That Influence Value

Not all collectors are fortunate enough to have a professional-level team, major concert hall or museum located in the city where they live. These collectors are forced to acquire most celebrity autographs indirectly, some of which will be purchased from dealers. In order to efficiently purchase celebrity autographs from dealers it is necessary to have an understanding of value. Understanding the key factors that influence value will help prevent you from being overcharged for an item.

There are five key factors that determine the value of a celebrity autograph: condition, scarcity (supply), demand, form, or what you have signed, and source from which you made the purchase.

Condition

The condition of an autographed celebrity collectible is considered by most dealers to be the paramount factor affecting an item's value. When assessing the value of an autographed celebrity collectible, the condition of the signature as well as the condition of the material that was signed, are both thoroughly examined. The signature should be bold, clear and unobstructed by any portion of the material that was signed or any other signatures that appear with it. The material that was signed should reflect, as much as possible, the original state of that object. The only exception would be some costumes and game/event-worn equipment that naturally would show some indications of wear. For those collectors of autographed game-worn equipment or costumes, it is important to understand that severe damage to the item, such as uniform tears or large pieces missing from certain items, can detract from the value of the autographed item.

It is not unusual for some autographed items to reflect certain aging characteristics. The aging characteristics of paper-based collectibles are probably the most familiar to collectors. They often include light stains, discoloration due to fading and inconsistent wear due to folding. Sports equipment, such as hockey sticks and baseball bats, will typically exhibit discoloration due to the aging of the finish applied to them during the final stages of production. Jerseys will exhibit loose threads and some fading. Certain aging characteristics are anticipated by collectors and thus have little to no affect on value. Any flaw that is not part of the normal aging process will have a negative impact on the value of the piece. For example, autographed baseballs, costumes or playbills that show excessive wear due to mishandling will be valued lower than a mint condition piece.

The type of ink and the writing device used for an autograph can affect an item's condition, thus impacting its value. All material has a level of porosity, or a degree to which fluids, air or light can pass through or into them. The higher the level of porosity, the greater the chance of a deterioration effect taking place in the item. Unfinished wood and certain fabrics are very porous, thus when certain inks are applied to them the fluid spreads into the surface. This is why so many collectors of autographed baseballs prefer ballpoint pen ink signatures over those produced by other porous tipped markers. Many inks react negatively to the surfaces they are in contact with, causing dramatic discoloration over a short period of time.

Supply/Scarcity

The supply or scarcity of a form of autographed celebrity memorabilia will typically have a reciprocal effect on the demand for the piece. This is particularly true with the signatures of deceased individuals and many of the pioneers in certain fields. In the sport of baseball, the autograph of Babe Ruth has always been in great demand. Even though he signed frequently, the supply continues to be insufficient to meet the demand in the market. Although "Shoeless" Joe Jackson is not a member of the Baseball Hall of Fame, his signature is highly sought, not only for the mystique created by the movies that have recently depicted him, but for the fact that he was considered illiterate for many years, and it wasn't until the later part of his life that he learned to sign his name.

The Jacksons owned a liquor store in Greenville, South Carolina. When accompanied by his wife, Joe never would never sign anything or, if forced, signed an "X." On the occasions where he was left alone, his wife would leave a piece of paper with his name written on it, just in case he needed to sign for merchandise or possibly an autograph. Mr. Jackson would essentially draw his autograph, sometimes taking close to a minute to complete. Today the autograph of "Shoeless" Joe Jackson is considered the most valuable sports autograph in history. The first Jackson clipped signature that entered the market was sold for $23,000. A few years ago, an 8" x 10" photograph of "Shoeless" Joe sold for $28,000 at a sale held by Odyssey Auctions of Corona, California.

Scarcity can often be difficult to determine. Many times the market will move based on a rumor, and a celebrity's signature will immediately skyrocket in value, even though there has been no confirmation that the information is indeed true. A few years ago a collector I knew began buying Stan Musial autographed baseballs at twice the current market price because he heard a rumor that he wasn't going to sign baseballs anymore. The rumor was incorrect and the collector ended up spending an awful lot of money foolishly.

Fluctuations in supply are often temporary, as is the case with most celebrities who are actively involved in their field. The demand for the signatures of the field's biggest stars or contributors builds during certain seasons, and is typically met during the "off" season when many celebrities are more accessible. Many entertainers do sign during tours, but at a lesser frequency. There are also occasions where a dealer has purchased a large amount of autographed checks or documents from an estate and offered them for resale to the market. This flooding of material will fill current demand and drive values down for that type of autographed item. In this case it may take many years for the market to replenish the demand and drive values back upward.

Demand

The current demand for many celebrity autographs has been so strong that athletes, entertainers and musicians have had to resort to facsimile (stamped), secretarial, or machine signed (autopen) autographs. The massive correspondence of celebrities like Michael Jordan, Tim Allen, Jay Leno, and Bill Clinton, if attended to personally, would leave little time for their own everyday needs. To reduce the response time to signature requests made by mail, some celebrities will only sign one item per person. This technique is used by many celebrities including Alan Alda, Shirley Temple-Black, and Norman Mailer. This helps meet current market demand without frustrating collectors, or resorting to non-authentic responses that only serve to confuse the public. Some television shows, such as the "Beverly Hills 90210," will try to hamper demand by responding to collectors requests for cast autographs with 4" x 6" color postcards, that bear facsimile signatures on the back. Although collectors are grateful that their requests are at least acknowledged, this method only serves to increase demand.

Significant achievements, such as reaching a career milestone, winning an Emmy, Oscar or Golden Globe can immediately affect demand. An example of this is certainly Tom Hanks, who was accessible to collectors for many years through both the mail and in person during his television days. It wasn't until his Oscar for best actor in "Philadelphia" (1993), that anyone saw a noticeable increase in the demand for his signature. This increase will remain until all public demand has been met.

Changes in a celebrity's popularity, for whatever the reason, also affect demand. Usually changes are triggered by a poor performance, poor judgment or career-threatening injuries, but they can also be brought about by an event that the public may consider distasteful. For example, Tonya Harding, Paul Ruebens, Mike Tyson, and Hugh Grant have all seen the demand for their signature decline because they have not met the public's performance expectations. These demand changes are often cyclical and as you can see by some of the names on this list, any of these celebrities has the potential to bounce back. For the contrarian in the autographed celebrity memorabilia market, this represents the best time to buy these individual's signatures, because they are probably at the lowest possible prices.

The signatures of recently deceased celebrities, especially former or current stars, are always in demand, often commanding two or three times what an average autograph from this individual would have commanded prior to his death. In the case of an unpredictable circumstances claiming a celebrity's life, demand can be enormous, as exemplified by the reaction of collectors following the deaths of Natalie Wood, River Phoenix, Princess Diana and Brandon Lee.

Form/Content

The type of material the collector has the celebrity sign and its relevance to that person has an impact on the item's value. This is why a Sylvester Stallone autographed boxing glove is worth more than having his signature on a photograph. This is not to say that you can't be creative, like having a baseball signed by Kevin Costner, Garth Brooks, and Michael Jordan. You can, but just try to restrict yourself from having foolish or unrelated items autographed. How many times have unprepared fans flocked to request the signature of a celebrity on a napkin? I have never in all my years of collecting ever met a collector of napkins, either the dinner or cocktail varieties. If you're going to collect autographed celebrity memorabilia, try to choose a form that is at least appealing and accepted by the majority of others already participating in the hobby. While popular forms of collecting may be less creative, they offer a greater range of acquisition possibilities. Adding to an autographed sports trading card, baseball, movie script or personal check collection is easier than more bizarre forms of collectibles, such as clocks, furniture and glassware.

Baseball collectors believe in having only "Official League" baseballs autographed, primarily because they are datable and subject to less authentication scrutiny. Additionally, "Official League" baseballs are identical to those used by the professionals. Because this has become an accepted form of collecting, "Official League" autographed baseballs have greater value than other varieties. Whenever an autographed sports collectible can be dated, it reduces a collector's concern for authenticity, and thus increases the value of that item. Collectors of autographed baseballs also prefer single-signature baseballs, or balls with only one autograph on the "sweet spot" (the side opposite the name of the league's president) over multiple signature balls. This is why a single-signature baseball of Lou Gehrig is worth more than an equivalent Gehrig signature on a baseball, accompanied by the names of Johnny Allen, Frank Crosetti, Bill Dickey and Doc Farrell. In this case "less is more" in terms of value.

Autographed letters containing "great," or extremely relevant or even controversial content are a highly sought after by collectors. A letter from Bob Hope discussing his style of golf is far more intriguing than a simple note thanking someone for an autograph request. Admittedly, most celebrities are not known for their letter-writing prowess, but if you pick this form to collect, remember that value is a function of content.

Source

When mentioning celebrity and sports autograph values in my other books, I have been reluctant to acknowledge that the source (where the item was acquired) could has any impact on the value of a piece. Increasing market concern for authenticity has forced me to reconsider its importance. Although the source of a signature can impact an autograph's value, I believe it has a lesser effect than any of the factors listed previously. Recently, advertisements in many of the autograph collecting periodicals have assigned an increased value to in-person signatures. Whether this trend continues or not remains to be seen, but it is certainly worth taking note of.

Additionally, it is getting extremely difficult for the average collector to authenticate many of the sports autographs he is buying, so he is more willing to spend the extra money to purchase an autographed Roger Staubach football directly from the Dallas Cowboys, the best source, for $129.99. Yes, he could have saved himself as much as $40 by choosing an alternative source, but his level of purchasing confidence would have been reduced. In this case, his lack of expertise in authentication determined his purchasing source.

What scares me about the inclusion of source as an impact on value is that I have already seen many larger companies intimidate smaller collectors into purchasing their products by using a "forgery fear" in their marketing tactics. Let me state it clearly to all collectors that the signature you receive in person, be it at a show, or in the arena, is of equal, if not greater value than a purchase you make from a major autograph memorabilia supplier. "Letter of Authenticity" or not, if a major company or dealer files for bankruptcy, what do you honestly think it's going to take in terms of time and finances to redeem your autographed Reggie Jackson baseball, that you paid $79.95 for, because you have authenticity concerns?

Subject

The demand for autograph-related items is not equal throughout all fields — Sports, Presidential, Entertainment, etc., or in forms — signed photographs, handwritten letters, etc. Not only is it not equal, it is also variable. Who and what was "hot" twenty years ago is probably is not in demand now. While this is of little concern to the casual autograph collector, it is paramount to dealers and investors. Collecting for value is another field of its own and, like speculating in stocks and mutual funds, it can be very volatile.

A Final Word on Value

Remember it is not the dealer, celebrity, or promoter who determines value; it is the collector. Your willingness, justifiable or not, to pay a certain price for an auto-graphed celebrity item has an impact on value. While there is little doubt in my mind that an autographed photograph of Bob Hope will eventually increase in value, there is a point at which the collector refuses to purchase an item. You, the collector, make that decision. These major dealers and companies are in business to make money, or they will not be around for long. If they cannot get the price they are asking for an autographed sports item, there is only one alternative — to lower it. Stagnant inventory doesn't pay bills or impress investors, but sales do. My father once told me, "An item is only worth what someone is willing to pay for it."

A Twenty-Year Market Analysis

Wouldn't it be fun to analyze each field of collecting in the market to see what ones showed the greatest gains in value, or even to determine what areas have been over-looked? Does the autograph market favor a particular form, such as handwritten letters over signed photographs? Is the market prejudiced toward race, religion or gender? Is George Washington the best autograph to collect?

To understand the answers to these questions, we need only look back twenty years to see where we have been and to determine some of the characteristics we have developed.

TOP TWELVE MARKET SEGMENTS IN VALUE, 1978-98	
Market Segment	**Rating***
1. Athletes & Sports Figures (all forms including SP)	17.54
2. Famous Women (all forms - AF)	17.40
3. Entertainment Personalities (all forms minus SP)	16.72
4. Entertainment Personalities (all forms with SP)	16.67
5. Athletes & Sports Figures (all forms minus SP)	15.95
6. Financiers, Philanthropists, Jurists & Lawyers (all forms with SP)	15.78
7. Financiers, Philanthropists, Jurists & Lawyers (all forms minus SP)	15.40
8. Inventors, Aviators, Explorers & Architects (AF)	12.40
9. Military Leaders (all forms with SP)	12.13
10. Black Leaders (AF)	11.27
11. Composers (all forms with SP)	11.02
12. Frontiersmen and Indians (AF)	10.88

Comments:

Not a surprise to those of us who participated in the autograph sports memorabilia boom of the 1980s and early 1990s; however, this market appears to be slowing down significantly. Whether this is the supply catching up to the demand, or forgery fear, remains to be seen. Famous Women was probably a surprise to many, but not when you really look at the area and see the significant increases in people such as Eva Peron and Susan B. Anthony, not to mention the increased respect we have grown to have for the many pioneers of human rights. Speaking of which, the increased interest in African-American culture and the many prominent black leaders of the '60s is certainly evident here. The respect this area has achieved has allowed its value to surpass that of American Authors and even the U.S. Presidents. It is particularly interesting to note how certain autographed forms impact value, if it were not for signed photographs, the first and second positions would be inverted.

*Ratings are arbitrary numbers derived from the author's calculations from source materials and are used mainly for the purpose of comparison among categories.

TOP TWELVE WORST MARKET SEGMENTS IN VALUE, 1978-98	
Market Segment	Rating*
1. Colonial and Revolutionary Leaders (All forms - AF)	4.29
2. Signers of the Declaration of Independence (AF)	5.17
3. Royalty (AF)	5.59
4. Nazi & Fascist Leaders (AF)	6.31
5. Continental Authors (AF)	6.64
6. Religious Leaders (AF)	6.98
7. British Authors (AF)	7.50
8. Artists and Photographers (AF)	7.84
9. Scoundrels (AF)	8.19
10. Scientists & Doctors (AF)	8.56

Comments:

No surprise here when you realize that these are the oldest and most established segments in the hobby. In many of these areas, autograph collecting has had hundreds of years of experience with the trials and tribulations associated with the particular segment. Twenty years ago, thanks to many of the outstanding dealers and collectors, our knowledge base was strong in these areas, and as such, many of the items were fairly and consistently priced. While it might be fair to say that the popularity of the subject may have waned slightly with time, my analysis also showed that these areas have had the most consistent value increases in all forms.

TOP TEN MARKET SEGMENTS IN VALUE, BY FORM, 1978-98	
Market Segment	Rating*
1. Athletes & Sports Figures (SP)	22.32
2. Famous Women (Sig.)	21.93
3. World Leaders and Politicians (SP)	21.32
4. Financiers, Philanthropists, Jurists & Lawyers (DS/LS)	20.88
5. Entertainment Personalities (Sig.)	20.06
6. Athletes & Sports Figures (ALS)	17.70
7. Inventors, Aviators, Explorers & Architects (DS/LS)	17.62
8. Athletes & Sports Figures (All forms)	17.54
9. Famous Women (All forms)	17.40
10. Financiers, Philanthropists, Jurists & Lawyers (SP)	16.92

Comments:

Worth noting is that half are, or include, photographs as a form. We have become a very visually oriented society even in our autograph collecting. The advances in photography has given collectors access to better and cheaper photographs to have signed, especially in the areas of Sports and Entertainment. Although ironically, in the latter segment, the form of appreciation is the Sig.! Keep sending out those index cards.

WORST TEN MARKET SEGMENTS IN VALUE, BY FORM, 1978-98	
Market Segment	Rating*
1. Colonial and Revolutionary Leaders (ALS)	2.61
2. Colonial and Revolutionary Leaders (All forms)	4.29
3. Colonial and Revolutionary Leaders (Sig.)	4.33
4. Royalty (ALS)	4.36
5. Signers of the Declaration of Independence (ALS)	4.51
6. Royalty (Sig.)	4.76
7. Scoundrels (ALS)	4.83
8. Signers of the Declaration of Independence (All forms)	5.17
9. Nazi & Fascist Leaders (ALS)	5.30
10. Signers of the Declaration of Independence (Sig.)	5.34

Comments:

Once again, older, consistent and established segments occupy the list. A contrarian thinker and investor would view all of these as bargains, layers in a market that has exploded in popularity, and perhaps this is indeed the case. Again, popularity, price and location could be factors. Certainly the signatures of Royalty are far better appreciated in Europe and Asia than in the United States. Another factor is familiarity. While many Americans can list twenty popular athletes or actors, few could even name five Signers of the Declaration of Independence.

Looking through this study, some market characteristics regarding value became clearly evident.

American Authors
Anticipated value variation (all forms): 18%
Range: 3.46 to 13.79
Stability factor: 10.33
Condition: Stable
Market drivers: Low in volatility with nice broad-based gains.

Artists and Photographers
Anticipated value variation (all forms): 18.47%
Range: 2.92 to 16.42
Stability factor: 13.5
Condition: Stable
Market drivers: Driven by modern artists, such as Andy Warhol, Jasper Johns and Andrew Wyeth, and photographers, such as Ansel Adams. Nineteenth century participants remain stable with broad-based gains.

Black Leaders
Anticipated value variation (all forms): 54.35%
Range: 2.6 to 27.46
Stability factor: 24.86
Condition: Uncertain
Market drivers: Some nice value gains led by an equal demand for autographs in the Sig. and DS/LS form. This segment is starting to see the values of traditional leaders, such as Booker T. Washington, pick up ground against the explosion of interest in modern-day leaders such as Martin Luther King and Malcolm X.

British Authors

Anticipated value variation (all forms): 21.29%

Range: 3.33 - 12.24

Stability factor: 8.91

Condition:Stable

Market drivers: Driven by the values of ALS sales, this segment has exhibited some attractive gains. Clearly a stable and well-understood market segment, despite its unimpressive gains against other segments over the past twenty years. This segment has lots of the characteristics of a stock that has been undervalued. There may be some very good buys here.

Colonial and Revolutionary Leaders

Anticipated value variation (all forms): 56.1%

Range: -0.90 to 9.45

Stability factor: 8.55

Condition: Stable

Market drivers: Driven by the values of DS/LS sales, this segment is highly volatile in the ALS form, exhibiting the majority of decreases. Best to stick with the bigger names in DS/LS form.

Composers

Anticipated value variation (all forms): 50%

Range: 3.83 to 27.04

Stability factor: 23.21

Condition: Uncertain

Market drivers: Driven by signed photographs, but not nearly as significant as that of "World Statesman and Political Leaders." Not driven by names as much as form.

Continental Authors

Anticipated value variation (all forms): 29.36%

Range: 2.5 - 12.25

Stability factor: 9.75

Condition: Stable

Market drivers: Driven by the values of ALS sales, this segment has exhibited some modest gains in both Sig. and DS/LS forms - both of which remain equal in demand. What it has lacked in value, has clearly been balanced by stability. Could be a sleeper!

Entertainment Personalities

Anticipated value variation (all forms): 25.6%

Range: 6 to 37.5

Stability factor: 31.5

Condition: Unstable

Market drivers: Key names such as Marilyn Monroe.

Famous Women

Anticipated value variation (all forms): 32.55%

Range: 5.16 to 25.29

Stability factor: 20.13

Condition: Uncertain/Stable

Market drivers: The entire segment posted nice broad-based gains and was not driven by a certain celebrity or form.

Financiers, Philanthropists, Jurists & Lawyers

Anticipated value variation (all forms): 45.35%

Range: 5 to 31.6

Stability factor: 26.60

Condition: Uncertain/Unstable

Market drivers: Driven by the values of DS/LS sales, this segment has exhibited some nice gains. Less interest in Sig. form versus DS/LS form. Has a tendency toward being driven by key names, such as Clarence Darrow.

Frontiersmen and Indians

Anticipated value variation (all forms): 43%

Range: 3.30 to 27.5

Stability factor: 24.2

Condition: Uncertain

Market drivers: Driven by names associated with the "Old West" over regional frontiersmen.

Inventors, Aviators, Explorers & Architects

Anticipated value variation (all forms): 43.7%

Range: 4.12 to 25.22

Stability factor: 21.1

Condition: Uncertain/Stable

Market drivers: Driven by the values of DS/LS sales, this segment has exhibited some nice gains in both Sig. and ALS forms, both of which remain equal in demand.

Jewish Leaders

Anticipated value variation (all forms): 36.67%

Range: 1.7 to 19.2

Stability factor: 17.50

Condition: Stable

Market drivers: Driven by the values of DS/LS sales, this segment has exhibited some nice gains in both Sig. and ALS forms, both of which remain equal in demand.

Military Leaders

Anticipated value variation (all forms): 49.15%

Range: 4 to 34.40

Stability factor: 30.4

Condition: Uncertain/Unstable

Market drivers: Driven by the values of SP sales, this segment has exhibited some nice broad-based gains. This segment is, however, driven by key names such as Robert E. Lee.

Nazi and Fascist Leaders

Anticipated value variation (all forms): 29.23%

Range: 2.27 to 9.99

Stability factor: 7.72

Condition: Stable

Market drivers: Driven by the values of DS/LS sales, this segment has exhibited some modest gains in both Sig. and ALS forms. Sig. demand is slightly higher than the demand for an ALS. What it has lacked in value, has clearly been balanced by stability.

Presidents
Anticipated value variation (all forms): 24.49 %
Range: 1.92 to 17.08
Stability factor: 15.16
Condition: Stable
Market drivers: The entire segment posted nice broad-based gains and is exemplary of a niche clearly understood in the autograph market.

Religious Leaders
Anticipated value variation (all forms): 36.15%
Range: 3.5 to 11.83
Stability factor: 8.33
Condition: Stable
Market drivers: Driven by the values of DS/LS sales, this segment has exhibited some attractive gains. While the stability factor is a comfort level to collectors, the anticipated value variations may be a sign that the market needs to better understand the availability of autographed material from these participants.

Royalty
Anticipated value variation (all forms): 43%
Range: 3.5 to 10.90
Stability factor: 7.4
Condition: Stable
Market drivers: Driven by the values of DS/LS sales, this segment has exhibited some modest gains in both Sig. and ALS forms, both of which remain equal in demand. While the stability factor is assuring, the somewhat higher-than-anticipated value variation is attributable to the market's lack of understanding in pricing autographs in the DS/LS format.

Scientists and Doctors
Anticipated value variation (all forms): 34.90%
Range: 3.37 to 15.83
Stability factor: 12.46
Condition: Stable
Market drivers: A surprise to many is that this segment is driven by the values of Sig. sales, especially those of key names such as Albert Einstein. Many dealers attribute this to the fact that some material, particularly that of Einstein, has exceeded the average collector's price capacity, particularly in DS/LS and ALS form. While this may indeed be the case, pricing for Einstein material in DS/LS and ALS form has been consistent with the market over the past two decades.

Scoundrels
Anticipated value variation (all forms): 60.31%
Range: 1.5 to 26.87
Stability factor: 25.37
Condition: Uncertain/Unstable
Market drivers: Driven by the values in DS/LS form, the high level of anticipated variation is an indication that pricing is not clearly understood in this area. An additional factor complicating this area is the lack of knowledge regarding the writing habits of many of its subjects. This segment also has a tendency to be driven by the traditional big names, such as Al Capone, and the latest popular "bad boy" or "bad girl."

Signers of the Declaration of Independence

Anticipated value variation (all forms): 20.59%

Range: 3.12 to 8.80

Stability factor: 5.68

Condition: Stable

Market drivers: Perhaps the most stable and well-understood segment of the autograph market, with demand nearly equal in all forms (slight ALS fallout). What it has lacked in value, has clearly been balanced by stability.

Sports Figures

Anticipated value variation (all forms): 35.88%

Range: 5 to 42.8

Stability factor: 37.8

Condition: Unstable

Market drivers: Driven by the values of SP sales, this segment has exhibited some enormous gains — primarily fueled by the boom in autographed sports memorabilia. With the exception of the enormous appeal of the SP format, gains have been broad-based. This segment is clearly driven by key traditional names and the "hottest" current athletes. Unfortunately, it is also the least stable market segment at 37.8.

World Statesmen and Political Leaders

Anticipated value variation (all forms): 62% (with SP), 22% (without)

Range: 3.20 to 35 (with SP), 3.2 to 19.1 (without)

Stability factor: 31.8 (with SP), 15.9 (without)

Condition: Unstable

Market drivers: Driven by signed photographs and the leaders such as Jefferson Davis, once you extract value increases for signed photographs the segment is very stable.

THE TEN MOST STABLE AUTOGRAPH MARKET SEGMENTS, 1978-98	
Market Segment	**Rating***
1. Signers of the Declaration of Independence	5.68
2. Royalty	7.4
3. Nazi and Fascist Leaders	7.72
4. Religious Leaders	8.33
5. Colonial and Revolutionary Leaders	8.55
6. British Authors	8.91
7. Continental Authors	9.75
8. American Authors	10.33
9. Scientists and Doctors	12.46
10. Artists and Photographers	13.5

THE FIVE LEAST STABLE AUTOGRAPH MARKET SEGMENTS, 1978-98	
Market Segment	**Rating***
1. Sports Figures	37.8
2. World Statesmen and Political Leaders	31.8
3. Entertainment Personalities	31.5
4. Military Leaders	30.4
5. Financiers, Philanthropists, Jurists & Lawyers	26.6

Over the last twenty years the hobby of autograph collecting has experienced phenomenal growth, with the value of autographed items increasing nearly tenfold. The influx of new hobbyists, fueled in many cases by the boom in autographed sports memorabilia, has contributed significantly to the demand for many items. As the sports market has slowed, many of its participants have migrated to other areas of autograph collecting. To what extent this will assist or detract from the hobby still remains to be seen. Most of the current participants in the traditional autograph market, while somewhat apprehensive about the changes, are also enticed by the new opportunities it brings.

Perhaps I'm bullish, but I believe the autograph market will thrive over the next decade. While the "forgery factor" has been detrimental to both the sports market and the hobby in general, the traditional market participants are older, wiser and less prone to the mistakes experienced in the sports market. Many of these dealers are much more well-versed on the autograph market, authentication methods and acceptable business practices. Additionally, traditional market participants will be integral in stabilizing many segments in the hobby, including sports. As has always been the case, "quality autographs," the cream of the hobby, will always rise to the top!

Notes on Study:

Anticipated value variation (all forms): Lower percentages indicate that the market is familiar with how to price items in this segment of the hobby. Higher percentages can be an indication of an unstable market, or a niche fueled by a significant demand and limited supply.

Range: A measurement range used to determine stability factor.

Stability factor: Low numbers indicate a stable or steadfast niche, well-understood and prone to consistent appreciation in value—the "blue chips" of the hobby. High numbers indicate instability; an area susceptible to volatile fluctuations.

Condition: An overall assessment of this niche, between 1978-1998—stable/uncertain/unstable.

Market drivers: What forms or individuals have had the greatest impact on the value of this niche between 1978-1998.

3
Colonial & Revolutionary Americana

As citizens, and even as autograph collectors, we often forget the length of the our country's colonial period prior to our independence. Generations of Americans existed before George Washington was even inaugurated. Our ancestors created a wealth of records, from diaries and journals to routine transactions before the American Revolution was even a consideration. Many of these items were relatively plentiful in the autograph market for decades, as were artifacts of the Revolution: orderly books, correspondence, pay receipts, promissory notes and signed currency.

During the past two decades, much of the quality material has been absorbed by both institutions and collectors. While important letters of Revolutionary leaders have always been in demand, few collectors could have anticipated the enormous appreciation for these pieces. For example, autographed material from William Penn and many other early figures in our history, which for decades had been exchanged regularly by major dealers, now commands between five and six times the original purchase price of twenty years ago.

Most dealers attribute this appreciation to earlier collectors' investment philosophy. During the '60s and '70s, this niche of collecting was viewed as a key market segment of the hobby, and an index relative to the strength of autograph collecting. However, the dilution of quality material, higher prices, and even preservation concerns, has done much to weaken this theory. An additional factor is the lack of its representation in most dealer and auction catalogs. With the exception of major dealers, material from this era typically represents between 5 and 10 percent of a market participant's inventory.

As the hobby has evolved, so has the philosophy of collecting and the collector. Some dealers state that collectors simply lack the historical knowledge to understand the significance of many documents, while others say that many key documents are out of the price range of most hobbyists. Add to these theories the variety of other accessible areas of collecting and you can understand some of the transition that has taken place in the hobby.

Large accumulations of this material have been offered for sale in the market, most from estates, and this trend will no doubt continue in the years that follow. Many of these significant collections are subdivided to make them more affordable to a larger base of collectors, but still profitable for dealers. Not surprisingly, most of the quality pieces have a provenance that can be traced to many earlier major collections. Collectors in this area can enhance their knowledge by picking up many of the major auction catalogs of the past that have focused on American colonial and Revolutionary autographs and manuscripts.

Like so many areas of collecting, perseverance, patience and creativity can be useful characteristics when it comes to building an impressive collection. While price may prohibit certain subjects and their related signed materials from your collection, this niche of collecting cannot exclude you. Options, such as collecting signed colonial currency, deeds, and receipts are still viable to many collectors. If George Washington and Ben Franklin are out of your price range, how about "association items," such as letters from family and friends about these great men. Topical collections are also extremely interesting—those manuscripts that deal with subjects such as printing and bookbinding can make for a very impressive collection. Regional collections, such as those found in many Historical Societies are also very popular with collectors. Whatever your personal preference for collecting, it won't take you long to realize that the pursuit for colonial and Revolutionary Americana can be challenging, but extremely rewarding.

Declaration of Independence

The Declaration of Independence, approved by the Continental Congress on July 4, 1776, and later signed by 56 members, is a statement of the principles that two days earlier had led Congress to vote for the independence of the American colonies from Great Britain. It was designed to influence public opinion, both at home and abroad as the United States pursued military support. On June 11, 1776, the creation of the document was entrusted, by the Continental Congress, to a committee consisting of John Adams (Mass.), Benjamin Franklin (Pa.), Thomas Jefferson (Va.), Roger Sherman (Conn.), and Robert R. Livingston (N.Y.). Jefferson's reputation as a literary scholar and craftsman encouraged the committee to assign him the task, and with minor exceptions it is his work.

Jefferson drew upon a long oppositionist tradition in Britain, as well as the English and French Enlightenments, as sources for the document's framework. While his language and the structure of his argument closely parallel the natural-rights theories of John Locke, his elaboration was characteristic of his style. Locke, in justifying England's Glorious Revolution of 1688, had advanced the contract theory of government, arguing that all "just" governments are founded on consent and are designed solely to protect people in their inherent rights to life, liberty and property. Radical proponents of this theory where contained by the more conservative Jefferson who declared that resistance is justified only when a consistent course of policy shows an unmistakable design to establish tyranny. While the monarchy was insulted, King George III bore the brunt of Jefferson's attack, although earlier protests had been directed at Parliament and the governing ministry. The emphasis placed by Jefferson was necessary for a contractual justification of independence, as the colonists had consistently maintained that their only agreement was with the Crown.

Of paramount importance to the declaration was Jefferson's use of "Natural Law" instead of natural-rights theory, substituting "the pursuit of happiness" for "property" in the trinity of inalienable rights. This alteration, derived from the Swiss legal philosopher Emerich de Vattel, emphasized public duty rather than (as the language seems to indicate) personal choice. The concept of natural-law theory is that happiness is attainable only by diligent cultivation of civic virtue. Two passages in Jefferson's draft were rejected by the Congress — an intemperate reference to the English people and a scathing denunciation of the slave trade. The document was otherwise adopted without significant change, and formal signing by 56 members of Congress began on Aug. 2, 1776.

The term "Signer" became synonymous with these 56 members, who risked committing an act of treason when they affixed their name to the document. Without question, had the tide turned against the Americans, these men would have been proclaimed "war criminals," rather than forefathers of freedom. A simple indication of this was the fact the their names were held secret until Jan. 18, 1777, when the victories of both Trenton and Princeton prompted their disclosure in the form of authenticated copies sent to each state. Additionally, both the fate of Richard Stockton and Francis Lewis, at the hands of the British, were exemplary of the degree to which this treasonist act was perceived.

Completing a set of "Signers," has been, and will forever remain, the ultimate task in autograph collecting. While this "ne plus ultra" task is out of the hands of many, primarily due to financial requirements, it has diminished little in the dreams of autograph collectors. In 1991, Superior Galleries manuscript sale included lot 325, a complete set of "Signers" whose provenance could be linked to the now legendary Louis Bamberger. The lot, which sold for $396,000 then, was once again offered by Superior on Nov. 3, 1993, only this time each piece was offered individually.

Worth noting was the construction of the set, which included 36 ALS (Autographed Letters Signed), 11 ADS (Autographed Documents Signed), 7 DS (Documents Signed), 3 LS (Letters Signed) and 1 cropped signature removed from a book. Additionally, nearly one-third were dated during the Revolutionary War, while seven were even dated 1776.

Some experts believe that between 40 and 50 complete sets of Signers exist, however no recent surveys have been taken. The completion of any set is based upon the limited availability of Button Gwinett (about 54), Thomas Lynch (about 85), Arthur Middleton, George Taylor, Joseph Hewes, William Hooper, and John Penn signatures. Many collections of Signers may also include John Alsop, George Clinton, Henry Wisner, Robert R. Livingston and Charles Thomson, all of whom were associated with the process. Many collectors chose alternative sets to the Signers, including signatures of the Stamp Act Congress, Continental Congress, presidents and generals of the American Revolution. Of these, the toughest acquisitions are William Murdock, Timothy Ruggles, Peyton Randolph, Henry Middleton, John Hanson, Charles T. Armand, Daniel Brodhead, Thomas Clark, Thomas Conway, John Crane, Johann DeKalb, Charles Du Coudray, Richard Humpton, John Laumoy, Andrew Lewis, Hugh Mercer, Richard Montgomery, James Moore, Francis Nash, John Neville, Casimir Pulaski, Israel Putnam, Matthias Rochfermoy, Joseph Vose, Frederick Woedtke, Ethan Allen, and Nicholas Herkimer respectfully.

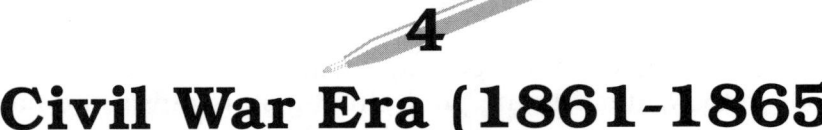

Civil War Era (1861-1865)

Introduction

The Civil War in America, also referred to as the "War Between the States," was fought between the Northern, or Union, states and the Southern, or Confederate, states of America from 1861 to 1865. The Confederacy wished to maintain certain "states' rights," which included the particularly controversial right to author and execute state law on the institution of slavery and the right to secede from the Union. The Union, fearing it's dissolution, fought for its existence and for slave emancipation, a secondary factor proclaimed in 1863.

The pure economic and social variances between both the North and the South, while always conspicuous, was brought to a pinnacle of confrontation over the issue of slavery. Newly admitted states were verbally crucified from both directions, opening old wounds while fueling cries for the succession by the South. Political parties splintered into various factions, undermining national political consensus and furthering the obvious difference in beliefs.

Many Southerners hoped that the threat of secession alone would force acceptance of the Southern demands. When South Carolina adopted an ordinance of secession on Dec. 20, 1860, the seed was planted for the other states to follow suit. In February of 1861, as the first Republican president was just beginning to familiarize himself with the task at hand, Abraham Lincoln now faced the secession of 6 states (later 11) from the Union. The Confederate States of America was formed from its capital in Richmond, Virginia, under the watchful eye of its own new president, Jefferson Davis.

The Confederate States of America

A West Point graduate who distinguished himself in the Mexican War, Jefferson Davis had served admirably in the U.S. Senate and as Secretary of War in Franklin Pierce's cabinet. With Alexander H. Stephens in place as vice-president, Davis quickly began to form his own cabinet and focus increasingly on Confederate control of public property — especially military installations such as Fort Pickens and Fort Sumter, the latter being the key to claiming Southern sovereignty. On April 12, 1861, Confederate cannons fired upon Fort Sumter, now forever considered the site of the first battle of the American Civil War.

Davis then collected an impressive number of volunteers and sent them to Virginia. The goal was to defend the northern border of the Confederacy, as well as to protect many key munitions factories in Richmond. Gen. P.G. T. Beauregard, who had led the assault on Fort Sumter, organized the Confederate troops in Richmond.

The Union

Lincoln, too, had his share of problems, the first of which was establishing himself as the leader of his party against such adversaries as Thurlow Weed and William H.

Seward, Lincoln's Secretary of State. Both had been entrenched in national politics, while Lincoln was still an outsider to the ways of Washington. The loss of Virginia was painful to Lincoln, who now felt that the border states, especially Kentucky, were the key to success. Since the new president had limited military experience, he turned to career soldiers for advice. The first was the ranking general in the U.S. Army, Winfield Scott. The aging soldier not only struggled to put together an overall strategy for the North, but also failed to lure a key leader to the Union side, Robert E. Lee. General Irvin McDowell then took command of the main federal army and positioned it for a Virginia offensive.

The First Modern War

As "the first modern war," the Civil War presents a wide variety of topics, from which autograph and document collectors still build impressive collections. For example, railroads were first used in large-scale movements of troops and supplies, technological advances in weaponry were noted, steam and ironclad warships were now in harbors, new military tactics were being honed and for the first time a war was being visually documented by photographers.

Key Battles and Campaigns

Understanding the key battles and campaigns of the Civil War is a necessity for autograph and document collectors, for without this information, no accurate value/significance could ever be placed on a particular item. An autographed letter signed by Stonewall Jackson describing in detail the battle of Bull Run would have far greater value than a handwritten and signed correspondence answering a mundane question. The first point to remember is that Northerners named battles after nearby bodies of water, while Southerners after nearby places. Therefore the Union fought at Bull Run Creek, while the Confederacy battled at Manassas. Some of this information is included next to the names of the generals in the pricing section.

Military Operations - A Brief, Non-comprehensive Overview

* First Bull Run
* On July 21, 1861, forces met near Manassas, Virginia, to wage the first major land battle. Gen. McDowell's army, later to be known as the "Army of the Potomac," confronted Beauregard's lines along Bull Run Creek. It was during this battle that Gen. Barnard E. Bee proclaimed, "There is Jackson standing like a stone wall."

Other Activities of 1861/Early 1862

* Wilson's Creek (Aug. 10, 1861), Pea Ridge, Ark. (March, 1862)
* Grant in the West, Spring 1862
* Fort Henry and Fort Donelson, on the Tennessee and Cumberland rivers (February 1862), Island No. 10 in the Mississippi (March 16-April 7, 1862), Shiloh Church (April 6, 7, 1862), Corinth (May 1862), and New Orleans (April 26, 1862).
* Peninsular (March, 1862)

★ Monitor and Merrimack (March 9, 1862), Shenandoah Valley (March to June 1862), Yorktown (May 4, 1862), Williamsburg (May 5, 1862), Seven Pines (May 31 - June 1, 1862) and Seven Days (June 26 - July 1, 1862)

★ Second Bull Run

★ Cedar Mountain (Aug. 9, 1862) and Manassas Junction (Aug. 29, 30, 1862)

★ Perryville and Antietam

★ Perryville, Kentucky (Oct.8, 1862) and Sharpsburg, Maryland, along Antietam Creek (Sept. 17-19, 1862)

★ Vicksburg

★ Grant failed (December 1862, January-March 1863), but was successful May - July 4, 1863.

★ Chancellorsville

★ Chancellorsville (May 1-4, 1863), Jackson mortally wounded.

★ Gettysburg

★ Gettysburg, Pennsylvania (July1-July 3, 1863)

★ Chickamauga and Chattanooga

★ Chattanooga (September, 1863), Chickamauga Creek (Sept. 19-20, 1863), Lookout Mountain and Missionary Ridge (Nov. 24-25, 1863)

★ Virginia Campaigns of 1864-65

★ Wilderness (May-June, 1864), Cold Harbor (June 3, 1864), Petersburg (June 15-18, 1864), Cedar Creek (October 19, 1864), Petersburg (March, 1865)

★ Georgia and Carolina

★ Kennesaw Mountain (June 27, 1864), Atlanta (September 1864), Savannah (Dec. 21, 1864), Franklin, Tennessee (November 30, 1864), Nashville, Tennessee (Dec. 15-16, 1864), Bentonville, North Carolina (March 19-21, 1865), Raleigh, North Carolina (April 13, 1865).

★ Surrender at Appomattox Court House (April 9, 1865)

War Correspondence

The Civil War was a young man's war, as generals whose average age was under 40 rose to the highest ranks at an unprecedented rate. While the majority of Union generals were, indeed, professional soldiers, such was not the case in the South (C.S.A.), where political considerations had a greater impact upon rank. Lawyers outnumbered soldiers, farmers and educators, albeit by a few. More than once, internal strife on both sides was fueled over confrontations between officers from West Point (WP) and those not trained as professional soldiers. As a collector of Civil War manuscripts, an understanding of the antebellum and post-war occupations of major participants will no doubt prove fruitful. Some of this information is included in the pricing section.

Autographs of the Confederate Commanders

On April 28, 1928, the final surviving general officer of the armies of the Confederacy passed away. His name was Felix Huston Robertson. While he outlived many, including lieutenant general Simon Bolivar Buckner, Major General Prince de Plignac and the last surviving full general, Kirby Smith, he could not outlive Confederate private Walter Washington Williams, the final man to hold the "Stars and Bars" of the lost Confederate States of America.

Thanks to a legion of scholars, and some outstanding resources, the lives of the Confederate commanders have evolved from nearly mythical status to a group of finite and rare individuals. Called from all walks of life, these commanders became the leaders of the New South and the first to wage a war that would spill American blood on her own soil.

While controversies have raged even decades after the Civil War as to who was, or wasn't, entitled to be called "General," such has been the case with nearly every war. As the line of demarcation in many individual cases still fluctuates, you as a collector may be forced to make an addition or deletion, but consider this your "Executive Privilege." The record, for what it's sometimes worth, states that 425 individuals received appointments by the President to one of the four grades of general. When the war ended, 126 had fallen prey to attrition, while 299 remained.

Acquiring the signatures of the Generals of the Confederacy has been a task undertaken for decades by many outstanding and dedicated collectors. While many collectors prefer "war-dated" signatures, many C.S.A. generals' signatures in any form have become so scarce that date simply doesn't matter. Similar to collecting the "Signers" of the Declaration of Independence, acquiring this finite set of 425 reflects one of the most difficult tasks in the hobby. Fortunately for collectors, many examples from this era have been preserved by both institutions and individuals, aspiring to chronicle this rich portion of our history.

Collectors are also fortunate that autograph dealers for years have recognized this portion of the hobby and routinely catered to it by offering fine examples for sale. While it is natural to suspect that some of the more obscure signatures have slipped out of the collecting arena, it is doubtful that many authentic examples of the primary players have been overlooked.

As the first war with many literate, or at least semi-literate participants, it is typical to find numerous forms of written or printed communication. Documentation was critical, with the primary source of interchange often handwritten. Collectors who wish to attack this area of collecting should familiarize themselves with the many routine forms used, and the anticipated signatures that would adorn these examples.

Additionally, collectors should acquaint themselves with the handwriting habits and idiosyncrasies of all the key individuals/generals, since besides often paying a hefty sum for their autograph, you may also find a fair amount of forged or "ghost-signed" examples. For example, it was common for Varina Davis, wife of the Confederate President, to routinely affix his signature to late-dated war documents.

Confederate-generated military documents are scarcer that those from the Union, precisely due to the destruction of the South, the need to destroy military information and the lack of resources. The advent of photography makes this form available, albeit expensive in some cases. While a collector may often find carte de vistes reflective of this era, other forms should parallel the life of the subject.

The signatures of Patrick Romayne Cleburne, James Dearing, John Herbert Kelly, William Dorsey Pender, John Calhoun and Horace T. Sanders should provide the most significant challenges of your conquest. As facsimiles of their signatures have been published in the market, anticipate encountering your fair share of forgeries. The two most commonly encountered forgeries in this niche of the market are Robert E. Lee and Thomas J. "Stonewall" Jackson.

Useful Resources

"Autographs of the Confederacy, A Collection of Handwriting of Men Who Led The Confederacy," compiled by Michael Reese II, Cohasco, Inc., 198; the Manuscript Division, Library of Congress; Military Archives Division, National Archives and Record Service, G.S.A.; "Generals in Gray, Lives of the Confederate Commanders," by Ezra J. Warner, Louisiana State University Press, 1959; Biographical Directory of the American Congress, 1774-1949, 1950; C.S.A. "General Orders from the Adjutant and Inspector General's Office, 1862-1863," 1864; C.S.A. War Department. "Regulations for the Army of the Confederate States, 1863," 1863; "Historical Register of the United States Army, from its Organization, September 29, 1789 to September 29, 1889" by Francis Bernard Heitman, 1903; "Army Register of 1860," USA, 1861; "Journal of the Congress of the Confederate States of America, 1861-1865," 7 vols, 1904; "List of Field Officers, Regiments, and Battalions in the Confederate States Army, 1861-1865," USA, n.d.; "List of Staff Officers of the Confederate States Army, 1861-1865," USA, 1891; "Memorandum Relative to the General Officers Appointed by the President in the Armies of the Confederate States, 1861-1865," USA, 1905.

5
Sports

Entire books have been written and published about sports autographs, including many by this author. Since 1980 it has become a world of its own, with many of the prominent dealers and auction houses choosing to separate themselves from the rest of the market. The boom in autographed sports memorabilia led to considerable fraud and deception, too. This then led to considerable negative press that tarnished this niche of the hobby as well as autograph collecting in general.

The mainstream of the autograph hobby, which typically deals only in the signatures of sports legends — Babe Ruth, Jack Dempsey, Joe Louis, Ty Cobb, Lou Gehrig, Jim Thorpe, etc., did much to distance themselves from this niche but as this market began to fade many of the sports autograph dealers have tried to migrate into other areas. The extent to which these dealers will survive depends on their ability to educate themselves on the necessary skills to compete effectively.

In comparison to the other niches of the autograph market, the value of sports autographs is extremely inflated, with few exceptions. Correct information, abundant supply — both of legitimate and fraudulent examples, frequent athlete signings, both public and private, and celebrity access will eventually bring prices back in line with the market. Like any niche in the hobby there will still be bargains and good deals, but they are far less frequent.

6

Entertainment Autographs

One of the most popular areas of autograph collecting is the field of entertainment. The ability to bring an actor or actress into our own world has evolved from theater to cinematography, from television to videotape, and now even through the Internet. Stars from the stage and screen have captured our hearts for decades now, creating images that have become larger than life. In an instant we can capture in our mind images of Judy Garland in "The Wizard of Oz," Clark Gable in "Gone with the Wind" and Humphrey Bogart in "Casablanca."

With the advent of television, another media introduced us to an entire new world of characters. From Lucille Ball in "I Love Lucy" and Jackie Gleason in "The Honeymooners," to Carroll O'Conner in "All In The Family" and Alan Alda in "M.A.S.H.," we've laughed, cried and even sympathized with numerous characters.

So powerful are these forces in our society that these forms of communication have altered the way we dress and act, and have even affected our vernacular. The entertainers most influential were those whose roles seemed to forever change our life. "Hawkeye Pierce," "Fonzie," "Kramer," "Scarlet," "Gilligan," "Captain Kirk," and "Count Dracula" evoke vivid memories and often even a phrase or two: "Beam me up Scotty!"

Understanding the impact of the medium, and even that of certain entertainers in pivotal roles, will help you gauge the demand for, and value of certain autographs. This is why you will quickly understand when a simple signed photograph of Clark Gable sells for $700 and a similar signed photograph of the actor, only this time as "Rhett Butler" sells for $1,200 to $1,400.

While the signed photograph is certainly the most popular form of collecting in this niche, other forms do enter the market. Contracts, canceled personal checks, signed movie posters, autographed scripts, and letters are often found in the catalogs of autograph dealers who specialize in the field of entertainment.

While collecting entertainment signatures can certainly be rewarding, it is also not without its share of pitfalls. First, unless you live in Hollywood or New York, direct access to your subject is typically limited. Therefore indirect methods, such as a request for a signature through the mail, are often your only sources. Knowing this, many dealers have begun placing a premium on in-person signatures. While some collectors may take issue with this concept, facsimile responses, including many "ghost" signature and machine signed examples received via mail requests may quickly vindicate these dealers.

Second, understanding the signing habits of entertainers will be critical to your success. For example, Marilyn Monroe often used secretaries to respond to her mail, Steve McQueen often utilized the services of his wife to answer his fan mail and some subjects, such as Barbra Streisand, are so elusive to autographs that they do nearly anything possible to avoid dealing with requests.

Third, like many areas of the hobby, success in this area of the autograph market requires that you develop a resource library, which should not only include every autograph book and catalog available, but also numerous facsimiles of known authentic signatures. Establishing good skills in unmasking a facsimile or forgery, as well as a good understanding of how an entertainer responds to indirect autograph requests is a must!

Fortunately, there are numerous excellent sources for you to utilize from books, such as "Signatures of the Stars" by Kevin Martin, "The Stein and Day Book of World Autographs" by Ray Rawlins, "Collector's Guide to Celebrity Autographs" by the author of this book, as well as some outstanding dealers such as Profiles in History, Steven Raab Autographs, University Archives, Max Rambod Autographs, just to name a few! Collectors participating in this area should also subscribe to numerous hobby publications including "The Autograph Collector's Magazine," "Autograph Times" and even "People" magazine to better understand their subject. Just like there will never be enough movies or television shows to satisfy public need, there will also never be enough resources to satisfy the needs of the collector of entertainment autographs.

7

Classical Music Autographs and Manuscripts

Pass me the baton, because this area of the autograph hobby is not only enjoyable to participate in but can also be extremely profitable. Always popular among autograph collectors have been those signatures and manuscripts of the world's premier composers. From Bartok to Brahams and from Prokofiev to Puccini, these eagerly sought materials consistently command top prices in the market. For example, in 1977, Christies sold an autographed letter from Mozart to his wife Constanze for an astounding $25,500.

Catalogs, such as those issued by University Archives (#139), are routinely filled with choice autographed classical music selections. For example, a signed portrait of Nikolay Rimsky-Korsakov is priced at $2,500, a musical score and signature on a picture postcard from Ruggero Leoncavallo offered at $250, and even an autographed letter from Richard Strauss is $800.

Noted autograph dealer Robert F. Batchelder routinely offers magnificent music pieces to the market. For example, in his 100th catalog he offered am AMQS (Autograph Musical Quotation Signed) — one of the most popular forms in this niche — of Italian operatic composer Giuseppe Verdi for $8,500. He also offered: a AMQS from Russian composer Serge Prokofier for $2,900; an AMQS from Nikolai Rimsky-Korsakov for $5,800; an ALS (Autograph Letter Signed) from German composer Carl Maria Von Weber for $1,800; an AMQS from Johannes Brahms for $7,500; and even an AMQS from French composer Hector Berlioz for $3,900.

Many attribute the interest in this area to music's universal appeal. An individual need not speak Russian to appreciate the talent of many of the country's finest composers. An important manuscript from an outstanding Russian composer appeals to a global autograph audience, instead of strictly a national market. The increased competition can also play a significant role in driving the price of many of these autographed items to new highs.

Highly sought forms in this area of the hobby include: original musical compositions in all forms from initial sketch to a final version; AMQS, attractive for display and commonly given out by composers; ALS (Autograph Letter Signed), as with all niches content is paramount; followed by scarcity, condition and length; SP (Signed Photograph) and all other forms, tickets, programs, etc.

Although interest in this area peaks at the Beethoven, Bach and Mozart level, many collectors can still enjoy autographed items from American composers at reasonable prices. Irving Berlin, Leonard Bernstein and Aaron Copland are still at affordable levels, as are many others. From orchestra conductors to soundtrack composers, this area is filled with treasures. Many composers are more than willing to throw an AMQS your way in answer to a courteous and polite request. No encore needed!

Notable Jazz & Blues Artists

At the turn of the 20th century a new form of polyphonic syncopated music developed, and it was called jazz. Characterized by solo virtuosic improvisation, jazz was initially a form of dance music, but as it evolved it grew increasingly intricate and even experimental. Various distinct forms of jazz quickly emerged. Pioneered by many seminal musicians such as Charlie Parker, Louis Armstrong, and John Coltrane, jazz not only gained the respect of music's toughest critics, but grew into a respected art form. Rooted in black American and other popular forms of music, jazz styles originated from many places across this country. Cities such as New Orleans, where Dixieland jazz was born, became increasingly popular and slowly migrated up the Mississippi River. Noted disciples of this form of music included King Oliver and Jelly Roll Morton. While popular among jazz enthusiasts, both Oliver and Morton were not household names; therefore, autograph requests didn't flood their mailboxes.

Autograph collectors were common in the '30s and it wasn't unusual to find numerous fans lingering outside jazz halls such as the Savoy Ballroom in Harlem. Signatures were easily obtained from jazz legends such as Count Basie, Billie Holiday and Duke Ellington. Fortunately for collectors, some autograph albums from this time period have found their way into the market, with many containing very scarce signatures. While autographs from Jimmie Lunceford, Ivie Anderson and Chick Webb are highly desirable and scarce, other individuals are even more difficult to find.

Blues was a form of African-American music that originated from the rural South in the late 19th century. Characterized by a twelve-bar construction and free-form lyrics, blues became popular with many of the war-torn regions of the former Confederacy. The pioneers of early blues were common folk who entertained and vented their emotions to those around them. While obscurity surrounds both the roots of these early musicians and the origination of many of their songs, no one can argue about the tremendous influence blues has had on American music. For example, the legendary bluesman of the '20s, Blind Lemon Jefferson, has influenced all the greats who have followed, including Joe Williams, T-Bone Walker and even B.B. King. Similar to jazz, the signatures of the pioneers of this music form are extremely scarce.

If you want an autograph-collecting challenge, jazz and blues could be the perfect niche.

From Country to Rock

The Country Music Hall of Fame was founded in 1961 and its inductees include some highly sought signatures, such as Hank Williams, Gene Autry, Original Carter Family, Bill Monroe, Patsy Cline and Roy Rogers. Completing a set of signatures from all inductees in still feasible and affordable when compared to other areas of the hobby.

The autographs of Rock 'n' Roll stars have always been popular, led by Elvis Presley, The Beatles, Jimi Hendrix and The Rolling Stones. Similar to sports autographs, many forged examples have found their way into the market, necessitating collectors to exercise caution in all purchases. I prefer in-person acquisition or signed legal documents, like certificates of authenticity, in this area.

8

Fine Artists, Illustrators, Architects, Art Theorists, Photographers & Art Critics

Over the past decade, attendance at art galleries and museums has increased, though perhaps not dramatically. According to the U.S. Bureau of the Census and American Demographics magazine, from 1982 to 1992, this pastime has seen an increase to over 12 million visitors. The increased attention has also led to a greater interest in collecting the autographs, illustrated letters, signed sketches and other various mediums of artisans worldwide.

Those choosing to collect in this area may want to familiarize themselves with the technical terms commonly used to describe the end result, or output. For example, painting is typically described in terms of acrylic, oil and tempera on canvas, panel or paper, while drawing is often referred to as chalk, gouache, charcoal, ink, pastel, wash and watercolor. Prints also come in many forms including acquaint, copper engraving, dry-point etching, etching, heliograph, lithograph, mezzotint, monotype, poster, silkscreen and soft ground. Sculptures are typically found in ceramic, bronze, ivory, ivory-bronze, plaster, marble, baked-burnt clay, or wood. Photographic prints are typically albumen, carbon, platinum, salt, silver, or gum bichromat.

While many artists learned to express themselves in their chosen medium, often it was not on paper and even more often it was not in words. Whatever the deterrent for the artist, be it the formal education level they attained or simply the accepted mode of communication of their era, not all turned to a correspondence by mail to express their feelings. While this may frustrate many collectors, the added benefit to collecting letters or documents from artists is that often they may be illustrated. For example, it's not uncommon for a letter from George Cruickshank (1792-1878) to include a drawing or two. Naturally this addition to a correspondence can add significant value to the piece.

As artwork has been a common form of investment for years, the market has had its fair share of monitoring resources. These tools can be particularly beneficial to the autograph collector for gauging value and demand. As absurd as it may sound, I have witnessed an autograph collector purchase a simple signed card by an artist for the same price he could have paid for a signed and numbered print (the latter of course being the wiser purchase). In addition to form, like other areas of autograph collecting, the content of a letter and its significance to the artist has considerable impact on value. For example, a letter from Andrew Wyeth discussing his trials and tribulations in dealing with tempera while painting "Christina's World" is of far greater value than a simple thank you note.

The dissolution of a major collection, period change, and forgery concerns are just some of the elements that will cause value fluctuation in this niche. Collectors are advised to purchase signed artwork from art galleries, rather than autograph dealers. Most autograph dealers have no idea about printing techniques or print runs, let alone key biographical material about the artist that may be crucial to the piece you wish to purchase.

9
Literary Autographs

Collecting literary autographs has been popular for over a century. Beginning first with book collectors who savored signed limited and first editions, literary autograph collecting then migrated toward the now-traditional forms. Increasingly, book dealers realized the value of letters associated with a certain body of work; therefore, it wasn't unusual to drop by a distinguished book store and find a letter written by an author tipped into one of his best-selling works. As no other occupation lends itself more toward the written form of communication, most authors are quite prolific autograph signers during their lifetime.

During this century, many very distinguished literary collections have been sold and resold for a very handsome profit. While these collections typically begin in private hands, they eventually find a home at major institutions or libraries. During the latter half of this century, it became increasingly evident that autographed letters and manuscripts had tremendous research value. Many major institutions began contacting both authors and collectors to persuade them to present or donate their manuscripts. Many universities, such as Harvard and Yale, now contain vast holdings of 20th century literary material, as does the New York Public Library.

While institutions have soaked up a considerable amount of material, changes in the tax laws have had a negative effect on many donations to these institutions, so the amount of material available to the autograph market has increased. Constantly in demand have been the works of contemporary writers. As the generations pass, Updike, Mailer, Kerouac and Bellow have replaced Eliot, Faulkner, Frost and Hemingway. It's not to say that the latter are in any lesser demand, only that both the supply and price have somewhat restricted the market for their material.

Many outstanding literary collections are still in private hands, thus when circumstance requires relinquishing these holdings, a flood of new material can be expected in the market. As literary collectors have matured, so have their collections, which can now include signed first and limited editions, published and unpublished letters, corrected manuscripts, associated literary criticisms, original magazine articles, advertisements, journals, posters, photographs, bank checks, cachets, contracts and even telegrams. I have seen private collections of Hemingway, Faulkner, Ginsburg and Fitzgerald that now rival many of the major institutional holdings in this country. With no end to this trend in sight, literary collections should continue to grow exponentially in the hobby during the decades ahead.

Many literary collectors, myself included, prefer to collect only unpublished letters or manuscripts. This is because they generally attract great market attention and value. While this fact certainly should not deter you from purchasing an important letter or manuscript, it is a factor that you should be aware of. As the letters of many famous authors have been published, these resources can be of tremendous benefit to the collector. These books typically source the whereabouts of the correspondence, and, should any ever turn up in the market, a quick phone call to a library or institution can usually determine an item's provenance.

As a literary collector, you should have a thorough knowledge of your subject, and, while it is tempting to choose an author such as Poe or Hawthorne to collect, an understanding of both price and availability of their material can alleviate considerable frustration. Few Hawthorne letters ever surface in the market, and should a major piece hit the auction block, you can expect fierce bidding for its acquisition. Collectors are best to choose contemporary writers whose material is moderately sought, yet common in the market.

While interest levels can vary by subject, primarily due to the availability of material, do not expect a downward spin in price for the letters and manuscripts of William Faulkner, Eugene O'Neill or John Steinbeck any time soon. Often a major movie or play can revive interest in an author, so as a collector you should be aware of these circumstances and anticipate the demand. The greater interest you have in the author and his work, the more enjoyment you can expect to receive from collecting.

10

Business Leaders, Economists, Financiers & Publishers

While it takes money to make money, it will probably also take a few bucks to add the signatures of many of the well-known business leaders to your collection. Popular with collectors in this niche of the hobby are the autographs of those business leaders who founded some of the most popular and recognizable corporations of our time.

Names such as William C. Durant (General Motors), Ray Kroc (McDonalds), and Henry Ford (Ford Motor Co.) are just some of the examples of businessmen whose lives have left a lasting impression on our society. Economists like John Maynard Keynes played a central role in British war finances during World War II. His economic theories are often quoted, such as advocacy of a government-sponsored policy of full employment as a key to the recovery from a recession. Financiers such as August Belmont, a leading private banker in his time, were critical to the success of many influential businessmen and to the international banking market. Publishers, such as Dewitt and Lila Acheson Wallace, founders of "The Reader's Digest," focused on the literary needs of Middle America with truncated articles published in a unique format.

Popular forms in this market segment include stock certificates, bank checks, business cards and letters on corporate letterhead. For example, an American Express Company stock certificate, signed by "Henry Wells" (President) and "Wm G. Fargo" (Secretary) can command a price as high as $1,600. A bank check signed by Frederick Weyerhaeuser can be priced at $2,125, while a business card and a typed letter signed by J.C. Penney on corporate letterhead is about $250. A word of caution, however. This segment of the market is prone to significant pricing variations, particularly in the DS form. For example, stock certificates and mortgage bonds signed by Wells & Fargo and Jay Gould have shown pricing variances of more than 40 percent! Stock certificates are a specialized area and are not reflected in the DS pricing listed in this book. Collectors are advised to consult major dealers for a better understanding of value.

While it's probably no surprise that autographed material from John D. Rockefeller, Cornelius Vanderbilt, and Meyer Guggenheim have exhibited consistent and strong gains over the past twenty years, it may startle you when you see some of the prices commanded by individuals such as Howard Hughes, J. Paul Getty and Aristotle Onassis.

As for the future of this segment of the autograph hobby, you won't have to run out and acquire the services of a financial planner to realize that the autographs of Bill Gates, H. Ross Perot, and Donald Trump might be undervalued.

11
Medicine, Science & Technology

This area of the hobby generally attracts collectors with similar backgrounds to those whose autographs they seek. Some of the signatures of notable participants in medicine, science and technology are not only extremely valuable, but are also difficult to find. While many scientists such as Niels Bohr, Humphry Davy, and Elihu Thomson are unfamiliar to most, the names of Thomas Edison, Isaac Newton, and Alexander Graham Bell are common to our vernacular. As a visual society, prone to association, most individuals are familiar with television and penicillin, but few could name the individuals whose contributions were significant to the end product.

The signatures of those individuals who have contributed significantly in the fields of medicine, science and technology are fascinating — and an interesting area to collect. Just think of the strides mankind has made in this century alone in these fields. From rockets to robots, or from computer chips to fat-free chips, many of the innovators of key products and processes have been overlooked in the autograph market.

Autographed material from individuals such as the Swiss psychiatrist Carl Jung have shown significant price appreciation in all forms. While Jung and Freud are probably no surprise, other notables, such as B.F. Skinner — an outstanding signer through the mail during his lifetime, have also shown increased interest.

This area, while showing strong, broad-based increases, is prone to having certain individuals, such as Albert Einstein, exhibit dramatic price increases in certain forms. The simple signature of Einstein appreciated nearly threefold to almost that of Louis Pasteur in the last twenty years.

Like so many areas of the hobby, form plays a significant factor in determining value. An original mathematical manuscript from French physicist Andre Marie Ampere or a document concerning the dosages of Mesothorium by PSI radiation signed by Marie Curie are always going to have a far greater value than a simple signature. While you're probably saying, "What's the likelihood that I would even encounter such items?" both of these items were offered by the prestigious Remember When Auctions, Inc., in March 1997.

A strong benefit of collecting in this area is that pricing is relatively consistent, as is the appreciation. Also worth noting is that there are many key contributors in these fields who are still alive and still making enormous strides.

12
Space, the Final Frontier

The launching of Sputnik 1 by the Soviet Union on Oct. 4, 1957, was the official dawn of the space age. Since this event, many thousands of spacecraft have been placed into the Earth's orbit, and numerous probes have been launched on lunar, planetary, and cometary missions. Most of these craft have been launched by the United States and the USSR. The early years of the space age were characterized as a "space race" between the United States and the Soviet Union, and soon other nations quickly began developing their own domestic programs.

Acquiring space autographs offers you many collecting options. You can collect all the astronauts who have flown in the U.S. or Russian space program, all who have been chosen (which is extremely difficult), all who have participated in certain programs, those who were first to achieve a certain feat in space, or just the twelve who have walked on the moon. The options are endless and the rewards are often great. To better understand this area of collecting, a brief overview of the space program is provided below for your benefit

SOVIET UNION

From its beginning with the launch of Sputnik 1, the Soviet venture into space has been characterized both by a slow, steady progress and by a determined, dedicated attempt to fulfill national goals. The Soviets possess a respectable array of spaceflight operational skills. With about a hundred space launches each year, a permanently manned space station, heavy space boosters, operational space weapons, and a bold program of interplanetary exploration, the Soviets are major contenders in space-flight technology.

Cosmonaut Program

The main cosmonaut training facility is at Zvyozdniy Gorodok, or "Starry Town" (sometimes translated as "Star City"). Located about 64 km (40 mi) northeast of Moscow, it is a complete training facility where military cosmonauts live in apartment complexes with their families at the center. The Soviet flight control center is located in the town of Kaliningrad, north of Moscow, where many of the leading spacecraft engineering and manufacturing facilities are also located.

Soviet cosmonauts are drawn almost entirely from two distinct groups: military jet pilots, and space engineers.

The jet pilots are generally selected at a young age — typically from 22 to 26 years old — and begin a lengthy apprenticeship that involves university training, physical conditioning, rigorous psychological and ideological screening, and actual spaceflight support. Approximately half of those selected complete the ten-year program. They are then assigned as mission commanders, the only flight assignment available to this group.

In the other cosmonaut group, civilian engineers come exclusively from the space-craft design bureaus and the flight control center, where they have already undergone extensive spacecraft familiarization and personal screening. Military flight engineers come from similar aviation backgrounds. The engineers are generally designated as cosmonaut-trainees at about the age of 30 and undergo a five-year program of general preparation before they are assigned a specific mission. Exceptions can be made to these criteria for special purposes. For example, several pilots associated with the Soviet shuttle program have made space missions as flight engineers.

Thus far, all Soviet cosmonauts have been ethnic Slavs, and all but a few have been men. The Soyuz spacecraft used in manned missions has a maximum mission duration of only six months, so short, simple replacement flights to space stations such as Mir afford the opportunity to place "guest cosmonauts" among the swap crews. Since 1978 more than a dozen non-Soviet guest cosmonauts have been used. The first nine came from Soviet-bloc nations, followed by French, Indian, and Syrian representatives. Plans exist for several other nations, as well. It has been a tradition among the cosmonauts to not sign an autograph until after his or her mission. Although there has been exceptions, this condition still applies.

In June 1971 the crew of Soyuz 11 perished during reentry. The signatures of all three aboard are highly sought by space autograph collectors, particularly Dobrovolski and Patsayev. Vladislav Volkov had flown previously aboard Soyuz 7. As a collector you will find acquiring the signatures of Dobrovolski and Patsayev nearly impossible. Other cosmonaut challenges include Vladimir Komarov, Yuri Gagarin, Pavel Belyayev and, of course, the ever-elusive Anatoli Levchenko.

Popular among cosmonaut collectors are signatures of Alexei Leonov, the first to walk in space, and Valentina Tereshkova, the first woman in space. Naturally, the latest group of cosmonauts who returns from space is always popular with collectors.

UNITED STATES

The contrast between the U. S. and the Soviet space programs has been substantial. Whereas the Soviet program was characterized above as slow and steady, the Americans have approached activity in space in a swift series of strong and consistent efforts slowed only by tragedy or triumph.

Astronaut Program

The achievements of the astronauts who took part in the first two decades of U.S. manned space exploration — the Mercury, Gemini, Apollo, Apollo-Soyuz and Skylab programs — have been enormous. The current professional corps of astronauts consists of about 100 men and women at the Johnson Space Center in Houston, Texas. Approximately half of them are pilots, most of whom are male, and almost all of whom are active or retired military officers. The other half are mission specialists. Of these, about half are military flight engineers, and the remaining are civilian scientists and engineers. In the past, astronaut selections have been made almost exclusively from the ranks of federal employees, whether members of the military or employees of NASA or the civil service, but it is likely that this mix will change.

Following the disaster of the Space Shuttle Challenger, there was concern over the wide variety of passengers carried in addition to the NASA flight crew. Although the term "payload specialist" was applied to almost all of them, they actually played a variety of roles. Commercial launch customers were allowed to send representatives into orbit — a marketing feature intended to enhance the Shuttle's image and viability. This option was exercised by the Defense Department, by satellite manufacturers, and by several foreign customers. The citizen-in-space program that was to involve teachers, journalists, and ordinary Americans was suspended following the death of the first such passenger in the Challenger disaster, and flights by various members of Congress and bureaucrats were temporarily shelved.

The U.S. Space program has its own share of difficult autographs to acquire. Of the astronauts who have flown, Roger Chaffee and his fellow Apollo 1 crewmates, Gus Grissom and Ed White, are highly sought, as are those who also were victims of terrible tragedies, such as the crew of the Challenger. Of the latter, the signature of rookie shuttle astronauts Mike Smith, Greg Jarvis and Christa McAuliffe remain the most-sought of the deceased crew.

OTHER COUNTRIES

Often forgotten by space collectors is that there are other programs throughout the world — an entire new realm for autograph targets. There is no better time than now to begin tracking the progress made by these countries and the names of the astronauts of tomorrow. A collection of autographs from the first flown space-farers of each country is also a collecting option. Both the Soviet and U.S. space programs have had their fair share of international representatives. While of all the first, Gagarin will be the most difficult, those of Akiyama (Japan), Mohamand (Afghanistan) and Tuan (Vietnam) will also prove challenging.

The ESA (European Space Agency) has an official astronaut program, which was originally designed to train candidates for Spacelab missions aboard the U.S. Space Shuttle. Three candidates were selected in 1980, two of whom flew actual missions until the Challenger disaster drastically curtailed the program. In addition, two West German physicists also flew aboard the Spacelab as payload specialists. In 1987, the West Germans selected five more astronauts — two women and three men — to train for flights aboard the Shuttle and, possibly, remaining Spacelab missions. The trainees have scientific research backgrounds but lack test pilot experience. In France, eight "spationautes" were selected to train for participation in possible Shuttle programs as well. Prior to that, a French pilot took part in the Soviet "guest cosmonaut" program aboard Salyut 7 in 1983, and his understudy took part in a seven-day Shuttle mission in 1985.

JAPAN

Japan's National Space Development Agency (NASDA) was formed in 1968. The Japanese are also playing a major role in the U.S. space station by developing a laboratory module. Ambitious programs in the further future include solar probes and, possibly, a reusable shuttle that would be used to service a manned space "factory" in the 21st century, keeping the nation at the forefront of advanced manufacturing techniques.

CHINA

Discussions of plans for manned space missions have been reported for several years, but any precise plans and schedules are unknown.

INDIA

India has an active space program that concentrates on the development of aerospace technology and on direct economic applications of such technology. It also makes use of communications satellites for nationwide educational systems. The Department of Space, established in the early 1970s, has the Indian Space Research

Organization (ISRO) as its major unit. In manned programs, an Indian pilot took part in a Soyuz visit to the Salyut 7 space station in 1984. Two other Indian engineers were selected in 1985 to train as payload specialists on a Space Shuttle mission, but the mission was subsequently canceled.

CANADA

In 1983, six Canadian astronaut trainees were selected to take part in Space Shuttle missions. One of the men flew aboard a mission in 1984, but the other missions were delayed or canceled after the Challenger disaster.

OTHER NATIONS

Several other nations have been involved in space activities. In manned space activities, nations that have taken part in the Soviet's guest cosmonaut program have included Poland, the former East Germany, Hungary, Vietnam, Cuba, Mongolia, Romania, Bulgaria, Syria, and Afghanistan. The first person in space who was neither from the United States nor the Soviet Union was the Czech spaceman Vladimir Remek, a guest aboard a 1978 Soyuz flight.

ASTRONAUTS, COSMONAUTS & AUTOGRAPHS

When the space program began, no one was quite certain what to expect from these modern-day, Buck Rogers "wannabes," who NASA had labeled astronauts. The original Mercury participants were even somewhat perplexed by their newfound celebrity status. Signing autographs to most astronauts was not only a pleasure, but an unexpected surprise.

With each new mission and accomplishment came a greater sense that something very special was happening. This extraordinary group of individuals was forging a new path in a frontier unfamiliar to us all. Thanks to television, and the increased media attention, most of the early astronauts quickly became celebrities. From ticker tape parades to White House visits, America now had a new group of heroes.

Deluged with autograph requests — both in-person and through the mail, each astronaut became a target for collectors. While some seemed unaffected by requests, others were noticeably bothered by the task. Eventually this led some astronauts to simply decline signing anything. Apollo 8's Bill Anders, for example, began sending out pre-printed cards stating that due to the sheer volume of requests and the commercialism surrounding autograph collecting, that he would no longer sign. His signature now is considered by many to be more scarce than the crew of the Challenger.

The advent of the Apollo program seemed to attract the attention of every souvenir collector and "quick-buck" artist. Actual space-flown trinkets of all types became highly sought by collectors. Not surprisingly, some astronauts fell prey to lucrative commercial offers presented by autograph and memorabilia dealers. The extent of this enterprise even sparked a senate investigation and cast a dark shadow on autograph collecting.

While many astronauts have resorted to facsimile, secretarial or machine-signed responses to comply with autograph requests, there has always been exceptions. Apollo 7's Walter Cunningham, who was receptive to autograph requests for years, finally stopped signing due to the commercialization of the hobby.

Collectors do have alternatives, however. Companies such as The SpaceSource (A Division of AVD Services) now offers astronauts' autographed photos from the Mercury, Gemini, Apollo and Apollo-Soyuz programs. Representing many astronauts, including seven out of the twelve moonwalkers and three of the original Mercury astronauts, the company offers photographs primarily from NASA archive negatives, as well as an occasional postal cover, or flown trinket. Prices typically range from $35 to $139 for single-signed photos, with some multiple combinations available at slightly higher prices.

Today's astronauts, most of whom are not under the same umbrella of notoriety as their predecessors, find it much easier to handle their mail personally. It is not unusual to receive an authentic signature with a sincere salutation from most of the current field of shuttle astronauts. Andrew M. Allen, James P. Bagian, Ellen S. Baker, Michael A. Baker, Robert D. Cabana and Kenneth D. Cockrell, are just a few of many outstanding signers.

MACHINE-SIGNED ASTRONAUT SIGNATURES

★ Be suspicious of any items, from different astronauts, returned in the same envelope, especially if they have the same mail code (Mail Code_____. The mail code appears in the upper left hand corner on envelope).

★ Irregular ink deposits, rough strokes (especially during machine-difficult combinations such as "ae"), and height-consistent ascenders — "h," "l" often match each other in height and the height of capital letters can be an indication of a machine-signed item.

★ Active astronauts often have machine-signed items processed at the same time and often even by the same person. Therefore, machine-signed index cards processed during the same session will be nearly identical.

★ Stockpiles of some items, such as machine-signed index cards and photographs are stored at the Johnson Space Center, so it is not unusual to receive an older example, with noticeable discoloration resulting from aging. Often these are sent to fill the autograph requests of inactive astronauts.

★ Active-astronaut, machine-signed index cards will typically begin or end 1" from the end of either side of the card. The common range is 7/8" to 1-1/8".

★ Always be wary of signatures signed parallel (90 degrees) to the edge of an item's surface!

Shuttle crew photos, which are often added to mail requests, are almost always machine-signed. As these photos exemplify all the typical characteristics of machine-generated autographs, they are not difficult to identify as such. While many astronauts, especially the flight commanders, typically add the crew photos to autograph requests, often they also add other fascinating photographs, brochures, stickers or flight data. All of these items, when combined, can make for a very attractive display.

MOONWALKERS

"Armstrong is on the moon"
Only eighteen months after the tragedy of Apollo 1, man conquered the most hazardous and greatest adventure that he has ever embarked upon — landing a man on the moon and safely returning him home. To date, only twelve individuals have had

the opportunity to look skyward from another world and see the beauty of their home, Earth. From 1967 to 1973, seven manned missions to the moon were conducted. Of those, six succeeded in lunar landings. Only the ill-fated Apollo 13, a "successful failure," did not complete its desired task.

Similar to a complete set of Presidents and Signers, this prestigious group of individuals has been one of the most sought-after autograph collections. Available in signed photographs and books, as well as an occasional typed or handwritten letter, a complete set of moonwalkers is still attainable. Of all the forms that enter the market, signed official NASA publicity photographs are by far the most common, followed by signed books.

Of the twelve moonwalkers, it's no surprise that Neil Armstrong remains the most desirable. As the first man to set foot on the moon, he has been deluged with autograph requests ever since. Following the mission Armstrong did respond to most autograph requests, but the volume of mail quickly became overwhelming. He no longer responds to autograph requests through the mail and has been selective with in-person requests. Now somewhat reclusive, his autograph on a photo can command upwards of $275 to $450.

The most difficult signatures of the moonwalkers are John Young, followed by David Scott, who has now agreed to a relationship with The SpaceSource.

THE SIX SUCCESSFUL APOLLO LUNAR LANDINGS	
Mission	**Moonwalkers**
APOLLO 11, July 16-24, 1969	Neil Armstrong, Buzz Aldrin
APOLLO 12, Nov. 14-24, 1969	Charles Conrad, Alan Bean
APOLLO 14, Jan. 31 - Feb. 9, 1971	Alan Shepard*, Edgar Mitchell
APOLLO 15, July 26 - Aug. 7, 1971	James B. Irwin*, David R. Scott
APOLLO 16, April 16 - 27, 1972	John Young, Charles Duke, Jr.
APOLLO 17, Dec. 7-19, 1972	Eugene Cernan, Harrison Schmitt
* deceased	

13
Heads of State

Take me to your leader, be it a king, queen or prime minister. The autographs of foreign heads of state, many of whom have had military experience, can have significant market value. In fact, according to my research, only signed photographs from athletes and signatures of prominent women have had greater market appreciation during the last two decades. According to dealers, autographed pictures of world leaders and politicians have definite appeal over a letter or document that may require a translation. Whatever the case, no one can argue the appeal of a quality color photograph.

Autograph dealers certainly understand the appeal of this area. Just look into a Gallery of History direct auction catalog (Sept. 17, 1997), where for sale is a photograph signed by David Ben-Gurion ($546), a philatelic envelope signed by both Moshe Dyan and Henry Kissinger ($316), a manuscript DS (Document Signed) from Edward, Duke of Kent ($230) and even a manuscript DS from Ferdinand II ($805). In fact, the same autographed photo I received in the mail from Yitzhak Rabin in response to my request for his signature sold for $230. Gallery of History is just one of many outstanding dealers serving the needs of Heads of State autograph collectors.

University Archives, under the watchful eye of John Reznikoff, is also one of the world's leaders in this area. Just glancing through their catalog (#129), a potential buyer can run across a DS (Document Signed) from Czar Alexander I of Russia offered at $1,200, a DS from Czarina Catherine II of Russia (Catherine The Great) for $2,500, a DS from King George II of England for $700, a DS from Emperor Hirohito of Japan for $6,900 and a DS from Prime Minister of England Winston Churchill for $1,900, just to name a few. Worth noting is University Archives specializes in many areas, one of which would certainly be Winston Churchill.

As a niche, including all forms minus SP, this area of the hobby outperformed many including American authors, U.S. Presidents and even scientists and doctors. If you can get past the language or cultural barriers, increased postage, and unique address formats, you may find yourself discovering a fascinating new area of collecting!

14
Presidents of the United States

One of the most popular, and perhaps logical, areas of autograph collecting in America is that of the individuals who have held our most prestigious office, Commander in Chief. Nowhere is the history of our great country better portrayed than through the office of the president. This finite group of leaders is a microcosm of the trials and tribulations of democracy at its finest.

As a collection, investing in a complete set of Presidential signatures is like buying a lot of "blue chip" stocks. There is limited volatility, with a strong basis on fundamentals. George Washington will always be our first president and our first truly great leader. In addition, it's worth noting that, should one wish to dispose of a complete set, like General Electric stock someone else will be there waiting to take it off your hands. Whether or not you make a profit will depend on the quality, condition and, of course, the length of time the collection has been in your possession.

Like the stock market, "institutional" investors have played an important role in this area of the autograph market. The institutions are the major museums and universities who have chosen to invest in presidential material as a part of their research holdings. Fortunately for collectors, often these holdings reappear in the market for financial reasons, or to simply make room for additional material. It is a common inference, however, that as the years roll along, instances of earlier presidential material will decrease exponentially as a result of the increased participation in the market.

While the choice of what particular form to collect will most often be determined by your finances, an individual entering this niche must have a clear understanding of what types of items are available on the subject and from what particular period. For example, putting together a complete set of handwritten letters from the presidents authored during their term is nearly impossible. One only need to remember that William Henry Harrison held the prestigious office for only about a month. While Harrison's presidential material is scarce, other mementos of his life are not.

Like many areas of collecting, certain forms are common, such as clipped signatures, autographed album pages, index cards, postcards, free franks, business cards, canceled checks, etc., while others may be unique to the office, such as ship's papers, land grants, pardons, military discharges and appointments. Naturally, not all these forms were available to all the presidents of the United States.

Popular among collectors have been associated items like the "The Executive Mansion" card (2-3/4" x 4-1/4"), which bore the office's title in the upper right-hand corner and offered the subject a quick and inexpensive solution to a note or autograph request. While this card was introduced by President Grant, it was later accompanied by a similar card bearing "White House, Washington" originated by Theodore Roosevelt. While these earlier cards became increasingly popular with collectors, following the Truman administration the likelihood of an autopenned (machine-signed) or secretarial response caused diminished interest in this form.

Machine-signed, or "autopenned" signatures have been prevalent since the Kennedy administration. Ironically it was John F. Kennedy, who himself was an autograph collector, who introduced a whole new element of intrigue into the oval office. Collectors not only had to fight for a presidential signature, put had to go to great lengths to prove that it was indeed genuine.

The modern-day collector of presidential autographs now faces the greatest challenges the hobby has been able to present him. From machine-generated signatures with devious multiple patterns, to increased security and, of course, presidential libraries, collecting a complete set in this niche will certainly present its fair share of obstacles.

Presidential Overview

George Washington

With his attractive calligraphy and prolific and insightful output, George Washington, who seldom signed his full name opting instead for "Go. Washington," was an awe-inspiring president. The variance in content of his letters is best reflected in the exponential price ranges they command. Thus each individual letter from Washington will necessitate some research to accurately determine price. Washington, extraordinary during his own era and extremely popular still, will not be as common as one might think in a clipped signature form. Generally these will only appear in the market when an established collector is trying to upgrade his set or a lazy forger is trying to pass off his latest creation. Washington forgeries are common, and often examples were done by Robert Spring (mid 1800's) or later Joseph Cosey. Collectors are advised to seek the tremendous research materials published by autograph sleuth and collecting pioneer Charles Hamilton for further information on bogus Washington examples.

Worth noting is that Alexander Hamilton acted as Washington's secretary during the Revolutionary War; therefore, many LS examples found were actually penned by the future president. Washington did personally sign all war discharges, however, finding an example in "investment" condition is difficult.

Although the language of diplomacy during this era was French, Washington never learned the language and did not attend a university.

John Adams

Prolific and insightful, the letters of John Adams typically exemplify an asymmetric quality in his calligraphy. Size and character formations vary regularly, with his signature decreasing in proportion and legibility with age. Considered by many to be the rarest of the early presidents, term-dated material is scarce, which is most certainly attributable to his single term in office. His hands shook with palsy by the time he became president. The transformation of his signature to nearly illegible prior to his death has led to much confusion among collectors. Adams was a voracious reader and often added handwritten notes in the margins of his books. He was also a prolific writer and diarist, recording the many details of the people he met and the places he visited. Common forms: "John Adams," "J. Adams."

Thomas Jefferson

Consistent and often fascinating in content, the letters of Thomas Jefferson are highly sought by both collectors and institutions. While his handwriting varied little throughout his life, his bold signature often casts confusion in determining an ALS from a DS. Similar to Washington, authentic clipped signatures remain scarce and enter the market typically when collections are upgraded. Forgeries are common — especially with regard to signatures and handwritten letters. Many of the Jefferson documents that appear in the market are land grants or ships' papers, some of which also bear the signature of James Madison. Although Jefferson also wrote in French, and sometimes Greek and Latin, few examples of such exist domestically. He was a meticulous record keeper and an avid book collector. In fact, a library of his books was sold to the government after the British destroyed the Library of Congress. Perfect copies of much of Jefferson's correspondence were created through the use of a polygraph that reproduced precisely the hand movements of a writer. Common form: "Th. Jefferson."

James Madison

The letters and documents of the "Father of the Constitution" are in great demand by both collectors and institutions. While insightful handwritten letters are rare, even his prolific and mundane correspondence is getting increasingly difficult to acquire. Later, tremulous examples are common as an arthritic Madison fought valiantly against the disease. His wife Dolley authored many a letter for her suffering husband during the latter years, most of which were adorned with his print like signature. Many ships' papers, bearing both Madison's and Monroe's signatures, have been available to collectors throughout the years, with even a few franks surfacing. Military commissions and land grants are two other viable alternatives for acquiring his authentic signature. Be wary of cuts and exercise all the typical cautions associated with such a purchase. Madison was crippled by rheumatism during the last six months of his life and confined to his room. He kept a comprehensive journal on the Constitutional Convention and was proficient in Latin. Common form: "J. Madison" (exception, legal documents), rare as "James Madison, Jr."

James Monroe

Succinct and often routine, the letters of James Monroe exhibit many handwriting variances throughout his lifetime. Examples of his authentic signature can still be found in many forms — especially documents such as land grants. It was common for land to be transacted in lieu of cash during his era. Monroe had the uncommon proclivity of having his handwriting increase in size over the body of a correspondence and, like many other presidents, his script lost legibility with age. Unlike many presidents, his writings rarely mentioned his religious faith. Common form: "James Monroe," also "J. Monroe," rare in other forms.

John Quincy Adams

Similar to his father, Adams' handwriting transformed with age due to illness. While his early correspondence is consistent, insightful, small and legible, the latter is a stark contrast. Adams was also a poet, and while an occasional manuscript poem may be unearthed, it is uncommon. The fact he was a single-term president lends itself to the rarity of associated material, although alternatives are certainly available to collectors in the form of documents, such as land grants, and even an occasional frank. Daniel Brent was Adams' secretary and his handwriting bore a stark similarity to the president. Thus, determining an ALS from a DS might provide collectors with a research challenge. Adams was proficient in a number of languages including Latin, Greek, Dutch, French and he knew some Spanish. He was also the only former president to serve as a U.S. representative. Common forms: "John Quincy Adams," "J.Q. Adams" and later "J.Q.A."

Andrew Jackson

Although the eloquence of his letters is far cry from his predecessors, Andrew Jackson's bold and succinct correspondence, with its large signature, is attractive to collectors. A truly charismatic figure, Jackson's candid letters often contained a fair share of spelling and grammatical errors; however, few could claim it detracted from his message. While his handwriting and typical full signature changed little throughout his life, he did much to alter the signing habits of the presidency. Jackson discontinued signing land grants during his second term and bequeathed much of his signatory power to liberate himself from administrative details. Andrew Jackson Donelson, the president's nephew and secretary, handled many of these tasks that over time have led to much identification confusion in the autograph market. From bank checks to land grants, Donelson adequately adorned the signature of his uncle as needed. Collectors are advised to exercise caution when purchasing any Jackson-autographed, second-term items. Common form: "Andrew Jackson" in bold.

Martin Van Buren

Although the first president born an American citizen had the capability to fire off an insightful correspondence, Van Buren seldom utilized this talent. Instead he opted for politically correct and often mundane communications. His script also transformed from small and legible to large and often unintelligible with age. Unfortunately for collectors, examples of his signatures are scarce in many forms and will require some patience before certain items find there way into the market. Likely this will be a document signed by Van Buren as Andrew Jackson's Secretary of State. In his youth, Van Buren studied at the law firm of Francis Sylvester and often had the duty of making copies of documents. Common forms: "M. Van Buren," "M.V.B." or "M.V. Buren."

William Henry Harrison

The most difficult signature to obtain on material authored while he was in the Oval Office, William Henry Harrison reflects a dichotomy of sorts as his non-presidential autographs are fairly common. Harrison's handwriting evolved during his life and reached its pinnacle in form and substance during his quest for the presidency. Common forms: "Wm. H. Harrison," "Willm. Henry Harrison" and "W.H. Harrison."

John Tyler

Following the death of William Henry Harrison, John Tyler became the first vice-president to assume the Oval Office. Tyler brought to the office greater administrative control and took great comfort in handling most of his correspondence. Typically his letters varied in length, legibility and content due to both his attitude and the materials he chose to write with. His often succinct and forceful script is best exemplified with documents written during his term in office, and the most revealing in content, his correspondence with his friends and relatives. While both handwritten letters and franks are somewhat common, documents and signed letters can be more elusive. Characteristic of his signature is the addition of a decorative line to which a date is often added nearby. During his last years he served as chancellor of his alma mater, the College of William and Mary. Tyler was the only president to join the Confederacy. Common form: "J. Tyler."

James Knox Polk

The eleventh president of the United States, James K. Polk, a former House Speaker and Governor of Tennessee, is perhaps most commonly associated with his elaborate, distinctive and often embellished signature. While the demand for his autographed material is far from impressive, the lack of consistency in availability contributes to the volatility in demand. Of the documents that have surfaced in the market, appointments that often include the signature of Secretary of State James Buchanan have drawn interest. Handwritten letters as Speaker of the House and congressman have also surfaced, while term-related pieces remain elusive. Dictated letters are also rare, but there are a few impressive multiple-page early legal documents that have found themselves in collector's hands in the past five years. Considered by many historians to be the greatest one-term president, it remains a shock to many that his writings do not command a greater price in the autograph market. Common form: "James K. Polk."

Zachary Taylor

Serving only fifteen months in office before his death, Zachary Taylor's presidential autographed material presents a significant acquisition-challenge for the collector. Pre-presidential autographed material that has surfaced has typically been signed documents. Bold, clean, and attractive handwritten letters, particularly those substantive in content, remain elusive and in demand. Taylor, at his literary finest, is represented best in correspondence during his Indian-fighting days. "Old Rough and Ready" fought in the War of 1812, the Black Hawk War and the Seminole War. He was a poor speller during his entire life. Common forms: "Z. Taylor."

Millard Fillmore

Upon Zachary Taylor's death in 1850, Whig party member and vice president Millard Fillmore became our 13th president. A prolific person who penned precise, prudent and prosaic communications, his lack of available presidential autographed materials is countered in the market by numerous non-presidential examples. Partly printed signed documents are perhaps the most common form offered, many of which relate to his days practicing law in Buffalo, New York. Fillmore also served in the House of Representatives (1833-35, 1837-43) and became the New York State Comptroller in 1848. Although other presidents had been photographed, even John Quincy Adams, Fillmore was the first president who regularly inscribed his name to a carte de viste. Common forms: "Millard Fillmore."

Franklin Pierce

Often illegible and seldom intriguing in content (with the exception of those to friends and relatives), the letters of Franklin Pierce were far from literary masterpieces. Collectors will find handwritten letters, naval commissions and even perhaps a "Warrant for a Pardon" before any other forms. Clipped signatures, franks and signed photographs have always been scarce. Because Pierce repealed the Missouri Compromise and passed the Kansas-Nebraska Act, which ultimately fueled the Civil War, he was not particularly popular after leaving office. Common forms: Franklin Pierce," also "Frank Pierce," "F. Pierce" and "Fr. Pierce"

James Buchanan

With his ornate calligraphy, Buchanan rivaled only Washington for the most attractive, yet precise handwriting of any president. Buchanan's signature varied little throughout his life, with perhaps the most notable example the increase in his signature's size as he grew in prominence. His typical single-page correspondences have been offered for years in the autograph market and, although examples have been exemplary of most of the periods of his life, with the slight exception being his term, interest has been generally moderate or below average. Now considered slightly controversial, as greater details of his personal life have been unearthed over the years, one can now anticipate some additional interest. During his retirement he was a very prolific writer. Common form: "James Buchanan."

Abraham Lincoln

Insightful and succinct, yet gracious and charming, the letters of Abraham Lincoln are the most sought-after form for inclusion in autograph collections. The demand for Lincoln material far exceeds the supply, as well as the demand for material from any other U.S. president. His pre-presidential material is also scarce as are his legal briefs. Many are signed with the firm's name, "Draft Calls" and "Military Appointments," and many include the signature of Edwin M. Stanton, Secretary of War, if they do surface in the market. But, like all Lincoln material, they carry a hefty price tag. Full signatures appear on official documents and formal papers signed as president, and 99 percent of all other examples in this form should be questioned. Most experts believe that not more than ten and as few as two authentic signed photographs of Lincoln are known to exist. If you understand the man you can certainly believe this to be true. Unfortunately, demand and the lack of significant variation in his handwriting has led to numerous forgeries since his death. Abraham Lincoln was the first president to introduce "Executive Mansion" stationery (octavo sheets). Collectors are advised to consult an expert before making any Lincoln autograph purchase. Common form: "A. Lincoln."

Andrew Johnson

Johnson assumed the office following the death of Abraham Lincoln, but although Johnson believed in the former president's policies, he lacked the efficiency and skills to fulfill them. His conflict with radical Republicans led to his impeachment. Following his term in office he was again elected to the Senate, which he had previously served in from 1957 to 1862. Johnson was also a former member of the House of Representatives (1843-54) and Governor of Tennessee (1853-57). Johnson's handwritten letters are typically routine and short in length, due to his lack of education and bad right arm, but nevertheless they're in demand because of their scarcity. He also used secretaries, his son and even a rubber stamp to fulfill the demand for his signature. Commissions, pardons and land grants typically enter the market and are good sources for an authentic example. While Johnson photographs (c.d.v's) are not common, they have occasionally appeared in the market with an appropriate hefty price tag. Collectors should familiarize themselves with all of Johnson's facsimile signatures before attempting to purchase an authentic example. Some forms, such as franks, were often signed by his son and can be tricky to identify. Common forms: "Andrew Johnson," and occasionally "A. Johnson" or "And. Johnson."

Ulysses S. Grant

The 18th president of the United States, Ulysses S. Grant, formerly "Cadet U.H. Grant," changed his name early in life. Grant's finest handwritten letters were authored during his war years, and as such have remained in demand for decades. A weak cabinet, disorganized policies and corrupt intimate associates scarred much of his presidential legacy. Common in all forms, collectors are most likely to first encounter handwritten letters and signed documents. Although Grant introduced the formal "Executive Mansion" card, no doubt for short and expedient notes, ironically only few examples with signature are known to exist. Signed Grant photographs, both cabinets and c.d.v.'s, also occasionally surface in the market. Near the end of his life he lost his voice and was forced to communicate by notes. Common form: "U.S. Grant."

Rutherford B. Hayes

Although much of his material has found its way into the hands of institutions, the autographed material of Rutherford B. Hayes has never been overly popular with collectors. Some of the institutional draw to artifacts of the Hayes administration has been attributed to interest in his economic recovery, civil service reform, and conciliation of the Southern states. Hayes' handwritten letters typically fill the page, with some variations in legibility. Hayes was also prone to use an occasional underline to emphasize a particular point. Collectors are more apt to encounter the president's signature on handwritten letters or commissions over many other forms. Hayes did occasionally make use of "Executive Mansion" cards for brief notes. Common forms: "R.B.Hayes," "Rutherford B. Hayes."

James A. Garfield

Having been assassinated just four months after taking office, Garfield's term-related letters and documents are extremely scarce. However, fortunately for collectors, his pre-presidential material is quite common in many forms. Numerous fine manuscript signed letters, on House of Representatives letterhead, have found their way into the market, as have a few franks. Garfield did employ a secretary by the name of J. Stanley Brown during the year prior to his election whose handwriting bore a stark resemblance to the president's. Collectors purchasing handwritten material from this era should exercise caution. Garfield is scarce on "Executive Mansion" cards, as well as all other examples authored during his term. Common forms: "J.A. Garfield."

Chester A. Arthur

Perhaps the easiest of all presidential handwriting to identify, Chester Arthur was not an advocate of lifting his pen off the paper once he began writing, therefore most of his words are connected. Non-presidential Arthur material is common, with many handwritten letters found on "Custom House, New York, Collector Office" letterhead or "Law Offices of Arthur, Phelps, Knevals & Ransom" stationery. Of the scarce presidential items collectors are likely to encounter, military appointments seem to be most common, along with signed manuscript letters or cards. The latter is the engraved depiction of the White House, which he introduced in a convenient card format. These cards were in addition to the already used "Executive Mansion" version. Worth noting is that Arthur was the first president to utilize a typewriter as part of his daily routine (1881-1885). He was bedridden in his final months and during this time he ordered all of his public and private papers in his possession to be burned. Common forms: "C. A. Arthur," "Chester A. Arthur."

Grover Cleveland

Both the 22nd and 24th president of the United States, Grover Cleveland was also an assistant district attorney, sheriff, mayor and governor. Although he wrote so small that many of his letters were difficult to read, he was always insightful, formal, polite and often charming. Abundant in many forms, collectors can anticipate finding signed appointments, handwritten letters and even photographs — the most prevalent is the profile bust cabinet photo by Gutekunst of Philadelphia. As president he also used "Executive Mansion" cards, which required a stamp since he never had franking privilege. Cleveland was said to have answered all of his mail personally into his final years, a statement confirmed by the numerous examples I have seen over the years. Cleveland also authored numerous articles for the "Saturday Evening Post" from 1900 to 1906. Common form: "Grover Cleveland."

Benjamin Harrison

Grandson of William Henry Harrison, Benjamin Harrison's pro-protection platform won him his seat as the 23rd president of the United States. Harrison served in the Union army, was active in Grant's presidential campaign, was involved in state politics and was elected a senator for Indiana. His handwriting varied significantly over his lifetime, losing much of its legibility in his later years. Handwritten letters by Harrison are fairly scarce with most pre-presidential on "Porter, Harrison & Fishback, Attorneys at Law" letterhead and signed "Benja. Harrison." Some pre-presidential personal checks drawn from "Fletcher's Bank" in Indianapolis, Ind., have also found their way to the autograph market over the past decade. Unlike Cleveland, signed photographs of Harrison are scarce and may command a significant price. Much of his post-presidential material is in TLS or LS form on his personal stationery: "BENJAMIN HARRISON, 874 NORTH DELAWARE STREET, INDIANAPOLIS, IND." During his retirement he also penned numerous articles for national magazines. Common form: "Benj. Harrison."

William McKinley

McKinley served in congress and was also governor of Ohio before becoming a Republican presidential candidate. Although Cleveland and Harrison were no strangers to the typewriter, McKinley seemed to be the first president truly comfortable with the machine, therefore many pre-presidential TLS's have turned up in the market. Handwritten letters by William McKinley as president are scarce, although some examples before he took office have been available. Collectors will typically encounter authentic signatures of McKinley in document form in the market. These will range from military commissions and appointments to simple appointments as Marshall of the United States. "Executive Mansion" cards and signed photographs can also be found. Common forms: "William McKinley."

Theodore Roosevelt

Despite the lack of gracefulness to his script, this "Roughrider" wrote clear, crisp and forceful letters. A prolific writer, whose handwriting varied little over his lifetime, Roosevelt spent time in the New York Legislature (1884), was president of the New York Police Board (1895-97), assistant secretary of the Navy (1898), governor of New York State (1898-1900) and vice president in 1901, before assuming the presidential office after the assassination of McKinley. His signature habits included the use of a rubber stamp as governor of New York, and he permitted his secretary to sign on his behalf as governor and vice president. While obtainable in all forms, collectors will typically cross paths with his signatures first on typed letters and documents. As president, he changed the format of the "Executive Mansion" cards to "White House" in hopes of presenting a different image. He was the first president to be known popularly by his initials. During 1910-1914 he was associate editor of "Outlook" magazine. The demand for his material has remained strong over the years, while exhibiting some nice price appreciation. Common forms: "Theodore Roosevelt," "T. Roosevelt."

William Howard Taft

The 27th president of the United States, William Howard Taft is perhaps best remembered as the only man to serve time both in the Oval Office and as the chief justice of the U.S. Supreme Court (1921-1930). A prolific man of letters, his material has been common in many forms for years — the only exception is handwritten letters as president and "White House" cards. Many signed photographs, which were initially thought to be scarce, have surfaced from private collections over the years.

These signed photographs depict Taft as both president and chief justice. Ironically, many collectors find his correspondence as chief justice far more interesting and appealing. After leaving the Oval Office, he accepted an appointment as Kent professor of law at Yale University (1913-1921). Since he was the first president to take up golf, keep your eye out for signed scorecards! Common forms: "Wm. H. Taft," and to friends and relatives "Bill," "Bill Taft."

Woodrow Wilson

A gifted wordsmith, who also happened to have legible handwriting, Wilson wrote magnificent letters, particularly early in his life. As his responsibilities increased, so did the demand on his correspondence. He began limiting himself to brief notes, while also seeking solace behind a typewriter. His signed, typed letters will be some of the first examples collectors will encounter in the market, followed by military appointments. As governor of New Jersey and during his run for the office, Wilson resorted to the use of a rubber stamp on correspondence. Wilson's signed photographs do occasionally appear in the market as have a couple of scarce canceled checks from his days at Princeton. Signed "White House" cards are also scarce and the ones that have entered the market have been signed at the top of the card. Following his 1919 stroke, his signature picked up a few slight variations. He was virtually blind in his final years. Common form: "Woodrow Wilson"

Warren G. Harding

An interest in journalism led Warren Harding to purchase the "Marion Star" and as its editor, the paper prospered. The prolific Harding quickly caught the attention of Republican politicians. As a lieutenant governor (1904-06), then senator (1914), he honed his political skills before becoming his party's dark-horse nominee. While he was easily elected to the presidency, the infrastructure of his cabinet was filled with ineptness and corruption. During his rise to prominence, his handwriting varied significantly, losing considerable legibility. While his autographed material is uncommon and even scarce in some forms, the demand for such items has been weak over the past decades. Harding did use a rubber stamp to answer correspondence and even employed a secretary who mimicked his handwriting. After Harding died unexpectedly in San Francisco, his wife burned his papers, which added much speculation as to her reasoning. Common forms: "W.G. Harding," almost always connected, "Warren G. Harding."

Calvin Coolidge

Coolidge was a man who believed that if you don't have anything good to say, well, why bother saying or even writing anything at all. Certainly one of the least profound and insightful presidents, his autographed material has been relatively common and in little demand. He had a knack for filling a page, even if it was far from necessary. His handwritten letters are scarce, as are term-authored documents. Coolidge did have secretaries signing his name, although most are easily distinguished as such. During his retirement he wrote numerous articles for many national magazines. Common form: "Calvin Coolidge."

Herbert Hoover

Common in numerous autographed forms, particularly signed, typed letters, Herbert Hoover will no doubt be one of the first signatures in your presidential collection. Handwritten letters are nearly impossible to acquire, as, according to Hoover himself, he wrote very, very few. While his letters in general were far from interesting, he was a prolific writer who authored many intriguing books. Hoover did authorize his secretary to sign his name, which causes some confusion for collectors who often confuse the facsimile with an authentic signature. "White House" cards are attainable, but not common. Franks are even more difficult to encounter. In his final years he resided often at the Waldorf-Astoria Hotel in New York and was virtually deaf and blind. Common form: "Herbert Hoover."

Franklin D. Roosevelt

Polite, yet platitudinous; amicable, yet aseptic: adjectives that perhaps best characterize Franklin Roosevelt's correspondence, with the only exception being the letters he wrote to intimate friends and relatives. Handwritten letters, particularly as president, are difficult to come by and when you do find one it is typically pre-presidential. Roosevelt also often signed his correspondence with initials only, and since he used proxy signers, many facsimiles can be difficult to distinguish. Roosevelt, also an autograph collector, varied his signature often and even used a rubber stamp as Governor of New York. Although "White House" cards and even "New York Sate" cards were commonly found in the market, they too have dissipated somewhat with the increased interest in the hobby. Common forms: "FDR," "Franklin D. Roosevelt."

Harry S. Truman

If you're just wild about Harry, it probably had little to do with the content of one his letters. Often formulaic, Truman rarely displayed his passionate feelings in written form, but when he did you knew he meant it. Handwritten letters are scarce, and when they do hit the market can command a significant price. Post-presidential typed letters signed have been common for years, with the demand increasing steadily over the past two decades. As senator, Truman authorized secretaries to sign his letters so exercise caution when purchasing material from this era. After the presidency, Truman dated nearly every autograph he signed, which can make for an interesting study on signature variations. Common forms: " Harry Truman," "Harry S. Truman," "HST," presidential memorandums.

Dwight D. Eisenhower

An extremely popular American general and the 34th president of the United States, Dwight Eisenhower has always been popular among autograph collectors. While dictated letters and typed letters signed have been generally available, those handwritten by "Ike" have not. The only exception is an occasional letter he wrote to his wife. Signed photographs, particularly those of him in uniform, seem never to fill the demand, while routine presidential poses meet with less appeal. Eisenhower was the first president to introduce facsimile signatures on "White House" cards and thankfully they were identified as such on the back of the card. A lot of war-dated correspondence bears secretarial signatures, so collectors beware! Common form: Dwight D. Eisenhower," "D.E.," to friends, "Ike" very rare, other than to his wife.

John F. Kennedy

Books have been written about the signature habits of John F. Kennedy, who is by far the most unpredictable signature in history. The irony, of course, is that Kennedy himself was an autograph collector. His signature was unpredictable — inconsistent in slant, character formation, signature breaks, etc. The only consistent element to his signature is the numerous machine-signed patterns, secretarial facsimiles and forgeries. Because the demand for authentic Kennedy material has always been high and the variables in his signature numerous, he has constantly been a target for forgeries. Even the finest handwriting experts in the country have been deceived by forgeries; therefore, collectors are at an incredible risk when purchasing his material. Handwritten letters are scarce as are examples found on "Air Force One" stationery. Collectors will typically encounter typed letters signed, signed photographs, or a variety of examples signed while Kennedy was campaigning. While some pre-presidential material was dictated, JFK often felt obligated to add a handwritten postscript. His prolific use of the autopen has frustrated many a collector. Those of you who wish to find further information on the device should purchase a copy of Charles Hamilton's book "The Robot That Helped to Make a President." Doodles and notes from Kennedy have also found their way to the market, but they, too, are difficult to authenticate. Common forms: "John Kennedy."

Lyndon B. Johnson

Following Kennedy's assassination, Johnson carried out many of JFK's policies including his philosophy on correspondence. Secretary-signed, machine-signed and facsimile examples of Johnson's signature are common in the market. Authentic Johnson signatures are scarcer than what collectors first thought. Post-presidential items found in the market are often dictated letters signed by "LBJ." Collectors wishing to purchase an authentic Johnson example might best turn to signed books or photographs. The lack of interest in his autographed material over the past two decades seems to be dissipating somewhat as more information regarding his administration becomes declassified. Johnson's image has as been enhanced greatly by the release of many of his taped phone conversations. Common forms: "Lyndon B. Johnson," "Lyndon" "LBJ."

Richard M. Nixon

Authentic letters from the first President to submit his resignation are scarce, with the few that have surfaced being from his later years. Secretarial and Autopen samples are common, particularly on "White House" cards. Most authentic signed pieces from his presidency have been with his initials. Collectors wishing to complete a set, may want to turn to a signed book authored by Nixon after leaving office. Common forms: "R. Nixon" early, "Richard Nixon," "R.N.," and "Dick" or "Dick Nixon" to friends.

Gerald R. Ford

Following the resignation of vice-president Spiro Agnew in October 1973, Ford was appointed his replacement. Ford then became president in August of 1974, when Nixon resigned. Gerald R. Ford had previously been a member of the House of Representatives (1949-73), and became minority leader in 1965. Like all modern presidents, Ford made extensive use of the autopen and secretarial signatures. While his handwritten letters are scarce, a few do occasionally enter the market. Collectors will most likely run across authentic signed photographs or books before any other forms. Common forms: "Gerald R. Ford," "Gerald Ford," and "Jerry," or "Jerry Ford" to friends.

Jimmy Carter

By the time Jimmy Carter was elected to office, machines were being created that could reproduce an entire handwritten letter. Both machine-generated and secretarial facsimiles of Carter's signature are commonly found in the market. Carter remains scarce in authentic handwritten letters, which typically began with a "To" salutation. Carter, who has become an outstanding humanitarian and prolific author, is probably best to obtain in a signed book form to complete a collection. Common forms: "Jimmy," "Jimmy Carter," "J. Carter" later.

Ronald Reagan

Former television and film star Ronald Reagan first became interested in politics while serving as president of the Screen Actors Guild (1947-52). As governor of California (1966-1974), he became increasingly popular and it was of little surprise that he had greater political aspirations. As both a film star and politician, Reagan utilized proxy signers. As the 40th president of the United States he signed very little, opting instead for all the now-accepted alternatives. Fortunately for collectors, Reagan was passionate about maintaining old relationships through handwritten correspondence, many examples of which found their way into the autograph market. Most of these are warm and friendly in content and often signed "RR," "Ron," or "Dutch". A few of his handwritten drafts as governor have also appeared in the market, and typically have a red slash drawn across the sheet to indicate that they have been typed in final form. Despite this alteration — a commonly accepted office procedure — these drafts are also extremely popular with collectors. Common forms: "Ronald Reagan."

George Bush

Before joining Reagan on the successful Republican ticket in 1980, Bush served in the House of Representatives (1966), as American ambassador to the United Nations (1971-73), Republican national chairman (1973-74), special envoy to China (1974-75), then director of the CIA (1976). While Bush is common in authentic post-presidential forms, many of his pre-presidential signatures are secretarial or autopenned. As president, all authentic forms are scarce. Bush seems to have always had a passion for note cards and as president even introduced a new form. Since leaving office he has even done private signings for dealers, thus his material is readily available to collectors. Common forms: "George Bush," "George."

Bill Clinton

The man who envied "Camelot" as a youngster, is now plagued by "Scandalot" as president. Despite the adversity, William Jefferson Clinton remains incredibly popular. In person he has always been charismatic, charming and even warm toward autograph requests; however, by mail it is a completely different story. Since the president receives about 15,000 letters a day, it's not hard to understand why he can't comply with all autograph requests. Clinton has always made excellent use of machine-signed signatures and it is likely that he will continue. Like most modern presidents it will take a few years out of office before a variety of material will surface in the marketplace. Common forms: "Bill Clinton," "Bill."

U.S. PRESIDENTS - Washington to Carter	
Ranking by Price Appreciation of Material, 1978-1998 *	
Most Appreciation	Least Appreciation
1. U.S. Grant	1. G. Ford
2. J. Tyler	2. L.B. Johnson
3. B. Harrison	3. J. Carter
4. A. Johnson	4. R. Nixon
5. F. Pierce	5. W. Harding

U.S. PRESIDENTS - Washington to Carter	
Ranking by Price Appreciation of Material, 1978-1998 *	
Most Appreciation	**Least Appreciation**
6. T. Roosevelt	6. W. Wilson
7. F. D. Roosevelt	7. C. Arthur
8. M. Van Buren	8. R. B. Hayes
9. H. Truman	9. D. D. Eisenhower
10. M. Fillmore	10. C. Coolidge

U.S. PRESIDENTS - Washington to Carter	
Ranking by Price Appreciation, Form - Sig., 1978-1998 *	
Most Appreciation	**Least Appreciation**
1. U. S. Grant	1. W. Harding
2. T. Jefferson	2. L. B. Johnson
3. F. Pierce	3. J. Carter
4. W. H. Harrison	4. G. Ford
5. A. Lincoln	5. W. Wilson
6. J. Tyler	6. R. Nixon
7. M. Van Buren	7. C. Arthur
8. A. Jackson	8. J. Madison
9. A. Johnson	9. J. Polk
10. B. Harrison	10. H. Hoover

U.S. PRESIDENTS - Washington to Carter	
Ranking by Price Appreciation, Form - LS/DS, 1978-1998 *	
Most Appreciation	**Least Appreciation**
1. F. D. Roosevelt	1. G. Ford
2. U. S. Grant	2. J. Carter
3. T. Roosevelt	3. L. B. Johnson
4. H. Truman	4. R. Nixon
5. J. Tyler	5. A. Lincoln
6. M. Van Buren	6. M. Van Buren
7. H. Hoover	7. W. Wilson

U.S. PRESIDENTS - Washington to Carter	
Ranking by Price Appreciation, Form - LS/DS, 1978-1998 *	
Most Appreciation	Least Appreciation
8. M. Fillmore	8. C. Arthur
9. B. Harrison	9. G. Washington
10. Z. Taylor	10. J. Polk

U.S. PRESIDENTS - Washington to Carter	
Ranking by Price Appreciation, Form - ALS, 1978-1998 *	
Most Appreciation	Least Appreciation
1. U. S. Grant	1. G. Ford
2. A. Johnson	2. L. B. Johnson
3. J. Adams	3. J. Carter
4. B. Harrison	4. C. Coolidge
5. J. Tyler	5. R. Nixon
6. T. Jefferson	6. F. D. Roosevelt
7. F. Pierce	7. W. McKinley
8. J. Buchanan	8. D. Eisenhower
9. M. Fillmore	9. H. Hoover
10. J. Garfield	10. R. B. Hayes

*Sig., DS/LS, ALS; no SP
Source: This book's database.

15
Politicians, Educators, Reformers, Lawyers & Labor Leaders

Although it seems an awkward title for this unstable area, this subject it an intriguing part of the autograph market. Autograph value increases tend to migrate toward very key contributors to their fields, such as Clarence Darrow to the legal profession, and Susan B. Anthony to temperance, anti-slavery and women's suffrage movements. In the area of politicians, considerable speculation has always revolved around individuals who may be future United States presidents.

With the advent of television and certainly Court TV, the names of numerous prominent attorneys are becoming household words and these people have risen to near-celebrity status. Take F. Lee Bailey, Melvin Belli, Robert Shapiro and Gloria Allred, for instance. As a society, we have done much to badmouth this profession, but we have also become intrigued by its participants.

"So as our society goes, so does the autograph hobby." If you look at the signatures of educators and the lack of interest we have for education, some parallels could certainly be drawn. In an era and area where educators seldom reach celebrity status, we do occasionally recognize the enormous achievements of some of these individuals, such as Marva Collins. An overlooked area on all accounts, certainly, but it may be a terrific area and a great opportunity for you to focus your autograph collecting.

Ironically, as a labor leader you don't always have to turn up missing in order for your autograph to be worth something. In fact, this area has done very well over the past two decades. As with the other fields, content and relevance means everything to the appreciation of an autographed item. A picket sign, autographed by AFL-CIO boss George Meany, is obviously more valuable than a simple signed index card.

The autographs of women and minority contributors to these fields have also shown significant appreciation and interest. This area should continue to exhibit significant and consistent price gains over the next decade. If it pleases the court, then this niche of the hobby should please you also!

16
Justices of the Supreme Court of The United States

While not everyone who collects autographs is familiar with the names George Shiras, Jr., Levi Woodbury, and Wiley B. Rutledge, many Supreme Court justices' names do seem to ring a bell. Do the names William Howard Taft, Oliver Wendell Holmes, Jr., and Thurgood Marshall sound familiar? This unique group is actually quite fascinating once you delve beneath the surface and begin exploring the backgrounds of the more than 100 very diverse individuals who have served our country with the utmost dedication.

These individuals have had the monumental task of interpreting the U.S. Constitution, a document that was written — in many cases — decades before they were even born. What this precious document means and doesn't mean is in their hands. From abortion to executive privilege, the Supreme Court is the final stop for the most controversial legal decisions our country faces. In some cases an individual's entire reputation as a Supreme Court justice can be associated with a single controversial ruling of a case. For example, Roger B. Taney is often the first name mentioned when the fateful Dred Scott v. Sanford decision of 1857 resurfaces. Taney, who wrote the decision, was actually blamed by many for starting the Civil War. Can you imagine having nearly three decades of dedicated service summarized by a single decision?

Taney is not alone, however. Charles Evan Hughes is often cited as the man who lost the presidency by a narrow margin to Woodrow Wilson, and William Howard Taft is typically labeled a former president. While justices can both agree and disagree, both decisions can also have a lasting impact. Oliver Wendell Holmes, Jr., Louis Brandeis, John Marshall Harlan and Earl Warren all made history with their dissents.

Entire eras of a country's history have often been associated with the name of the chief justice, the Marshall Court, the Warren Court and the Burger Court. Yet ironically, the chief justice, who presides over the Court, has only an equal vote. Nine justices, all with equal votes.

While many of these unique individuals share law as a similar fascination, most have backgrounds in stark contrast to one another. They come from all walks of life, from all areas of this great land, raised from families of diverse economic, ethnic and religious backgrounds. William Johnson was the son of a blacksmith, Joseph P. Bradley was born into a very large and poor agricultural family, and Samuel F. Miller was a medical doctor for nearly a decade before he turned toward the bar. Other justices simply migrated from other areas of the legal system, Harold H. Burton came from the U.S. senate and Earl Warren was a former governor.

As our country evolved, the Supreme Court echoed those changes. Roger B. Taney became the first Catholic justice, Thurgood Marshall was the first African-American justice and Sandra Day O'Conner our first woman to hold the office. In addition to these firsts, which are always intriguing to autograph collectors, the length of service and the age a justice begins to serve are also important. Thomas Johnson had the shortest term, while William O. Douglas had his sights on longevity — 36 years, 7 months. William Johnson and Joseph Story were just 32 years of age when they put their robes on, while Horace Lurton was 65. While there are no age restrictions for either appointment or retirement, there are also no qualifications to meet for appointment. Essentially, there is no job description.

While some justices were political, such as those of the 19th century, generally our modern-day participants refrain from partisan activity. Similar to our presidents, their diverse backgrounds — from the military to medicine — have contributed to some very intriguing and thought-provoking views. Just like the men who have appointed them, Supreme Court justices vary considerably in their writing habits and the content that fills the page. Oliver Ellsworth hated to write anything, while William Strong was a skilled wordsmith whose correspondence can be fascinating.

Collecting an entire set of signatures on official stationery, or about a specific legal viewpoint, can present collectors with a significant challenge. Many therefore begin a Supreme Court collection with just the signatures of the chief justices. Other popular methods involve correspondence around a particular case associated with the justice or a form, such as a signature on a "Chambers" card. Naturally, those justices who have had significant public careers lend themselves to more diverse forms of collecting. Earlier justices rode circuit and were far less formal with correspondence than a modern-day appointee. Occasionally even an informal note, perhaps to a familiar face in the audience during an argument, surfaces in the market. And, since many prestigious lawyers were often familiar faces in front of the court, it is rare, but not unheard of for such pleasantries to be exchanged.

Many collectors prefer photographs signed by the entire court, most of which can be found in the market dating back to the Chase Court. In some instances photographs may not be available. For example, in 1924 no official group photograph was taken because James C. McReynolds refused to sit next to Louis D. Brandeis. McReynolds' personal behavior during his tenure was often controversial. Since 1900, virtually everything imaginable has been signed by one justice or another, however, judicial papers are, of course, sacred. While it was customary to destroy the judicial papers of a justice upon death, this tradition slowly gave way to the university or institution donation concept. For security reasons certain papers will have restricted access. Collectors may want to contact The Supreme Court Historical Society for further information on this topic.

During the past twenty years all but three market segments — royalty, Signers of the Declaration of Independence and Colonial and Revolutionary Leaders — have outperformed Supreme Court Justices in terms of value. While it is considered a stable market, based on my analysis, its anticipated value variation of 34.84 (all forms minus SP) indicates that the hobby isn't as familiar with the pricing in various forms as one might think. This can be verified with a quick glance through dealer catalogs over the past five to ten years. The greatest increases in form have been handwritten letters, outperforming the DS/LS category by nearly twofold. This market is clearly driven by the autographs of the greatest justices, such as Oliver Wendell Holmes, Jr., and John Marshall. Collectors participating in this are advised to consult many different dealers, for on a given day I have been quoted prices that have varied by as much as 200 percent for very similar items!

Completing a full set of autographs from the Supreme Court, similar to Signers, has its fair share of elusive subjects. James Iredell and Howell E. Jackson come to mind as they were short-termed. Alfred Moore is nearly impossible, while Robert Trimble, John McKinley and Thomas Todd can also be incredibly difficult to find. Forgeries in this area thus far have been scarce, however, it always better to be safe than sorry. For those of you who wish to start an autograph collection, this area is a terrific place to begin. Case closed!

17
Religious Leaders/Clergy

Since the existence of mankind as a civilization, religion has played a paramount role in people's lives. While the definition of a "religious" manuscript or autograph is often vague — as it could include parchment, papyrus, cloth, paper and even stone — most tend to limit the term to our modern era. Since many of our earliest religious texts are considered sacred, most have found permanent homes in museums (Vatican, the British Library, the Boodleian, etc.), shrines, or institutions and it is highly unlikely that they would ever be found in a public sale.

While documents such as the Dead Sea Scrolls, found in 1947, are not likely to face the autograph market, the letters of popes, saints, cardinals and numerous other eminent religious personages do. Renaissance popes have enjoyed some level of interest, as have many popular modern day religious leaders.

Looking through noted dealer Steven S. Raab Autograph catalogs (#20), one could find a fine signature of Cardinal John Henry Newman offered for $195, a bank check from Elijah Muhammad, founder of the Nation of Islam, for $225 and even a large signed photo of Albanian nun Mother Teresa for $450.

While the appreciation in value of signatures of religious leaders and figures has been significant, it was far from that of other areas. The lack of substantive material and interest in this area has affected this niche. Should significant material find its way into the market, it might be a perfect opportunity to buy!

18
The Infamous

Controversy sells, as do the autographs of the controversial. The infamous have always intrigued historians. How ironic it is that in our civilized world, a signature of a cold-blooded murderer is worth more than their victim. A comparable letter from Lee Harvey Oswald can command twice as much as President John F. Kennedy's. Granted Kennedy, a popular public figure, signed his name far more often that Oswald, but considering the sheer prominence of the presidency, many would still be surprised.

Fundamental issues in collecting the infamous are authenticity, availability and even risk. Few authentic examples of many infamous people are even known to exist, while others are so rare that they seldom enter the market. Complicating the issue has also been the signing habits of the incarcerated, which can also be extremely volatile. While a few of the infamous are prolific, most are not. Individuals such as the serial killer Jeffrey Dahmer rarely, if at all, answered mail. He did however, like many inmates, have to sign numerous legal and mandatory prison forms. While some of these documents have found there way into the autograph market, they are extremely scarce. Risk is also a consideration when contacting some of the infamous, particularly incarcerated murderers and felons. While maximum security prisons have been enormously successful in holding inmates, the thought of an exception with your address can't be too comforting.

Many of the infamous are in the spotlight only briefly; therefore, the demand for their signature can have radical fluctuations. Pricing in this area has also been highly subjective over the years, with many major dealers differing in opinion regarding the scarcity of an item. Collectors are advised to exercise caution when pursuing subjects and materials in this area. Also, don't be surprised when an officer of the law pays your residence or place of employment a visit. Although you know that your intentions are sincere and are only in the pursuit of an autograph, a sheriff or a FBI agent may not.

19
First Ladies

History is living proof that behind every good United States president has been a charming "first lady," and if you were smart, over the past twenty years you would have spent more time acquiring her signature than that of the Chief Executive. In fact signatures (Sig.) of these distinguished women have outpaced the autographs of the presidency by nearly twofold. As an entity in the autograph market, signatures of the first ladies have outpaced all but four popular areas of collecting.

While this may or may not be a shock to you, further research into this segment can support such claims. Similar to the presidents, the popularity of the first lady varies with each administration, as do her signing habits. While some have been prolific, such as Eleanor Roosevelt, others have been reclusive. While the ratification of the 19th Amendment in 1920, which gave U.S. women the right to vote, may have added a new dimension to the position of first lady, the impact of the charm, sophistication, and elegance of those who have filled this position has done much more.

Administration-dated autograph material has only genuinely impacted the value of Jacqueline Kennedy and Eleanor Roosevelt correspondence. Whether or not this slow trend will continue, or migrate into other administrations, remains to be seen. But since it has been so distinct (in the case of Jacqueline Kennedy alone the price increased about twofold), it is my guess this trend will continue.

Not all presidential widows were granted the franking privilege. In fact, Mrs. Lincoln was so disliked by congress, that it took her years for approval. On Dec. 18, 1973, congress finally permitted every living presidential widow to have the franking privilege.

Similar to their husbands, many first ladies utilized the services of machines to sign their name. Both Betty Ford and Pat Nixon were notorious for having their correspondence machine signed.

A Brief Overview of First Ladies

Washington, Martha Dandridge Custis

Martha was a widow of a prominent planter Daniel Parke Custis. She was a gracious hostess and first lady. Her signature is scarce in all forms.

Adams, Abigail Smith

A prolific writer, Abigail corresponded often with her husband during the Revolution. As the first lady she was the first to preside over the White House. Although thousands of her letters are known to exist, few find their way into the autograph market.

Jefferson, Martha Wayles Skelton

Few, if any, written examples exist. She died 19 years before her husband's term as president.

Madison, Dorothea "Dolley" Payne Todd

A widow, Dolley Payne Todd met Thomas Jefferson through a mutual friend, Aaron Burr. Charming and vivacious, she occasionally served as official hostess during the Jefferson administration. After her husband's death at Montpelier, she returned to Washington and its social circuit. To pay her creditors she sold Madison's papers to congress.

Monroe, Elizabeth Kortright

Elizabeth Kortright was the daughter of an officer in the British army. As first lady she suffered from an unidentified chronic ailment that forced her into seclusion. Her eldest daughter, Eliza often acted for her as official hostess. Elizabeth, in stark contrast to Dolley Madison, did nothing to cultivate the Washington social circuit, and as such was unpopular and reclusive. Her writings in any form are considered scarce.

Adams, Louisa Catherine

Louisa Adams, the only foreign-born first lady, suffered from numerous physical problems including migraine headaches and bouts with depression. Similar to her predecessor she became withdrawn and reclusive. Although she was a prolific journal writer, she seemed to correspond only to close friends.

Jackson, Rachel Donelson Robards

Rachel Jackson was a controversial, popular, and dynamic woman. She suffered from heart trouble and her sudden death in 1828 seemed to have been brought about by her and husband's battles with the press over her controversial past.

Van Buren, Hannah Hoes

Shy and occasionally withdrawn, Hannah Hoes Van Buren contracted tuberculosis and died at the young age of 35. Her writings in any form are considered extremely scarce!

Harrison, Anna Tuthill Symmes

An extremely intelligent woman, Anna Harrison was the only woman to be the wife of one president and the grandmother of another. Because of her husband's sudden death she never occupied the White House, and became the first recipient of a president's widow pension.

Tyler, Letitia Christian

Devoted to her family, Letitia Tyler was quiet, shy and often withdrawn. She suffered a paralytic stroke in 1839 that left her an invalid. Her first lady duties were confined to the upstairs quarters of the White House where she remained a recluse.

Tyler, Julia Gardiner

Julia Tyler, in stark contrast to her predecessor, was a young and vivacious first lady who adored her social role in Washington.

Polk, Sarah Childress

Charming and intelligent, yet conservative, Sarah Polk welcomed her role as first lady. In her role, Sarah hosted the first Thanksgiving dinner at the White House.

Taylor, Margaret Mackall Smith

A reclusive first lady, "Peggy" Taylor was a semi-invalid who found solace in the confines of the second floor of the White House. Her daughter, Mrs. Betty Bliss, attended to the role of official hostess. Perhaps the scarcest of all first lady signatures, less than a handful are known to exist.

Fillmore, Abigail Powers

Abigail Fillmore was a teacher and former instructor of her husband. The Fillmores shared a love for books and were responsible for the establishment of the first permanent library at the White House. Susceptible to sickness, her role as first lady was often filled by her daughter. Little autographed material of hers has found its way into the market, no doubt because much of it was burned.

Fillmore, Caroline McIntosh

Caroline Fillmore was the widow of a prominent businessman. She married and settled with the former president in Buffalo, New York. Her autograph is scarce in all forms.

Pierce, Jane Means Appleton

Shy and somewhat melancholy, Jane Pierce became depressed and reclusive following the death of her son Bennie in 1853. Resentful of her husband's ambition, the two were often at odds with one another. She withdrew from the role of first lady and opted for the seclusion of the upstairs quarters at the White House for nearly two years. Some letters occasionally surface exhibiting a deteriorating script due to old age.

(Buchanan) Lane (Johnston), Harriet

President Buchanan did not marry, and the role of the first lady was given to his orphaned niece, Harriet Lane. Occasional letters do surface but she is considered scarce in all forms.

Lincoln, Mary Todd

Although she was personable, popular and articulate, Mary Lincoln suffered mental instability throughout her life. Her irrational behavior, no doubt enhanced by the death of two of her sons, led to hallucinations and commitment to a mental institution. She was a prolific letter writer, but few find their way into the autograph market.

Johnson, Eliza McCardle

Marrying at a younger age than any other first lady, Eliza Johnson became a semi-invalid in middle age. Too ill to handle the role of first lady, she joined her husband at the White House, but remained in a room on the second floor. She appeared publicly on only two occasions. Her autograph is scarce in all forms.

Grant, Julia Boggs Dent

Julia Grant loved the role of first lady and entertained lavishly at the White House. Her letters routinely surface in the autograph market.

Hayes, Lucy Ware Webb

An extremely active first lady, Lucy Hayes was the first in her position to have graduated from college. "Lemonade Lucy" was active in the temperance movement and instituted the customary White House Easter egg roll. Her autographs also surface routinely in the market.

Garfield, Lucretia Rudolph

Lucretia "Crete" Garfield was a teacher whose appetite for knowledge seemed endless. Her plans to restore the White House and its furnishings ended when she contracted malaria. She became withdrawn following her husband's assassination. Her autographs do surface in many forms in the autograph market.

Arthur, Ellen Lewis Herndon

Ellen "Nell" Arthur, daughter of a distinguished naval officer, had a passion for music that was hampered often by her poor health. She died of pneumonia at the young age of 42. She didn't live long enough to see her husband become president. Her autograph in any form is scarce as most were destroyed.

Cleveland, Frances Folsom

Frances Cleveland was the only first lady married in the White House, the youngest ever in her role, the only first lady to preside at two nonconsecutive administrations, and the first presidential widow to remarry. Among first ladies in check form, she is perhaps the most common.

Harrison, Caroline Lavina Scott

Caroline Harrison renovated the White House, installed electricity and even put up the first Christmas tree in her new residence. Her signature is scarce in all forms.

Harrison, Mary Scott Lord

A widow, Mary Harrison married the former president and survived him by nearly a half century. Her signature can be found periodically in the autograph market.

McKinley, Ida Saxton

Polished and charming, Ida McKinley developed epilepsy and became fully dependent on her husband. As an invalid she passed time by sewing. Her first lady role fell to that of the wife of the vice president, Mrs. Garret Hobart. Her signature occasionally surfaces in frank form or on mourning stationery.

Roosevelt, Alice Hathaway Lee

Intelligent and charming, Alice Roosevelt died from Bright's disease and childbirth complications at the young age of 22. Her signature in any form is incredibly scarce.

Roosevelt, Edith Kermit Carow

Edith Roosevelt, had a gift for organization and used it to remodel the White House. Her signature is found periodically in the autograph market.

Taft, Helen Herron

Helen "Nellie" Taft was the first wife of a president to ride alongside him down Pennsylvania Avenue on Inauguration Day. The Washington Tidal Basin is also a monument to her memory as it was she who arranged for the planting of 3,000 Japanese cherry trees. Two months into Taft's term, she suffered a stroke that greatly impaired her speech. She is the only woman to be the wife of both a president and Supreme Court justice. Examples of her signature in numerous forms periodically can be found in the autograph market.

Wilson, Ellen Louise Axson

Cultured in the fine arts, Ellen Wilson spent many hours in an art studio set up on the third floor of the White House. She succumbed to Bright's disease at the White House in 1914. Relatively scarce in all autograph forms.

Wilson, Edith Bolling Galt

A gallant example during World War I, Edith Wilson was a respected and active first lady. Following the president's stroke in 1919, she became pivotal in his recovery and essential as his "office manager." (She screened his work.) Her post-White House correspondence surfaces periodically in the market.

Harding, Florence King De Wolfe

Florence "Flossie" Harding, with her somewhat "rough edges," managed to be an effective circulation manager for her husband's successful newspaper. As first lady she hosted elegant parties and felt comfortable mingling with guests, all the while living through a rough marriage. Her autographs can be found on visiting cards and on typed letters.

Coolidge, Grace Anna Goodhue

Well-educated and charming, Grace Coolidge was a popular hostess, effective first lady and altruistic in her crusading on behalf of the deaf and the Red Cross. Her autograph is common in all forms.

Hoover, Lou Henry

Multilingual, intelligent, charming and often spontaneous, Lou Hoover was an effective first lady. She was always gracious to autograph collectors.

Roosevelt, Anna Eleanor Roosevelt

One of the most loved and respected first ladies, Eleanor Roosevelt was well-educated, articulate and extremely active in government affairs. When her husband was stricken with polio, she became the cornerstone to his recovery. She transformed the role of first lady to a role of substance over distinction. Her signature is available in numerous forms, especially TLS, and is abundant in the autograph market.

Truman, Elizabeth Virginia "Bess"

Reluctantly accepting the role of first lady, during a time when we were at war and the White House was under repair, Bess Truman toned down much of the activities held in tradition by previous administrations. When she died at the age of 97, she was the longest living first lady. She was always extremely gracious to autograph collectors.

Eisenhower, Mamie Geneva Doud

Private, gracious and conforming, Mamie Eisenhower effectively carried out the role of first lady. She was a guarded woman, and occasionally reluctant to autograph requests.

Kennedy, Jacqueline Lee Bouvier

Intelligent, graceful, sophisticated and articulate, Jacqueline Kennedy was one of the most popular first ladies. She remodeled the White House, became a fashion trendsetter and created the "Camelot" ambiance and legacy of the Kennedy administration. As her popularity transcended all the previous bounds for her position, she was hounded by the media and in particular the tabloid photographers. Since her death, everything she owned, touched, gave away or wrote has become collectible. She often wrote brief handwritten notes of appreciation to acquaintances, many of which have found there way into the autograph market.

Johnson, Claudia "Lady Bird" Alta Taylor

A very active and intelligent first lady, Lady Bird Johnson campaigned on behalf of the beautification of America. She fought gallantly against poverty and numerous other issues while creating "an island of peace" at the White House. Although subdued in her later years, she spent much of her life happily complying to request for her signature.

Nixon, Thelma Catherine Patricia Ryan*

A gifted actor and teacher, Pat Nixon promoted certain issues as first lady, but for the most part avoided publicity. Although not reluctant, she was somewhat elusive toward autograph requests.

Ford, Elizabeth Bloomer Warren "Betty"*

A gifted dancer and model, Betty Ford tackled many issues as first lady. From the liberalization of abortion laws to the Equal Rights Amendment, she was always direct and candid with her feelings. Forever linked to the Betty Ford Clinic, the premier chemical dependency recovery center, she is certainly one of the most outspoken of all the first ladies. She is approachable and extremely warm to autograph requests.

Carter, Rosalynn Smith*

From interior decorating to keeping the books for the peanut business, Rosalynn Carter was an intelligent and active voice for the president. She testified before congress on behalf of improved funding for mental health programs and fought alongside her husband on numerous humanitarian issues. In recent years, her patience toward autograph seekers has worn thin.

Reagan, Anne Frances "Nancy" R. Davis*

A gifted actress, Nancy Reagan returned opulence to the White House, while playing a pivotal but subdued role as first lady. Her flair for fashion and formality, while in contrast to her predecessors, became a distinct part of her legacy. She has always been reluctant and elusive toward autograph seekers.

Bush, Barbara Pierce*

Intellectual, candid, organized and energetic, Barbara Bush turned attention away from the first lady and toward the issues. Literacy and the plight of the homeless became the key benefactors from her role as first lady. She remains a prolific writer and is extremely warm to autograph requests.

Clinton, Hillary Rodham*

The first lawyer to become First Lady, Hillary Clinton is a strategic thinker of tremendously high intellect. She has been active in campaigning for the rights of America's children, while also fighting for other issues, such as national health care reform. She has been somewhat guarded and elusive to autograph requests.

*Made extensive use of machine-signed signatures.

Size References For Autographs

Duodecimo

Often designated as 12mo - approximately 3" by 4" or half octavo

Sextodecimo

Often designated as 16mo - approximately 1-1/2" x 2" or 1/4 octavo

Octavo

Often designated as 8vo - 5" x 7" to 6" x 9"

Quarto

Often designated as 4vo - 7" x 9" to 9" x 12"

Folio

Often designated as fol. - 12" x 16", legal stationery

Giant Folio

Four to eight times as large as the folio size

Elephant or Atlas Folio

Terms used to designate very large sheets or pages

Pricing Categories

The Four Basic Pricing Categories

SIG

A signature in its most basic form, on an index card, trimmed from a letter or simply one removed from an autograph album. While it may or may not be accompanied by an additional date, place or title, only the title's addition — particularly in reference to the military — typically adds value to the signature.

LS/DS

A letter (LS) or document (DS), not penned by the subject, only signed. Prior to the advent of enhanced writing devices such as the typewriter, personal secretaries, clerks and even relatives often prepared this form for a subject's signature. A typed letter signed (TLS) would fall into this category, as would many routine documents. Stock certificates do not fall into this category.

ALS

An "autograph letter signed" is one entirely written and signed by the subject — a handwritten letter. At times dealers have included the abbreviation (ANS) — a note signed — as part of this category, but typically these are well below the normal value.

SP

A signed photograph. Vintage photographs, as well as those depicting the subject in a significant role (particularly in the entertainment niche), are of additional value. Military collectors are also partial to signed photographs of officers in uniform and in battle, both of which can add additional value. Opera collectors also prefer signed photographs of artists in key roles.

Note:

The prices quoted in this volume are retail prices. When selling to a dealer, anticipate about half of book value. Many dealers give preferred pricing to regular customers. The prices indicated here are based on the extensive database that I had to create for the foundation of this book, my knowledge of the market, the world's most extensive autograph resource library and public domain information. For additional pricing information, consult other price guides. While all the listings and prices have been checked for accuracy, the author and publisher cannot be responsible for any errors that may have occurred, nor for any losses or profits that may be incurred while using this book.

Abbreviations

AA — Auction Item

ADC — Aide-de-camp

AMQS — A Musical Quotation Signed

ANS — Autographed Note Signed

AOC — Articles of Confederation

AOTP — Army of the Potomac

APT — Appointment

BB — Signed Basketball

BC — Bank Check or Business Card

CC — Continental Congress

CEO — Chief Executive Officer

CSA — Confederate States of America

D — Daughters

d. — Deceased, Year

DOI — Declaration of Independence

ESPV — Exhibits Significant Pricing Variation

F — Featherweight

FA — Forgery/Facsimile Alert

FB — Signed Football

FE/SB — First Edition Signed Book

FF — Free Frank

FHTE — From Here to Eternity

GWTW — Gone With the Wind

H — Heavyweight

HOF — Hall of Fame, Induction Year

IAWL — It's a Wonderful Life

KIA — Killed in Action

KS — Key Signature

KW — Korean War

L — Lightweight

LG — Land Grant

MA — Military Appointment

MAW — Mexican American War

Mhelm — Signed Mini Helmet

MW — Moonwalker

NYPL — New York Public Library

PD — Presidential Term-dated

RS — Responsive Signer

S — Sons

SALS — Significant Autographed Letter Signed

SA/CD — Signed Album or CD

SB — Signed Book

SB (sports section) — Signed Baseball

Sbat — Signed Bat

SC — Supreme Court

SDS — Significant Document Signed

SG — Signed Boxing Glove

SL — State Legislature

SPC — Signed Postcard

Spuck — Signed Hockey Puck

SS — Secretary Signed

TGOW — The Grapes of Wrath

TWOO — The Wizard of Oz

TLS — Typed Letter Signed

TS — Typed Script

USHR — United States House of Representatives

USS — United States Senate

VP — Vice president

W1812 — War of 1812

WD — War-dated

WHCC — White House Christmas Card

WH/EMC — White House or Executive Mansion Card

WP — West Point

* — Fought in various other campaigns

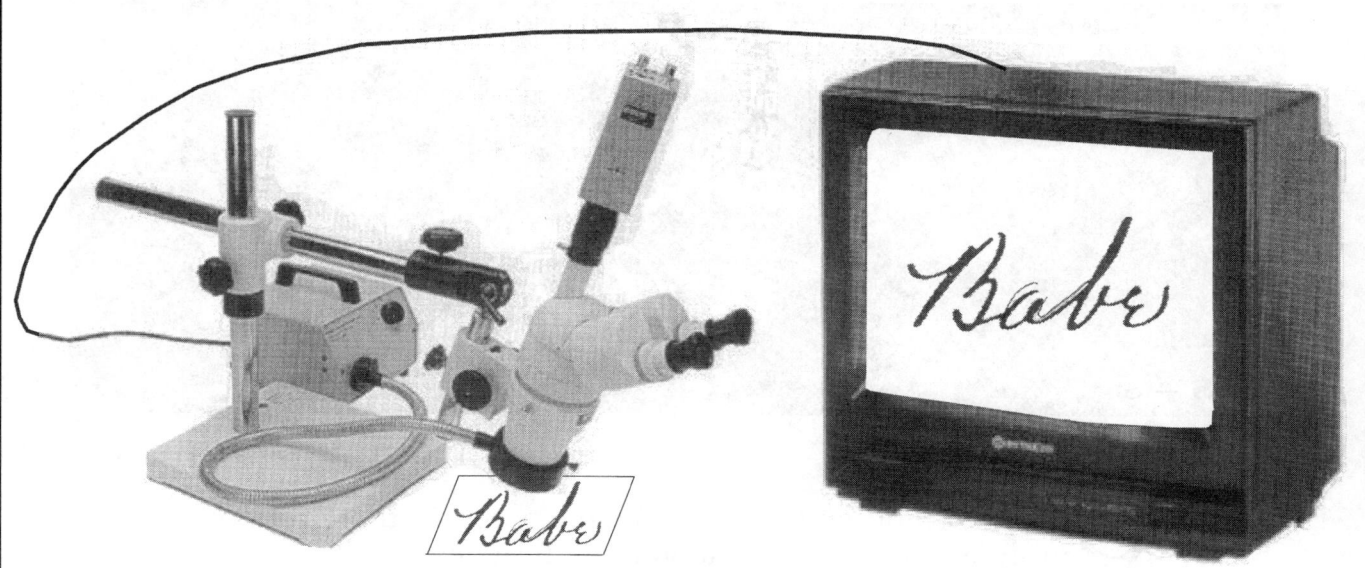

THE 1ST TIME IN HOBBY HISTORY

THAT YOU WILL BE ALLOWED TO VIEW YOUR ITEMS THROUGH THE LENS OF A POWERFUL STEREO ZOOM MICROSCOPE. INSTEAD OF BLIND TRUST AND OPINIONS, YOU WILL RECEIVE VIDEO PROOF.

FORENSIC AUTOGRAPH AUTHENTICATORS, INC.

NOW OFFERS A VSH VIDEO TAPE OF YOUR ITEM AS IT GOES THROUGH ITS FORENSIC EXAMINATION. EACH ITEM GOES THROUGH A FOUR PART EXAMINATION CONSISTING OF MICROSCOPIC, ULTRA-VIOLET, DATE / MEDIUM AND SIGNATURE COMPARISON. YOU WILL RECEIVE A WRITTEN REPORT THAT LISTS SPECIFIC DETAILS OF WHY YOUR ITEM HAS PASSED OR FAILED.

HERE ARE TWO OTHER GREAT REASONS TO GIVE US A TRY...

<u>1ST:</u> YOU PAY ONLY ONE PRICE FOR YOUR MULTI SIGNED ITEMS (UP TO 3 SIGNATURES ARE INCLUDED). PLEASE ADD $10 FOR EACH ADDITIONAL SIGNATURE (MAXIMUM OF $75 PER ITEM).

<u>2ND:</u> YOU PAY THE SAME PRICE FOR YOUR BABE RUTH AUTHENTICATION AS YOU WILL FOR YOUR MICKEY MANTLE. YOU'RE PAYING FOR THE EXAM SERVICE, NOT FOR HOW EXPENSIVE YOUR ITEM IS!

F.A.A. SUBMISSION FORM

MasterCard · VISA · NOVUS

Name _____

Address _____

Phone # _____

Credit Card # and exp. date _____
(for credit card orders only)

Signature _____
(for credit card orders only)

Please accurately describe each item submitted and list its insurance value, so that we can properly insure your item's safe return.

* Please Note: Please add a total of $15.00 for the video tape service (up to 5 exams).

Item	Insured Value	Authentication Fee
Example: Babe Ruth signed baseball	*$3,500*	*$35.00*

Item	Insured Value	Authentication Fee
1. _____	_____	$35.00
2. _____	_____	$35.00
3. _____	_____	$35.00
4. _____	_____	$35.00
5. _____	_____	$35.00

Total: Number of items _____ **Ins. value $** _____ **Auth. fee $** _____

YOU MAY LIST ADDITIONAL ITEMS ON A SEPARATE PIECE OF PAPER.

Video Tape $15.00

Total $ _____

Please include $10 for return S&H plus an additional $.35 per each $100 of insured value. (Example for a $1,000 autographed baseball you will need to include $3.50 + the $10 shipping fee for a total of $13.50. Packages weighing more than 4 pounds or oversized items such as bats etc...shipping is $15 + $.35 for each $100 of insured value.

+S&H _____

+Ret. Ins _____

Total $ _____

Please ship insured to:

FORENSIC AUTOGRAPH AUTHENTICATORS, INC.
Phone: 609-787-0202 • FAX 609-802-0814
590 S. Lenola Rd. #3-101 • Maple Shade, NJ 08052

Autograph Authentication, Handwriting & Document Analysis

Entertainment & Celebrities

Popular, trend-setting and in the spotlight, this group of unique and talented individuals touches our lives daily through their contributions to movies, television, commercials, music and literature. These are names we recognize, people we idolize, whose signatures we collect and cherish. Categories of entertainers and celebrities covered in this section are:

- Classical musicians
- Authors and poets
- Infamous—those whose fame is a result of controversy
- Entertainers of the movies and television

Entertainment & Celebrity Guide

NAME	DOB/DOD	SIG	DS/LS	ALS	SP	COMMENTS
Aames, Willie (Willie Upton)	1960-	5	15			"Eight Is Enough"-TV
Abbado, Claudio	1933-	15	35		30	Music conductor
☆ **Abbott, Bud**	**1895-1974**	**225**	**325**		**450**	**Comedy team member, "Buck Privates"**
Abbott, George	1887-1995	35	50	60	125	Producer, director, screenwr., "Damn Yankees"
Abel, Walter	1898-1987	20	30	45	40	"Raintree County"
Abraham, F. Murray	1939-	20	35	40	30	"Amadeus," elusive signer
AC/DC		125			225	Bon Scott (KS); "Back in Black," "Highway To Hell"; SA/CD-300
Achebe, Chinua	1930-	15	25	45	20	Nigerian writer, "Things Fall Apart"
Acquanetta	1920-	30			40	Cheyenne Indian actress, "Jungle Woman"
Acuff, Roy		15	25		30	Country Music Hall of Fame
Adam, Adolphe	1803-1856	45	150	275	125	Composer
Adams, Alice	1926-	10	20	30	15	U.S. writer, RS
Adams, Brooke	1949-	5	10	15	12	"Invasion of the Body Snatchers"
Adams, Bryan		25			45	"Cuts Like a Knife," "Have You Ever Really..."; SA/CD-65
Adams, Don	1926-	5	10	15	20	"Get Smart"-TV
Adams, Edie (Elizabeth Edith Enke)	1929-	5	10	15	10	"The Ernie Kovacs Show"
Adderley, Julian "Cannonball"	1928-1975	40	65		85	Alto sax player
Addingell, Richard	1904-1977	20	45		40	Composer
Adjani, Isabelle	1955-	15	30	60	30	"Camille Claudel"
Adler, Larry	1914-	15	30		35	Musician
Adler, Luther	1903-1984	15	20	30	25	"The Last Angry Man"
Adler, Richard	1921-	20	40	75	35	U.S., "Damn Yankees"
Aerosmith		125	225		225	Entire band good signers! "Sweet Emotion," "Dream On"; SA/CD-400
Agar, John	1921-	5	10	15	10	"The Sands of Iwo Jima," RS
Ager, Milton	1893-1979	25	40	50	40	U.S. songwriter, "Ain't She Sweet?"

NAME	DOB/DOD	SIG	DS/LS	ALS	SP	COMMENTS
Agutter, Jenny	1952-	5	10	15	10	"Logan's Run"
Aherne, Brian	1902-1986	20	30	40	45	"Juarez"
Aiello, Danny	1933-	10	20	30	20	"Moonstruck," writer
Aiken, Conrad	1889-1973	35	100	165	50	U.S. poet, critic, "Ushant"
Ailey, Alvin	1931-1989	25	50	75	50	Dancer, choreographer
Aimee, Anouk (Francoise Soyra Dreyfus)	1932-	5	10	15	10	"A Man and a Woman"
Albee, Edward	1928-	10	30	55	20	U.S. writer, very RS
Alberghetti, Anna Maria	1936-	25	45		40	Fifties sex symbol, sig. can be illegible
Albert, Eddie (Eddie Albert Heimberger)	1908-	10	20	40	35	"Roman Holiday," "Green Acres"-TV, charges
Albert, Edward	1951-	5	10	15	10	"Midway," son of Eddie
Albertson, Frank	1909-1964	25	35	45	30	"Psycho," "IAWL," "Alice Adams"
Albright, Lola	1925-	10	20	30	20	"Champion," "Kid Galahad"
Alcott, Louisa May	**1832-1888**	**220**	**300**	**450**		**U.S. novelist, "Little Women"**
Alda, Alan (Alphonso D'Abruzzo)	1936-	10	15	30	35	"M * A * S * H"-TV, writer, director, FA
Alda, Frances	1883-1952	30	60	125	80	Opera: Soprano
Alda, Robert	1914-1986	10	15	25	20	"Rhapsody in Blue," stage actor
Aleichem, Sholom	1859-1916	800	2000	4000		Russian, Yiddish writer, "The Old Country", ESPV
Alexander, Ben	1911-1969	55	60	65	110	"All Quiet on the Western Front," TV actor
Alexander, Jane (Jane Quigley)	1939-	5	10	15	10	"All The President's Men"
Alexander, Jason	1959-	15	25	40	25	"Seinfeld"-TV, can be elusive signer
Alexandre, Vicente	1898-1984					Spanish poet, "La destruccion o el amor"
Alger, Horatio	1832-1899	150	200	350	250	U.S. author, clergyman
Allan, Elizabeth	1910-1990	20	25	35	25	"David Copperfield," "Camille," illegible sig.
Allen, Debbie	1950-	5	10	15	10	"Fame," choreographer, sister Phylicia Rashad
Allen, Gracie	1902-1964	65	200		150	TV star w/George Burns, "Damsel in Distress"
Allen, Joan	1956-	5	10	15	10	"Comromising Positions"
Allen, Karen	1951-	10	20	30	20	"Raiders of the Lost Ark"

NAME	DOB/DOD	SIG	DS/LS	ALS	SP	COMMENTS
Allen, Nancy	1950-	5	10	15	10	"Robocop"
Allen, Peter		30			60	Musician, composer
Allen, Red	1908-1967	50	125		100	Jazz trumpeter
Allen, Rex	1922-	15	20	25	25	"The Legend of Lobo," TV actor, narrator
Allen, Steve	1921-	10	20	25	20	"The Steve Allen Show," writer, h/J. Meadows, RS
Allen, Tim	1953-	15	30	75	50	"Home Improvement"-TV, tough via mail.
Allen, Woody	1935-	20	40	65	40	"Annie Hall," director, writer, RS
Alley, Kirstie	1955-	20	45	60	50	"Cheers," often elusive
Allgood, Sara	1883-1950	20	30	40	45	Irish stage actress, "How Green Was My Valley"
Allman Brothers Band, The		125			240	(1995), D. Allman (KS), B. Oakley (KS)-+$400; "Ramblin Band," 'One Way Out"; SA/CD-300
Allyson, June	1918-	10	20	30	15	"Little Women," "The Glenn Miller Story"
Alonso, Alicia	1921-	15	30		25	Dancer, choreographer
Alonso, Maria Conchita	1957-	5	10	15	10	"The Running Man," RS
Alt, Carol	1960-	10	20	25	15	Supermodel
Althouse, Paul	1889-1954	35	75	150	100	Opera: Tenor
Altman, Arthur	1910-1994	20	30	40	35	U.S. "All or Nothing at All"
Altman, Robert	1925-	10	20	30	20	"The Player," director, writer, producer
Alvarado, Trini	1969-	5	10	15	10	"Rich Kids"
Amado, Jorge	1912-	20	30	50	25	Brazilian writer, "The Violent Land"
Amato, Pasquale	1878-1942	45	100	200	130	Opera: Baritone
Ambler, Eric	1909-	25	50		40	Writer
Ameche, Don	1908-1993	25	45	50	50	"Swanee River," was RS
Ames, Adrienne	1909-1947	25	40	65	45	"The Avenger," rare in SP
Ames, Leon	1903-1993	25	30	40	30	Character actor, "Little Women"
Amis, Kingsley	1922-1995	20	30	75	35	British novelist and critic, "Lucky Jim"
Amis, Martin	1949-	15	20	40	20	British writer, "Success"
Amis, Suzy	1961-	5	10	15	10	"Blown Away"

NAME	DOB/DOD	SIG	DS/LS	ALS	SP	COMMENTS
Amos & Andy		165	260		325	Signed by both
Amos, John	1941-	10	15	20	15	"Good Times", FA
Amos, Tori		20			50	Rock diva
Amsterdam, Morey		20	35		50	Dick Van Dyke show
Andersen, Hans Christian	1805-1875	500	1175	1750		Danish fairy tale author, "The Ugly Duckling"
Anderson, Eddie "Rochester"	1905-1977	55	200	235	170	GWTW, assoc. w/Jack Benny on radio & TV
Anderson, Gillian	1968-	25	50	75	50	"The X-Files"-TV, often elusive
Anderson, Harry	1952-	5	10	15	20	"Night Court"
Anderson, Judith	1898-1992	25	45	60	50	"The Ten Commandments," "Rebecca"
Anderson, Kevin	1960-	5	10	15	10	"Sleeping with the Enemy"
Anderson, Leroy	1908-1975	30	75	150	50	U.S. "Syncopated Clock"
Anderson, Loni	1946-	10	20	30	15	"WKRP in Cincinnati," often elusive
Anderson, Lynn		10	25		15	Country & Western
Anderson, Marion	1902-1993	175	220	275	365	Opera: Contralto
Anderson, Maxwell	1888-1959	35	50	150	60	U.S. playwright, "Key Largo"
Anderson, Melissa Sue	1962-	10	15	25	20	"Little House on the Prairie"
Anderson, Melody	1955-	5	10	15	10	"Flash Gordon"
Anderson, Richard	1926-	5	10	15	10	"The Six Million Dollar Man"
Anderson, Richard Dean	1950-	5	10	15	15	"MacGyver"
Anderson, Sherwood ☆	**1876-1941**	**50**	**100**	**175**	**65**	**U.S. short-story writer, "Winesburg, Ohio"**
Andersson, Bibi	1935-	5	10	15	15	"The Seventh Seal"
Andress, Ursula	1936-	10	20	30	25	"Dr. No"
Andrews, Anthony	1948-	5	10	15	10	"Brideshead Revisited"
Andrews, Dana	1912-	20	35	60	40	"The Best Years of Our Lives"
Andrews, Julie	1935-	35	45	75	50	"Mary Poppins," often elusive, FA
Angel, Heather	1909-1986	20	25	30	40	"The Informer," "Lifeboat," "Suspicion"
Angeles, Victoria de las	1923-	15	40		30	Lyric soprano
Angeli, Pier	1932-1971	65	80	215	125	"Teresa," distinctive signature
Angelou, Maya	1928-	30	35	50	30	U.S. writer, poet

NAME	DOB/DOD	SIG	DS/LS	ALS	SP	COMMENTS
Animals, The		200			350	(1994), E. Burden (KS), C. Chandler (KS); "House of the Rising Sun," "See See Rider"; SA/CD-400
Aniston, Jennifer	1969-	25	50	65	50	"Friends"-TV, often evasive, FA
Anka, Paul	1941-	10	15	30	15	Pop singer & songwriter, responsive
Ankers, Evelyn	1918-1985	20	35	60	40	"Queen of the Horror Movies," screamer
Ann-Margret (Ann-Margret Olsson)	1941-	10	20	35	30	"Viva Las Vegas"
Annabella	1909-	20	30	40	45	"Wings of the Morning"
Annaud, Jean-Jacques	1943-	5	10	15	10	"Quest for Fire"; "The Lover," writer, director
Anspach, Susan	1945-	5	10	15	10	"Five Easy Pieces"
Anton, Susan	1950-	5	10	15	15	"Goldengirl," actor, singer
Anwar, Gabrielle	1970-	15	25	30	35	"Scent of a Woman"
Applegate, Christina	1972-	10	20	30	35	"Married With Children"
Arbuckle, Minta Durfee	1897-1975	65	125	230	115	m. "Fatty," comic leading lady
Arbuckle, Roscoe "Fatty"	1887-1933	380	445	795	800	Comic actor of the silent screen, scandal vict.
Archer, Anne	1947-	10	20	30	15	"Fatal Attraction"
Archer, Robyn	1948-	10			20	Singer, actress
Arden, Eve	1912-1990	20	35	40	40	"Mildred Pierce," "Our Miss Brooks"-TV
Arenholz, Stephen	1969-	5	10	15	10	Actor
Arias Sanchez, Oscar	1941-	40	50	75	40	Costa Rican writer
Arkin, Alan	1934-	5	10	20	15	"The In-Laws," actor, director, folk singer
Arlen, Harold	1905-1986	145	240		125	U.S. composer, "Stormy Weather"
Arlen, Richard	1899-1976	25	45	80	45	"Wings," pilot
Arliss, Florence	1871-1950	25	40	50	45	British charcter actress, "The Devil"
Arliss, George	1868-1946	35	60	70	75	"House of Rothschild," sig. often illegible
Armani, Giorgio	1935-	20	35		40	Fashion designer
Armetta, Henry	1888-1945	25	35	45	75	"A Farewell to Arms,"
Armitage, Karole	1954-	15	30		20	Dancer, choreographer
Armstrong, Bess	1953-	5	10	15	10	"On Our Own"

NAME	DOB/DOD	SIG	DS/LS	ALS	SP	COMMENTS
Armstrong, Louis "Satchmo"	**1900-1971**	**225**	**500**	**725**	**500**	**Singer, trumpet player, "scat" vocalist**
Armstrong, Robert	1890-1973	70	80	100	200	"King Kong," "Son of Kong"
Arnaz, Desi	1917-1986	45	110	.	160	"I Love Lucy"-TV, a.leaf w/Lucy-$200
Arnaz, Desi, Jr.	1953-	5	10	15	10	"Here's Lucy," singer
Arnaz, Lucie	1951-	5	10	15	10	"Here's Lucy"
Arness, James	1923-	25	55	75	60	"Gunsmoke," brother of Peter Graves, RS
Arno, Sig	1895-1975	15	25	40	25	German comedian, "Up in Arms"
Arnold, Edward	1890-1956	45	50		80	"Diamond Jim," "Meet Nero Wolfe"
Arnold, Matthew	1822-1888	45	70	130		British poet, critic, "Thrysis"
Arnold, Sir Malcolm	1921-	20	40		45	Composer
Arnold, Tom	1959-	20	40	60	40	"Roseanne"-TV, FA
Arquette, Patricia	1968-	5	10	15	20	"True Romance," sister of Rosanna
Arquette, Rosanna	1959-	15	25	40	30	"Desperately Seeking Susan," song subject
Arthur, Beatrice (Bernice Frankel)	1926-	5	15	25	15	"Maude", RS
Arthur, Jean	1905-1991	60	120	225	140	"Mr. Smith Goes to Washington," scarce ALS
Ashbery, John	1927-	10	20	30	20	U.S. writer, "Flow Chart"
Ashkenazy, Vladimir	1937-	15	35		30	Pianist, conductor
Ashley, Elizabeth	1939-	5	10	20	15	"Evening Shade", RS
Ashman, Howard	1950-1991	50	100	130	80	U.S. lyricist, "The Little Mermaid", scarce
Asimov, Issac	1920-1992	50	100	225	100	U.S. science-fiction writer, "I Robot"
Asner, Edward	1925-	5	10	15	10	"Lou Grant", RS
Assante, Armand	1949-	20	40	75	40	"The Doctors"
Association, The		20			35	"Cherish," "Windy," "Never My Love"; SA/CD-50
Astaire, Fred	1899-1987	75	175	250	185	"Top Hat," dance partner of Ginger Rogers
Astin, John	1930-	5	10	20	15	"The Addams Family," father of Sean Astin
Astor, Mary	1905-1987	50	100	225	150	"Beau Brummel," "Don Juan," "The Maltese Falcon"
Ates, Roscoe	1892-1962	35	40	70	70	"The Champ," "GWTW," "Freaks"

NAME	DOB/DOD	SIG	DS/LS	ALS	SP	COMMENTS
Atkins, Chet		5	10		15	Country & Western
Atkins, Christopher	1946-	5	10	15	10	"The Blue Lagoon"
Attenborough, Richard	1923-	30	50	70	60	"Ghandi," producer, director
Atwill, Lionel	1885-1946	100	200	425	200	Horror film star
Atwood, Margaret	1939-	10	20	50	25	Canadian writer, "Surfacing," RS!
Auberjonois, Rene	1940-	5	10	15	10	"Deep Space Nine"
Auchincloss, Louis	1917-	10	25	60	25	U.S. writer, "A World of Profit," RS
Auden, Wyston Hugh	1907-1973	150	300	550		British poet, playwright, critic, ESPV
Auer, Mischa	1905-1967	20	40	50	45	"My Man Godfrey"
Auermann, Nadja	1971-	5	10	15	15	Supermodel
August, Billie	1948-	15	35		30	Film director
Aumont, Jean-Pierre	1909-	15	30	40	50	"Assingment in Brittany," French leading man
Austen, Jane	1775-1817	830	2500	4000		British novelist, "Emma," ALS-2X, ESPV
Autry, Alan	1952-	5	10	15	10	"In the Heat of the Night"
Autry, Gene	1907-	35	75	135	65	Singing cowboy, songwriter, FA
Avalon, Frankie	1939-	15	25	35	30	Fifties teen idol, "Venus"
Avery, Tex	1908-1980	75	125		125	Cartoonist
Axton, Hoyt	1938-	5	10	15	10	"Gremlins," singer, songwriter, RS
Aykroyd, Dan	1952-	15	30	40	20	"Ghostbusters," SNL-TV, responsive
Ayres, Lew	1908-1996	15	20	40	30	"All Quiet on the Western Front"
Babel, Issac	1894-1941					Russian short-story writer, "Odessa Tales"
Bacall, Lauren	1924-	15	30	40	30	"To Have and Have Not," RS
Bach, Barbara	1947-	5	10	15	10	"The Spy Who Loved Me," Mrs. Ringo Starr
Bach, Carl P. E.	1714-1788					German composer
Bach, Johann Christian	1735-1782					German composer
☆ **Bach, Johann Sebastian**	**1685-1750**	**3875**	**24650**	**37600**		**German composer, ALS can vary significantly!, ESPV**
Bacharach, Burt	1928-	20	40	50	35	U.S., "Raindrops Keep Fallin' on My Head"
Bacon, Kevin	1958-	20	40	50	45	"Footloose," "Apollo 13," elusive signer

Louie Armstrong

Ingrid Bergman

Lauren Bacall

Irving Berlin

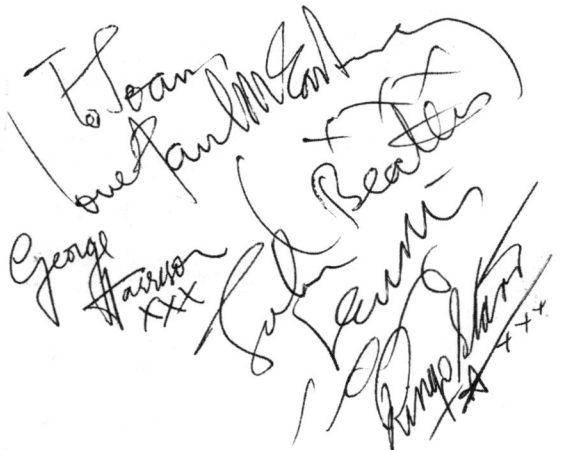

The Beatles

Hector Berlioz

Sarah Bernhardt

L.B. Beiderbeche

The Beatles

Shirley Temple Black

NAME	DOB/DOD	SIG	DS/LS	ALS	SP	COMMENTS
Baez, Joan	1941-	10	25		20	Folksinger, RS
Bailey, Mildred	1907-1951					Blues singer
Bailey, Pearl	1918-1990	20	35	45	40	"Porgy and Bess"
Bain, Barbara	1934-	10	25	30	30	"Mission: Impossible"
Bainter, Fay	1892-1968	60	80	125	120	"Jezebel," can be scarce in vintage SP
Baio, Scott	1961-	5	10	15	10	"Happy Days," "Charles in Charge"
Bairnstather, Bruce	1888-1959	55			110	Cartoonist
Baker, Aaron	1958-	5	10	10	10	'Wayne's World"
Baker, Carroll	1931-	10	20	30	20	"Kindergarten Cop"
Baker, Chet	1929-1988	30	65		60	Trumpet player
Baker, Dame Janet	1933-	15	30		30	Mezzo-soprano
Baker, Elizabeth	1968-	10	15	20	20	"Titanic"
Baker, Joe Don	1936-	5	10	15	10	"Walking Tall"
Baker, Josephine	1906-1975	175	350	400	600	Music hall diva,seductress
Baker, Kathy	1950-	5	10	15	15	"Picket Fences"
Baker, LaVerne	1929-1997	20			35	(1991); "I Cried a Tear," "Jim Dandy"; SA/CD-45
Baker, Rebecca	1909-	15	20	25	30	"Wizard of Oz"
Bakshi, Ralph	1938-	5	10	15	10	"Fritz the Cat," animator, director
Bakula, Scott	1955-	5	10	20	35	"Quantum Leap," RS
Balaban, Bob	1945-	5	10	15	10	"Midnight Cowboy"
Balanchine, George	1904-1983	150		275	275	Ballet
Baldwin, Adam	1962-	10	15	20	15	"My Bodyguard"
Baldwin, Alec	1958-	20	40	50	45	"The Hunt for Red October," elusive signer
Baldwin, James	1924-1987	100	350	425	200	Author, "Just Above My Head," ALS-2X
Baldwin, Stephen	1966-	15	30	45	40	"Threesome"
Baldwin, William	1963-	15	30	45	40	"Backdraft"
Ball, Lucille ☆	**1911-1989**	**180**	**400**	**650**	**500**	**"I Love Lucy," often elusive in later years**
Ball, Suzan	1933-1955	175	325	400	345	"Untamed Frontier," "East of Sumarta"
Ballard, Kaye (Catherine Gloria Balotta)	1926-	5	10	15	10	Actress, singer

NAME	DOB/DOD	SIG	DS/LS	ALS	SP	COMMENTS
Balsam, Martin	1919-	20	25	30	40	"A Thousand Clowns"
Balzac, Honore de	1799-1850	800	1650	3000		French novelist, "Le Pere Goriot," ESPV
Bancroft, Anne	1931-	10	20	30	20	"The Graduate," married to Mel Brooks
Band, The		175			200	(1994), R. Manuel (KS); "The Weight," "Up on Cripple Creek"; SA/CD-225
Banderas, Antonio	1960-	25	50	80	60	"Philadelphia," "Evita," elusive signer
Bankhead, Tallulah	1903-1968	65	130	200	210	"Lifeboat"
Banks, Tyra		10	20	25	30	Model, actress, FA
Banner, John		125	165		200	"Hogan's Heroes"
Bara, Theda	1890-1955	170	375	360	300	Silent era "vamp," "Under Two Flags"
Baranski, Christine	1952-	10	20	30	20	"Cybill," "The Real Thing"
Barbeau, Adrienne	1945-	5	10	15	10	"Maude," RS
Barber, Samuel	1910-1981	50	250	300	100	U.S. composer, "Vanessa"
Bardot, Brigitte	1934-	35	50	65	70	"And God Created Woman," seductress, FA
Bari, Lynn	1913-1989	5	10	20	15	"The Bridge of San Luis Rey"
Barker, Lex	1919-1973	75	100	165	130	"Tarzan" film series
Barkin, Ellen	1954-	5	10	20	15	"Sea of Love"
Barnes, Binnie	1905-	5	10	15	15	"The Private Life of Henry VIII"
Barnett, Vince	1902-1977	20	30	40	40	Character actor, "Scarface," "The Killers"
Barrie, James M.	1860-1937	85	250	350	300	British playwright, novelist, "Peter Pan," SB-$250
Barrie, Wendy	1912-1978	30	50	60	50	"The Private Life of Henry VIII," e. B. Siegel
Barrow, Clyde	1909-1934	2000	4500			Bonnie & Clyde, criminals, ESPV
Barrymore, Diana	1921-1960	45	50	60	50	"Eagle Squadron," daughter of John
Barrymore, Drew	1975-	25	50	60	50	"E.T., the Extra-Terrestrial," unpredictable
Barrymore, Ethel	1878-1959	100	170	350	200	"None But the Lonely Heart," stage star
Barrymore, John	1882-1942	185	275	325	500	"Grand Hotel," stage actor
Barrymore, John Drew	1932-	20	35	45	35	Actor, father of Drew
Barrymore, Lionel	1878-1954	100	200	300	200	IAWL, " Key Largo"

NAME	DOB/DOD	SIG	DS/LS	ALS	SP	COMMENTS
Bart, Lionel	1930-	10	30		25	"Oliver," composer, lyricist
Bartel, Paul	1938-	5	10	15	10	"Eating Raoul," director, writer
Barth, John	1930-	20	40	100	35	U.S. writer, "The End of the Road"
Barthelme, Donald	1931-1989	20	35		40	Novelist, RS
Bartholomew, Freddie	1924-1992	35	45	50	70	"David Copperfield," child star
Bartok, Bela	1881-1945	400	750	2000	1500	Hungarian composer
Barty, Billie	1925-	10	15	20	15	"Footlight Parade," "Roman Scandels"
Baryshnikov, Mikhail	1948-	80	100	200	175	"White Nights," elusive signer, tough in-person
Basehart, Richard	1914-1984	20	40	25	40	"He Walked By Night," TV actor, narrator
Basie, Count	1904-1984	80	225		250	Orchestra leader, piano player
Basinger, Kim	1953-	15	25	45	40	" 9 1/2 Weeks," RS
Basquette, Lina	1907-1994	20	30	45	30	"Ziegfeld Follies" star, "The Godless Girl"
Bassett, Angela	1948-	15	25	35	25	"Waiting to Exhale"
Bateman, Jason	1969-	10	20	30	25	"The Hogan Family"
Bateman, Justine	1966-	10	20	30	20	"Family Ties"
Bates, Alan	1934-	5	10	15	10	"An Unmarried Woman"
Bates, Barbara	1925-1969	150	260	325	275	"All About Eve," "The Caddy," com. suicide
Baudelaire, Charles	1821-1867	475	1200	2500		French symbolist poet, "Les Fleurs du Mal"
Bauer, Steven	1956-	5	10	15	10	"Wiseguy"
☆ **Baum, Lyman Frank**	**1856-1919**	**1265**	**2500**			**U.S. writer, "The Wizard of Oz," ALS-2X, ESPV**
Bausch, Pina	1940-	15	30		25	Choreographer, dancer
Bavier, Frances		125	250		200	"Andy Griffith"
Baxter, Anne	1923-1985	25	40	55	50	"The Razor's Edge," "All About Eve"
Baxter, Keith	1933-	5	10	15	10	Actor
Baxter, Meredith	1947-	5	10	15	10	"Family Ties"
Baxter, Warner	1889-1951	50	90		130	"In Old Arizona"
Beach Boys, The		250			450	(1988), B. Wilson (KS), D. Wilson (KS); "Good Vibrations"; SA/CD-500
Beach, Amy	1867-1944	50	150	460	200	U.S. composer

NAME	DOB/DOD	SIG	DS/LS	ALS	SP	COMMENTS
Beach, Sylvia	1887-1962	60	140	200	125	"Shakespeare and Co."
Beacham, Stephanie	1947-	5	10	15	10	"The Colbys"
Beals, Jennifer	1963-	10	20	30	20	"Flashdance," elusive signer
Beard, Daniel C.		125	200		250	Boy Scouts founder
Beasley, Allyce	1954-	5	10	15	10	"Moonlighting"
Beastie Boys		25			35	"(You Gotta) Fight for Your Right (to Party)"; SA/CD-50
Beatles, The		**1750**			**3000**	**(1988), FA; "Penny Lane," "Let It Be," "Hey Jude"; SA/CD-3500**
Beattie, Ann	1947-	10	20	35	15	U.S. writer, Love Always," RS!
Beatty, Ned	1937-	10	15	20	15	"Deliverance"
Beatty, Warren	1937-	35	100	225	45	"Shampoo," "Reds," elusive signer
Beauvior, Simone de	1908-1986	35	70	150		French novelist, essayist, "The Second Sex"
Beavers, Louise	1902-1962	95	200	285	215	"Beulah"-TV series, "Imitation of Life"
Bechet, Sidney	1897-1959	135	600		200	Soprano sax player, jazz pioneer
Beck	1970-	20			30	"Loser"; SA/CD-40
Beck, John	1943-	5	10	15	10	"Dallas"
Beck, Michael	1949-	5	10	15	10	"Xanadu"
Beckett, Samuel	1906-1989	175	500	425	400	Irish novelist, "Waiting for Godot," TS- $450
Beckett, Scotty	1929-1968	60	160	225	110	child actor, "Our Gang" member
Bedelia, Bonnie	1946-	5	10	15	10	"Presumed Innocent"
Bee Gees, The		35			70	(1997); "Stayin' Alive"; SA/CD-100
Beene, Geoffrey	1927-	15	35		30	Fashion designer
Beery, Noah, Sr.	1884-1946	85	150	250	170	"Beau Geste," silent film star, scarce sig.
Beery, Wallace	1885-1949	110	175	350	275	"The Champ," "Grand Hotel," many others
Beethoven, Ludwig van	**1770-1827**	**5500**	**21000**	**40000**		**German composer, ESPV, ALS-$49,500**
Begley, Ed, Jr.	1949-	5	10	15	10	"St. Elsewhere"
Behan, Brendan	1923-1964	175	365	700	400	Irish playwright, "The Hostage"
Behrman, S.N.	1893-1973	20	40	75	40	"The Second Man," playwright

NAME	DOB/DOD	SIG	DS/LS	ALS	SP	COMMENTS
Beiderbecke, Bix	1903-1931	5500				Composer, cornet and piano player, scarce
Bejart, Maurice	1927-	20	50		45	Choreographer
Bel Geddes, Barbara	1922-	20	40	50	30	"Vertigo," "I Remember Mama", RS
Bel Geddes, Norman	1893-1958	25	50		50	Theatrical designer
Belafonte, Harry	1927-	15	30	50	35	"Island in the Sun," singer, elusive signer
Belafonte, Shari	1954-	5	10	15	10	"Hotel"
Bellamy, Madge	1900-1990	15	25	45	30	"The Most Beautiful Girl on Broadway"
Bellamy, Ralph	1904-1991	17	25	35	45	"The Awful Truth," numerous others
Belasco, David	1853-1931	40	80		80	Playwright
Bellini, Vincenzo	1801-1835	500	1250			Italian composer, ESPV
Bellow, Saul	1915-	30	100	100	50	U.S. writer, "Humboldt's Gift"- $175 (FE, SB), elusive signer
Belmondo, Jean-Paul	1933-	60	100	150	75	"The Professional," tough signature
Belushi, Jim	1954-	5	10	15	15	"K-9"
Belushi, John	1949-1982	225	500		550	SNL, "Blues Brothers"
Benatar, Pat	1953-	15			30	"Hit Me With Your Best Shot," "We Belong"; SA/CD-50
Benben, Brian		5	10	15	10	"Dream On"
Benchley, Robert	1889-1945	55	95	180	80	Critic, "How to Sleep"
Benchly, Peter	1940-	20	55	140	45	U.S. writer, "Jaws," responsive, shark sk.- $30
Bendix, William	1906-1964	40	85	75	140	"The Babe Ruth Story," "Life of Riley"-TV
Benedict, Dirk	1945-	5	10	15	10	"The A-Team"
Benet, Stephen Vincent	1898-1943	100	175	240	150	U.S. poet, novelist, "John Brown's Body"
Benford, Tommy	1906-1994	20	50		40	Drummer
Bening, Annette	1958-	15	30	45	40	"The Grifters," Mrs. Warren Beatty
Benjamin, Richard	1938-	5	10	15	10	"Love at First Bite"
Bennett, Bruce	1909-	20	25	30	40	Herman Brix, "Tarzan," "The Treasure of..."
Bennett, Constance	1904-1964	40	65	125	75	"Three Faces East," silent star
Bennett, Joan	1910-1990	20	35	40	40	"Little Women," "Father of the Bride"
Bennett, Richard R.	1936-	30	60		50	Composer

NAME	DOB/DOD	SIG	DS/LS	ALS	SP	COMMENTS
Benny, Jack	**1894-1974**	**100**	**275**	**400**	**175**	**"To Be or Not to Be," radio & TV pioneer**
Benson, Robbie	1956-	5	10	15	12	"Ice Castles," "Beauty and the Beast"
Benson, Sir Frank	1858-1939	30	45		50	Actor-manager, ESPV
Berenger, Tom	1950-	20	30	40	50	"Platoon"
Berenson, Marisa	1947-	10	15	20	20	"Barry Lyndon"
Berg, Alban	1885-1935	150	415	600		Austrian composer, "Lulu", ESPV-ALS
Bergen, Candice	1946-	15	20	30	40	"Murphy Brown"-TV, can be elusive, FA
Bergen, Edgar	1903-1978	75	100	145	150	Partner with dummy "Charley McCarthy"
Bergen, Polly	1930-	10	20	30	40	"The Winds of War"
Berger, Thomas	1924-	10	25	40	15	U.S. writer, "Killing Time"
Bergman, Ingmar	1918-	40	50	60	115	"The Silence," writer, director
Bergman, Ingrid	1913-1982	150	200	300	400	"Gaslight," "Anastasia," "Notorious"
Bergner, Elizabeth	1898-1986	15	30	45	30	"Escape Me Never," sig. often illegible
Berigan, Bunny	1909-1942					Trumpet player, singer
Beresford, Bruce	1940-	20	40		35	"Driving Miss Daisy," director
Berlioz, Hector	1803-1869	250	1325	2000		French comp., "Dam...Faust," AMQS-$3900
Berkeley, Busby	1895-1976	150	200	275	300	"42nd Street," "Babes on Broadway"
Berkoff, Steven	1937-	10	20		20	Playwright
Berkowitz, David, "Son of Sam"		50	75	200		"Son of Sam" serial killer, ESPV
Berle, Milton	1908-	20	30	40	35	"Always Leave Them Laughing," TV pioneer
Berlin, Irving	1888-1989	200	960		1290	Gifted composer
Bernardi, Herschel	1923-1986	30	60	110	75	"Fiddler on the Roof," voice over star
Bernhard, Sandra	1955-	5	10	15	10	"Roseanne"
Bernhardt, Sarah	1844-1923	160	275	500	750	Actress, ALS-$750, ESPV
Bernsen, Corbin	1954-	15	20	40	35	"L.A. Law"
Bernstein, Carl	1944-	10	25		20	Journalist, SDS-ESPV
Bernstein, Leonard	1918-1990	100	300	575	200	U.S. composer, "Mass," RS, SCC-$75
Berri, Claude (Claude Langmann)	1934-	10	20	30	20	Actor, director, producer

NAME	DOB/DOD	SIG	DS/LS	ALS	SP	COMMENTS
Berry, Chuck	1926-	50			100	(1986), has always been an elusive signer; "Johnny B. Goode"; SA/CD-150
Berry, Halle	1968-	15	25	35	35	"Boomerang," model, RS, FA
Berryman, John	1914-1972	30	75	150		U.S. poet, "Homage to Mistress Bradstreet"
Bertinelli, Valerie	1960-	10	20	25	20	"One Day at a Time," Mrs. Eddie Van Halen
Bertolucci, Bernoardo	1940-	20	45		40	"The Last Emperor," director
Berwald, Franz	1796-1868	465	600			Composer
Bessmertnova, Natalia	1941-	35			70	Ballerina, ESPV
Best, Edna	1900-1974	25	30	40	50	British stage actress, "Escape"
Best, Willie	1913-1962	65	125	200	130	"Sleep 'n Eat," TV actor
Bialik, Mayim	1975-	5	10	15	10	"Blossom"
Bickford, Charles	1889-1967	55	110	125	100	"Anna Christie," "The Song of Bernadette"
Biehn, Michael	1956-	10	15	25	45	"The Terminator"
Bierce, Ambrose	1842-1914	300	600	600		U.S. short-story writer, "The Devil's Dictionary"
Big Bopper, The (J.P. Richardson)		275			350	Died in plane crash with Buddy Holly; "Chantilly Lace"; SA/CD-450
Bigard, Barney	1906-1980	70	135		170	Clarinet player
Biggs, Ronald	1929-	40			75	"The Great Train Robbery"
Bilge, Mary J.		10			15	"Real Love," "Be Happy"; SA/CD-20
Bille Haley and the Comets		400			725	B. Haley was an elusive signer! "Rock Around the Clock"; SA/CD-750
Billingsley, Barbara	1922-	5	10	15	10	"Leave it to Beaver"
Billingsley, Peter	1972-	5	10	15	10	"A Christmas Story"
Bing, Herman	1889-1947	32	55	100	60	"Dinner at Eight," "The Merry Widow"
Bing, Sir Rudolf	1902-	10	25	40	25	Opera administrator
Binoche, Juliette	1964-	20	60	75	60	"The English Patient," popular in France
Birney, David	1939-	5	10	15	10	"St. Elsewhere"
Bishop, Elizabeth	1911-1979	40	130	200	50	U.S. poet
Bishop, Joey	1918-	5	15	25	20	"The Joey Bishop Show," RS
Bissell, Whit	1919-1981	12	20	30	25	Character actor, "Destination Tokyo"

Ray Bolger

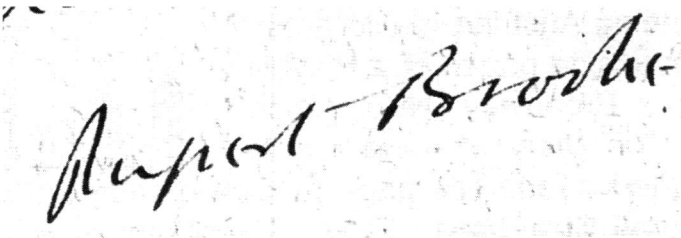

Rupert Brooks

John Wilkes Booth

Louise Brooks

Johannes Brahms

Robert Browning

Humphrey Bogart

NAME	DOB/DOD	SIG	DS/LS	ALS	SP	COMMENTS
Bisset, Jacqueline	1944-	5	20	30	20	"The Deep"
Bisset, Josie	1969-	15	30	40	45	"Melrose Place"
Bizet, Georges	1838-1875	400	1150	1600		French composer, ESPV
Bjorling, Jussi	1911-1960	520	675	1000	950	Opera: Tenor
Bjornson, Bjornstjerne	1832-1910	60	75	150		Writer, NP
Bjornson, Maria	1949-	10	25		25	Stage designer
Black Sabbath		55			125	Catch them at a reunion concert! "Paranoid"; SA/CD-175
Black, Karen	1942-	5	10	15	15	"Easy Rider"
Blackmer, Sidney	1895-1973	20	30	35	40	"Little Caesar," "Heidi," and many others
Blackstone, Harry, Sr.		150		475	250	Magician
Blackwell, Ed	1929-1992	25	40		40	Drummer
Blades, Ruben	1948-	5	10	15	10	"The Milagro Beanfield War"
Blaine, Vivian	1921-	10	20	30	25	"State Fair," "Guys and Dolls"
Blair, Janet	1921-	15	20	25	25	"My Sister Eileen"
Blair, Linda	1959-	10	20	25	30	"The Exorcist"
Blake, Eubie	1883-1983	75	200	250	150	U.S., "I'm Just Wild About Harry"
Blake, Robert	1933-	5	10	15	15	"Baretta"
Blakely, Susan	1950-	5	10	15	10	"Rich Man, Poor Man"
Blakey, Art	1919-1990	30	50		50	Jazz drummer
Blanc, Mel	1908-1989	70	100	150	200	Voice of Warner Brothers cartoon characters
Bland, Bobby "Blue"	1930-	25			60	(1992), reclusive and evasive signer! "Turn On Your Love Light," "Farther Up..."; SA/CD-75
Blandick, Clara	1880-1962	425	830		800	"TWOO," "Tom Sawyer," scarce
Blane, Sally	1910-	10	15	20	20	The Vagabond Lover," s. Loretta Young
Blanton, Jimmy	1921-1942					Bass player
Blasoo-Ibanez, Vicente	1867-1928	75	150	260		Novelist, ESPV-SP
Bledsoe, Tempestt	1973-	5	10	15	10	"The Cosby Show"
Blind Faith		200			400	Grech (1946-90, KS); "Can't Find My Way Home"; SA/CD-500
Bliss, Sir Arthur	1891-1975	30	80		70	Composer

NAME	DOB/DOD	SIG	DS/LS	ALS	SP	COMMENTS
Blitzstein, Marc	1905-1964	50	100		125	Composer
Bloch, Ernest	1880-1959	55	115	200	75	Swiss/U.S. composer, "Macbeth"
Blondell, Joan	1909-1979	35	45	75	65	"The Blue Veil," "Stage Struck"
Blondie		30			60	"Heart of Glass"; SA/CD-75
Blondin, Charles	1824-1897	30	65		70	Acrobat
Blood, Sweat and Tears		30			55	D.C. Thomas (KS); "Spinning Wheel," "You've Made Me..."; SA/CD-85
Bloom, Claire	1931-	10	15	20	15	"Richard III"
Blore, Eric	1887-1959	33	40	75	60	The "Sullivan's Travels," "The Lady Eve"
Blue, Ben	1901-1975	35	40	65	60	Vaudevillian, "For Me and My Gal"
Blue, Monte	1890-1963	35	45	60	70	Silent star, "Dodge City"
Blume, Judy	1938-	15	25	50	20	U.S. writer, "Are You There God?..."
Bly, Nellie	c.1865-1922	100	150	200		Journalist
Bly, Robert	1926-	15	30		25	Poet
Blyth, Ann	1928-	10	20	30	15	"Mildred Pierce," singer, very RS
Blythe, Betty	1893-1972	45	75	100	150	"The Queen of Sheba," silent star
Boccherini, Luigi	1743-1805	140	300			Italian composer, chamber music
Bochco, Steven	1943-	5	10	20	10	"NYPD Blue," producer, screenwriter, RS
Bock, Jerry	1928-	35	50	75	60	U.S., "Fiddler on the Roof"
Bogarde, Dirk	1921-	10	20	30	20	"Death in Venice"
☆ **Bogart, Humphrey**	**1899-1957**	**925**	**1500**	**2350**	**2725**	**C, often forged, numerous secretarial, ESPV**
Bogart, Mayo Methot	1904-1951	30	50	65	50	"Marked Woman," H.Bogart's third wife
Bogdanovich, Peter	1939-	15	40		30	Director
Bogosian, Eric	1953-	5	10	15	10	"Talk Radio"
Böhm, Karl	1894-1981	25	60	100	60	Conductor
Boland, Mary	1880-1965	20	45	90	55	"Ruggles of Red Gap"
Boles, John	1895-1969	28	35	60	50	"Stella Dallas," "King of Jazz"
Bolger, Ray	1904-1987	75	135	300	225	TWOO, "April in Paris," SP- TWOO role 1-2X
Boll, Heinrich	1917-1985	50	100	175	75	German novelist, "Group Portrait With Lady"

NAME	DOB/DOD	SIG	DS/LS	ALS	SP	COMMENTS
Bolm, Adolph	1884-1951	40	75		50	Dancer, choreographer
Bologna, Joseph	1938-	5	10	15	10	"Chapter Two," can be unresponsive
Bolt, Robert	1924-1995	25	50		45	Playwright, "Dr. Zhivago"
Bon Jovi		55			125	J. Bon Jovi (KS); "Livin' on a Prayer"; SA/CD-175
Bonaduce, Danny	1959-	5	10	15	10	"The Partridge Family," RS
Bonanova, Fortunio	1893-1969	25	45	65	50	"Citizen Kane," "For Whom the Bell Tolls"
Bond, Carrie Jacobs	1862-1946	40	100	145	50	U.S., I Love You Truly"
Bond, Michael	1926-	15	25		25	Writer, "Paddington Bear"
Bond, Ward	1903-1960	125	155	200	250	Western film star, fav. of John Wayne, GWTW
Bondi, Beulah	1892-1981	25	40	50	45	"Gorgeous Hussey," IAWL, consist. demand
Bonds, Gary U.S.		10			15	RS! "Quarter to Three," "School is Out"; SA/CD-25
Bonet, Lisa	1967-	5	10	12	10	"The Cosby Show," RS
Bonham-Carter, Helena	1966-	5	10	15	10	"A Room with a View"
Bonner, Frank	1942-	5	10	15	10	"WKRP in Cincinnati"
Bonney, W.H. "Billy the KId"	c.1859-1881			17000		Legendary outlaw, scarce
Bono, Sonny	1935-1998	35	65	125	65	"The Sonny and Cher Comedy Hour," USHR
Bonsall, Brian	1982-	5	10	15	10	"Family Ties"
Booker T. and the MG's		50			115	(1992), Booker T. Jones (KS), A. Jackson (KS); "Green Onions"; SA/CD-125
Boone, Pat	1934-	5	10	15	10	"The Pat Boone Show," very RS
Boorman, John	1933-	10	25		25	Film director
Booth, Edwin	1833-1895	125	210	300	275	Actor, b. John Wilkes
Booth, Shirley	1898-1992	25	50	65	50	"Hazel"-TV, "Come Back, Little Sheba"
Boothe, Powers	1949-	5	10	15	10	"Guyana Tragedy: The Story of Jim Jones"
Borden, Lizzie	1860-1927	1250	2500	5250		Alleged ax murderer, ESPV
Bordoni, Irene	1895-1953	25	35	45	55	"Louisiana Purchase," stage comedian
Borge, Victor	1909-	20	40		50	Entertainer

NAME	DOB/DOD	SIG	DS/LS	ALS	SP	COMMENTS
Borges, Jorge Luis	1900-1986	100	375	525		Short-story writer, poet, "Labyrinths"
Borgnine, Ernest	1915-	15	25	30	25	"Marty," "From Here To Eternity," US
Bori, Lucrezia	1887-1960	45	100	125	100	Opera: Soprano
Borodin, Aleksandr	1833-1887	260	500	1000		Russian composer
Borzage, Frank	1893-1962	45	100	225	165	The "great romanticist" director
Bosson, Barbara	1939-	5	10	15	10	"Hill Street Blues"
Bostic, Earl		15			35	(1913-1965); "Flamingo," "Sleep"; SA/CD-45
Bostwick, Barry	1945-	10	15	20	20	"The Rocky Horror Picture Show"
Boswell, James	1740-1795	1000	2000	4500		Biographer, "The Life of Samuel Johnson"
Bottoms, Joseph	1954-	5	10	15	10	"The Black Hole"
Bottoms, Sam	1955-	5	10	15	10	"Apocalypse Now"
Bottoms, Timothy	1951-	5	10	15	15	"Johnny Got His Gun," RS
Boulez, Pierre	1925-	35	60	80	30	French composer
Boulle, Pierre	1913-1994	15	25	45	25	French novelist, "Planet of the Apes"
Bow, Clara	1905-1965	225	400	500		Actress, ESPV, SP-$895
Bowie, David (David Jones)	1947-	100	150		125	(1996), often illegible signature; "Space Oddity," "Fame," "Diamond Dogs"; SA/CD-180, FA
Boxleitner, Bruce	1950-	5	10	15	10	"Scarecrow and Mrs. King," RS
Boyd, William	1895-1972	185	300	425	375	Hop-a-long Cassidy, sig. as both BB & Hoppy
Boyer, Charles	1897-1978	35	50	85	110	"Gaslight," French actor
Boyle, Lara Flynn	1970-	10	15	20	15	"Twin Peaks"
Boyle, Peter	1933-	5	10	15	10	"Young Frankenstein"
Boyz II Men		60	100		125	"I'll Make Love to You," "On Bended Knee"; SA/CD-150
Bracco, Lorraine	1955-	5	10	20	15	"GoodFellas"
Bracken, Eddie	1920-	5	10	15	10	"The Miracle of Morgan's Creek," RS
Brackett, Charles	1892-1969	25	50	75	60	Drama critic, producer, Pres. AMPAS
Bradbury, Ray	1920-	25	125	200	35	U.S. writer, "Fahrenheit 451", RS
Braden, Benard	1916-1993	25	40		45	Television journalist
Bradford, Barbara Taylor	1933-	10	20	30	25	British writer, "Angel," RS
Bradna, Olympe	1920-	15	45	75	30	"Souls at Sea," French actress

NAME	DOB/DOD	SIG	DS/LS	ALS	SP	COMMENTS
Brady, Alice	1892-1939	80	150	230	160	"In Old Chicago," "Young Mr. Lincoln"
Brady, Pat, Sons of the Pioneers	1914-1972	140	250		300	Roy Rogers sidekick, singing group
Brady, Scott	1924-1985	20	45	50	35	"Canon City," "Johnny Guitar"
☆ **Brahms, Johannes**	**1833-1897**	**1250**	**1650**	**3300**		**German composer, AMQS-$7500, ESPV**
Branagh, Kenneth	1960-	25	50		40	"Henry V"
Brand, Neville	1921-1992	90			150	Decorated G.I., "D.O.A.," "The Untouchables"
Brandauer, Klaus Maria	1944-	10	20		30	"Out of Africa"
Brando, Marlon	1924-	225	575		630	"On The Waterfront," "The Godfather"
Brasselle, Keefe	1923-1981	25	45		40	"The Eddie Cantor Story"
Braxton, Toni	1968-	20	40	50	40	"Un-Break My Heart"; SA/CD-60
Brecht, Bertolt	1898-1956	500	1725	2675		German dramatist, poet, "The Threepenny..."
Breen, Bobby	1927-	15	25	30	35	"Make a Wish," "Hawaii Calls," child star
Brendel, El	1890-1964	25	40		70	Vaudeville team member, "Sunny Side Up"
Brennan, Eileen	1935-	10	15	20	15	"Private Benjamin"
Brennan, Walter	1894-1974	100	150	225	175	First actor to win 3 Academy Awards, TV actor
Brenneman, Amy	1964-	5	10	20	15	"NYPD Blue"
Brenner, David	1945-	5	10	20	15	"Nightlife," comedian
Brent, George	1904-1979	35	40	45	60	"Jezebel," "42nd Street," "Front Page Woman"
Brian, Mary	1908-	12	25	30	25	"Peter Pan," "Beau Geste"
Brice, Fanny	1891-1951	150	260	325	350	"Ziegfeld Follies" star, "Baby Snooks"
Bridges, Beau (Lloyd Vernet Bridges III)	1941-	10	25		30	"The Fabulous Baker Boys"
Bridges, Jeff	1949-	10	25		30	"The Fabulous Baker Boys"
Bridges, Lloyd	1913-	25	55		55	"Sea Hunt"
Bridges, Todd	1966-	10	20		20	"Diff'rent Strokes"
Brimley, Wilford	1920-	15	30	40	25	"Cocoon", elusive signer
Brinkley, Christie	1954-	10	25	35	40	Supermodel, RS
Brinkley, David		10	20		25	Journalist, broadcaster

NAME	DOB/DOD	SIG	DS/LS	ALS	SP	COMMENTS
Britt, May	1933-	20	35	40	45	"Murder, Inc.," Swedish actress
Brittany, Morgan	1951-	10	20	25	25	"Dallas"
Britten, Benjamin	1913-1976	125	280	450	240	British composer
Britton, Barbara	1919-1980	15	35	35	30	"Captain Kidd," The Revlon Lady
Brod, Max	1884-1968	50	80		75	Writer
Broderick, Helen	1891-1959	40	75		75	"Top Hat," "Swing Time"
Broderick, Matthew	1962-	10	25		30	"Ferris Bueller's Day Off," "Brighton Beach...", RS
Brodsky, Joseph	1940-1996	20	30	55	25	Russian-U.S. poet, "To Urania," RS
Brokaw, Tom		10			20	Journalist, broadcaster
Brolin, James	1940-	10	20		40	"Marcus Welby, M.D.", RS
Bromfield, Louis	1896-1956	40	80	125	75	"Early Autumn" author
Bronson, Charles	1921-	10	40		50	"Death Wish", RS
Brook, Clive	1887-1974	45	65	70	80	"Sherlock Holmes," "Shanghai Express"
Brook, Peter	1925-	15	30		25	Director
Brooke, Hillary	1914-	15	20	30	30	"Jane Eyre," "My Little Margie"-TV
Brooks, Albert	1947-	10	20		25	"Defending Your Life," director, writer
Brooks, Garth		15	30		45	Country music, baseball player
Brooks, Geraldine	1925-1977	15	30	25	30	"Possessed," "Cry Wolf," m. B. Schulberg
Brooks, Gwendolyn	1917-	25	45	60	30	U.S. writer, "Primer For Blacks"- $75 (FE,SB), RS
Brooks, James L.	1940-	10	20		20	"Mary Tyler Moore Show"-creator, producer
Brooks, Mel	1926-	10	35	40	25	"Blazing Saddles," director, FA
Brooks, Phyllis	1914-	10	20		20	"The Unseen," "High Powered"
Broonzy, Big Bill	1893-1958	40	55		65	Blues singer, guitar player
Brosnan, Pierce	1952-	20	50		50	"Remington Steele", elusive signer
Brown, Blair	1948-	5	15	20	15	"The Days and Nights of Molly Dodd"
Brown, Bryan	1947-	5	10		10	Actor, married to Rachel Ward
Brown, George Stanford	1943-	5	10		15	"Colossus: The Forbin Project"
Brown, James	1933-	20	40	50	45	(1986), RS; "Papa's Got a Brand New Bag"; SA/CD-65
Brown, Joe E.	1892-1973	42	50	50	80	"Show Boat," "Some Like It Hot"

NAME	DOB/DOD	SIG	DS/LS	ALS	SP	COMMENTS
Brown, Johnny Mack	1904-1974	60	125		150	"Billy the Kid," "B" movie western star
Brown, Nacio Herb	1896-1964	50	125	150	75	U.S., "Singing in the Rain"
Brown, Ruth	1928-	20	30		35	(1993); "Lucky Lips," "This Little Girl..."; SA/CD-50
Brown, Vanessa	1928-	15	25		30	"Margie," "The Ghost and Mrs. Muir"
Browne, Jackson	1948-	15	30		30	"Doctor My Eyes," "Stay"; SA/CD-45
Browning, Elizabeth Barrett	1806-1861	525	1250	3250		British poet, "Aurora Leigh"
Browning, Robert	1812-1889	425	750	1450	1550	Brit. poet, "The Ring... Book," AMsS-$3250
Brownlee, John	1900-1969	20	50		45	Baritone
Brubeck, Dave	1920-	10	20		20	Pianist, composer, RS
Bruce, Lenny	1925-1966	275	325		865	Comedian
Bruce, Nigel	1895-1953	165		300	300	"Sherlock Holmes"-Dr. Watson
Bruce, Virginia	1910-1982	20	35		35	"Jane Eyre," "Born to Dance"
Bruckner, Anton	1824-1896	1400	2800	4250	2750	Austrian composer, ALS-ESPV
Bryan, Jane	1918-	10	20	25	20	"Kid Galahad," "The Old Maid"
Bryant, William Callen	1794-1878	125	259	420		Poet
Brynner, Yul	1915-1985	50	100	100	125	"The King and I," sig. often illegible
Buchanan, Edgar	1903-1979	40	50	60	80	"Move Over, Darling!," "Judge Roy Bean"
Buck, Frank	1888-1950	30	75	150	80	"Bring 'Em Back Alive," hunter, explorer
Buck, Pearl S.	1892-1973	50	175	225	65	U.S. novelist, "The Good Earth," RS
Buckley, Betty	1947-	5	10	15	10	"Eight is Enough"
Buddy Holly and the Crickets		875			1250	B. Holly (KS); "That'll Be the Day"; SA/CD-1550, FA
Buffalo Springfield		85			125	(1997), N. Young (KS), S. Stills (KS); "For What It's Worth"; SA/CD-175
Bujold, Genevieve	1942-	10	20	25	25	"Dead Ringers"
Bukowski, Charles	1928-1994	25	75	100	50	Cult writer, poet, RS
Bulgakov, Mikhail	1891-1940					Russian novelist, "The Heart of a Dog", PU
Bullock, Sandra	1967-	25	50	50	60	"Speed"
Bundy, Ted	1954-1989	50	100	150	150	Convicted murderer, ESPV
Bunin, Ivan	1870-1953	35	75		65	Writer, NP

William Cullen Bryant

Johannes Brahms

Edgar Rice Burroughs

Johannes Brahms

Edgar Rice Burroughs

Richard Burton

Robert Browning

Lenny Bruce

Enrico Caruso

NAME	DOB/DOD	SIG	DS/LS	ALS	SP	COMMENTS
Burgess, Anthony	1917-1993	50	90		100	British author, "A Clockwork Orange"
Burghoff, Gary	1943-	10	25		30	"M * A * S * H"
Burke, Billie	1885-1970	150	250		250	TWOO, "Merrily We Live"
Burke, Delta	1956-	5	10		20	"Designing Women"
Burke, Johnny	1908-1984	25	65	100	50	U.S. lyricist, "Misty"
Burleigh, Henry T.	1866-1949	35	70	140	50	Baritone, composer
Burneet, Frances Hodgson	1849-1924	100	200	300		British-U.S. novelist, "The Secret Garden"
Burnett, Carol	1933-	15	25	40	35	"The Carol Burnett Show"
Burnette, "Smiley"	1911-1967	50	60		80	"Frog Millhouse," western film star
Burns, Ed	1968-	15	30		45	"The Brothers McMullen"
Burns, George	1896-1996	30	75		75	Radio & TV pioneer, w/Gracie-$175-a. leaf, FA
Burns, Robert	1759-1796	750	1500	3000		Poet, "Auld Lang Syne," ESPV-ALS
Burr, Raymond	1917-1993	40	50		75	"Rear Window," "Perry Mason"-TV
Burroughs, Edgar Rice	1875-1950	275	500	800	750	U.S. novelist, "Tarzan of the Apes," TLS-4X
Burroughs, William S.	1914-1997	35	55	100	50	U.S. novelist, "Naked Lunch," elusive signer
Burrows, Darren E.	1966-	5	10		15	"Northern Exposure"
Burstyn, Ellen (Edna Rae Gillolly)	1932-	5	15	25	20	"Alice Doesn't Live Here Anymore", RS
Burton, LeVar	1957-	25	50		50	"Star Trek: The Next Generation", FA
Burton, Richard	1925-1984	125	225		210	"Beckett," "Who's Afraid of Virginia Wolff"
Burton, Virginia Lee	1909-1968	35	75	125		U.S. children's author, "Mike Mulligan and ..."
Busey, Gary	1944-	10	20		25	"The Buddy Holly Story", RS
Busfield, Timothy	1957-	10	20		20	"thirtysomething"
Bush		35			50	"Glycerine"; SA/CD-65
Bushman, Francis X.	1883-1966	60	120	125	125	"Ben Hur," "Romeo and Juliet"
Bushnell, Nolan	1943-	20	40		35	Inventor of video games
Butler, Brett	1958-	5	10		15	"Grace Under Fire," comedian
Butlin, Billy	1899-1980	25	35		45	Holiday camp enthusiast
Buttafuoco, Joey		5	20	30		Mechanic

NAME	DOB/DOD	SIG	DS/LS	ALS	SP	COMMENTS
Butterley, Nigel H.	1935-	15			25	Composer, pianist
Buttrose, Ita	1942-	10	20		20	Journalist
Buttons, Red	1918-	10	20		25	"Sayonara," TV and club comic
Buttram, Pat	1917-1994	30	30		65	"The Gene Autry Show," "Green Acres"-TV
Buzzi, Ruth	1936-	5	10		15	"Laugh-In", RS
Byas, Don	1912-1972	25	45		45	Tenor sax
Byington, Spring	1893-1971	40	50		60	"Little Women," "Meet John Doe"
Byrds, The		300			575	(1991), G. Clark (1941-1991); "Turn! Turn! Turn!"; SA/CD-600
Byron, Lord (George Gordon)	1788-1824	1750	3000	3000		British poet, "Don Juan," ESPV-ALS
Caan, James	1939-	5	15	25	25	"The Godfather", RS
Caballe, Montserrat	1933-	10	25		25	Soprano
Cabot, Bruce	1905-1972	70	85	100	150	"King Kong," "Fury"
Cabot, Sebastian	1918-1977	40	50	120	80	British character actor, "Family Affair"-TV
Caesar, Irving	1895-1996	25	60	100	50	U.S. lyricist, "Just a Gigolo"
Caesar, Sid	1922-	10	20	35	25	"Your Show of Shows"
Cage, John	1912-1992	50	130	175	75	U.S. composer
Cage, Nicolas	1964-	15	40	80	40	"Raising Arizona," RS, FA
Cagney, James	1899-1986	85	125	225	250	"Yankee Doodle Dandy," RS
Cagney, Jeanne	1919-1984	20	30	40	30	Sister of James, "Yankee Doodle Dandy"
Cahn, Sammy	1913-1993	25	75	130	50	Composer of "High Hopes," "Three Coins...", RS
Cain, Dean	1966-	20	40	75	45	"Lois & Clark"-TV, FA
Cain, James M.	1892-1977	30	50	75	50	Writer
Caine, Michael	1933-	10	20	30	25	"Hannah and Her Sisters," RS
Cairoli, Charlie	1910-1980	25	50		50	Circus clown
Calabro, Thomas	1959-	5	10	15	10	"Melrose Place"-TV
Caldwell, Erskine	1903-1987	40	120	200	80	Writer, "Tobacco Road"
Calhern, Louis	1895-1956	40	50	65	50	"Duck Soup," "Notorious," character actor
Calhoun, Rory	1922-	10	20	25	20	"The Spoilers," "The Texan"-TV
Calisher, Hortense	1911-	10	20	40	15	U.S. writer, "Collected Stories"

NAME	DOB/DOD	SIG	DS/LS	ALS	SP	COMMENTS
Callaghan, Morley	1903-	10	20	40	20	Writer
Callas, Maria	1923-1977	325	875	900	1200	Opera: Soprano
Callow, Simon	1949-	5	10	15	10	"A Room with a View"
Calloway, Cab	1907-1994	35	50	75	150	Band leader
Calve, Emma	1858-1942	65	125	200	475	Opera: Soprano
Calvet, Corinne	1925-	10	15	20	15	"La Part de l'Ombre," "Rope of Sand"
Calvino, Italo	1923-1985	35				Italian novelist, "If On a Winter's Night..."
Cameron, Kirk	1970-	10	20	30	20	"Growing Pains"
Camp, Colleen	1953-	10	20	25	20	"Dallas"
Campbell, Bill	1960-	5	10	15	10	"The Rocketeer"
Campbell, Bruce	1958-	5	10	15	10	"The Adventures of Briscoe County, Jr."
Campbell, Glen	1936-	5	10	15	15	"The Glen Campbell Goodtime Hour"
Campbell, Mrs. Patrick	1865-1940	40	70		75	Actress
Campbell, Naomi	1970-	20	35	40	40	Supermodel
Campbell, Neve	1973-	15	25	45	40	"Party of Five," "Scream"
Campbell, Sir Malcolm	1885-1948	60	115		100	Speed-record holder
Campbell, Tisha	1970-	5	10	15	10	"Martin"
Campion, Jane	1954-	10	20	25	20	"The Piano," director, screenwriter
Camus, Albert	1913-1960	100	275	600		French writer, "The Stranger"
Cannon, Dyan (Samille Diane Friesen)	1937-	10	15	20	25	"Bob & Carol & Ted & Alice", "Ally McBeal"
Canova, Judy	1916-1983	20	30	35	30	"In Caliente," "Chatterbox"
Cantinflas	1918-1994	55	75	115	100	Mexican actor, "Around the World in Eighty..."
Cantor, Eddie	1892-1964	70	145	215	150	Vaudeville and radio star, "Whoopee", FA
Capone, Al	1899-1947	3000	11500		4250	Chicago gangster
Capote, Truman	1924-1984	150	350	1000	300	U.S. author, "In Cold Blood"
Capra, Frank	1897-1991	45	150	285	90	Famed director, IAWL, RS
Capshaw, Kate	1953-	5	10	15	20	"Indiana Jones and the Temple of Doom"
Cara, Irene	1959-	5	10	15	10	"What a Feeling," "Fame" singer

NAME	DOB/DOD	SIG	DS/LS	ALS	SP	COMMENTS
Caray, Harry	1921-1998	30	55	65	50	Announcer for the Chi. Cubs, 7th Inn. singer, RS
Cardin, Pierre	1922-	20	40		40	French fashion designer
Cardinale, Caludia	1939-	5	10	15	10	"The Pink Panther"
Carey, Drew	1958-	10	20	25	25	"The Drew Carey Show," RS
Carey, Harry	1878-1947	140	175	200	275	Pioneer of Westerns, both silent & sound
Carey, MacDonald	1913-1994	15	30	60	30	"Dream Girl," "The Great Gatsby"
Carey, Mariah	1970-	30			75	"Vision of Love," "Honey," "Fantasy"; SA/CD-65, FA
Carlin, George	1937-	5	10	15	20	"Seven Dirty Words", RS
Carlisle, Kitty	1914-	10	15	20	15	"A Night at the Opera," "To Tell the Truth"-TV
Carlisle, Mary	1912-	10	15	25	20	"College Humor," "Double or Nothing"
Carlson, Richard	1914-1977	30	50	60	60	"Creature from the Black Lagoon"
Carmichael, Hoagy	1899-1981	50	175	300	225	U.S., "Stardust," AMQS- $325
Carne, Judy	1939-	5	10	15	10	"Laugh-In"
Carnegie, Dale	1888-1955	50	100	160	100	Lecturer, author
Carney, Art	1918-	10	30	60	25	"The Honeymooners," RS
Carney, Harry	1910-1974	30	70		60	Baritone sax
Caron, Leslie	1931-	10	20	30	30	"Lili"
Carpenter, John	1948-	10	20	45	25	"Halloween," director, writer
Carpenter, Karen		170	325		300	"The Carpenters," sig. by both-$265
Carradine, David	1936-	5	10	15	20	"Kung Fu"
Carradine, John	1906-1988	75	100	150	150	"Stagecoach," "The Grapes of Wrath"
Carradine, Keith	1949-	5	10	15	15	"Nashville," b. of David
Carradine, Robert	1954-	5	10	15	15	"Revenge of the Nerds," b. of Keith
Carrera, Barbara	1951-	5	10	15	25	Model, "Dallas"
Carreras, Jose Maria	1946-	10	20		25	Lyric tenor
Carrey, Jim	1962-	40	100	200	65	"Ace Ventura: Pet Detective," elusive signer
Carrillo, Leo	1880-1961	60	100	175	150	Pancho in "Cisco Kid" films and TV series
Carroll, Diahann	1935-	5	10	15	15	"I Know Why the Caged Bird Sings"
Carroll, Leo G.	1892-1972	50	60	75	80	"Wuthering Heights," "Rebecca"

NAME	DOB/DOD	SIG	DS/LS	ALS	SP	COMMENTS
Carroll, Lewis (Charles Dodgson)	1832-1898	300	825	1650		British writer, "Alice's Adventures ..."
Carroll, Madeline	1906-1987	30	75	150	65	"The Thirty-Nine Steps"
Carroll, Nancy	1904-1965	20	25	30	40	"The Shopworn Angel," "The Devil's Holiday"
Carry, Julius		5	10	15	10	"Murphy Brown"
Cars, The		40			50	R. Ocasek (KS); "Shake It Up"; SA/CD-55
Carson, Jack	1910-1963	20	30	40	40	"Mildred Pierce," "Cat on a Hot Tin Roof"
Carson, Johnny	1925-	15	30	40	50	"The Tonight Show," elusive signer, FA
Carter, Benny	1907-	30	65		75	Alto saxophonist
Carter, Dixie	1939-	5	10	15	10	"Designing Women"
Carter, Elliott Cook, Jr.	1908-	20	45		40	Composer
Carter, Lynda	1951-	5	10	20	20	"Wonder Woman"
Carter, Nell	1948-	5	10	15	10	"Gimme a Break," singer
Carteris, Gabrielle	1961-	10	20	30	20	"Beverly Hills 90210"
Cartland, Barbara	1901-	15	40	75	50'	Novelist, RS
Cartwright, Veronica	1950-	5	10	15	10	"Alien"
Caruso, David	1956-	10	20	30	35	"NYPD Blue", RS
Caruso, Enrico	**1873-1921**	**300**	**575**	**700**	**1000**	**Opera: Tenor, noted for drawing self-caricatures**
Carvey, Dana	1955-	10	25	30	35	"Wayne's World," SNL
Casals, Pablo	1876-1973	75	150		400	Cellist
Casanova, Giacomo		165				Author
Cash, Johnny	1942-	20	50		40	(1992); "I Walk the Line," "A Boy Named Sue"; SA/CD-50
Cass, Peggy (Mary Margaret Cass)	1924-1999	10	15	20	15	"To Tell the Truth"
Cassidy, David	1950-	10	20	25	30	"The Partridge Family"
Cassidy, Joanna	1944-	5	10	20	15	"Buffalo Bill"
Cassidy, Ted		200			500	"Addams Family," scarce
Cates, Phoebe	1963-	10	15	25	30	"Fast Times at Ridgemont High"
Cather, Willa	1873-1947	300	450	800	260	U.S. novelist, "O Pioneers!," ALS-2-2.5X
Catlett, Walter	1889-1960	15	25	30	30	Vaudeville and stage comedian

NAME	DOB/DOD	SIG	DS/LS	ALS	SP	COMMENTS
Cattrall, Kim	1956-	5	10	15	10	"The Bonfire of the Vanities"
Caulfield, Joan	1922-1991	15	25	35	30	"Blue Skies," "Dear Ruth"
Cavett, Dick	1936-	5	10	20	10	"The Dick Cavett Show," RS
Chabrier, Emmanuel	1841-1894	100	200	400		French composer
Chaliapin, Fyodor	1873-1938	225	275	525	575	Opera: Bass
Chamberlain, Richard (George)	1935-	10	20	30	25	"Dr. Kildare"
Chan, Jackie	1954-	10	20	25	30	"Rumble in the Bronx", RS
Chancellor, John		20			40	Journalist, broadcaster, FA
Chandler, Helen ₰	1906-1965	40	50	65	80	"Outward Bound," "The Last Flight"
Chandler, Jeff	1918-1961	60	75	150	120	"Broken Arrow," Western & action actor
Chandler, Raymond	1888-1959	320	600	1000		U.S. writer, "Philip Marlowe" series, scarce
Chaney, Lon ☆	**1883-1930**	**1200**	**3000**	**3250**	**2000**	**"The Man of a Thousand Faces," scarce, ESPV**
Chaney, Lon, Jr.	1906-1973	350	740		640	"Of Mice and Men," "The Wolf Man", ESPV
Channing, Carol	1921-	5	15	20	10	"Thoroughly Modern Millie," sig. often illegible, RS
Channing, Stockard	1944-	5	10	15	10	"Grease" (Susan Williams Antonia Stockard)
Chao, Rosalind		5	10	15	10	M*A*S*H*
Chaplin, Charlie ☆	**1889-1977**	**350**	**775**	**800**	**850**	**Screen legend, elusive signer, FA**
Chaplin, Geraldine	1944-	10	20	30	25	"Doctor Zhivago"
Chaplin, Lita Grey	1909-1995	30	35	50	40	Married to Charlie Chaplin
Chaplin, Sydney	1885-1965	20	25	40	40	Half brother of Charlie, "Charley's Aunt"
Chapman, Mark David		100	175	200		Shot John Lennon
Charisse, Cyd	1921-	5	10	15	25	"Brigadoon"
Charles, Ray	1930-	135	275		200	(1986), DS-$300; "Georgia on My Mind"; SA/CD-175, FA
Charo	1951-	5	10	15	10	"The Love Boat," singer
Charpentier, Gustave	1860-1956	80	180	300	250	French composer
Charters, Spencer	1875-1943	25	40	45	50	"Whoopee," "Tobacco Road"
Chase, Chevy	1943-	5	10	20	30	SNL, "The Blues Brothers," "Vacation," "Caddyshack"

NAME	DOB/DOD	SIG	DS/LS	ALS	SP	COMMENTS
Chatterton, Ruth	1893-1961	20	25	35	50	"Madame X," "Sarah and Son"
Chayefsky, Paddy	1923-1981	75	150	200	150	Playwright, "Marty"
Cheap Trick		35			40	RSs! "Surrender," "The Flame," "I Want You To..."; SA/CD-45
Cheatham, Doc	1905-1997	15	30		30	Big band trumpeter
Checker, Chubby		10	30		25	RS, "The Twist"; SA/CD-30
Cheever, John	1912-1982	55	125	265	125	U.S. poet, short-story writer, "The Wapshot..."
☆ **Chekhov, Anton**	**1860-1904**	**1000**	**2500**	**5500**		**Russian short-story writer, ALS-2X, ESPV**
Cher (Cherilyn Sarkisan La Piere)	1946-	25	50	50	60	"Moonstruck," "Sonny & Cher", FA
Cherry, Don	1937-1995	20	40		45	Lyrical jazz trumpeter
Chessman, Caryl	1921-1960	225	450	500		American criminal
Chesterton, Gilbert Keith	1874-1936	100	200	300	200	British critic, "Father Brown" series, STLS-2X
Chevalier, Maurice	1888-1972	55	150	175	150	Popular Frenchman, "The Love Parade"
Chicago		85			150	T. Kath (1946-1978), P. Cetera (KS); "Saturday in the Park"; SA/CD-175
Child, Julia	1912-	5	10	15	10	"Mastering the Art of French Cooking," chef
Chiles, Lois	1950-	5	10	15	20	"The Way We Were," model
Chong, Rae Dawn	1962-	5	10	15	15	"The Color Purple," d. Thomas Chong
Chong, Tommy	1938-	10	20	25	20	"Up in Smoke," former partner Cheech Marin
☆ **Chopin, Frederic**	**1810-1849**	**2000**	**4500**			**Polish composer, ans-$24800, ESPV**
Christian, Linda	1923-	10	20	25	20	"Battle Zone," "Athena"
Christie, Agatha	1890-1976	265	550	750	600	British mystery writer, "Murder on the ..." ESPV
Christie, Julie	1941-	30	40	40	65	"Dr. Zhivago"
Christoff, Boris	1914-1993	25	60	125	80	Opera: Bass
Christopher, William	1932-	5	10	15	10	"M*A*S*H," RS
Churchill, Marguerite	1909-	10	20	25	20	"The Big Trail," "The Valiant"
Churchill, Sarah	1914-1982	25	40	45	45	"Royal Wedding," daughter of Winston
Ciannelli, Eduardo	1887-1969	30	35	40	55	"Reunion in Vienna," "Gunga Din"

KAREN CARPENTER

RICHARD L. CARPENTER

Karen & Richard Carpenter

Agatha Christie

Agatha Christie

Edgar Cayce

Edgar Cayce

Samuel Clemens

Charlie Chaplin

Samuel Clemens, Mark Twain

Charlie Chaplin

Patsy Cline

NAME	DOB/DOD	SIG	DS/LS	ALS	SP	COMMENTS
Claiborne, Craig	1920-	10	20		15	Chef, writer
Clancy, Tom	1947-	10	20	30	15	U.S. writer, "The Hunt for ..." RS
Clapton, Eric	1945-	50			60	RS! "Tears in Heaven," "Layla"; SA/CD-75
Clark, Dane	1913-	5	10	20	15	"Whiplash," "Moonrise," RS
Clark, Dick	1929-	5	15	25	20	"American Bandstand"
Clark, Fred	1914-1968	30	40	50	60	"A Place in the Sun," "Sunset Boulevard"
Clark, Mary Higgins	1931-	10	20	35	20	U.S. writer, "Remember Me," RS
Clark, Petula	1932-	10	25	35	20	"Dance Hall," singer, actress
Clark, Roy	1933-	5	10	15	10	"Hee Haw," RS
Clarke, Arthur C.	1917-	20	40	80	40	"2001: A Space Odyssey"
Clarke, Kenny	1914-1985	30	60		60	Modern drum pioneer
Clash, The		40			100	"Rock the Casbah," "Train in Vain..."; SA/CD-120
Clavell, James	1925-1994	20	40	65	30	British-U.S. novelist, "Shogun," RS
Clay, Andrew Dice	1958-	5	10	15	10	"The Adventures of Ford Fairlane"
Clayburgh, Jill	1944-	10	15	20	20	"An Unmarried Woman"
Clayton, Buck	1911-1991	30	55		50	Trumpet player, arranger
Cleary, Beverly	1916-	10	20	30	20	U.S. writer, "Ramona" series, RS
Cleese, John	1939-	10	20	30	20	"Monty Python's Flying Circus," res. signer
Cleveland, James	1931-1991	25	40		45	Gospel singer
Cliburn, Van	1934-	30	60		60	Pianist
Clift, Montgomery	1920-1966	250	375	600	725	Talented actor, FHTE, FA, died young
Cline, Patsy	1932-1962	600		1200	1500	Country music legend
Clooney, George	1961-	25	50	65	70	"ER," elusive signer, sig. often illegible
Clooney, Rosemary	1928-	5	15	20	10	"White Christmas," TV star
Close, Glenn	1947-	20	45	60	70	"Fatal Attraction," FA, mail ghost-signed
Clute, Chester	1891-1956	20	35	40	35	"Yankee Doodle Dandy," "Guest Wife"
Clyde, Andy	1892-1967	60	100	125	155	"Annie Oakley," "The Green Years"
Coasters, The		50			125	(1987); "Yakety Yak"; SA/CD-150
Cobb, Joe	1917-	15	30	35	35	"Our Gang" member

NAME	DOB/DOD	SIG	DS/LS	ALS	SP	COMMENTS
Cobb, Lee J.	1911-1976	60	75	100	120	"On The Waterfront," "Coogan's Bluff"
Coburn, Charles	1877-1961	45	100	120	130	"The More the Merrier," "The Green Years"
Coburn, James	1928-	10	20	25	20	"The Magnificent Seven"
Coca, Imogene	1908-	10	20	25	20	"Your Show of Shows"
Cochran, Eddie	1938-1960	450	600		750	(1987), (1938-1960); "Summertime Blues"; SA/CD-1000
Cocker, Joe	1944-	20			30	Can be an elusive signer; "With a Little Help From My Friends"; SA/CD-35
Cocteau, Jean	1889-1963	150	300	850	600	French writer, "The Beauty and the Beast"
Coen, Ethan	1958-	5	10	15	10	"Raising Arizona," director, writer
Coen, Joel	1955-	5	10	15	10	"Raising Arizona," b. Ethan
Cohan, George M.	1878-1942					See composers
Cohan, George M.	1878-1942	125	200	350	275	U.S., "Give My Regards to Broadway"
Cohen, Leonard	1934-	15	25	50	30	U.S. lyricist, "Suzanne"
Cohn, Al	1925-1988	25	50		45	Tenor sax player, composer
Cohn, Roy	1927-1986	25	60		50	Lawyer
Colbert, Claudette	1905-	25	150	200	100	"It Happened One Night," "Cleopatra"
Cole, Cozy	1909-1981	20	40		35	Drummer
Cole, Nat King	1919-1965	200	300		375	
Coleman, Cy	1929-	10	20	30	25	U.S., "Sweet Charity," RS!
Coleman, Dabney	1932-	10	20	20	15	"Buffalo Bill"
Coleman, Gary	1968-	5	10	10	10	"Diff'rent Strokes," FA
Coleman, Nancy	1917-	5	10	10	10	"Kings Row," "Edge of Darkness," RS
Coleman, Ornette	1930-	15			30	Alto saxophonist
Coleridge, Samuel Taylor	1772-1834	300	600	1200		British poet, "Kubla Khan," ESPV
Colette, (Sidonie)	1873-1954	100	275	400		French novelist, "Gigi"
Collins, Cora Sue	1927-	5	10	10	10	Child star, "Treasure Island"
Collins, Gary	1938-	5	10	10	10	"Home"
Collins, Joan	1933-	25	30	35	50	"The Girl in the Red Swing," "Dynasty"-TV

NAME	DOB/DOD	SIG	DS/LS	ALS	SP	COMMENTS
Collins, Phil	1951-	20			40	A RS; "Against All Odds"; SA/CD-50
Collins, Stephen	1947-	5	10	10	10	"Tales of the Gold Monkey"
Collins, Wilkie	1824-1889	125	275	300		English novelist, "Antonina"
Collyer, June	1907-1968	15	20	25	25	"The Trouble With Father"-TV
Colman, Ronald	1891-1958	65	150	150	150	"A Double Life," "Lost Horizon," FA
Colonna, Jerry	1903-1986	15	25	25	30	"Road to Singapore," Bob Hope's sidekick
Coltrane, John	1926-1967	350	700		1250	Innovative tenor sax player, rare, ESPV
Columbo, Russ	1908-1934	60	100	175	125	"Dynamite," "Moulin Rouge"
Columbus, Chris	1958-	10	20	20	10	"Home Alone," director
Combs, Sean "Puff Daddy"		15			35	"I'll Be Missing You"; SA/CD-40
Comden, Betty & Green, Adolph	1919-, 1915-	20	40	65	40	U.S. lyricist, "New York, New York"
Compson, Betty	1897-1974	20	25	45	50	"The Miracle Man," "The Barker"
Compton, Fay	1894-1978	20	35		40	Actress
Conaway, Jeff	1950-	5	10	10	10	"Taxi"
Condon, Eddie	1904-1973	45	100		75	Band leader, guitar player
Congreve, William	1670-1729	220	615	1000		English dramatist "Double Dealer"
Conklin, "Heinie"	1880-1959	45	60	65	75	"All Quiet on the Western Front"
Conklin, Chester	1888-1971	115	125	225	250	"Modern Times," "The Great Dictator"
Conlin, Jimmy	1885-1962	25	35	45	40	Vaudeville star, "Sharps and Flats"
Connell, Evan S.	1924-	10	25	35	15	U.S. writer, "Mr. Bridge"
Connelly, Jennifer	1970-	5	10	15	25	"The Rocketeer"
Connelly, Marc	1890-1980	25	60		40	Playwright
Conners, Mike (Krekor Ohanian)	1925-	10	20	25	20	"Mannix"
Connery, Sean	1930-	60	150	325	130	"James Bond" series-SP-2X, elusive signer
Connolly, Walter	1887-1940	80	100	100	100	"It Happened One Night"
Conrad, Joseph	1857-1924	200	875	1250		British novelist, "Lord Jim"
Conried, Hans	1917-1982	20	25	30	40	"The 5,000 Fingers of Dr. T"
Conroy, Kevin	1955-	5	10	10	10	Actor, voice "Batman:The Animated Series"
Conroy, Pat	1945-	12	30	45	20	U.S. writer, "The Prince of Tides," RS!

NAME	DOB/DOD	SIG	DS/LS	ALS	SP	COMMENTS
Constantine, Michael	1927-	10	15	20	15	"Room 222"
Conte, Richard	1914-1975	15	20	25	20	"Under the Gun," "A Walk in the Sun"
Conti, Tom	1941-	5	10	10	10	"Reuben Reuben"
Conway, Kevin	1942-	5	10	10	10	"Slaughterhouse-5"
Conway, Tim (Thomas Conway)	1933-	5	10	10	10	"The Carol Burnett Show," RS
Conway, Tom	1904-1967	60	120	150	150	"Sky Murder," "The Falcon's Brother"
Coogan, Jackie	1914-1984	25	35	40	50	Silent child star, "Oliver Twist"
Cook, Elisha, Jr.	1906-1995	25	30	45	65	"The Maltese Falcon"
Cook, Robin	1940-	10	15	25	15	U.S. writer, RS
Cooke, Alistair	1908-	25	75		60	Journalist
Cooke, Sam	1935-1964	300			600	(1986), (1935-1964); "You Send Me," "Shake"; SA/CD-650
Cooley, Denton	1920-	15	40		30	Cardiac surgeon
Coolio	1963-	15			25	"Gangsta's Paradise"; SA/CD-40
Cooper, Alice	1948-	20			40	"Elected," "School's Out," "You and Me"; SA/CD-75
Cooper, Dame Gladys	1888-1971	40	75	85	70	Actress
☆ **Cooper, Gary**	**1901-1961**	**225**	**400**	**500**	**595**	**Screen legend, "High Noon," "Sergeant York", FA**
Cooper, Gladys	1888-1971	40	50	75	65	British actress, "Rebecca," "My Fair Lady"
Cooper, Jackie	1923-	20	30	40	50	"Our Gang" series, "Skippy"
Cooper, James Fenimore	1789-1851	80	175	750		U.S. novelist, "The Last ...," ALS-2-3X
Coote, Robert	1909-1982	20	35	45	45	British actor, "Gunga Din," "Forever Amber"
Coots, John Frederick	1897-?	40	65	135	50	U.S., "For All We Know"
Copland, Aaron	1900-1990	75	200	550	165	U.S. composer, "Appalachian Spring," RS
Copperfield, David	1956-	5	10	15	20	Magician, RS
Coppola, Francis Ford	1939-	40	100	100	75	"The Godfather," recent elusive signer
Corbin, Barry	1940-	5	10	15	10	"Northern Exposure"
Corday, Mara	1932-	5	10	20	10	"Sea Tiger," "The Naked Gun"
Cordobes, El	1936-	25	50		60	Matador

NAME	DOB/DOD	SIG	DS/LS	ALS	SP	COMMENTS
Corey, Wendell	1914-1968	40	55	75	80	"Rear Window," "The Rainmaker"
Corley, Pat	1930-	5	10	10	10	"Murphy Brown"
Cornell, Katharine	1893-1974	25	50		65	Actress
Cort, Bud	1950-	5	10	10	10	"Harold and Maude"
Cortez, Ricardo	1899-1977	30	40	40	45	"The Torrent," "The Maltese Falcon"
Cosby, Bill	1937-	10	15	25	25	"The Cosby Show"-TV, RS
Costello, Dolores	1905-1979	30	35	55	60	"The Sea Beast," "Little Lord Fauntleroy"
Costello, Elvis	1954-	10			25	RS; "Alison"; SA/CD-35
Costello, Frank	1893-1973	1565				Mafia boss
Costello, Lou	**1906-1959**	**265**	**550**	**600**	**500**	**"Abbott & Costello," sheet w/BA-$600**
Costner, Kevin	1955-	40	100	200	75	"The Untouchables," FA, elusive signer
Cottee, Kay	1954-	75	40		35	Yachting record holder
Cotten, Joseph	1905-1994	25	35	60	45	"Citizen Kane," "Gaslight," "Under Capricorn"
Coulier, David		5	10	15	10	"Full House"
Couric, Katie	1957-	5	10	15	10	"Today," RS, FA
Courtney, Tom	1937-	15	35		30	Actor
Cowan, Jerome	1897-1972	35	50		55	"The Maltese Falcon"
Coward, Noel	1899-1973	150	250	375	300	British, "Bitter Sweet," composer, actor
Cowley, Malcolm	1898-1989	25	50		50	Critic, editor, ESPV-DS
Cox, Courtney	1964-	20	45	65	50	"Friends," elusive signer, FA
Cox, Ronny	1938-	5	10	10	10	"Beverly Hills Cop"
Coyote, Peter	1942-	5	10	15	10	"Jagged Edge"
Crabbe, Larry "Buster"	1907-1983	40	75	65	80	"Tarzan," "Flash Gordon," 1932 Olympics
Crain, Jeanne	1925-	20	25	35	50	"Pinky," "State Fair," "Margie"
Crane, Bob		150	260		240	"Hogan's Heroes," scarce
Crane, Hart	1899-1932	200	500	1250		U.S. poet, "The Bridge"
Crane, Stephen	1871-1900	500	1000	4500		U.S. novelist, "The Red Badge of Courage"
Craven, Wes	1939-	10	20	25	20	"Nightmare on Elm Street"

NAME	DOB/DOD	SIG	DS/LS	ALS	SP	COMMENTS
Crawford, Broderick	1911-1986	40	145	145	100	"All The King's Men," "Born Yesterday"
Crawford, Cindy	1964-	5	20	30	40	Supermodel, "House of Style," RS
Crawford, Joan	1904-1977	65	175	200	200	"Mildred Pierce," "Sudden Fear," "Possessed"
Crawford, Michael (Michael Dumble-Smith)	1942-	25	40	45	75	"The Phantom of the Opera," singer
Cream		150		175	200	(1993), E. Clapton (KS); "Sunshine of Your Love"; SA/CD-300
Creedence Clearwater Revival		175			325	(1993), T. Fogerty (1941-1990); "Proud Mary"; SA/CD-350
Cregar, Laird	1916-1944	110	125	250	300	Character actor, "Charley's Aunt," died young
Creeley, Robert	1926-	10	25		20	Writer, "Words"
Crenna, Richard	1927-	10	15	15	25	"Rambo: First Blood Part I"
Crews, Harry	1935-	12	20	40	20	U.S. writer, "Where Does One..." $75 (FE,SB)
Crews, Laura Hope	1880-1942	200	350	375	400	GWTW-Aunt Pittypat, scarce in all forms
Crichton, Michael	1942-	10	40	100	25	U.S. writer, "Jurrasic Park," RS, FA
Crisp, Donald	1881-1974	75	100	125	150	Silent film director, "How Green Was My Valley"
Cristal, Linda	1936-	15	20	25	25	"The Alamo," "The High Chaparral"-TV
Croce, Jim	1943-1973	175	300		395	"Bad, Bad Leroy Brown," killed in plane crash
Cromwell, Richard	1910-1960	20	25	30	35	"Jezebel," "Young Mr. Lincoln"
Cronenberg, David	1943-	10	25		25	Director, "The Fly"
Cronkite, Walter		15	30	50	30	TV pioneer news anchor
Cronyn, Hume	1911-	15	25	35	40	"The Seventh Cross," w/J. Tandy on leaf-$45
Crooks, Richard	1900-1972	25	50	60	75	Opera: Tenor
Crosby, Bing	1901-1977	70	350	400	175	"Going My Way," "Hoilday Inn," the "High Society", RS
Crosby, Cathy Lee	1949-	5	10	15	20	"That's Incredible!"
Crosby, Denise	1958-	5	10	15	20	"Star Trek: The Next Generation"
Crosby, Stills and Nash		50	150		150	(1997); "Suite: Judy Blue Eyes"; SA/CD-175
Cross, Ben	1948-	10	20		25	"Chariots of Fire"

NAME	DOB/DOD	SIG	DS/LS	ALS	SP	COMMENTS
Crouse, Lindsay	1948-	5	10	10	10	"The Verdict"
Crow, Sheryl		25	25	35	45	"All I Want to Do"; SA/CD-50
Cruise, Tom	1962-	50	200	400	95	"Top Gun," "Jerry Maguire," SDS-2X
Cryer, Jon	1965-	5	10	10	10	"The Famous Teddy Z"
Crystal, Billy	1947-	10	20	25	20	"When Harry Met Sally...," RS
Crystals, The		50			75	"Da Doo Ron Ron," "Then He Kissed Me"; SA/CD-80
Cugat, Xavier	1900-1990	35	50	75	125	Bandleader, "Rhumba King," "Stage Door ..."
Cui, Cesar	1835-1918	125	250	300		Russian composer
Cukor, George	1899-1983	50	100		125	Director, "My Fair Lady"
Culkin, Macauly	1980-	25	35	35	50	"Home Alone," elusive signer
Cullen, Countée	1903-1946	200	400	500	375	Writer, scarce, ESPV
Cullom, John	1930-	5	10	10	10	"Northern Exposure"
Culp, Robert	1930-	10	15	20	20	"I Spy"
Cummings, E.E.	1894-1962	225	400	500	600	U.S. fiction writer, "Tulips and Chimneys"
Cummings, Irving	1888-1959	40	65	55	80	Director, "Curly Top," "The Johnstown Flood"
Cummings, Robert	1910-1990	20	35	40	40	"King's Row," "Bob Cummings Show"-TV
Cunningham, Merce	1919-	25	60		50	Dancer
Cure, The		40			60	"Love Song," "Friday I'm in Love"; SA/CD-80
Curry, Tim	1946-	25	35	45	50	"The Rocky Horror Picture Show"
Curtin, Jane	1947-	10	20	25	20	"Kate & Allie," SNL
Curtis, Jamie Lee	1958-	30	45	50	60	"A Fish Called Wanda," "True Lies"
Curtis, Tony	1924-	20	40	50	30	"Some Like It Hot," f. Jamie L. Curtis
Cusack, Cyril	1910-	5	10	15	10	"Farenheit 451"
Cusack, Joan	1962-	5	10	10	10	"Working Girl"
Cusack, John	1966-	20	30	40	45	"Say Anything"
Cusack, Sinead	1948-	5	10	15	10	Actor, m. Jeremy Irons
Cushman, Charlotte	1816-1876	25	45		60	Actress
Cypress Hill		20			30	"Insane in the Brain"SA/CD-35
Czolgosz, Leon	1873-1901					Assassin of William McKinley, scarce, PU

Wilkie Collins

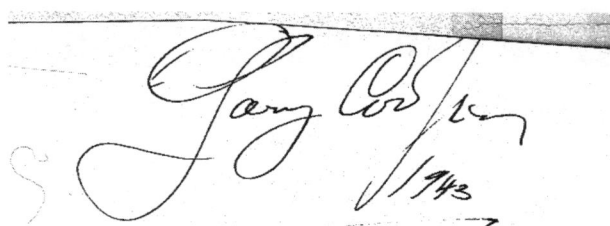

Gary Cooper

William "Buffalo Bill" Cody

Gary Cooper

Joseph Conrad

Lou Costello

Joseph Conrad

Arthur Conan Doyle

Noel Coward

NAME	DOB/DOD	SIG	DS/LS	ALS	SP	COMMENTS
DaCosta, Morton	1914-1989	20	25	35	30	"The Music Man," "Auntie Mame," director
Dafoe, Willem	1955-	10	15	30	40	"Mississippi Burning"
Dahl, Arlene	1925-	5	10	25	10	"Journey to the Center of the Earth"
Dahl, Roald	1916-1990	30	50	80	50	British-U.S. writer, "James and the Giant ..."
Dahmer, Jeffrey		600	800	3250		Serial killer
Dailey, Dan	1914-1978	20	30	50	40	"The Best Things in Life Are Free," dancer
Dailey, Janet	1944-	10	20	35	15	U.S. writer, "Aspen Gold"
Daley, Rosie	1961-	5	10	10	10	"In the Kitchen with Rosie"
Dall, John	1918-1971	25	30	45	40	"The Corn is Green," "Rope"
Dalton, Emmett		750	2000	4500	2750	American outlaw, scarce, ESPV
Dalton, Frank		900	2275			U.S. Marshal
Dalton, Grat		1000	5000	3000		American outlaw, scarce, ESPV
Dalton, Robert	1867-1892	1000	5000	3000		American outlaw, scarce, ESPV
Dalton, Timothy	1944-	10	20	30	45	"The Living Daylights"
Daly, Timothy	1956-	5	10	15	10	"Wings"
Daly, Tyne (Ellen Tyne Daly)	1946-	5	10	15	10	"Cagney & Lacey"
Dameron, Tadd	1917-1965	35	60		60	Piano player, composer
Damita, Lily	1901-	45	75	100	75	French actress, Mrs. Errol Flynn
Dana, Richard	1815-1882	60	165	225		Writer
Dana, Viola	1898-1987	15	20	30	25	Silent era star, "The Stone Heart"
Dance, Charles	1946-	5	10	10	10	"The Jewel in the Crown"
Dandridge, Dorothy	1923-1965	60	70	75		"A Day at the Races," "Carmen Jones"
Danes, Claire	1979-	20	35	65	50	"My So-Called Life," "Romeo and Juliet"
D'Angelo, Beverly	1954-	5	10	15	10	"Hair," "Every Which Way But Loose"
Dangerfield, Rodney (Jacob Cohen)	1921-	5	15	20	15	"Back to School"
Daniels, Bebe	1901-1971	25	30	65	60	Silent era star, "Rio Rita"
Daniels, Jeff	1955-	15	25	40	50	"The Purple Rose of Cairo," "Dumb and ..."
Daniels, William	1927-	5	10	10	20	"St. Elsewhere"

NAME	DOB/DOD	SIG	DS/LS	ALS	SP	COMMENTS
Danner, Blythe	1943-	5	10	15	15	"The Prince of Tides"
D'Annunzio, Gabriele	1863-1938	85	125	165		Poet, novelist, "The Victim"
Danny and the Juniors		25			50	D. Rapp (KS), responsive via mail! "At the Hop," "Rock and Roll Is Here To Stay"; SA/CD-65
Danson, Ted	1947-	25	40	50	60	"Cheers"-TV, elusive signer
Dante, Michael (Ralph Vitti)	1935-	5	10	10	10	"Custer"
Danza, Tony	1951-	10	20	25	20	"Who's the Boss?"
D'Arcy, Alexander	1908-	10	15	20	15	"Fifth Avenue Girl"
Darin, Bobby	1936-1973	100	150	225	250	"Come September," pop singer, teen idol, FA
Darnell, Linda	1921-1965	50	150		175	"Song of Bernadette," died young
Darrieux, Danielle	1917-	10	15	15	20	"Mayerling," "The Rage of Paris"
Davenport, Harry	1866-1949	160	275		300	GWTW, "The Hunchback of Notre Dame"
David, Felicien-Cesar	1810-1876	125	500			French composer, "Le Desert"
David, Hal	1921-	15	30	75	40	U.S. lyricist, "What the World Needs ...," RS
Davidovich, Lolita	1961-	5	10	10	10	"Blaze"
Davidson, Jaye	1967-	5	10	15	10	"The Crying Game"
Davidson, John	1941-	5	10	10	15	"Hollywood Squares," game show host, singer
Davies, Marion	1893-1961	45	75	175	150	"The Patsy," "Show People"
Davies, Robertson	1913-1995	20	35	60	25	Canadian novelist, playwright
Davis, Bette	1908-1989	60	175		200	"Dangerous," SP from "Jezebel"- $325
Davis, Clifton	1945-	5	10	10	10	"Never Can Say Goodbye," singer, composer
Davis, Dwight	1879-1945	50	100			"The Davis Cup"
Davis, Eddie "Lockjaw"	1921-1986	30	50		50	Tenor sax player
Davis, Geena	1957-	10	45	50	45	"Thelma and Louise," 'The Accidental Tourist"
Davis, Joan	1907-1961	30	60	50	60	"I Married Joan"- TV
Davis, Judy	1955-	15	30		30	Actress
Davis, Miles	1926-1991	175	350		400	Trumpet player, pioneer of "cool" jazz
Davis, Ossie	1917-	10	15	20	20	"Evening Shade"
Davis, Sammy, Jr.	1925-1990	50	80	125	160	"Porgy and Bess," elusive signer, FA

NAME	DOB/DOD	SIG	DS/LS	ALS	SP	COMMENTS
Davison, Wild Bill	1906-1989	40	100		85	Cornet player, Chicago jazz pioneer
Day, Doris	1924-	10	50	65	45	"The Doris Day Show," animal act., SDS-6X
Day, Laraine	1917-	15	30		35	"Dr. Kildare" series
Day-Lewis, C.	1904-1972	35	50		50	Poet
Day-Lewis, Daniel	1957-	25	60		80	"My Left Foot," "The Boxer"
De Luca, Giuseppe	1876-1950	45	85	120	135	Opera: Baritone
De Reszke, Edouard	1853-1917	115	200		215	Opera: Bass
De Reszke, Jean	1850-1925	130	200		300	Opera: Tenor
De Sylva, Buddy	1895-1950	60	100	145	100	U.S. lyricist, "April Showers"
De Vries, Peter	1910-1993	25	40	60	30	U.S. journalist, "The Tunnel of Love," RS
☆ **Dean, James**	**1931-1955**	**2200**	**7000**		**5250**	**Screen legend, "Rebel Without a Cause"**
Dean, Jimmy	1928-	5	10	15	15	"The Jimmy Dean Show"
Dean, Laura	1945-	15	25		25	Dancer
Debussy, Claude	1862-1918	500	1750	2000	2250	French composer, AMQS-$4250
DeCamp, Rosemary	1914-	10	25	35	20	"Yankee Doodle Dandy," "Life of Riley," RS
DeCarlo, Yvonne	1922-	10	25	35	30	"McLintock!," "The Munsters"- TV
DeCordoba, Pedro	1881-1950	30	50		50	Carmen," "For Whom the Bell Tolls"
Dee, Francis	1907-	10	15	20	20	"Playboy in Paris," "Little Women"
Dee, Ruby	1924-	5	10	10	25	"Do the Right Thing"
Dee, Sandra (Alexandra Zuck)	1942-	5	10	10	15	"Gidget"
Deep Purple		50		75	80	"Smoke on the Water," "Strange Kind of ..."; SA/CD-125
Def Leppard		75		100	150	S. Clark (1960-1991); "Photograph"; SA/CD-175
Defoe, Daniel	1660-1731	1650				British writer, "Robinson Crusoe", scarce
Deforest, Calvert	1923-	5	10	10	10	Actor, Larry "Bud" Melman
Degeneres, Ellen	1958-	20	35	60	45	"Ellen," controversial
DeHaven, Gloria	1924-1993	10	15	20	25	"Best Foot Forward," "Three Little Words"
DeHavilland, Olivia	1916-	35	150	275	125	"GWTW, STLS/ALS, inc.GWTW-X2, var. sig.

NAME	DOB/DOD	SIG	DS/LS	ALS	SP	COMMENTS
Dekker, Albert	1905-1968	15	20	25	25	"The Killers," "East of Eden"
Del Rio, Dolores	1905-1983	35	45	60	70	"Madame Du Barry," "I Live For Love"
Delany, Dana	1956-	10	20	25	25	"China Beach," RS
DeLaurentis, Dino	1919-	10	25	35	25	"King Kong," producer
Delius, Frederick	1862-1934	225	400			Composer, ESPV
Dell, Gabriel	1919-1988	20	25	30	35	"Dead End Kids" member
Delon, Alain	1935-	5	10	10	10	"Is Paris Burning?"
Deluise, Dom	1933-	5	10	10	10	"The Dom Deluise Show," RS
Deluise, Peter	1967-	5	10	10	10	"21 Jump Street"
Demarest, William	1892-1985	20	35	30	40	"The Jolson Story," "My Three Sons"-TV
DeMille, Agnes	1905-1993	65	225		150	Choreographer
DeMille, Cecil B.	1881-1959	75	225		300	"The Ten Commandments," producer, director
Demme, Jonathan	1944-	10	25	30	25	The Silence of the Lambs"
Demornay, Rebecca	1962-	20	35	50	50	"The Hand That Rocks the Cradle"
Dempsey, Patrick	1966-	10	15	15	15	"Loverboy"
Dench, Judi	1934-	15	30		30	Actress
Deneuve, Catherine (Catherine Dorleac)	1943-	20	35	50	60	"Belle de Jour"
DeNiro, Robert	1943-	25	50		60	"Taxi Driver," "Raging Bull," RS
Dennehy, Brian	1939-	5	10	15	15	"Cocoon"
Denning, Richard	1914-	10	15	20	20	"Union Pacific," "Hawaii Five-O"-TV
Denny, Regginald	1891-1967	20	25	25	30	"Private Lives," "Love Letters"
Denver, Bob	1935-	10	20	15	25	"Gilligan's Island"
Depardieu, Gerard	1948-	10	20	25	30	"Green Card"
Depeche Mode		40			50	"Enjoy the Silence"; SA/CD-65
Depp, Johnny	1963-	25	55	65	70	"Edward Scissorhands"
Derek, Bo (Mary Cathleen Collins)	1956-	15	25	30	35	"10" SP- 2X, m. John Derek, elusive signer
Derek, John	1926-1998	25	30	35	40	"The Ten Commandments," m. Bo Derek
Dern, Bruce	1936-	10	15	20	20	"Coming Home"
Dern, Laura	1967-	15	25	35	50	"Jurassic Park," d. Bruce Dern

NAME	DOB/DOD	SIG	DS/LS	ALS	SP	COMMENTS
Desmond, Paul	1924-1977	35	50		60	Alto sax player
Destinn, Emmy	1878-1930	125	185	225	230	Opera: Soprano
DeVane, William	1937-	5	10	10	25	"Knots Landing"
Devine, Andy	1905-1977	40	50	100	130	A Star is Born," "Stagecoach"
Devito, Danny	1944-	10	20	35	30	"Taxi," RS, "Batman" SP- 2-3X
Dewhurst, Colleen	1926-1991	15	25	35	35	"The Nun's Story," Mrs. George C. Scott
Dexter, Anthony	1919-	10	15	10	10	"Valentino"
Dey, Susan	1952-	10	20	25	25	"L.A. Law"
Deyoung, Cliff	1945-	5	10	15	10	"The Hunger"
Diamond, Neil	1941-	30	100	150	75	U.S., "I'm a Believer," songwriter, singer, FA
Diaz, Cameron	1972-	15	25	35	50	"There's Something About Mary," model
Dicaprio, Leonardo	1975-	50	100	250	125	"Titanic" SP w/Winslet- $265
☆ **Dickens, Charles**	**1812-1870**	**585**	**1250**	**1225**	**1600**	**British novelist, "Oliver Twist," ALS cont.- 2.5X**
Dickens, Jimmy		10	25		25	Country Music Hall of Fame
Dickenson, Vic	1906-1984	30	50		50	Trombone player, composer
Dickey, James	1923-1997	20	40	75	50	U.S. poet, novelist, "Deliverance," RS
Dickinson, Angie	1932-	5	15	20	20	"Police Woman," RS
☆ **Dickinson, Emily**	**1830-1886**	**800**	**2400**			**U.S. lyric poet, ESPV, scarce**
Didion, Joan	1934-	10	25	45	25	U.S. writer, "Run River"
Didley, Bo	1928-	25			40	(1987); "Who Do You Love"; SA/CD-50
Dietrich, Marlene	1901-1992	60	160	250	175	"Morocco," "The Blue Angel," seductress
Dietz, Howard	1896-1983	25	65	80	50	U.S. lyricist, "Dancing in the Dark"
Diller, Phyllis (Phyllis Driver)	1917-	5	10	10	10	"The Phyllis Diller Show," RS
Dillinger, John	1902-1934		2650			Bank robber
Dillon, Kevin	1965-	5	10	15	10	"The Doors"
Dillon, Matt	1964-	10	25	25	30	"The Outsiders"
Dinesen, Isak (Karen Blixen)	1885-1962	125				Danish author, "Winter's Tales", ESPV
Dion and the Belmonts		25			40	(1989); "A Teenager in Love," "Runaround Sue"; SA/CD-60

NAME	DOB/DOD	SIG	DS/LS	ALS	SP	COMMENTS
Dion, Celine	1968-	30			65	"Because You Love Me," "My Heart Will ..."; SA/CD-75
Dior, Christian	1905-1957	125			250	Fashion designer, ESPV-DS
Dire Straits		30			65	M. Knopfler (KS); "Money For Nothing"; SA/CD-80
Dix, Richard	1894-1949	30	45	55	75	Silent film star, "Cimarron"
Dixon, Donna	1957-	10	15	20	20	"Bosom Buddies," m. Dan Aykroyd
Dixon, Willie	1915-1992	75				Songwriter, blues player, "You Shook Me"
Dobson, Kevin	1943-	5	10	15	15	"Knots Landing"
Doctorow, E.L.	1931-	10	40	75	25	U.S. writer, "Billy Bathgate"- $75 (FE,SB)
Dodds, Johnny	1892-1940	50	80		75	Clarinet player
Dodds, Warren "Baby"	1898-1959	40	50		50	Drummer
Doherty, Shannen	1971-	20	40	50	50	"Beverly Hills 90210"
Doi, Takako	1928-					Japanese writer
Domingo, Placido	1941-	25	50		50	Tenor
Domino, Fats	1929-	25			40	(1986), a RS; "Blueberry Hill," "Blue Monday," "I'm Walkin'"; SA/CD-50
Donahue, Phil	1935-	10	20	25	20	Talk show host, reluctant signer
Donahue, Troy	1936-	10	20	20	25	"Hawaiian Eye"
Donaldson, Walter	1893-1947	75	150	250	150	U.S., "Main' Whoopee"
Donat, Robert	1905-1958	70	100		250	Rare SP from "Goodbye Mr. Chips"- $600
Donizetti, Gaetano	1797-1848	600	1200	2100		Italian composer, ESPV
Donleavy, J.P.	1926-	10	30	50	25	Writer
Donlevy, Brian	1899-1972	35	75	100	85	"Beau Geste," "Destry Rides Again"
Donnelly, Ruth	1896-1982	15	25	35	30	"The Snake Pit"
Donovan (Leitch)	1946-	15			20	"Mellow Yellow"; SA/CD-35
Donovan, Jason	1968-	5	10	10	10	Singer, actor
Doobie Brothers, The		45			75	"What a Fool Believes," "China Grove"; SA/CD-85
Doors, The		1750			2500	(1993), J.Morrison- $700- $1,500; "Light My Fire," "The End"; SA/CD-3000
Doran, Ann	1911-	10	20	25	20	"Blondie," character actress, RS

Hart Crane

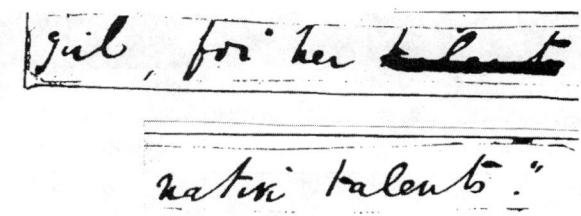

Charles Dickens

Laura Hope Crews

Charles "Lewis Carroll" Dodgson

E. E. Cummings

Arthur Conan Doyle

Emmett Dalton

Alexandre Dumas

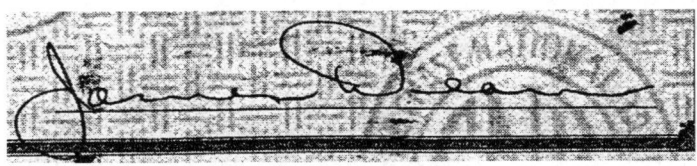

James Dean

T. S. Eliot

Claude Debussy

Thomas S. Eliot

NAME	DOB/DOD	SIG	DS/LS	ALS	SP	COMMENTS
Dorn, Philip	1905-1975	20	30	30	35	"I Remember Mama"
Dors, Diana	1931-1984	30	65		100	Actress, ESPV-SP
D'Orsay, Fifi	1904-1983	20	25	30	30	"They Had to See Paris"
Dorsey, Jimmy	1904-1957	40	150	300	270	Band leader, clarinet & alto sax player
Dorsey, Tommy	1905-1956	50	150	250	175	Band leader, trombone player
Dos Passos, John	1896-1970	30	50	100	50	U.S. novelist, "U.S.A."
☆ **Dostoyevsky, Fyodor**	**1821-1881**	**2000**				**Russian novelist, "Crime and Punishment"**
Douglas, Donna (Dorothy Bourgeois)	1935-	5	10	15	15	"The Beverly Hillbillies," RS
Douglas, Kirk	1916-	25	35	40	50	"The Bad and the Beautiful"
Douglas, Melvyn	1901-1981	20	25	30	55	"Hud," "Being There"
Douglas, Michael	1944-	20	40	35	50	"Wall Street," "Fatal Attraction," elusive signer
Douglas, Paul	1908-1959	15	25	35	40	"Born Yesterday"
Dove, Rita	1952-	20	30	60	25	U.S. writer, "Mandolin," SB- $60
Dow, Peggy	1928-	10	15	15	20	"Undertow," "Harvey"
Dow, Tony	1945-	5	10	15	15	"Leave It to Beaver"
Dowell, Anthony	1943-	10	30		25	Dancer
Down, Lesley-Ann	1954-	5	10	15	15	"Dallas"
Downey, Morton	1933-	10	15	20	20	Controversial talk show host
Downey, Robert, Jr.	1965-	25	40	55	60	"Chaplin"
Downey, Roma	1963-	20	30	35	45	"Touched by an Angel"
Downs, Hugh	1921-	10	20	25	20	"20/20," RS
Downs, Johnny	1913-1994	25	45	45	55	"Our Gang" series, "Rhapsody in Blue"
☆ **Doyle, Arthur Conan**	**1859-1930**	**500**	**700**	**1500**	**1850**	**British novelist, "Sherlock Holmes," rare full sig.**
Drake, Tom	1918-1982	5	10	10	10	"Meet Me in St. Louis"
Draper, Ruth	1884-1956	20	45	80	60	Monologue performer
Dreiser, Theodore	1871-1945	75	175	280	300	U.S. novelist, "Sister Carrie"
Drescher, Fran	1957-	20	40	50	55	"The Nanny"
Dresser, Louise	1880-1965	40	50	65	70	"The Eagle," "Mammy," "A Ship Comes In"
Dressler, Marie	1869-1934	120	200	200	240	"Min and Bill," character actress

NAME	DOB/DOD	SIG	DS/LS	ALS	SP	COMMENTS
Drew, Ellen (Terry Ray)	1915-	5	10	15	10	"Christmas in July," "My Favorite Spy"
Dreyfuss, Richard	1947-	10	30	50	45	"Mr. Holland's Opus"
Drifters, The		500			800	Four key lineups, all various prices; "Save the Last Dance for Me," "Money Honey"; SA/CD-1000
Drinkwater, John	1882-1937	25	50		40	Poet
Driscoll, Bobby	1936-1968	150	175	200	365	Child star, "Song of the South"
Dru, Joanne	1923-	10	20	25	20	"All the King's Men," Red River"
du Pré, Jacqueline	1945-1987	25	50		50	Cellist
Dubin, Al	1891-1945	40	75	75	65	U.S. lyricist, "Tiptoe Through the Tulips"
DuBois, W.E.B.	1868-1963	325	675		400	U.S. educator, editor, writer
Duchovny, David	1960-	45	100	265	115	"The X-Files"
Dudikoff, Michael	1954-	5	10	15	10	"American Ninja"
Duff, Howard	1917-1990	20	25	30	40	"Naked City," m. Ida Lupino
Duffy, Julia	1950-	5	10	10	10	"Newhart"
Duffy, Patrick	1949-	10	20	20	20	"Dallas"
Dukakis, Olympia	1931-	20	35	50	45	"Moonstruck"
Dukas, Paul	1865-1935	70	140	300	150	French composer
Duke, Patty	1946-	15	20	25	25	"The Miracle Worker," child star
Duke, Vernon	1903-1969	35	50	110	50	U.S., "April in Paris"
Dukes, David	1945-	5	10	10	10	"Sisters"
Dullea, Keir	1936-	10	15	20	25	"2001: A Space Odyssey"
Dumas, Alexandre	1802-1870	150	300	750	1000	French novelist, "The Three Musketeers"
Dumas, Alexandre, Jr.	1824-1895	35	150	200	75	French dramatist, novelist, "The Lady of the Camillas"
Dumont, Margaret	1889-1965	210	300	340	375	Known for work with Marx Brothers, tough sig.
Dunaway, Faye	1941-	10	25	40	35	"Mommie Dearest," "Bonnie and Clyde"
Dunbar, Dixie	1919-1991	10	15	15	20	"Rebecca of Sunnybrook Farm"
Duncan, Isadora	1877-1927	500	750		1000	Dancer, choreographer, ESPV
Duncan, Sandy	1946-	5	10	10	15	"Funny Face"
Dunham, Katherine	1910-	20	35		45	Dancer, choreographer

NAME	DOB/DOD	SIG	DS/LS	ALS	SP	COMMENTS
Dunn, James	1905-1967	65	100	125	130	"A Tree Grows in Brooklyn"
Dunn, Josephine	1906-1983	20	30	35	40	"The Singing Fool," "Big Time"
Dunne, Griffin	1955-	5	10	15	10	"After Hours"
Dunne, Irene	1901-1990	30	25	50	60	Popular actress, nominated for 5 Oscars
Dunne, John Gregory	1932-	15	25	50	25	U.S. writer, "True Confessions"
Dunnock, Mildred	1904-1991	15	20	25	30	"Cat On A Hot Tin Roof," "Baby Doll"
Dupond, Patrick	1959-	10	20		25	Dancer
Duprez, June	1918-1984	25	35	35	45	"The Four Feathers"
Duran Duran		45			100	"Hungry Like the Wolf," "The Reflex"; SA/CD-135
Durante, Jimmy	1893-1980	30	75	120	85	Comedian, "Little Miss Broadway"
Durbin, Deanna	1921-	20	25	45	35	"That Certain Age," "It Started with Eve"
Durning, Charles	1933-	10	15	15	20	"Evening Shade"
Duryea, Dan	1907-1968	20	25	35	40	"Scarlet Street," "The Little Foxes"
Due, Eleonora	1858-1924	2225	450		300	Italian actress, ESPV
Dutton, Charles	1951-	5	10	10	10	"Roc"
Duvall, Robert	1931-	25	50	75	60	"Tender Mercies"
Duvall, Shelly	1949-	10	15	20	20	"The Shining"
Dvorak, Antonin	1841-1904	500	1000	2000		Czech composer
Dylan, Bob	**1941-**	**275**	**750**	**1250**	**500**	**U.S., "Blowin' in the Wind," singer, songwriter, scarce, SA/CD-500, ESPV**
Dysart, Richard	1929-	10	20	30	20	"L.A. Law"
Eagles, The		150			200	Some RSs here! "Hotel California"; SA/CD-250
Eames, Emma	1865-1952	40	75	120	85	Opera: Soprano
Earp, Wyatt, B.S.	1848-1929	5000				American lawman, ESPV, scarce
Earth, Wind and Fire		30			60	"Shining Star"; SA/CD-75
Eastwood, Clint	1930-	25	125		60	"Unforgiven," RS, SDS-2X
Ebb, Fred	1936-	10	25	40	25	U.S. lyricist, "Cabaret," RS!
Eberhart, Richard	1904-	15	30	50	30	Poet, "Undercliff"
Ebsen, Buddy	1908-	15	60	50	35	"Breakfast at Tiffany's," "Beverly Hillbillies"

NAME	DOB/DOD	SIG	DS/LS	ALS	SP	COMMENTS
Eckstine, Billy	1914-1995	25	50		65	"That Old Black Magic" singer
Eddy, Duane	1938-	30			60	(1994); "Rebel-Rouser"; SA/CD-65
Eddy, Nelson	1901-1967	55	150	150	130	"Naughty Marietta," singer
Eden, Barbara	1934-	10	20	30	35	"I Dream of Jeannie"
Edgar, David	1948-	10	20		25	Playwright
Edwards, Anthony	1963-	15	50		60	"ER"
Edwards, Blake	1922-	10	30		30	The "Pink Panther" series, director
Edwards, Cliff, "Ukelele Ike"	1895-1971	60	75	125	135	Vaudeville headliner, GWTW, Pinocchio"
Edwards, Gus	1879-1945	50	125	150	100	U.S., "School Days"
Edwards, Sherman	1919-1981	30	50	70	60	U.S., "See You In September"
Edwards, Vince	1928-	10	20	15	20	"Ben Casey"- TV
Eggar, Samantha	1939-	5	10	15	10	"The Collector"
Eikenberry, Jill	1947-	10	15	15	15	"L.A. Law"
Eilers, Sally	1908-1978	20	25	30	40	"Bad Girl," "State Fair"
Ekberg, Anita	1931-	10	15	20	25	"La Dolce Vita"
Ekland, Britt	1942-	10	15	20	30	"After the Fox"
Eldridge,Roy	1911-1989	30	60		75	Trumpet player, drummer, singer
Elgar, Edward	1857-1934	150	300	750	500	British composer
Eliot, George (Mary Ann, Marian Evans)	1819-1880	175	550	1100		British novelist
Eliot, Thomas Stearns	1888-1965	200	650	2250	750	British poet, "Dante"- $1250 (FE, SB)
Elizondo, Hector	1936-	5	10	10	10	"Freebie and the Bean"
Elkin, Stanley	1930-1995	15	30	50	30	U.S. novelist, short-story writer
Ellington, Duke	**1899-1974**	**225**	**500**	**1000**	**500**	**Band leader, composer, piano player**
Elliott, Chris	1960-	5	10	10	10	"Get a Life," comedy writer, actor
Elliott, Gordon "Wild Bill"	1903-1965	55	100	125	150	"The Great Adventures of Wild Bill Hickok"
Elliott, Sam	1944-	15	30	50	40	"Tombstone," a tough signature
Ellis, Patricia	1916-1970	40	65	65	100	"42nd Street"
Ellison, Ralph	1914-1994	75	250	475	100	U.S. writer, "Invisible Man"
Eltz, Theodore von	1894-1964	50	65	70	100	Character actor, "The Big Sleep"
Elvard, Paul (Eugene Grindel)	1895-1952	125	250	400		French poet, surrealist

☆ (star marking next to Ellington, Duke row)

NAME	DOB/DOD	SIG	DS/LS	ALS	SP	COMMENTS
Elvira (Cassandra Peterson)	1951-	10	15	25	30	Horror film hostess
Elwes, Cary	1962-	5	10	15	10	"The Princess Bride"
Elytis, Odysseus	1911-	15	40		35	Poet
Emerson, Hope	1897-1960	20	30	35	40	"Caged"
Emerson, Lake and Plamer		100			150	Have done private signings! "Lucky Man"; SA/CD-200
Emerson, Ralph Waldo	**1803-1882**	**225**	**375**	**750**		**U.S. poet, essayist, ALS-4-5X**
En Vogue		25			40	"Hold On"; SA/CD-50
Enescu, Gheorghe	1881-1955	150	300	600	500	Romanian violinist, composer
Englund, Robert	1949-	10	20	25	30	"Nightmare on Elm Street"
Ephron, Nora	1941-	15	20	25	25	"Sleepless in Seattle," screenwriter, director
Erdich, Louise	1954-	10	20	30	15	U.S. writer
Erickson, Leif	1911-1986	25	30	45	50	"Conquest," "On the Waterfront"
Errol, Leon	1881-1951	50	70	75	80	vaudeville star, comedy shorts star
Erskine, John	1879-1951	50	100	200	100	Educator, novelist
Erwin, Stuart	1903-1967	25	35	45	50	"Pigskin Parade," TV star
Esmond, Jill	1908-1990	45	65	75	90	British actress, "The White Cliffs of Dover"
Esposito, Giancarlo	1958-	5	10	10	10	"Do the Right Thing"
Esquivel, Laura	1950-	15	25	45	20	Mexican writer
Estevez, Emilio	1962-	10	20	25	25	"Repo Man," writer
Estrada, Erik	1949-	5	10	10	10	"CHIPS"- TV
Eurythmics, The		50			75	"Sweet Dreams (Are Made of This)"; SA/CD-100
Evangelista, Linda	1965-	10	20	25	30	Supermodel
Evans, Bill	1929-1980	25	50		45	Piano player
Evans, Dale	1912-	15	30	45	35	"The Yellow Rose of Texas"
Evans, Dame Edith	1888-1976	25	40	50	45	Actress
Evans, Gil	1912-1988	20	45		40	Composer, arranger, piano player
Evans, Linda (Linda Evanstad)	1942-	10	20	30	40	"Dynasty," RS
Evans, Madge	1909-1981	20	25	30	45	"David Copperfield," child star
Evans, Maurice	1901-1989	40	35	65	60	"Scrooge," "Planet of the Apes"
Evans, Mike	1949-	5	10	10	10	"The Jeffersons"- TV

NAME	DOB/DOD	SIG	DS/LS	ALS	SP	COMMENTS
Evans, Sir Geraint	1922-1992	20	40		40	Baritone
Everett, Chad	1936-	10	15	25	20	"Medical Center"
Everly Brothers, The		40			75	(1986); "Wake Up, Little Susie"; SA/CD-80
Evigan, Greg	1953-	5	10	10	10	"B.J. and the Bear," RS
Ewell, Tom	1909-1994	25	30	30	40	"The Seven Year Itch," comic actor
Eythe, William	1918-1957	15	25	25	30	"Special Agent," died at 38, scarce
Fabares, Shelley (Michelle Marie Fabares)	1944-	10	15	15	20	Actor, m. Mike Farrell
Fabian (Fabian Forte)	1943-	10	25		25	"North to Alaska," "Hound Dog Man," pop star
Fabio (Fabio Lanzoni)	1961-	20	50	60	75	Model, "I Can't Believe It's Not Butter"
Fabray, Nanette (Ruby Nanette Fabares)	1920-	5	10	15	20	"One Day at a Time"
Fain, Sammy	1902-1989	20	40	45	40	U.S., "I'll Be Seeing You"
Fairbanks, Douglas	**1883-1939**	**165**	**325**	**400**	**365**	**Screen legend, "Mr. Robinson Crusoe"**
Fairbanks, Douglas, Jr.	1909-	15	25	30	30	"Little Caesar," "Gunga Din"
Fairchild, Morgan	1950-	10	15	25	30	"Falcon Crest"
Falco, Louis	1942-1993	25	50		50	Modern dancer
Falk, Peter	1927-	5	15	20	20	"Columbo"
Falkenburg, Jinx	1919-	10	25	30	30	Fashion model, "Meet Me on Broadway"
Falla, Manuel de	1876-1946	200	400	725		Spanish composer, "The Three-Cornered Hat"
Farantino, James	1938-	10	15	20	25	"Dynasty"
Farina, Dennis	1944-	10	15	25	20	"Crime Story"
Farley, Chris	1964-1998	25	50	75	70	SNL, "Tommy Boy," died young, FA
Farmer, Fannie M.	1857-1915	200			265	American cookery expert
Farmer, Francis	1914-1970	165	200	275	335	"Rhythm on the Range," "Ebb Tide," SSP-2X
Farr, Jamie (Jameel Joseph Farah)	1934-	5	10	15	20	"M*A*S*H" SP-2X, RS!
Farrakhan, Louis	1933-	60			125	Black Muslim leader, FA
Farrar, Geraldine	1882-1967	75	120	125	125	Opera: Soprano
Farrell, Charles	1901-1990	20	30	35	45	"My Little Margie"- TV

NAME	DOB/DOD	SIG	DS/LS	ALS	SP	COMMENTS
Farrell, Glenda	1904-1971	30	40	65	75	"I Am a Fugitive From a Chain Gang"
Farrell, James T.	1904-1979	20	35	50	25	U.S. novelist, "Studs Lonigan"
Farrell, Mike	1939-	5	10	15	20	"M*A*S*H," RS
Farrow, Mia	1945-	15	30	25	30	"Rosemary's Baby"
Fast, Howard	1914-	15	45	60	25	U.S. writer, "Spartacus," RS!
Faulkner, William	**1897-1962**	**425**	**1250**	**2550**		**U.S. novelist, "The Sound and the Fury"**
Faure, Gabriel	1845-1924	125	250	250	465	French composer
Fawcett, Farrah	1947-	10	15	25	30	"Charlie's Angels"
Fay, Frank	1894-1961	25	35	35	50	Vaudeville star, "Harvey"- Broadway
Faye, Alice	1912-1998	20	25	25	40	"Alexander's Ragtime Band"
Fazenda, Louise	1895-1962	35	70	75	80	Silent film star, "Alice in Wonderland"
Feld, Eliot	1942-	10	25		20	Dancer
Feld, Fritz	1900-1993	12	15	25	25	Character actor, "At the Circus"
Feldman, Corey	1971-	10	20	25	25	"Stand By Me"
Feldon, Barbara	1941-	5	10	10	20	"Get Smart"
Feldshuh, Tovah	1953-	5	10	15	10	"The Idolmaker"
Fell, Norman	1924-	5	10	10	10	"Three's Company"
Fellini, Federico	1920-1995	70	200		150	Film director
Fenley, Molissa	1954-	10	20		25	Dancer
Fenn, Sherilyn	1965-	15	20	15	30	"Twin Peaks"
Ferber, Edna	1887-1968	125	225	450		U.S. novelist, "Show Boat," SDS-2X
Ferlinghetti, Lawrence	1919-	15	55	100	25	Beat poet, RS
Ferrer, Jose	1912-1992	30	50	75	60	"Cyrano de Bergerac," "Joan of Arc"
Ferrer, Mel (Melchor Gaston Ferrer)	1912-	5	10	20	15	"Falcon Crest," producer, director
Ferrer, Miguel	1954-	5	10	15	15	"Twin Peaks" s. Jose Ferrer & Rose. Clooney
Ferrigno, Lou	1952-	10	15	40	20	"The Incredible Hulk," body builder
Ferris, Barbara	1940-	5	10	10	10	"The Strauss Family"
Fetchit, Stepin	1902-1985	40	85	150	175	"In Old Kentucky," "Stand Up and Cheer"
Fibber McGee & Molly" (J. & M. Jordan)	1897-1988, 1897-1961	45	70	60	100	Radio team, "This Way Please"

Ralph Ellison

Ralph Waldo Emerson

incerely,
W. C. Fields

W. C. Fields

F. Scott Fitzgerald

Errol Flynn

Clark Gable

Greta Garbo

Judy Garland

George Gershwin

George Gershwin

NAME	DOB/DOD	SIG	DS/LS	ALS	SP	COMMENTS
Fidler, Jimmie	1900-1988	10	20	25	20	Hollywood gossip reporter
Fiedler, Arthur	1894-1979	30	100		125	Conductor Boston Pops
Field, Betty	1918-1973	20	35	35	40	"What a Life!," "Of Mice and Men"
Field, Eugene	1850-1895	125	250	425	225	American poet, journalist
Field, Sally	1946-	15	30	45	35	"The Flying Nun," "Norma Rae," elusive signer, FA
Field, Virginia	1917-1992	10	15	20	20	"Waterloo Bridge"
Fields, Dorothy	1905-1974	25	60	75	50	U.S. lyricist, "Don't Blame Me"
Fields, Gracie	1898-1979	25	35	50	60	"Molly and Me," singer, comedienne
Fields, Kim	1969-	5	10	10	10	"The Facts of Life"
Fields, Stanley	1883-1941	30	45	50	55	"Little Caesar," "Show Boat"
☆ **Fields, W.C.**	**1879-1946**	**375**	**750**	**1250**	**1500**	**Screen legend, comedian, SSP-.5-1X**
Fiennes, Ralph	1962-	20	35	50	55	"Schindler's List," "Hamlet"- stage
Fierstein, Harvey	1954-	5	10	15	10	"Mrs. Doubtfire"
Finney, Albert	1936-	10	20	25	20	"Shoot the Moon"
Fiorentino, Linda (Clorinda Fiorentino)	1960-	15	25	35	60	"The Last Seduction"
Firth, Colin	1960-	5	10	15	10	"Another Country"
Fishburne, Laurence	1961-	15	25	40	40	"Boyz N the Hood," "Tribeca"
Fisher, Amy		25		150		Shot M.J. Buttafuoco
Fisher, Carrie	1956-	15	25	30	40	"Star Wars," d. Debbie Reynolds
Fisher, Eddie	1928-	10	15	25	20	"The Eddie Fisher Show"
Fisher, Fred	1875-1942	60	115	150	125	U.S., "Chicago"
Fitzgerald, Barry	1888-1961	140	165	225	275	"Going My Way," "And Then There Were None"
Fitzgerald, Ella	1918-1996	50	75	125	100	Jazz vocalist, often elusive, FA
☆ **Fitzgerald, F. Scott**	**1896-1940**	**425**	**1500**	**3000**	**2600**	**U.S. nov., ALS 2X-3X, ANS-$1500, ESPV**
Fitzgerald, Geraldine	1912-1992	15	30	35	40	"Wuthering Heights," "Dark Victory"
Five Satins, The		20			40	"In the Still of the Night," "Shadows"; SA/CD-55
Flagstad, Kirsten	1895-1962	100	185	250	275	"The Big Broadcast of 1938," opera singer
Flatt and Scruggs		60	125		150	Country Music Hall of Fame

NAME	DOB/DOD	SIG	DS/LS	ALS	SP	COMMENTS
Flaubert, Gustave	1821-1880	200	575	1350		French novelist, "Madame Bovary"
Fleetwood Mac		175			250	"Rumours" lineup; "Dreams," "Don't Stop," "Hold Me"; SA/CD-300
Fleiss, Heidi		10	25	50	30	Hollywood Madame, RS
Fleming, Ian	1908-1964	460	700	1400		British novelist, creator of James Bond, scarce
Fleming, Rhonda	1922-	15	25	30	45	"Spellbound," "Gunfight at the O.K. Corral"
Fletcher, Bramwell	1904-1988	40	50	65	80	"The Mummy," "The Scarlet Pimpernel"
Fletcher, John G.	1886-1950	25	45	75	50	Writer, "Selected Poems"
Fletcher, Louise	1934-	10	20	25	20	"One Flew over the Cuckoo's Nest", RS
Flynn, Errol	**1909-1959**	**300**	**575**	**800**	**645**	**Screen legend, FA, "...Robin Hood", ESPV**
Foch, Nina	1924-	10	15	12	15	"Executive Suite," "The Ten Commandments"
Follows, Megan	1968-	5	10	15	10	"Anne of Green Gables"
Fonda, Bridget	1964-	20	35	40	45	"Singles," d. Peter Fonda
Fonda, Henry	1905-1982	50	125	175	150	Screen legend, "The Grapes of Wrath", RS
Fonda, Jane	1937-	10	55	40	35	"Barbarella," "On Golden Pond," m. Ted Turner, RS
Fonda, Peter	1939-	10	40	45	40	"Easy Rider," s. Henry Fonda, RS
Fontaine, Joan	1917-	10	15	35	25	"Suspicion"
Foote, Horton	1916-	10	20	25	15	U.S. writer, "Night Seasons"
Foran, Dick	1910-1979	20	25	40	40	"Stand Up and Cheer," "Four Wives"
Ford, Faith	1964-	5	10	15	15	"Murphy Brown"
Ford, Glenn	1916-	40	70	100	85	"The Blackboard Jungle"
Ford, Harrison	1942-	60	175	300	140	"Indiana Jones" SP-2X, series, elusive signer
Ford, John	1894-1973	150	275		300	Film director
Ford, Tennessee Ernie		10	25		35	Country Music Hall of Fame
Ford, Wallace	1898-1966	25	35	40	50	"Possessed," "Freaks," "The Informer"
Forman, Milos	1932-	15	35		50	Film director, RS
Forster, Edward Morgan	1879-1970	75	200	300	150	British novelist, "Howards End"
Forster, Margaret	1938-	10	25	40	20	Writer, "Georgy Girl"

NAME	DOB/DOD	SIG	DS/LS	ALS	SP	COMMENTS
Forster, Robert	1941-	5	10	10	10	"Banyon"
Forsyth, Bill	1947-	10	20		20	Film maker
Forsyth, Bruce	1928-	10	25		25	Entertainer
Forsyth, Frederick	1938-	15	40	75	25	British writer, "The Day of the Jackal"
Forsythe, John	1918-	20	30	35	35	"In Cold Blood," TV actor, "Dynasty"
Fosse, Bob	1927-1987	35	125	125	75	Choreographer
Foster, Jodie	1962-	45	125	250	80	"The Silence of the Lambs," elusive signer
Foster, Meg	1948-	10	25	25	20	"Cagney and Lacey"
Foster, Preston	1901-1970	25	60	65	60	"My Friend Flicka"
Foster, Stephen Collins ☆	**1826-1864**	**1150**	**3000**			**U.S., "My Old Kentucky Home", scarce**
Four Seasons, The		40			100	(1990), F. Valli (KS)- $20-$50; "Sherry"; SA/CD-115
Four Tops, The		60			125	(1990); "I Can't Help Myself (Sugar Pie, Honey ...)"; SA/CD-150
Fowles, John	1926-	20	45	110	35	Writer, RS
Fox, James	1939-	5	10	10	10	"The Loneliness of the Long Distance Runner"
Fox, Matthew	1966-	10	15	25	20	"Party of Five"
Fox, Michael J.	1961-	20	30	40	40	"Family Ties"
Fox, Paula	1923-	10	35	55	15	U.S. writer, "A Place Apart," RS
Foxworth, Robert	1941-	5	10	10	10	"Falcon Crest"
Foxworthy, Jeff	1958-	5	10	25	20	"You Might Be a Redneck If...," RS
Foy, Eddie, Jr.	1905-1983	25	30	35	50	"Yankee Doodle Dandy," "Wilson"
Foy, Eddie, Sr.	1854-1928	30	45	50	60	
Frakes, Jonathan	1952-	10	15	20	35	"Star Trek: The Next Generation"
France, Anatole	1844-1924	60	125	200		French writer, "Penguin Island"
Franciosa, Anthony (Anthony Papaleo)	1928-	5	10	10	15	"The Long Hot Summer"
Francis, Anne	1930-	5	10	15	15	Former child model, actor
Francis, Connie	1938-	5	10	15	25	"Where the Boys Are," popular singer, RS
Francis, Dick	1920-	20	50	75	35	Novelist, jockey
Francis, Kay	1903-1968	30	40	60	75	"Living On Velvet," "Stranded"

NAME	DOB/DOD	SIG	DS/LS	ALS	SP	COMMENTS
Franck, Cesar	1822-1890	425	1200	2000		Belgian composer, SALS-2-3X
Frankie Lymon and the Teenagers		450			600	(1993), prices can vary significantly! "Why Do Fools Fall in Love?"; SA/CD-700
Franklin, Aretha		25			50	(1987); "Respect"; SA/CD-55
Franz, Dennis	1944-	20	30	35	45	"NYPD Blue"
Fraser, Brendan	1967-	5	10	10	10	"Encino Man"
Frawley, William	1887-1966	300	400	450	500	"I Love Lucy"- TV, a tough signature
Freeman, Kathleen	1919-	10	15	20	20	"Singin' in the Rain," "Artists and Models"
Freeman, Morgan	1937-	25	85	75	55	"Driving Miss Daisy"
Freeman, Nora	1926-	10	20	30	20	"Black Beauty," "Dear Ruth"
Fremstad, Olive	1871-1951	110	200	350	400	Opera: Soprano
French, Marilyn	1929-	12	25	50	25	U.S. writer, "The Women's Room"
Frewer, Matt	1958-	5	10	15	10	"Max Headroom"
Fricker, Brenda	1945-	15	30	45	60	"My Left Foot"
Friedan, Betty	1921-	10	30	50	30	Feminist leader
Friml, Rudolf	1879-1972	125	250	350	250	Czech./U.S. "The Firefly"
Fromme, Lynette "Squeaky"		60	150	200	100	Manson family member
☆ **Frost, Robert**	**1874-1963**	**175**	**650**	**2000**	**600**	**poet, $500 (FE, SB), TLS-2X, ANS-$250**
Frost, Sir David	1939-	10	25	40	20	Broadcaster
Fuentes, Carlos	1928-	25			40	Mexican writer, "Aura", ESPV
Fuller, Charles	1939-	10	25	40	25	U.S. writer, "A Soldier's Play," RS!
Funicello, Annette	1942-	10			40	"Beach Blanket Bingo," RS, ESPV, 2X full
Funt, Allen	1914-	10	15	15	15	"Candid Camera," elusive signer
Furness, Betty	1916-1994	20	25	30	40	TV commercial queen
Furtwangler, Wilhelm	1886-1954	325	500		750	Controversial conductor, ESPV
Gabin, Jean	1904-1976	25	35	40	50	French actor, "Grand Illusion"
Gable, Clark	1901-1960	375	450	900	900	Screen legend, GWTW, FA, SP w/CL- $1200
Gable, John Clark	1961-	10	15	20	15	Actor, son of Clark Gable
Gabor, Eva	1921-	30	35	45	40	"A Royal Scandal," "Green Acres"-TV

NAME	DOB/DOD	SIG	DS/LS	ALS	SP	COMMENTS
Gabor, Zsa Zsa	1917-	10	15	25	20	"Moulin Rouge"
Gabriel, Peter		25			50	Former member of Genesis; "Red Rain," "Sledgehammer," "Big Time"; SA/CD-50
Gacy, John Wayne		75	150	200	200	Serial killer
Gaddis, William	1922-	10	20	35	20	U.S. writer, "The Recognitions"
Gail, Maxwell	1943-	5	10	15	10	"Barney Miller"
Gallagher, Peter	1955-	5	10	10	10	"sex, lies and videotape"
Galli-Curci, Amelita	1882-1963	75	150	300	250	Opera: Soprano
Galsworthy, John	1867-1933	50	100	200	200	British novelist, "The Forsyte Saga"
Galway, James	1939-	10	20		25	Flautist, RS
☆ **Garbo, Greta**	**1905-1990**	**1785**	**3500**		**9350**	**Screen legend, reclusive, FA, ESPV, scarce**
Garcia, Andy	1956-	10	20	25	35	"The Godfather Part III"
Garden, Mary	1874-1967	40	70	100	150	Opera: Soprano
Gardiner, Reginald	1903-1980	20	35	30	40	British actor, "A Yank in the RAF"
Gardner, Ava	1922-1990	60	135	150	150	"Mogambo," "The Barefoot Contessa"
Gardner, Erie Stanley	1889-1970	100	200	300	200	Mystery writer, creator of Perry Mason
Garfield, John	1913-1952	85	120		400	"Body and Soul," died at age 39.
Gargan, William	1905-1979	20	30	40	45	"They Knew What They Wanted"
Garland, "Red"	1923-1984	25	50		35	Piano player
Garland, Beverly	1930-	5	10	10	10	"My Three Sons"
☆ **Garland, Judy**	**1922-1969**	**425**	**860**	**1000**	**925**	**TWOO, FA, autograph varied significantly**
Garner, Erroll	1921-1977	85	150		165	Piano, composer
Garner, James	1928-	10	15	30	25	"The Rockford Files"
Garofalo, Janeane	1964-	15	25	35	40	"The Truth About Cats and Dogs"
Garr, Teri	1949-	15	25	30	45	"Tootsie"
Garrett, Betty	1919-	10	15	15	20	"All In The Family"
Garson, Greer	1908-1996	30	80	130	80	"Mrs. Miniver," "Madame Curie"
Garth, Jennie	1972-	20	30	50	40	"Beverly Hills 90210," FA
Gatty, Harold	1903-1957	100	250		200	Aviator, author

NAME	DOB/DOD	SIG	DS/LS	ALS	SP	COMMENTS
Gaye, Marvin		150			300	(1939-1984), Sheet music- $350; "I Heard It Through the Grapevine"; SA/CD-400, FA
Gaynor, Janet	1906-1984	35	65	100	100	Won first Oscar for best actress in 1927
Gaynor, Mitzi	1930-	10	15	20	15	"South Pacific," charges $5 for SP
Gazzara, Ben	1930-	5	10	15	15	"Inch On," RS
Geary, Anthony	1947-	10	15	15	20	"General Hospital," FA, elusive signer
Geary, Cynthia	1966-	5	10	10	15	"Northern Exposure"
Geldof, Bob	1954-	20			40	Musician
Genesis		75			100	"Genesis Live" lineup; P. Collins (KS); "Invisible Touch," "Misunderstanding"; SA/CD-125
Genet, Jean	1911-1986	200	350	500		French playwright, novelist, "The Maids"
George, Gladys	1900-1954	50	65	75	75	"The Maltese Falcon," uncommon sig.
Gerard, Gil	1943-	10	15	20	25	"Buck Rogers in the 25th Century"
Gere, Richard	1948-	25	125	150	60	"An Officer and a Gentleman," SP (5x7)- .5V
German, Sir Edward	1862-1936	40	80	160	80	Composer
☆ **Gershwin, George**	**1898-1937**	**1000**	**1750**		**3650**	**U.S., "I've Got a Crush on You"**
Gershwin, Ira	1896-1983	100	200	300	200	U.S. lyricist, "Embraceable You"
Gertz, Jami	1965-	5	10	10	10	"Less Than Zero"
Getty, Balthazar	1975-	5	10	10	10	"Where the Day Takes You"
Getty, Estelle	1923-	5	10	15	15	"The Golden Girls," RS
Getz, Stan	1927-1991	100	200		250	Tenor sax player
Ghostley, Alice	1926-	5	10	10	15	"Bewitched"
Giannini, Giancarlo	1942-	20	30	45	40	"Seven Beauties"
Givvon, Edward	1737-1794	280		1500		English historian, ESPV
Gibbons, Leeza	1957-	5	10	15	10	"Entertainment Tonight," FA
Gibbs, Marla	1933-	5	10	10	10	"The Jeffersons"
Gibran, Kahill	1883-1931	175	400	800		Mystical novelist, "The Prophet"
Gibson, Henry	1935-	5	10	10	10	"Laugh-In"
Gibson, Hoot	1892-1962	140	175	225	250	Cowboy, silent and sound star
Gibson, Mel	1956-	45	150	275	125	"Lethal Weapon," elusive signer, FA

NAME	DOB/DOD	SIG	DS/LS	ALS	SP	COMMENTS
Gide, Andre	1869-1951	200	400	600		French writer, "The Immoralist"
Gielgud, John	1904-	30	50	75	70	British stage actor, TV and film star
Gielgud, Maina	1945-	10	25		25	Dancer
Gifford, Frances	1920-1994	10	15	15	15	"Jungle Girl," "The Glass Key"
Gifford, Kathie Lee	1953-	5	10	15	10	"Live with Regis and Kathie Lee," RS
Gigli, Benjamino	1890-1957	110	225	275	300	Opera: Tenor
Gilbert, Billy	1894-1971	25	35	45	50	"Snow White and the Seven Dwarfs"
Gilbert, Melissa	1964-	5	10	15	35	"Little House on the Prairie"
Gilbert, Sara	1975-	10	15	20	20	"Roseanne," s. Melissa Gilbert
Gilbert, William S.	1836-1911	200	400	750	650	British, "H.M.S. Pinafore"
Gilchrist, Connie	1901-1985	10	20	25	20	"Barnacle Bill," "A Letter to Three Wives"
Gillespie, Dizzy	1917-1993	75	100	250	125	Composer, trumpet player
Gillette, William	1855-1937	65	200	225	150	"Sherlock Holmes"
Gilliam, Terry	1940-	5	10	10	10	"Monty Python and the Holy Grail"
Gillis, Ann	1927-	10	15	20	25	Child actress, "Little Orphan Annie"
Gilmore, Gary		25	50	100	75	criminal
Gilroy, Frank	1925-	15	35	60	25	U.S. writer, "Little Ego"
Ginsberg, Allen	1926-1997	55	200	300	110	U.S. Beat poet, elusive signer
Ginty, Robert	1948-	5	10	10	10	"Baa Baa Black Sheep"
Giordano, Umberto	1867-1948	230	330			Italian composer, "Siberia"
Girardot, Etienne	1856-1939	45	85	115	100	"Go West, Young Man," "Charley's Aunt"
Gish, Dorothy	1898-1968	70	100	125	130	Best remembered for wearing blue jeans!
Gish, Lillian	1896-1993	30	75	140	75	"Duel in the Sun"
Givenchy, Hubert J.M.T.	1927-	20	65	100	50	Fashion designer, RS
Givens, Robin	1964-	5	10	10	15	"Head of the Class"
Gladys Knight and the Pips		25			55	(1996), G. Knight (KS)- RS; "Midnight Train to Georgia"; SA/CD-70
Glaser, Paul Michael	1943-	5	10	15	20	"Starsky and Hutch"
Glass, Phillip	1937-	25	50	100	45	U.S. composer, "The Voyage," RS
Glass, Ron	1945-	5	10	10	10	"Barney Miller"

Aleksaor Glazunov

William Golding

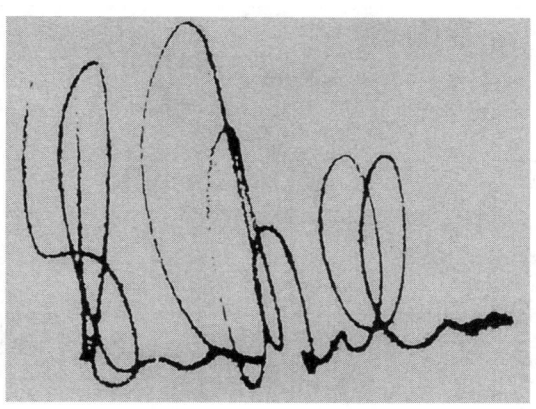

Glenn Miller

Horace Greeley

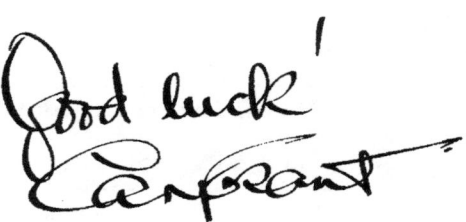

Cary Grant

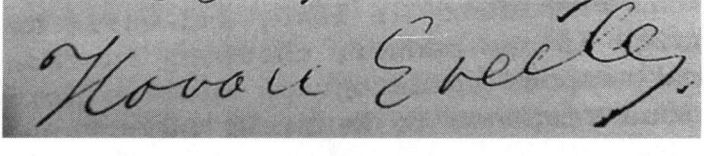

Horace Greeley

Cary Grant

Zane Grey

NAME	DOB/DOD	SIG	DS/LS	ALS	SP	COMMENTS
Glazunov, Aleksandr	1865-1936	200	400		225	Russian composer
Gleason, Jackie	1916-1987	80	185		185	"The Honeymooners"-TV
Gleason, James	1882-1959	50	75	75	80	"Meet John Doe," "A Free Soul"
Gleason, Joanna	1950-	5	10	10	15	"Into the Woods," d. Monty Hall
Glenn, Scott	1942-	25	55	65	50	"The Right Stuff"
Gless, Sharon	1943-	10	15	20	25	"Cagney and Lacey"
Glover, Crispin	1964-	5	10	10	10	"Back to the Future"
Glover, Danny	1947-	10	25	45	30	"Lethal Weapon", FA
Glover, John	1944-	10	15	20	20	"Shamus"
Glover, Savion	1973-	10	20	25	30	"The Tap Dance Kid," "Bring in 'Da Noise,..."
Gluck, Christoph W.	1714-1787	825	2450	4250		German composer, "Alceste"
Gobbi, Tito	1913-1984	35	70	100	125	Opera: Baritone
Godard, Jean-Luc	1930-	15	35		30	Film director
Goddard, Paulette	1911-1990	30	65	130	110	"So Proudly We Hail," author
Godwin, Gail	1937-	15	30	50	20	U.S. writer, "Violet Clay," RS
Goehr, Alexander	1932-	20	45		40	Composer
Goethe, Johann Wolfgang von	1749-1832	1500	3000	6000		German poet, novelist, "Faust"
Goetz, Bernhard		20	40	50	35	Subway shooter
Goffin, Gerry	1939-	15	40	50	30	U.S. lyricist, "Up on the Roof"
Gogol, Nikolai	1809-1852	800	3000	6000		Short-story writer, novelist, "Dead Souls"
Gold, Tracey	1969-	5	10	15	15	"Growing Pains"
Goldberg, Whoopi	1949-	10	20	30	30	"Ghost," RS
Goldblum, Jeff	1952-	15	30	40	35	"The Big Chill," reluctant signer
Golding, Louis	1895-1958	30	75	100	60	Writer, ESPV-ALS & SP
Golding, William	1911-1993	75	250	500		British novelist, "Lord of the Flies"
Goldman, William	1931-	20	35	80	50	U.S. writer, "Marathon Man"
Goldsmith, Jerry		10	25	50	20	U.S. composer, movie soundtracks
Goldthwait, Bobcat	1962-	5	10	10	10	"Police Academy"
Goldwyn, Tony	1960-	5	10	10	10	"Ghost," RS!
Golino, Valeria	1966-	10	20	25	35	"Rain Man"
Gomez, Thomas	1905-1971	30	40	50	60	"Ride The Pink Horse," "Key Largo"

NAME	DOB/DOD	SIG	DS/LS	ALS	SP	COMMENTS
Gooding Jr., Cuba	1968-	10	20	30	40	"Jerry Maguire," "Show me the money!"
Goodman, Benny	1909-1986	75	175	265	185	Band leader, clarinet player
Goodman, John	1952-	15	25	35	45	"Roseanne"
Gorcey, Leo	1915-1969	130	150	200	175	"Dead End Kids," "Bowery Boys"
Gordimer, Nadine	1923-	30	50	75	35	South African writer, "A Guest of Honour"
Gordon, Bert	1922-	25	35	40	45	Horror film star, "Cyclops"
Gordon, Dexter	1923-1990	30	50		60	Tenor sax player
Gordon, Mack	1905-1959	40	65	125	50	U.S. lyricist, "You'll Never Know"
Gordon, Mary	1949-	10	20	30	15	U.S. writer, "Men and Angels"
Gordon, Noele	1922-1985	30	65		60	Actress
Gordon, Ruth	1896-1985	20	25	30	40	"Rosemary's Baby"
Goring, Marius	1912-	20	40		35	Actor, "The Expert"
Gorky, Maxim	1868-1936	500	1100	2000	1000	Russian dramatist, novelist, "The Lower ..."
Gorshin, Frank	1933-	10	20	25	25	"Batman" SP- 2X
Gossett, Louis Jr.	1936-	15	25	45	30	"An Officer and a Gentleman," RS
Gotti, John		50	125	150	125	Mafia Don
Gottschalk, Louis M.	1829-1969	450	925			Composer, ESPV
Gould, Elliott	1938-	10	15	20	20	"Bob & Carol & Ted & Alice"
Gould, Morton	1913-1996	25	50	75	50	U.S., "Fall River Suite"
Goulet, Robert	1933-	5	10	10	10	"Blue Light", RS
Gounod, Charles	1818-1893	175	400		500	French composer, "Romeo and Juliet"
Grable, Betty	1916-1973	110	150	225	250	World War II pin-up, "Mother Wore Tights"
Grafton, Sue	1940-	15	25	40	20	U.S. writer
Grahame, Gloria	1925-1981	60	120	200	165	IAWL, "Crossfire," 'The Bad and the Beautiful"
Grahame, Kenneth	1859-1932	60	120	175		Writer
Grainger, Percy	1882-1961	45	100	200	125	Composer
Grammer, Kelsey	1955-	15	25	50	45	"Frasier," reluctant signer, FA
Grand Funk Railroad		30			75	"We're an American Band"; SA/CD-100

NAME	DOB/DOD	SIG	DS/LS	ALS	SP	COMMENTS
Grand Master Flash and the Furious Five		10			25	"The Message"; SA/CD-30
Grandy, Fred	1948-	5	10	10	10	"The Love Boat"
Granger, Farley	1925-	5	10	15	20	"Rope," "Strangers on a Train"
Granger, Stewart	1913-1993	25	45	50	50	"Waterloo Road," "Captain Boycott"
Grant, Cary	1904-1986	230	450	540	465	Screen icon, "Suspicion," "North By Northwest"
Grant, Hugh	1960-	25	40	55	65	"Four Weddings and a Funeral"
Grant, Lee	1927-	10	20	30	30	"Plaza Suite"
Granville, Bonita	1923-1988	20	25	30	40	"These Three," "Lassie"-TV, child star
Grapewin, Charley	1875-1956	260	525		500	"The Petrified Forest," "The Grapes of Wrath"
Grappelli, Stephane	1908-	20	45		40	Jazz violinist
Grass, Gunter	1927-	45	100	200	100	German writer, "Dog Years"
Grateful Dead, The		300			550	J. Garcia (KS), Mckernan- $100-325- scarce; "Uncle John's Band"; SA/CD-700
Grau, Shirley Ann	1929-	10	25	40	20	U.S. writer, "The Condor Passes," RS!
Grauman, Sid	1879-1950	50	60	100	100	Theater owner, "Star Dust"
Graves, Peter	1926-	10	15	20	25	"Mission: Impossible," b. James Arness
Graves, Ralph	1900-1977	25	30	40	45	"Sporting Life," "Out of Luck"
Graves, Robert	1895-1985	70	150	350	125	British poet, novelist, "The White Goddess"
Gray, Coleen	1922-	15	25	40	35	"Kiss of Death," "Red River"
Gray, Gilda	1901-1959	55	110	125	150	Polish dancer, "Cabaret," "Rosemarie"
Gray, Linda	1940-	10	20	20	25	"Dallas"
Gray, Spalding	1941-	10	20	25	20	"The Killing Fields," writer
Gray, Thomas	1716-1771	1000	2000			British poet, "The Progress of Poesy", scarce
Gray, Zane	1872-1939	125	300	600		U.S. Western writer
Grayson, Kathryn	1922-	10	15	20	15	"Show Boat," "Kiss Me, Kate," RS
Greeley, Horace	1811-1872	75	300	275	800	Journalist
Green, Al	1946-	15			35	(1995), a RS! "Let's Stay Together"; SA/CD-40
Green, Mitzi	1920-1969	25	35	35	45	"Tom Sawyer," child star

NAME	DOB/DOD	SIG	DS/LS	ALS	SP	COMMENTS
Greenaway, Peter	1942-	5	10	15	10	"The Cook, the Thief, His Wife...," director
Greene, Graham	1904-1991	100	300	500	300	British novelist, "The Heart of the Matter"
Greene, Richard	1914-1985	20	35	65	45	"The Hound of the Baskervilles"
Greene, Sir Hugh C.	1910-1987	25	40	50	35	Journalist
Greenstreet, Sydney	1879-1954	235	450	500	575	"The Maltese Falcon," C, scarce
Greenwood, Joan	1921-1987	25	40	40	45	"Tom Jones," "Stage Struck"
Greer, Germaine	1939-	15	30	60	25	Feminist, writer
Greer, Jane	1924-	10	15	20	20	"Out of the Past," "Against All Odds"
Grey, Dame Beryl	1927-	25	50		50	Ballerina
Grey, Jennifer	1960-	10	25	35	50	"Dirty Dancing," d. Joel Gray
Grey, Joel (Joel Katz)	1932-	5	10	15	20	"Cabaret," RS
Grey, Nan	1918-1993	10	15	20	20	"Three Smart Girls," "Margie"
Grey, Virginia	1917-	10	15	15	20	"Back Street," "The Rose Tattoo"
Grey, Zane	1875-1939	100	200	325		Novelist, SALS-$750
Grieg, Edvard	1843-1907	415	895	1700	1299	Norwegian composer
Grier, David Alan	1955-	10	15	15	15	"In Living Color"
Griffith, Andy	1926-	20	30	50	45	"The Andy Griffith Show"
Griffith, Corinne	1894-1979	40	60	100	110	Silent era star, "Black Oxen," "The Garden..."
Griffith, D.W.	1875-1948	320	300			American director, producer, SB-$500, ESPV
Griffith, Hugh	1912-1980	160	250		400	Actor, "Ben Hur," ESPV, scarce
Griffith, Melanie	1957-	25	40	50	65	"Working Girl"
Grimm, Jakob	1785-1863	650	1600	3500		German folklorist, "Grimm's Fairy Tales"
Grimm, Wilhelm	1786-1859	675	1725	3650		German folklorist, "Grimm's Fairy Tales"
Grisham, John	1955-	25	110		35	U.S. writer, "The Firm," RS
Grissi, Givlia	1811-1869	225			250	Italian singer
Grodin, Charles	1935-	5	10	15	15	"Midnight Run," RS
Grofe, Ferde	1892-1972	125	230	275	125	U.S., "Grand Canyon Suite"
Gross, Mary	1953-	5	10	15	15	SNL, s. Michael Gross
Gross, Michael	1947-	10	15	15	15	"Family Ties," b. Mary Gross, no longer signs

NAME	DOB/DOD	SIG	DS/LS	ALS	SP	COMMENTS
Guardino, Harry	1925-	10	15	15	20	"Dirty Harry"
Guare, John	1938-	15	30	60	25	U.S. writer, "Two Gentleman of Verona"
Guest, Christopher	1948-	5	10	10	10	"This Is Spinal Tap," writer, m. Jamie L. Curtis
Guest, Lance	1960-	5	10	10	10	"Knots Landing"
Guillame, Robert (Robert Williams)	1937-	5	10	10	10	"Soap"
Guiness, Alec	1914-	35	40	50	60	"The Bridge on the River Kwai"
Guiteau, Charles J.	1842-1882	500	1000			Garfield assassin
Gulager, Clu	1928-	5	10	15	15	"The Last Picture Show"
Gumbel, Bryant	1948-	5	10	12	10	"Today," RS
Guns N' Roses		150			175	"Sweet Child o' Mine," "Welcome to ... Jungle"; SA/CD-200
Gurley Brown, Helen	1922-	5	10	25	15	U.S. writer, editor
Gustafson, Karin	1959-	5	10	10	10	"Taps"
Guthrie, Woody	1912-1967	300	600			Folksinger, scarce, ESPN
Guttenberg, Steve	1958-	10	15	20	25	"Three Men and a Baby," RS
Guy, Jasmine	1964-	10	15	20	25	"A Different World"
Gwenn, Edmund	1875-1959	85	150	175	200	"Mister 880," "Miracle on 34th Street"- SP-7X
Haas, Lukas	1976-	5	10	10	10	"Witness"
Hack, Shelley	1952-	5	10	15	20	"Charlie's Angels"-TV
Hackett, Bobby	1915-1976	30	50		60	Trumpet and cornet player
Hackett, Buddy	1924-	5	10	15	20	"The Love Bug," RS
Hackman, Gene	1930-	25	75	65	50	"The French Connection," "Unforgiven"
Haden, Sara	1897-1981	15	25	25	30	"Spitfire," "Andy Hardy" series
Hagerty, Julie	1955-	5	10	10	10	"Airplane!"
Haggard, Merle	1937-	10			25	Country singer
Haggard, Sir H. Rider	1856-1925	75	150	300	250	Novelist, "She," ESPV-SP
Hagman, Larry	1931-	10	20	20	25	"Dallas," son of Mary Martin
Haid, Charles	1943-	5	10	10	10	"Hill Street Blues," director, producer
Hailey, Arthur	1920-	20	40	60	30	U.S. writer, "Airport," RS
Haim, Corey	1972-	10	15	15	20	"The Lost Boys"

NAME	DOB/DOD	SIG	DS/LS	ALS	SP	COMMENTS
Haines, William	1900-1973	20	30	35	40	"The Tower of Lies," "Brown of Harvard"
Hale, Alan	1892-1950	60	65	100	115	"Robin Hood," "The Sea Hawk"
Hale, Alan, Jr.	1918-1990	60	110	125	115	The Skipper on "Gilligan's Island"
Hale, Barbara	1922-	20	35	35	40	"Perry Mason"-TV
Haley, Alex	1921-1992	65	150	225	150	U.S. author, "Roots," ALS content-10-12X
Haley, Jack	1899-1979	125	150	265	300	TWOO, "Rebecca of Sunnybrook Farm"
Hall and Oates		40			50	"Kiss on My List," "Maneater," "Out of Touch"; SA/CD-55
Hall, Anthony Michael	1968-	5	10	10	10	"Sixteen Candles"
Hall, Arsenio	1959-	5	10	15	15	Actor, talk show host
Hall, Bridget	1977-	10	15	20	40	Supermodel
Hall, Deidre	1947-	5	10	10	15	"Days of Our Lives," RS
Hall, Huntz	1920-	15	20	25	35	"Dead End Kids," "The Bowery Boys"
Hall, Jon	1913-1979	40	50	75	60	"Ramar of the Jungle"-TV
Hall, Juanita	1901-1968	80	125		130	"South Pacific," may add Bloody Mary to sig.
Hall, Monty	1924-	5	10	10	10	"Let's Make a Deal"
Hall, Porter	1888-1953	25	35	30	40	"The Plainsman," "His Girl Friday"
Hamel, Veronica	1943-	10	35	25	25	"Hill Street Blues"
Hamill, Mark	1952-	5	10	20	25	"Star Wars" trilogy SP-2X
Hamilton, George	1939-	5	10	10	10	"Love at First Bite"
Hamilton, Linda	1956-	20	30	25	55	"The Terminator"
Hamilton, Margaret	1902-1985	120	275	435	300	TWOO, very RS
Hamlin, Harry	1951-	10	15	20	20	"L.A. Law"
Hamlisch, Marvin	1944-	10	25	50	20	U.S., "The Way We Were"
Hammerstein, Oscar II	**1895-1960**	**200**	**250**	**500**	**275**	**U.S. lyricist, "Ol' Man River", SDS-2X**
Hammett, Dashiell	1894-1961	425	1200	2500		U.S. detective-story writer, "The Maltese ..."
Hampshire, Susan	1941-	5	10	10	10	"The Forsythe Saga"
Hampton, Lionel	1909-	20	50		40	Jazz musician, RS
Hamsun, Knute	1859-1952	45	125	175	100	Novelist, "Hunger"

☆ (Hammerstein, Oscar II)

NAME	DOB/DOD	SIG	DS/LS	ALS	SP	COMMENTS
☆ **Handel, George Frederic**	**1685-1759**	**1250**	**7500**			**German/british composer, "Messiah", ESPV, SALS-AA**
Handy, W.C.	1873-1958	300	500		625	Composer, "St. Louis Blues"
Hank Ballard and the Midnighters		40			75	(1990), a scarce signature; "Work With Me Annie," "Let's Go, Let's Go..."; SA/CD-150
Hanks, Tom	1956-	45	150		100	"Forrest Gump," "Apollo 13", FA
Hannah, Daryl	1960-	10	30	45	60	"Splash"
Hanson		30			60	Very reluctant and evasive signers! "MMMBop"; SA/CD-75
Hanson, Howard	1896-1981	25	50	100	50	U.S. composer
Harburg, E.Y. (Yip)	1898-1981	150	300	300	250	U.S. lyricist, "Over the Rainbow"
Harding, Ann	1902-1981	20	25	30	35	"Holiday," "The Animal Kingdom"
Hardison, Kadeem	1966-	5	10	10	10	"A Different World"
Hardwicke, Cedric	1893-1964	40	70	100	110	"Les Miserables," "Victory"
☆ **Hardy, Oliver**	**1892-1957**	**300**	**350**	**555**	**650**	**"Laurel & Hardy," SP (both)-$900**
Hardy, Thomas	1840-1928	275	750	1500	1475	British novelist, poet, "Jude the Obscure"
Harewood, Dorain	1950-	5	10	10	10	"Roots-The Next Generation"
Harlow, Jean	1911-1937	1200	2125	3365	2675	30s screen star, very scarce in any form, FA
Harmon, Mark	1951-	10	15	20	25	"St. Elsewhere"
Harnick, Sheldon	1924-	15	30		25	Songwriter
Harper, Jessica	1949-	5	10	10	10	"Pennies from Heaven"
Harper, Tess	1950-	10	15	20	20	"Crimes of the Heart"
Harper, Valerie	1940-	5	10	15	15	"The Mary Tyler Moore Show," RS
Harrelson, Woody	1961-	20	40	50	60	"Indecent Proposal," "Cheers"-TV
Harrington, Pat	1929-	5	10	10	10	"One Day at a Time"
Harris, Barbara (Sandra Markowitz)	1937-	5	10	10	15	"Family Plot"
Harris, Ed	1950-	15	30	40	45	"Apollo 13," "The Right Stuff"
Harris, Joel Chandler	1848-1908	200	350	700		U.S. short-story writer, Uncle Remus series
Harris, Julie	1925-	5	10	15	15	"Knots Landing," "Member of the Wedding"
Harris, Mel	1957-	5	10	10	15	"thirtysomething"

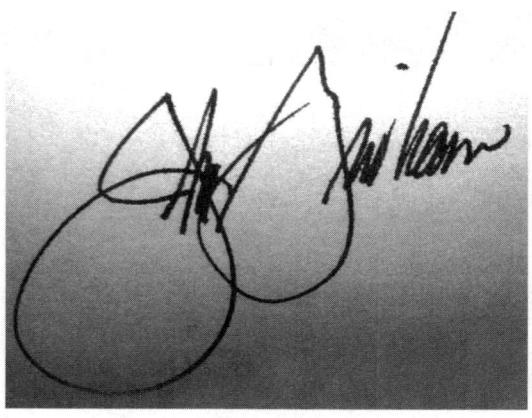

John Grisham

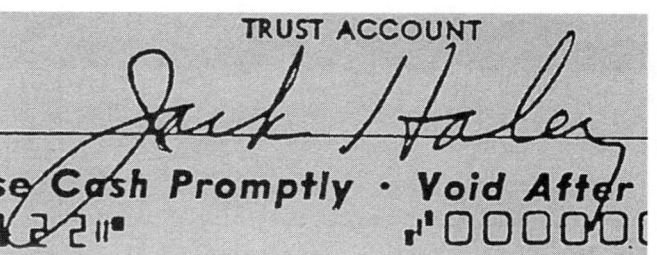

Jack Haley

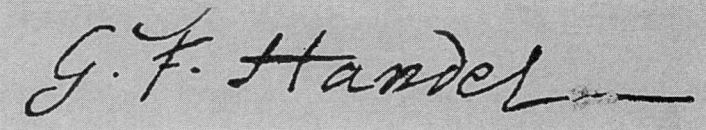

George F. Handel

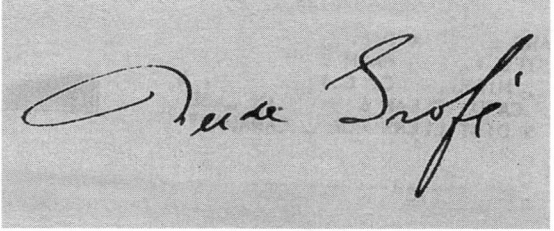

Ferde Grofe

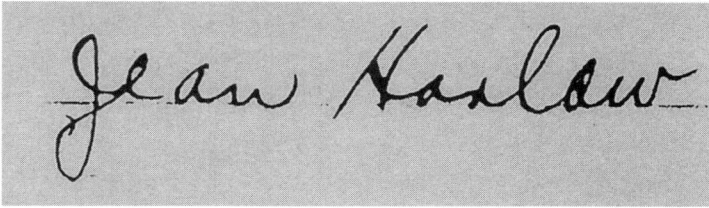

Jean Harlow

Charles Guiteau

Jean Harlow

Charles Guiteau

Francis "Brett" Harte

NAME	DOB/DOD	SIG	DS/LS	ALS	SP	COMMENTS
Harris, Mrs. Jean		35	70	150	75	Scarsdale diet killer
Harris, Richard	1933-	20	45	35	45	"A Man Called Horse"
Harris, Rosemary	1930-	20	40		40	Actress
Harris, Roy	1898-1979	60	125		75	U.S. composer
Harrison, Gregory	1950-	5	10	15	15	"Trapper John, MD"
Harrison, George	1943-	200	1100	3500	350	The Beatles, FA
Harrison, Jenilee	1959-	5	10	10	15	"Dallas"
Harrison, Noel	1935-	5	10	12	15	"The Girl from U.N.C.L.E."
Harrison, Rex	1908-1990	45	75	100	80	"My Fair Lady," "Dr. Doolittle"-SP-2X
Hart, John		20	25	35	40	The first Lone Ranger
Hart, Lorenz	1895-1943	500				U.S. lyricist, "Blue Moon," Rogers & Hart, scarce
Hart, Mary	1944-	5	10	15	20	"Entertainment Tonight"
Hart, Melissa Joan	1976-	25	40	50	60	"Sabrina, the Teenage Witch"
Hart, Moss	1904-1961	30	55	120	40	U.S. playwright, "The Man ... Dinner"
Hart, Richard	1915-1951	25	35	50	60	"B.F.'s Daughter," died at age 36
Hart, William S.	1870-1946	150	225	255	450	Early western star
Harte, Bret	1836-1902	100	175	200		U.S. short-story writer, poet
Hartley, Mariette	1940-	5	10	15	15	"Peyton Place"
Hartman, David	1935-	5	10	15	10	"Good Morning America," talk show host
Hartman, Phil	1948-1998	35	50	100	80	SNL, writer, "Talk Radio"
Hasselhoff, David	1952-	20	50	50	50	"Knight Rider," "Baywatch"
Hasso, Signe	1910-	10	15	15	20	"Karriar," "The Story of Dr. Wassell"
Hatcher, Teri	1964-	25	50	60	75	"Lois & Clark: The New Advent ... Superman"
Hauer, Rutger	1944-	10	15	20	35	"Blade Runner"
Hauptmann, Gerhart	1862-1946	125	300	500	325	writer, NP
Hauptmann, Bruno Richard	?-1936	600				Lindbergh baby kidnapper
Havel, Vaclav	1936-	25	100	150	50	Czech. writer
Haver, June	1926-	5	10	10	15	"The Dolly Sisters," RS
Havoc, June	1916-	10	15	15	20	"Four Jacks and a Jill," "My Sister Eileen"
Hawke, Ethan	1970-	15	30	45	40	"Dead Poets Society"

NAME	DOB/DOD	SIG	DS/LS	ALS	SP	COMMENTS
Hawkes, John	1925-	20	40	60	25	U.S. writer, "Lunar Landscape"
Hawkins, Coleman	1904-1969	150	250		265	Tenor sax player
Hawkins, Erick	1909-1994	25	50		50	Dancer, choreographer
Hawkins, Jack	1910-1973	50	80	75	120	"The Fallen Idol," "Ben-Hur"
Hawks, Howard	1896-1977	80	175		200	Film director
Hawn, Goldie	1945-	20	40	45	50	"Private Benjamin"
☆ **Hawthorne, Nathaniel**	**1804-1864**	**500**	**1275**	**2250**		**U.S. novelist, "The Scarlet Letter", ESPV**
Hayakawa, Sessue	1889-1973	150	200	200	265	"The Bridge on the River Kwai"
Hayden, Russell	1912-1981	30	50	60	80	"Hopalong Rides Again"
Hayden, Sterling	1916-1986	30	40	40	55	"The Asphalt Jungle," "Dr. Strangelove"
Haydn, Franz Joseph	1732-1809	650	3000	4275		Austrian composer
Hayes, Gabby	1885-1969	140	175		475	Western film sidekick, "Don't Fence Me In"
Hayes, Helen	1900-1994	25	50	60	75	"Airport," Signed autobiography-$40, FA
Hays, Robert	1947-	5	10	10	10	"Airplane!"
Hayward, Louis	1909-1985	15	25	40	50	"The Man in the Iron Mask"
Hayward, Susan	1918-1975	180	275	500	475	"I Want To Live," FA, often ghost-signed
Hayworth, Rita	1918-1987	165	300	400	440	"Only Angels Have Wings," FA, ALS-scarce
Head, Edith	1898-1981	35	70	130	145	Hollywood costume designer
Headly, Glenne	1955-	5	10	10	10	"Dirty Rotten Scoundrels"
Healy, Ted	1896-1937	40	50	50	75	"Soup to Nuts," "Bombshell"
Heard, John	1946-	5	10	10	10	"Home Alone"
Heart		30			55	Ann & Nancy Wilson (KS); "Barracuda"; SA/CD-60
Heche, Ann	1969-	15	20	25	30	"Volcano"
Heckart, Eileen	1919-	12	20	20	25	"The Bad Seed," "Butterflies Are Free"
Hedren, Tippi (Nathalie Hedren)	1935-	10	20	25	30	"The Birds," requests $25 donation for Sig.
Heflin, Van	1910-1971	40	80	75	80	"Johnny Eager," "Shane"
Heifetz, Jascha	1901-1987	150	265		500	Violinst, ESPV, SIG-$195

NAME	DOB/DOD	SIG	DS/LS	ALS	SP	COMMENTS
Heine, Heinrich	1797-1856			7000		German poet, "Book of Songs", ESPV, scarce
Heiss, Carol	1940-	15	30	30	30	Olympic skater, "Snow White and the Three..."
Heller, Joseph	1923-	20	40	55	30	U.S., resp. sig., "God Knows"- $150 (FE, SB)
Hellman, Lillian	1905-1984	50	150	275	115	U.S. playwright, "The Little Foxes"
Helpmann, Sir Robert	1909-1986	25	50		50	Dancer, choreographer
Helprin, Mark	1947-	15	30	60	25	U.S. writer, "Swan Lake"
☆ **Hemingway, Ernest**	**1899-1961**	**1000**	**2750**	**4500**	**2750**	**U.S. , "For Whom the Bell Tolls"- $2500 (SB), FA, CS&ALS-ESPV**
Hemingway, Mariel	1961-	20	55	40	40	"Manhattan"
Hemingway, Marqaux		40			80	Granddaughter of E.H.; actress / model
Hemingway, Mary		25	50	100		Mrs. Ernest Hemingway, SPS, SALS-2X
Hempel, Frieda	1885-1955	30	75	100	100	Opera: Soprano
Hemsley, Sherman	1938-	5	10	10	10	"The Jeffersons"
Henderson, Fletcher	1898-1952	25	50		45	Orchestra leader, arranger
Henderson, Florence	1934-	5	10	10	10	"The Brady Bunch"
Henderson, Ray	1896-1970	30	50	60	45	U.S., "Five Foot Two Eyes of Blue"
☆ **Hendrix, Jimi**	**1942-1970**	**850**	**1850**		**2000**	**(1992), FA; "Purple Haze"; SA/ CD-2250, ESPV**
Henie, Sonja	1912-1969	35	40	50	65	"One in a Million," "Thin Ice," RS
Henner, Marilu	1952-	15	25	30	40	"Taxi"
Henning, Doug	1947-	5	10	10	10	"The Magic Show," magician
Henreid, Paul	1908-1992	30	85		90	"Casablanca," "Goodbye, Mr. Chips"
Henriksen, Lance	1940-	5	10	10	10	"Aliens"
Henry, Buck (Buck Zuckerman)	1930-	5	10	10	10	"The Man Who Fell to Earth"
Henry, Justin	1971-	5	10	10	10	"Kramer vs. Kramer"
Henry, O. (W.S. Porter)	1862-1910	325	750	1500		U.S. short-story writer, "The Gift of the Magi"
Hensley, Pamela	1950-	5	10	10	15	"Matt Houston"
Henson, Jim	1936-1990	125	200		300	Puppeteer, CC-$200, ESPV
Hepburn, Audrey	1929-1993	125	350	500	270	"Roman Holiday," "Sabrina," "My Fair Lady"

NAME	DOB/DOD	SIG	DS/LS	ALS	SP	COMMENTS
Hepburn, Katharine	1907-	165	600	450	895	Screen legend, signed program- $375, FA, v. rare in photos
Herbert, Hugh	1887-1952	15	20	35	30	Character actor, "Footlight Parade"
Herbert, Victor	1859-1924	100	200	400	350	Irish/U.S., "Babes in Toyland"
Herman, Jerry	1933-	10	30	45	25	U.S., "Hello Dolly," RS!
Herman, Pee-Wee (Paul Reubens)	1952-	10	15	25	20	"Pee-Wee's Playhouse"
Herman, Woody	1913-1987	25	100		75	Band leader, clarinet and alto sax player
Herman's Hermits		30			75	P. Noone (KS); "Mrs. Brown, You've Got a Lovely Daughter"; SA/CD-100
Herriot, James (James Wright)	1916-1995	25	45	90	35	British novelist, "All Creatures Great and ..."
Herrmann, Edward	1943-	5	10	10	10	"The Paper Chase"
Hersey, John	1914-1993	25	60	125	30	U.S. novelist, "Hiroshima," RS
Hershey, Barbara (Barbara Herzstein)	1948-	10	20	25	25	"Hannah and Her Sisters"
Hersholt, Jean	1886-1956	25	35	80	55	"Greed," "The Greater Glory"
Hervey, Jason	1972-	5	10	10	10	"The Wonder Years"
Herzog, Werner	1942-	15	25		30	Film director
Hesse, Hermann	1877-1962	175	375	500	350	German novelist, "Steppenwolf," SDS/LS-2X
Hesseman, Howard	1940-	5	10	15	10	"WKRP in Cincinnati"
Heston, Charlton	1923-	10	30	50	30	"Ben-Hur," very RS
Hewett, Dorothy	1923-	15	30		25	Writer
Heydt, Louis Jean	1905-1960	45	80	135	85	"Test Pilot," GWTW
Heyward, DuBose	1885-1940	150	400	300	275	U.S. lyricist, "Summertime"
Hickman, Darryl	1931-	5	10	10	15	Child star, "If I Were King"
Hickman, Dwayne	1934-	10	20	20	20	"The Many ... Dobie Gillis," sends price list!
Hicks, Catherine	1951-	5	10	15	15	"Peggy-Sue Got Married"
Higginbotham, Jay C.	1906-1973	40	50		60	Trombone player
Higgins, George	1939-	15	25		20	Novelist
Higgins, Jack	1929-	15	25		30	Writer
Hightower, Rosella	1920-	15	30		35	Ballerina
Hill, Arthur	1922-	5	10	10	10	"Who's Afraid of Virginia Wolff?"

NAME	DOB/DOD	SIG	DS/LS	ALS	SP	COMMENTS
Hill, Benny	1925-1992	20	45		40	Comedian
Hill, Steven	1922-	5	10	10	15	"Law and Order"
Hiller, Wendy	1912-	20	35	35	30	"Separate Tables," "Pygmalion"
Hillerman, John	1932-	5	10	15	20	"Magnum P.I."
Hilliard, Harriet	1914-	20	25	25	35	"The Adventures of Ozzie and Harriet"
Hilton, James	1900-1954	50	150	265	75	British novelist, "Lost Horizon"
Hindemith, Paul	1895-1963	125	275	450	175	German composer
Hines, Earl "Fatha"	1905-1983	140	250		275	Piano player
Hines, Gregory	1946-	10	15	20	25	"The Cotton Club," dancer
Hingle, Pat (Martin Patterson Hingle)	1923-	5	10	10	15	"Gunsmoke"
Hinton, S.E.	1948-	10	20	35	15	U.S. writer, "Rumble Fish"
Hirsch, Judd	1935-	5	10	20	20	"Taxi"
Hitchcock, Alfred ☆	**1899-1980**	**275**	**550**	**620**	**625**	**Legendary director, "The Birds," FA**
Hodge, Patricia	1946-	5	10	10	10	"The Elephant Man"
Hodges, Eddie	?	25	35	40	45	Child star, "A Hole In The Head"
Hodges, Johnny	1906-1970	40	60		55	Alto sax player
Hodiak, John	1914-1955	25	35	40	50	"Lifeboat," "The Harvey Girls"
Hoey, Dennis	1893-1960	80	175	200	210	British character actor, "Sherlock Holmes"
Hoffman, Dustin	1937-	35	80	125	65	"The Graduate," "Rain Man," FA
Hofstadter, Richard	1916-1970	20	35	45	30	Historian
Hogan, Paul	1939-	10	20	25	20	"Crocodile Dundee"
Holbrook, Hal	1925-	10	20	25	25	"All The President's Men"
Holden, Fay	1895-1973	25	45	45	50	"Andy Hardy" film series
Holden, Gloria	1908-1991	20	40	35	45	"Dracula," "Dodge City"
Holden, William	1918-1981	50	100	200	175	"Stalag 17," "Sunset Boulevard"
Holiday, Billie ☆	**1915-1959**	**625**	**1000**		**1750**	**Blues singer, "Strange Fruit", ESPV**
Holland, B., Dozier, L., Holland, E.	1941-, 1941-, 1939-	125				U.S., "Heat Wave," "Stop! In the Name..."
Holliday, Judy	1923-1966	135	300	400	350	"Born Yesterday," rare in all forms
Holliman, Earl	1928-	5	10	10	10	"Police Woman"

NAME	DOB/DOD	SIG	DS/LS	ALS	SP	COMMENTS
Holloway, Stanley	1890-1982	20	40		50	Entertainer
Holloway, Sterling	1905-1992	30	50	55	60	Voice of numerous cartoon characters
Holly, Lauren	1966-	20	45	75	65	"Picket Fences"
Holm, Celeste	1919-	10	15	20	25	"Gentleman's Agreement," "All About Eve"
Holm, Hanya	1893-1992	15	35		30	Dancer, choreographer
Holm, Ian	1931-	10	30		25	Actor
Holmes, Oliver Wendell	1809-1894	100	225	450		U.S. poet, novelist, ESPV-ALS
Holmes, Phillips	1909-1942	75	150	325	175	"Nana," "The Man I Killed," KIA
Holst, Gustav	1874-1934	50	160	400	225	British composer, "The Planets"
Honegger, Arthur	1892-1955	60	175	425	75	French composer
Hooker, John Lee		50			120	(1991), no longer signs via mail; "Boogie Chillun"; SA/CD-150
Hooks, Jan	1957-	5	10	10	15	"Designing Women"
Hootie and the Blowfish		35			80	D. Rucker (KS); "Hold My Hand," "Let Her Cry"; SA/CD-110
Hope, Bob	1903-	40	165	300	115	Screen legend, comedian, "Road" series, FA
Hopkins, Anthony	1937-	30	55	125	65	"Silence of the Lambs," "The Bunker", FA
Hopkins, Miriam	1902-1972	40	100	125	125	"Becky Sharp," "Dr. Jekyll and Mr. Hyde"
Hopkins, Sam "Lightnin"	1912-1982	40	75		125	Guitarist and blues singer
Hopper, Dennis	1936-	25	40	60	50	"Easy Rider"
Hopper, Hedda	1890-1966	25	50	30	45	"Topper," "Sunset Boulevard," columnist
Hordern, Sir Michael	1911-1995	15	30		35	Actor, "Jumpers"
Horne, Lena	1917-	15	25	25	30	"Stormy Weather," "Ziegfeld Follies", RS
Horne, Marilyn	1934-	15	30		30	Mezzo-soprano, RS
Horner, James		15	30	55	25	U.S. composer, movie soundtracks
Horowitz, Vladimir	1904-1989	50	100		115	Pianist
Horton, Edward Everett	1886-1970	25	45	65	80	"Top Hat," "Lost Horizon," "Holiday"
Hoskins, Bob	1942-	5	10	10	15	"Who Framed Roger Rabbit"
☆ **Houdini, Harry**	**1874-1926**	**825**	**2000**		**3000**	**Magician, ESPV in all forms, FA**
Houseman, John	1902-1989	20	40		45	Stage director, actor

Nathaniel Hawthorne

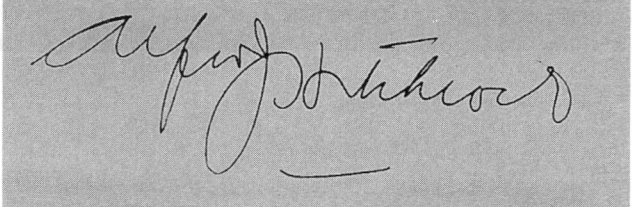

Alfred Hitchcock

Ernest Hemingway

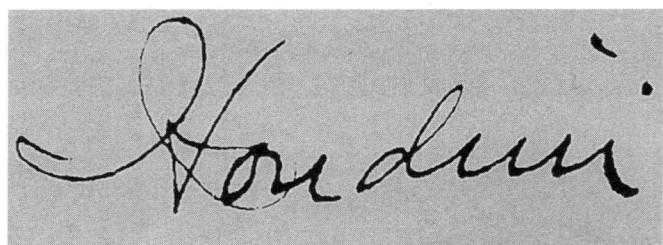

Buddy Holly

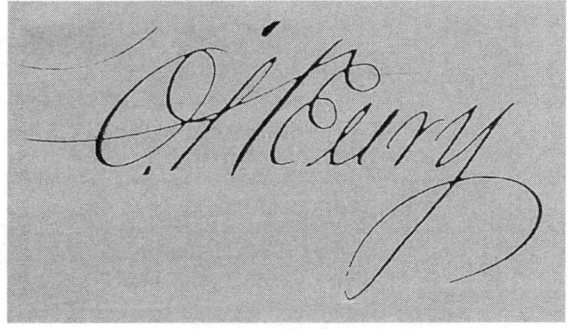

O. Henry

Harry Houdini

Katharine Hepburn

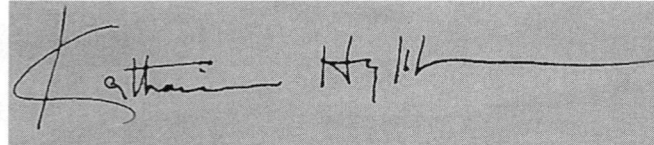

Katharine Hepburn

Alfred E. Housman

DuBose (Heyward)

Julia W. Howe

NAME	DOB/DOD	SIG	DS/LS	ALS	SP	COMMENTS
Housman, Alfred	1859-1936	75	180	350		British poet, "A Shropshire Lad," ALS-2X
Houston, Whitney	1963-	35			75	She can be an elusive signer; "I Will Always Love You"; SA/CD-100, FA
Hovhaness, Alan	1911-	40	100	225	100	U.S. composer
Howard, Arliss	1955-	5	10	10	15	"Full Metal Jacket"
Howard, Curly		500	1000		1000	Three Stooges
Howard, John	1913-	10	20	30	35	"Lost Horizon," "The Philadelphia Story"
Howard, Ken	1944-	5	10	10	10	"The White Shadow"
Howard, Leslie	1893-1943	300	500		500	"Pygmalion," GWTW, died at age 50, ESPV
Howard, Moe	1895-1975	225	300		500	Three Stooges
Howard, Ron	1954-	20	40	65	50	"Cocoon," "Apollo 13," director, elusive sig.
Howard, Shemp	1891-1955	500	600		600	Three Stooges
Howard, Sidney	1891-1939	55	125	240	100	Hollywood screenplay author
Howard, Trevor	1916-1988	15	35		30	Actor, "The Third Man"
Howard, William K.	1899-1954	55	115	175	100	"Sherlock Holmes," director
Howe, James Wong	1899-1976	45	50	60	75	Cinematographer, "The Thin Man"
Howe, Julia Ward	1819-1910	110	200	300		American writer, reformer
Howells, William Dean	1837-1920	60	150			U.S. novelist, "The Rise of Silas Lapham"
Howlin' Wolf	1910-1976	300	500		850	Guitarist, harmonica player, blues singer
Howlin, Olin	1896-1959	35	70	80	70	"So Big," GWTW
Hubbard, L. Ron	1911-1986	150				Religious leader, ESPV
Hudlin, Reginald	1961-	5	10	10	10	"House Party"
Hudlin, Warrington	1952-	5	10	10	10	"House Party," b. Reginald Hudlin
Hudson, Rochelle	1914-1972	35	40	50	50	"Rebel Without a Cause"
Hudson, Rock	1925-1985	65	150	300	125	"Giant," "Pillow Talk," FA, ESPV-ALS
Hughes, Langston	1902-1967	265	425	900		U.S. poet, "One-Way Ticket," SB-$865, ESPV
Hughes, Mary Beth	1919-	10	15	10	15	"The Great Profile"
Hughes, Ted	1930-	20	35	65	35	Poet, author, "A Dancer to God"

NAME	DOB/DOD	SIG	DS/LS	ALS	SP	COMMENTS
Hugo, Victor	1802-1885	250	500	1000	1000	French poet, dramatist, "Les Miserables", ESPV-ALS
Hulce, Tom	1953-	10	15	20	25	"Amadeus"
Hull, Henry	1890-1977	65	100	115	120	"Werewolf of London," "High Sierra"
Hull, Warren	1903-1974	30	40	55	60	"The Spider," "The Green Hornet"
Humperdinck, Engelbert	1854-1921	100	210	425	225	German composer, "Hansel and Gretel"
Humphreys, Emyr	1919-	15	30		25	Writer
Hunt, Helen	1963-	25	50	60	75	"Mad About You," "Twister," now very elusive!
Hunt, Linda	1945-	10	15	15	20	"The Year of Living Dangerously"
Hunt, Marsha	1917-	10	15	15	20	"Pride and Prejudice"
Hunter, Holly	1958-	25	50	75	75	"Broadcast News"
Hunter, Jeffrey	1925-1969	50		100	75	"The True Story of Jesse James", ESPV
Hunter, Kim	1922-	15	25	25	25	"A Streetcar Named Desire"
Hunter, Tab (Arthur Gelien)	1931-	10	15	20	25	"Damn Yankees"
Huppert, Isabelle	1955-	5	10	10	10	"Violette Noziere"
Hurley, Elizabeth	1965-	20	40	50	75	Actress, model, "Austin Powers"
Hurt, John	1940-	10	20	20	25	"The Elephant Man"
Hurt, Mary Beth (Mary Beth Supinger)	1948-	5	10	10	10	"The World According to Garp"
Hurt, William	1950-	25	50	75	65	"Children of a Lesser God"
Hussey, Ruth	1914-	10	20	20	25	"The Philadelphia Story," "Northwest Pass..."
Huston, Anjelica	1951-	10	25	40	30	"Prizzi's Honor", RS
Huston, John	1906-1987	45	100	100	100	Legendary director, screenwriter, "The Maltese Falcon"
Huston, Walter	1884-1950	115	200	175	230	Gifted character actor, "Dodsworth"
Hutton, Betty	1921-	10	15	20	25	"The Greatest Show on Earth"
Hutton, Lauren (Mary Hutten)	1943-	5	10	15	25	"American Gigolo," model, RS
Hutton, Timothy	1960-	15	30	45	40	"Ordinary People"
Huxley, Aldous	1894-1963	75	250	375	450	Brit. writer, "Brave New World," TLS-2-6X, ESPV
Hyer, Martha	1929-	10	15	20	30	"Some Came Running," "Sabrina"
Ibsen, Henrik	1828-1906	225	500	1350		Dramatist, poet, "A Doll's House"

NAME	DOB/DOD	SIG	DS/LS	ALS	SP	COMMENTS
Ice-T (Tracy Morrow)	1958-	10	20	25	35	"New Jack City," rap artist
Ice Cube (O'Shea Jackson)	1969-	10	20	25	30	"Boyz N the Hood," rap artist
Idle, Eric	1943-	10	20	25	30	"Monty Python's Flying Circus"
Ike and Tina Turner		50			125	(1991); "Proud Mary"; SA/CD-175
Iman	1955-	10	20	25	30	Model, m. David Bowie
Impressions, The		30			75	(1991), C. Mayfield (KS); "For Your Precious Love," "Amen"; SA/CD-100
Imus, Don	1940-	5	10	15	10	"Imus in the Morning," radio talk-show host
Inge, William	1913-1973	60	140	215		U.S. playwright, "Bus Stop"
Ingels, Marty	1936-	5	10	10	10	"The Pruitts of Southhampton"
Ingram, Rex	1895-1969	140	250	300	340	"The Green Pastures," one of first black actors
INXS	1960-1997	50			100	M. Hutchence (deceased); "Need You Tonight"; SA/CD-125
Ionesco, Eugene	1910-1994	40	100	225		French surrealist dramatist, "The Chairs"
Ireland, John	1914-1992	15	25	25	30	"All the King's Men"
Ireland, Kathy	1963-	10	20	25	30	Model
Irons, Jeremy	1949-	15	25	40	40	"The French Lieutenant's Woman"
Irving, Amy	1953-	5	10	10	15	"Yentl"
Irving, John	1942-	10	25	40	50	U.S. writer, "The World According to Garp"
Irving, Washington	1783-1859	200	450	600		U.S. writer, "Rip Van Winkle", ESPV, SALS=2X
Irving, Sir Henry	1838-1905	40	75	100	80	Actor
Irwin, Bill	1950-	5	10	10	15	"Eight Men Out"
Isherwood, Christopher	1904-1986	50	150	250	200	British novelist, playwright, "Goodbye to Berlin"
Islam, Kazi Nazrul	1899-1976	30	50		50	Poet
Isley Brothers, The		30			100	(1992), values without J. Hendrix; "It's Your Thing," "This Old Heart of Mine"; SA/CD-125
Issak, Chris	1956-	15	25	40	40	Singer, songwriter, actor
Ives, Burl	1909-	15	30	40	45	"The Big Country," ballad singer
Ives, Charles	1874-1954	225	850	1750	450	U.S. composer
Ivey, Judith	1951-	5	10	15	15	"Designing Women"

NAME	DOB/DOD	SIG	DS/LS	ALS	SP	COMMENTS
Ivory, James	1928-	10	15	25	20	"Howard's End," director, producer
Jackee (Jackee Harry)	1956-	5	10	10	15	"227"
Jackson Five, The		275			350	(1997), M. Jackson (KS); "ABC," "I'll Be There," "Dancing Machine"; SA/CD-400
Jackson, Alan		10	25		25	Country Music
Jackson, Glenda	1936-	10	20	20	20	"Women in Love"
Jackson, Janet	1966-	40	75		70	"Control," "When I Think of You"; SA/CD-75, FA
Jackson, Kate	1948-	10	25	25	50	"Charlie's Angels"
Jackson, Mahaila	1911-1972	100	200		185	Gospel singer
Jackson, Michael	1958-	150	400		275	Can be a RS; "Rock With You," "Billie Jean," "Thriller"; SA/CD-350, ESPV, FA
Jackson, Milton	1923-	15	30		25	Vibraphone player
Jackson, Samuel L.	1949-	20	45	50	70	"Pulp Fiction"
Jackson, Victoria	1958-	5	10	10	10	SNL
Jacobi, Derek	1938-	5	10	10	10	"The Day of the Jackal"
Jacobi, Lou	1913-	5	10	10	15	"Irma La Douce"
Jacobs, David	1926-	15	30		25	British radio & T.V. broadcaster
Jacques, Hattie	1924-1980	25			45	Comic actress
Jaffe, Sam	1897-1984	25	35	40	50	"The Asphalt Jungle," "Gunga Din"
Jagger, Dean	1903-1991	20	25	30	40	"Twelve O'Clock High"
Jakes, John	1932-	10	20	30	15	U.S. writer, very RS!
Jamal, Ahmad	1930-	15	30		25	Jazz pianist
James, Clifton	1925-	5	10	10	10	"Cool Hand Luke," RS
James, Etta	1938-	20			40	(1993), RS; "Roll With Me, Henry," "At Last"; SA/CD-45
James, Frank	1844-1915	1100	2000	3625		Outlaw, ESPV
James, Henry	1843-1916	125	375	750		U.S. novelist, "Daisy Miller"
James, P.D.	1920-	25	50	100		British crime writer, "The Black Tower"
Jamison, Judith	1943-	10	25		20	Dancer
Janis, Conrad	1928-	5	10	10	10	"Mork and Mindy," RS
Jason, Sybil	1929-	10	15	15	15	"The Singing Kid," "The Blue Bird"

NAME	DOB/DOD	SIG	DS/LS	ALS	SP	COMMENTS
Jay and the Americans		25			50	"This Magic Moment," "Cara Mia," "She Cried"; SA/CD-65
Jean, Gloria	1928-	5	10	15	20	"Never Give a Sucker An Even Break," RS
Jeffers, Robinson	1887-1962	75	280	400	100	U.S. poet, dramatist, "Tamar"
Jefferson Airplane		125			200	(1996), RSs; "White Rabbit"; SA/CD-250
Jefferson, Blind Lemon	1897-1930	1250	2500		2500	Guitarist, blues singer, scarce, ESPV
Jeffries, Lionel	1926-	5	10	10	10	"The Water Babies"
Jenkins, Allen	1900-1974	30	40	45	50	"42nd Street," "Dead End"
Jeritza, Maria	1887-1982	25	50	75	100	Opera: Soprano
Jerome, Jerome K.	1859-1927	35	70	100	75	Writer
Jessel, George	1898-1981	35	75	80	100	"The Jazz Singer," "Toastmaster General"
Jeter, Michael	1952-	5	10	10	15	"Evening Shade"
Jethro Tull		40			60	I. Anderson (KS) $15-$30; "Thick as a Brick," "Aqualung"; SA/CD-80
Jett, Joan	1960-	15			20	"I Love Rock 'n' Roll"; SA/CD-35
Jewel		15			50	RS; "You Were Meant for Me"; SA/CD-55
Jewell, Isabel	1909-1972	55	70	100	100	"Blessed Event," GWTW
Jhabvala, Ruth	1927-	10	25		20	Writer
Jillian, Anne	1951-	5	10	10	20	"It's a Living"
Jobim, Antonio Carlos	1927-1994	25	40	75	50	Brazil, "One Note Samba"
Joel, Billy	1949-	20			60	FA; "Piano Man," "Just The Way You Are"; SA/CD-60
Joffrey, Robert	1930-1988	20	50		60	Dancer, ESPV
Johansen, David	1950-	10	15	20	20	"Scrooged"
John, Elton	1947-	50			85	(1994); "Candle in the Wind," "Crocodile Rock"; SA/CD-125, FA
John, Little Willie	1937-1968	225			500	Singer, songwriter, "Sleep," "Fever"
Johns, Glynis	1923-	10	15	25	30	"Glynis"
Johnson, Artie	1929-	5	10	10	15	"Laugh-In"
Johnson, Beverly	1952-	5	10	15	15	Model, actress
Johnson, Bunk	1879-1949	225	450		600	Cornet and trumpet player
Johnson, Dame Celia	1908-1982	25	50			Actress

NAME	DOB/DOD	SIG	DS/LS	ALS	SP	COMMENTS
Johnson, Don	1949-	15	25	45	50	"Miami Vice"- TV, FA
Johnson, James P.	1891-1955	140	500		225	Composer, piano player
Johnson, Kay	1904-1975	35	45	45	50	"Thirteen Women," "Dynamite"
Johnson, Samuel	1709-1784	1800	4500			British author, scholar, "Vanity of Human Wishes", scarce, ESPV
Johnson, Van	1916-	10	20	25	25	"The Caine Mutiny," "Battleground", RS
Johnston, Eric	1896-1962	10	20	25	25	Pres. Motion Picture Assoc. of America
Jolson, Al	1886-1950	150	425		450	Popular stage star, "The Jazz Singer" SP-.5X
Jones, Allan	1908-1992	15	20	30	40	"A Night At The Opera"
Jones, Buck	1889-1942	185	255	325	370	Cowboy star, "Hearts and Spurs", ESPV-ALS
Jones, Carolyn	1929-1983	60	125	100	100	"The Bachelor Party," "The Addams Family", ESPV
Jones, Dame Gwyneth	1936-	15			25	Soprano
Jones, Dean	1931-	5	10	10	15	"The Shaggy D.A."
Jones, George		10	20		20	Country Music Hall of Fame
Jones, Grace	1952-	20	30	35	40	"A View to Kill"
Jones, Grandpa		20	40		50	Country Music Hall of Fame
Jones, James	1921-1977	50	125		100	Novelist, FHTE
Jones, James Earl	1931-	10	25	30	25	"The Great White Hope"
Jones, Jeffrey	1947-	5	10	10	10	"Ferris Bueller's Day Off"
Jones, Jennifer	1919-	135	275	300	300	"Song of Bernadette," m. D. O. Selznick, ES
Jones, Jo	1911-1985	30	50		50	Drummer
Jones, Marcia Mae	1924-	5	10	10	15	child actr., "These Three," "The Champ," RS
Jones, Philly Joe	1923-1985	25	40		40	Drummer
Jones, Sam J.	1954-	5	10	10	15	"Flash Gordon"
Jones, Shirley	1934-	5	15	25	20	"The Partridge Family"
Jones, Spike	1911-1965	30	50	60	65	"Bring On the Girls," bandleader
Jones, Terry	1942-	10	15	15	20	"Monty Python's Life of Brian"
Jones, Thad	1923-1986	25	40	75	60	Trumpet and cornet player
Jones, Tommy Lee	1946-	45	85		50	"The Fugitive," elusive signer

Engelbert Humperdinck

Washington Irving

Al Jolson

Aldous Huxley

Boris Karloff

Washington Irving

Gene Kelly

Washington Irving

Grace Kelly

NAME	DOB/DOD	SIG	DS/LS	ALS	SP	COMMENTS
Jong, Erica	1942-	10	20	25	15	U.S. writer, "Fear of Flying"
Jonson, Ben	1572-1637	3000				British dramatist, "Volpone"
Joplin, Janis	1943-1970	725	1650	2650	2000	(1995); "Me and Bobby McGee," "Piece of My Heart"; SA/CD-2250
Joplin, Scott	1868-1917	700	1125	2210		U.S., "Treemonisha"
Jordan, Louis	1908-1975	35	70		70	Singer, alto sax player
Jordan, Neil	1950-	10	30		25	Film maker
Jory, Victor	1902-1982	60	125	225	165	GWTW, "The Adventures of Tom Sawyer"
Jourdan, Louis	1919-1993	30	55	125	75	"Three Coins in the Fountain", BC-$25
Joy, Leatrice	1896-1985	15	25	40	35	"Ten Commandments," "Manslaughter"
Joyce, Brenda	1915-	25	40	40	45	"Tarzan," retired at age 34
Joyce, Eileen A.	1912-1991	20	45		40	Concert pianist
☆ **Joyce, James**	**1882-1941**	**450**	**600**	**2750**		**Irish writer, "Ulysses", scarce-SP, ESPV**
Judge, Arlene	1912-1974	20	25	35	40	"Are These Our Children?"
Jump, Gordon	1932-	5	10	10	15	"WKRP in Cincinnati," RS
Justin, John	1917-	40	50	50	75	"Thief of Baghdad," RAF pilot in WWII
K.C. and the Sunshine Band		25			35	RSs! "Get Down Tonight," "I'm Your Boogie Man"; SA/CD-40
Kafka, Franz	1883-1924	1100				Austrian novelist, "The Castle", scarce
Kagel, Mauricio R.	1931-	15			25	Composer
Kahn, Gus	1886-1941	55	70	80	75	U.S. lyricist, "Memories"
Kahn, Madeline	1942-	10	15	20	40	"Blazing Saddles"
Kain, Karen	1951-	10			25	Dancer
Kander, John	1927-	10	20	40	20	U.S., "Cabaret," RS!
Kane, Carol	1952-	5	10	10	15	"Taxi"
Kane, Helen	1903-1966	30	45	50	75	"Good Boy," "Sweetie"
Kanin, Garson	1912-	15	20	25	30	"The True Glory," director, screenwriter
☆ **Kant, Immanuel**	**1724-1804**	**1250**				**German philosopher, ESPV**
Kaprisky, Valerie	1963-	5	10	10	15	"Breathless"

NAME	DOB/DOD	SIG	DS/LS	ALS	SP	COMMENTS
Karloff, Boris	1887-1969	315	550	500	575	"Frankenstein," horror ALS-2-3X, SP-2X
Karpis, Alvin		100			130	Criminal
Karras, Alex	1935-	10	20	25	25	"Webster," former football player
Katt, William	1955-	5	10	10	10	"The Greatest American Hero"
Kaufman, George	1889-1961	40	80	160	65	"Animal Crackers," screenwriter, playwright, SDD-2-3X, TLS-225
Kaufman, George S.	1889-1961	35	70	150	40	U.S. playwright, "The Man Who Came to Dinner"
Kavner, Julie	1951-	5	10	10	15	Voice of Marge Simpson, "Rhoda" SP-2X
Kay, Ulysses	1917-	15			30	Composer
Kaye, Danny	1913-1987	75	125	200	135	"The Secret Life of Walter Mitty"
Kaye, Nora	1920-1987	20	50		55	Ballerina
Kaye, Stubby	1918-	10	20	20	20	"Guys and Dolls"
Kazan, Elia	1909-	20	45		40	Director
Kazantzakis, Nikos	1885-1957					Greek novelist, "Zorba the Greek", scarce
Kazurinsky, Tim	1950-	5	10	15	15	SNL, actor
Keach, Stacy (William Keach, Jr.)	1941-	10	20	25	20	"Mickey Spillane's Mike Hammer"
Keaton, Buster	1895-1966	235	375		550	Silent film star, "Sunset Boulevard", ESPV
Keaton, Diane	1946-	20	40	50	60	"Annie Hall"
Keaton, Michael (Michael Douglas)	1951-	25	40	75	65	"Batman" SP-$75
Keel, Howard	1917-	10	15	20	20	"Dallas," unresponsive via mail
Keeler, Ruby	1909-1993	30	40	50	60	"42nd Street," "Gold Diggers of 1933"
Keene, Tom	1896-1963	30	45	50	55	"Sundown Trail," "Our Daily Bread"
Keeshan, Bob	1927-	5	10	20	25	"Captain Kangaroo"
Keighley, William	1889-1984	20	40	50	40	Director, "G-Men"
Keillor, Garrison	1942-	10	20	30	15	U.S. writer, very RS!
Keith, David Lemuel	1954-	5	10	10	10	"An Officer and a Gentleman"
Kellaway, Cecil	1893-1973	30	50	75	80	"The Luck of the Irish," "Harvey"
Keller, Marthe	1945-	5	10	10	10	"Marathon Man"
Kellerman, Sally	1937-	10	15	20	25	"M*A*S*H"

NAME	DOB/DOD	SIG	DS/LS	ALS	SP	COMMENTS
Kelley, Deforest	1920-	10	20	25	30	"Star Trek"
Kelley, Kitty		10	25		20	Biographer
Kelly, Gene	1912-1996	50	225	200	100	"Singin' in the Rain" SP-+ 25%, dancer, ESPV
Kelly, Grace (Grace de Monaco)	**1928-1982**	**265**	**740**	**845**	**530**	**"High Noon," GdM sig. 75% of value, SP-50%**
Kelly, Moira	1968-	10	20	25	30	"The Cutting Edge"
Kelly, Nancy	1921-	10	20	25	20	"The Bad Seed," "Jesse James"
Kemke, Rudolf	1916-1976	40	75		75	Conductor
Kendal, Felicity	1947-	10	25		25	Actress
Keneally, Thomas	1935-	12	30		25	Author, "Schindler's List," SDS-2-3X
Kennedy, Arthur	1914-1990	35	45	75	70	"Champion," "Bright Victory," "Trial"
Kennedy, Edgar	1890-1948	140	250	250	265	Keystone Kop, "San Francisco"
Kennedy, George	1925-	10	20	25	35	"Cool Hand Luke," FA
Kennedy, Madge	1891-1987	10	20	25	30	"Poppy," "Lust for Life"
Kennedy, Nigel	1956-	10	25		20	Violinist
Kennedy, William	1928-	10	25	35	20	U.S. writer, "Ironweed"
Kensit, Patsy	1968-	15	20	30	50	"Lethal Weapon 2"
Kenton, Stan	1912-1979	50	100		125	Orchestra leader, composer, piano player
Kern, Jerome	1885-1945	450	825		2000	U.S., "Show Boat", ESPV
Kerns, Joanna (Joanna De Varona)	1953-	5	10	10	15	"Growing Pains," FA
Kerouac, Jack	**1922-1969**	**500**	**2000**	**5000**		**U.S. author, Beat poet, "On The Road", ESPV**
Kerr, Deborah	1921-	20	25	25	30	"From Here To Eternity"
Kesey, Ken	1935-	30	50		60	Author, can be elusive!
Kevorkian, Dr. Jack		30	50	100	75	Assisted suicide doctor, controversial
Key, Francis Scott	1779-1843	300	725	1000		American lawyer, poet, ESPV
Keyes, Evelyn	1919-	20	50	40	50	GWTW, "The Jolson Story"
Khachaturian, Aram	1903-1978	150	300	600	600	Russian composer, ESPV
Kibibble, Ish	1908-	10	15	20	20	Merwyn Bogue, Trumpeter, "You'll Fnd Out"
Kidd, Michael	1919-	10	25		25	Dancer, choreographer
Kidder, Margot	1948-	10	15	20	25	"Superman"

NAME	DOB/DOD	SIG	DS/LS	ALS	SP	COMMENTS
Kidman, Nicole	1967-	20	40	50	50	"To Die For," "Days of Thunder"
Kiel, Richard	1939-	10	15	15	20	"The Spy Who Loved Me"
Kietel, Harvey	1939-	15	20	25	35	"Bad Lieutenant"
Kilbride, Percy	1888-1964	90135	200	265	325	"Ma and Pa Kettle," character actor
Kilburn, Terry	1926-	10	15	20	20	"A Christmas Carol," "Goodbye, Mr. Chips"
Kiley, Richard	1922-1999	10	15	20	25	"Man of La Moncha," "The Blackboard Jungle"
Kilmer, Joyce	1886-1918	225	500	750		U.S. poet, "Trees"
Kilmer, Val	1959-	40	100	200	100	"Batman Forever," "The Doors"
King, Alan	1927-	5	10	15	15	The Anderson Tapes," producer, comedian
King, Albert	1923-1992	20	50		50	Blues guitarist
King, B.B.	1925-	20			60	(1987), RS; "The Thrill is Gone"; SA/CD-85
King, Carole	1942-	15	50	60	25	U.S., "Up on the Roof," RS!, SA/CD-25
King, Carole		15			20	A RS; "It's Too Late," "Jazzman";
King, Henry	1888-1982	35	50	60	70	Director, "Tol'able David," "The Sun Also Rises"
King, Larry	1933-	5	10	30	15	"Larry King Live", RS
King, Perry	1948-	5	10	15	15	"Riptide"
King, Stephen	1947-	50	125	400	100	U.S. writer, "Carrie," elusive signer!
Kingsley, Ben (Krishna Bhanji)	1943-	15	25	50	40	"Gandhi"
Kingsley, Charles	1819-1975	50	100	150		Author, "Westward Ho!"
Kingsolver, Barbara	1955-	10	20	30	15	U.S. writer, "Animal Dreams," elusive signer!
Kingston, Maxine Hong	1940-	10	25	35	15	U.S. writer, "The Woman Warrior:..."
Kinks, The		75			125	(1990); "You Really Got Me," "Lola"; SA/CD-150
Kinnear, Greg	1964-	5	10	15	15	"Talk Soup"
Kinnell, Galway	1927-	15	30	50	25	U.S. writer, "Selected Poems"- $150 (FE, SB)
Kinski, Klaus	1929-1991	25	45		50	Actor
Kinski, Nastassja (Nastassja Nakszynski)	1960-	15	45	40	50	"Cat People," "Tess"

NAME	DOB/DOD	SIG	DS/LS	ALS	SP	COMMENTS
Kipling, Rudyard	1865-1936	240	460	600		British author, poet, "The Jungle Book"
Kipnis, Alexander	1891-1978	50	100	125	125	Opera: Bass
Kirby, Bruno (Bruce Kirby)	1949-	5	10	10	10	"City Slickers"
Kirk, Phyllis	1926-	15	30	35	40	"The Thin Man"-TV
Kitkland, Gel sey	1952-	10	20		25	Dancer
Kirkland, Sally	1944-	5	10	10	15	"Anna"
Kiss		100			150	Values for original lineup; "Rock 'n' Roll All Night," "Beth"; SA/CD-175
Kitt, Eartha	1928-	10	20	20	20	"The Mark of the Hawk," singer
Klein, Robert	1942-	5	10	15	15	"Comedy Tonight", RS
Klemperer, Otto	1885-1973	50	100		150	Conductor
Klemperer, Werner	1920-	10	20	25	30	"Hogan's Heroes", RS
Kline, Kevin	1947-	15	25	40	40	"The Big Chill," m. Phoebe Cates
Klugman, Jack	1922-	10	20	25	25	"Twelve Angry Men," "The Odd Couple"-TV
Kneale, Nigel	1922-	20	40		35	Writer, playwright
Knight, "Fuzzy"	1901-1976	65	115	125	150	Nightclub musician, "She Done Him Wrong"
Knight, Michael E.	1959-	5	10	10	15	"All My Children"
Knight, Shirley	1937-	10	15	20	20	"The Dark at the Top of the Stairs"
Knotts, Don	1924-	15	25	30	25	"The Andy Griffith Show"
Knowles, John	1926-	20	35	60	30	U.S. writer, "A Separate Peace"
Knowles, Patric (Reginald L. Knowles)	1911-	10	20	20	25	"How Green Was My Valley"
Knox, Alexander	1907-	15	20	25	30	"The Sea Wolf"
Koch, Kenneth	1925-	15	25	45	20	U.S. writer, "The Red Robins," RS!
Kodaly, Zoltan	1882-1967	150	350	800	400	Hungarian composer
Koenig, Walter	1936-	15	30	40	35	"Star Trek," writer, director, producer
Koestler, Arthur	1905-1983	20	40		40	Writer, journalist
Kolb, Clarence	1875-1964	30	40	45	55	"My Little Margie"-TV
Koontz, Dean	1945-	10	20	40	20	U.S. writer, RS, "Winter Moon"
Kopell, Bernie	1933-	5	10	10	10	"The Love Boat"
Korda, Alexander	1893-1956	55	70	100	100	Gifted director, "The Private Life of Henry VIII"

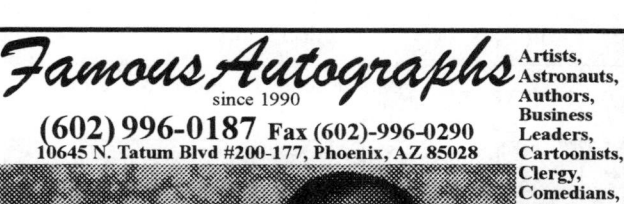

NAME	DOB/DOD	SIG	DS/LS	ALS	SP	COMMENTS
Korman, Harvey	1927-	5	10	15	20	"The Carol Burnett Show"
Korngold, Erich	1897-1957	100	200	300	160	Composer
Kotto, Yaphet	1937-	5	10	10	15	"Live and Let Die"
Krabbe, Jeroen	1944-	10	15	15	20	"The Fugitive"
Krantz, Judith	1928-	10	20	40	20	U.S. writer, RS, "Scruples"
Kreisler, Fritz	1875-1962	125	225	300	250	Austrian composer
Krige, Alice	1955-	5	10	10	10	"Chariots of Fire"
Kruger, Otto	1885-1974	35	45	50	85	"High Noon," "Dracula's Daughter"
Krupa, Gene	1909-1973	50	200		120	Band and combo leader, drummer
Kruschen, Jack	1922-	10	20	25	20	"The Apartment," "Cape Fear"
Kschessinskaya, Mathilde	1872-1971	125	235	400		Russian dancer
Kubrick, Stanley	1928-1999	25	50	75	100	"2001: A Space Odyssey"
Kudrow, Lisa	1963-	20	40	45	50	"Friends"
Kumin, Maxine	1925-	15	25	45	25	U.S. writer, "Up Country: Poems of New ..."
Kunitz, Stanley	1905-	15	35		30	Poet, RS
Kurtz, Swoosie	1944-	5	10	15	22	"Sisters," RS
Kwan, Nancy	1939-	10	15	35	40	"The World of Suzie Wong"
Kyser, Kay	1897-1985	20	40	40	35	Band leader, "Playmates," "Carolina Blue"
L.L. Cool J	1968-	20			30	(James Todd Smith); "Mama Said Knock You Out"; SA/CD-40
La Rue, Jack	1900-1984	15	20	25	30	"A Farewell to Arms," "Lady Killer"
Ladd, Alan	1913-1964	65	110	175	200	"This Gun For Hire," "Shane"
Ladd, Cheryl	1951-	10	15	25	45	"Charlie's Angels"
Ladd, Diane (Diane Ladner)	1932-	5	10	10	15	"Alice Doesn't Live Here Anymore"
Lagerkvist, Par	1891-1974	40	80	160	75	Swedish poet, dramatist, "The Sybil"
Lagerlof, Selma	1858-1940	100	275	500	150	Swedish novelist, "Jerusalem"
Lahr, Bert	1895-1967	320	500		565	TWOO, "Always leave Them Laughing"
Lahti, Christine	1950-	5	10	15	15	"Swing Shift"
Lake, Arthur	1905-1987	20	35	40	45	"Blondie" film series
Lake, Ricki	1968-	5	10	15	20	"Hairspray," talk show host, RS
Lake, Veronica	1919-1973	145	300	180	345	"Star-Spangled Rhythm", scarce

NAME	DOB/DOD	SIG	DS/LS	ALS	SP	COMMENTS
Lamarr, Hedy	1916-	35	70	100	115	"Extase," "Samson and Delilah"
Lamartine, Alphonse de	1790-1869	120	225	300		French poet, "Meditations poetiques"
Lamas, Fernando	1915-1982	25	35	45	50	"Rich Young and Pretty"
Lamas, Lorenzo	1958-	10	15	20	25	"Falcon Crest"
Lamb, Charles	1775-1834	125	275	700		British essayist, "Essays of Elia"
Lambert, Christopher	1957-	15	25	30	40	"Greystroke: The Legend of Tarzan"
Lamour, Dorothy	1914-	20	40	60	40	"Road" series w/Bob Hope & Bing Crosby
L'Amour, Louis	1908-1988	80	250	500	165	U.S. western author, screenwriter, "Hondo"
Lancaster, Burt	1913-1994	65	150	265	100	"Elmer Gantry," "From Here To Eternity"
Lanchester, Elsa	1902-1986	30	65		65	"Come to the Stable," "Witness ... Prosecution"
Landau, Martin	1931-	15	30	35	40	"Mission: Impossible"
Lander, Harald	1905-1971	40	75		70	Ballet dancer
Landers, Ann	1918-	10	20		15	Journalist
Landers, Audrey	1959-	5	10	10	15	"Dallas"
Landesberg, Steve	1945-	5	10	10	15	"Barney Miller"
Landi, Elissa	1904-1948	50	70	75	80	"London," "Underground"
Landis, Carole	1919-1948	110	300		230	"A Day at the Races," died at age 29, scarce
Landis, Jessie R.	1904-1972	35	55	60	75	"Moon Over Miami"
Landis, John	1950-	15	25	30	30	"Twilight Zone- The Movie," director
Lane, Abbe	1935-	10	20	20	20	"Xavier Cugat Show," m. Xavier Cugat
Lane, Burton	1912-1997	15	25	30	25	U.S., "Finian's Rainbow"
Lane, Charles	1953-	10	15	15	20	"Sidewalk Stories," director
Lane, Diane	1965-	10	15	15	15	"Rumble Fish"
Lane, Lola	1906-1981	20	25	25	30	"Four Daughters," one of three Lane sisters
Lane, Nathan	1956-	20	35	40	50	"The Birdcage," FA
Lane, Rosemary	1914-1974	20	25	30	35	"Four Wives," one of three Lane sisters
Lang, Fritz	1890-1976	85	280		155	German film director, "Metropolis," "M"
Lang, June	1915-	15	20	25	20	"Wee Willie Winkie"

NAME	DOB/DOD	SIG	DS/LS	ALS	SP	COMMENTS
Langdon, Harry	1884-1944	125	250	300	250	"Tramp, Tramp, Tramp," "The Strong Man"
Landon, Michael		125	150		225	"Bonanza"
Lange, Hope	1931-	5	15	25	25	"Peyton Place"
Lange, Jessica	1950-	20	40	50	75	"Frances," "Tootsie"
Lange, Ted	1947-	5	10	10	10	"The Love Boat"
Langella, Frank	1940-	10	20	25	25	"Dracula"- SP- 2X
Langford, Frances	1914-	10	20	25	25	"The Glenn Miller Story"
Lanier, Sidney	1842-1881	275	500	775		American poet, "Sunrise"
Lansbury, Angela	1925-	10	25	40	45	"Murder She Wrote"- TV, RS
Lansing, Robert	1929-	5	10	10	10	"The Man Who Never Was"
Lansky, Meyer	1902-1983	375	1100			Mobster, signed check $2750, scarce
Lanza, Mario	1921-1959	155	410	500	675	"The Great Caruso," "That Midnight Kiss"
Lardner, Ring	1885-1933	75	175	300	100	U.S. short-story writer, humorist
Larroquette, John	1947-	10	20	20	25	"Night Court"
Lasser, Louise	1939-	5	10	15	15	"Bananas"
Latifah, Queen	1970-	15	20	25	40	"Jungle Fever," rap artist
Lauder, Sir Harry	1870-1950	45	90		75	Comis singer
Lauer, Matt	1957-	10	20	25	20	"Today," very RS
Laughton, Charles	1899-1962	100	200		250	"The Private Life of Henry VIII"
☆ Laurel, Stan	**1890-1965**	**200**	**350**	**475**	**400**	**Screen comedy legend, SP (both)- $900-$1475**
Laurence, Margaret	1926-1987	20			40	Novelist
Laurie, Piper	1932-	5	10	10	15	"Carrie"
Lavin, Linda	1937-	5	10	10	15	"Alice," singer
Lawford, Peter	1923-1984	35	75		75	"Mrs. Miniver," "The White Cliffs of Dover"
Lawless, Lucy	1968-	20	40	50	75	"Xena: Warrior Princess," FA
Lawrence, Carol	1935-	5	10	15	15	"West Side Story," singer
Lawrence, David Herbert	1885-1930	285	675	2500		British novelist, "Sons and Lovers"
Lawrence, Gertrude	1898-1952	25	50	50	50	British stage actor, "The Glass Menagerie"
Lawrence, Joey	1976-	5	10	15	15	"Blossom"

NAME	DOB/DOD	SIG	DS/LS	ALS	SP	COMMENTS
Lawrence, Martin	1965-	10	10	15	20	"Martin"
Lawrence, Vicki	1949-	5	10	10	15	"Mama's Family"
Lawson, Leigh	1945-	5	10	10	15	"Tess"
Laxness, Halldor	1902-	20	45		40	Novelist, NP
Lazarus, Emma	1849-1887	1250	2150			American poet, essayist, ESPV, scarce
Le Carre, John	1931-	20	40	80	25	British writ., "The Honourable Schoolboy," RS
Leach, Robin	1941-	5	10	10	10	"Lifestyles of the Rich and Famous"
Leachman, Cloris	1930-	10	20	25	20	"The Mary Tyler Moore Show"
Lean, Sir David	1908-1991	40	85		75	Film director, "Dr. Zhivago"
Lear, Norman	1922-	10	20	50	20	"All in the Family," producer, director
Learned, Michael	1939-	5	10	10	10	"The Waltons," RS
Leblanc, Matt	1967-	15	25	35	40	"Friends"- TV, "Lost in Space"
Led Zeppelin		750			1200	(1995), J. Bonham (1948-1980); "Stairway to Heaven"; SA/CD-1250; 3 living-$500
Ledbetter, Huddie "Leadbelly"	1888-1949				5000	Guitarist, blues singer, scarce
Lederer, Francis	1906-	15	20	25	25	"Pandora's Box," "Midnight"
Lee, Brandon	1965-1993	300	800		625	"The Crow", ESPV, FA
Lee, Brenda	1944-	10			20	RS; "I'm Sorry"; SA/CD-30
Lee, Bruce	1940-1973	350	850	1750	1100	"Enter the Dragon", FA
Lee, Christopher	1922-	30	60	150	100	Horror film legend
Lee, Gypsy Rose	1913-1970	75	150	225	265	"Belle of the Yukon," Burlesque SP-2X
Lee, Harper		125	300		300	U.S. novelist, "To Kill a Mockingbird"
Lee, Jason Scott	1966-	10	20	20	20	"Dragon: The Bruce Lee Story"
Lee, Laurie	1914-	10	25		20	Writer
Lee, Michele	1942-	5	10	10	15	"Knots Landing"
Lee, Pamela Anderson	1967-	15	25	35	40	"Baywatch," sexy SP- 2X
Lee, Peggy	1920-	10	15	20	20	"The Jazz Singer", RS
Lee, Spike (Shelton Lee)	1957-	10	25	25	20	"Do the Right Thing," director, RS
Leeds, Andrea	1914-1984	10	15	15	25	"Stage Door," "Come and Get It"
Leeves, Jane	1963-	5	10	15	15	"Frasier"

of his sincerely

Jerome Kern

Stan Laurel & Oliver Hardy

Rudyard Kipling

David H. Lawrence

Bruce Lee

Rudyard Kipling

Vivian Leigh

Bert Lahr

Jack Lemmon

NAME	DOB/DOD	SIG	DS/LS	ALS	SP	COMMENTS
LeGuin, Ursula	1929-	15	25	45	25	U.S. writer, The Dispossessed"
Leguizamo, John	1965-	5	10	15	20	"Carlito's Way"
Lehar, Franz	1870-1948	100	200	475	300	Hungarian composer, "Merry Widow"
Lehmann, Lilli	1848-1929	100	200	325	300	Opera: Soprano, scarce
Lehmann, Lotte	1888-1976	35	75	150	150	Opera: Soprano
Leiber, J. & Stoller, M.	1933-, 1933-	150				U.S., " Hound Dog," "Yakety Yak"
Leibman, Ron	1937-	5	10	10	10	"Kaz," RS
Leigh, Janet (Jeannette Helen Morrison)	1927-	5	15	20	15	"Psycho," RS
Leigh, Jennifer Jason (Jennifer Morrow)	1962-	15	20	30	45	"Fast Times At Ridgemont High"
Leigh, Mitch	1928-	20	30	40	35	U.S., "Man of La Mancha"
Leigh, Vivien	1913-1967	400	600	750	600	GWTW, SP- 2X, "A Streetcar Named Desire"
Leighton, Laura	1968-	15	25	30	40	"Melrose Place"
Leighton, Margaret	192201976	20	40		45	Actress
Leinsdorf, Erich	1912-1993	25	50		60	Conductor, RS
Leisen, Mitchell	1898-1972	35	55	60	65	"Hands Across the Table," "Easy Living"
Leitch, Donovan	1968-	5	10	10	10	Actor, son of folk singer
Lemat, Paul	1952-	5	10	10	10	"American Graffiti"
Lemmon, Chris	1954-	5	10	10	15	"Swing Shift," s. Jack Lemmon
Lemmon, Jack	1925-	15	50	75	40	"Some Like It Hot," "Missing"
L'Engle, Madeleine	1918-	15	25	50	25	U.S. writer, "Wintersong"
Lennon, John	**1940-1980**	**700**	**2500**	**6000**	**1200**	**FA, was responsive in-person; "Imagine," "Whatever Gets You Thru the Night"; SA/CD-1450, ESPV**
Leno, Jay (James Leno)	1950-	10	25	25	40	"The Tonight Show," FA
Lenya, Lotte	1900-1981	50	85		100	Actress
Leonard, Elmore	1925-	10	20	30	20	U.S. writer, "Get Shorty", RS
Leonard, Robert Sean	1969-	5	10	10	15	"Dead Poets Society"
Leonard, Robert Z.	1889-1968	30	45	40	55	Director, "The Great Ziegfeld"
Leonard, Sheldon	1907-	10	15	20	20	"Guys and Dolls," IAWL, "Lucky Jordan"
Leoncavallo, Ruggero	1857-1919	200	425	750	500	Italian composer

☆ (star marker next to Lennon, John)

NAME	DOB/DOD	SIG	DS/LS	ALS	SP	COMMENTS
Leoni, Tea	1966-	15	25	35	45	"The Naked Truth"
Leopold, Nathan	1905-1971	130	400	600	150	Loeb & Leopold case, ESPV
Lermontov, Mikhail	1814-1841	615	2000	4500		Russian novelist, poet, "Hero of Our Time", scarce
Lerner, Alan J.	1918-1986	50	100	235	150	U.S. lyricist, "My Fair lady"
Lerner, Michael	1941-	5	10	10	10	"Barton Fink"
Leslie, Joan	1925-	5	10	10	15	"High Sierra," "Sergeant York," res. signer
Lessing, Doris	1919-	20	40	60	30	English novelist, "The Grass is Singing"
Letterman, David	1947-	25	45	50	50	"Late Show with David Letterman," elusive
Levant, Oscar.	1906-1972	30	50	65	55	Pianist, "Rhapsody in Blue"
Levin, Ira	1929-	20	35	50	25	U.S. writer, "Rosemary's Baby," RS!
Levine, James	1943-	15	30		25	Conductor
Levy, Eugene	1946-	5	10	10	10	"SCTV," writer
Lewis, Al	1910-	10	20	20	25	"The Munsters"
Lewis, Clive Staples	1898-1963	250	500	1250		British critic, novelist, "Out of the Silent Planet", ESPV
Lewis, Emmanuel	1971-	5	10	10	10	"Webster"
Lewis, Jerry	1926-	20	25	45	30	"My Friend Irma," RS
Lewis, Jerry Lee	1935-	35			50	(1986), charges for his signature; "Whole Lotta Shakin' Going On"; SA/CD-85
Lewis, Juliette	1973-	20	35	40	45	"Cape Fear," "Kalifornia"
Lewis, Mel	1929-1990	20	40	75	55	Orchestra leader, drummer
Lewis, Sinclair	1885-1951	120	275	600	275	U.S. novelist, "Babbitt"
Liberace	1919-1987	50	150		150	Entertainer
Light, Judith	1949-	5	10	10	15	"Who's the Boss?," RS
Lillie, Beatrice	1898-1989	30	40	50	40	"Thoroughly Modern Millie"
Limbaugh, Rush	1951-	10	20	30	25	"The Rush Limbaugh Show," talk show host
Lincoln, Abbey (Anna Marie Woolridge)	1930-	5	10	10	15	"For Love of Ivy"
Lincoln, Elmo	1889-1952	480	875		1200	"The Birth of a Nation," "Tarzan" film series, scarce
Lind, Jenny	1820-1887	100	200	300	800	Opera: Soprano

NAME	DOB/DOD	SIG	DS/LS	ALS	SP	COMMENTS
Linden, Hal (Hal Lipschitz)	1931-	10	20	20	20	"Barney Miller"
Lindsay, Margaret	1910-1981	20	40	50	45	"Cavalcade," "Ellery Queen" film series
Lindsay, Vachel	1879-1931	65	150	475	115	U.S. poet, "The Congo"
Linkletter, Art	1912-	5	10	10	15	"People Are Funny"
Linn-Baker, Mark	1954-	5	10	15	15	"Perfect Strangers"
Linville, Larry	1939-	10	20	20	25	"M*A*S*H"
Liotta, Ray	1955-	20	30	50	45	"GoodFellas"
Lipman, Maureen	1946-	10	25		20	Actress, writer
Lippman, Walter	1889-1974	15	55		30	Journalist
Liszt, Franz	**1811-1886**	**500**	**915**	**1000**	**925**	**Hungarian composer. ESPV, scarce, in SP, SALS-2-3X, ALS-$1275**
Lithgow, John	1945-	10	20	35	20	"3rd Rock from the Sun," RS
Little Anthony and the Imperials		30			50	"Tears on My Pillow"; SA/CD-55
Little Richard	1932-	65			125	(1986), an elusive signer; "Tutti Frutti"; SA/CD-150
Littlefield, Lucien	1895-1960	30	40	40	45	"The Torrent," "Henry Aldrich" film series
Live		25			30	E. Kowalczyk (KS); "Lightning Crashes," "I Alone," "Freaks"; SA/CD-45
Livermore, Mary Ashton	1820-1905	70	100	165	125	Suffragette, reformer
Lloyd, Christopher	1938-	15	25	25	30	"Taxi", FA
Lloyd, Emily	1970-	10	15	20	25	"Wish you Were Here"
Lloyd, Harold	1893-1971	185	240	500	365	"Safety Last," "The Freshman"
Locke, Sondra	1947-	10	20	20	20	"The Gauntlet"
Lockhart, Gene	1891-1957	30	45	50	60	"Algiers," "Going My Way"
Lockhart, June	1925-	10	20	25	20	"Meet Me in St. Louis," charges for signature
Locklear, Heather	1961-	20	40	50	55	"Dynasty," "Melrose Place," FA
Lockwood, Gary	1937-	10	15	15	15	"2001: A Space Odyssey"
Lockwood, Harold A.	1887-1918	100	200	200	250	Silent era star, "The House of a Thousand..."
Lockwood, Margaret	1916-1990	20	40	50	45	"The Lady Vanishes"
Loden, Barbara	1932-1980	40	100		115	Actress, film director

NAME	DOB/DOD	SIG	DS/LS	ALS	SP	COMMENTS
Loesser, Frank	1910-1969	125	200	375	225	U.S., "Guys and Dolls", ESPV
Loewe, Frederick	1901-1988	50	80	150	75	U.S./Austrian, "My Fair Lady"
Lofting, Hugh	1896-1947	115	265	500		British writer, Dr. Doolittle series
Logan, Joshua	1908-1988	30	45	40	50	"Picnic," "Bus Stop," director
Loggia, Robert	1930-	5	10	10	15	"Mancuso, FBI"
Lollobrigida, Gina	1927-	10	20	25	30	"Solomon and Sheba"
Lom, Herbert	1917-	15	20	30	30	"Spartacus"
Lombard, Carole	1908-1942	345	775	1000	775	"My Man Godfrey," died tragically at age 34, scarce, ESPV
London, Jack	**1876-1916**	**315**	**750**	**2400**		**U.S. novelist, "Call of the Wild", ESPV-ALS**
Long, Alison	1960-	10			30	Mezzo-soprano
Long, Shelley	1949-	10	20	25	25	"Cheers"
Longfellow, Henry Wadsworth	1807-1882	175	350	500	840	U.S. poet, "The Song of Hiawatha"
Loos, Anita	1893-1981	25	40	65	40	Playwright, novelist, screenwriter
Lopukhov, Fyodor	1886-1973	35	55		65	Dancer
Lord, Jack	1930-1998	25	40	75	40	"Hawaii Five-O," FA, elusive signer
Lord, Pauline	1890-1950	30	55	75	65	"Anna Christie," great stage actress
Lords, Traci	1968-	5	15	25	30	"Melrose Place," porn star SP- 2-4.5X
Loren, Sophia	1934-	25	40	50	50	"Two Women", RS, FA
Lorre, Peter	1904-1964	175	350		355	"M," "The Maltese Falcon" SP-2X, C
Louis-Dreyfus, Julia	1961-	15	30	35	40	"Seinfeld," FA
Louise, Anita	1915-1970	20	30	35	40	"My Friend Flicka"
Louise, Tina (Tina Blacker)	1934-	10	20	25	25	"Gilligan's Island"
Love, Courtney	1964-	20	40	50	60	"Straight to Hell," m. Kurt Cobain
Lovin' Spoonful, The		35			65	"Summer in the City," "Do You ... Magic"; SA/CD-75
Lovitz, Jon	1957-	10	20	30	25	SNL
Lowe, Arthur	1914-1982	35	55		60	Actor
Lowe, Chad	1968-	5	10	10	10	"Life Goes On," b. Rob Lowe
Lowe, Edmund	1890-1971	25	40	65	50	"The Cisco Kid"
Lowe, Rob	1964-	20	30	35	40	"St. Elmo's Fire"
Lowell, Amy	1874-1925	40	110	225		U.S. poet, "Lilacs"

NAME	DOB/DOD	SIG	DS/LS	ALS	SP	COMMENTS
Lowell, James Russell	1819-1891	60	150	250	325	U.S. poet, editor, "The Biglow Papers"
Lowell, Robert	1917-1977	40	125	200	150	U.S. poet, "Lord Weary's Castle"
Loy, Myrna	1905-1993	25	50	50	60	"The Thin Man," "The Best Years of Our Lives"
Lubitsch, Ernst	1892-1947	65	130	175	125	Film director
Lucas, George	1944-	30	75	100	60	"Star Wars" all forms-2X, director, FA
Lucci, Susan	1950-	10	20	25	25	"All My Children," FA
Luckinbill, Laurence	1934-	5	10	10	15	"The Boys in the Band", Star Trek-3X
Ludlom, Robert	1927-	10	20	30	15	U.S. writer, "The Scarlatti Inheritance"
Luft, Lorna	1952-	5	10	10	10	"Where the Boys Are," d. Judy Garland
Lugosi, Bela	1888-1956	365	1775	2175	1500	Hungarian horror film star, "Dracula," FA, ESPV
Lukas, Paul	1895-1971	50	85	120	100	"Watch on the Rine," "Little Women"
Luke, Keye	1904-1991	20	35	50	45	"Kung Fu"- TV
Lumet, Sidney	1924-	15	30	35	30	"Twelve Angry Men," director, RS
Lunceford, Jimmie	1902-1947	45	100		150	Band leader, sax player
Lund, John	1911-1992	10	15	20	20	"High Society"
Lunden, Joan	1950-	5	10	10	10	"Good Morning America"
Lundgren, Dolph	1959-	10	20	25	40	"Rocky IV"
Lunt, Alfred	1892-1977	35	50	75	60	"The Guardsman," Sigs. w/L. Fontanne- $40
Lupino, Ida	1918-	20	50	75	65	"The Adventures of Sherlock Holmes"
Lupone, Patti	1949-	5	10	10	10	"Life Goes On," RS
Lupus, Peter	1937-	10	20	20	20	"Mission: Impossible"
Lurie, Alsion	1926-	10	25	40	15	U.S. writer, "Love and Friendship," RS
Lynch, David	1946-	10	30		25	Film director
Lyndon, Jimmy	1923-	25	40	40	50	Known for character Henry Aldrich
Lynn, Diana	1924-1972	35	40	40	50	"Bedtime for Bonzo," died at age 48
Lynn, Jeffrey	1909-	10	15	20	20	"Four Wives"
Lynn, Loretta		10	20		20	Country Music Hall of Fame, RS

NAME	DOB/DOD	SIG	DS/LS	ALS	SP	COMMENTS
Lynyrd Skynyrd		225			250	Values for original lineup, R. Van Zant (KS); "Sweet Home Alabama"; SA/CD-275
Lytell, Bert	1885-1954	40	50	100	75	Silent era star, "The First Legion"-stage
Lyttelton, Humphrey	1921-	15	30		30	Jazz trumpeter, ESPV
Ma, Yo-Yo	1955-	10	30		25	Cellist, RS
Maazel, Lorin	1930-	15	30		30	Conductor
Mabley, Jackie Moms		80			175	Entertainer
MacArthur, James	1937-	5	10	15	20	"Hawaii Five-O," "Kidnapped," RS
Macchio, Ralph	1962-	5	10	10	10	"The Karate Kid"
MacCorkindale, Simon	1952-	5	10	10	10	"Falcon Crest"
MacDonald, Jeanette	1901-1965	75	175	300	150	"Love Me Tonight," teamed w/Nelson Eddy
MacDonald, Ross	1915-1983	50	125		85	Thriller writer
MacDowell, Andie (Rosalie MacDowell)	1958-	10	20	15	25	"sex, lies and videotape"
MacDowell, Edward	1861-1908	175	300	600	375	U.S. composer, "To a Wild Rose"
MacGraw, Ali	1938-	5	10	15	25	"Love Story"
Mack, Helen	1913-1986	15	30	45	30	"King Kong," radio producer
Mackintosh, Sir Lameron	1946-	15	40		35	British impressario
MacLachlan, Kyle	1959-	10	20	25	20	"Twin Peaks"
MacLaine, Shirley (Shirley Beaty)	1934-	10	25	50	35	"Terms of Endearment," RS
Maclean, Alistair	1922-1987	25			50	Writer
Macleish, Archibald	1892-1982	40	125	150	50	U.S. poet "Conquistador"
MacMurray, Fred	1908-1991	35	100	165	70	"My Three Sons"- TV, "The Apartment"
MacNaughton, Robert	1966-	5	10	10	20	"E.T., the Extra-Terrestrial"
MacNee, Patrick	1922-	10	20	35	30	"The Avengers"
MacNichol, Peter	1954-	5	10	10	10	"Sophie's Choice"
MacPherson, Elle	1965-	5	20	25	35	Supermodel, actress, RS!
MacRae, Gordon	1921-1986	20	50	100	45	"Oklahoma," singer
Madigan, Amy	1951-	10	15	20	20	"Places in the Heart"
Madonna (Madonna Louise V. Ciccone)	1958-	150	1000		300	FA; SA/CD-375, ESPV, elusive signer

NAME	DOB/DOD	SIG	DS/LS	ALS	SP	COMMENTS
Madsen, Michael	1959-	10	15	20	30	"Reservoir Dogs"
Madsen, Virginia	1963-	5	10	15	15	"Electric Dreams"
Maeterlinck, Maurice	1862-1949	40	100	200		Playwright, NP, ESPV-SP
Magnani, Anna	1908-1973	275	445	500	575	"The Rose Tattoo," "Rome, Open City"
Magnuson, Ann	1956-	5	10	10	10	"Anything but Love"
Maher, Bill	1956-	10	20	25	25	"Politically Incorrect"- TV
Mahfouz, Naguib	1911-	20	35	55	25	Egyptian writer
Mahler, Gustav	**1860-1911**	**600**	**1350**	**3200**		**Austrian composer, scarce, ESPV**
Mahoney, John	1940-	5	10	10	20	"Cheers," "Frasier"
Mailer, Norman	1923-	15	100	200	60	U.S. writer, RS, "An Amer .."
Majors, Lee (Harvey Lee Yeary II)	1940-	5	10	15	15	"The Six Million Dollar Man"
Makarova, Nataliya	1940-	10	20		25	Ballerina, RS
Makeba, Miriam	1932-	15			30	Singer
Makepeace, Chris	1964-	5	10	10	10	"My Bodyguard"
Mako (Makoto Iwamatsu)	1933-	5	10	15	20	"The Sand Pebbles"
Malamud, Bernard	1914-1986	30	55	125	30	U.S. short-story writer, novelist, "The Magic..."
Malden, Karl (Mladen Sekulovich)	1914-	5	10	20	25	"A Streetcar Named Desire," RS!
Malkovich, John	1953-	15	30	30	45	"Dangerous Liaisons"
Mallarme, Stephane	1842-1898	165	400	950		French poet, "Poesies", ESPV, scarce
Malone, Dorothy	1925-	30	55	110	60	"Written on the Wind"
Malthus, Thomas R.	1766-1834	250	950			English economist, ESPV
Mamas and the Papas, The		350			450	C. Elliott (KS)- $150; "Monday, Monday," "California Dreamin'"; SA/CD-500
Mamet, David	1947-	5	10	15	20	U.S. writer, "Glengarry Glen Ross," RS!
Manchester, William	1922-	5	15	25	15	Novelist, RS
Mancini, Henry	1924-1994	25	100	125	75	U.S., "Moon River," RS!
Mandel, Howie	1955-	5	10	20	25	"St. Elsewhere," "Bobby's World"
Manen, Hans van	1932-	10	25		20	Ballet dancer
Manetti, Larry	1947-	5	10	10	10	"Magnum P.I."
Mankowitz, Wolf	1924-	10	25		30	Writer

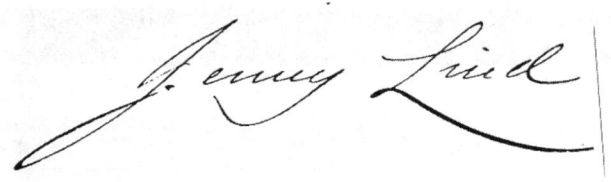

Jenny Lind

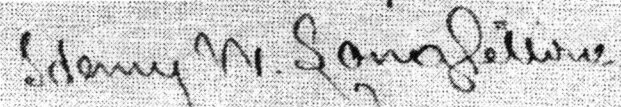

Henry Wadsworth Longfellow

Jack London

Amy Lowell

Henry Longfellow

James Russell Lowell

Henry Longfellow

Bela Lugosi

Henry Longfellow

Erotica

whats beautiful
whats exciting
what wakes you up inside
what pierces your senses
makes you taste & feel & hear for
the 1st time.
forget yourself
forget the rules
forget your fears
forget the fools.

Henry Longfellow

Madonna (song lyrics)

NAME	DOB/DOD	SIG	DS/LS	ALS	SP	COMMENTS
Mann, Barry & Weil, Cynthia	1939-, 1937-	50			75	U.S., "You've Lost That Loving Feeling"
Mann, Terrence	1945-	5	10	15	15	"Les Miserables"
Mann, Thomas	1875-1955	150	400	1100	800	German novelist, "The Magic Mountain"
Manners, David	1901-	22	50	100	50	"Dracula," horror film hero
Mannoff, Dinah	1958-	5	10	15	15	"Empty Nest"
Mansfield, Jayne	1933-1967	165	400		480	"Will Success Spoil Rock Hunter," sex symbol, ESPV
Mansfield, Katherine	1888-1923	115	250	460		British short-story writer, "Bliss"
Manson, Charles		125	250	500	200	Hippie cult leader
Mantegna, Joe	1947-	10	15	20	200	"The Godfather, Part III"
Marceau, Marcel	1923-	25	60	200	100	Pantomimist, "Bip"
March, Frederic	1897-1975	50	165	225	110	"Dr. Jekyll and Mr. Hyde," "Victory"
Marchand, Nancy	1928-	5	10	10	10	"Lou Grant," RS!
Marchesi, Bianche	1863-1940	60	150	175	200	Opera: Soprano
Marcovicci, Andrea	1948-	5	10	10	10	"Trapper John, MD"
Margo	1917-1985	20	30	35	40	"Lost Horizon," m. Eddie Albert (1945-85)
Margulies, Julianna	1966-	15	25	30	35	"ER"
Marin, Cheech (Richard Marin)	1946-	5	15	15	20	"Up in Smoke"
Marinaro, Ed	1950-	10	20	30	20	"Hill Street Blues"
Markey, Enid	1890-1981	100	115	200	275	"Tarzan," the first screen "Jane"
Markova, Came Alicia	1910-	25	55		60	Prima ballerina
Marley, Bob (and the Wailers)	1945-1981	1250			2250	(1994). B. Marley (KS)- $1,000; "No Woman No Cry," "Exodus"; SA/CD-3000
Marlowe, Hugh	1911-1982	30	50	75	55	Character actor, "All About Eve," "Monkey Bus."
Marquez, Gabriel Garcia	1928-	125	200		250	Novelist, NP, ESPV, elusive
Marriner, Sir Neville	1924-	20	45		45	Conductor
Marsalis, Wynton	1961-	15	35		25	Trumpeter, RS
Marsh, Mae	1895-1968	40	50	75	70	"The Birth of a Nation," "TGOW"
Marshall, Brenda	1915-1992	15	30	30	35	"The Sea Hawk," m. William Holden
Marshall, E.G.	1910-	10	25	45	30	"Twelve Angry Men"

NAME	DOB/DOD	SIG	DS/LS	ALS	SP	COMMENTS
Marshall, Herbert	1890-1966	30	65	160	70	"The Letter," "The Little Foxes"
Marshall, Paule	1929-	25	55		40	Writer, ESPV-SP
Marshall, Penny	1942-	5	10	20	20	"Laverne and Shirley"
Marshall, Peter	1930-	5	10	10	10	"The Hollywood Squares"
Martha and the Vandellas		25			65	(1995), M. Reeves (KS); "Dancin' in the Streets," "Heat Wave"; SA/CD-75
Martin du Gard, Roger	1881-1958	60	125		100	Novelist, NP
Martin, Andrea	1947-	5	10	10	12	"SCTV"
Martin, Dean	1917-1996	35	165	200	115	"Bells Are Ringing," com. partner J. Lewis, FA
Martin, Dick	1923-	5	25	20	20	"Laugh-In"
Martin, Mary	1914-1990	40	75	100	65	"The Birth of the Blues," "Night and Day"
Martin, Pamela Sue	1953-	10	15	20	25	"Dynasty"
Martin, Steve	1945-	15	20	45	25	"All of Me," "Father of the Bride", RS
Martindale, Wink	1934-	5	10	10	10	"Tic Tac Dough"
Martinson, Harry	1904-1978	40	100			Poet, novelist, NP
Marvelettes, The		35			60	G. Dobbins (KS); "Please, Mr. Postman," "Playboy"; SA/CD-75
Marx, Chico	1887-1961	200	270	350	400	"Animal Crackers," member Marx Brothers
Marx, Groucho	1890-1977	260	525	400	300	Member Marx Brothers, FDC, all sigs.- $1825, RS
Marx, Harpo	1888-1964	400	750		665	Member Marx Brothers, often adds drawing
Marx, Zeppo	1901-1979	85	120	150	125	"Marx Brothers," "Duck Soup"
Mascagni, Pietro	1863-1945	175	355	710	575	Italian composer
Mason, Bobbie Ann	1940-	10	25	30	15	U.S. writer, "Feather Crowns," RS!
Mason, Jackie	1934-	5	10	10	10	"Chicken Soup"
Mason, James	1909-1984	35	65	75	80	"A Star Is Born," "Evil Under the Sun"
Mason, Marsha	1942-	5	10	10	20	"The Goodbye Girl," RS!
Massenet, Jules	1842-1912	75	150	300	300	French composer
Massey, Ilona	1912-1974	30	40	35	40	"Northwest Outpost"
Massey, Raymond	1896-1983	40	85	145	80	"Abe Lincoln in Illinois," "Dr. Kildare"- TV
Massine, Leonide	1896-1979	40			100	Ballet dancer, scarce, ESPV

NAME	DOB/DOD	SIG	DS/LS	ALS	SP	COMMENTS
Masters, Edgar Lee	1869-1950	60	175	225	60	U.S. poet, "Spoon River ...," AMS-$600
Masterson, Mary Stuart	1966-	5	10	10	25	"Fried Green Tomatoes"
Masterson, Peter	1934-	5	10	10	15	"The Exorcist"
Mastrantonio, Mary Elizabeth	1958-	15	40	50	60	"The Color of Money"
Mastroianni, Marcello	1924-	30	80		65	Actor, "Dark Eyes"
Masur, Richard	1948-	5	10	15	15	"One Day at a Time"
Mathers, Jerry	1948-	10	20	30	25	"Leave It to Beaver," signs at shows
Matheson, Tim	1947-	5	10	20	15	"National Lampoon's Animal House", RS
Mathews, Denise	1963-	5	10	10	10	"The Last Dragon"
Matthau, Walter	1920-	10	25	20	20	"The Odd Couple"
Matthiessen, Peter	1927-	20	50		40	Novelist
Mature, Victor	1915-	10	20	25	25	"Samson and Delilah"
Maugham, William Somerset	1874-1955	75	175	350	380	British author, "The Moon and Sixpence"
Maupassant, Guy de	1850-1893	300	700	1000		French, short-story writer, "The Necklace"
Maxwell, Marilyn	1921-1972	15	25	30	30	"Summer Holiday," singer
May, Elaine	1932-	5	10	10	15	"Ishtar," director, writer
Maynard, Ken	1895-1973	100	125	150	150	Cowboy star, "Texas Gunfighter"
Mayo, Virginia	1920-	10	20	25	25	"The Best Years of Our Lives"
Mazar, Debi	1964-	5	10	10	15	"Civil Wars: L.A. Law"
Mazursky, Paul	1930-	5	10	15	15	"Down and Out in Beverly Hills"
McBain, Ed	1926-	10	25	50	20	Novelist, "The Blackboard Jungle"
McCallum, David	1933-	10	15	20	25	"The Great Escape"
McCambridge, Mercedes	1918-	50	60	70	60	"All the King's Men," "Suddenly, Last Summer"
McCarey, Leo	1898-1969	50	100	100	75	Director, "Duck Soup," "Going My Way"
McCarthy, Andrew	1962-	5	10	10	10	"Less Than Zero"
McCarthy, Cormac	1933-	10	20	35	20	U.S. writer, "All the Pretty Horses"
McCarthy, Jenny	1972-	25	45	50	60	"Singled Out", FA
McCarthy, Kevin	1914-	10	20	25	20	"Invasion of the Body Snatchers"
McCarthy, Mary	1912-1989	50	100	165	65	U.S. critic, novelist, "Memories of a Catholic..."

NAME	DOB/DOD	SIG	DS/LS	ALS	SP	COMMENTS
☆ **McCartney, Paul**	1942-	200	625	4000	350	**"Band on the Run," "Maybe I'm ...";** **SA/CD-450, SDS-2X, FA**
McClanahan, Rue	1934-	5	10	20	15	"The Golden Girls," RS!
McClellan, William "Scrugs"	1907-1931	75	150		200	Guitar player, scarce
McClurg, Edie	1950-	5	10	10	10	"The Hogan Family"
McConaughey, Matthew	1970-	20	40	55	65	"A Time To Kill," "Dazed and Confused"
McCormack, John	1884-1945	55	175	335	200	Opera: Tenor, ESPV
McCormick, Myron	1907-1962	30	50	55	60	"Jolson Sings Again," "No Time for Sergeants"
McCourt, Frank	1930-	10	25	40	20	U.S. writer
McCoy, Tim	1891-1978	60	100	130	125	"The Indians Are Coming," "War Paint"
McCracken, James	1927-1988	15	40		35	Tenor
McCrea, Joel	1905-1990	20	40	40	40	"Dead End," "Bird of Paradise"
McCullers, Carson	1917-1967	50	175	440	75	U.S. novelist, "Clock Without ..."-$125 (SB)
McCullough, Colleen	1937-	20			55	U.S. writer, "The Grass Crown"
McDaniel, Hattie	1895-1952	620	1100	2000	2120	GWTW, "Beulah," often stamped signature
McDonald, Marie	1923-1965	45	60	75	90	"It Started With Eve," model, controversial
McDonnell, Mary	1952-	5	10	25	20	"Dances with Wolves," RS!
McDormand, Frances	1957-	10	20	20	20	"Fargo"
McDowall, Roddy	1928-1998	15	25	45	30	"How Green Was My Valley," "Lassie Come Home"
McDowell, Malcolm	1943-	10	25	40	30	"A Clockwork Orange"
McFarland, George "Spanky"	1928-1993	30	45	50	60	Child star, "Our Gang" series
McGavin, Darren	1922-	20	40	35	40	"The Court Martial of Billy Mitchell"
McGillis, Kelly	1957-	10	20	30	40	"Witness"
McGovern, Elizabeth	1961-	5	10	20	20	"Ragtime"
McGraw, Tim		10	25		30	Country Music
McGregor, Ewan	1971-	5	10	10	10	"Trainspotting"
McGuane, Thomas	1939-	10	20	30	15	U.S. writer, "Missouri Breaks," responsive sig.
McGuire, Dorothy	1918-	15	30	35	35	"Gentleman's Agreement"

NAME	DOB/DOD	SIG	DS/LS	ALS	SP	COMMENTS
McHugh, Frank	1898-1981	25	50	50	60	Character actor, "A Midsummer Night's Dream"
McHugh, Jimmy	1894-1969	30	60	120	60	U.S., "Don't Blame Me"
McIntyre, Sir Donald	1934-	15	40		35	Opera singer
McKean, Michael	1947-	5	10	10	10	"Laverne & Shirley"
McKellar, Danica		5	10	10	10	"The Wonder Years"
McKellen, Sir Ian	1939-	15	40		30	Actor, RS
McKenna, Siobhan	1923-1986	15	35		30	Actress
McKenzie, Julia	1941	10	25		20	Actress, singer
Mckeon, Nancy	1966-	5	10	15	20	"The Facts of Life"
McLaglen, Victor	1886-1959	140	240	250	280	"The Informer," "Gunga Din"
McLean, Don	1945-	15			25	"American Pie," "Vincent," "Crying"; SA/CD-15
McMahon, Ed	1923-	5	10	15	10	"The Tonight Show," "Star Search"
McMurtry, Larry	1936-	10	25	40	20	U.S. writer, "Terms of Endearment"
McNichol, Kristy	1962-	5	10	15	20	"Empty Nest"
McPartland, Jimmy	1907-1991	30	50		55	Trumpet player
McPhatter, Clyde		600			1150	(1987), (1932-1972); "A Lover's Question"; SA/CD-1275, scarce
McQueen, Butterfly	1911-	50	100	125	115	GWTW, "Mildred Pierce"
McQueen, Steve	**1930-1980**	**275**	**500**	**640**	**400**	**"Bullitt," FA, elusive signer!, ESPV, FA**
McRae, Carmen	1920-1994	20	35		45	Jazz singer
McRaney, Gerald	1948-	5	10	10	15	"Major Dad," FA
McWhirter, Norris & Ross	1925- 1925-1975	100				Both, ESPV, Publisher, "The Guiness Book…"
Meadows, Audrey		20	35	50	50	"The Honeymooners", RS
Meadows, Jayne (Jayne Cotter)	1920-	5	10	10	10	Actress, quiz show regular
Meaney, Colm	1953-	15	25	25	30	"Star Trek: The Next Generation"
Meara, Anne	1929-	5	10	10	15	"The Out-of-Towners"
Meatloaf (Marvin Aday)	1947-	15			25	A RS! "Paradise by the Dashboard Light"; SA/CD-35
Medina, Patricia	1919-	5	10	15	15	"The Foxes of Harrow," "Botany Bay"
Meek, Donald	1880-1946	40	70	75	80	"Stagecoach," "State Fair"
Meeker, Ralph	1920-1988	30	40	45	50	"Picnic"- stage, "Kiss Me Deadly"

NAME	DOB/DOD	SIG	DS/LS	ALS	SP	COMMENTS
Melba, Nellie	1861-1931	100	200	325	500	Opera: Soprano, ESPV
Melchior, Lauritz	1890-1973	40	85	135	165	"Thrill of a Romance"
Melchior, Lauritz	1890-1973	50	125	200	200	Opera: Tenor
Mellencamp, John (Cougar)		20			35	"Jack and Diane," "Hurts So Good"; SA/CD-50
☆ **Melville, Herman**	**1819-1891**	**700**	**2500**	**10000**		**U.S. novelist, "Billy Budd," ALS content- 2-4X scarce in all forms, FA, ESPV**
Men at Work		15			25	"Who Can It Be Now?," "Down Under"; SA/CD-30
Mencken, Henry Lewis	1880-1956	100	200	400	425	U.S. author, "Prejudices"
☆ **Mendelssohn, Felix**	**1809-1847**	**850**	**2250**	**4750**		**German composer, "A Midsummer Night's...", ESPV**
Menjou, Adolphe	1890-1963	25	50	60	70	"The Front Page," autobiography- $40
Menken, Alan	1950-	20	50	55	40	U.S., "Beauty and the Beast"
Menotti, Gian-Carlo	1911-	165	265		320	Italian/U.S. composer, "The Medium"
Menuhin, Yehudi M.	1916-	15	45		40	Violinist, RS
Mercer, David	1928-1980	30			50	Playwright
Mercer, Johnny	1909-1976	50	125	200	125	U.S. lyricist, "That Old Black Magic"
Mercouri, Melina	1923-1994	20	35		55	Film actress
Meredith, Burgess	1908-1997	25	40	50	45	"Of Mice and Men," "Batman," "Rocky"
Merkel, Una	1903-1986	20	30	30	35	"Destry Rides Again"
Merman, Ethel	1909-1984	40	125	135	100	"There's No Business Like Show Business"
Merrick, David	1911-	40	75		85	"The Great Gatsby", scarce
Merrill, Bob	1921-	10	20	35	25	U.S. lyricist, "People"
Merrill, Gary	1915-1990	20	30	40	40	"Young Dr. Kildare"- TV, "All About Eve"
Merrill, James	1926-1995	25	40	55	35	U.S. poet, "Divine Comedies," responsive sig.
Merrill, Robert	1917-	1-	15		20	Baritone, RS
Merwin, W.S.	1926\7-	15	30		25	Poet
Metallica		75			160	J. Hetfield (KS), C. Burton (1962-1986); "Enter Sandman," "One"; SA/CD-200

NAME	DOB/DOD	SIG	DS/LS	ALS	SP	COMMENTS
Metcalf, Laurie	1955-	5	10	15	20	"Roseanne"
Methot, Mayo	1904-1951	25	40	50	45	"Mr. Deed Goes to Town," m. H. Bogart
Meyer, Joseph	1894-1987	25	50	60	50	U.S., "If You Knew Susie"
Meyerbeer, Giacomo	1791-1864	200	300			German composer
Meyers, Ari	1970-	5	10	10	10	"Kate & Allie"
Michael, George	1963-	25			50	"Faith," "Father Figure," ; SA/CD-65
Michaels, Lorne	1944-	20	35	40	40	SNL, producer, writer
Michener, James	1907-1998	25	250	300	70	U.S. writer, "Tales ... South Pacific," RS
Middler, Bette	1945-	25	50	75	60	"The Rose," "Beaches"
Mifune, Toshiro	1920-	20	30	50	40	"Throne of Blood"
Milano, Alyssa	1972-	20	35	40	55	"Who's the Boss?" "Melrose Place"
Milanov, Zinka	1906-1989	30	75	125	125	Opera: Soprano
Miles, Sarah	1941-	10	15	25	20	"Ryan's Daughter"
Miles, Sylvia	1932-	5	10	25	20	"Midnight Cowboy"
Miles, Vera	1930-	5	10	15	15	"Psycho"
Milhaud, Darius	1892-1974	200	300	375	400	French composer
Mill, John Stuart	1806-1873	165	345	780		English philosopher, economist
Milland, Ray	1905-1986	35	60	70	75	"The Lost Weekend," "Beau Geste"
Millay, Edna St. Vincent	1892-1950	150	300	725	1000	U.S. poet, "A Few Figs From Thistles," ESPV
Miller, Ann (Lucille Ann Colier)	1923-	10	20	30	25	"On the Town"
Miller, Arhur	1915-	20	100	200	50	U.S. writer, "Death of a Salesman," SB- $75
Miller, Dennis	1953-	10	15	25	20	SNL
Miller, Glenn	1904-1944	200	450	500	450	Band leader, trombone player, SDS-2X
Miller, Henry	1891-1980	100	200	350	130	U.S. erotic novelist, "Tropic of Cancer," scarce
Miller, Patsy Ruth	1905-	30	40	50	50	"The Hunchback of Notre Dame"
Miller, Penelope Ann	1964-	15	30	40	40	"Carlito's Way"
Miller, Roger		10			20	Country Music Hall of Fame
Milligan, Spike	1918-	10	20		20	Humorist
Mills, Hayley	1946-	10	15	20	20	"The Parent Trap"

Gustav Mahler

Norman Mailer

Marx Brothers

Jayne Mansfield

Eugene O'Neil

Jules Massenet

Charles Manson

W. Somerset Maugham

Margaret Mitchell Marsh

Nellie Melba

NAME	DOB/DOD	SIG	DS/LS	ALS	SP	COMMENTS
Mills, John	1908-	15	25	35	30	"Ryan's Daughter"
Mills, Juliet	1941-	5	10	15	10	"Nanny and the Professor"
Mills, Stephanie	1957-	5	10	15	15	"The Wiz"
Milne, Alan Alexander	1882-1956	225	500	900	400	British author, "Winnie-the-Pooh"
Milosz, Czeslaw	1911-	30	75		50	Poet, NP
Mimiuex, Yvette	1939-	5	10	10	15	"The Black Hole"
Minnelli, Liza	1946-	20	35	45	35	"Cabaret," typically signs only "Liza"
Minnelli, Vincente	1910-1986	25	50		65	Film director
Mingus, Charles	1922-1979	200				Composer, bass player
Minter, Mary Miles	1902-1984	100	150	175	200	Leading silent film star, controversial
Miou-Miou	1950-	5	10	10	10	"Going Places"
Miranda, Carmen	1909-1955	120	200	300	400	"The Brazilian Bombshell," died at age 46
Mistral, Frederic	1830-1914	35	70	125	60	Poet, NP
Mistral, Gabriela	1889-1957	30	50	75	35	Poet, "Sonnets of Death"
Mitchell, Arthur	1934-	15			30	Dancer, choreographer
Mitchell, Cameron	1918-	10	25	30	30	"Death of a Salesman," "The High Chapparal"
Mitchell, Grant	1874-1957	45	80	75	80	TGOW, "Tobacco Road," "Laura"
Mitchell, Joni		25			50	(1997), a RS; "Big Yellow Taxi"; SA/CD-75
Mitchell, Margaret	**1900-1949**	**600**	**3000**	**3250**		**U.S., "Gone With the Wind"- $7500 (FE, SB)**
Mitchell, Thomas	1892-1962	250	500	500	525	"Stagecoach," "The Hurricane," GWTW, IAWL
Mitchum, James	1941-	5	10	10	10	"Thunder Road"
Mitchum, Robert	1917-1997	25	50	75	55	"The Story of G.I. Joe," FA
Mitford, Jessica	1917-	15	30		30	Writer
Mitropoulos, Dimitri	1896-1960	30	65		100	Conductor
Mix, Tom	1880-1940	125	200	325	400	Cowboy star, "Sky High," "Desert Love"
Modine, Matthew	1959-	5	10	20	20	"Vision Quest"
Moffat, Donald	1930-	5	10	10	15	"Clear and Present Danger"
Moll, Richard	1942-	10	15	20	20	"Night Court"
Molnar, Ferenc	1878-1952	85	150	300		Hungarian novelist, "The Swan"

NAME	DOB/DOD	SIG	DS/LS	ALS	SP	COMMENTS
Monk, Thelonius	1920-1982	100	200		200	Piano player, composer, bop developer
Monkees, The		150			200	M. Nesmith (KS)- $35-$55; "I'm a Believer," "Valerie," "D. W. Washburn"; SA/CD-225
Monroe, Bill		40	80		100	Country Music Hall of Fame, RS
Monroe, Marilyn ☆	**1926-1962**	**1850**	**3000**	**6250**	**5575**	**FA, many SS- $7400, TBC-$3000, DS "NJD"-signed Norma…**
Montalban, Ricardo	1920-	10	20	25	20	"Sayonara," "Fantasy Island"- TV
Montale, Eugenio	1896-1981	15	40	75	25	Italian poet
Montez, Maria	1920-1951	55	85		125	"Arabian Nights," "Cobra Woman"
Montgomery, George	1916-	5	10	15	15	"Riders of the Purple Sage"
Montgomery, Robert	1904-1981	20	30	30	30	"Night Must Fall," sig. often illegible
Montgomery, Wes	1925-1968	40	60		50	Guitarist
Montana, Patsy		15			40	Country Music Hall of Fame
Moody Blues		100			175	Scarce with D. Laine (vintage); "Nights in White Satin," "Question"; SA/CD-200
Moore, Clayton	1908-	5	20	40	45	"Lone Ranger," RS
Moore, Clement C.	1779-1863	200	450	1250		U.S. poet, "A Visit From Saint Nicholas," RSPV
Moore, Colleen	1900-1988	12	25	30	35	Silent star,"The Scarlet Letter," "Sally," "Irene"
Moore, Demi (Demetria Guynes)	1962-	55			145	"Ghost," elusive, DS & ALS- varies sig.
Moore, Dickie	1925-	10	15	20	20	Child actor, "Oliver Twist," "Miss Annie Rooney"
Moore, Dudley	1935-	10	20	20	25	"Arthur," FA
Moore, Grace	1901-1947	75	140	230	150	"One Night of Love," opera singer
Moore, Marianne	1887-1972	75	175	300	100	U.S. poet, "The Absentee"- $250 (FE, SB)
Moore, Mary Tyler	1937-	15	30	45	25	"The Mary Tyler Moore Show," FA
Moore, Roger	1928-	25	80	150	75	"Live and Let Die"
Moore, Sara Jane		45	75	250	100	Shot at Gerald Ford
Moore, Terry	1929-	10	15	15	30	Child model, "Mighty Joe Young," "Peyton Pl."
Moore, Thomas	1779-1852	50	100			Poet
Moore, Victor	1876-1962	30	50	60	60	"Make Way for Tomorrow," "Swing Time"

NAME	DOB/DOD	SIG	DS/LS	ALS	SP	COMMENTS
Moran, Erin	1961-	5	10	10	10	"Happy Days"
Moran, Jackie	1923-1990	25	50	50	50	"Adventures of Tom Sawyer," GWTW
Moranis, Rick	1954-	5	10	15	20	"Honey, I Shrunk the Kids"
Moreau, Jeanne	1928-	5	10	10	25	"Jules et Jim"
Moreno, Rita	1931-	5	10	15	20	"West Side Story"
Morgan, Dennis	1910-	10	15	15	15	"Kitty Foyle," "In This Our Life"
Morgan, Frank	1890-1949	400	685	1120	625	TWOO, hardest of all characters to obtain, ESPV, scarce MALS
Morgan, Harry	1915-	10	20	25	25	"Dragnet"- TV, "M*A*S*H"- TV
Morgan, Helen	1900-1941	60	150	265	200	"Show Boat"- stage, "Applause"
Morgan, Michele	1920-	15	25	25	30	French actress, "Joan of Paris"
Morgan, Ralph	1882-1956	40	55	60	70	"The Power and the Glory"
Moriarity, Cathy	1960-	5	10	15	20	"Raging Bull"
Moriarity, Michael	1941-	10	20	25	30	"Law and Order"
Morissette, Alanis	1974-	50			75	An elusive signer! "Ironic"; SA/CD-100
Morita, Noriyuki "Pat"	1932-	5	10	10	15	"The Karate Kid"
Morley, Christopher	1890-1957	50	100	150		Novelist
Morley, Robert	1908-1992	40	65	70	75	"Marie Antoinette," "The African Queen"
Morris, Chester	1901-1970	40	50	60	70	"Alibi," known for "Boston Blackie"
Morris, Wright	1910-	20	35	50	25	U.S. writer, "My Uncle Dudley"
Morrison, Toni	1931-	25	35	100	30	U.S. writer, "Beloved," can be elusive signer!
Morrison, Van	1945-	45			75	(1993); "Brown-Eyed Girl," "Domino," "Gloria"; SA/CD-125
Morrow, Rob	1962-	20	30	40	40	"Northern Exposure"
Morrow, Vic	1932-1982	120	160		200	"Combat"
Morse, David	1953-	5	10	15	10	"St. Elsewhere"
Mortimer, John	1923-	15			30	Playwright
Morton, "Jelly Roll"	1885-1941	500	750			Composer, singer, piano player, scarce
Morton, Joe	1947-	5	10	12	15	"Terminator 2: Judgement Day"
Moss, Kate	1974-	10	20	15	25	Supermodel
Most, Donny	1953-	5	10	10	10	"Happy Days"

NAME	DOB/DOD	SIG	DS/LS	ALS	SP	COMMENTS
Mostel, Josh	1946-	5	10	10	10	"City Slickers"
Mostel, Zero	1915-1977	75	180	265	200	"Fiddler on the Roof," "The Producers"
Mott, Lucretia	1793-1880	75	150		260	Feminist
Movita (Movita Castenada)	1915-	10	20	20	20	"Mutiny on the Bounty," m. Marlon Brando
Mowbray, Alan	1896-1969	50	65	70	85	Character actor, "Becky Sharp," "The King and I"
Mozart, Wolfgang Amadeus	**1756-1791**		**15500**	**45000**		**Austrian composer, SALS-2X, ESPV**
Mtshali, Oswald M.	1940-	15	40		30	Poet
Muir, Edwin	1887-1959	45	100			Poet, critic
Muldaur, Diana	1938-	10	15	15	20	"Star Trek: Voyager"
Mulgrew, Kate	1955-	5	10	10	15	"Ryan's Hope"
Mulhall, Jack	1887-1979	30	50	55	60	Silent star, "The Three Musketeers"
Mulhern, Matt	1960-	5	10	10	10	"Major Dad"
Mull, Martin	1943-	5	10	12	15	"Mary Hartman, Mary Hartman"
Mulligan, Gerry	1927-1996	20	40	50	35	Baritone sax player, songwriter
Mulligan, Richard	1932-	5	10	10	10	"Empty Nest"
Mumy, Billy	1954-	5	10	12	15	"Lost in Space"
Muni, Paul	1895-1967	70	100	135	185	"The Story of Louis Pasteur"
Munro, Alice	1931-	15	25	40	20	Canadian writer, "Lives of Girls..."
Munsel, Patrice	1925-	20	30	50	45	"Melba," operatic soprano
Munson, Ona	1906-1955	155	215	265	300	GWTW, "The Shanghai Gesture," ESPV
Murdoch, Iris	1919-	20	35	50	25	Irish writer, "The Bell"
Murphy, Audie	1924-1971	140	280	515	300	"To Hell and Back," war hero, died at age 46
Murphy, Eddie	1961-	10	25	45	40	"Beverly Hills Cop," SNL
Murphy, George	1902-1992	20	30	30	30	"Show Business," "Step Lively"
Murphy, Michael	1938-	5	10	10	10	"Manhattan"
Murphy, Turk	1915-1987	25	40	50	65	Band leader, trombone player, RS
Murray, Bill	1950-	15	30	50	40	"Ghostbusters," SNL
Murray, Ken	1903-1988	10	10	15	20	"The Man Who Shot Liberty Valence," prod.

NAME	DOB/DOD	SIG	DS/LS	ALS	SP	COMMENTS
Murray, Mae	1885-1965	40	50	60	70	silent star, "The Merry Widow"
Murrow, Edward R.		150	300		275	T.V. journalist
Musgrave, Thea	1928-	15			25	Composer
Music, Lorenzo	1937-	5	10	10	10	"Rhoda"
Myers, Mike	1963-	15	30	35	40	"Wayne's World," SNL, "Austin Powers"
Nabokov, Vladimir	1899-1977	300	850		850	Russian-U.S. novelist, ESPV
Nabors, Jim	1932-	5	10	15	20	"Gomer Pyle"
Nagel, Anne	1912-1966	30	55	50	60	"The Green Hornet" series
Nagel, Conrad	1897-1970	25	40	50	60	"The Impossible Mrs. Bellows"
Naipaul, V.S.	1932-	25	40	65	30	Trinidadian novelist, "The Mystic Masseur"
Naish, J. Carrol	1897-1973	30	55	60	75	"Sahara," "A Medal for Benny"
Naldi, Nita	1899-1961	32	55	50	60	"Blood and Sand," reclusive
Narayan, R.K.	1906-	10	25		20	Writer
Nash, Clarence	1904-1985	120	170	150	175	Voice of Donald Duck, "The Wise Little Hen"
Nash, Ogden	1902-1971	50	100	150	60	U.S. poet
Nast, Condé	1873-1942	30	50		60	Publisher
Nation, Carry	1846-1911	100	200			Temperance agitator
Natwick, Mildred	1908-	15	25	30	25	"Barefoot in the Park"
Naughton, David	1951-	5	10	15	20	"An American Werewolf in London"
Naughton, James	1945-	5	10	10	10	"The Good Mother"
Nazimova, Alla	1879-1945	50	80	90	110	"In Our Time," AQS- $80
Neagle, Anna	1904-1986	15	25	30	35	"Victoria the Great," "Nell Gwyn"
Neal, Patricia	1926-	20	40	50	45	"Breakfast at Tiffany's"
Neeson, Liam	1952-	25	50	60	50	"Schindler's List," FA
Neff, Hildegard	1925-	25	35	40	45	"The Snows of Kilimanjaro"
Negri, Pola	1894-1987	35	65	75	100	Silent film star
Negus, Arthur	1903-1985	20	40		35	Broadcaster
Neill, Sam	1947-	20	35	40	40	"Jurassic Park"
Nelligan, Kate	1951-	10	15	20	20	"The Prince of Tides"
Nelson, Craig	1946-	10	15	20	25	"Coach"

NAME	DOB/DOD	SIG	DS/LS	ALS	SP	COMMENTS
Nelson, David	1936-	10	20	25	25	"The Adventures of Ozzie and Harriet"
Nelson, Gene	1920-1996	20	50	60	75	"Oklahoma!," director
Nelson, Harriet Hilliard	1914-	25	40	45	50	TV actress w/husband, both sigs. on a. leaf- $95
Nelson, Judd	1959-	5	10	10	10	"The Breakfast Club"
Nelson, Ozzie	1906-1975	40	65	70	80	"Here Come the Nelsons"
Nelson, Ricky	1940-1985	130	275		225	(1987), was a RS; "Hello, Mary Lou," "Travelin' Man"; SA/CD-300
Nelson, Willie		15	30		25	Country Music
Nemerov, Howard	1920-1991	20	40	45	35	Poet
Neumeier, John	1942-	15	25		25	Ballet dancer
Newhart, Bob	1929-	5	15	15	20	"The Bob Newhart Show"
Newley, Anthony	1931-	5	10	15	20	"Sweet November"
Newman, Nanette	1939-	20			35	British actress
Newman, Paul	1925-	100	200	365	250	"The Sting," very reluctant signer, FA
Newton, Robert	1905-1956	50	75	145	100	Treasure Island," "Oliver Twist"
Nguyen, Dustin	1962-	5	10	10	10	"21 Jump Street"
Nichols, Mike	1931-	25				Director, "The Graduate"
Nichols, Red	1905-1965	40	70		75	Cornet player
Nicholson, Jack	1937-	25	125		50	"One Flew Over the Cuckoo's Nest"
Nielsen, Brigitte	1963-	5	10	15	25	"Red Sonja"
Nielsen, Carl August	1865-1931	225	500	650		Danish composer
Nielsen, Leslie	1926-	10	20	25	25	"The Naked Gun," FA
Nietzsche, Friedrich	**1844-1900**	**600**				**German philosopher, poet, scarce, ESPV**
Niijnska, Bronislava	1891-1972	25	50		60	Ballet dancer
Nijinsky, Vaslav F.	1890-1950	625				Russian dancer, choreographer, scarce, ESPV
Nilsson, Anna Q.	1888-1974	20	30	40	40	Silent screen star, "Sunset Boulevard"
Nimoy, Leonard	1931-	30	70	75	65	"Star Trek"
Nin, Anais	1903-1977	50	100		100	Writer, RS
Nine Inch Nails (NIN)	1965-	35			50	(Trent Reznor); "Closer"; SA/CD-65

Herman Melville

Marilyn Monroe

Henry L. Mencken

Frank Morgan

Felix Mendelssohn

Christopher Morley

Margaret Mitchell Marsh

Jim Morrison

Margaret Mitchell Marsh

Tom Mix

Vladimir Nabokov

NAME	DOB/DOD	SIG	DS/LS	ALS	SP	COMMENTS
Nirvana		400			500	K. Cobain (KS); "Smells Like Teen Spirit," "Floyd the Barber"; SA/CD-600, FA
Niven, David	1909-1993	40	85	150	80	"Wuthering Heights"
Noiret, Philippe	1931-	5	10	10	10	"Cinema Paradiso"
Nolan, Lloyd	1902-1985	25	65	115	50	"Peyton Place"
Nolte, Nick	1940-	10	25	40	40	"48 Hrs."
Noonan, Tommy	1922-1968	50	75	100	85	"Gentlemen Prefer Blondes"
Nordica, Lillian	1857-1914	75	150	230	275	Opera: Soprano
Normand, Mabel	1894-1930	190	325	600	435	"Tillie's Punctured Romance," scarce
Norris, Chuck	1940-	10	25	50	40	"Good Guys Wear Black," RS
Norris, Frank	1870-1902	100	2520	420		American novelist
Norton, Edward	1969-	15	25	30	35	"Primal Fear"
Norworth, Jack	1879-1959	150	275	250	250	U.S. lyricist, "Shine On Harvest Moon"
Nouri, Michael	1945-	10	15	15	20	"Flashdance"
Novak, Kim	1933-	15	40	50	75	"Picnic," "Vertigo"
Novarro, Ramon	1899-1968	30	60	75	100	"Mata Hari"
Noyes, Alfred	1880-1958	20	45	60	35	Poet
Nugent, Elliott	1899-1980	15	25	25	25	Stage actor, playwright, "The Male Animal"
Nureyev, Rudolf	1938-1993	75	130	165	150	Ballet dancer, elusive signer
Nuyen, France	1939-	10	20	20	22	"South Pacific"
Oakie, Jack	1903-1978	20	60	115	45	"The Great Dictator"
Oasis		50			120	Liam & Noel Gallagher (KS); "Wonderwall"; SA/CD-135
Oates, Joyce Carol	1938-	10	30	40	25	U.S. writer, "The Poisoned Kiss"
Oberon, Merle	1911-1979	50	100	175	85	"The Scarlet Pimpernel," " Wuthering Heights"
O'Brian, Hugh	1925-	15	25	25	30	"Wyatt Earp"- TV, RS
O'Brien, Conan	1963-	5	10	15	10	"NBC's Late Night with Conan O'Brien," RS
O'Brien, Edmond	1915-1985	25	45	60	50	"The Hunchback of Notre Dame"
O'Brien, George	1900-1985	25	40	50	55	Boxer, "Fort Apache," "Sunrise"
O'Brien, Margaret	1937-	20	40	35	40	"Little Women," "The Secret Garden," Sig. (child)- 2X

NAME	DOB/DOD	SIG	DS/LS	ALS	SP	COMMENTS
O'Brien, Pat	1899-1983	40	125	200	100	"Angels With Dirty Faces"
O'Brien, Virginia	1922-	10	20	20	15	"Miss Red Hot Frozen Face," scat-singer
O'Casey, Sean	1884-1964	125	200	400	250	Irish dramatist, "The Plough and the Stars"
O'Connor, Carroll	1924-	10	20	25	25	"All in the Family"- TV
O'Connor, Donald	1925-	20	35	40	25	"Singin' In the Rain," SP (vintage)-2X
O'Connor, Flannery	1925-1964	350	1000			U.S. novelist, 'Wise Blood," ESPV
O'Connor, Una	1880-1959	45	100	160	90	"Cavalcade," "The Informer"
Odets, Clifford	1903-1963	60	115	200	125	"None But the Lonely Heart," U.S. playwright
O'Donnell, Cathy	1925-1970	40	65		75	"The Best Years of Our Lives," died at age 45
O'Donnell, Chris	1970-	20	50	70	55	"Scent of a Woman," SP as "Robin"-$70
O'Donnell, Rosie	1962-	10	20	45	25	"The Rosie O'Donnell Show," FA
Offenbach, Jacques	1819-1880	150	300	550		French composer, ESPV
O'Hara, Catherine	1954-	5	10	10	12	"Home Alone"
O'Hara, John	1905-1970	150	400	700		U.S. novelist, "Pal Joey," was elusive signer
O'Hara, Maureen	1920-	15	30	45	30	"How Green Was My Valley"
Oistrakh, David	1908-1974	30			75	Violinist, ESPV
O'Keefe, Dennis	1908-1968	10	15	20	20	"B" picture star
Oland, Warner	1880-1938	175	265		300	"The Jazz Singer," "Dishonored," C.Chan films, ESPV
Olcott, Chauncey	1858-1932	50	75	125	100	U.S., "Mother Machree"
Oldman, Gary	1958-	15	30	35	45	"Bram Stoker's Dracula" SP- $55
Olin, Ken	1954-	5	10	10	10	"thirtysomething"
Olin, Lena	1955-	15	25	25	30	"Havana"
Oliver, Edna May	1883-1947	50	100	165	110	"Little Women," "Drums Along the Mohawk"
Oliver, King	1885-1938	400	800			Cornet player, band leader, scarce
Oliver, Sy	1910-1988	35	70		80	Composer, conductor, arranger
Oliver, Vic	1898-1964	25	50	65	50	"Room For Two," comedian, conductor
Olivier, Laurence	1907-1989	45	150	175	200	Stage legend, "Hamlet"

NAME	DOB/DOD	SIG	DS/LS	ALS	SP	COMMENTS
Olmos, Edward James	1947-	5	10	15	15	"Miami Vice," slow, but RS!
Olsen, Ashley	1986-	5	15		20	"Full House," FA, both on SP- $35
Olsen, Mary-Kate	1986-	5	15		20	"Full House," FA, both on SP- $35
Olsen, Moroni	1889-1954	40	80	145	85	"Annie Oakley," "Mildred Pierce"
Olsen, Ole	1892-1963	20	40	40	50	"Hellzapoppin'," vaudeville act
Olson, Nancy	1928-	10	15	20	25	"Sunset Boulevard," "Airport"
Ondaatje, Michael	1943-	15	30		24	Author, "The English Patient"
O'Neal, Ryan (Patrick Ryan O'Neal)	1941-	10	20	30	30	"Love Story"
O'Neal, Tatum	1963-	10	15	25	25	"Paper Moon," elusive signer
O'Neil, Barbara	1908-1980	175	340	620	360	"All This and Heaven Too," "GWTW," ESPV
O'Neill, Ed	1946-	5	10	15	15	"Married ...with Children"
O'Neill, Eugene	1888-1953	265	400	500		U.S. playwright, "Long Day's Journey ..."
O'Neill, Jennifer	1949-	5	10	20	15	"Summer of '42"
Ontkean, Michael	1946-	5	10	10	15	"Twin Peaks"
Opatoshu, David	1918-	10	15	25	20	"The Naked City," "Exodus"
Oppenheimer, Alan	1930-	5	10	10	10	"Murphy Brown"
Orbach, Jerry	1935-	10	20	30	30	"Law and Order," voice "Beauty and the Beast"
Orbison, Roy	1936-1988	125			250	(1987), responsive in-person! "Oh, Pretty Woman," "Crying," "Only the..."; SA/CD-350
Orezy, Emma	1865-1947	30	60	100	115	Author, "The Scarlet Pimpernel"
Orff, Carl	1895-1982	25	50		125	Composer
Ormandy, Eugene	1899-1985	25	50	100	75	Conductor, RS
Ormond, Julia	1965-	20	50	75	65	"Legends of the Fall"
Ornstein, Leo	1895-	20	50		45	Composer
Orsted, Niels-Henning	1946-	15			30	Jazz double-bassist
Ory, Kid	1886-1973	125	250		230	Trombone player, "Muskrat Ramble"
Osborne, John	1929-1994	15	30	50	25	British dramatist, "The Entertainer"
Osbourne, Lloyd	1868-1947	70			125	Writer
Osbourne, Ozzy	1948-	25			45	Former member of Black Sabbath; "Crazy Train"; SA/CD-50

NAME	DOB/DOD	SIG	DS/LS	ALS	SP	COMMENTS
O'Shea, Milo	1925-	5	10	10	10	"The Verdict," RS
O'Sullivan, Maureen	1911-1998	20	35	50	40	"Tarzan" movies
Oswald, Lee Harvey	**1939-1963**	**2000**	**8500**	**11000**		**J.F.K. assassin, ESPV, FA, scarce**
Otis, Carre		5	10	15	20	Model, actor
O'Toole, Annette	1953-	5	20	15	20	"Superman III"
O'Toole, Peter	1932-	30	75	125	65	"Lawrence of Arabia"
Ouspenskaya, Maria	1876-1949	130	300		375	Russian actress, "Love Affair," scarce, ESPV
Overman, Lynne	1887-1943	25	50	65	50	"Little Miss Marker," "Union Pacific"
Ovitz, Michael	1946-	10	20	45	25	Studio executive
Owen, Reginald	1887-1972	35	50	60	65	Sherlock Holmes," "A Christmas Carol"
Owens, Buck		10	20		25	Country Music Hall of Fame
Oxenberg, Catherine	1961-	15	25	25	30	"Dynasty"
Oz, Frank	1944-	5	20	25	20	"The Muppet Show," FA
Ozawa, Seiji	1935-	15	30		30	Conductor, RS
Ozick, Cynthia	1928-	15	25	45	25	U.S. writer, "Fame and Folly"
Pacino, Al	1940-	25	100		65	"The Godfather," DS-$475, FA
Pacula, Joanna	1957-	10	15	20	20	"Gorky Park"
Paderewski, Ignacy	1860-1941	200	450	600	500	Polish composer, ESPV-DS
Paganini, Niccolo	1782-1840	215	750	895		Italian composer, SALS-2-3X, ESPV
Page, Geraldine	1924-1987	25	55	80	65	"The Trip to Bountiful," "Hondo"
Paget, Debra	1933-	25	40	35	55	"Broken Arrow," "The Terror"
Paige, Elaine	1951-	20	45		45	Actress, "Evita"
Paige, Janis	1922-	10	15	15	15	"The Pajama Game"-stage, "Trapper John, M.D."
Palance, Jack	1920-	20	45	60	50	"City Slickers"
Paley, Grace	1922-	10	25	40	20	U.S. writer, "Later the Same Day," RS
Palin, Michael	1943-	10	20	25	25	"Monty Python's Flying Circus," writer
Pallette, Eugene	1889-1954	70	110	160	115	"The Three Musketeers," "Mr. Smith..."
Palmer, Betsy	1926-	5	10	10	10	"I've Got a Secret," RS
Palmer, Lilli	1914-1986	20	45	50	60	"The Secret Agent"

NAME	DOB/DOD	SIG	DS/LS	ALS	SP	COMMENTS
Palmer, Nettie	1885-1964	25			40	Writer, critic
Palminteri, Chazz	1951-	10	20	20	20	"A Bronx Tale," playwright
Paltrow, Gwyneth	1973-	20	45	50	50	"Emma"
Pangborn, Franklin	1893-1958	60	75	80	80	"A Star is Born," "My Man Godfrey"
Panov, Valeri	1938-	15	30		30	Ballet dancer
Papp, Joe	1921-1991	25	45		50	Stage director, RS
Paquin, Anna	1982-	50	60		80	"The Piano," very reluctant signer, ESPV
Pare, Michael	1959-	5	10	10	15	"Eddie and the Cruisers"
Parillaud, Anne	1961-	10	15	20	20	"La Femme Nikita"
Parish, Mitchell	1901-1993	25	40	75	50	U.S. lyricist, "Stardust"
Parker, Cecilia	1915-1993	25	40	40	45	"Andy Hardy" films
Parker, Charlie	1920-1955	375	1200		3250	Composer, alto sax player, improviser, ESPV
Parker, Dorothy	1893-1967	40	65	100	55	"A Star Is Born," screenwriter, author
Parker, Eleanor	1922-	5	10	15	15	"Caged," "Detective Story," "Interrupted ...," RS
Parker, Fess	1925-	10	25	30	30	"Daniel Boone," RS
Parker, Jameson	1947-	5	10	10	15	"Simon and Simon"
Parker, Jean	1912-	20	30	35	35	"Little Women," "Sequoia"
Parker, Mary-Louise	1964-	5	10	15	25	"Fried Green Tomatoes"
Parker, Sarah Jessica	1965-	10	25	30	35	"Honeymoon in Vegas"
Parks, Larry	1914-1975	35	65		75	"The Jolson Story"
Parliament Funkadelics		60			125	(1997); "One Nation Under a Groove"; SA/CD-150
Parsons, Estelle	1927-	5	10	15	15	"Roseanne," RS
Parsons, Louella	1893-1972	25	35	65	50	Gossip columnist, appeared in some films
Parton, Dolly	1946-	5	20	30	25	"9 to 5," RS
Pascal, Gabriel	1894-1954	50	70	100	85	Director, "Pgymalion," "Major Barbara"
Pass, Joe	1929-1994	20	35		45	Guitarist
Pasternak, Boris	1890-1960	400	800	1650		Russian, "Doctor Zhivago," SB-$1500
Patinkin, Mandy	1952-	25	40	45	45	"Yentl"
Patric, Jason	1966-	5	10	15	15	"Rush"

NAME	DOB/DOD	SIG	DS/LS	ALS	SP	COMMENTS
Patrick, Gail	1911-1980	12	20	20	25	"Stage Door," "Love Crazy"
Patrick, Lee	1911-1982	25	45	55	50	"The Maltese Falcon," "Mildred Pierce"
Patrick, Robert	1959-	10	15	20	20	"Terminator 2: Judgment Day," SP-$25
Patterson, Elizabeth	1874-1966	30	40	45	55	"Tobacco Road," "Little Women," "I Love Lucy"
Patterson, Lorna	1957-	5	10	10	10	"Private Benjamin"
Patterson, Melody	1947-	5	10	15	10	"F Troop," SP-$15
Patti, Adelina	1843-1919	125	250	350	445	Opera: Soprano
Patton, Will	1954-	5	10	10	10	"No Way Out"
Paul, Alice	1885-1977	40			75	Feminist, reformer
Paul, Les	1915-	15	35		40	Musician, RS
Pauley, Jane	1950-	5	10	15	15	"Dateline NBC," m. Garry Trudeau
Pavarotti, Luciano		25	125	165	75	Opera singer, RS
Pavlova, Anna	1881-1931	300	450		500	Ballerina, ESPV-SP
Paxton, Bill	1955-	20	50	50	55	"Twister"
Payne, John	1912-1989	25	40	50	65	"Miracle on 34th Street"
Pays, Amanda	1959-	5	10	15	15	"The Flash"
Paz, Octavio	1914-	30	50	65	40	Mexican writer
Pearce, Alice	1913-1966	25	40	40	45	"On The Town," "Bewitched"-TV
Pearl Jam		150			275	E. Vedder (KS); "Jeremy," "Go"; SA/CD-350
Pearl, Jack	1895-1982	12	20	20	25	"The Jack Pearl Show"-radio
Pearl, Minnie		15	45		40	Country Music Hall of Fame
Pears, Peter	1910-1986	25	50	60	60	Opera: Tenor
Peary, Harold	1908-1985	25	40	45	50	"The Great Gildersleeve"
Peck, Gregory	1916-	30	150	300	65	"To Kill A Mockingbird"
Peckinpah, Sam	1925-1984	40	80	120	80	Film director
Peerce, Jan	1904-1984	25	50	75	70	Opera: Tenor
Pena, Elizabeth	1961-	5	10	10	15	"La Bamba"
Pendercki, Krzystof	1933-	25	50	100	50	Polish composer
Pendleton, Austin	1940-	5	10	10	10	"What's Up Doc?," RS
Pendleton, Nat	1895-1967	40	50	55	50	"At the Circus," "Dr. Kildare" films

NAME	DOB/DOD	SIG	DS/LS	ALS	SP	COMMENTS
Penn, Sean	1960-	20	30	50	40	"Dead Man Walking," reluctant signer
Pennington, Michael	1943-	15	30		30	Actor
Penny, Joe	1956-	10	20	10	20	"Jake and the Fatman"
Peppard, George	1928-1994	25	40		50	"Breakfast at Tiffany's"
Pepper, Art	1925-1982	35	50		70	Alto sax player
Percy, Walker	1916-1990	45	100	200	75	Novelist
Perelman, S.J.	1904-1979	60	125	150		Screenwriter, "Monkey Business"
Perez, Rosie	1964-	10	25	30	35	"Do the Right Thing"
Perkins, Anthony	1932-1992	50	75	100	85	"Friendly Persuasion," "Psycho," SP-$210
Perkins, Carl	1932-	25			50	(1987), was a very RS; "Blue Suede Shoes," "Matchbox"; SA/CD-100
Perkins, Elizabeth	1961-	5	10	10	10	"Big"
Perkins, Maxwell	1884-1947	35				Editor, publisher, ESPV-DS & ALS
Perlman, Rhea	1948-	10	15	20	25	"Cheers," m. Danny DeVito
Perlman, Itzhak	1945-	20	45		40	Violinist, RS
Perlman, Ron	1950-	5	10	15	15	"Beauty and the Beast," SP-$25
Perreau, Gigi	1941-	5	10	15	10	Child actress, "Bonzo Goes to College"
Perrine, Valerie	1944-	5	10	15	20	"Lenny"
Perry, Antoinette	1888-1946	50	110			Actress, director
Perry, Luke (Perry Coy III)	1966-	20	40	50	50	"Beverly Hills 90210"
Perry, Matthew	1969-	25	50	55	60	"Friends," FA, reluctant signer
Pesci, Joe	1943-	10	25	35	35	"My Cousin Vinny," RS
Pescow, Donna	1954-	5	10	10	10	"Saturday Night Fever," SP-$20
Peter, Paul & Mary		25			50	"Leavin' on a Jet Plane," "Puff the Magic..."; SA/CD-60
Peters, Bernadette (Bernadette Lazzara)	1948-	5	10	25	30	"Pennies from Heaven"
Peters, Brock	1927-	5	10	15	15	"To Kill a Mockingbird"
Peters, Jean	1926-	65	100	100	100	"Captain from Castile," "A Man Called Peter"
Peters, Susan	1921-1952	100	130	150	125	"Random Harvest"
Petersen, William	1953-	5	10	10	10	"To Live and Let Die in L.A."

Eugene O'Neill

Cole Porter

Eugene O'Neill

Elvis Aaron Presley

Elvis Presley

Lee Harvey Oswald

Elvis Presley

Niccolo Paganini

Sergi Prokofieff

Boris Pasternak

James R. Randall

Alexander Pope

James R. Randall

NAME	DOB/DOD	SIG	DS/LS	ALS	SP	COMMENTS
Peterson, Oscar	1925-	20	40		50	Jazz pianist
Pettiford, Oscar	1922-1960	45	75		60	Bop bassist
Petty, Lori		5	10	10	10	"A League of Their Own"
Pfeiffer, Michelle	1957-	25	65	75	100	"The Fabulous Baker Boys"
Philbin, Regis	1933-	5	10	10	10	"Live With Regis and Kathie Lee," RS
Phillips, Lou Diamond	1962-	10	20	25	25	"La Bamba," "Courage Under Fire
Phillips, Mackenzie	1959-	10	20	25	30	"One Day at a Time"
Phillips, Michelle	1944-	15	30	35	40	"Knots Landing"
Phlower		30			45	"Jingle Your Bells," "Trying to Find the …"; SA/CD-50
Phoenix, River	1971-1993	210	445		360	"Stand By Me," tragic death, ESPV
Piaf, Edith	1915-1963	130	265		250	Singer
Piatigorsky, Gregor	1903-1976	100	200	300	300	Cellist, AMQS-$95
Piccaver, Alfred	1884-1958	75	150		200	Tenor
Pichel, Irving	1891-1954	55	80	75	100	"An American Tragedy," "Oliver Twist"
Pickens, Slim	1919-1983	85	165	175	195	"Dr. Strangelove," "Blazing Saddles"
Pickett, Wilson	1941-	20			45	(1991); "Land of 1,000 Dances," "In the Midnight…"; SA/CD-50
Pickford, Mary	1893-1979	65	150	280	160	Silent legend, "Coquette"
Picon, Molly	1898-1992	20	30	40	60	"Fiddler On The Roof"
Pidgeon, Walter	1897-1984	25	50	75	70	"Mrs Miniver," "Madame Curie"
Pierce, David Hyde	1959-	10	20	25	35	"Frasier"
Piercy, Marge	1936-	10	30	50	20	U.S. writer, "Available Light"
Pilger, John	1939-	15	35		30	Journalist
Pinchot, Bronson	1959-	5	10	10	10	"Perfect Strangers"
Pink Floyd		150			300	(1996), original lineup- $600- $700; "Money," "Us & Them," "Sorrow"; SA/CD-325
Pinkett, Jada	1971-	10	20	25	25	"The Nutty Professor"
Pinsky, Robert	1940-	10	20	30	20	U.S. writer, "The Want Bone"
Pinter, Harold	1930-	25			50	Playwright
Pinza, Ezio	1892-1957	75	150		185	Opera: Bass, ESPV-SP
Pirandello, Luigi	1867-1936	75	200	365	300	Italian novelist, "Six Characters in Search…"

NAME	DOB/DOD	SIG	DS/LS	ALS	SP	COMMENTS
Piscopo, Joe	1951-	10	25	25	30	SNL
Pitt, Brad	1964-	40	225	450	85	"Legends of the Fall," reluctant signer
Pitts, ZaSu	1898-1963	40	60	70	85	"Oh, Susannah"-TV
Place, Mary Kay	1947-	5	10	15	15	"The Big Chill"
Plater, Alan	1935-	15	30		30	Playwright
Platters, The		100			200	(1990), D. Lynch & T. Williams (KS); "The Great Pretender"; SA/CD-275
Pleshette, John	1942-	5	10	10	15	"Knots Landing"
Pleshette, Suzanne	1937-	5	10	15	15	"The Bob Newhart Show"
Plisetskaya, Maya	1925-	20	45		45	Ballerina
Plowwright, Joan	1929-	10	15	20	20	"Enchanted April"
Plumb, Eve	1958-	5	10	10	15	"The Brady Bunch"
Plummer, Amanda	1957-	10	15	20	20	"The Fisher King"
Plummer, Christopher	1927-	10	15	20	25	"The Sound of Music"
Poco		25			40	"Crazy Love," "Heart of the Night"; SA/CD-60
Poe, Edgar Allan	**1809-1849**	**5500**	**5000**			**U.S. poet, "The Raven," FA, ESPV, scarce**
Pohl, Frederik	1919-	15	35		30	Sci-Fi writer
Poitier, Sidney	1927-	20	40	45	50	"Guess Who's Coming to Dinner?," FA
Polanski, Roman	1933-	35	70	130	100	"Rosemary's Baby," director, writer
Poliakoff, Stephen	1952-	10	25		25	Playwright
Police, The		50			85	Sting (KS); "Every Breath You Take," "Roxanne," "King..."; SA/CD-115
Pollack, Sydney	1934-	15	30	35	30	"The Way We Were," director, producer
Pollan, Tracy	1960-	10	20	25	30	"Family Ties"
Pomus, Jerome "Doc"	1925-1991	20	40	50	40	U.S., "A Teenager in Love"
Ponchielli, Amilcare	1834-1886	225				Italian composer, "Clarina"
Pons, Lily	1898-1976	50	100	200	150	Opera: Soprano
Ponselle, Rosa	1897-1981	50	75	125		Opera: Soprano, ESPV-SP
Pop, Iggy	1947-	15			30	"Lust for Life"; SA/CD-40
Pope, Alexander	1688-1744	650	1600	2250		British poet, "An Essay on Man," scarce, ESPV

NAME	DOB/DOD	SIG	DS/LS	ALS	SP	COMMENTS
Porter, Cole	1892-1964	250	590		625	Gifted composer, "Anything Goes," ESPV-SP
Porter, Eric	1928-1995	15	35		35	Actor
Porter, Jane	1776-1850	125	250			English novelist, "The Scottish Chiefs"
Potter, Beatrix	1866-1943	275	550	800		English writer, illustrator
Porter, Katherine Anne	1890-1980	75	150	350	125	U.S. novelist, "Ship of Fools"
Post, Emily	1872-1960	50	100		100	Etiquette expert
Post, Markie	1950-	5	10	10	10	"Night Court," RS
Potok, Chaim	1929-	15	25	45	25	U.S. writer, "The Promise"
Potter, Carol	1948-	10	15	20	20	"Beverly Hills 90210"
Potter, Dennis	1935-1994	20			40	Playwright
Potts, Annie	1952-	10	15	20	25	"Designing Women"
Poulenc, Francis	1899-1963	150	300	600	400	French composer, ESPV
Pound, Ezra	1885-1972	200	890	1135		U.S. poet, "Cantos," ESPV
Poundstone, Paula	1960-	5	10	10	15	"Actor, comedian
Povich, Maury	1939-	5	10	10	15	"Maury Povich," m. Connie Chung
Powell, Anthony	1905-	20	40		40	Novelist
Powell, Bud	1924-1966	100	200		200	Piano player, modern jazz pioneer
Powell, Dick	1904-1963	30	45	60	75	"42nd Street," "Murder My Sweet"
Powell, Eleanor	1910-1982	15	20	40	50	"Born to Dance," tap dancer
Powell, William	1892-1984	65	75	100	120	"My Man Godfrey," "The Thin Man"
Power, Tyrone	1913-1958	120	200	400	265	"Nightmare Alley," "The Long Gray Line," ESPV
Powers, Mala	1931-	5	10	10	10	Child star, "Rose of Cimarron," RS
Powers, Stephanie	1942-	10	15	20	25	"Hart to Hart," FA
Powter, Susan	1957-	5	10	10	10	"Stop the Insanity!"
Powys, John Cowper	1872-1964	30	60		65	Writer
Preisser, June	1923-1984	20	25	30	35	Babes in Arms," "Strike Up the Band"
Preminger, Otto	1906-1986	60	100	125	110	"The Man With The Golden Arm," director
Prentiss, Paula	1939-	5	10	15	15	"What's New Pussycat?"
☆ **Presley, Elvis**	**1935-1977**	**575**	**1300**		**950**	**(1986), SP- $600-$3,500, FA; "Love Me Tender"; SA/CD-1200, ESPV**

NAME	DOB/DOD	SIG	DS/LS	ALS	SP	COMMENTS
Presley, Lisa Marie	1968-	5	10	20	25	Daughter of Elvis Presley
Presley, Priscilla	1945-	10	25	40	35	Married and divorced from Elvis Presley
Preston, Kelly	1962-	10	20	25	25	"52 Pick-Up," m. John Travolta
Preston, Robert	1918-1987	45	100	150	100	"The Music Man," SP- $125
Pretenders, The		50			150	Values for original lineup, C. Hynde (KS); "Back in the Chain Gang," "Middle of the ..."; SA/CD-200
Previn, André	1929-	20	40		50	Conductor, RS
Prey, Hermann	1929-	10	20		25	Baritone
Price, Leontyne	1927-	15	30		40	Soprano, RS
Price, Lloyd	1934-	10			35	"Stagger Lee," "Lawdy Miss Clawdy"; SA/CD-45
Price, Ray		10	20		20	Country Music Hall of Fame
Price, Reynolds	1933-	10	20	40	20	U.S. writer, "A Long and Happy Life"
Price, Vincent	1911-1994	50	365	260	115	Horror film star, "House of Wax," SBC-$120
Priestley, J.B.	1894-1984	30	60	125	100	Writer
Priestley, Jason	1969-	20	30	35	40	"Beverly Hills 90210"
Prince (Symbol)	1958-	100	225		175	Elusive signer! "Purple Rain," "7," "U Got the Look"; SA/CD-225
Prince, Hal	1928-	10	25		20	Stage director, producer
Principal, Victoria	1950-	10	15	25	35	"Dallas"
Pringle, Aileen	1895-1989	20	25	30	30	Silent era star, "Three Weeks"
Pritchett, Sir V.S.	1900-	20	45		40	Writer, critic
Procol Harum		40			60	"A Whiter Shade of Pale," "Conquistador"; SA/CD-75
☆ **Prokofieff, Sergi**	**1891-1953**	**575**	**1200**	**2175**	**1500**	**Russian Composer, AMQS-$2900, SALS-2-3X, ESPV**
Proulx, E. Annie	1935-	10	20	35	15	U.S. writer, "The Shipping News," RS
Proust, Marcel	1871-1922	550	750	2150		French novelist, "Rememberance...Past," ESPV
Pryce, Jonathan	1947-	5	10	10	10	"Miss Saigon"
Pryor, Nicholas	1935-	5	10	10	10	"Risky Business"
Pryor, Richard	1940-	10	25	60	30	"Stir Crazy," signature varies significantly

ENT
CELEB
P

NAME	DOB/DOD	SIG	DS/LS	ALS	SP	COMMENTS
Public Enemy		35			45	"Fight the Power," "Can't Truss It"; SA/CD-50
Puccini, Giacomo	1858-1924	500	1000	1675	1000	Italian composer, AMQS-$1950, ALS-$775, ESPV
Pullen, Don	1942-1995	20	40		40	Percussive piano player
Pullman, Bill	1954-	25	40	50	65	"While You Were Sleeping"
Purcell, Sarah	1948-	5	10	10	10	"Real People"
Purdom, Edmund	1924-	10	20	20	20	""The Student Prince," "The Prodigal"
Purdy, James	1923-	20	40	50	30	Writer, RS
Pushkin, Aleksander	1799-1837	850	2750	14650		Russian poet, "Evgeni Onegin," ESPV, scarce
Puttnam, David	1941-	10	25		20	Film maker
Puzo, Mario	1920-	15	60	115	35	U.S. writer, "The Godfather," RS
Pyle, Ernie	1900-1945	175	300		330	Journalist
Pynchon, Thomas	1937-	10	25	40	20	U.S. writer, "V"
Quaid, Dennis	1954-	20	30	40	45	"The Big Easy"
Quaid, Randy	1953-	10	20	25	25	"The Last Picture Show," b. Dennis Quaid
Qualen, John	1899-1987	20	25	30	35	Character actor, "The Long Voyage Home"
Quayle, Sir Anthony	1913-1989	25	50		50	Actor, director
Queen		400			600	F. Mercury (KS)- $225-$650; "Bohemian Rhapsody," "Killer Queen"; SA/CD-750
Queen, Ellery	1905-1982	45	125	250	150	"Frederick Dannay"
Quillan, Eddie	1907-1990	25	50	55	50	Character actor, "Mutiny on the Bounty"
Quinlan, Kathleen	1954-	5	10	15	15	"Clara's Heart"
Quinn, Aidan	1959-	5	10	10	10	"The Playboys"
Quinn, Anthony	1915-	20	40	65	50	"Viva Zapata," "Lust For Life"
Quirk, Randolph	1920-	20	45		40	Grammarian
Quivers, Robin	1953-	5	10	10	15	"The Howard Stern Show"- radio
R.E.M.		120			150	M. Stipe (KS)- an elusive signer; "Losing My Religion," "Stand,"; SA/CD-165
Ra, Sun	c.1915-1993	25	50		60	Bandleader, composer, pianist

NAME	DOB/DOD	SIG	DS/LS	ALS	SP	COMMENTS
Rabe, David	1940-	10	25	30	15	U.S. writer, "Streamers"
Rachmaninoff, Sergei	1873-1943	335	975	865	550	Russian composer, SALS-2-3X, ESPV
Racine, Jean	1639-1699	5000				French dramatist, "Britannicus," scarce
Radner, Gilda		100	165		175	SNL
Raffin, Deborah	1953-	5	10	10	15	"Once Is Not Enough"
Raft, George	1895-1980	50	135	150	150	"Scarface"
Rainer, Luise	1912-1993	25	35	45	50	"The Great Ziegfeld," "The Good Earth"
Rainer, Yvonne	1934-	15	30		30	Experimental dancer
Raines, Ella	1921-1988	10	15	20	20	"Corvette K-225," "Phantom Lady"
Rainey, Gertrude "Ma"	1886-1939	475			1275	Blues singer, scarce, ESPV
Rains, Claude	1889-1967	140	385	500	255	"Mr. Smith Goes to Washington,"
Ralph, Sheryl Lee	1956-	5	10	10	15	"The Distinguished Gentleman"
Ralston, Esther	1902-1994	12	20	45	40	"American Venus" of silent films
Ralston, Vera	1921-	10	15	25	25	Olympic skater, "Ice Capades," RS
Rambeau, Marjorie	1889-1970	30	35	50	50	"Primrose Path," "Torch Song"
Rambert, Dame Marie	1888-1982	30	55		60	Ballet dancer
Ramis, Herald	1944-	5	10	10	15	"Ghostbusters," SP- $20
Ramones, The		65			75	"I Wanna Be Sedated," "Blitzkrieg Bop"; SA/CD-85
Rampling, Charlotte	1946-	5	10	15	20	"Farewell, My Lovely"
Rand, Ayn	1905-1982	525	1100		700	Russian-U.S. novelist "Atlas Shrugged," ESPV
Rand, Sally	1903-1979	50	80	75	100	Fan dance queen
Randall, James R.	1839-1908	60	125	200		Poet, ESPV
Randall, Tony	1920-	5	10	20	25	"The Odd Couple," RS!
Ransome, Arthur	1884-1967	55	110			Writer
Raphael, Sally Jessy	1943-	5	10	10	10	"Sally Jesse Raphael," RS
Rasche, David	1944-	5	10	10	10	"Sledge Hammer"
Rashad, Phylicia	1948-	5	10	10	15	"The Cosby Show"
Rasputin, Grigory Y.	1872-1916	2250		9500		Russian mystic, scarce, ESPV
Rathbone, Basil	1892-1967	255	500	680	450	"Sherlock Holmes," SP- $500
Ratzenberger, John	1947-	5	10	20	20	"Cheers"

NAME	DOB/DOD	SIG	DS/LS	ALS	SP	COMMENTS
Ravel, Maurice	1875-1937	550	1500	2490	1600	French composer, "Bolero," ESPV
Rawlings, Marjorie	1896-1953	50	100	150		Author, "The Yearling"
Rawlinson, Herbert	1885-1953	25	30	55	75	Silent screen idol, "The Sea Wolf"
Ray, James Earl		50	175	350	200	Martin Luther King assassin
Raye, Martha	1916-	20	60	50	40	"Hellzapoppin'"
Raymond, Gene	1908-	10	15	20	25	"B" movie star, "Smilin' Through"
Rayner, Claire	1931-	15	30		25	British writer, broadcaster
Razaf, Andy	1895-1973	50	100	200	100	U.S. lyricist, "Honeysuckle Rose"
Reagan, Ronald, Jr.	1958-	5	10	10	10	Son of Ronald Reagan
Reason, Rex	1928-	10	15	20	20	"This Island Earth"
Red Hot Chilli Peppers		45			100	H. Slovak (scarce); "Brass in Pocket"; SA/CD-110
Redding, Otis	1941-1967	375			750	(1989), a scarce signature; "(Sittin' on) The Dock of the Bay"; SA/CD-800
Redford, Robert	1937-	60	200	400	135	"Butch Cassidy and the Sundance Kid," FA
Redgrave, Corin	1939-	5	10	10	10	"A Man for All Seasons"
Redgrave, Lynn	1943-	5	15	15	20	"House Calls"
Redgrave, Michael	1908-1985	25	50	50	60	"Mourning Becomes Electra"
Redgrave, Vanessa	1937-	15	30	50	60	"Playing for Time"
Redman, Don	1900-1964	20	30		60	Composer, arranger
Redpath, Jean	1937-	20	40		35	Folk singer
Reed, Donna	1921-1986	50	75	225	185	"The Donna Reed Show"- TV
Reed, Ishmael	1938-	10	20	35	15	U.S. writer, "Yellow Back Radio Broke-down"
Reed, Jimmy	1925-1976	25			50	(1991), (1925-1976); "Honest I Do," "Big Boss Man"; SA/CD-100
Reed, John	1887-1920	165		285		American journalist, poet
Reed, Lou	1942-	25			40	"Walk on the Wild Side"; SA/CD-55
Reed, Oliver	1938-	10	15	20	25	"The Three Musketeers"
Reed, Pamela	1953-	5	10	10	15	"The Right Stuff"
Reed, Sir Carol	1906-1976	35	75		150	Film director
Reems, Harry	1947-	20	40	50	50	"Deep Throat"
Reeve, Christopher	1952-	55	150	265	135	"Superman"

Basil Rathbone

Ginger Rogers

George Reeves

Will Rogers

James W. Riley

Will Rogers

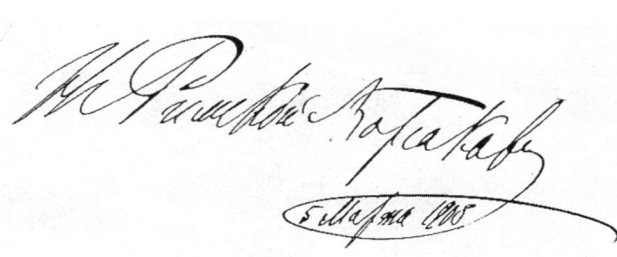

Nikolai Rimsky-Korsakov

Will Rogers

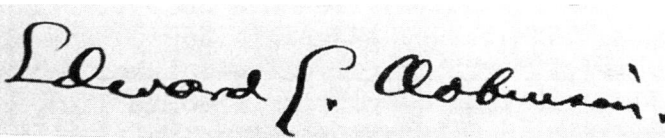

Edward G. Robinson

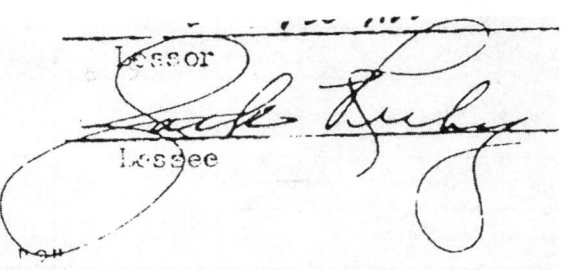

Jack Ruby

NAME	DOB/DOD	SIG	DS/LS	ALS	SP	COMMENTS
Reeves, George	1914-1959	900	2000	6275	1250	"Adven....Superman," DS GWTW-$6000, FA, SDS-2X, ESPV
Reeves, Keanu	1964-	20	50	50	65	"Speed"
Reeves, Steve	1926-	15	25	30	40	"Hercules," charges for signature!
Regalbuto, Joe		5	10	10	10	"Murphy Brown"
Regan, Phil	1906-	15	50	30	30	"Singing Policeman"
Reger, Max	1873-1916	100	200	325		Composer, ESPV-ALS
Reich, Steve	1936-	15	30		30	Composer
Reid, Tim	1944-	5	10	10	10	"WKRP in Cincinnati"
Reid, W. Wallace	1891-1923	225	540		625	"The King of Paramount," "Birth of a Nation"
Reiner, Carl	1922-	5	10	20	20	"The Dick Van Dyke Show," RS
Reiner, Fritz	1888-1963	60	125		175	Conductor
Reiner, Rob	1945-	5	10	25	25	"All in the Family," SP- $30, RS
Reinhardt, Django	1910-1953	65	125		125	Influential European guitarist
Reinhardt, Max	1873-1943	100	200		300	Theater director, ESPV
Reinhold, Judge	1957-	5	10	15	20	"Beverly Hills Cop"
Reinking, Ann	1949-	5	10	15	20	"Annie," dancer
Reiser, Paul	1957-	10	20	30	30	"Mad About You"
Reitman, Ivan	1946-	5	10	15	15	"Ghostbusters," director, producer
Reitz, Dana	1948-	10	25		20	Dancer, choreographer
Remarque, Erich Maria	1898-1970	60	135	400	75	German-U.S. novelist, "All Quiet on the..."
Remick, Lee	1935-1991	40	50	60	75	"Days of Wine and Roses," died at age 56
Renaldo, Duncan	1904-1980	30	100	125	200	"Cisco Kid"
Rennie, Michael	1909-1971	100	145	165	200	"The Day the Earth Stood Still"
Renoir, Jean	1894-1979	100	200		250	Film director, ESPV
Revere, Anne	1907-1990	20	35	35	40	"National Velvet"
Reynolds, Burt	1936-	15	30	50	35	"Smokey and the Bandit"
Reynolds, Debbie	1932-	10	30	50	25	"Singin' In The Rain," SP- $50, "The Unsink..," RS
Reynolds, Gene	1925-	5	10	10	15	"Dianna," "Heidi," RS!
Reynolds, Margorie	1921-	5	10	10	15	"Holiday Inn"
Rhett, Alice		250				GWTW, scarce in all forms, FA

NAME	DOB/DOD	SIG	DS/LS	ALS	SP	COMMENTS
Rhodes, Erik	1906-1990	25	35	35	50	Broadway and radio comedian, "Top Hat"
Rhys, Jean	1894-1979	35	75		60	Writer, ESPV
Ribeiro, Alfonso	1971-	5	10	10	10	"Fresh Prince of Bel Air," dancer
Ricci, Christina		15	30	40	50	"Casper"
Rice, Anne	1941-	10	20	40	15	U.S. writer, "Interview... Vampire," resp. sig.
Rice, Elmer	1892-1967	100	200		125	American playwright, "Street Scene"
Rice, Grantland	1880-1954	30	60		60	Sportswriter
Rice, Tim	1944-	20	40		45	Lyricist, writer, ESPV
Rich, Adam	1968-	5	10	10	10	"Eight Is Enough"
Rich, Adrienne	1929-	15	20	40	20	U.S. writer, "Diving into the Wreck"
Rich, Buddy	1917-1987	40	75		150	Band leader, drummer
Rich, Irene	1891-1988	10	15	20	20	"Craig's Wife," "The Certain Age"
Richard, Cliff	1940-	20	40		40	Pop singer
Richards, Michael	1948-	15	25	30	35	"Seinfeld"
Richardson, Miranda	1958-	20	40	40	50	"The Crying Game"
Richardson, Natasha	1963-	20	35	40	50	"The Handmaid's Tale"
Richardson, Ralph	1902-1993	35	45	50	60	British stage actor, "The Heiress"
Richardson, Susan	1952-	5	10	10	10	"Eight Is Enough"
Richardson, Tony	1928-1991	20	50		45	Director, "Tom Jones"
Richler, Mordecai	1931-	15	30		30	Writer
Richter, Sviatoslav	1915-	25			50	Pianist
Rickles, Don	1926-	5	10	15	15	"The Don Rickles Show"
Rickman, Alan	1946-	5	10	15	20	"Die Hard"
Riding, Laura	1901-1991	20	40		35	Writer, critic, RS
Riegert, Peter	1947-	5	10	10	10	"Crossing Delancey"
Rigby, Cathy	1952-	5	10	15	20	Actress, gymnast
Rigg, Diana	1938-	10	25	35	40	"The Avengers"
Righteous Brothers, The		45			100	"You've Lost That Lovin' Feelin'," "Ebb Tide"; SA/CD-125
Riley, James Whitcomb	1849-1916	125	200		325	Poet, ESPV, SP-$500, AQS-$600
Rilke, Rainer Maria	1875-1926	150	300	1000		German poet, "Life and Songs"
Rimsky-Korsakov, Nikolai	1844-1908	500	2200	3425	2125	Russian composer, AMQS-$5800

NAME	DOB/DOD	SIG	DS/LS	ALS	SP	COMMENTS
Ringwald, Molly	1968-	20	40	50	50	"Sixteen Candles"
Ritter, John	1948-	5	10	15	20	"Three's Company"
Ritter, Tex	1907-1974	100	200	325	265	Recording star, actor, and cowboy
Ritter, Thelma	1905-1969	50	100	200	140	"The Misfits," "Pillow Talk," "All About Eve"
Ritz Brothers: Al (1901-65); Jim (1903-85); Harry (1906-86		100	150		150	Popular comedians, "The Three Musketeers"
Rivera, Geraldo	1943-	10	20	25	25	"Geraldo," FA
Rivers, Joan	1937-	5	10	20	20	"Can We Talk...," RS
Rivers, Johnny	1942-	10			20	"Poor Side of Town," "Memphis"; SA/CD-25
Roach, Hal	1892-1992	125	400		175	Industry comedy pioneer
Roach, Hal, Jr.	1921-1972	15	25	45	25	Producer, "Of Mice and Men"
Roach, May	1924-	20			40	Jazz drummer
Robards, Jason Jr.	1922-	20	25	30	30	"All The President's Men," m. Lauren Becall
Robbins, Harold	1916-	20	60		40	Writer, "The Carpetbaggers"
Robbins, Jerome	1918-1998	60	100	150	100	"Fiddler on the Roof," choreographer
Robbins, Marty		20	50		50	Country Music Hall of Fame
Robbins, Tim	1958-	20	40	50	45	"The Player"
Roberts, Eric	1956-	10	20	25	25	"The Pope of Greenwich Village," b. Julia
Roberts, Julia	1967-	45	200	250	85	"Pretty Woman," FA, ESPV
Roberts, Tanya	1955-	5	10	15	25	"Charlie's Angels"
Roberts, Tony	1939-	5	10	15	15	"Play It Again, Sam"
Robertson, Cliff	1925-	15	25	45	35	"The Two Worlds of Charly Gordon"
Robeson, Paul	1898-1976	140	245	325	500	"'Ole Man River," singer
Robin, Leo	1900-1984	25	45	50	40	U.S. lyricist, "Diamonds Are a Girl's Best ..."
Robinson, Bill "Bojangles"	1878-1949	115	225	500	450	"The Little Colonel"
Robinson, Edward G.	1893-1973	65	200	165	225	"Little Caesar," "Scarlet Street," BC-$80
Robinson, Edwin Arlington	1869-1935	50	135	200		U.S. poet, "Merlin"
Robinson, Jay	1930-	5	10	10	15	"The Robe"
Robinson, Smokey	1940-	30	125	225	60	U.S., "Shop Around"

NAME	DOB/DOD	SIG	DS/LS	ALS	SP	COMMENTS
Robson, Flora	1902-1984	30	50	75	85	British stage actress, "Saratoga Trunk"
Robson, May	1858-1942	50	85	125	90	"Lady For A Day," "A Star Is Born"
Rock, Chris	1966-	15	25	30	35	"The Chris Rock Show," "Lethal Weapon 4"
Roddenberry, Gene	1921-1991	100	200		200	Writer, "Star Trek," ESPV
Rodgers, Richard	1902-1979	100	300	440	175	Gifted composer, "Oklahoma," RS
Rodney, Red	1928-1994	20	35		40	Trumpeter
Rodzinski, Artur	1892-1958	40	80		60	Conductor
Roethke, Theodore	1908-1963	45	150	250	50	U.S. poet, "The Far Field"
Rogers, Charles "Buddy"	1904-	20	25	50	50	"America's Boy Friend," "Wings," "My Best Girl"
Rogers, Fred "Mr."	1928	5	10	15	20	"It's a beautiful day in the neighborhood!," RS
Rogers, Ginger	1911-1995	45	190	300	200	Fred Astaire's dance partner, "Top Hat," VA
Rogers, Kenny	1938-	10	15	25	25	"The Gambler"
Rogers, Mimi	1956-	10	15	20	25	"Someone To Watch Over Me"
Rogers, Roy	1912-1998	50	175	250	100	"Under Western Skies," singer
Rogers, Wayne	1933-	5	10	10	10	"M*A*S*H," RS!
Rogers, Will	1879-1935	305	1000	1250	1150	"State Fair," comedian, died in plane crash
Rogers, Will Jr.	1912-	10	20	25	25	"The Story of Will Rogers"
Roland, Gilbert	1905-1994	25	30	40	45	"Camille," fourth "Cisco Kid"
Rolland, Romain	1866-1944	35	100	150	40	French novelist, biographer
Rolle, Esther	1922-	15	30	55	25	"Driving Miss Daisy," RS!
Rolling Stones, The		500			1250	(1989), values for original lineup, Jones (KS); "Satisfaction," "Jumping Jack Flash"; SA/CD-1300
Rollins, Sonny	1930-	20	50		50	Jazz saxophonist
Roman, Ruth	1923-	15	30	45	40	"Strangers on a Train"
Romberg, Sigmund	1887-1951	110	225	340	250	Composer, "The Desert Song," illegible sig.
Rome, Harold	1908-1993	20	50	100	40	U.S., "Pins and Needles"
Romero, Cesar	1907-1993	30	50	100	75	"Cisco Kid," "Batman"- TV
Ronettes, The		30		.	40	R. Spector (KS); "Be My Baby," "Baby I Love You"; SA/CD-50

NAME	DOB/DOD	SIG	DS/LS	ALS	SP	COMMENTS
Ronstadt, Linda		25			30	Responsive in-person; "You're No Good," "Blue Bayou"; SA/CD-45
Rooney, Mickey	1920-	20	80	100	30	"Boys Town," "Babes in Arms," RS
Rose, Vincent	1880-1944	50	75	150	115	U.S., "Blueberry Hill"
Roseanne	1953-	15	30	35	40	"Roseanne," FA
Rosolino, Frank	1926-1978	25	40		40	Trombone player
Ross, Katharine	1943-	15	25	30	35	"The Graduate," " Butch Cassidy and the Sundance Kid"
Ross, Marion	1928-	5	10	10	15	"Happy Days"
Ross, Shirley	1909-1975	25	40	45	50	"The Big Broadcast of 1938"
Rossellini, Isabella	1952-	10	20	30	40	"Blue Velvet," model, cosmetics
Rossini, Gioacchino	1792-1868	640	1500	2450		Italian composer, "William Tell," ESPV
Rossiter, Leonard	1926-1984	20	45		40	Actor
Rostand, Edmond	1868-1918	75	200	500	750	French playwright, "Cyrano de Bergerac"
Rostropovich, Mstislav L.	1927-	35	100		75	Cellist, composer, elusive
Roth, Henry	1906-	15				Novelist
Roth, Lillian	1910-1980	40	65	80	100	"The Love Parade," "Animal Crackers"
Roth, Philip	1933-	10	25	60	20	U.S. writer, "Portnoy's Complaint"-$315 (TS)
Roth, Tim	1961-	5	10	10	15	"Reservoir Dogs"
Roundtree, Richard	1942-	5	10	15	15	"Shaft"
Rourke, Mickey	1953-	15	30	30	40	"9 1/2 Weeks"
Rowan, Carl	1925-	10	25		20	Journalist, RS
Rowlands, Gena	1934-	5	10	10	15	"Gloria," RS!
Rowles, Jimmy	1918-1996	15	25		30	Composer, accompanist
Rozsa, Miklos	1907-1995	25	60		60	Composer
Rubinstein, Anton	1829-1894	100	200	300		Pianist, composer, ESPV
Rubinstein, Artur	1887-1982	75	160	300	200	Pianist, SB-$250, ALS-$165, ESPV
Ruby, Harry	1895-1974	25	100	200	50	U.S., "Who's Sorry Now?"
Ruby, Jack	1911-1967	300	525			Shot Lee Harvey Oswald, ESPV, DS-$1200
Rudner, Rita	1955-	5	15	10	15	Actor, comedian
Ruehl, Mercedes	1948-	20	35	40	40	"Lost in Yonkers"

NAME	DOB/DOD	SIG	DS/LS	ALS	SP	COMMENTS
Ruggles, Charles	1886-1970	50	65	75	80	"It Happened on Fifth Avenue," b. Wesley
Ruggles, Wesley	1889-1972	25	30	50	50	Director, "True Confession," "I'm No Angel"
Run-D.M.C.		30			45	"Walk This Way," "Sun City"; SA/CD-50
Runyon, Damon	1880-1946	150	375	450	200	U.S. short-story writer, "Guys and Dolls"
Rush, Barbara	1927-	5	10	10	15	"Bigger Than Life," "It Came From Outer Space"
Rush, Geoffrey	1951-	10	20	25	30	"Shine"
Rushdie, Salman	1947-	30	60	120	45	Indian writer, "The Satanic Verses"
Rushing, Jimmy	1903-1972	30	60		50	Blues singer
Ruskin, John	1819-1900	40	125	275		British critic, "Modern Painters"
Russell, Harold	1914-	20	30	25	25	"The Best Years of Our Lives," war hero
Russell, Jane	1921-	10	15	25	30	"Gentlemen Prefer Blondes," RS
Russell, Ken	1927-	20	40		40	Film director
Russell, Kurt	1951-	15	25	35	40	"Stargate"
Russell, Nipsey	1924-	5	10	10	10	"Car 54, Where Are You?"
Russell, Pee Wee	1906-1969	25	50		50	Clarinet player
Russell, Rosalind	1908-1976	55	70	100	125	"My Sister Eileen," "Auntie Mame"
Russell, Theresa	1957-	10	15	20	20	"Black Widow"
Russell, Willy	1947-	15	30		30	Playwright, "Blood Bros."
Russo, Rene	1954-	15	30	45	45	"Lethal Weapon 3," "Tin Cup"
Rutherford, Ann	1922-	15	25	30	45	"Andy Hardy" series, GWTW
Rutherford, Margaret	1892-1972	60	145	200	200	"The VIPs," "Murder She Said"
Ruttan, Susan	1948-	5	10	10	15	"L.A. Law"
Ryan, Meg	1961-	30	50	100	75	"When Harry Met Sally..."
Ryan, Peggy	1924-	10	15	30	30	Teenage singer, dancer, D. O'Connor's partner
Ryan, Robert	1909-1973	25	40	75	70	"Crossfire," "Setup," "The Dirty Dozen"
Rydell, Bobby	1942-	10	20	25	20	"Bye Bye Birdie," singer, teen idol
Ryder, Winona	1971-	25	50	100	85	"Beetlejuice"
Sabu	1924-1963	70	165		175	"Elephant Boy," "Jungle Book"

NAME	DOB/DOD	SIG	DS/LS	ALS	SP	COMMENTS
Sacher-Masoch, Leopold	1836-1895	165	300			German novelist
Sachs, Nelly	1891-1970	50				Poet, playwright, NP
Sade, Marquis de	1740-1814	265	700	2150		French writer
Sagal, Katey	1956-	5	10	10	15	"Married ...with Children"
Saget, Bob	1956-	5	10	10	10	"Full House"
Saint-Exupery, Antoine de	1900-1944	75	150	250	150	French writer, "The Little Prince"
Saint-John, Perse	1887-1975	25	50			Poet, diplomat, NP
Saint-Saens, Camille	1835-1921	150	400	575	400	French composer
Saint James, Susan	1946-	10	15	20	20	"Kate & Allie"
Saint, Eva Marie	1924-	15	20	25	30	"On The Waterfront," "North By Northwest"
Sajak, Pat	1946-	5	10	10	10	"Wheel of Fortune, RS!"
Sales, Soupy (Milton Supman)	1930-	5	10	10	10	"The Soupy Sales Show"
Salinger, J.D.	**1919-**	**1275**	**3250**	**4000**		**U.S. writer, reclusive, "The Catcher in the Rye," FA, ESPV**
Salt, Jennifer	1944-	5	10	10	15	"Midnight Cowboy"
Salt-N-Pepa		25			35	"Shoop," "Whatta Man," "Let's Talk About..."; SA/CD-50
Salten, Felix	1869-1945	70	135	200		Novelist, "Bambi"
Sam and Dave		100			150	(1992), D. Prater (1937-1988); "Soul Man," "I Thank You"; SA/CD-175
Samms, Emma	1960-	10	20	25	30	"Dynasty"
San Giacomo, Laura	1961-	10	15	20	30	"sex, lies and videotape"
Sand, George	1804-1876	125	250	600		French novelist, "Indiana"
Sandburg, Carl	**1878-1967**	**100**	**250**	**325**	**500**	**U.S. poet, "The People"**
Sanders, George	1906-1972	75	120	150	160	"The Saint in London," "All About Eve"
Sanders, Lawrence	1920-	15	20	50	20	U.S. writer, "The Anderson Tapes"
Sanders, Richard	1940-	5	10	10	10	"WKRP in Cincinnati"
Sandler, Adam	1966-	10	20	25	30	"Happy Gilmore" SNL, FA
Sands, Julian	1958-	5	10	10	10	"A Room with a View"
Sandy, Gary	1946-	5	10	10	10	"WKRP in Cincinnati"
Sanford, Isabel	1917-	5	10	10	12	"The Jeffersons"

J.D. Salinger

The Proprietor

J.D. Salinger

Rod Serling

Jean Sibelius

John Phillip Sousa

John Phillip Sousa

G. Bernard Shaw

John Steinbeck

G. Bernard Shaw

Rod Serling

Mary Shelley

Robert Louis Stevenson

NAME	DOB/DOD	SIG	DS/LS	ALS	SP	COMMENTS
Santana/Carlos Santana	1947-	35			40	Can be an elusive signer; "Black Magic Woman," "Oye Como Va"; SA/CD-50
Sarandon, Chris	1942-	5	10	10	12	"Dog Day Afternoon"
Sarandon, Susan	1946-	20	50	125	65	"Thelma and Louise"
Sardou, Victorien	1831-1908	30	60	100	120	Playwright
Saroyan, William	1908-1981	75	200	300	100	U.S. playwright, novelist, "The Human Comedy"
Sarton, May	1914-1995	15	25	50	25	Belg/U.S. poet, novelist, "Anger"
Sartre, Jean-Paul	1905-1980	125	250	360		French writer, philosopher, illegible signature, FA
Satie, Erik-Alfred-Leslie	1866-1925	275	645			French composer, ESPV
Savage, Fred	1976-	5	10	10	15	"The Wonder Years," FA
Savage, John	1949-	5	10	10	10	"The Deer Hunter"
Savant, Doug	1964-	5	10	10	15	"Melrose Place"
Sayers, Dorothy L.	1893-1957	225	400	600	130	British mystery writer
Scacchi, Greta	1960-	5	10	15	30	"Presumed Innocent"
Scalia, Jack	1951-	5	10	15	20	"Wolf"
Scarlatti, Alessandro	1660-1725		7250	15000		Italian composer, scarce, ESPV
Scarpelli, Glenn	1968-	5	10	10	12	"One Day at a Time"
Scarry, Richard	1920-1994	25	40	75	45	U.S. author of children's books
Schaeffer, Rebecca	1967-1989	100			250	TV, "My Sister Sam," killed by stalker
Schary, Dore	1905-1980	20	25	30	35	"Boy's Town," writer, producer
Scheider, Roy	1935-	10	20	20	25	"Jaws"
Schell, Maximilian	1930-	10	20	25	30	"Judgement at Nuremberg"
Schepisi, Fred	1939-	10	25		25	Film director
Schiffer, Claudia	1971-	10	25	30	35	Supermodel
Schildkraut, Joseph	1895-1964	70	150	150	175	"The Life of Emile Zola"
Schlesinger, Arthur M. Jr.	1917-	10	30		25	Historian, RS
Schlesinger, John	1926-	10	25		25	Film director
Schneider, Maria	1952-	5	10	15	20	"Last Tango in Paris"
Schoenberg, Arnold	1874-1951	350	1275	2500	600	Austrian composer
Schroder, Rick	1970-	10	10	10	25	"Lonesome Dove"

NAME	DOB/DOD	SIG	DS/LS	ALS	SP	COMMENTS
☆ **Schubert, Franz**	**1797-1828**	**2850**	**6500**	**1275 0**		**Austrian composer, scarce, ESPV-ALS**
Schultz, Dwight	1947-	5	10	10	10	"The A-Team"
Schuman, William	1910-1992	25	50		50	Composer
Schumann, Elisabeth	1885-1952	50	100		125	Operatic soprano
Schumann, Robert	1810-1856	1000	2000	4000		German composer, scarce, ESPV
Schumann-Heink, Ernestine	1861-1936	60	125		150	Contralto
Schwartz, Arthur	1900-1984	40	100	250	75	U.S., "That's Entertainment"
Schwarzenegger, Arnold	1947-	25	175	240	75	"The Terminator," SP as "Mr. Freeze"-$125
Schwarzkopf, Elisabeth	1915-	20	45		40	Soprano
Schwimmer, David	1966-	20	45	75	55	"Friends"
Schygulla, Hanna	1943-	5	10	10	10	"Dead Again"
Sciorra, Annabella	1964-	10	15	20	25	"The Hand that Rocks the Cradle"
Scofield, Paul	1922-	10	25	60	25	"A Man For All Seasons"
Scolari, Peter	1954-	5	10	10	10	"Bosom Buddies"
Scorsese, Martin	1942-	30	175	230	60	"Taxi Driver"
Scott, George C.	1926-	35	225		75	"Patton," first actor to refuse the Acad. Award
Scott, Gordon	1927-	15	30	25	30	"Tarzan's Hidden Jungle"
Scott, Lizabeth	1922-	10	15	15	20	"You Came Along," "Desert Fury"
Scott, Martha	1914-	10	15	20	25	"Our Town," "Ben Hur," RS!
Scott, Randolph	1903-1987	55	100	115	130	"Jesse James," "Abilene Town"
Scott, Ridley	1937-	10	15	15	20	"Thelma and Louise," director
Scott, Ronnie	1927-	15	30		25	Jazz saxophonist
Scott, Sir Walter	1771-1832	125	550	800		Novelist, poet "Ivanhoe," ESPV
Scott, Willard	1934-	5	10	10	10	"Today," weatherman
Scott, Zachary	1914-1965	30	50	110	60	"Mildred Pierce"
Seagal, Steven	1952-	20	50	75	45	"Under Seige," FA
Seal	1963-	15			25	(Sealhenry Samuel); "Kiss From a Rose," "Don't Cry"; SA/CD-30
Seal, Elizabeth	1933-	5	10	10	15	"Irma La Douce"
Secombe, Sir Harry	1921-	15			25	Comedian

NAME	DOB/DOD	SIG	DS/LS	ALS	SP	COMMENTS
Sedaka, Neil	1939-	10	25	30	20	U.S., "Breaking Up is Hard to Do," RS
Seeger, Pete	1919-	15	45		30	Folk singer, RS
Sedgwick, Kyra	1965-	15	35	35	40	Actress, m. Kevin Bacon
Segal, George	1934-	5	10	15	20	"Look Who's Talking"
Segovia, Andres		125	230		150	Classical guitarist
Seinfeld, Jerry	1955-	25	75	140	60	"Seinfeld," FA
Sellecca, Connie	1955-	10	20	25	25	"Hotel," m. John Tesh
Selleck, Tom	1945-	15	25	65	35	"Magnum, P.I.," FA, RS!
Sellers, Peter	1925-1980	120	200	300	275	"Inspector Clouseau" in Pink Panther films
Sembrich, Marcella	1858-1935	100	200	275	275	Opera: Soprano
Sennett, Mack	1880-1960	250	450			Film director, ESPV-SP
Serkin, Peter	1947-	20	40		40	Pianist
Serkin, Rudolf	1903-1991	50	100	175	125	Pianist
Serling, Rod	1924-1975	150	300	400	400	"The Twilight Zone," "Requiem For a ..."
Sessions, Almira	1888-1974	20	35	40	40	"Little Nellie Kelly," "Rosemary's Baby"
Seuss, Dr. (Theodor Geisel)	1904-1991	100	450	500	325	U.S. , "The Cat in the Hat"- $745 (SBP), ESPV
Sevareid, Eric	1912-1992	30	65		75	CBS anchor, FA
Sex Pistols, The		550			800	Values for original lineup, S. Vicious (KS); "Anarchy in the U.K.," "Holidays in the Sun"; SA/CD-900
Seymour, Jane	1950-	15	30	40	45	"Dr. Quinn, Medicine Woman," FA
Seymour, Stephanie	1968-	15	25	35	45	Supermodel
Shaffer, Paul	1949-	5	10	10	10	"Late Show with David Letterman"
Shaffer, Peter	1926-	10	20		25	Playwright
Shakespeare, William	1564-1616	RARE	RARE	RARE	RARE	British dramatist, poet, "Hamlet," only 6 known, FA
Shalit, Gene	1932-	5	10	10	10	"Today," film critic
Shandling, Garry	1949-	15	25	35	40	"Larry Sanders Show"
Shankar, Ravi	1920-	20	40		35	Sitarist
Shannon, Del	1939-1990	45			75	(1939-1990); "Runaway," "Hats Off to Larry"; SA/CD-85

NAME	DOB/DOD	SIG	DS/LS	ALS	SP	COMMENTS
Sharif, Omar	1932-	20	50	70	75	"Dr. Zhivago"
Shatner, William	1931-	25	50	75	65	"Star Trek"
Shaughnessy, Mickey	1920-1985	20	40	40	45	"From Here To Eternity"
Shaver, Helen	1951-	10	15	15	20	"The Amityville Horror"
Shaw, Artie	1910-	20	45		50	Clarinet player, RS
Shaw, George Bernard ☆	**1856-1950**	**425**	**700**	**850**		**Playwright, critic, "Pygmalion," SDS & SALS-2X**
Shawn, Dick	1928-1987	55	100	150	125	"The Producers"
Shawn, Wallace	1943-	10	15	15	15	"My Dinner with Andre," playwright
Shea, John	1949-	5	10	10	10	"Lois & Clark"
Shean, Al	1868-1949	65	120	110	125	"San Francisco," partner w/Gallagher
Shearer, Harry	1943-	5	10	10	10	"This Is Spinal Tap"
Shearer, Moira	1926-	30	50	50	65	"The Red Shoes," ballet dancer
Shearer, Norma	1900-1983	100	300	350	265	"The Divorcee," nominated for 6 Oscars.
Sheedy, Ally	1962-	5	10	10	10	"WarGames"
Sheen, Charlie	1965-	15	25	25	25	"Platoon," FA
Sheen, Martin	1940-	12	25	30	30	"Apocalypse Now," RS!, producer
Sheldon, Sidney	1917-	10	20	30	15	U.S. writer, "Bloodline," RS
Shelley, Carole	1939-	5	10	10	10	"The Elephant Man"
Shelley, Mary W.	1797-1851	750	1000	1400		Novelist, "Frankenstein," ESPV
Shelley, Percy Bysshe	1792-1822	1250	2500	2625		British poet, "Ode to the West Wind," SALS-2x
Shepard, Cybill	1950-	20	35	40	50	"Cybill"
Shepard, Sam	1943-	30	55	100	45	U.S. writer, "Chicago," elusive signer
Sheridan, Ann	1915-1967	60	115	100	125	"King's Row," "Shine On Harvest Moon"
Sheridan, Jim	1949-	10	15	20	20	"My Left Foot," director
Sheridan, Nicollette	1963-	10	25	25	30	"The Sure Thing"
Sheridan, Richard B.	1751-1816	75	125	300		British dramatist, "The Rivals"
Sherriff, R.C.	1896-1975	40	110	150	100	British screenwriter, "Goodbye Mr. Chips"
Sherrin, Ned	1931-	10	25		20	Producer, director
Sherwood, Robert	1896-1955	35	100	215	45	U.S. playwright, "Abe Lincoln in Illinois"

NAME	DOB/DOD	SIG	DS/LS	ALS	SP	COMMENTS
Shields, Brooke	1965-	20	40	50	50	"Pretty Baby"
Shields, Carol	1935-	15	20	40	20	U.S. writer, "The Box Garden," RS!
Shire, Talia (Talia Rose Coppola)	1946-	25	75	100	50	"Rocky I-V," (S)DS-2X, elusive signer
Shirelles, The		40			110	(1996), A. Harris (1940-1982); "Soldier Boy," "Will You Love Me Tomorrow"; SA/CD-125
Shirer, William	1904-1993	15	30		30	Historian, journalist, RS
Shirley, Anneta	1918-1993	20	25	40	40	"Stella Dallas"
Shoemaker, Ann	1891-1978	20	35	35	40	"Sunrise at Campobello"
Shore, Dinah	1917-1994	25	50	100	60	"Thank Your Lucky Stars"
Short, Martin	1950-	10	20	25	25	SNL
Shorter, Wayne	1933-	15	25		30	Jazz saxophonist
Shostakovich, Dmitri D.	1906-1975	400	700	1200	2000	Russian composer, SDS & SALS-2X, ESPV
Show, Grant	1962-	20	35	35	45	"Melrose Place"
Showalter, Max	1917-	5	10	10	10	"Leave It to Beaver," RS!
Shue, Andrew	1967-	15	30	30	40	"Melrose Place"
Shue, Elisabeth	1963-	20	40	50	65	"Leaving Las Vegas"
Sibelius, Jean	1865-1957	450	875	1125	1100	Finnish composer, SALS-2X, ESPV
Sibley, Dame Antoinette	1933-	15	25		30	Dancer
Siddons, Sarah	1755-1831	225	350	475		Actress
Sidney, Sylvia	1910-	10	20	25	25	"City Streets," "Summer Wishes, Winter ..."
Sikking, James B.	1934-	5	10	10	15	"Hill Street Blues"
Sillanpaa, Frans E.	1888-1964	50	110			Novelist, NP
Sills, Beverley	1929-	20	50		40	Operatic soprano, RS
Silva, Henry	1928-	10	15	15	15	"Johnny Cool," "Sharky's Machine"
Silver, Ron	1946-	15	25	25	30	"Reversal of Fortune"
Silverheels, Jay	1919-1980	160	350		400	Played "Tonto" in "The Lone Ranger"
Silverman, Jonathan	1966-	5	10	10	10	"The Single Guy," RS!
Silvers, Phil	1912-1985	50	100	215	185	"You'll Never Get Rich"
Silverstein, Shel	1932-	25	45	75	35	U.S. writer, "Drain My Brain," elusive signer!
Silverstone, Alicia	1976-	25	55	75	80	"Clueless"

NAME	DOB/DOD	SIG	DS/LS	ALS	SP	COMMENTS
Sim, Alastair	1900-1976	25			50	Actor
Simmons, Jean	1925-	15	20	25	30	"Hamlet," "The Happy Ending"
Simmons, Richard	1948-	5	10	10	10	"Sweatin' to the Oldies"
Simms, Larry	1934-	5	10	10	15	"Blondie" film series
Simon and Garfunkel		65			150	(1990); "Bridge Over Troubled Water," "The Boxer"; SA/CD-175
Simon, Carly	1945-	20			35	"You're So Vain," "Nobody Does It Better"; SA/CD-50
Simon, Neil	1927-	20	50	100	25	U.S. writer, RS, "The Odd Couple"
Simon, Paul	1941-	25	100		60	FA, can be an elusive and illegible signer; "50 Ways to Leave Your Lover," "Graceland"; SA/CD-75
Simon, Simone	1914-	40	100		80	"Cat People," ESPV
Simone, Nina	1933-	20			40	Jazz singer
Simpson, Russell	1880-1959	65	120	150	130	Character actor, TGOW, "Billy the Kid"
Sims, Zoot	1925-1985	30	50		60	Tenor, alto sax and clarinet player
Sinatra, Frank	**1915-1998**	**225**	**675**	**1250**	**300**	**"From Here To Eternity," FA, sec. sigs., SALS-2-3X**
Sinbad (David Adkins)	1956-	10	15	20	25	"A Different World"
Sinclair, Upton	1878-1968	50	100	150	120	U.S. novelist, "The Jungle"
Sinden, Donald	1923-	15			30	Actor, ESPV
Singer, Isaac Bashevis	1904-1991	45	165	275	145	Pol./U.S. novelist
Singer, Lori	1962-	5	10	10	12	"Fame"
Singleton, John	1968-	10	15	15	20	"Boyz N the Hood"
Singleton, Penny	1908-	12	15	20	20	"Good News"-stage, "Boy Meets Girl"
Singleton, Zutty	1898-1975	25	45		40	Drummer
Sirhan Sirhan		225			400	Shot Robert F. Kennedy, ESPV, scarce
Siskel, Gene	1946-1999	10	20	10	10	"Siskel & Ebert & The Movies"
Sitwell, Dame Edith	1887-1964	50	100	200		Poet
Skelton, Red	1913-1997	40	100	160	125	"Whistling in the Dark," television star
Skerritt, Tom	1933-	10	15	25	25	"Picket Fences," "Top Gun"
Skye, Ione	1971-	5	10	10	10	"Say Anything"
Slater, Christian	1969-	15	25	30	45	"Heathers"

NAME	DOB/DOD	SIG	DS/LS	ALS	SP	COMMENTS
Slater, Helen	1965-	10	20	20	30	"Supergirl"
Sloane, Everett	1909-1965	30	50	50	60	"Citizen Kane"
Sly and the Family Stone		85			175	(1993), S. Stone (KS); "Everyday People," "Dance to the Music"; SA/CD-200
Smashing Pumpkins		40			80	B. Corgan (KS); "Today"; SA/CD-115
Smeaton, Bruce	1938-	15			30	Composer
Smetana, Bedrich	1824-1884	2000		10000		Czech composer, scarce, ESPV
Smiley, Jane	1949-	10	20	30	15	U.S. writer, "At Paradise Gate," RS!
Smirnoff, Yakov	1951-	5	10	10	10	"What a Country!"
Smith, Alexis	1921-1993	20	50	40	40	"Dive Bomber," "Rhapsody in Blue"
Smith, Bessie	1894-1937	550	1150		2000	Blues singer, scarce, ESPV
Smith, Bob	1917-1998	25	35	50	60	"Howdy Doody," often signed at shows
Smith, C. Aubrey	1863-1948	40	80	130	80	British stage actor, "Queen Christina"
Smith, Charles Martin	1953-	10	20	20	25	"American Graffiti"
Smith, Jaclyn	1947-	5	15	20	25	"Charlie's Angels"
Smith, Jeff	1939-	5	10	10	10	"The Frugal Gourmet"
Smith, Kate	1909-1986	50	165	175	130	"This Is The Army," singer, hockey fan!
Smith, Liz	1923-	5	10	15	10	Gossip columnist
Smith, Maggie	1934-	10	20	25	25	"Sister Act"
Smith, Patti	1946-	35			75	SA/CD: for "Horses"; "Because the Night," "Gloria"; SA/CD-11
Smith, Will	1968-	30	165	300	75	"Independence Day," rap artist
Smith, Willie "The Lion"	1897-1973	85	150		140	Stride pianist
Smits, Jimmy	1955-	10	25	30	30	"L.A. Law," RS!
Smokey Robinson and the Miracles		30			55	(1987), S. Robinson (KS), DS- $150; "Shop Around," "Going to a Go-Go"; SA/CD-65
Smothers, Dick	1939-	5	10	10	12	"The Smothers Brothers Comedy Hour"
Smothers, Tom	1937-	5	10	10	12	"The Smothers ...," SP both-$30
Snipes, Wesley	1962-	20	120	175	70	"New Jack City"
Snodgrass, Carrie	1946-	5	10	10	12	"Diary of a Mad Housewife," RS!

James Stewart

Harriet Beecher Stowe

Johann Strauss

Richard Strauss

Igor Stravinsky

Elizabeth Taylor

Piotr I. Tchaikovsky

Shirley Temple (vintage)

Virgil Thomson

Henry David Thoreau

NAME	DOB/DOD	SIG	DS/LS	ALS	SP	COMMENTS
Snow, Charles Percy	1905-1980	30	65	130	45	British novelist
Snyder, Gary	1930-	10	25		20	Poet
Snyder, Tom	1936-	5	10	10	10	"Late Late Show with Tom Snyder," RS
Soderstrom, Elisabeth A.	1927-	15	30		30	Soprano
Sokolow, Anna	1912-	15			30	Dancer, choreographer
Solti, Sir Georg	1912-	25	50		50	Conductor
Solzhenitsyn, Aleksandor	1918-	100	300	400	150	Russian writer, "Cancer Ward"
Somers, Suzanne	1946-	10	20	30	50	"Three's Company"
Sommer, Elke	1940-	5	10	10	15	"A Shot in the Dark," RS!
Sondergaard, Gale	1900-1985	35	60	60	70	"The Life of Emile Zola"
Sondheim, Stephen	1930-	25	100	200	100	U.S., "A Little Night Music"
Sorbo, Kevin	1958-	25	50	130	65	"Hercules"
Sorvino, Mira	1969-	20	40	50	65	"Mighty Aphrodite"
Sorvino, Paul	1939-	15	30	40	40	"GoodFellas"
Sothern, Ann	1909-	20	40	50	55	"Ann Sothern Show," "Maisie" series
Soul, David	1943-	5	10	10	10	"Starsky and Hutch," SP-$15
Soundgarden		35			70	C. Cornell (KS); "Outshined"; SA/CD-80
☆ Sousa, John Phillip	**1854-1932**	**175**	**300**	**500**	**1000**	**U.S., "Stars and Stripes Forever"**
Soyinka, Wole	1934-	30	65	100	40	Nigerian writer, "The Interpreter," elusive sig.
Spacek, Sissy	1949-	20	40	50	50	"Coal Miner's Daughter"
Spacey, Kevin	1959-	15	30	40	45	"Wiseguy," RS!
Spader, James	1960-	5	10	10	10	"sex, lies, and videotape"
Spanier, Muggsy	1906-1967	40	75		65	Band leader, coronet player
Spano, Joe	1946-	5	15	15	15	"Hill Street Blues"
Spano, Vincent	1962-	5	10	10	10	"Rumble Fish"
Sparks, Ned	1883-1957	30	35	55	65	"42nd Street," "Magic Town"
Spelling, Aaron	1923-	10	15	25	25	"Beverly Hills 90210"
Spelling, Tori	1973-	20	30	40	55	"Beverly Hills 90210"
Spencer Davis Group		40			100	S.Winwood (KS); "Gimme Some Lovin"; SA/CD-125
Spender, Stephen	1909-1995	60	150	200	100	British poet, critic, novelist

NAME	DOB/DOD	SIG	DS/LS	ALS	SP	COMMENTS
Spice Girls		70			150	G. Spice (KS); "Wannabe"; SA/CD-175
Spielberg, Steven	1947-	75	230	465	150	"Schindler's List," director, FA
Spillane, Mickey	1918-	10	20	30	15	U.S. writer, "The Deep"
Spontini, Gaspare	1774-1851	135				Italian composer
Springsteen, Bruce	1946-	65			195	RS in-person; "Born to Run," "Glory Days," "Born in ... U.S.A."; SA/CD-225
Squeeze		25			35	P. Carrack (KS); "Tempted," "Hourglass"; SA/CD-55
St. John, Jill	1940-	10	15	20	25	"Diamonds Are Forever"
Stack, Robert	1919-	15	25	30	30	"Written on the Wind,""The Untouchables"
Stafford, Jean	1915-1979	20	50		45	Writer, RS
Stallone, Sylvester	1946-	32	150	300	85	"Rocky," reluctant signer
Stamos, John	1963-	10	15	15	20	"Full House"
Stamp, Terence	1939-	10	20	20	25	"Superman, The Movie"
Stander, Lionel	1908-	10	15	15	20	"Mr. Deeds Goes to Town"
Standings, Guy	1873-1937	35	100	215	75	British stage actor, "Death Takes..."
Stang, Arnold	1925-	5	10	15	20	"The Man With The Golden Arm"
Stanislavsky, Konstantin	1863-1938	300				Russian actor, director, ESPV
Stanton, Harry Dean	1926-	5	10	10	10	"Paris, Texas"
Stanwyck, Barbara	1907-1990	35	85	125	100	"Ball of Fire," TV star
Stapleton, Jean	1923-	5	10	20	20	"All in the Family," RS!
Stapleton, Maureen	1925-	10	20	25	25	"Lonelyhearts," "Airport," "Reds"
Starr, Ringo	1940-	125	250	2500	225	Beatle, SDS-4X
Steber, Eleanor	1916-1990	25	50	100	85	Opera: Soprano
Steel, Danielle	1947-	10	20	35	15	U.S. writer, "Wings," very RS!
Steele, Bob	1906-1988	28	35	50	60	"Of Mice and Men," "F Troop"-TV
Steele, Richard	1672-1729	240	575	1150		British essayist, playwright
Steely Dan		75			125	Elusive signers; "Do It Again," "Reeling in the Years," "FM"; SA/CD-150
Steenburgen, Mary	1954-	15	40	40	40	"Parenthood"
Steffens, Lincoln	1866-1936	35	100	150	50	U.S. editor, writer

NAME	DOB/DOD	SIG	DS/LS	ALS	SP	COMMENTS
Steiger, Rod	1925-	10	20	25	35	"In the Heat of the Night"
Stein, Gertrude	1874-1946	500	600	1000	650	U.S. writer, "Three Lives," ESPV
☆ **Steinbeck, John**	**1902-1968**	**425**	**1825**	**2650**	**1000**	**U.S. novelist, "East of Eden"-$2875 (FE,SB)**
Steinberg, David	1942-	10	20	20	25	"Paternity," director
Steinem, Gloria	1934-	10	25		25	Feminist
Steiner, Max	1888-1971	225	430			Composer, ESPV, GWTW
Sten, Anna	1910-1993	20	25	35	40	"Nana," "The Yellow Passport"
Steppenwolf		35			65	"Born to Be Wild," "Magic Carpet Ride"; SA/CD-75
Sterling, Jan	1923-	10	20	25	25	"Caged," "The High and the Mighty"
Sterling, Robert	1917-	10	20	25	25	"Only Angels Have Wings," "Topper"-TV
Stern, Daniel	1957-	10	20	20	25	"The Wonder Years"
Stern, Howard	1954-	5	20	40	25	Radio shock-jock
Stern, Isaac	1920-	20	50		50	Violinist, RS
Stern, Richard	1928-	10	25	30	15	U.S. writer, "Golk," RS!
Sterne, Laurence	1713-1768	100	250	325		British novelist, "Tristram Shandy"
Sternhagen, Frances	1930-	5	10	15	10	"Driving Miss Daisy," RS!
Stevens, Andrew	1955-	5	10	15	15	"Dallas"
Stevens Bernard	1916-1983	20	40		40	Composer
Stevens, Connie	1938-	5	10	20	20	"Hawaiian Eye"
Stevens, Craig	1918-	10	15	20	20	"Peter Gunn"-TV
Stevens, Fisher	1963-	5	10	10	10	"Short Circuit"
Stevens, George	1904-1975	25			50	Film director
Stevens, K.T.	1919-	5	10	10	10	"Kitty Foyle," "Vice Squad"
Stevens, Ray	1939-	5	10	10	10	"Andy Williams Presents Ray Stevens"
Stevens, Rise	1908-	15	30	35	40	"Going My Way," opera singer
Stevens, Stella	1936-	5	10	15	15	"Santa Barbara"
Stevens, Wallace	1879-1955	225	800	1275		U.S. poet, "Harmonium," ESPV
Stevenson, Parker	1952-	5	10	10	15	"Falcon Crest"
☆ **Stevenson, Robert Louis**	**1850-1894**	**350**	**1125**	**2000**		**British novelist, "Treasure Island," ESPV**

NAME	DOB/DOD	SIG	DS/LS	ALS	SP	COMMENTS
Stevenson, Ronald	1928-	15	30		30	Composer
Stewart, James	1908-1997	45	225	400	160	IAWL, "Harvey," sketch-$375, BC-$200
Stewart, Jon	1963-	5	10	10	15	"The Jon Stewart Show"
Stewart, Martha	1942-	5	10	10	10	"Martha Stewart Living," RS!
Stewart, Martha	1922-	5	10	10	15	"Holocaust"
Stewart, Mary	1916-	25	45	70	40	British writer, "The Ivy Tree," elusive signer
Stewart, Patrick	1940-	25	50	130	70	"Star Trek: The Next Generation"
Stewart, Rod	1945-	35			60	(1994), a RS! "Maggie Mae," "Tonight's the Night..."; SA/CD-75
Stiers, David Ogden	1942-	40	175	280	150	"M*A*S*H," very reluctant signer
Stiller, Ben	1966-	10	20	25	30	"Reality Bites"
Stiller, Jerry	1931-	5	10	15	15	Actor, f. Ben Stiller
Sting	1951-	25			60	"If You Love Somebody, Set Them Free"; SA/CD-75
Stitt, Sonny	1924-1982	20	40		30	Alto, tenor sax player
Stockhausen, Karlheinz	1928-					German composer, PU
Stockwell, Dean	1935-	10	20	20	25	"Quantum Leap"
Stockwell, John	1961-	5	10	10	10	"My Science Project"
☆ **Stoker, Bram**	**1847-1912**	**400**	**675**	**750**	**1000**	**British writer, "Dracula," ESPV**
Stokowski, Leopold	1882-1977	75	150		150	American conductor
Stolz, Eric	1961-	10	20	25	25	"Mask"
Stone, Dee Wallace	1948-	5	10	10	12	"E.T., the Extra-Terrestrial"
Stone, George E.	1904-1967	25	50	50	50	"Seventh Heaven," "Little Caesar"
Stone, Irving	1903-1989	25	50	100	50	Writer, RS
Stone, Lewis	1878-1953	40	50	75	75	"The Trial of Mary Dugan"
Stone, Oliver	1946-	25	65	50	40	"Platoon," RS!
Stone, Robert	1937-	10	25	30	15	U.S. writer, "Dog Soldiers," RS!
Stone, Sharon	1958-	30	100	180	60	"Basic Instinct"
Stooges, Three		1350	4000		3375	Larry sig. $130, SP, final lineup-$650
Stoppard, Tom	1937-	25	45	60	30	U.K. Writer, "Billy Bathgate"
Storch, Larry	1923-	5	10	15	15	"F Troop"
Storm, Gale	1922-	5	10	15	20	"My Little Margie"

NAME	DOB/DOD	SIG	DS/LS	ALS	SP	COMMENTS
Stout, Rex	1886-1975	30	65	165	45	U.S. mystery writer
Stowe, Harriet Beecher	1811-1896	275	475	775		U.S. novelist, "Uncle Tom's Cabin," ESPV
Stowe, Madeleine	1958-	15	25	30	40	"The Last of the Mohicans"
Strachey, Lytton	1880-1932	80	150	450		British biographer, critic
Strasberg, Lee	1901-1982	25	45		70	Actor, director, RS
Strassman, Marcia	1948-	5	10	10	10	"Welcome Back Kotter"
Strathairn, David	1949-	5	10	10	10	"Matewan"
Stratton, Charles	1838-1883	225	450		450	"General Tom Thumb," ESPV-DS
Straus, Oskar	1870-1954	150	225	250	225	Austrian, "Chocolate Soldier"
Strauss, Johann	**1825-1899**	**500**	**1000**	**1450**		**Austrian, "Blue Danube," ESPV, scarce-SP**
Strauss, Johann B.	1804-1849	250	500			Violinist, composer, ESPV
Strauss, Peter	1947-	10	20	25	30	"The Jericho Mile"
Strauss, Richard	1864-1949	275	750	800	750	German composer
Strauss, Robert	1913-1975	32	50	50	60	"Stalag 17"
Stravinsky, Igor	1882-1971	350	700	1150	750	Russian composer, ESPV-ALS
Streep, Meryl	1950-	25	50	60	65	"Sophie's Choice"
Streisand, Barbra	1942-	200	300		300	"Funny Girl," SLP-$350, FA, sec. sigs.
Strindberg, August	1849-1912	300		800	1000	Swedish dramatist, novelist, "The Father," ESPV
Stringfield, Sherry	1967-	15	25	30	35	"ER"
Stritch, Elaine	1925-	5	10	10	10	"September"
Stroheim, Erich von	1885-1957	195	400		475	Director, "Greed," "Sunset Boulevard"
Stroud, Robert	1890-1963	225		600		Criminal, Birdman of Alcatraz Bird-Man
Strouse, Charles	1928-	20	50	100	40	U.S., "Bye Bye Birdie"
Struther, Jan	1901-1953	100				Writer, ESPV
Struthers, Sally	1948-	5	10	15	15	"All in the Family"
Stuart, Gloria	1909-	15	30	30	30	"Titanic," "Time Out For Murder," FA
Sturges, Preston	1898-1959	30	55	50	60	"The Great McGinty," "The Palm Beach Story"
Styne, Jule	1905-1994	30	75	135	60	British/U.S., "Funny Girl," composer
Styron, William	1925-	15	30	100	45	U.S. writer, "Sophie's Choice"- $150 (FE,SB)

NAME	DOB/DOD	SIG	DS/LS	ALS	SP	COMMENTS
Sugar Hill Gang, The		10			15	"Rapper's Delight"; SA/CD-20
Sullavan, Margaret	1911-1960	55	100	200	165	"Three Comrades," committed suicide at 49
Sullivan, Arthur S.	1842-1900	200	400	750	1000	British, "Pirates of Penzance"
Sullivan, Barry	1912-	10	20	20	25	"Lady in the Dark," "The Great Gatsby"
Sullivan, Ed	1902-1974	30	60	75	150	Broadcaster, RS
Sullivan, Susan	1944-	5	10	15	15	"Falcon Crest"
Sullivan, Tom	1947-	5	10	10	10	Actor, singer
Summer, Donna	1948-	15			20	"Bad Girls"; SA/CD-25
Supremes, The		250			500	(1988), D. Ross (KS), F. Ballard (1943-1976); "Stop! In the Name of Love"; SA/CD-600
Sutherland, Donald	1935-	10	20	25	25	"Ordinary People"
Sutherland, Kiefer	1966-	10	25	25	30	"Flatliners"
Susann, Jacqueline	c.1926-1974	25	50	50	50	Novelist
Sutton, Grady	1908-	10	20	20	20	Character actor, "Alice Adams"
Sutton, Willie	1901-1980	65		325	100	Bank robber, ESPV
Suzman, Janet	1939-	5	10	10	12	"Nicholas and Alexandra"
Svenson, Bo	1941-	5	10	10	10	"Walking Tall"
Swann, Donald	1923-1994	20	40		45	Composer
Swanson, Gloria	1899-1983	50	200	430	150	"Sunset Boulevard," silent star, RS
Swarthout, Gladys	1904-1969	30	65	70	70	"Champagne Waltz," opera singer
Swayze, Patrick	1952-	20	50	50	65	"Dirty Dancing"
Sweeney, D.B.	1961-	10	15	15	20	"The Cutting Edge"
Sweet, Blanche	1895-1986	30	45	40	50	"The Lonedale Operator," m. Marshall Neilan
Swenson, Inga	1932-	5	10	10	10	"Benson"
Swift, Jonathan	1667-1745	2650	6500	12500		British satirist, poet, "Gulliver's Travels," ESPV
Swinburne, Algernon C.	1837-1909	200	300	575		British writer, "Atalanta in Calydon," ESPV
Swit, Loretta	1937-	10	20	25	25	"M*A*S*H"
Switzer, Carl "Alfalfa"	1927-1959	325	500		725	"Our Gang" member, ESPV
Sydow, Max von	1929-	20	40		40	Actor, elusive signer!

NAME	DOB/DOD	SIG	DS/LS	ALS	SP	COMMENTS
T, Mr. (Lawrence Tero)	1952-	5	10	10	15	"The A-Team"
T. Rex		150			400	(Marc Bolan); "Bang a Gong (Get It On)," "Jeepster"; SA/CD-450
Taglioni, Marie	1804-1884	350				Ballerina
Tagore, Rabindranath	1861-1941	130	275	425	300	Author, poet, "Sadhana"
Takei, George	1939-	15	20	25	25	"Star Trek"
Takei, Kei	1939-	15			25	Dancer
Talbot, Lyle	1904-1994	15	30	30	35	"The Bob Cummings Show"- TV
Talese, Gay	1932-	10	25		20	Journalist, RS
Talking Heads		40			80	D. Byrne (KS); "Psycho Killer," "Burning Down the House"; SA/CD-90
Talmadge, Constance	1900-1973	40	60	75	80	"Intolerance," "Lessons of Love"
Talmadge, Norma	1897-1957	60	175	260	150	"Secrets," "Camille"
Tamblyn, Russ	1934-	5	10	20	20	"West Side Story"
Tambor, Jeffrey	1944-	5	10	10	15	"Hill Street Blues"
Tamiroff, Akim	1899-1972	40	50	75	80	"The General Died at Dawn," "For Whom the..."
Tan, Amy	1952-	20	30	50	30	U.S. writer, "The Moon Lady"
Tandy, Jessica	1909-1994	40	50	65	75	"Driving Miss Daisy," SP w/ m.Cronyn- $115
Tarantino, Quentin	1963-	25	50	75	60	"Pulp Fiction," director, writer
Tarkington, Booth	1869-1946	45	140	200	100	U.S. novelist, "Seventeen"
Taylor, Art	1929-1995	20	40		35	Bandleader, drummer
Taylor, Cecil	1933-	10			25	Pianist
Taylor, Deems	1885-1966	25	75	100	50	U.S., "Peter Ibbetson," "Fantasia" narrator
Taylor, Elizabeth	1932-	185	550		425	"Cleopatra," FA, sec. sig. are common
Taylor, Estelle	1899-1958	20	30	45	50	"The Ten Commandments," "Don Juan"
Taylor, James	1948-	30			50	A RS in-person; "You've Got a Friend," "Fire and Rain"; SA/CD-75
Taylor, Lili	1967-	5	10	10	10	"Mystic Pizza"
Taylor, Paul	1930-	20			40	Choreographer
Taylor, Peter	1917-1994	25	40	60	30	U.S. novelist, "A Summons to Memphis"

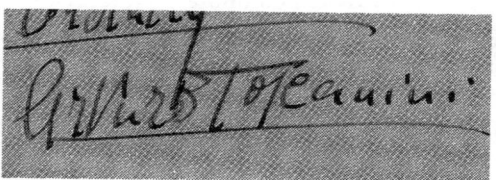

J. R. R. Tolkien

Arturo Toscanini

Spencer Tracy

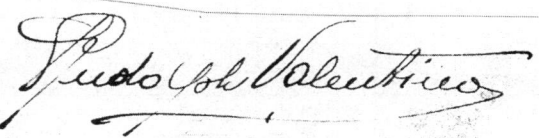

John Travolta

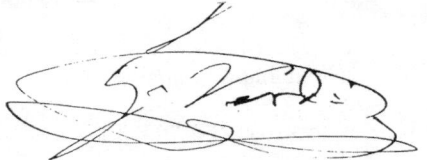

Rudolph Valentino

Giuseppe Verdi

Giuseppe Verdi

Jules Verne

Voltaire

Richard Wagner

Thomas "Fats" Waller

John Wayne

NAME	DOB/DOD	SIG	DS/LS	ALS	SP	COMMENTS
Taylor, Robert	1911-1969	40	150	170	200	"Magnificent Obsession," m. B. Stanwyck
Taylor, Rod	1929-	5	10	10	10	"The Time Machine," RS!
☆ **Tchalkovsky, Pyotr I.**	**1840-1893**	**2500**	**4000**	**7000**		**Russian composer, "Nutcracker"**
Teagarden, Jack	1905-1964	75	100		135	Trombone player, singer
Tebaldi, Renata	1922-	15			35	Soprano
Temple, Shirley	1928-	25	50	75	65	"Little Colonel," early 1936 FDC-$275, vintage 6-10X
Temptations, The		200			300	(1989), varies by lineup, E. Kendricks (KS); "My Girl," "Get Ready," "All I Need"; SA/CD-350
Tennant, Victoria	1950-	10	20	20	25	"L.A. Story"
☆ **Tennyson, Alfred, Lord**	**1809-1892**	**225**	**650**	**800**		**British poet, "Idylls of the King," ESPV**
Terkel, Studs	1912-	10	25		20	Writer, RS
Terry, Dame Ellen	1847-1928	40	75		80	Actress
Tetley, Glen	1926-	15	35		30	Ballet dancer
Tetrazzini, Luisa	1871-1940	100	150	250	250	Opera: Soprano
Thackeray, William Makepeace	1811-1863	125	400	650		British novelist, "Vanity Fair"
Thalberg, Irving	1899-1936	300	600	850	625	MGM artistic dir., scarce in all forms
Tharp, Tayla	1942-	20	40		45	Choreographer
Theodorakis, Mikis	1925-	20	40		35	Composer
Theroux, Paul	1941-	20	35	50	25	U.S. writer, "The Family Arsenal"
Thicke, Alan	1947-	5	10	10	10	"Growing Pains," RS!
Thiessen, Tiffany Amber		20	40	35	50	"Saved by the Bell," "Beverly Hills 90210"
Thomas, Betty	1948-	5	10	10	15	"Hill Street Blues," RS!
Thomas, Danny	1914-1991	25	50	50	60	"The Jazz Singer," TV actor
Thomas, Dave	1949-	5	10	10	12	"SCTV"
☆ **Thomas, Dylan**	**1914-1953**	**525**	**1250**	**1650**		**Welsh poet, "Under Milk Wood"**
Thomas, Henry	1972-	5	10	10	15	"E.T., the Extra-Terrestrial"
Thomas, Jay	1948-	5	10	10	15	"Murphy Brown"
Thomas, Jonathan Taylor	1981-	25	50	50	50	"Home Improvement"
Thomas, Kristin Scott	1960-	20	40	40	45	"The English Patient"
Thomas, Marlo	1938-	5	10	20	20	"That Girl"

NAME	DOB/DOD	SIG	DS/LS	ALS	SP	COMMENTS
Thomas, Philip Michael	1949-	20	35	30	40	"Miami Vice"
Thomas, Richard	1951-	5	10	20	20	"The Waltons"
Thomas, William T. "Buckwheat"	1931-1980	60	150	200	125	"Our Gang" member
Thompson, Emma	1959-	20	50	45	65	"Howards End," RS
Thompson, Hunter	1939-	25	60		65	Journalist, ESPV
Thompson, Lea	1951-	15	10	15	40	"Back to the Future"
Thompson, Sada	1929-	5	10	10	10	"Family"
Thomson, Virgil	1896-1989	35	100	150	125	U.S. composer
Thoreau, Henry David	**1817-1862**	**2425**	**4750**	**8000**		**U.S. writer, philosopher, "Walden," ESPV**
Thorne-Smith, Courtney	1968-	15	30	30	35	"Melrose Place," "Ally McBeal"
Thornton, Billy Bob	1955-	30	60	135	75	"Sling Blade," screenwriter, director, RS
Three Dog Night		45			100	"Joy to the World," "Liar," "Eli's Coming"; SA/CD-125
Thurber, James	1894-1961	125	265	475		U.S. humorist, cartoonist, "The Secret Life of Walterb Mitty"
Thurman, Uma	1970-	25	60	50	60	"Dangerous Liaisons"
Tibbett, Lawrence	1896-1960	60	125	125	150	Opera: Baritone
Tiegs, Cheryl	1947-	10	15	20	25	Model, RS!
Tierney, Gene	1920-1991	25	45	50	50	"Tobacco Road," "Leave Her to Heaven"
Tierney, Lawrence	1919-	10	20	25	25	"Dillinger," "Born to Kill"
Tilly, Meg	1960-	10	15	15	20	"The Big Chill"
Tilton, Charlene	1958-	10	20	25	30	"Dallas"
Tiomkin, Dimitri	1894-1980	50	100	165	115	Composer
TLC		30			45	"Waterfalls"; SA/CD-50
Tobias, George	1901-1980	60	130	185	145	"Sinbad the Sailor," "Mildred Pierce"
Tobias, Harry	1905-1994	20	40	60	45	U.S., "I'll Keep the Lovelight Burning"
Tobin, Genevieve	1901-	15	30	30	30	"Easy to Love," "Zaza"
Todd, Ann	1909-1993	25	40	45	45	"The Seventh Veil," "Madeleine"
Todd, Richard	1919-	80	125	220	150	"The Hasty Heart," "The Dam Busters"
Todd, Thelma	1905-1935	215	275	430	585	"Monkey Business," died at age 30

NAME	DOB/DOD	SIG	DS/LS	ALS	SP	COMMENTS
Tolkan, James	1931-	5	10	10	12	"Back to the Future"
Tolkien, J.R.R.	1892-1973	500	1200	1500		British writer, "The Hobbit"
☆ **Tolstoy, Leo**	**1828-1910**	**1000**	**2350**	**3150**	**2250**	**Russian novelist, short-story writer, "War and Peace," ESPV-DS & ALS**
Tom Petty and the Heartbreakers		40			70	T. Petty (KS); "Refugee," "Breakdown," "American Girl"; SA/CD-110
Tomei, Marisa	1964-	20	40	40	45	"My Cousin Vinny"
Tomlin, Lily	1939-	10	20	25	25	"Rowan & Martin's Laugh-In"
Tommy James and the Shondells		45			70	T. James (KS); "Crimson and Clover," "Hanky Panky"; SA/CD-100
Tone, Franchot	1905-1968	35	100	100	85	"Mutiny on the Bounty," "Ben Casey"- TV
Toomey, Regis	1902-1991	20	40	40	45	"G-Men," "Dive Bomber," "The Big Sleep"
Torn, Rip	1931-	15	25	20	25	"Sweet Bird of Youth"
Toscanimi, Arturo	1867-1957	300	500	700	625	Italian conductor
Totter, Audrey	1918-	10	20	20	20	"The Postman Always Rings Twice"
Toumanova, Tamara	1917-	30	80	125	125	"Torn Curtain," Russian ballerina
Townsend, Robert	1957-	10	20	25	25	"Hollywood Shuffle"
Tracey, Stan	1926-	15	30		30	Jazz pianist
Tracy, Lee	1898-1968	18	30	35	35	"The Best Man," "Bombshell"
☆ **Tracy, Spencer**	**1900-1967**	**175**	**375**	**600**	**350**	**"Boy's Town," sig. w/m. Hepburn- $800, ESPV-DS & ALS**
Traubel, Helen	1899-1972	45	90	100	110	"Deep in my Heart"
Travanti, Daniel J.	1940-	5	10	15	20	"Hill Street Blues"
Travers, Bill	1922-	5	10	10	10	"Born Free"
Travers, Henry	1874-1965	265	375	545	400	"Mrs. Miniver," IAWL, scarce, ESPV
Travolta, John	1954-	35	225	250	60	"Saturday Night Fever," RS, FA
Treacher, Arthur	1894-1975	25	45	50	60	"Mary Poppins," TV sidekick to M. Griffin
Trebek, Alex	1940-	5	10	10	10	"Jeopardy!," RS!
Trevor, Claire	1909-	25	50	100	50	"Key Largo," "Dead End," "Stagecoach"
Tripplehorn, Jeanne	1959-	20	35	40	50	"The Firm"
Tristano, Lennie	1919-1978	30	55		50	Piano player, composer

NAME	DOB/DOD	SIG	DS/LS	ALS	SP	COMMENTS
Trollope, Anthony	1815-1882	100	250	750		British novelist, "The Warden"
Truffaut, Francois	1932-1984	60	125		150	Director, critic, elusive
Trump, Marla Maples	1963-	5	10	15	25	"The Will Rogers Follies"
Tucker, Forrest	1919-1986	30	45	50	50	"The Yearling," "F Troop"- TV
Tucker, Michael	1944-	5	10	10	15	"L.A. Law"
Tucker, Richard	1913-1975	50	50	100	125	Opera: Tenor
Tucker, Sophie	1884-1966	50	80	75	100	"Honky Tonk"
Tudor, Antony	1908-1987	25	50		75	Dancer
Tune, Tommy	1939-	10	15	15	25	Actor, director, dancer, RS!
Turgenev, Ivan	1818-1883	225	500	1250		Russian novelist, "First Love"
Turlington, Christy	1969-	5	10	15	25	Supermodel
Turner, Big Joe	1911-1985	100			200	(1987), (1911-1985); "Shake, Rattle & Roll," "Sweet Sixteen"; SA/CD-225
Turner, Janine	1963-	20	40	50	50	"Northern Exposure"
Turner, Joe	1911-1985	50	120		150	Blues singer
Turner, Kathleen	1954-	10	25	30	40	"Romancing the Stone"
Turner, Lana	1920-	40	150	125	100	"Peyton Place"
Turner, Tina		25			50	(1991); "What's Love Got to Do With It?"; SA/CD-60
Turow, Scott	1949-	25	50	75	30	U.S. writer, "The Burden of Proof"
Turtles, The		40			65	Volman & Kaylan (KS); "Happy Together," "Elenore"; SA/CD-75
Turturro, John	1957-	5	10	10	10	"Barton Fink"
Tutuola, Amos	1920-1997	30	50	60	40	Nigerian novelist
Twain, Mark (Samuel Clemens)	**1835-1910**	**1100**	**1560**	**2000**	**2000**	**U.S. novelist, "Tom Sawyer," ESPV**
Twiggy (Lesley Hornby)	1949-	20	25	30	35	"The Boy Friend"
Tyler, Ann	1941-	10	25	50	25	U.S. writer, "Breathing Lessons," res. signer
Tyler, Liv	1977-	25	50	50	70	"Armageddon"
Tyson, Cicely	1942-	10	15	20	20	"The Autobiography of Miss Jane Pittman"
U2		165			225	"(Pride) In the Name of Love," "One"; SA/CD-250
Uecker, Bob	1935-	5	10	15	15	"Mr. Belvedere"

NAME	DOB/DOD	SIG	DS/LS	ALS	SP	COMMENTS
Uggams, Leslie	1943-	5	10	15	15	"Roots," singer
Ulanova, Galma S.	1910-	20			40	Ballerina
Ullman, Tracey	1959-	10	20	25	30	"The Tracey Ullman Show"
Ullmann, Liv	1939-	5	10	25	30	"Persona," RS!
Umeki, Miyoshi	1929-	250	400	450	500	"Sayonara," "Flower Drum Song," "Courtship of Eddie's Father" TV show
Underwood, Blair	1964-	10	15	20	20	"L.A. Law"
Undset, Sigrid	1882-1949	80	160		260	Novelist
Updike, John	1932-	25	100	175	50	U.S. writer, responsive signer, "The Coup"
Urich, Robert	1946-	10	20	25	25	"Spenser: For Hire"
Uris, Leon	1924-	15	40	60	30	U.S. writer, "Exodus," RS
Ustinov, Peter	1921-	35	100	65	70	"Spartacus," "Topkapi"
Vaccaro, Brenda	1939-	5	10	10	12	"Midnight Cowboy," RS!
Vadim, Roger	1928-	15	25	30	35	Movie director
Valens, Ritchie		450			800	High school yearbook- $2,500-$3,000; "La Bamba," "Come On, Let's Go"; SA/CD-750
Valentine, Scott	1958-	5	10	10	10	"Family Ties"
Valentino, Rudolph	**1895-1926**	**800**	**2120**		**2100**	**Silent film legend, ESPV**
Valery, Paul	1871-1945	50	125	200	75	French poet, critic
Vallee, Rudy	1901-1986	20	40	40	40	"The Bachelor and the Bobby Soxer," singer
Valli, Alida	1921-	25	40	45	50	Italian actress, "The Third Man," signs "Valli"
Vallone, Raf	1917-	5	10	10	10	"A View from the Bridge"
Van Alstyne, Egbert	1882-1951	45	90	120	75	U.S., "Pretty Baby"
Van Ark, Joan	1943-	5	10	10	10	"Knots Landing"
Van Damme, Jean-Claude	1960-	25	130	215	60	"Kickboxer," FA
Van Devere, Trish	1945-	5	10	10	10	"The Day of the Dolphin"
Van Doren, Carl	1885-1950	20	45		40	Critic
Van Doren, Mamie	1933-	15	20	25	35	"Girls Town"
Van Dyke, Dick	1925-	10	20	25	25	"The Dick van Dyke Show"- TV, RS
Van Dyke, Jerry	1931-	5	10	15	20	"Coach"

NAME	DOB/DOD	SIG	DS/LS	ALS	SP	COMMENTS
Van Fleet, Jo	1919-	10	20	35	40	"East of Eden"
Van Halen		150			175	E. Van Halen (KS); 'Running With the Devil," "Dreams," "Panama"; SA/CD-200
Van Heusen, Jimmy	1913-1990	60	100	175	100	U.S., "Love and Marriage"
Van Patten, Dick	1928-	5	10	10	10	"Eight Is Enough," RS
Van Peebles, Mario	1957-	5	10	15	15	"Posse," s. of Melvin
Van Peebles, Melvin	1933-	5	10	15	15	Actor, writer, composer
Van, Bobby	1930-1980	20	40	55	40	Singer, dancer, TV actor, "Kiss Me, Kate"
Vance, Vivian	1913-1979	175	250		300	"I Love Lucy"
Varney, Jim	1949-	10	15	15	20	"Ernest Goes..."
Vaughan, Sarah	1924-1990	50	100	200	150	Singer
Vaughan, Stevie Ray		450			500	"Crossfire"; SA/CD-550
Vaughn, Robert	1932-	10	15	15	15	"The Man From U.N.C.L.E."- TV
Veidt, Conrad	1893-1943	100	150	150	300	"Casablanca"
Velez, Eddie	1958-	5	10	10	10	"Extremities"
Velez, Lupe	1908-1944	80	140	165	200	"Mexican Spitfire," Mexican actress
Velijohnson, Reginald	1952-	5	10	10	10	"Family Matters"
Velvet Underground, The		150			250	(1996), original lineup; "Sweet Jane," "Rock and Roll"; SA/CD-275
Vendela (Kirsebom)	1967-	10	20	20	30	Supermodel
Venuti, Joe	1904-1978	55	125		100	Pioneer jazz violinist
Vera, Ellen	1926-1981	25	40	40	50	"On the Town," "Three Little Words"
☆ **Verdi, Giuseppe**	**1813-1901**	**1275**	**2000**	**3640**		**Italian composer, AMQS-$8500, ESPV**
Verdon, Gwen	1925-	10	15	20	20	"Damn Yankees"
Verdy, Violette	1933-	10	25		25	Dancer
Vereen, Ben	1946-	5	15	20	20	"Roots"
Verne, Jules	1828-1905	200	700	1275		French novelist, "Twenty Thousand..."
Veruschka	1943-	5	10	15	25	"Blow Up," model
Viardot, Pauline	1821-1910	50	125	200	150	Opera: Mezzo-soprano
Vidal, Gore	1925-	25	40	75	30	U.S. writer, "Washington D.C."
Vider, King	1894-1982	45			100	Film director

NAME	DOB/DOD	SIG	DS/LS	ALS	SP	COMMENTS
Villa-Lobos, Heitor	1887-1959	125	250	650	250	Brazilian composer
Villella, Edward	1936-	15			30	Dancer
Vincent, Jan-Michael	1944-	5	10	15	15	"The Mechanic"
Vinson, Helen	1907-	15	25	35	40	"Torrid Zone," "Private Words"
Visconti, Luchino	1906-1976	35			50	Director
Voight, Jon	1938-	20	40	40	50	"Midnight Cowboy"
Voltaire (F.M. Arouet)	1694-1778	500	1725	3125		French writer, philosopher, "Candide," ESPV
Von Stade, Frederica	1945-	10	20		25	Mezza-soprano
Von Stroheim, Erich	1885-1957	165	350	450	500	"Sunset Boulevard," director
Von Sydow, Max	1929-	10	20	25	25	"The Exorcist"
von Tilzer, Albert	1878-1956	50	100	200	75	U.S., "Take Me Out to the Ball Game"
von Tilzer, Harry	1872-1946	40	100	150	60	U.S., "On a Sunday Afternoon"
Vonnegut, Jr., Kurt	1922-	25	125	150	60	U.S. writer, "Slapstick"- $215 (TS), RS
Waggoner, Lyle	1935-	5	10	10	10	"Wonder Woman"
Wagner, Jack	1959-	5	10	10	15	"General Hospital," "Melrose Place"
Wagner, Lindsay	1949-	10	15	20	20	"The Bionic Woman," FA
Wagner, Richard	**1813-1883**	**1950**	**3540**	**4575**		**German composer, "Rienzi," ESPV**
Wagner, Robert	1930-	15	20	25	30	"The Longest Day"
Wagoner, Dan	1932-	10	25		25	Dancer
Wahl, Ken	1956-	5	10	10	10	"Wiseguy"
Wajda, Andrzej	1926-	15			35	Film director
Walburn, Raymond	1887-1969	15	20	25	30	"The Laughing Lady"
Walcott, Derek	1930-	20	45		40	Poet, playwright, NP
Walken, Christopher	1943-	10	20	25	30	"The Deer Hunter"
Walker, Alice	1944-	25	60	80	50	U.S. writer, "The Color Purple"
Walker, Clint	1927-	5	10	10	15	"Cheyenne"
Walker, Helen	1920-1968	20	35	40	40	"Nightmare Alley," "Lucky Jordan"
Walker, Jimmie	1948-	5	10	10	10	"Good Times"
Walker, Robert	1918-1951	50	100	175	150	"Strangers on a Train"
Walker, T-Bone	1910-1975	50	125		100	Electric guitar pioneer

Henry Wells

Hank Williams

Walt Whitman

Hank Williams

Walt Whitman

Robin Williams

Walt Whitman

Thomas Wolfe

Walt Whitman

John Whittier

Virginia Woolf

Oscar Wilde

Brigham Young

NAME	DOB/DOD	SIG	DS/LS	ALS	SP	COMMENTS
Wallach, Eli	1915-	5	10	15	15	"The Good, the Bad and the Ugly"
Waller, Fats	1904-1943	150	300		450	U.S., "Honeysuckle Rose," ESPV
Waller, Robert James	1939-	15	30	50	25	U.S. writer, "The Bridges of Madison County"
Walsh, M. Emmet	1935-	5	10	15	15	"Blodd Simple," RS!
Walston, Ray	1917-	10	20	25	25	"My Favorite Martian"
Walter, Bruno	1876-1962	60	120			Conductor, ESPV
Walter, Jessica	1940-	5	10	10	15	"Play Misty for Me"
Walter, Tracey		10	15	15	20	"Batman"
Wambaugh, Joseph	1937-	15	25	45	20	U.S. writer, "The Onion Field," RS
Wanamaker, Sam	1919-	15	30	35	35	"Death on the Nile"
Wanger, Walter	1894-1968	40	130	125	125	Producer, "The Trail of the Lonesome Pine"
Ward, Burt	1946-	15	25	30	30	"Batman"
Ward, Fred	1942-	5	10	10	10	"Henry and June"
Ward, Rachel	1957-	10	20	25	30	"Against All Odds"
Ward, Sela	1956-	15	30	45	65	"Sisters"
Warden, Jack	1920-	5	10	15	20	"Crazy Like a Fox"
Warfield, Marsha	1955-	5	10	15	20	"Night Court"
Warfield, William	1920-	15	30		35	Bariton
Warner, David	1941-	5	10	10	10	"The Omen"
Warner, H.B.	1876-1958	35	50	75	75	"King of Kings," "Lost Horizon"
Warner, Julie	1965-	5	10	10	10	"Doc Hollywood"
Warner, Malcolm-Jamal	1970-	10	20	20	20	"The Cosby Show"
Warren, Harry	1893-1981	35	75	150	50	U.S., "We're in the Money"
Warren, Leonard	1911-1960	100	200	225	250	Opera: Baritone
Warren, Lesley Ann	1946-	5	10	15	20	"Mission: Impossible"
Warren, Robert Penn	1905-1989	35	125	150	70	U.S. poet, critic, "All the King's Men," RS
Warrick, Ruth	1915-	15	20	25	25	"Citizen Kane"
Warwick, Dionne	1940-	10			15	"I Say a Little Prayer," "Love Power"; SA/CD-20
Warwick, Robert	1878-1964	25	50	50	55	Silent era actor, "The Sea Hawk"
Washington, Denzel	1954-	25	145	150	65	"Malcolm X," FA

NAME	DOB/DOD	SIG	DS/LS	ALS	SP	COMMENTS
Washington, Dinah	1924-1963	140	200		225	Singer
Wasserstein, Wendy	1950-	15	25	35	20	U.S. writer, "The Heidi Chronicles"
Waters, Ethel	1896-1977	50	135	175	175	Jazz and blues singer
Waters, John	1946-	10	20	20	25	"Hairspray," director, writer
Waters, Muddy	1915-1983	200			400	(1987); "I Can't Be Satisfied"; SA/CD-450
Waterson, Sam	1940-	10	15	15	20	"The Killing Fields"
Watson, "Tex"		35			50	Manson family member
Watson, Johnny	1935-1996	25	50	125	60	Guitarist (R&B)
Watts, Andre	1946-	10	25		25	Pianist
Waugh, Evelyn	1903-1966	50	225	300	65	British novelist, "The Loved One"
Waxman, Al	1934-	5	10	10	10	"Cagney and Lacey"
Wayans, Damon	1961-	10	25	25	25	"In Living Color"
Wayne, David	1914-	5	10	15	20	"The American Way"
Wayne, John ☆	**1907-1979**	**425**	**950**	**800**	**725**	**Screen legend, "True Grit," FA, SDS-2X**
Wayne, Patrick	1939-	5	10	10	15	"McClintock"
Weathers, Carl	1948-	10	15	20	20	"Rocky"
Weaver, Dennis	1925-	5	10	15	20	"McCloud"
Weaver, Fritz	1926-	5	10	10	10	"Marathon Man"
Weaver, Sigourney	1949-	15	30	40	50	"Alien," "Ghostbusters"
Webb, Clifton	1891-1966	35	50	60	70	"The Razor's Edge"
Webb, Jack	1920-1982	50	105	150	130	"Dragnet," FA
Webb, Jimmy	1946-	25	50	100	50	U.S., "Up, Up and Away"
Webber, Andrew Lloyd	1948-	100	250	425	235	Composer, prod., The Phantom of the Opera," ESPV, elusive signer
Weber, Karl Maria von	1786-1826	325	1015	1100		German composer
Webster, Ben	1909-1973	140			250	Tenor sax player
Webster, Paul F.	1907-1984	25	50	75	50	U.S. lyricist, "Secret Love"
Weidler, Virginia	1927-1967	25	40	40	50	"The Philadelphia Story," died at age 40
Weill, Kurt	1900-1950	250	700	1150	400	German/U.S., "Threepenny Opera"
Weir, Peter	1944-	15	30		30	Film director

NAME	DOB/DOD	SIG	DS/LS	ALS	SP	COMMENTS
Weissmuller, Johnny	1904-1984	150	260		280	Swimmer, "Tarzan," SP- $265, SDS- $500
Weitz, Bruce	1943-	5	10	10	15	"Hill Street Blues"
Welch, Raquel (Raquel Tejada)	1940-	10	25	25	50	"One Million Years B.C."
Weld, Tuesday	1943-	10	15	20	25	"Looking for Mr. Goodbar"
Welland, Colin	1934-	15	30		35	Actor, playwright
Weller, Paul	1947-	5	10	10	15	"Robocop"
Welles, Orson	1915-1985	100	500	350	300	"Citizen Kane," SP- $325
Wellman, William	1896-1975	40	75	75	80	"Men With Wings," " "The High and the Mighty"
Wells, H.G.	1866-1946	160	350	550	800	British novelist, "The Invisible Man"
Wells, Kitty		10	20		20	Country Music Hall of Fame
Wells, Mary	1943-1992	25			35	(1943-1992); "My Guy," "Two Lovers"; SA/CD-45
Welty, Eudora	1909-	40	125	200	75	U.S. writer, "The Ponder Heart"
Wenders, Wim	1945-	10	20		25	Film director
Wendt, George	1948-	10	20	25	30	"Cheers"
Wenrich, Percy	1887-1952	60	125	320	130	U.S., "Moonlight Bay"
West, Adam	1929-	10	25	30	30	"Batman"
West, Mae	1892-1980	75	150	300	250	"My Little Chickadee," FA
West, Morris	1916-	20	40		40	Novelist
West, Rebecca	1892-1983	20	50	100	35	British novelist, "Black Lamb and Grey Falcon"
Westbrook, Mike	1936-	15			35	Jazz composer
Westheimer, Ruth	1928-	5	10	15	10	"Ask Dr. Ruth"
Westley, Helen	1875-1942	50	125	175	100	Character actor, "Dimples," "Heidi"
Whalen, Michael	1902-1974	20	35	35	40	"Ten Little Indians," "Country Doctor"
Whaley, Frank	1963-	10	15	15	15	"The Doors"
Whalley, Joanne	1964-	5	10	10	12	"Willow"
Wharton, Edith	1862-1937	215	500	1350		U.S. novelist, "Ethan Frome"
Wheeler, Bert	1895-1968	30	60	100	75	"Ziegfeld" star, comedy team member
Whelan, Arleen	1915-1993	12	25	25	25	"Kidnapped," "Dear Wife"
Whelchel, Lisa	1963-	5	10	10	10	"The Facts of Life"
Whitaker, Forest	1961-	5	10	10	10	"The Crying Game"

NAME	DOB/DOD	SIG	DS/LS	ALS	SP	COMMENTS
Whitaker, Johnny	1959-	5	10	10	15	"Family Affair"
White, Betty	1922-	10	15	20	25	"The Golden Girls"
White, E.B.	1899-1985	35	125	265	75	U.S. essayist, novelist, "Charlotte's Web"
White, Jaleel	1976-	5	10	10	10	"Family Matters"
White, Jesse	1918-	15	20	20	25	Maytag repair man, "Harvey"
White, Pearl	1889-1938	100	200	300	260	Film actress
White, Vanna	1957-	5	10	10	15	"Wheel of Fortune"
Whitelaw, Billie	1932-	10	15	15	20	"Charlie Bubbles"
Whiteman, Paul	1890-1967	70	150		300	Orchestra leader
Whiting, Richard A.	1891-1938	50	100	150	100	U.S., "Beyond the Blue Horizon"
Whitman, Stuart	1926-	5	10	10	15	"The Mark," "Cimarron Strip"-TV
☆ **Whitman, Walt**	**1819-1892**	**1000**	**2750**	**3075**	**3250**	**U.S. poet, "Leaves of Grass," ESPV**
Whitmore, James	1921-	10	15	15	20	"Battleground"
Whitney, Eleanor	1917-	5	10	10	15	"Millions in the Air"
Whittier, John Greenleaf	1807-1892	85	300	450		U.S. poet, "Snow-Bound"
Whitty, Dame May	1865-1948	40	60	75	80	"Night Must Fall"
Who, The		600			1000	(1990), K. Moon (KS)- $200-$250; "My Generation," "Pinball Wizard"; SA/CD-1250
Whorf, Richard	1906-1966	20	35	40	40	"Yankee Doddle Dandy," TV actor
Wideman, John Edgar	1941-	10	20	30	20	U.S. writer, "Sent For You Yesterday," RS
Widmark, Richard	1914-	10	25	25	25	"Kiss of Death," "The Alamo"
Wiest, Dianne	1948-	10	20	25	35	"Hannah and Her Sisters"
Wilbur, Crane	1889-1973	30	50	60	75	"The Perils of Pauline," "House of Wax"
Wilbur, Richard	1921-	10	20		20	Poet
Wilcox, Larry	1947-	5	10	10	10	"CHiPS"
Wilcoxon, Henry	1905-1984	25	35	40	50	"Cleopatra," associate producer
Wilde, Cornel	1915-1989	20	30	35	40	"A Song To Remember"
☆ **Wilde, Oscar**	**1854-1900**	**850**	**1700**		**2750**	**Irish novelist, playwright, ESPV**
Wilder, Billy	1906-	25	50		50	Film maker
Wilder, Gene	1935-	10	25	40	25	"Young Frankenstein"

NAME	DOB/DOD	SIG	DS/LS	ALS	SP	COMMENTS
Wilder, Thornton	1897-1975	75	185	435	225	U.S. playwright, "Our Town," responsive sig.
Williams, Barry	1954-	5	10	10	12	"The Brady Bunch"
Williams, Billy Dee	1937-	10	20	25	25	"Lady Sings the Blues"
Williams, Cindy	1947-	5	10	15	15	"Laverne & Shirley"
Williams, Clarence III	1939-	5	10	10	12	"The Mod Squad"
Williams, Emlyn	1905-1067	25	50		50	Playwright
Williams, Esther	1923-	10	20	25	25	"Bathing Beauty"
Williams, Hank	1923-1953	700	1500		1500	Country legend, "Cold Cold Heart," scarce, ESPV-SP
Williams, Jobeth	1953-	10	15	15	20	"The Big Chill"
Williams, John	1932-	25	50	100	50	U.S., "Star Wars" series, movie soundtracks
Williams, Montel	1956-	5	10	15	15	"The Montel Williams Show"
Williams, Rhys	1892-1969	25	45	40	45	Charcter actor, The Bells of St. Mary"
Williams, Robin	1952-	25	225	250	65	"Mork and Mindy," RS
Williams, Tennessee	1911-1983	175	365	585	300	U.S. playwright, "Cat on a Hot Tin Roof," TMS- $550
Williams, Treat	1951-	5	10	15	15	"Prince of the City"
Williams, Vanessa	1963-	20	40	50	50	"Kiss of the Spider Woman," singer
Williams, William Carlos	1883-1963	250	350	425	300	U.S. poet
Williamson, Nicol	1938-	5	10	10	15	"Excalibur"
Willis, Bruce	1955-	55	150		85	"Die Hard," FA, elusive signer
Wills, Chill	1903-1978	60	75	85	100	"The Alamo," voice of mule "Francis"
Wilson, August (Frederick Kittel)	1945-	10	20	20	25	Playwright, "The Piano Lesson"
Wilson, Colin	1931-	15	30		25	Novelist
Wilson, Demond	1946-	10	15	20	25	"Sanford and Son"
Wilson, Don		10	15	15	15	radio/TV announcer for Jack Benny Show
Wilson, Edmund	1895-1972	30	100	160	65	U.S. critic, novelist
Wilson, Flip	1933-	20	40		40	"The Flip Wilson Show," FA, RS
Wilson, Jackie		275			500	(1987), (1934-1984), prices can vary sign; "That's Why," "Lonely Teardrops"; SA/CD-525
Wilson, Lanford	1937-	15	25	40	20	U.S. writer, "Angels Fall"

NAME	DOB/DOD	SIG	DS/LS	ALS	SP	COMMENTS
Wilson, Marie	1916-1972	20	40	50	65	"Boy Meets Girl"
Wilson, Meredith	1902-1984	30	60	100	70	U.S., "The Music Man"
Wilson, Teddy	1912-1986	50	100	125	100	Composer, piano player
Winchell, Paul	1922-	15	30	35	40	"The Paul Winchell... Show," ventriloquist
Windom, William	1923-	5	10	15	15	"Murder She Wrote"
Windsor, Claire	1897-1972	15	20	25	25	"Rich Men's Wives," "Money Talks"
Windsor, Marie	1922-	5	10	15	20	"B" movie star, "Force of Evil"
Winfield, Paul	1940-	5	10	15	15	"Sounder"
Winfrey, Oprah	1954-	20	50	100	50	"The Oprah Winfrey Show," FA
Wing, Toby	1915-	10	20	25	30	Singer, dancer, "42nd Street"
Winger, Debra	1955-	15	100	30	35	"Terms of Endearment"
Winkler, Henry	1945-	5	10	20	25	"Happy Days," FA
Winnder, Michael	1935-	10	25		20	Film producer
Winninger, Charles	1884-1969	35	70	60	70	"Show Boat," "Destry Rides Again"
Winningham, Mare	1959-	5	10	20	30	"St. Elmo's Fire," RS!
Winslet, Kate	1975-	55	250		125	"Titanic," FA, very elusive signer!
Winters, Jonathan	1925-	5	10	10	15	"The Jonathan Winters Show"
Winters, Shelley	1922-	10	25	25	25	"The Diary of Ann Frank"
Winwood, Estelle	1883-1984	20	40	40	50	British stage actor, "The Swan"
Withers, Jane	1926-	10	15	20	25	Actress, "Handle With Care"
Wodehouse, P.G.	1881-1975	150	225	325	400	British/U.S. humorist
Wogan, Terry	1938-	15	30		30	Broadcaster
Wolf, Hugo P.J.	1860-1903	275				Austrian composer, scarce
Wolf, Scott	1968-	15	30	40	40	"Party of Five"
☆ **Wolfe, Thomas**	**1900-1938**	**450**	**2250**			**U.S. novelist, scarce, ESPV**
Wolfe, Tom	1931-	20	45	100	40	U.S. writer, "The Right Stuff"
Wolff, Tobias	1945-	10	20	30	15	U.S. writer, "The Barracks Thief"
Wolley, Monty	1888-1963	75	150	175	165	"The Pied Piper," teacher
Wonder, Stevie	1950-	200				(1989), Has used thumbprint signature! "You Are the Sunshine of My Life," ESPV
Wong, Anna May	1907-1961	100	175	175	225	"The Shanghai Express"

NAME	DOB/DOD	SIG	DS/LS	ALS	SP	COMMENTS
Wong, B.D.	1962-	5	10	10	12	"M. Butterfly"
Wood, Elijah	1981-	10	20	25	30	"The War"
Wood, Natalie	1938-1991	125	525		560	"Miracle on 34th Street," RS
Woodard, Alfre	1953-	5	10	10	10	"Cross Creek"
Woods, James	1947-	15	25	35	50	"Ghosts of Mississippi"
Woodward, Edward	1930-	10	15	15	15	"The Equalizer"
Woodward, Joanne	1930-	20	75	70	35	"The Three Faces of Eve," m. Paul Newman
Woolf, Virginia	1882-1941	350	1500	2000		British novelist, "The Waves," ESPV, scarce
Woolley, Monty	1888-1963	30	45	45	50	Charcter actor, "The Man Who Came to ..."
Woollsey, Robert	1889-1938	35	50	50	70	"Rio Rita"- stage, "High Flyers"
Wordsworth, William	1770-1850	230	1225	1720		British poet
Worley, Jo Anne	1937-	5	10	10	10	"Laugh-In"
Worth, Irene	1916-	15	30		30	Actress
Wouk, Herman	1915-	25	100	150	100	U.S. writer, "The Caine Mutiny"
Wray, Fay	1907-	30	60	125	65	"King Kong"
Wright, Max	1943-	5	10	10	10	"ALF"
Wright, Richard	1908-1960	75	200		280	Novelist, short-story writer, ESPV
Wright, Steven	1955-	5	10	10	15	Comedian
Wright, Teresa	1918-	25	50	75	65	"The Pride of the Yankees," "Mrs. Miniver"
Wuhl, Robert	1951-	5	10	10	15	"Bull Durham"
Wyatt, Jane	1911-	5	10	15	15	"Lost Horizon"
Wycherly, Margaret	1881-1956	30	50	60	60	"White Heat," stage actress
Wyle, Noah	1971-	20	40	40	45	"ER"
Wyler, William	1902-1981	25	45		65	Film director, RS
Wyman, Jane	1914-	20			55	"Johnny Belinda," SB, "The Yearling"- $45
Wynn, Ed	1886-1966	75	125		150	"The Diary of Anne Frank," comedian
Wynn, Keenan	1916-1986	20	30	40	40	"Kiss Me Kate," s. of Ed Wynn
Wynter, Dana	1930-	10	15	15	15	"Invasion of the Body Snatchers"
Yardbirds, The		200			275	(1992), values vary by lineup; "For Your Love"; SA/CD-300

NAME	DOB/DOD	SIG	DS/LS	ALS	SP	COMMENTS
Yeats, William Butler	1865-1939	225	725	800		Irish poet, playwright
Yellen, Jack	1892-1991	15	35	50	30	U.S. lyricist, "Happy Days Are Here Again"
Yes		150			250	Values for original lineup or (8/71-7/72) group; "Roundabout," "Owner of a Lonely Heart"; SA/CD-300
York, Michael	1942-	10	15	20	20	"Logan's Run," illegible signature!
Youmans, Vincent	1898-1946	60	150	275	150	U.S., "No, No, Nanette"
Young Rascals, The/The Rascals		45			100	(1997), F. Cavaliere (KS); "Good Lovin'," "Groovin'"; SA/CD-125
Young, Carlton	1907-1971	15	25	25	25	"Wyatt Earp"- TV
Young, Clara Kimball	1890-1960	50	100	150	85	"Camille," "Trilby"
Young, Gig	1913-1978	35	65	125	75	"They Shoot Horses, Don't They?"
Young, Lester "Pres"	1909-1959	90		160	175	Composer, tenor sax player
Young, Loretta	1913-	30	60	100	65	"The Farmer's Daughter"
Young, Neil	1945-	40			75	(1995); "Down by the River," "Heart of Gold"; SA/CD-100
Young, Robert	1907-1998	25	40	65	50	"Marcus Welby, M.D."
Young, Roland	1887-1953	20	40	45	50	"Topper"
Young, Sean	1959-	5	10	10	10	"No Way Out," RS
Younger, Bob		2650				American desperado, ESPV, scarce
Younger, Cole	1844-1916	2250				American desperado, ESPV, scarce
Younger, James		2500				American desperado, ESPV, scarce
Youngman, Henny	1906-1998	10	20	25	30	Actor, comedian
Yurka, Blanche	1887-1974	30	50	75	55	"A Night to Remember," opera singer
Zadora, Pia	1956-	5	10	15	20	"Naked Gun 33 1/3"
Zal, Roxana	1969-	5	10	10	15	"Something About Amelia"
Zanuck, Darryl F.	1902-1979	60	275	500	100	Producer, "The Grapes of Wrath"
Zappa, Frank/The Mothers of Invention	1944-1993	150			225	(1995), (1940-1993); "Dancin' Fool"; SA/CD-300
Zellweger, Renee	1969-	20	50	65	75	"Jerry Maguire"
Zemeckis, Robert	1951-	10	25	30	30	"Forrest Gump"
Ziering, Ian	1964-	15	30	30	30	"Beverly Hills 90210"
Zimbalist, Efrem	1889-1985	50	100	150	125	Violinist, composer

NAME	DOB/DOD	SIG	DS/LS	ALS	SP	COMMENTS
Zimbalist, Efrem, Jr.	1923-	10	15	20	25	"77 Sunset Strip"- TV, "The F.B.I."- TV
Zimbalist, Stephanie	1956-	10	20	25	25	"Remington Steele"
Zmed, Adrian	1954-	5	10	15	15	"T.J. Hooker"
Zola, Emile	1840-1902	175	425	675		French novelist, "Nana"
Zorina, Vera	1917-	20	35	35	45	"Follow the Boys," opera director
Zuckerman, Pinchas	1948-	15	3-		35	Violinist
Zukor, Adolph	1873-1976	75	155	220	165	Pioneer movie executive
Zuniga, Daphne	1962-	15	30	45	55	"Melrose Place," FA
ZZ Top		60			100	Very RSs; "Legs," "Sleeping Bag," "Velcro Fly"; SA/CD-125

ENT CELEB Z

Sports

They've kicked, slammed, pounded, scored, and soared to the top of their games. They've drawn us in, made fans of us, and we can't get enough of them — the professional athletes. Their talent and personalities have propelled them to superstar status, and there's nothing quite like a ball or puck signed by a favorite athlete to take us back to that final, winning point. Celebrities in their own right, sports stars have become one of the hottest autograph collecting areas.

Sports Guide

NAME	SPORT	SIG	SP	S.MEMO/MISC.	COMMENTS
☆ **Aaron, Hank**	**base**	**15**	**25**	SB-50, Sbat-200	**HOF 1982, Canc. check-35, Gold HOF s. post.-30, Perez-Steele s. post.-30, FA**
Abel, Sid	hock	5	15	Spuck-30	HOF 1969
Adams, Jack	hock	100	250		HOF 1959, d. 1968
Adderley, Herb	foot	5	15	SB-75, Mhelm-50	HOF 1980, RS
Agassi, Andre	tennis	10	30	TB-40	FA
Aikman, Troy	foot	25	45	FB-200	FA
Alexander, Grover Cleveland	base	350	725	SB-3500	HOF 1938, FA, d. 1950, b&w HOF s. post.-1500
☆ **Ali, Muhammad, 1942-**	**box**	**25**	**60**	**SG-155**	**USA, H, "Cassius Clay," sig. variations, FA**
Alston, Walter	base	40	100	SB-850	HOF 1983, Canc. check-75, Gold HOF s. post.-150 (scarce), RS, d. 1984
Alworth, Lance	foot	10	20	SB-100, Mhelm-50	HOF 1978, elusive signer
Ambers, Lou, 1913-1995	box	12	40	SG-130	USA, L, was responsive to requests
Ameche, Alan	foot	50	150		d. 1988
Andretti, Mario	auto	10	20		Auto Racing, RS
Angott, Sammy, 1915-1980	box	65	150	SG-600	USA, L
Anson, Cap	base	1500		S. doc.-3000, SB-AA	HOF 1939, FA, d. 1922
Aparicio, Luis	base	10	20	SB-25, Sbat-75	HOF 1984, Gold HOF s. post.-15, Perez-Steele s. post.-15
Appling, Luke	base	5	25	SB-75	HOF 1964, Gold HOF s. post.-20, Perez-Steele s. post-50, shaky sig. later in life, RS, d. 1991
Apps, Sr., Syl	hock	15	35	Spuck-50	HOF 1961
Arcel, Ray, 1899-1994	box	12	25	SG-125	USA, trainer, RS
Archibald, Nate	bask	5	15	SB-100	HOF 1991, RS
Arguello, Alexis, 1952-	box	7	15	SG-65	Nicaragua, L, F, SF, RS
Arizin, Paul	bask	10	20	SB-125	HOF 1977, RS
Armstrong, George	hock	15	35	Spuck-50	HOF 1975
Armstrong, Henry, 1912-1988	box	80	175	SG-750	USA, W, L, F, RS
Ashburn, Richie	base	10	20	SB-30, Sbat-75	HOF 1995, Canc. check-30, Gold HOF s. post.-20, Perez-Steele s. post.-30, RS, d. 1997
☆ **Ashe, Arthur, 1943-1993**	**tennis**	**25**	**75**	**TB-100**	
Atkins, Doug	foot	5	15	SB-125, Mhelm-50	HOF 1982, Canc. check-20, RS
Attell, Abe, 1884-1970	box	115	175	SG-700	USA, F, was responsive to requests

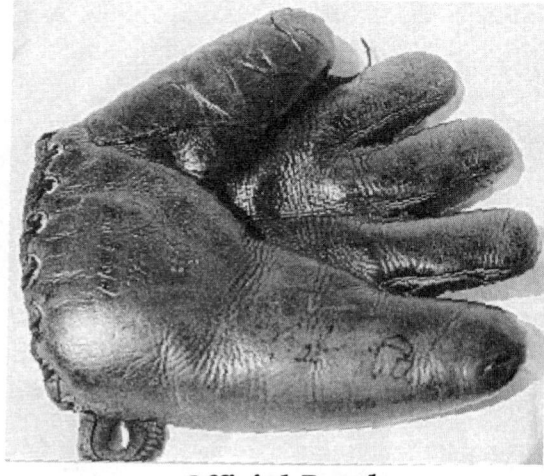

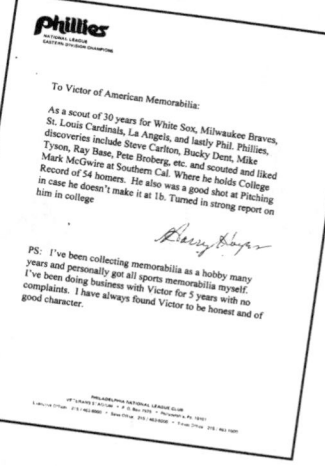

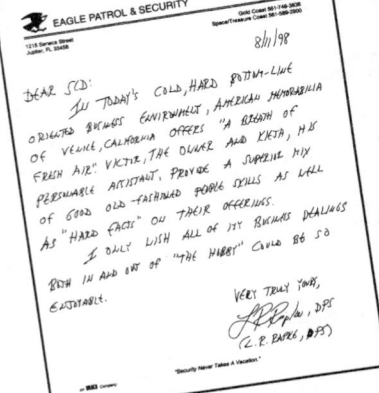

NAME	SPORT	SIG	SP	S.MEMO/MISC.	COMMENTS
Averill, Earl	base	15	75	SB-400	HOF 1975, Gold HOF s. post.-30, RS, shaky sig. later in life, d. 1983
Badgro, Red	foot	10	20	SB-75, Mhelm-50	HOF 1982, d. 1998
Baer, Max, 1909-1959	box	110	300	SG-1250	USA, H, was responsive to requests
Bailey, Ace	hock	50	125	Spuck-200	HOF 1975, d. 1992
Bain, Dan	hock	100	200		HOF 1945, d. 1962
Baker, Frank	base	200	600	SB-3625, b&w HOF s. post.-1250	HOF 1955, d. 1963
Baker, Hobey	hock	350			HOF 1945, d. 1918
Bancroft, Dave	base	150	300	SB-3500	HOF 1971, Gold HOF s. post.-625, RS, d. 1972
Banks, Ernie	base	10	20	SB-35, Sbat-175	HOF 1977, Canc. check-50, Gold HOF s. post.-20, Perez-Steele s. post.-30
Barber, Bill	hock	5	15	Spuck-20	HOF 1990
Barkley, Charles	bask	25	45	BB-225	
Barlick, Al	base	10	25	SB-55	HOF 1989, Canc. check-30, Gold HOF s. post.-15, Perez-Steele s. post.-15, d. 1995, RS
Barney, Lem	foot	5	15	SB-75, Mhelm-50	HOF 1992, RS
Barrow, Ed	base	75	250	SB-3500	HOF 1953, Canc. check-150, common on contracts, d. 1953
Barry, Marty	hock	75	200		HOF 1965, d. 1969
Barry, Rick	bask	10	20	SB-125	HOF 1987, RS
Basilio, Carmen, 1927-	box	5	12	SG-60	USA, W, M, RS
Bathgate, Andy	hock	5	15	Spuck-20	HOF 1978
Battles, Cliff	foot	80	200	SB-375	HOF 1968, d. 1981
Bauer, Bobby	hock	100	250		HOF 1996, d. 1964
Baugh, Sammy	foot	25	75	SB-300, Mhelm-100	HOF 1963
Baylor, Elgin	bask	10	20	SB-125	HOF 1976, RS
Beckley, Jake	base	1500		S. doc.-3500, SB-AA	HOF 1971, FA, d. 1918, scarce
Bednarik, Chuck	foot	10	20	SB-125, SGLA-30, Mhelm-50	HOF 1967, Canc. check-15, RS
Beliveau, Jean	hock	10	20	Spuck-30	HOF 1972
Bell, Bert	foot	100	400		HOF 1963, d. 1959
Bell, Bobby	foot	5	15	SB-75, SGLA-20, Mhelm-50	HOF 1983
Bell, Cool Papa	base	25	65	SB-300	HOF 1974, Gold HOF s. post.-35, Perez-Steele s. post.-75, RS, FA-SB, ESPV, d. 1991
Bellamy, Walt	bask	5	15	SB-100	HOF 1993, can be elusive
Belov, Sergei	bask	8	15	SB-100	HOF, d. 1992
Bench, Johnny	base	10	25	SB-40, Sbat-175	HOF 1989, Perez-Steele s. post.-30, Gold HOF s. post.-25, reluctant signer

NAME	SPORT	SIG	SP	S.MEMO/MISC.	COMMENTS
Bender, Chief	base	150	350	SB-3750	HOF 1953, Canc. check-750, d. 1954
Benedict, Clint	hock	50	150		HOF 1965, d. 1976
Benitez, Wilfred	box	10	20	SG-90	USA, JW, W, RS
Bentley, Doug	hock	50	175		HOF 1964, d. 1972
Bentley, Max	hock	30	125		HOF 1966, d. 1984
Benvenuti, Nino, 1938-	box	15	60	SG-250	Italy, JM, M, often elusive
Berg, Jackie "Kid", 1909-1991	box	30	65	SG-275	England, JW
Berg, Moe	base	350	100	SB-1250, ALS-$295	d. 1972
Berra, Yogi	base	8	20	Gold HOF s. post.-20, SB-50, Sbat-150	HOF 1972, Gold HOF s. post.-20, Perez-Steele s. post.-25
Berry, Raymond	foot	5	15	SB-100, SGLA-20, Mhelm-50	HOF 1973, RS
Bidwill, Charles	foot	250	600	SB-AA	HOF 1967, owner & pres. Cardinals, d. 1947
Biletnikoff, Fred	foot	5	15	SB-100, SGLA-15, Mhelm-60	HOF 1988
Bing, Dave	bask	10	20	SB-100	HOF 1990
Bird, Larry	bask	15	50	SB-175	HOF 1998, FA
Blackburn, Jack, 1883-1942	box	100	250		USA, trainer, "Chappie"
Blake, Toe	hock	25	100	Spuck-150	HOF 1966, d. 1995
Blanda, George	foot	5	15	SB-125, Mhelm-60	HOF 1981
Blazejowski, Carol	bask	5	15		HOF 1994
Bledsoe, Drew	foot	20	35	FB-175	
Blount, Mel	foot	5	15	SB-75, Mhelm-60	HOF 1989
Bobek, Nicole	skate	10	25		U.S. Figure Skating
Boitano, Brian	skate	10	25		U.S. Figure Skating, RS
Boivin, Leo	hock	5	15	Spuck-25	HOF 1986
Boon, Dickie	hock	100			HOF 1952, d. 1961
Borg, Bjorn	tennis	10	30	TB-40	
Bossy, Mike	hock	5	15	Spuck-25	HOF 1991
Bottomley, Jim	base	200	400	SB-3500	HOF 1974, d. 1959
Bouchard, Butch	hock	20	35	Spuck-75	HOF 1966
Boucher, Frank	hock	100	250		HOF 1958, d. 1977
Boucher, George	hock	50	150		HOF 1960, d. 1960
Boudreau, Lou	base	5	12	SB-20, Sbat-50	HOF 1970, Canc. check-40, Gold HOF s. post.-10, Perez-Steele s. post.-25, RS
Bower, Dubbie	hock	125			HOF 1945, d. 1959
Bower, Johnny	hock	5	15	Spuck-25	HOF 1976
Bowman, Christopher	skate	15	30		U.S. Figure Skating
Boyer, Ken	base	35	75	SB-300	d. 1982
Bradley, Bill	bask	15	40	SB-200	HOF, FA

NAME	SPORT	SIG	SP	S.MEMO/MISC.	COMMENTS
Bradshaw, Terry	foot	10	30	SB-175, Mhelm-100	HOF 1989
Brenner, Teddy, 1917-	box	5	10	SG-45	USA, matchmaker
Bresnahan, Roger	base	400		SB-7500, s. doc.-1500	HOF 1945, d. 1944
Brett, George	base	15	30	SB-50, Sbat-150	HOF 1999, FA
Brimsek, Frank	hock	10	30	Spuck-50	HOF 1966
Britton, Jack, 1885-1962	box	80	160	SG-600	USA, W
Broadbent, Punch	hock	100	200		HOF 1962, d. 1971
Brock, Lou	base	5	20	SB-30, Sbat-75	HOF 1985, Perez-Steele s. post.-15, Gold HOF s. post.-15
Broda, Turk	hock	100	200		HOF 1967, d. 1972
Brouthers, Dan, 1858-1932	base		1650	S. doc.-3275, SB-AA	HOF 1945, FA
Brown, Jim	foot	10	30	SB-200, Mhelm-100	HOF 1971
Brown, Joe	box	10	20	SG-65	USA, L
Brown, Mordecai	base	300	1150	SB-425	HOF 1949, Canc. check-750, d. 1948
Brown, Panama Al, 1902-1951	box	125	280		Panama, B
Brown, Paul	foot	25	50	SB-300	HOF 1967, d. 1991
Brown, Roosevelt	foot	5	15	SB-100, Mhelm-50	HOF 1975
Brown, Willie	foot	5	15	SB-75, Mhelm-50	HOF 1984, Canc. check-15
Buchanan, Buck	foot	20	50	SB-250	HOF 1990, d. 1992
Bucyk, John	hock	10	20	Spuck-30	HOF 1981
Bunning, Jim	base	10	20	SB-30, Sbat-50	HOF 1996, Gold HOF s. post.-15, FA
Burch, Billy	hock	100	250		HOF 1974, d. 1950
Burkett, Jesse	base	500	1200	SB-4525, b&w HOF s. post.-1500	HOF 1946, d. 1953
Burley, Charley, 1917-1992	box	20	40	SG-150	USA, M, RS
Burns, Tommy, 1881-1955	box	275	750	SG-2500	Canada, H
Butkus, Dick	foot	10	20	SB-125, Mhelm-75	HOF 1979
Cameron, Harry	hock	125	340		HOF 1962, d. 1953
Campanella, Roy	base	300	750	SB-3500	HOF 1969, d. 1993, significant signature variations, FA
Campbell, Earl	foot	5	15	SB-125, Mhelm-60	HOF 1991, RS
Canadeo, Tony	foot	5	15	Mhelm-50, Canc. check-20	HOF 1974
Canto, Miguel, 1949-	box	10	20	SG-60	Mexico, FL
Canzoneri, Tony, 1908-1959	box	65	130	SG-600	USA, F, L, JW, was responsive to requests
Carew, Rod	base	10	20	SB-40, Sbat-150	HOF 1991, Perez-Steele s. post.-25, Gold HOF s. post.-20, RS
Carey, Max	base	25	125	SB-500, b&w HOF s. post.-75	HOF 1961, Canc. check-75, Gold HOF s. post.-60 , d. 1976

NAME	SPORT	SIG	SP	S.MEMO/MISC.	COMMENTS
Carlton, Steve	base	10	25	SB-30, Sbat-75	HOF 1994, Perez-Steele s. post.-35, Gold HOF s. post.-20
Carpentier, Georges, 1894-1975	box	115	225	SG-1000	France, LH, was responsive to requests
Carr, Joe	foot	250		SS-440	HOF 1963, d. 1939
Cartwright, Alexander	base	750		S. doc.-2500	HOF 1938, d. 1892, ESPV
Cash, Norm, 1934-1986	base	40	30	SB-325	
Cerdan, Marcel, 1916-1949	box	300	775	SG-3225	Algeria, M, scarce signature
Cervantes, Antonio, 1945-	box	12	25	SG-65	Columbia, JW
Chadwick, Henry	base	1500		S. doc.-3500	HOF 1938, d. 1908, FA
Chamberlain, Wilt	bask	30	75	SB-250	HOF 1978
Chamberlin, Guy	foot	50	150		HOF 1965, d. 1967
Chance, Frank	base	600		SB-6250, s. doc.-2000	HOF 1946, d. 1924
Chandler, Happy	base	15	30	SB-100	HOF 1982, Canc. check-125, Gold HOF s. post.-20, Perez-Steele s. post.-25, d. 1991
Charles, Ezzard, 1921-1975	box	115	240	SG-975	USA, H
Charleston, Oscar	base	1000		SB-AA, s. doc.-3000	HOF 1976, d. 1954
Cheevers, Gerry	hock	5	15	Spuck-25	HOF 1985
Chesbro, Jack	base	1250		S. doc.-3250	HOF 1946, FA, d. 1931
Chocolate, Kid, 1910-1988	box	70	150	SG-600	Cuba, JL, F
Christiansen, Jack	foot	50	150		HOF 1970, d. 1986
Cicotte, Eddie	base	350			d. 1969
Clancy, Gil, 1922-	box	5	10	SG-45	USA, trainer, manager, RS
Clancy, King	hock	50	100	Spuck-175	HOF 1958, d. 1986
Clapper, Dit	hock	50	150		HOF 1947, d. 1978
Clark, Dutch	foot	50	175		HOF 1963, d. 1978
Clarke, Bobby	hock	5	15	Spuck-25	HOF 1987
Clarke, Fred	base	150	400	SB-3000, b&w HOF s. post.-650	HOF 1945, d. 1960
Clarkson, John	base	1500		S. doc.-3500	HOF 1963, FA
Cleghorn, Sprague	hock	150	300		HOF 1987, d. 1956
Clemens, Roger	base	25	35	SB-50	
Clemente, Roberto	base	250	700	SB-4000	HOF 1973, Canc. check-1200, d. 1972
☆ **Cobb, Ty**	**base**	**300**	**2150**	**SB-7200, b&w HOF s. post.-1500**	**HOF 1936, Canc. check-625, FA, LS-$2000, ALS-$1500, $1700, ESPV, d. 1961**
Cochrane, Mickey	base	75	400	SB-5750, b&w HOF s. post.-350	HOF 1947, Canc. check-200, d. 1962
Coffroth, James W., 1872-1943	box	80	150		USA, promoter
Colavito, Rocky	base	10	20	SB-50	Canc. check-25

NAME	SPORT	SIG	SP	S.MEMO/MISC.	COMMENTS
Collins, Eddie,	base	100	500	SB-3500, b&w HOF s. post.-1200	HOF 1939, signed numerous contracts, d. 1951
Collins, Jimmie	base	800	2000	SB-6250	HOF 1945, d. 1943, FA
Colville, Neil	hock	40	100		HOF 1967
Combs, Earle	base	30	250	SB-1785	HOF 1970, Canc. check-10, Gold HOF s. post.-75, d. 1976
Comiskey, Charles	base	450	1200	SB-6000	HOF 1939, d. 1931, ESPV
Conacher, Charlie	hock	75	200		HOF 1961
Conigliaro, Tony	base	75	175	SB-600	d. 1990
Conlan, Jocko	base	15	35	SB-150	HOF 1974, Gold HOF s. post.-15, Perez-Steele s. post.-50, d. 1989
Conn, Billy, 1917-1993	box	25	65	SG-275	USA, LH, RS
Connelly, Tom	base	350	750	SB-3500, b&w HOF s. post.-1500	HOF 1953
Conners, Jimmy	tennis	10	30	TB-40	
Connor, George	foot	5	15	SB-75	HOF 1975
Connor, Roger	base	1000		SB-7500, s. doc.-3000	HOF 1976, d. 1931
Conzelman, Jimmy	foot	125	200		HOF 1964, d. 1970, ESPV
Cook, Bill	hock	40	100		HOF 1952, d. 1986
Corbett, James J., 1866-1933	box	425	800	SG-3500	USA, H
Coulter, Art	hock	15	40		HOF 1974
Cournoyer, Yvan	hock	5	15	Spuck-20	HOF 1982
Court, Margaret	tennis	10	30	TB-N/A	
Cousy, Bob	bask	10	30	SB-125	HOF 1970
Coveleski, Stan	base	15	50	SB-500	HOF 1969, Gold HOF s. post.-25, d. 1984
Cowens, Dave	bask	5	15	SB-100	HOF 1991
Cowley, Bill	hock	40	100	Spuck-150	HOF 1968, d. 1993
Crawford, Rusty	hock	50			HOF 1962, d. 1971
Crawford, Sam	base	125	450	SB-2000, b&w HOF s. post.-300	HOF 1957, Gold HOF s. post.-350, d. 1968
Creekmur, Lou	foot	5	15	SB-75, Mhelm-50	HOF 1996
Cronin, Joe	base	30	100	SB-750, b&w HOF s. post.-50	HOF 1956, Canc. check-125, Gold HOF s. post.-35, RS, d. 1984
Csonka, Larry	foot	8	20	SB-125, Mhelm-75	HOF 1987
Cummings, Candy	base	1800		S. doc.-5000	HOF 1939, ESPV, FA, d. 1924
Cunningham, Billy	bask	10	20	SB-100	HOF 1886
Cuyler, Kiki	base	250	600	SB-3750	HOF 1968, RS, d. 1950
D'Amato, Cus, 1908-1985	box	75	150	SG-575	USA, manager
Dandridge, Ray	base	10	25	SB-75	HOF 1987, Canc. check-35, Perez-Steele s. post.-15, Gold HOF s. post.-20, RS, d. 1994
Davies, Bob	bask	25	50	SB-275	HOF 1969, d. 1990
Davis, Al	foot	20	50	SB-125	HOF 1992

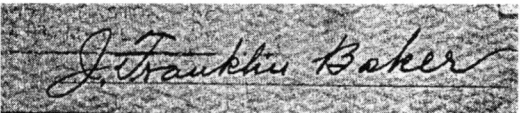

Franklin Baker

Mickey Cochrane

Charles Albert "Chief" Bender

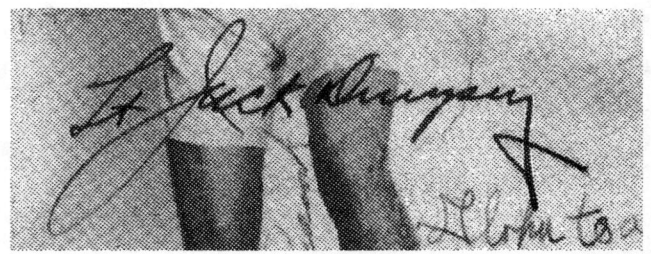

Jack Dempsey

Morgan G. Bulkeley

Joe DiMaggio

Henry Chadwick

Ty Cobb

Jimmie Foxx

NAME	SPORT	SIG	SP	S.MEMO/MISC.	COMMENTS
Davis, Willie	foot	5	15	SB-175, Mhelm-60	HOF 1981
Dawson, Len	foot	10	25	SB-125, Mhelm-75	HOF 1987
Day, Hap	hock	40	125		HOF 1961, d. 1990
Day, Leon	base	10	40	SB-150	HOF 1995, Canc. check-100, d. 1995
Dean, Dizzy	base	75	200	SB-750, b&w HOF s. post.-150	HOF 1953, Gold HOF s. post.-175, d. 1974
DeBusschere, Dave	bask	10	20	SB-125	HOF 1982
Delahanty, Ed	base	2000		S. doc.-5500	HOF 1945, FA, d. 1903
Delaney, Jack, 1900-1948	box	100	240		Canada, LH
Delvecchio, Alex	hock	5	15	Spuck-20	HOF 1977
☆ **Dempsey, Jack, 1895-1983**	**box**	**100**	**200**	**SG-750**	**USA, H, RS**
Denneny, Cy	hock	75	200		HOF 1959, 1970
Dickey, Bill	base	25	70	SB-300, b&w HOF s. post.-75	HOF 1954, Canc. check-250, Perez-Steele s. post.-75, Gold HOF s. post.-35, RS, d. 1993
Dierdorf, Dan	foot	5	15	SB-75, Mhelm-50	HOF 1996, MNF
Dihigo, Martin	base	600	1575	SB-4000, s. doc.-2500	HOF 1977, FA, d. 1971
Dillon, Jack, 1891-1942	box	115	320	USA, LH	
DiMaggio, Dom	base	10	20	SB-100	Canc. check-50
☆ **DiMaggio, Joe, 1914-1999**	**base**	**100**	**150**	**SB-300, Sbat-2000, b&w HOF s. post.-225**	**HOF 1955, Perez-Steele s. post.-250, Gold HOF s. post.-150, FA, ESPV**
DiMaggio, Vince	base	35	100	SB-300	d. 1986
Dionne, Marcel	hock	5	15	Spuck-20	HOF 1992
Ditka, Mike	foot	10	25	SB-125, Mhelm-75	HOF 1988
Doby, Larry	base	10	25	SB-40, Sbat-100	HOF 1998
Doerr, Bobby	base	5	15	SB-25, Sbat-75	HOF 1986, Canc. check-25, Perez-Steele s. post.-10, Gold HOF s. post.-7, RS
Donovan, Art	foot	10	15	SB-125	HOF 1968
Dorsett, Tony	foot	10	30	SB-125, Mhelm-70	HOF 1994
Douglas, J.S., Marquess of Queensberry	box	180	415		England, patron
Drillon, Gordie	hock	30	110		HOF 1975, d. 1986
Drinkwater, Graham	hock	200			HOF 1950, d. 1946
Driscoll, Paddy	foot	125	250		HOF 1965, d. 1968, ESPV
Dryden, Ken	hock	10	50		HOF 1983
Drysdale, Don	base	25	60	SB-200	HOF 1984, Perez-Steele s. post.-50, Gold HOF s. post.-45, d. 1993
Dudley, Bill	foot	5	15	SB-75, Mhelm-50	HOF 1966
Duffy, Hugh	base	300	1000	SB-3250, b&w HOF s. post.-1500	HOF 1945, d. 1954
Duman, Bill	hock	75	100		HOF 1958, d. 1964

NAME	SPORT	SIG	SP	S.MEMO/MISC.	COMMENTS
Dumart, Woody	hock	5	15	Spuck-25	HOF 1992
Dundee, Angelo, 1923-	box	5	10	SG-50	USA, trainer, RS
Dundee, Chris, 1908-	box	20	75	SG-100	USA, manager, promoter
Dundee, Johnny, 1893-1965	box	50	110	SG-420	Italy, F, JL
Dunderdale, Tommy	hock	125			HOF 1974, 1960
Dunphy, Don, 1911-	box	5	10	SG-50	USA, broadcaster
Durocher, Leo	base	25	40	SB-150	HOF 1994, d. 1991
Dutton, Red	hock	40	100		HOF 1958, d. 1987
Duva, Lou, 1922-	box	5	10	SG-50	USA, trainer, manager
Dye, Babe	hock	150	300		HOF 1970, d. 1962
☆ **Earnhardt, Dale**	**auto**	**10**	**40**		**Auto Racing, RS**
Edwards, Turk	foot	150	400		HOF 1969, d. 1973
Eldridge. Todd	skate	10	20		U.S. Figure Skating
Elliot, Bill	auto	10	20		Auto Racing
Elorde, Gabriel "Flash", 1935-1985	box	30	65	SG-250	Philippines, JL, RS
Elway, John	foot	25	35	FB-200	
Erving, Julius	bask	15	60	SB-200	HOF 1993
Esposito, Phil	hock	5	15	Spuck-25	HOF 1984
Esposito, Tony	hock	8	20	Spuck-30	HOF 1988
Evans, Billy	base	225	750	SB-3725	HOF 1973, d. 1956, ESPV
Evers, Johnny	base	400	1200	SB-4500	HOF 1946, d. 1947
Evert, Chris	tennis	10	30	TB-40	FA
Ewbank, Weeb, 1907-1998	foot	10	25	Mhelm-50	HOF 1978, Canc. check-60, RS
Ewing, Buck	base	1500		S. doc.-5000, SB-AA	HOF 1939, FA, d. 1906
Ewing, Patrick	bask	25	45	BB-225	FA
Faber, Red	base	50	125	SB-1500	HOF 1964, Gold HOF s. post.-100, often signed in red ink, RS, d, 1976
Favre, Brett	foot	25	40	FB-200	FA
Fears, Tom	foot	5	15	SB-100, Mhelm-50	HOF 1970
Fedorov, Sergei	hock	20	35	Puck-45	FA
Feller, Bob	base	5	15	SB-25, b&w HOF s. post.-25	HOF 1962, Gold HOF s. post.-10, Perez-Steele s. post.-20, RS
Ferrell, Rick	base	12	25	SB-75	HOF 1984, Canc. check-30, Gold HOF s. post.-10, Perez-Steele s. post.-15, d. 1995, RS
Fingers, Rollie	base	5	15	SB-25, Sbat-50	HOF 1992, Perez-Steele s. post.-20, Gold HOF s. post.-15, Canc. check-35
Finks, Jim	foot	30	125		HOF 1995, d. 1994
☆ **Fitzsimmons, Bob, 1863-1917**	**box**	**2250**	**6000**	**SG-14500**	**England, M, H, LH , ESPV**
Flaherty, Ray	foot	20	50	SB-200	HOF 1976, d. 1995

NAME	SPORT	SIG	SP	S.MEMO/MISC.	COMMENTS
Flaman, Fern	hock	5	15	Spuck-20	HOF 1990
Fleischer, Nat S., ?-1972	box	20	35	SG-130	USA, writer, publisher
Fleming, Peggy	skate	10	20		U.S. Figure Skating
Flick, Elmer	base	50	150	SB-1500, b&w s. post.-350	HOF 1963, Gold HOF s. post.-500, d. 1971
Flowers, Tiger, 1895-1927	box	425	1000		USA, M, scarce
Ford, Len	foot	200	500		HOF 1976, d. 1972
Ford, Whitey	base	10	20	SB-35, Sbat-100	HOF 1974, canc. check-35, Perez-Steele s. doc.-25, gold HOF s. doc.-20
Fortmann, Dan	foot	30	60	SB-200	HOF 1965, d. 1995
Foster, Bob, 1938-	box	5	15	SG-60	USA, LH, RS
Foster, Rube	base	2500		S. doc.-8000, SB-AA	HOF 1981, , FA, d. 1930
Fouts, Dan	foot	10	25	SB-100, Mhelm-60	HOF 1993
Fox, Nellie	base	180	400	SB-2000	HOF 1997, Canc. check-600, d. 1975
Fox, Richard K., 1846-1922	box	85	120		Ireland, writer, publisher, ESPV
Foxx, Jimmie	base	250	700	SB-3000, b&w HOF s. post.-1000	HOF 1951, d. 1967
Foyston, Frank	hock	50	150		HOF 1958
Foyt, A.J.	auto	10	20		Auto Racing, RS
Fratianne, Linda	skate	10	25		U.S. Figure Skating
Frazier, Joe, 1944-	box	8	20	SG-75	USA, H, RS
Frazier, Walt	bask	10	20	SB-100	HOF
Frederickson, Frank	hock	50	175	8x10 Photo	HOF 1958, d. 1979
Frick, Ford	base	50	150	SB-1500	HOF 1970, gold HOF s. post.-125, RS, d. 1978
Frisch, Frankie	base	50	175	SB-1725, b&w s. post.-250	HOF 1947, Canc. check-250, Gold HOF s. post.-250, RS, d. 1973
Fulks, Joe	bask	35	115		HOF, d. 1976
Fullmer, Gene, 1931-	box	5	12	SG-55	USA, M, RS
Furillo, Carl	base	25	80	SB-375	d. 1980
Futch, Eddie, 1911-	box	5	10	SG-50	USA, trainer, manager
Gadsby, Bill	hock	5	15	Spuck-20	HOF 1970
Gainey, Bob	hock	5	15	Spuck-20	HOF 1992
Galvin, Pud	base	1500	3000	S. doc.-4000	HOF 1965, d. 1902, FA
Gans, Joe, 1874-1910	box	575	1500		USA, L, scarce
Gardiner, Herb	hock	50	150		HOF 1958, d. 1972
Garner, Jimmy	hock	250			HOF 1962, d. 1940
Gatski, Frank	foot	5	15	SB-75, Mhelm-50	HOF 1985
Gavilan, Kid, 1926-	box	15	25	SG-100	Cuba, W, RS, sig. variations
☆ **Gehrig, Lou**	**base**	**1000**	**5750**	**SB-AA**	**HOF 1939, ESPV, FA, SP-$1800, $2500, d. 1941**

NAME	SPORT	SIG	SP	S.MEMO/MISC.	COMMENTS
Gehringer, Charley	base	15	50	SB-200, b&w s. post.-35	HOF 1949, Perez-Steele s. post.-75, gold HOF s. post.-25, RS, d. 1993
Genaro, Frankie, 1901-1966	box	100	150	SG-575	USA, F
Geoffrion, Boom Boom	hock	10	15	Spuck-30	HOF 1972
George, Bill	foot	75	150		HOF 1974, d. 1982
Gerard, Eddie	hock	300			HOF 1945, d. 1937
Giacomin, Eddie	hock	10	20	Spuck-25	HOF 1987
Giamatti, A. Bartlett	base	50	165		Baseball com., 1938-1989, TLS-$125
Giardello, Joey, 1930-	box	5	12	SG-55	USA, M, RS
Gibbons, Mike, 1887-1956	box	75	150		USA, M
Gibbons, Tommy, 1891-1960	box	80	175	SG-1400	USA, H
Gibbs, Joe	foot	5	15	SB-75	HOF 1996
Gibson, Athea	tennis	15	50	TB-N/A	
Gibson, Bob	base	5	20	SB-30, Sbat-100	HOF 1981, Perez-Steele s. post.-20, gold HOF s. post.-15
Gibson, Josh	base	600		SB-AA, s. doc.-2000	HOF 1972, FA, d. 1947
Gifford, Frank	foot	10	20	SB-125, Mhelm-60	HOF 1977, MNF
Gilbert, Red	hock	5	15	Spuck-25	HOF 1982
Giles, Warren	base	30	100	SB-250	HOF 1979, RS, d. 1979
Gilliam, Jim	base	20	75	SB-600	d. 1978
Gillman, Sid	foot	5	15	SB-75, Mhelm-50	HOF 1983
Gilmour, Billy	hock	150			HOF 1962, d. 1959
Goheen, Moose	hock	65			HOF 1952, d. 1979
Gola, Tom	bask	10	20	SB-100	HOF 1975
Goldman, Charley, 1888-1968	box	125	215	SG-600	Poland, trainer
Goldstein, Ruby, 1907-1984	box	60	100		USA, referee
Gomez, Lefty	base	25	50	SB-275	HOF 1972, Canc. check-125, Perez-Steele s. post.-75, gold HOF s. post.-20, d. 1988
Gomez, Wilfredo, 1956-	box	10	22	SG-70	Puerto Rico, SB, F, JL, elusive signer
Goodfellow, Ebbie	hock	30	100		HOF 1963, d. 1985
Gordon, Jeff	auto	15	30		Auto Racing, FA
Goslin, Goose	base	100	300	SB-2210	HOF 1968, Gold HOF s. post.-400, d. 1971
Graf, Steffi	tennis	10	30	TB-45	FA
Graham, Billy, 1922-1992	box	30	50	SG-200	USA, W
Graham, Otto	foot	15	40	SB-175, Mhelm-60	HOF 1965
☆ **Grange, Red, 1903-1991**	**foot**	**75**	**200**	**SB-825**	**HOF 1963**
Grant, Bud	foot	5	20		HOF 1994
Grant, Mike	hock	150			HOF 1950, d. 1955
Graziano, Rocky, 1922-1990	box	35	60	SG-250	USA, M, prolific

NAME	SPORT	SIG	SP	S.MEMO/MISC.	COMMENTS
Greb, Harry, 1894-1926	box	500	1250		USA, M
Green, Shorty	hock	115			HOF 1962, d. 1960
Greenberg, Hank	base	50	200	SB-900, b&w HOF s. post.-150	HOF 1956, Perez-Steele s. post.-300, gold HOF s. post.-100, d. 1986, TLS-$500
Greene, Joe	foot	10	25	SB-125, Mhelm-60	HOF 1987
Greer, Hal	bask	5	15	SB-75	HOF
Gregg, Forrest	foot	10	20	SB-75, Mhelm-50	HOF 1977
Gretzky, Wayne	**hock**	**35**	**65**	**Puck-75**	**FA, ESPV**
Griese, Bob	foot	10	25	SB-125, Mhelm-75	HOF 1990
Griffey, Jr., Ken	base	25	45	OLB-60	
Griffis, Si	hock	150			HOF 1950, d. 1950
Griffith, Clark	base	200	600	SB-3275, b&w s. post.-750	HOF 1946, d. 1955
Griffith, Emile, 1938-	box	5	10	SG-50	Virgin Islands, W, M, RS
Grimes, Burleigh	base	20	75	SB-325	HOF 1964, Canc. check-60, Gold HOF s. post.-25, Perez-Steele s. post.-200, d. 1985
Grove, Lefty	base	40	150	SB-2000, b&w HOF s. post.-150	HOF 1947, Canc. check-125, Gold HOF s. post.-125, d. 1975
Groza, Lou	foot	8	20	SB-100, SGLA-15, Mhelm-25	HOF 1974
Guyon, Joe	foot	150	300		HOF 1966, d. 1971
Hafey, Chick	base	50	150	SB-2000	HOF 1971, Gold HOF s. post.-400, ESPV, d. 1973
Hagan, Cliff	bask	8	20	SB-100	HOF
Hagler, Marvelous Marvin, 1954-	box	12	30	SG-100	USA, M, can be elusive, lives in Italy
Haines, Jesse	base	25	125	SB-1200	HOF 1970, Canc. check-175, BC-$250, Gold HOF s. post.-100, d. 1978
Hainsworth, George	hock	100	250		HOF 1961, d. 1950
Halas, George	foot	75	150	SB-825	HOF 1963, d. 1983
Hall, Glenn	hock	5	15	Spuck-20	HOF 1975
Ham, Jack	foot	5	15	SB-75, Mhelm-50	HOF 1988
Hamill, Dorothy	skate	10	20		U.S. Figure Skating
Hamilton, Billy	base	1100	2250	SB-6000	HOF 1961, d. 1940
Hamilton, Scott	skate	10	25		U.S. Figure Skating, FA
Hannah, John	foot	5	15	SB-75, SGLA-20, Mhelm-50	HOF 1991
Harada, Masahiko, 1943-	box	10	22	SG-65	Japan, FL, B, RS
Hardaway, Anfernee	bask	25	45	BB-225	
Harding, Tonya	skate	5	10		U.S. Figure Skating
Harridge, Will	base	50	200	SB-2750	HOF 1972, d. 1971

NAME	SPORT	SIG	SP	S.MEMO/MISC.	COMMENTS
Harris, Bucky	base	50	200	SB-1600	HOF 1975, Gold HOF s. post.-150, d. 1977
Harris, Franco	foot	10	25	SB-125, SGLA-20, Mhelm-75	HOF 1990
Hartnett, Gabby	base	75	180	SB-2100, b&w HOF s. post.-250	HOF 1955, Canc. check-250, Gold HOF s. post.-400, d. 1972
Harvey, Doug	hock	60	150	Spuck-200	HOF 1973, d. 1989
Havlicek, John	bask	10	25	SB-150	HOF 1983
Hawerchuk, Dale	hock	5	20	Spuck-15	
Hawkins, Connie	bask	5	15	SB-100	HOF 1992
Hay, George	hock	50	150		HOF 1958, d. 1975
Hayes, Elvin	bask	10	20	SB-100	HOF 1990, d. 1990
Heilmann, Harry	base	350	800	SB-3600	HOF 1952, d. 1951
Hein, Mel	foot	25	80	SB-200, SGLA-150	HOF 1963, d. 1992
Heinsohn, Tom	bask	10	30	SB-150	HOF 1986
Hendricks, Ted	foot	10	20	SB-75, SGLA-25, Mhelm-50	HOF 1990
Henry, Pete	foot	150	420	Canceled Check-500, SB-AA	HOF 1963, d. 1952
Herber, Arnie	foot	100	200	SB-AA	HOF 1966, d. 1969
Herman, Billy	base	10	35	SB-100	HOF 1975, Canc. check-60, Gold HOF s. post.-15, Perez-Steele s. post.-25, signature variations, d. 1992
Herman, Pete, 1896-1973	box	80	150		USA, B
Hern, Riley	hock	250			HOF 1962, d. 1929
Hewitt, Bill	foot	160	325	SB-AA	HOF 1971, d. 1947
Hextall, Bryan	hock	20	50	Spuck-150	HOF 1969, d. 1984
Hill, Grant	bask	30	50	BB-225	FA
Hingis, Martina	tennis	10	30	TB-40	FA
Hirsch, Elroy	foot	12	30	SB-150	HOF 1968
Hodges, Gil	base	110	400	SB-1300	d. 1972
☆ **Hogan, Ben**	**golf**	**100**	**200**	**GB-150**	**FA, signature variations**
Holman, Nat	bask	10	25	SB-225	HOF 1964
Holmes, Hap	hock	150			HOF 1972, d. 1940
Hooper, Harry	base	35	125	SB-800	HOF 1971, Canc. check-100, Gold HOF s. post.-150, d. 1974
Hooper, Tom	hock	125	230		HOF 1962, d. 1963
Hornsby, Rogers	base	250	1000	SB-3750, b&w HOFs. post.-500	HOF 1942, d. 1963
Hornung, Paul	foot	10	25	SB-125, SGLA-20, Mhelm-60	HOF 1986, FA
Horton, Tim	hock	100	225		HOF 1977, d. 1974

NAME	SPORT	SIG	SP	S.MEMO/MISC.	COMMENTS
Houston, Ken	foot	5	15	SB-75, SGLA-15, Mhelm-50	HOF 1986, RS
Howard, Elston	base	100	350	SB-1000	d. 1980
Howe, Gordie	**hock**	**10**	**25**	**Spuck-30**	**HOF 1972**
Howe, Syd	hock	60	150		HOF 1965, d. 1976
Howell, Harry	hock	5	15	Spuck-20	HOF 1979
Hoyt, Waite	base	25	125	SB-475	HOF 1969, Canc. check-125, Gold HOF s. post.-50, d. 1984, RS
Hubbard, Cal	foot/base	50	200	SB-1000	HOF 1963, HOF 1976, d. 1977
Hubbell, Carl	base	20	50	SB-250, b&w HOF s. post.-50	HOF 1947, Canc. check-75, Gold HOF s. post.-25, Perez-Steele s. post.-100, d. 1988
Hubbs, Ken	base	45	150	SB-700	d. 1964
Huff, Sam	foot	10	20	SB-100, Mhelm-50	HOF 1982
Huggins, Miller	base	600	2000	SB-5000	HOF 1964, d. 1929
Hull, Bobby	hock	10	25	Spuck-30	HOF 1983
Humphreys, Joe, 1872-1936	box	55	115		USA, announcer
Hunt, Lamar	foot	10	25	SGLA-20	HOF 1972
Hunter, Catfish	base	10	20	SB-40, Sbat-65	HOF 1987, Gold HOF s. post.-7, Perez-Steele s. post.-10
Hutson, Don	foot	15	50	SB-175, SGLA-50, Mhelm-75	HOF 1963, d. 1997
Hutton, Bouse	hock	150	300		HOF 1962, d. 1962
Hyland, Harry	hock	125			HOF 1962, d. 1969
Iba, Henry	bask	25	50	SB-350	HOF 1968, d. 1993
Indurain, Miguel	cycle	15	35		Cycling
Irvin, Dick	hock	100	200		HOF 1958, d. 1957
Irvin, Monte	base	10	20	SB-30, Sbat-75	HOF 1973, Canc. check-25, Gold HOF s. post.-10, Perez-Steele s. post.-15
Issel, Dan	bask	10	20	SB-100	HOF, d. 1993
Jabbar, Kareem Abdul	bask	25	50	SB-175	HOF 1995, FA
Jack, Beau, 1921-	box	10	20	SG-60	USA, L, RS, sig. variations
Jackson, Busher	hock	75	200		HOF 1971, d. 1966
Jackson, Joe	base	5500	AA	SB-AA	d, 1951, a very tough signature, FA
Jackson, Reggie	base	10	35	SB-55, Sbat-225	HOF 1993, Gold HOF s. post.-40, Perez-Steele s. post.-65
Jackson, Travis	base	25	125	SB-350	HOF 1982, Gold HOF s. post.-40, Perez-Steele s. post.-75, d. 1987, RS
Jacobs, Jimmy, 1930-1988	box	50	100		USA, manager, film historian
Jacobs, Mike, 1880-1953	box	75	150		USA, promoter
Jagr, Jaromir	hock	20	30	Puck-50	RS. FA
Jarrett, Ned	auto	10	20		Auto Racing, RS
Jeannette, Buddy	bask	5	15	SB-100	HOF 1994, d. 1998

NAME	SPORT	SIG	SP	S.MEMO/MISC.	COMMENTS
Jeannette, Joe, 1879-1958	box	130	325		USA, H
Jeffries, James J., 1875-1953	box	380	850	SG-3400	USA, H
Jenkins, Ferguson	base	5	15	SB-25, Sbat-75	HOF 1991, Canc. check-25, Gold HOF s. post.-10, Perez-Steele s. post.-15
Jennings, Hughie	base	700	2000	SB-7200	HOF 1945, d. 1928
Jensen, Jackie	base	30	65	SB-200	Canc. check-100, d. 1982
Jeter, Derek	base	25	35	SB-50, Sbat-130	
Jofre, Eder, 1936-	box	10	25	SG-80	Brazil, B, F, RS
Johnson, Ban	base	350	1000	SB-3650	HOF 1937, d. 1931
Johnson, Ching	hock	125	250		HOF 1958, d. 1979
Johnson, Ernie	hock	150			HOF 1952, d. 1963
Johnson, Harold, 1928-	box	5	15	SG-55	USA, LH, RS
Johnson, Jack, 1878-1946	box	800	1500	SG-6250	USA, H
Johnson, Jimmy	foot	5	15	SB-75, Mhelm-50	HOF 1994
Johnson, John Henry	foot	5	15	SB-75, Mhelm-50	HOF 1987
Johnson, Judy	base	25	100	SB-275	HOF 1975, Gold HOF s. post.-40, Perez-Steele s. post.-75, d. 1989
Johnson, Junior	auto	10	20		Auto Racing
Johnson, Magic	bask	20	50	SB-175	
Johnson, Randy	base	20	35		
Johnson, Tom	hock	5	15	Spuck-20	HOF 1970
Johnson, Walter	base	500	1500	SB-5250, b&w HOF s. post.-1300	HOF 1936, Canc. check-1000, d. 1946
Joinier, Charlie	foot	5	15	SB-75, Mhelm-50	HOF 1996
Joliat, Aurel	hock	125	200	Spuck-225	HOF 1947, d. 1986
☆ **Jones, Bobby**	**golf**	**500**	**2000**	**GB-N/A**	**SP-$2000, TLS-$1500, SC-$550, SIG-$800**
Jones, Deacon	foot	5	15	SB-100, SGLA-20, Mhelm-50	HOF 1980
Jones, K.C.	bask	5	15	SB-10	HOF 1989
Jones, Sam	bask	8	20	SB-150	HOF
Jones, Stan	foot	5	15	SB-75, Mhelm-50	HOF 1991
Jordan, Henry	foot	225	400		HOF 1995, d. 1977
☆ **Jordan, Michael**	**bask**	**100**	**175**	**BB-200**	**FA, a tough signature!**
Joss, Addie	base	2000		S. doc.-4000, SB-AA	HOF 1978, scarce in all forms, d. 1911
Jurgensen, Sonny	foot	10	20	SB-100, Mhelm-60	HOF 1983
Kaline, Al	base	10	20	SB-30, Sbat-100	HOF 1980, Gold HOF s. post.-15, Perez-Steele s. post.-20
Karras, Alex	foot	5	15	SB-75	
Kearns, Jack	box	35	70	SG-260	USA, manager
Keats, Duke	hock	100	250		HOF 1958, d. 1972

James "Pud" Galvin

Rogers Hornsby

Lou Gehrig

Joe Jackson

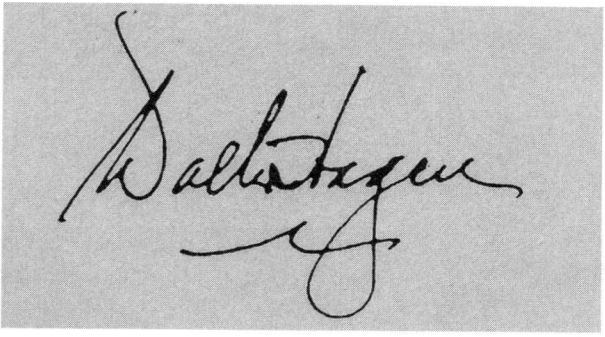
Walter Hagen

James J. Jeffries

Ben Hogan

Walter Johnson

Rogers Hornsby

Larry Lajoie

NAME	SPORT	SIG	SP	S.MEMO/MISC.	COMMENTS
Keefe, Tim	base	1250		SB-AA, s. doc.-3000	HOF 1964, scarce in all forms, d. 1933
Keeler, Willie	base	1000		SB-AA s. doc.-3200	HOF 1939, d. 1923
Kell, George	base	5	12	SB-20, Sbat-75	HOF 1983, Gold HOF s. post.-7, Perez-Steele s. post.-15
Kelly, George	base	15	50	SB-250	HOF 1973, Canc. check-100, Gold HOF s. post.-30, Perez-Steele s. post.-300, d. 1984
Kelly, Jim	foot	10	25	SB-125, Mhelm-100	
Kelly, Joe	base	1200	3000	SB-AA	HOF 1971, scarce, d. 1943
Kelly, Leroy	foot	5	15	SB-75, Mhelm-50	HOF 1994
Kelly, Mike "King"	base	2000		S. doc.-5000, SB-AA	HOF 1945, FA, d. 1894
Kelly, Red	hock	5	15	Spuck-25	HOF 1969
Kemp, Jack	foot	10	25	SB-100	FA
Kennedy, Teeder	hock	10	20	Spuck-40	HOF 1966
Keon, Dave	hock	10	15	Spuck-25	HOF 1986
Ketchel, Stanley, 1886-1910	box	700	1500		USA, M, scarce in all forms
Kiesling, Walt	foot	150	300		HOF 1966, d. 1962
Kilbane, Johnny, 1889-1957	box	100	265		USA, F
Killebrew, Harmon	base	10	20	SB-35, Sbat-50	HOF 1984, Gold HOF s. post.-15, Perez-Steele s. post.-20
Kinard, Frank "Bruiser"	foot	100	200		HOF 1971, d. 1985
Kiner, Ralph	base	5	15	SB-25, Sbat-50	HOF 1975, Canc. check-25, Gold HOF s. post.-10, Perez-Steele s. post.-15
King, Billie Jean	tennis	10	25	TB-35	
King, Don, 1931-	box	5	10	SG-40	USA, promoter
Klein, Chuck	base	250	750	SB-2500	HOF 1980, d. 1958
Klem, Bill	base	300	750	SB-2750	HOF 1953, d. 1951
Kluszewski, Ted	base	20	50	SB-150	Canc. check-100, d. 1988
Koufax, Sandy	base	20	50	SB-75, Sbat-125	HOF 1972, Gold HOF s. post.-50, Perez-Steele s. post.-50
Kryzewski, Mike	bask	10	20	SB-80	Duke basketball coach, RS
Labarba, Fidel, 1905-1981	box	20	35	SG-100	USA, FL
Lach, Elmer	hock	5	15	Spuck-25	HOF 1966
Lafleur, Guy	hock	10	20	Spuck-25	HOF 1988
Lajoie, Nap	base	350	1000	SB-4000	HOF 1937, b&w HOF s. post.-750, d. 1959
Lalonde, Newsy	hock	100	225		HOF 1950, d. 1971
Lambeau, Curly	foot	125			HOF 1963, d. 1965
Lambert, Jack	foot	10	25	SB-125, SGLA-25, Mhelm-75	HOF 1990
LaMotta, Jake, 1921-	box	15	25	SG-75	USA, M, charges for signatures

NAME	SPORT	SIG	SP	S.MEMO/MISC.	COMMENTS
Landis, Kenesaw	base	250	750	SB-3750	HOF 1939, illegible signature, TLS-$450, d. 1944
Landry, Tom	foot	10	25	SB-100, SGLA-20	HOF 1990
Lane, Dick	foot	15	30	SB-125, Mhelm-50	HOF 1974
Langer, Jim	foot	5	15	SB-75, Mhelm-50	HOF 1987
Langford, Sam, 1883-1956	box	225	500		Canada, H, scarce
Lanier, Bob	bask	5	15	SB-75	HOF
Lanier, Willie	foot	5	15	SB-75, Mhelm-75	HOF 1986
Laperriere, Jacques	hock	5	15	Spuck-20	HOF 1987
Lapointe, Guy	hock	5	15	Spuck-20	HOF 1993
Laprade, Edgar	hock	10	20	Spuck-30	HOF 1993
Largent, Steve	foot	10	20	SB-125, Mhelm-60	HOF 1995, FA
Lary, Yale	foot	5	15	SB-75, Mhelm-50	HOF 1979, Canc. check-20
Lavelli, Dante	foot	5	15	SB-75, Mhelm-50	HOF 1975
Layne, Bobby	foot	75	150	SB-800	HOF 1967, d. 1986
Lazzeri, Tony	base	325	850	SB-3500	HOF 1991, d. 1946
Leemans, Tuffy	foot	75	150	SB-700	HOF 1978, d. 1979
Lemaire, Jacques	hock	5	15	Spuck-20	HOF 1984
Lemieux, Mario	hock	20	50	Spuck-100	FA, HOF
Lemon, Bob	base	5	12	SB-25	HOF 1976, Gold HOF s. post.-7, Perez-Steele s. post.-15
Leonard, Benny, 1896-1947	box	45	115	SG-475	USA, L, was responsive to requests
Leonard, Buck	base	15	45	SB-80	HOF 1972, Canc. check-20, Gold HOF s. post.-20, Perez-Steele s. post.-35, d. 1997
Leonard, Sugar Ray, 1956-	box	10	25	SG-75	USA, W-LH, RS
LeSueur, Percy	hock	150	300		HOF 1961, d. 1962
Lewis, Carl	track	10	25		U. S. Track & Field, RS, signs "Carl" only!
Lewis, John Henry, 1914-1974	box	70	170	SG-700	USA, LH
Lewis, Ted "Kid", 1894-1970	box	60	125		England, W
Liebling, A.J., ?-1963	box	45	75		USA, writer
Lilly, Bob	foot	10	20	SB-100, Mhelm-50	HOF 1980
Lindros, Eric	hock	25	35	Puck-50	
Lindsay, Ted	hock	5	15	Spuck-25	HOF 1966
Lindstrom, Fred	base	30	125	SB-500	HOF 1976, Gold HOF s. post.-50, d. 1981
Liston, Charles "Sonny", 1932-1970	box	275	750	SG-3400	USA, H, very scarce in all forms, FA
Little, Larry	foot	5	15	SB-75, Mhelm-50	HOF 1993
Lloyd, John Henry	base	750	2500	SB-5200	HOF 1977, FA, d. 1964
Lombardi, Ernie	base	50	150	SB-1200	HOF 1986, d. 1977
☆ **Lombardi, Vince, 1913-70**	**foot**	**200**	**400**	**SB-AA**	**HOF 1971, Canc. check-300**

	NAME	SPORT	SIG	SP	S.MEMO/MISC.	COMMENTS
	Lopez, Al	base	15	40	SB-125, Sbat-150	HOF 1977, Gold HOF s. post.-30, Perez-Steele s. post.-75
	Lott, Ronnie	foot	10	20	SB-100, Mhelm-275	
	Loughran, Tommy, 1902-1982	box	40	90	SG-350	USA, LH
☆	**Louis, Joe, 1914-1981**	**box**	**200**	**400**	**SG-1500**	**USA, H, prolific**
	Lovellette, Clyde	bask	5	15	SB-75	HOF 1988
	Lucas, Jerry	bask	5	15	SB-100	HOF 1979
	Luckman, Sid	foot	10	30	SB-150, Mhelm-50	HOF 1965, d. 1998
	Lumley, Harry	hock	5	15	Spuck-20	HOF 1980
	Luyendyk, Arie	auto	10	20		Auto Racing
	Lyman, Link	foot	100	225		HOF 1964, d. 1972
	Lynch, Benny, 1913-1946	box	355	750		Ireland, FL
	Lyons, Ted	base	25	110	SB-325, b&w HOF s. post.-45	HOF 1955, Canc. check-80, Gold HOF s. post.-35, Perez-Steele s. post.-225, d. 1986
	MacCauley, Ed	bask	10	15	SB-125	HOF
	Mack, Connie	base	150	350	SB-2500, b&w HOF s. post.-850	HOF 1937, signed book-$260, TLS-$500, d. 1956
	MacKay, Mickey	hock	150	300		HOF 1952, d. 1940
	Mackey, John	foot	5	15	SB-75, Mhelm-50	HOF 1992
	MacPhail, Larry	base	100	250	SB-1500	HOF 1978, d. 1975
	Maddux, Greg	base	25	45	SB-60	
	Maglie, Sal	base	30	50	SB-250	Canc. check-60, d. 1992
	Mahovlich, Frank	hock	5	15	Spuck-20	HOF 1981
	Malone, Joe	hock	100			HOF 1950, d. 1969
	Malone, Karl	bask	25	35	BB-200	
	Mandell, Sammy, 1904-1967	box	25	45	SG-200	USA, L
	Mantha, Sylvio	hock	60	150		HOF 1960, d. 1974
☆	**Mantle, Mickey**	**base**	**75**	**150**	**SB-250, Sbat-2000**	**HOF 1974, Gold HOF s. post.-150, Perez-Steele s. post.-250, d. 1995, FA**
	Manush, Heinie	base	50	200	SB-1500	HOF 1964, Canc. check-400, Gold HOF s. post.-200, d. 1971
	Mara, Tim	foot	125	275		HOF 1963, d. 1959
	Maranville, Rabit	base	200	500	SB-1500	HOF 1954, b&w HOF s. post.-750, d. 1954
	Maravich, Pete, 1947-1977	bask	125	300	SB-920	HOF 1987
	Marchetti, Gino	foot	5	15	SB-75, Mhelm-50	HOF 1972
☆	**Marciano, Rocky, 1923-1969**	**box**	**250**	**650**	**SG-2250**	**USA, H, was a very RS, SC-$195**
	Marichal, Juan	base	10	20	SB-30, Sbat-50	HOF 1983, Gold HOF s. post.-10, Perez-Steele s. post.-10
	Marino, Dan	foot	30	50	FB-225	FA
	Maris, Roger	base	200	500	SB-2000	d. 1985

SPORTS L

NAME	SPORT	SIG	SP	S.MEMO/MISC.	COMMENTS
Markson, Harry	box	5	10	SG-45	USA, publicist, promoter
Marquard, Rube	base	40	125	SB-750	HOF 1971, Gold HOF s. post.-40, d. 1980
Marshall, George	foot	100	200		HOF 1963, d. 1969
Marshall, Jack	hock	125	250		HOF 1965, d. 1965
Martin, Billy	base	25	60	SB-200	d. 1989
Martin, Pepper	base	75	250	SB-900	d. 1965
Martin, Slater	bask	10	20	SB-125	HOF
Mathews, Eddie	base	10	20	SB-30, Sbat-100	HOF 1978, Gold HOF s. post.-10, Perez-Steele s. post.-20
Mathewson, Christy	base	1250	4000	SB-AA	HOF 1936, d. 1925
Matson, Ollie	foot	10	20	SB-125, Mhelm-50	HOF 1972
Mattingly, Don	base	12	30	SB-50, Sbat-125	RS
Maxim, Joey, 1922-	box	10	20	SG-65	USA, LH, RS
Maxwell, Steamer	hock	125	250		HOF 1962, d. 1975
Maynard, Don	foot	5	15	SB-75, Mhelm-50	HOF 1987
Mays, Willie	base	20	40	SB-50, Sbat-150	HOF 1979, Gold HOF s. post.-30, Perez-Steele s. post.-50, FA
McAfee, George	foot	5	15	SB-75, Mhelm-50	HOF 1966
McAuliffe, Jack, 1866-1937	box	150	400		Ireland, L
McCarthy, Joe	base	50	150	SB-1250	HOF 1957, Gold HOF s. post.-75, b&w HOF s. post.-100, d. 1978, RS
McCarthy, Tom	base	1200	4000	SB-AA	HOF 1946, d. 1922, scarce
McCormack, Mike	foot	5	15	SB-75, Mhelm-50	HOF 1984
McCovey, Willie	base	10	20	SB-40, Sbat-80	HOF 1986, Canc. check-40, Gold HOF s. post.-25, Perez-Steele s. post.-30
McCoy, Charles "Kid", 1872-1940	box	120	200		USA, M
McDonald, Lanny	hock	5	15	Spuck-20	HOF 1992
McElhenny, Hugh	foot	10	20	SB-125, Mhelm-60	HOF 1970
McEnroe, John	tennis	10	30	TB-40	FA
McFarland, Packey, 1888-1936	box	125	250		USA, L
McGee, Frank	hock	350	825		HOF 1945, d. 1916
McGimsie, Billy	hock	125	250		HOF 1962, d. 1968
McGinnity, Joe	base	1000	3750	SB-AA, s. doc.-5000	HOF 1946, FA, d. 1929
McGovern, Terry, 1880-1918	box	400	1200		USA, F, B
McGowan, Bill	base	350	1200	SB-4250	HOF 1992, d. 1954
McGraw, John	base	750	2100	SB-6225	HOF 1937, d. 1934
McGuire, Dick	bask	5	15	SB-100	HOF 1993
☆ **McGwire, Mark**	**base**	**75**	**150**	**SB-200, SC-175**	**FA, ESPV, RS in-person**
McKechnie, Bill	base	150	400	SB-3000	HOF 1962, b&w HOF s. post.-400, d. 1965

NAME	SPORT	SIG	SP	S.MEMO/MISC.	COMMENTS
McLarnin, Jimmy, 1906-	box	20	40	SG-110	Ireland, W, refuses mail
McNally, Johnny "Blood"	foot	25	150		HOF 1963, d. 1985
McNamara, George	hock	150	300		HOF 1958, d. 1952
Medwick, Joe	base	50	150	SB-725	HOF 1968, Gold HOF s. post.-150, d. 1975
Mercante, Arthur, 1920-	box	5	10	SG-45	USA, referee, RS
Messier, Mark	hock	35	55	Puck-75	
Michalske, Mike	foot	50	150		HOF 1964, d. 1983
Mikan, George	bask	10	25	SB-160	HOF 1959
Mikita, Stan	hock	10	20	Spuck-35	HOF 1983
Mikkelsen, Vern	bask	5	15	SB-75	HOF 1995
Miller, Cheryl	bask	5	15	SB-75	HOF 1995
Miller, Freddie, 1911-1962	box	65	130		USA, F
Millner, Wayne	foot	70	270		HOF 1968, d. 1976
Mitchell, Bobby	foot	5	15	SB-75, Mhelm-50	HOF 1983
Mix, Ron	foot	5	15	SB-75, Mhelm-50	HOF 1979
Mize, Johnny	base	15	35	SB-125, Sbat-200	HOF 1981, Gold HOF s. post.-15, Perez-Steele s. post.-25, d. 1993, RS
Monk, Art	foot	10	20	SB-125, Mhelm-75	
Monroe, Earl	bask	5	15	SB-100	HOF 1990
Montana, Joe	**foot**	**15**	**40**	**SB-175, Mhelm-125**	**FA, RS**
Montgomery, Bob, 1919-	box	10	20	SG-70	USA, L, RS
Monzon, Carlos, 1942-1995	box	75	150	SG-300	Argentina, M, elusive signer, "tough" sig.
Moore, Archie, 1913-1998	box	15	25	SG-110	USA, LH, RS
Moore, Dickie	hock	5	15	Spuck-20	HOF 1974
Moore, Lenny	foot	10	20	SB-100, Mhelm-50	HOF 1975
Moran, Paddy	hock	125	250		HOF 1958, d. 1966
Morenz, Howie	hock	500	1500		HOF 1945, d. 1937
Morgan, Joe	base	8	15	SB-150, Sbat-150	HOF 1990, Gold HOF s. post.-15, Perez-Steele s. post.-20
Morrissey, John, 1831-1878	box	600			Ireland, scarce
Mosienko, Bill	hock	20	40	Spuck-150	HOF 1965
Motley, Marion	foot	10	20	SB-100, Mhelm-50	HOF 1968
Muhammad, Matthew Saad, 1954-	box	5	12	SG-50	USA, LH, "Matthew Franklin," responsive sign.
Muldoon, William, 1845-1933	box	50	115	USA, trainer, official	
Munson, Thurman	base	200	400	SB-1500	Canc. check-600, d. 1979
Murphy, Calvin	bask	5	15	SB-100	HOF 1993
Murphy, Stretch	bask	10	25	SB-250	HOF 1960, d. 1992
Musial, Stan	base	15	30	SB-50, Sbat-225	HOF 1969, Canc. check-100, Gold HOF s. post.-25, Perez-Steele s. post.-50

NAME	SPORT	SIG	SP	S.MEMO/MISC.	COMMENTS
Musso, George	foot	10	20	SB-100, Mhelm-50	HOF 1982
Nagurski, Bronko	foot	50	150	SB-400	HOF 1963, Canc. check-150, d. 1990
Namath, Joe	foot	20	50	SB-175, Mhelm-125	HOF 1985
Napoles, Jose, 1940-	box	10	25	SG-75	Cuba, W, elusive signer
Navratilova, Martina	tennis	15	35	TB-45	
Neale, Greasy	foot	125	250		HOF 1969, d. 1973
Nelson, Battling, 1882-1954	box	85	185	SG-775	Denmark, L
Nelson, Byron	golf	10	40	GB-60	
Nevers, Ernie	foot	75	150	SB-500	HOF 1963, d. 1976
Newhouser, Hal, 1921-1998	base	5	15	SB-30, Sbat-60	HOF 1992, Canc. check-35, Gold HOF s. post.-7, Perez-Steele s. post.-25
Nichols, Kid	base	300	600	SB-7000	HOF 1949, b&w HOF s. post.-1500, d. 1953
Nicklaus, Jack	**golf**	**20**	**50**	**GB-60**	**RS**
Nighbor, Frank	hock	100	225		HOF 1947, d. 1966
Nitschke, Ray, 1936-1998	foot	10	20	SB-150, Mhelm-50	HOF 1978
Noble, Reg	hock	100	250		HOF 1962, d. 1962
Noll, Chuck	foot	5	15	SB-100	HOF 1993
Nomellini, Leo	foot	5	15	SB-100, Mhelm-50	HOF 1969
Norman, Greg	golf	10	30	GB-40	
Norton, Ken, 1943-	box	10	25	SG-70	USA, H, RS
O'Brien, Philadelphia Jack, 1878-1942	box	125	200		USA, LH
O'Connor, Buddy	hock	50	150		HOF 1988, d. 1977
Odd, Gilbert, 1902-	box	30	70		England, writer, prolific
O'Doul, Lefty	base	75	200	SB-1500	d. 1969
Olajuwon, Hakeem	bask	25	35	BB-200	
Olivares, Ruben, 1947-	box	5	10	SG-45	Mexico, B, F, RS
Oliver, Harry	hock	25	175		HOF 1967, d. 1985
Olmstead, Bert	hock	5	15	Spuck-25	HOF 1985
Olsen, Merlin	foot	10	20	SB-100, SGLA-20, Mhelm-60	HOF 1982
O'Neal, Shaquille	bask	25	40	BB-200	FA
O'Rourke, Jim	base	1200		S. doc.-3500, SB-AA	HOF 1945, d. 1914
Orr, Bobby	hock	20	75	Spuck-100	HOF 1979
Ortiz, Carlos, 1936-	box	5	10	SG-45	Puerto Rico, JW, L, RS
Ortiz, Manuel, 1916-1970	box	70	150		USA, B
Ott, Mel	base	250	750	SB-7250	HOF 1951, b&w HOF s. post.-800, Canc. check-350, d. 1958
Otto, Jim	foot	5	15	SB-100, Mhelm-50	HOF 1980
Owen, Steve	foot	150	300		HOF 1966, d. 1964

SPORTS

M

NAME	SPORT	SIG	SP	S.MEMO/MISC.	COMMENTS
Owens, Jesse	track	100	300		U.S. Track & Field, RS, ESPV
Page, Alan	foot	10	25	SB-100, Mhelm-60	HOF 1988
Paige, Satchel	base	100	400	SB-1650	HOF 1971, Gold HOF s. post.-200, d. 1982
☆ **Palmer, Arnold**	**golf**	**20**	**50**	**GB-60**	**RS, FA**
Palmer, Jim	base	10	20	SB-30, Sbat-70	HOF 1990, Gold HOF s. post.-15, Perez-Steele s. post.-20
Parent, Bernie	hock	10	20	Spuck-35	HOF 1984
Park, Brad	hock	5	15	Spuck-25	HOF 1988
Parker, Clarence	foot	5	15	SB-150	HOF 1972
Parker, Dan, 1893-1967	box	35	60		USA, sports editor, columnist
Parker, Jim	foot	5	15	SB-75, Mhelm-50	HOF 1973
Parnassus, George, 1897-1975	box	35	70		Greece, promoter
Parrish, Robert	bask	10	20	SB-75	
Parsons, Benny	auto	10	20		Auto Racing
Paterno, Joe	foot	10	30		College football coach, FA
Patterson, Floyd, 1935-	box	10	20	SG-75	USA, H, reluctant, yet RS
Payton, Walter	foot	20	45	SB-175, Mhelm-100	HOF 1993
Pennock, Herb	base	250	650	SB-3200	HOF 1948, Canc. check-1200, d. 1948
Pep, Willie, 1922-	box	5	10	SG-50	USA, F, RS, perhaps the best!
Perez, Pascual, 1926-1977	box	65	175		Argentina, FL
Perreault, Gil	hock	5	15	Spuck-25	HOF 1990
Perry, Gaylord	base	5	15	SB-25, Sbat-50	HOF 1991, Canc. check-25, Gold HOF s. post.-7, Perez-Steele s. post.-15
Perry, Joe	foot	5	15	SB-75, Mhelm-50	HOF 1969
Pettit, Bob	bask	10	20	SB-150	HOF 1970
Petty, Lee	auto	20	65		Auto Racing
☆ **Petty, Richard**	**auto**	**10**	**25**		**Auto Racing, RS**
Phillip, Andy	bask	10	20	SB-150	HOF 1961
Phillips, Tommy	hock	350	700		HOF 1945, d. 1923
Piazza, Mike	base	25	35	SB-50	
Piccolo, Brian	foot	200	500		ESPV, d. 1979
Pihos, Pete	foot	5	15	SB-75, Mhelm-50	HOF 1970
Pilote, Pierre	hock	5	15	Spuck-20	HOF 1975
Pippen, Scottie	bask	25	35	BB-200	
Pitre, Didier	hock	300	600		HOF 1962, d. 1934
Plank, Eddie	base	1000	3500	SB-10,000	HOF 1946, d. 1926
Plante, Jacques	hock	100	250	Spuck-250	HOF 1978, d. 1986
Pollard, Jim	bask	25	50	SB-250	HOF 1977, d. 1993
Potvin, Denis	hock	5	15	Spuck-20	HOF 1991
Primeau, Joe	hock	125	275		HOF 1963, d. 1989

Tony Lazzeri

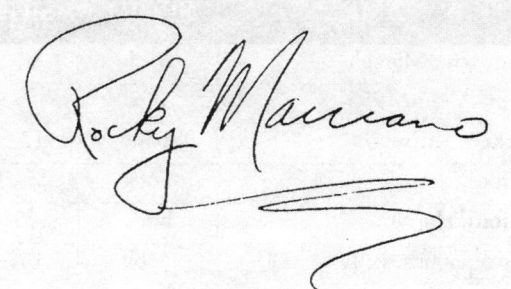

Rocky Marciano

Benny Leonard

Rocky Marciano

Joe Louis

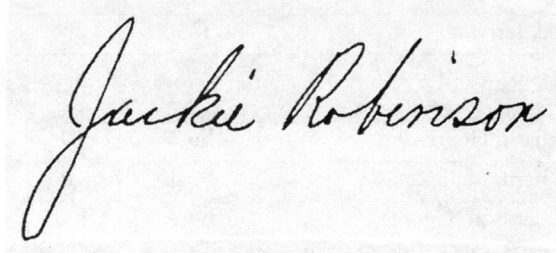

Jackie Robinson

Connie Mack

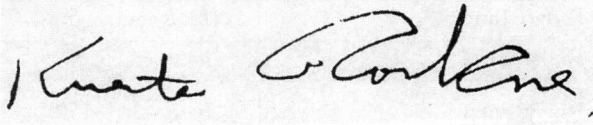

Knute Rockne

Connie Mack

George H. "Babe" Ruth

NAME	SPORT	SIG	SP	S.MEMO/MISC.	COMMENTS
Pronovost, Marcel	hock	5	15	Spuck-25	HOF 1978
Pryor, Aaron, 1955-	box	5	10	SG-45	USA, JW, RS
Puckett, Kirby	base	12	30	SB-50, Sbat-125	RS
Pulford, Bob	hock	5	15	Spuck-25	HOF 1991
Pulford, Harry	hock	175	400		HOF 1945, d. 1940
Quackenbush, Bill	hock	10	20		HOF 1976
Radbourne, Hoss	base	2000		S. doc.-5500	HOF 1939, ESPV, FA, d. 1897, scarce
Rahal, Bobby	auto	10	25		Auto Racing
Ramsey, Frank	bask	5	20	SB-100	HOF 1981
Rankin, Frank	hock	225	500		HOF 1961, d. 1932
Ratelle, Jean	hock	5	15	Spuck-20	HOF 1985
Ray, Shorty	foot	150	400		HOF 1966, d. 1956
Rayner, Chuck	hock	5	15	Spuck-20	HOF 1973
Reardon, Ken	hock	10	20	Spuck-40	HOF 1966
Reed, Willis	bask	5	15	SB-100	HOF 1981
Reese, Pee Wee	base	15	35	SB-65, Sbat-150	HOF 1984, Gold HOF s. post.-40, Perez-Steele s. post.-35
Reeves, Dan OWN	foot	75			HOF 1967, d. 1971
Renfro, Mel	foot	5	15	SB-75, Mhelm-50	HOF 1996
Rice, Jerry	foot	25	35	SB-175	
Rice, Sam	base	40	200	SB-1500, b&w HOF s. post.-125	HOF 1963, Gold HOF s. post.-150, d. 1974
Richard, Henri	hock	10	20	Spuck-30	HOF 1979
Richard, Maurice	hock	10	20	Spuck-25	HOF 1961
Richardson, George	hock	400			HOF 1950, d. 1916
Rickard, George "Tex", 1871-1929	box	175	375	SG-1700	USA, promoter
Rickey, Branch	base	150	400	SB-2000	HOF 1967, Canc. check-800, d. 1965
Riggins, John	foot	15	40	SB-125, Mhelm-75	HOF 1992
Ringo, Jim	foot	5	15	SB-100, Mhelm-50	HOF 1981
Ripken, Cal	base	30	50	SB-75, Sbat-200	FA
Rixey, Eppa	base	150	500	SB-2750	HOF 1963, Canc. check-150, d. 1964
Rizzuto, Phil	base	10	15	SB-30, Sbat-100	HOF 1994, Gold HOF s. post.-20, Perez-Steele HOF s. post.-25, RS
Roberts, Gordon	hock	75	200		HOF 1971, d. 1966
Roberts, Robin	base	10	15	SB-30, Sbat-75	HOF 1976, Gold HOF s. post.-7, Perez-Steele s. post.-15
Robertson, Oscar	bask	20	40	SB-175	HOF 1979
Robinson, Brooks	base	5	20	SB-30, Sbat-50	HOF 1983, Canc. check-25, Gold HOF s. post.-10, Perez-Steele s. post.-15

NAME	SPORT	SIG	SP	S.MEMO/MISC.	COMMENTS
Robinson, Frank	base	10	25	SB-35. Sbat-175	HOF 1982, Gold HOF s. post.-15, Perez-Steele s. post.-15
☆ **Robinson, Jackie**	**base**	**275**	**700**	**SB-4250**	**HOF 1962, Canc. check-465, GHOFPP-$390, Gold HOF s. post.-350, b&w HOF s. post.-800, d. 1972**
Robinson, Sugar Ray, 1920-1989	box	45	160	SG-750	USA, W, M, was responsive to requests
Robinson, Wilbert	base	800	2300	SB-AA	HOF 1945, d. 1934
Robustelli, Andy	foot	5	15	SB-75, Mhelm-50	HOF 1971
Rockne, Knute	foot	400	1500		d. 1931
Rodman, Dennis	bask	25	40	BB-225	
Rodriguez, Alex	base	20	35	SB-50	
Rodriguez, Luis, 1937-1996	box	20	45	SG-145	Cuba, W
Rooney, Art	foot	30	125		HOF 1964, d. 1988
Rose, Pete	base	15	30	SB-40, Sbat-125	
Rosenbloom, Maxie, 1904-1976	box	45	90	SG-360	USA, LH, was responsive to requests
Ross, Art	hock	250	500		HOF 1945, d. 1964
Ross, Barney, 1909-1967	box	45	100	SG-375	USA, W, JW, L
Roush, Edd	base	20	50	SB-325	HOF 1962, Gold HOF s. post.-25, Perez-Steele s. post.-75, b&w HOF s. post.-40, d. 1988
Roy, Patrick	hock	25	40	Puck-60	
Rozelle, Pete	foot	20	50	SB-175	HOF 1985, d. 1998
Ruffing, Red	base	30	115	SB-500	HOF 1967, Gold HOF s. post.-85, d. 1986
Rusie, Amos	base	1000	3000	SB-AA	HOF 1977, d. 1942, scarce in all forms
Russell, Bill	bask	100	200	SB-500	HOF 1974, ESPV, tough signature, FA
Russell, Blair	hock	100	200		HOF 1965, d. 1961
Russell, Ernie	hock	80	175		HOF 1965, d. 1963
☆ **Ruth, Babe**	**base**	**800**	**2650**	**SB-8000**	**HOF 1936, Canc. check-1750, ESPV, FA, d. 1948, sign. w/Gehrig-$3750**
Ruttan, Jack	hock	50	150		HOF 1962, d. 1973
Ryan, Nolan	base	20	40	SB-65, Sbat-200	HOF 1999, FA
Ryan, Tommy, 1870-1948	box	165	370		USA, W, M
Sabatini, Gabriela	tennis	10	30	TB-40	
Saddler, Sandy, 1926-	box	10	25	SG-70	USA, F, JL, RS, sig. variations
Sampras, Pete	tennis	15	35	TB-45	FA
Sarazan, Gene	golf	10	25	GB-40	
Savard, Denis	hock	5	15	Spuck-20	
Savard, Serge	hock	5	15	Spuck-25	HOF 1986

S P O R T S

R

NAME	SPORT	SIG	SP	S.MEMO/MISC.	COMMENTS
Sawchuk, Terry	hock	200	400		HOF 1971 d. 1970, ESPV
Sayers, Gale	foot	10	20	SB-125, Mhelm-75	HOF 1977
Schalk, Ray	base	65	165	SB-1325	HOF 1955, Gold HOF s. post.-400, b&w HOF s. post.-300, d. 1970
Schayes, Dolph	bask	10	20	SB-150	HOF 1972
Schmeling, Max, 1905-	box	20	35	SG-175	Germany, H, RS
Schmidt, Joe	foot	5	15	SB-75, Mhelm-50	HOF 1973
Schmidt, Mike	base	10	25	SB-60, Sbat-150	HOF 1995, Gold HOF s. post.-50, Perez-Steele s. post.-60
Schmidt, Milt	hock	5	15	Spuck-25	HOF 1961
Schoendienst, Red	base	5	15	SB-25, Sbat-75	HOF 1989, Gold HOF s. post.-10, Perez-Steele s. post.-15
Schramm, Tex	foot	10	25		HOF 1991
Schriner, Sweeney	hock	50	125		HOF 1962, d. 1990
Seaver, Tom	base	10	20	SB-50, Sbat-100	HOF 1992, Gold HOF s. post.-20, Perez-Steele s. post.-40
Seibert, Oliver	hock	200	400		HOF 1961, d. 1944, ESPV
Seles, Monica	tennis	10	35	TB-45	FA
Selmon, Lee Roy	foot	5	15	SB-75, Mhelm-50	HOF 1995
Sewell, Joe,	base	15	40	SB-125	HOF 1977, Canc. check-50, Gold HOF s. post.-20, Perez-Steele s. post.-50, d. 1990
Sharkey, Jack, 1902-1994	box	80	165	SG-600	USA, H
Sharman, Bill	bask	10	20	SB-125	HOF 1975
Shell, Art	foot	10	20	SB-100, Mhelm-50	HOF 1989
Shore, Eddie	hock	125	300		HOF 1947, d. 1985
Shutt, Steve	hock	5	15	Spuck-20	HOF 1993
Siebert, Babe	hock	325			HOF 1964, d. 1939
Simmons, Al	base	200	500	SB-2000, b&w HOF s. post.-600	HOF 1953, Canc. check-175, d. 1956
Simms, Phil	foot	10	20	SB-125, Mhelm-75	MNF
Simpson, Joe	hock	65	150		HOF 1962, d. 1973
Simpson, O.J.	foot	15	40	SB-175, Mhelm-75	HOF 1985, ESPV
Singletary, Mike	foot	10	20	SB-125, Mhelm-75	HOF 1998
Sisler, George	base	60	150	SB-1500, b&w HOF s. post.-150	HOF 1939, Gold HOF s. post.-150, d. 1973
Sittler, Darryl	hock	5	15	Spuck-25	HOF 1989, RS
Slaughter, Enos	base	5	15	SB-25, Sbat-75	HOF 1985, Canc. check-35, Gold HOF s. post.-7, Perez-Steele s. post.-15
Smith, Al	hock	150	300		HOF 1962, d. 1953
Smith, Billy	hock	5	15	Spuck-20	HOF 1993
Smith, Clint	hock	5	15	Spuck-25	HOF 1991
Smith, Emmitt	foot	25	40	FB-200	

NAME	SPORT	SIG	SP	S.MEMO/MISC.	COMMENTS
Smith, Hooley	hock	100	250		HOF 1972, d. 1963
Smith, Jackie	foot	5	15	SB-75, Mhelm-50	HOF 1994
Smith, Ozzie	base	15	30	SB-35, Sbat-100	
Smith, Tommy	hock	100			HOF 1973, d. 1966
Snead, Sam	golf	15	35	GB-30	
Snider, Duke	base	10	25	SB-35, Sbat-100	HOF 1980, Canc. check-40, Gold HOF s. post.-15, Perez-Steele s. post.-25
Solomons, Jack, ?-1979	box	50	100		England, promoter, PU
Sosa, Sammy	base	60	75	SB-175	
Spahn, Warren	base	10	20	SB-30, Sbat-75	HOF 1973, Canc. check-20, Gold HOF s. post.-10, Perez-Steele s. post.-20
Spalding, Al	base	1000		SB-AA, S. doc-3000	HOF 1939, d. 1915
Speaker, Tris	base	300	850	SB-5150, b&w HOF s. post.-800	HOF 1937, d. 1958
Spinks, Michael, 1956-	box	10	20	SG-75	USA, LH, H, can be elusive, FA
Spitz, Mark, 1950-	swim	20	50		U.S. swimmer, elusive signer!, FA
St. Clair, Bob	foot	5	15	SB-75, Mhelm-50	HOF 1990
Stanley, Allan	hock	10	20	Spuck-30	HOF 1981
Stanley, Barney	hock	15			HOF 1962, d. 1971
Stargell, Willie	base	5	20	SB-25, Sbat-100	HOF 1988, Gold HOF s. post.-7, Perez-Steele s. post.-15
Starr, Bart	foot	10	20	SB-125, Mhelm-100	HOF 1977
Staubach, Roger	foot	10	35	SB-150, Mhelm-100	HOF 1985, RS
Stautner, Ernie	foot	5	15	SB-100, Mhelm-50	HOF 1969
Stenerud, Jan	foot	5	15	SB-75, Mhelm-50	HOF 1991
Stengel, Casey	base	75	200	SB-1000	HOF 1966, Gold HOF s. post.-150, d. 1975
Steward, Emanuel, 1944-	box	5	10	SG-45	USA, trainer, manager
Stewart, Jack	hock	100	150		HOF 1964, d. 1983
Stewart, Jackie	auto	10	25		Auto Racing, RS
Stewart, Nels	hock	200	300		HOF 1962, d. 1957
Stribling, Young, 1904-1933	box	500	1250		USA, LH, H
Strong, Ken	foot	65	150		HOF 1967, Canc. check-100, d. 1979
Stuart, Hod	hock	550			HOF 1945, d. 1907, ESPV
Stydahar, Joe	foot	65	150		HOF 1967, d. 1977
☆ **Sullivan, John L., 1858-1918**	**box**	**1100**	**1800**		**USA, H**
Tarkenton, Fran	foot	10	25	SB-125, Mhelm-100	HOF 1986
Taub, Sam, ?-1979	box	50	110		USA, broadcaster
Taylor, Charley	foot	10	20	SB-100, Mhelm-60	HOF 1984
Taylor, Cyclone	hock	175			HOF 1947, d. 1979

NAME	SPORT	SIG	SP	S.MEMO/MISC.	COMMENTS
Taylor, Herman, 1887-1980	box	35	85		USA, promoter
Taylor, Jim	foot	8	20	SB-100, Mhelm-50	HOF 1976
Taylor, Lawrence	foot	10	20	SB-125, Mhelm-75	HOF 1999
Terry, Bill	base	20	50	SB-300, b&w HOF s. post.-40	HOF 1954, Canc. check-60, Gold HOF s. post.-25, Perez-Steele s. post.-75, d. 1989
Thomas, Frank	base	25	50	SB-60	
Thomas, Isiah	bask	10	20	SB-75	
Thompson, Sam	base	1500		S. doc.-4000, SB-AA	HOF 1974, ESPV, FA, scarce, d. 1922
Thompson, Tiny	hock	125	250		HOF 1959, d. 1981
Thomson, Bobby	base	5	15	SB-30, Sbat-60	Canc. check-30
Thorpe, Jim	foot	500	1325		HOF 1963, d. 1953
Thurmond, Nate	bask	5	15	SB-100	HOF 1984
Tiger, Dick, 1929-1971	box	85	220	SG-900	Nigeria, M, LH
Tilden, Bill	tennis	150	350	TB-AA	
Tinker, Joe	base	450	1200	SB-4250	HOF 1946, d. 1948
Tittle, Y.A.	foot	10	20	SB-125, Mhelm-60	HOF 1971
Torres, Jose, 1936-	box	5	10	SG-50	Puerto Rico, LH, RS
Trafton, George	foot	100	300		HOF 1964, Canc. check-150, d. 1971
Traynor, Pie	base	150	500	SB-2000, b&w HOF s. post.-300	HOF 1948, Gold HOF s. post.-500, d. 1972
Tretiak, Vladislav	hock	15	25	Spuck-40	HOF 1989
Trevino, Lee	golf	10	25	GB-40	FA
Trihey, Harry J.	hock	250			HOF 1950, d. 1942
Trippi, Charley	foot	5	15	SB-100, Mhelm-50	HOF 1968, Canc. check-20
Tunnell, Emlen	foot	60	175		HOF 1967, d. 1975
Tunney, Gene, 1897-1978	box	85	200	SG-800	USA, H, RS
Turner, Clyde, 1919-1990	foot	10	25		HOF 1966, Canc.check-15
Twyman, Jack	bask	5	15	SB-75	HOF 1982
Ullman, Norm	hock	10	20	Spuck-30	HOF 1982
Unitas, Johnny	foot	10	30	SB-150, Mhelm-100	HOF 1979
Unseld, Wes	bask	5	15	SB-75	HOF 1988
Unser, Al	auto	10	20		Auto Racing, RS
Unser, Al, Jr.	auto	10	20		Auto Racing, RS
Unser, Bobby	auto	10	20		Auto Racing, RS
Upshaw, Gene	foot	5	15	SB-75, Mhelm-50	HOF 1987
VanBrocklin, Norm	foot	60	125	SB-400	HOF 1971, d. 1983
VanBuren, Steve	foot	8	20	SB-125, Mhelm-50	HOF 1965
Vance, Dazzy	base	200	500	SB-2000	HOF 1955, d. 1961
VanderMeer, Johnny	base	15	40	SB-60	Canc. check-30, d. 1997
Vaughan, Arky	base	300	600	SB-3000	HOF 1985, d. 1952

NAME	SPORT	SIG	SP	S.MEMO/MISC.	COMMENTS
Veeck, Bill	base	30	75	SB-825	HOF 1991, Canc. check-100, d. 1987
Villa, Pancho, 1901-1925	box	600	1350		Philipines, FL, extremely scarce signature
Waddell, Rube	base	1400		S. doc.-4000, SB-AA	HOF 1946, d. 1914
Wagner, Honus	base	400	1000	SB-4250	HOF 1936, Canc. check-2000, d. 1955
Waitz, Grete	mara	15	25		Marathon champion
Walcott, Jersey Joe, 1914-1994	box	30	75	SG-300	USA, H, was responsive to requests
Walker, Doak, 1927-1998	foot	10	30	SB-150, Mhelm-50	HOF 1986
Walker, Jack	hock	175			HOF 1960, d. 1950
Walker, James J., 1881-	box	35	50		USA, politician
Walker, Mickey, 1901-1981	box	60	175	SG-700	USA, W, M, was responsive to requests
Wallace, Bobby	base	500	1500	SB-3000	HOF 1953, b&w HOF s. post.-1500, d. 1960, ESPV
Wallace, Rusty	auto	10	25		Auto Racing, RS
Walsh, Bill	foot	5	15	SB-75	HOF 1993
Walsh, Ed	base	250	750	SB-4000	HOF 1946, b&w HOF s. post.-400, d. 1959
Walton, Bill	bask	5	15	SB-75	HOF 1993
Waner, Lloyd	base	25	150	SB-525	HOF 1967, Gold HOF s. post.-30, Perez-Steele s. post.-AA, RS, d. 1982
Waner, Paul	base	175	300	SB-2000	HOF 1952, b&w HOF s. post.-350, d. 1965
Ward, John	base	2000		S. doc.-4000, SB-AA	HOF 1964, d. 1925
Warfield, Paul	foot	5	15	SB-75, Mhelm-50	HOF 1983
Waterfield, Bob	foot	50	125	SB-350	HOF 1965, d, 1983
Watson, Harry	hock	10	25	Spuck-30	HOF 1994
Watson, Harry E.	hock	150			HOF 1962, d. 1957
Watson, Tom	golf	10	25	GB-35	RS
Weaver, Earl	base	5	20	SB-30, Sbat-75	HOF 1996, Gold HOF s. post.-15
Weiland, Cooney	hock	75	175	8x10 Photo	HOF 1971, d. 1965
Weinmeister, Arnie	foot	5	15	SB-75, Mhelm-50	HOF 1984
Welch, Mickey	base	1500	5000	SB-25000	HOF 1973, d. 1941, scarce
West, Jerry	bask	12	35	SB-150	HOF 1979
Westwick, Harry	hock	165			HOF 1962, d. 1957
Wheat, Zack	base	50	150	SB-2000	HOF 1959, Canc. check-600, Gold HOF s. post.-350, b&w HOF s. post.-250, d. 1972
Whitcroft, Fred	hock	300			HOF 1962, d. 1931
White, Randy	foot	5	15	SB-75, Mhelm-50	HOF 1994
Wilde, Jimmy, 1892-1969	box	130	225		Wales, FL

Babe Ruth

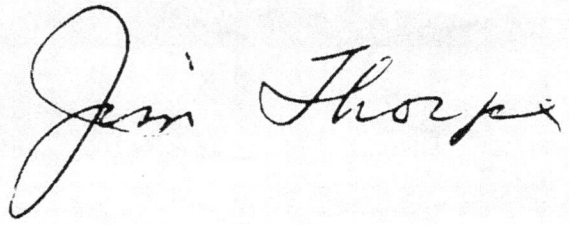

Jim Thorpe

William Tilden

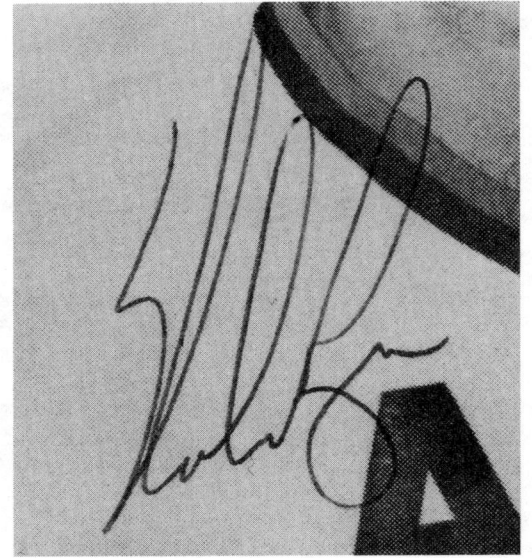

Nolan Ryan

Gene Tunney

Al Simmons

John Sullivan

Honus Wagner

NAME	SPORT	SIG	SP	S.MEMO/MISC.	COMMENTS
Wilhelm, Hoyt	base	5	15	SB-24, Sbat-65	HOF 1985, Canc. check-25, Gold HOF s. post.-5, Perez-Steele s. post.-10
Wilkens, Lenny	bask	5	20	SB-75	HOF 1989
Williams, Billy	base	5	15	SB-25, Sbat-60	HOF 1987, Gold HOF s. post.-10, Perez-Steele s. post.-10
Williams, Ike, 1923-1994	box	20	30	SG-140	USA, L, RS
Williams, Kid, 1893-1963	box	80	165		Denmark, B
Williams, Ted	**base**	**50**	**150**	**SB-200, Sbat-1500**	**HOF 1966, Gold HOF s. post.-125, Perez-Steele s. post.-200, ESPV, FA**
Willis, Bill	foot	5	15	SB-75, Mhelm-50	HOF 1977
Willis, Vic	base	1000		S. doc.-4000, SB-AA	HOF 1995, d. 1947
Wills, Harry, 1889-1958	box	125	260		USA, H
Wills, Helen	tennis	40	80	TB-N/A	
Wilson, Hack	base	450	1000	SB-4650	HOF 1979, Canc. check-700, ESPV, d. 1948
Wilson, Larry	foot	10	15	SB-100, Mhelm-50	HOF 1978
Wilson, Phat	hock	60	225		HOF 1962, d. 1970
Winslow, Kellen	foot	5	15	SB-75, Mhelm-50	HOF 1995
Wojciechowicz, Alex	foot	15	40	SGLA-1000	HOF 1968, d. 1992
Wood, Joe	base	20	100	SB-500	Canc. check-50, 1985
Wood, Willie	foot	5	15	SB-75, Mhelm-60	HOF 1989
Wooden, John	bask	10	30	SB-125	HOF 1960, RS
Woods, Tiger	golf	35	75	GB-100	ESPV, FA
Worsley, Gump	hock	10	15	Spuck-25	HOF ESPV, FA1980
Worthy, James	bask	8	20	SB-75	
Wright, Chalky, 1912-1957	box	70	150		Mexico, F
Wright, George	base	725	2500	SB-8000	HOF 1937, d. 1937, ESPV
Wright, Harry	base	1500		S. doc.-5000, SB-AA	HOF 1953, d. 1895, ESPV, scarce in all forms
Wynn, Early	base	5	20	SB-35, Sbat-100	HOF 1972, Canc. check-35, Gold HOF s. post.-15, Perez-Steele s. post.-20
Yastrzemski, Carl	base	10	30	SB-50, Sbat-175	HOF 1989, Gold HOF s. post.-25, Perez-Steele s. post.-25
Young, Cy	base	375	1500	SB-5000, b&w HOF s. post.-1000	HOF 1937, d. 1955
Youngs, Ross	base	725		S. doc.-2600, SB-AA	HOF 1972, scarce, d. 1927
Yount, Robin	base	10	30	SB-45, Sbat-100	HOF 1999
Yzerman, Steve	hock	20	30	Puck-40	
Zaharias, Babe D.	golf	250	750	GB-N/A	
Zale, Tony, 1913-	box	20	40	SG-165	USA, M, RS
Zarate, Carlos, 1951-	box	15	30	SG-100	Mexico, B, can be an elusive signer
Zivic, Fritzie, 1913-1984	box	25	50	SG-170	USA, W, RS

S
P
O
R
T
S

W

General & Political

This broad category covers the great many people whose faces may not be so easily recognizable, but whose contributions to history, our political system, technology and business are awe-inspiring. The world would not be the place it is today had it not been for the work of these ground-breaking individuals and leaders, from history-makers through today's brightest minds. This category includes:

- Colonial and Revolutionary America
- Civil War era
- Artists, Illustrators, Architects
- Art Theorists, Art Critics and Photographers
- Business leaders, Economists, Financiers and Publishers
- Medicine and technology
- Astronauts, Cosmonauts
- Heads of State
- Presidents and First Ladies
- Politicians, Educators, Reformers, Lawyers and Labor Leaders
- Supreme Court Justices
- Religious Leaders and Clergy

General & Political Guide

NAME	DATES	SIG	DS	ALS	SP	COMMENTS
Aalto, Alvar	**1898-1976**	**20**				**Finnish architect, designer, sculptor, painter**
Abbey, Edwin Austin	1852-1911	25	50	70		American painter, etcher, D-$1600
Abbot, Charles G.	1872-1973	20	45		40	Astrophysicist
Abbott, Lyman	1835-1922	30	55	80	50	U.S. clergyman, reformer
Abercrombie, John Joseph	1798-1877	65	100	250		Son-in-law of Gen. R.Patterson, SALS-2X; MW; Seven Pines, Malvern Hill, Falling Waters
Abernathy, Ralph D.	1926-1990	25	75	125	75	Baptist clergyman, civil rights activist, SDS, ALS, 2X
Aboville, Francois Marie, Count d'	1730-1817	240	510	1250		French officer; Yorktown
Abrams, Creighton Williams, Jr.	1914-1974	20	40	60	70	American general, WWII, KW, VW
Abzug, Bella	1920-1988	15		50	25	Congresswoman
Acheson, Dean	1893-1971	20	60	110	50	U.S. sec. of state, SP-$150, ESPV
Acton, Loren W.		5	15	25	10	Challenger, 7/29/85
Adam, Henri-Georges	1904-1967	10	20	40	30	French sculptor, graphic artist, D-$250
Adami, Valerio	1935-	20	35	60		Italian pop artist
Adams, Abigail Smith	1744-1818	525	1825	7000		(1772); MA; S-3; D-2
Adams, Ansel Easton	1902-1984	150	300	525	350	U.S.landscape photo., SB-$300, STLS-$1400, RS
Adams, Brooks	1848-1927	75	130	220	100	U.S. historian
Adams, Charles Francis	1807-1886	40	130	200		Political leader, diplomat, s. J.Q. Adams
Adams, Daniel Wesiger	1821- 1872	215	300	450		Killed in a duel, SALS-2X; Practiced law in New Orleans; Shiloh, Chickamauga
Adams, Henry	1838-1918	125	250	350	150	U.S. historian, TLS - 1.5 - 2X
☆ **Adams, John**	**1735-1826**	**1850**	**5000**	**15500**		**First pres. to live in the White House; FF:3350, MA-2900, ESPV, ALS**
Adams, John	1825-1864	400	890	2500		KIA; WP; MW; Vicksburg, Atlanta, ESPV

NAME	DATES	SIG	DS	ALS	SP	COMMENTS
Adams, John Quincy	1767-1848	375	1450	2650		ALS of content 7x-9x, s. engraving-$5500, LG-825
Adams, Louisa Catherine	1775-1852	240	500	1000		(1797); MD; b. London; S-3; D-1, First Lady
Adams, Samuel	1722-1803	750	2025	4750		Signer of DOI; patriot; agitator; gov., SALS, 2X, ESPV
Adams, Scott	1957-	20	40		55	Cartoonist, "Dilbert"
Adams, William Wirt	1819-1888	300	600	900		Killed in a street quarrel; SL, Postmaster of Jackson; Vicksburg
Adamson, James C.		8	20	30	15	Columbia, 8/9/89, Atlantis, 8/3/91, FA
Addams, Charles	1912-1988	60	125			Macabre cartoons, "The Addams Family"
Addams, Jane	1860-1935	75	175	325	275	Cofounder of Hull House
Addison, Joseph	1672-1719	100	200	300		English essayist, poet, statesman, critic
Adenauer, Konrad	1876-1967	50	175	250	150	W. German chancellor, ESPV, ALS
Adler, Alfred	1870-1937	125	550	600	200	Austrian psychologist, SALS=2X, ESPV
Afansev, Viktor		15	40	40	20	Soyuz TM-11, 12/2/90
Agam, Yaacov (Jacob Gipstein)	1928-	20	30	50		Israeli sculptor, D-$4000
Agassiz, Jean Louis Rodolphe	1807-1873	100	125	300	650	Swiss-born US paleontologist, geologist
Agnew, Spiro Theodore	1918-1996	30	150	260	75	Political leader, vice president, FA
Aguinaldo, Emilio	1869-1964	125	150	200	150	Philippines revolutionary
Aiken, Howard	1900-1973	30	50	145	75	U.S. mathematician
Akers, Thomas D.		5	10	20	10	Discovery, 10/6/90, Endeavour, 5/7/92, RS
Akiyama, Toyohiro		20	30	45	25	Soyuz TM-11, 12/2/90, Japanese journalist
Albers, Josef	1888-1976	30	45	70		German-American painter, P-$6000
Albert I (Belgium)	1875-1934	40	100	150		
Albright, Adam Emery	1862-1957	30	50	80		American painter
Albright, Ivan Le Lorraine	1897-1983	15	20	35		American painter, P-$1200
Albright, Malvin Marr	1897-1983	10	15	30		American painter, D-$550
Aldrich, Nelson W.	1841-1915	15	20	40	20	Political leader
Aldrin, Edwin E., Jr.		65	225	300	150	Gemini 12, 2nd MW, TSS, ESPV, SP

NAME	DATES	SIG	DS	ALS	SP	COMMENTS
Alechinsky, Pierre	1927-	20	30	50		Belgian painter & graphic artist
Alexander I (Pavlovich)	1777-1825	400	750	1000		Russian czar, SDS, 2X
Alexander II (Russia)	1818-1881	400	750	875		LS-$750, ESPV, ALS
Alexander of Tunis	1891-1969	75	125	175	120	British field marshal
Alexander, "Stirling" William	1726-1783	225	700	1600		Cont'l. general; papers in NYPL
Alexander, Edward Porter	1835-1910	450	875			One of Three artillery Brigadier-Generals; WP, Distinguished post-war career; First Manassas, Gettysburg, Chickamauga*, ESPV
Alexanderson, Ernst	1878-1975	50	125	225	175	High frequency alternator inventor
Alford, Andrew	1904-	20	35	70	40	Localizer antenna system inventor
Alken, Samuel	1750-1815	125	165	300		British sporting artists
Allaire, Paul A.	1938-	5	15		10	Xerox CEO
Allen, Andrew M.		5	10	20	10	Atlantis, 7/31/92, Columbia, 3/4/94, RS
☆ **Allen, Ethan**	**1738-1789**	**700**	**1750**	**3000**		**American officer; author of many rare books**
Allen, Henry Watkins	1820-1866	260	450	750		Established newspaper in Mexico City; Lawyer, SL, TW, Governor of Louisiana; Shiloh
Allen, Joseph P.		10	15	30	20	Columbia, 11/11/82, Discovery, 11/8/84
Allen, Martin A.		5	15		10	Computervision CEO
Allen, Robert	1811-1886	45	55	110		MW; Quartermaster duties
Allen, William Wirt	1835-1894	215	450	600		SALS-2X; Princeton, U.S. Marshall; Shiloh, Kentucky Invasion, Atlanta
Allenby, Edmund Henry Hyman, 1st Viscount	1861-1936	75	160	200		British field marshal, ESPV
Allende Gossens, Salvador	1908-1973	50	140	275	100	Chilean Marxist pres., ousted
Alley, William J.		5	20		10	American Brands CEO
Allison, William B.	1829-1908	15	25	40	20	Political leader, USS
Allston, Washington	1779-1843	300	450	750		American painter and writer
Alma-Tadema, Sir Lawrence	1836-1912	30	60	140		Dutch painter, m. Laura, D-$1200
Almond, Edward Mallory	1892-1979	45	120	150		American general, WWI, WWII, KW, ESPV
Alsop, John	?-1794	190	375	875		Congressman; patriot; s. Richard; John

Abigail Adams

John Adams

Ansel Adams

John Quincy Adams

John Adams

John Quincy Adams

John Adams

John Quincy Adams

John Adams

John Quincy Adams

John Adams

John Quincy Adams & Louisa Catherine Adams

NAME	DATES	SIG	DS	ALS	SP	COMMENTS
Altgeld, John P.	1847-1902	10	40	50	20	Political leader, governor (IL)
Alvarez, Luis Walter	1911-1988	20	40	100	35	Radio distance & direct. indicator dev.
Alvord, Benjamin	1813-1884	35	50	75		WP, MW, reasearcher & writer
Ames, Adelbert	1835-1933	50	80	250		Last full-rank general survivor on either side; USS, gov. Miss.; First Manassas, Peninsular, Gettysburg
Amherst, Jeffery	1717-1797	525	1125	1650		British general; controversial; popular in U.K., SALS=2X
Ammen, Jacob	1806-1894	25	40	100		College professor, civil engineer; Shiloh, Corinth
Ampere, Andre-Marie	1775-1836	185	450	1500		Electrodynamics scientist, ESPV, ALS
Anders, William A.		45	100		100	Apollo 8
Anderson, Bill		5	10		10	Publisher, "The Atlantic Monthly"
Anderson, Brad	1924-	10	15	20	25	Cartoonist, "Marmaduke," RS!
Anderson, George Burgwyn	1831-1862	275	540			Tough fighter! Williamsburg, Sharpsburg, ESPV
Anderson, George Thomas "Tige"	1824-1901	125	250	400		Chief of Police in Atlanta; MW, Atlanta Chief of Police; Second Manassas, Gettysburg, Chickamauga
Anderson, J. Reid		5	10		5	Verbatim CEO
Anderson, James Patton	1822-1872	365				MW, SL, U.S. Marshall, tax collector; Shiloh, Murfreesboro, Chickamauga, ESPV
Anderson, Joseph Reid	1813-1892	175	400	650		WP, Tredegar Iron Works - Richmond; Seven Days
Anderson, Richard Heron	1821-1879	80	200	300		Poverty stricken after war; WP, MW; Sayler's Creek
Anderson, Robert	1805-1871	150	300	400		MW; Charleston Harbor
Anderson, Robert Houstoun	1835-1888	150	275	325		WP, Chief of Police - Savannah; Numerous engagements under Wheeler
Anderson, Samuel Read	1804-1883	150	300	400		MW, Postmaster - Nashville; Western Virginia
Andre, Carl	1935-	40	45	85		American Minimal sculptor, controversial
Andre, John	1751-1780	1750				British officer and spy; executed for latter, ESPV
Andreas, Dwayne O.	1918-	6	15		10	Honeymead Products CEO

NAME	DATES	SIG	DS	ALS	SP	COMMENTS
Andrews, Christopher Columbus	1829-1922	30	50	225		Lawyer, Harvard, newspaper writer, diplomat; Murfreesboro, Arkansas, Mobile
Andrews, George Leonard	1828-1899	40	60	100		WP, professor, US marshal; Cedar Mt., Sharpsburg, Port Hudson
Andriessen, Jurriaen	1742-1819	125				Dutch artist, D-$1000
Anne, Princess (England)		100	200		150	Daughter of Elizabeth II
Anthony, Susan B.	**1820-1906**	**200**	**1225**	**1750**	**1500**	**U.S. temperance, anti-slavery leader, ESPV**
Appel, Karel	1921-	50				Dutch abstract painter, sculptor, graphic artist
Applebaum, Irwyn	1955-	5	10		8	Bantam Books president
Apt, Jay		5	10	25	10	Endeavour, 9/12/92, 4/9/94, RS
Apt, Jerome		10	15	30	15	Atlantis, 4/5/91
Arafat, Yassir		125			250	
Archer, James Jay	1817-1864	285	400	675		Princeton, Univ. of Maryland, MW.; Numerous with the Army of Northern Virginia
Arden, Elizabeth (F.N. Graham)	1884-1966	35	55	120	50	Founder of cosmetics empire
Arledge, David A.	1945-	5	10		5	Coastal Corporation president
Arman (Armand Fernandez)	1928-	25				French-born assemblages artist
Armistead, Lewis Addison	1817-1863	600		1185		KIA, Pricing undetermined; WP, MW; Gettysburg, ESPV
Armitage, Kenneth	1916-	10				British sculptor, D-$1000
Armour, Philip D.	1832-1901	50			80	Industrialist, evolved meat packing
Armstrong, Edwin Howard	1890-1954	80	225	450	275	Dev. method of receiving high freq. oscil.
Armstrong, Frank Crawford	1835-1909	200	400		750	Holy Cross, U.S. Indian Inspector; First Manassas, Pea Ridge
Armstrong, John	1717-1795	220	360	800		Cont'l B.G.; USHR; father of John
Armstrong, John	1758-1843	60	200	400		American officer; USS; sec. of war; ALS-2X
Armstrong, Neil A.		**250**	**750**	**1500**	**400**	**Gemini 8, Apollo 11, TLS-$1,000, 1st MW**
Arno, Peter	1904-1968	25	40	60	50	New Yorker contributor
Arnold, Benedict	1741-1801	1800	3250	5000		Cont'l general; traitor; SALS-2X, SDS-2X
Arnold, Henry Harley "Hap"	1886-1950	65	350	475	225	American general, WWI, WWII

NAME	DATES	SIG	DS	ALS	SP	COMMENTS
Arnold, Lewis Golding	1817-1871	40	80	200		MW; Fort Pickens
Arnold, Richard	1828-1882	50	80	150		Son of RI gov., WP; First Manassas, Peninsular, Savage's Station
Arp, Jean (Hans)	1887-1966	60	120	200		French sculptor and painter
Arrow, Kenneth	1921-	15	30		20	Economist
☆ **Arthur, Chester Alan**	**1830-1886**	**350**	**800**	**1250**	**700**	**U.S. President, SALS (term)-$3750, MA-750, WH/EMC-425**
Arthur, Ellen Lewis Herndon	1837-1880	600	1000	1200		(1859); VA; S-2; D-1, First Lady
Artukhin, Yuri P.		35	75		70	Soyuz 14
Artzt, Edwin L.	1930-	5	15		10	Procter & Gamble director
Asboth, Alexander Sandor	1811-1868	55	140	200		Diplomat; Elkhorn Tavern, Marianna
Ash, Mary Kay	1915-	5	15	20	10	Mary Kay Cosmetics founder
Ashby, Turner	1828-1862	500	1000	1250		KIA, brilliant cavalry leader, SALS-2-3X; Shenandoah Valley
Ashe, John	1720-1781	125	315	565		Patriot; politician and militia B.G.
Ashley, William Henry	1778-1838	25	40	65		Political leader, USHR
Asquith, Herbert H.	1852-1928	40	75	125	150	British liberal prime minister
Astor, John Jacob	1763-1848	350	1750	5000		Real estate magnate, banker
Astor, William B.	1792-1875	150		325		Heir of J.J. Astor, ANS-$145
Atanasoff, John V.	1903-1995	20	40	80	50	U.S. (ABC) computer pioneer, physicist
Atchison, David R.		500	1000	1150		
Attlee, Clement	1883-1967	50	150	225	100	British labor party ldr., prime minister
Auchinleck, Sir Claude John Ayre	1884-1981	50	100			British field marshal, "The Auk", ESPV-ALS
☆ **Audubon, John James**	**1785-1851**	**800**	**2000**	**1500**		**Amer. painter, SALS-2X, DS-$2200 w/wife**
Audubon, John Woodhouse	1812-1862	350				American painter-naturalist, s. of John
Audubon, Victor Gifford	1809-1860	175				American painter-naturalist, s. of John
Auerbach, Frank	1931-	50			685	German-born painter
Augereau, Pierre Francois Charles	1757-1816	150	400	500		French Marshal of the Empire, PU
Augur, Christopher Columbus	1821-1898	60	110	150		MW, WP; Peninsular, Cedar Mt., Port Hudson
Augustine, Norman R.	1935-	5	10		10	Lockheed Martin Chairman

Louisa Catherine Adams

Susan B. Anthony

Louisa Catherine Adams

Benedict Arnold

Sam Adams

Benedict Arnold

Jeffrey Amherst

H. H. ARNOLD,
General, U. S. Army,
Commanding General, Army Air Forces.

Susan B. Anthony

H.H. "Hap" Arnold

NAME	DATES	SIG	DS	ALS	SP	COMMENTS
Augustus II of Poland	1670-1733		375			
Austin, Stephen F.	1793-1836	1000	2500	6000		Political leader, Texas, MDS-$1800
Averill, William Woods	1832-1900	75	140	200		Drug clerk, WP inventor, diplomat; First Manassas, Peninsular, Sharpsburg*
Avery, Tex	1908-1980	50	110		150	Animator of Bugs Bunny, Porky Pig
Avogardo, Amedeo	1776-1856	110	300	1100		Chemist, physicist
Ayer, Francis W.	1848-1923	15	30	65	30	Ad industry pioneer
Ayres, Romeyn Beck	1825-1888	50	100	200		WP, MW; First Manassas, Army of the Potomac*
Babbitt, Arthur	1907-1992	15	30			Disney cartoonist
Bacon, Francis	**1561-1626**	**4000**	**8000**	**15000**		**English philosopher, statesman, ESPV-all forms**
Baden-Powell, Robert S.S., 1st Baron	1857-1941	175	350	400		British general, "B-P,"
Bader, Sir Douglas Robert S.	1910-1982	50	150		125	British air force officer, PU
Badoglio, Pietro	1871-1956	45	100		80	Italian field marshal, PU
Baekeland, Leo Hendrik	1863-1944	40	60	150	75	Synthetic resins developer, "Bakelite"
Baer, George F.	1842-1914	20	30	50	35	Financier
Bagian, James P.		5	20	25	10	Discovery, 3/13/89, Columbia, 6/5/91, RS
Bailey, Joseph	1825-1867	110	200			Civil engineer, sheriff; Red River
Bainbridge, William	1774-1833	165	350	725		Amer. naval officer, QW, TW, W1812, ESPV-ALS
Baird, Absalom	1824-1905	40	65	115		Washington College, WP, inspector general; First Manassas, Peninsular, Chickamauga*
Baird, John L.	1888-1946	160	300	500		Scientist, television pioneer, SALS-2X
Baker, Alpheus	1828-1891	150	300	500		Lawyer; Vicksburg, Baker's Creek, Atlanta
Baker, Edward Dickinson	1811-1861	120	150	250		Weaver, lawyer, USHR, MW, USS; Ball's Bluff (Leesburg)
Baker, Ellen S.		5	20	25	10	Atlantis, 10/18/89, Columbia, 6/25/92, RS
Baker, George	1915-1975	35	70		175	Cartoonist, "The Sad Sack"
Baker, James A., III	1930-	5	15	30	20	Lawyer, politician, White House chief of staff
Baker, La Fayette Curry	1826-1868	150	175	250		Spy, provost marshal

GEN
POLIT
B

NAME	DATES	SIG	DS	ALS	SP	COMMENTS
Baker, Laurence Simmons	1830-1907	100	200	325		Wounded in battle several times; WP; Peninsular, Gettysburg, Bentonville
Baker, Michael A.		5	20	25	10	Atlantis, 8/3/91, Columbia, 10/22/92, RS
Baker, Newton D.	1871-1937	15	60	85	40	Political leader, sec. of war (Wilson)
Baker, Ray S.	1870-1946	15	30	50	20	Journalist, reformer, "Wilson: Life and..."
Bakst, Leon (Lev)	1866-1925	150	400	675		Russian painter, theater designer
Balbo, Italo	1896-1940	150	200	225		Italian air marshal, PU
Baldwin, Abraham	1754-1807		3500			CC, v. rare in all forms, GA, "Abr. Baldwin"
Baldwin, Henry	1780-1844	35	75	165		SC: 1830-1844, PA, ALS-2X
Baldwin, Loammi	1740-1807	425	750	1750		Civil engineer; Cont'l officer; apple developer, SALS-2X
Baldwin, William Edwin	1827-1864	500	1000	3000		Had fatal fall from a horse, ESPV - DS; Vicksburg
Balfour, Arthur J.	1848-1930	60	125	125	100	British foreign sec. under Lloyd George
Balfour, Nisbet	1743-1832	285	540	800		British officer; Parliament member, ESPV
Balla, Giacomo	1871-1958	100				Italian painter and sculptor
Ballivian, Jose	1804-1852					Bolivian general, statesman, PU
Balthus (Count Balthaser K. de Rola)	1908-	175				French painter, very reclusive
Bancroft, Edward (Edwards)	1744-1820			1750		Double agent; writer & inventor; "E. Bancroft", ESPV, scarce
Bancroft, George	1800-1891	35	70	125		Historian, political leader
Banks, Nathaniel Prentiss	1816-1894	100	200	400		SL, USHR, gov. Mass., US marshal; Valley, Cedar Mt., Vicksburg, Red River, ESPV-DSX, ALS
Banting, Fredrick Grant	1891-1941	600	700	1500	1000	Canadian physician, insulin developer
Barbe'-Marbois, Francois, Marqui de	1745-1837	50	100	225		French politician; author; neg. LA Purchase
Barbey, Daniel Edward	1889-1969	20	45	60	70	American admiral, WWII
Bardeen, John	1908-1991	35	60	120	45	Transistor developer
Barksdale, William	1821-1863	500	1000	1750		KIA; Lawyer, editor, USHR; First Manassas, Fredericksburg, Gettysburg, ESPV

NAME	DATES	SIG	DS	ALS	SP	COMMENTS
Barlow, Francis Channing	1834-1896	60	150	250		Harvard, lawyer, Sec. of State NY, marshal; Peninsular, Sharpsburg, Chancellorsville*
Barnard, Christiaan	1922-	30	45	125	50	S. African surgeon, first human heart transplant
Barnard, Henry	1811-1900	20	50	110		U.S. public school reformer
Barnard, John Gross	1815-1882	35	50	180		WP, writer; Corps of Engineers, Chief engineer AOTP
Barnardo, Thomas	1845-1905	30				British social reformer
Barnes, James	1801-1869	60	100	150		WP, civil engineer; Army of the Potomac (AOTP)*, Gettysburg
Barnes, Joseph K.	1817-1883	165	400			At the deathbeds of Lincoln & Garfield; Harvard, UPA, MW; Surgeon General
Barnum, Henry Alanson	1833-1892	50	100	175		Teacher, lawyer; First Manassas, Gettysburg, Lookout Mt.*
Barnum, Phineas T.	1810-1891	180	450	550	1100	Impresario, museum pass-$800
Barr, Alfred H. jun.	1902-1981	20	35	75		American art historian, director MOMA
Barringer, Rufus	1821-1895	150	300	500		Brother-in-law S. Jackson & D.H. Hill; Univ. of N.C., lawyer; Numerous with the Army of Northern V.A.
Barrios, Justo Rufino	1835-1885	65	150			Guatemalan dictator
Barry, John	1745-1803	1125	2250			Cont'l naval officer; first battle Br. ship capture
Barry, William Farquhar	1818-1879	70	140	175		WP, MW, writer; First Manassas, Army of the Potomac (AOTP)
Barth, Karl	1886-1968	45	110	140	80	Swiss theologian
Bartholdi, Frederic Auguste	1834-1904	300	600	850		Sculptor, PS-Statue of Liberty-$975-$1295
Bartlett, Joseph Jackson	1834-1893	40	80	160		Lawyer, US minister to Sweden, pen. comm.; Army of the Potomac (AOTP), Second Man.
Bartlett, Josiah	1729-1795	400	750	1210		Signer (Mass.); CC; first gov. NH; FF-$1050
Bartlett, William Francis	1840-1876	60	115	175		Harvard, Tredegar Iron Works; Peninsular, Wilderness
Bartoe, John-David F.		5	15	30	20	Challenger, 7/29/85
Barton, Bruce	1886-1967	20	45	50	30	Advertising executive, writer

Chester A. Arthur

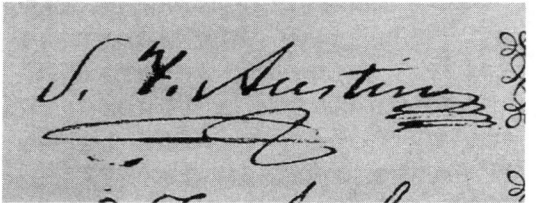

Stephen F. Austin

Chester A. Arthur

John L.Baird

Chester A. Arthur

Abraham Baldwin

John Jacob Astor

Samuel Barber

John James Audubon

Josiah Bartlett

NAME	DATES	SIG	DS	ALS	SP	COMMENTS
☆ **Barton, Clara**	**1821-1912**	**150**	**525**	**750**	**675**	**U.S. Amer. Red Cross org., ALS-$700-$975**
Barton, Seth Maxwell	1829-1900	165	250	500		SALS & SDS/LS - 2X; Vicksburg
Barton, William	1748-1831	300	600			Militia officer; captor Gen. Richard Prescott
Baruch, Bernard	1870-1965	45	150	250	125	Financier, advisor, TLS-$150
Bassett, Richard	1745-1815	400	800			CC, v. rare, ESPV, DE, full
Bate, William Brimage	1826-1905	100	200	300		ESPV, SALS & SDS/LS-3X; USS, MW, SL, editor, Gov. of TN.; Shiloh, Tullahoma, Chickamauga*
Bates, Edward		40	130	260		
Batista y Zaldivar, Fulgencio	1901-1973	175	325	400	200	Cuban president, dictator
Battle, Cullen Andrews	1829-1905	200	400	600		Lawyer, USHR, editor.; Sharpsburg, Fredericksburg, Gettysburg*
Baudelaire, Charles	1821-1867	350	750	1500		Art critic, PU
Baudry, Patrick		10	20	40	25	Discovery, 6/17/85
Baxter, Henry	1821-1873	30	80	175		Milling & lumber business, diplomat; Peninsular, Fredericksburg, Gettysburg
Bayard, George Dashiell	1835-1862	225	300	600		Killed in action, SALS-2X; WP, Indian fighter; Valley, Port Republic, Cedar MT, Fredericks.
Beal, George Lafayette	1825-1896	45	100	150		Book binder, adjutant general of ME; Cedar Mt., Sharpsburg, Red River
Beale, Richard Lee Tuberville	1819-1893	125	250	450		Univ of VA, USHR. lawyer; Numerous with Army of Northern Virginia
Beall, William Nelson Rector	1825-1883	200	400	700		General commission merchant; Western frontier
Bean, Alan		50	150	200	80	Apollo 12, Skylab 3, MW, TLS content - $500
Bean, Roy, Judge		2250	5000			Western
Beard, Charles A.	1874-1948	15	40	75	20	U.S. historian, author
Beard, Mary R.	1876-1958	40	85	125	50	Reformer, historian
Beardsley, Aubrey	1872-1898	150	300	425		English illustrator
Beatty, Clyde	1903-1965	50	110	200	175	
Beatty, David, 1st Earl	1871-1936	40	80	135		British admiral

NAME	DATES	SIG	DS	ALS	SP	COMMENTS
Beatty, John	1828-1914	35	60	115		Banker, USHR, historian; Perryville, Murfreesboro, Chickamauga*
Beatty, Samuel	1820-1885	40	65	120		MW, sheriff, farmer; Shiloh, Corinth, Perryville, Murfreesboro*
Beaufre, Andre	1902-1973	125	300	400		French general, nuclear advo., PU
Beauregard, Pierre Gustave Toutant	1818-1893	500	1000	1600	1000	One of the Confederacy's best generals; WP, MW, President of two railroads; First Manassas, Shiloh., ESPV, SPWD-2-3SX
Beaverbrook, Lord	1879-1964	40	100		50	British financier, statesman
Beck, C.C.	1910-1989	25	50		50	Cartoonist, "Captain Marvel"
Beckman, Arnold O.	1900-	30	45	85	50	Developed acidity testing equipment
Beckwith, George (K.B.)	1753-1823	225	430			British officer; gov. Bermuda; St. Vincent
Becquerel, A.C.	1788-1878	375	800	1000		Electrochemical pioneer, physicist
Becquerel, A.H.	1852-1908	200	500	600		Physicist, uranium radioactivity specialist
Bedford, Gunning	1742-1797	235	400			Cont'l. officer; gov. (DE); USHR
Bedford, Gunning, Jr.	1747-1812	350	725			CC, v. rare ALS & LS
Bee, Barnard Elliott	1824-1861	400	800	1750		Possibly the rarest of all Southern generals; WP, MW; Manassas
Bee, Hamilton Prioleau	1822-1897	100	200	400		SL, MW; Red River
Beecher, Henry W.	1813-1887	75	150	225	200	Religious leader
Beechey, Sir William	1753-1839				550	English portrait painter, PU
Beerbohm, Sir Max	1872-1956	35	75	150	80	English caricaturist
Begin, Menachem	1913-1992	100	200		200	Israeli prime minister, was RS
Belasco, David	1853-1931	30	40	60	75	Theatrical producer
Belcher, Jonathan	1682-1757	250	400	750		Col. gov. Mass. also NJ; merchant; Princeton
Belknap, William Worth	1829-1890	50	125	150		Controversial; Princeton, lawyer, SL, Sec. of War--Grant; Shiloh, Atlanta
Bell, Alexander Graham	**1847-1922**	**400**	**1200**	**3000**	**3000**	**U.S. telephone pioneer, inventor**
Bell, Clive	1881-1964	25				English critic and art writer
Bell, Henry H.	1808-1868	75	150			
Bell, Tyree Harris	1815-1902	70	150	250		Belmont, Shiloh, Richmond
Bellamy, Edward	1850-1898	30	60	165		Reformer, writer

NAME	DATES	SIG	DS	ALS	SP	COMMENTS
Bellmer, Hans	1902-1975	75	150			Polish-French painter, graphic artist
Bellows, George Wesley	1882-1925	100	200	400		American painter, lithographer
Belmont, August	1816-1890	50	100	200	200	Financier
Ben-Gurion, David	1886-1973	225	500	1250	500	First prime minister of Israel, SDS-2X
Benedict XV	1854-1922	150	300	450		Pope of Roman Catholic Church-1914
Benedict, Ruth	1887-1948	40	80	140		U.S. anthropologist
Benes, Eduard	1884-1948	75	100	175	200	Czech. president, PU, ESPV
Benham, Henry Washington	1813-1884	36	60	110		Yale, WP, MW; Corps of Engineers, W. Virginia, AOTP
Benjamin, Judah P.	1811-1884	300	1000	1000		CSA general-SALS XDS-2X
Bennett, James G.	1795-1872	50	150	225		Editor
Bennett, James G., Jr.	1841-1918	35	60	100	40	Publisher
Bennett, Willard H.	1903-1987	20	40	110	50	Dev. radio freq. mass spectrometer
Benning, Henry Lewis	1814-1875	150	300	400		Lawyer, Georgia Supreme Court; Second Manassas*
Benois, Aleksandr	1870-1960	50	150			Russian painter, stage designer
Bentham, Jeremy	1748-1832	100	225	450		British philosopher, reformer
Benton, Samuel	1820-1864	350	600	875		Nephew of Thomas Hart Benton, ESPV; Lawyer, SL; Atlanta
Benton, Thomas Hart	1889-1975	125	275	700		American painter, ALS-2X
Benton, Thomas Hart	1782-1858	65	100	200		U.S. Missouri senator
Benton, William Plummer	1828-1867	135	200	300		MW, lawyer, dist. atty.; W. Virginia, Vicksburg
Ben-Zvi, Hzhak	1884-1963	100	200	300		Israeli President
Berdeen, John	1908-1991	30	50	150	45	Co-inventor of transistor
Berenson, Bernard	1865-1959	50	100			American art critic, Renaissance authority
Beresford, Charles W. de la Poer, Lord	1846-1919	25	50	100	100	British admiral
Berger, Victor Louis	1860-1929	55	100	160	75	Political leader, newspaper editor
Bergson, Abram	1912-	5	10	20	15	Economist
Berle, Adolf A, Jr.	1895-1971	30	75	140	45	Lawyer
Berliner, Emile	1851-1929	60	100	235	100	Dev. microphone & gramophone
Berman, Eugene	1899-1972	50	125	200		Russian-born American painter

Clara Barton

Alexander Graham Bell

Richard Bassett

Alexander Graham Bell

Pierre G.T. Beauregard

Edvard Benes

Gunning Bedford Jr.

Hugo Black

Henry Ward Beecher

John Blair

Menachem Begin

Samuel Blodget Jr.

NAME	DATES	SIG	DS	ALS	SP	COMMENTS
Bernard, Sir Francis	1712-1779	200	400	700		Royal gov. NJ & Mass.
Bernoulli, Daniel	1700-1782	800	2200	2750		Swiss mathematician, gas & fluid expert
Berry, Clifford	1918-1963	40	75	180	60	Co-inventor first digital computer (ABC).
Berry, Hiram Gregory	1824-1863	400	600	1150		killed in action; SL, mayor of Rockland, bank pres., contractor; First Manassas, Army of the Potomac*
Berry, Jim	1932-	10	20	25		Cartoonist, "Berry's World"
Berthier, Louis Alexandre	1753-1815	100	200	400		French Lt.; Marshal of France; PU
Berzellus, Jons Jakob	1779-1848	80	170	525		Chemist, developed chemical symbols
Bessemer, Henry	1813-1898	40	65	225	100	U.S. inventor, Bessemer steel-making proc.
Bethune, Mary M.	1875-1955	140	300	600	200	Educator
Bettleheim, Bruno	1903-1990	50	100	200	100	Aust./U.S. psychoanalyst
Beveridge, Albert J.	1862-1927	10	25	50	25	Political leader, historian
Bevin, Ernest	1881-1951	30	50	100	50	British labor party leader, foreign minister
Bewick, Thomas	1753-1828	125	300	600		English wood engraver
Biddle,Nicholas	1786-1844	115	400	535	250	Banker
Bidwell, Daniel David	1819-1864	300	600	750		Killed in action, SALS-2X; police justice; Peninsular, Seven Pines, Gettysburg*
Bieriot, Louis	1872-1936	300	500	600		Aviator, first flight across the English Channel, ESPV
Bierstadt, Albert	1830-1902	150	275	600		German-born American painter
Bill, Max	1908-1994	50	100			Swiss painter, sculptor, architect, writer
Binning, Gerd Karl	1947-	20	50	100	50	Dev,. scanning tunneling microscope
Bird, Forrest	1921-	15	40	85	40	Dev. medical respirators
Birdseye, Clarence	1886-1957	225	400		300	Businessman, inventor
Birge, Henry Warner	1825-1888	45	130			Merchant, cotton planter, lumber business; Vicksburg, Red River
Birney, David Bell	1825-1864	250	375	1000		Somewhat controversial; Andover, lawyer; Peninsular, Seven Pines, Chantilly, AOTP*

NAME	DATES	SIG	DS	ALS	SP	COMMENTS
Birney, James G.	1792-1857	55	100	200		Reformer, antislavery movement
Birney, William	1819-1907	30	75	100		US atty. for Wash. D.C.; lawyer, newspaper writer, prolific writer; Army of the Potomac (AOTP)*
Bismarck, Otto von	1815-1898	300	600	800		German statesman, "Iron Chancellor"
Black, Harold Stephen	1898-	30	40	85	40	Negative feedback amplifier
Black, Hugo L.	1886-1971	45	110	255	100	SC: 1937-1971, AL, serv. over 30 yrs. TLS - $150
Blackmun, Harry A.	1908-1999	30	275	300	100	SC: 1970-1994, MN
Blaha, John E.		8	20	25	15	Discovery, 3/13/89, 11/22/89, Atlantis, 8/3/91
Blaine, James G.	1830-1893	30	50	130	50	U.S. Republican politician, diplomat
Blair, John	1732-1800	225	850	1250		CC, v. rare ALS, currency appears occas., Signer of Constitution
Blair, Jr., Francis Preston	1821-1875	40	60	100		Princeton, Transylvania, MW, atty. gen., USS; Georgia, Carolinas
Blanc, Louis	1811-1882	25	65	100		French socialist leader, historian
Blanchard, Albert Gallatin	1810-1891	70	175	500		ESPV; WP, MW
Blanchard, Claude	1742-1802					Chief Commissary to Rochambeau; PU
Bland, Theodorick	1742-1790	200	375	750		Cont'l officer; Pocahontas desc.; USHR
Blanding, Sarah G.	1899-1985	10	20	35	25	U.S. head of Vassar College, 1946-1964
Blandy, William Henry George	1890-1954	25	30	55	35	American admiral, WWI, WWII
Blatchford, Samuel	1820-1893	45	135	210		SC: 1882-1893, NY, prolific, hard-working
Blenker, Louis (Ludwig)	1812-1863	130	300	600		SLS/DS-2X; wine business, farmer; First Manassas, Cross Keys
Bleriot, Louis	1872-1936	300	500	600		Aviator. First flight across English Channel
Bligh, William	c.1754-c.1817	2000	4000			Naval Officer, HNS Bounty
Bliss, Tasker Howard	1853-1930	20	30	60		American general, WWI, SAW
Bloch, Henry W.	1922-	15	30	100	40	H & R Block founder
Block, Herb (Herblock)	1909-	10	25	125		Political cartoonist
Blodget, Samuel, Jr.		300	650	1275		Inventor

NAME	DATES	SIG	DS	ALS	SP	COMMENTS
Bloomer, Amelia	1818-1894	300	350	550		U.S. suffragette, social reformer
Bloomfield, Leonard	1887-1949	20	75	150	45	U.S. linguist
Blount, William	1749-1800	350	1000			CC, v. rare ALS & LS, DS on occas., NC
Blücher, Gebhard L. von	1742-1819	225	500	2000		Prussian field marshal
Bluford, Guion S., Jr.		15	30	35	25	Challenger, 8/30/83, 1st black Amer. in space
Blum, Leon	1872-1950	30	60	125	50	French socialist leader, writer
Blumberg, Baruch S.	1925-	25	40	65	40	Dev. hepatitis B vaccine
Blunt, James G.	1826-1881	40	60	120		Doctor, claims agent; Indian Territory, Old Fort Wayne
Bobko, Karol J.		10	20	25	20	Challenger, 4/4/83, FA
Bock, Fedor von	1880-1945	115	300		165	German field marshal
Boggs, William Robertson	1829-1911	125	250	400		WP, taught at VPI; Trans-Mississippi
Bohlen, Henry	1810-1862	150	400	575		Killed in action; MW, liquor dealer; Cross Keys, Cedar Mountain
Bohr, Niels	1885-1962	325				Danish physicist, quantum theorist, ESP-all forms
Bolden, Charles F., Jr.		5	25	30	15	Discovery, 4/24/90, 2/3/94, Atlantis, 3/24/92
Bolivar, Simon	1783-1830	500	3250	5000		South American revolutionary, ESPV
Bonaparte, Caroline	1782-1839	40	100	300		Youngest sister of Napoleon
Bonaparte, Elisa	1777-1820	300	525	600		Eldest surving sister of Napoleon I
Bonaparte, Jerome	1784-1860	70	140	275		Youngest brother of Napoleon I
Bonaparte, Joseph (Spain)	1768-1844	125	250	400		LS-$225, Eldest brother of Napoleon
Bonaparte, Lucien	1775-1840	60	120	175		Second surviving brother of Napoleon I
Bondar, Roberta L.		5	15	25	10	Discovery, 1/22/92, RS, send sm. SP
Bonham, Milledge Luke	1813-1890	150	225	450		Lawyer, MW, SL, Gov. (S.C.)
Bonheur, Rosa	1822-1899	125	200	300		French animal painter, f. Raymond
Bonnard, Pierre	1867-1947	125	300	600		French painter, graphic artist
☆ **Boone, Daniel**	**1734-1820**	**7550**	**12500**			**Frontiersman, scarce in all forms, ESPV**
Booth, George	1926-	10	25		45	New Yorker cartoonist
Booth, William	1829-1912	150	200	375	200	British Salvation Army founder

William Blount

Niels Bohr

Simon Bolivar

Napoleon Bonaparte

Napoleon Bonaparte

Napoleon Bonaparte

Heil Hitler !

Martin Bormann

James Bowen

Louis D. Brandeis

Carter Braxton

David Brearley

Jacob Broom

NAME	DATES	SIG	DS	ALS	SP	COMMENTS
Borah, William E.	1865-1940	15	25	50	25	U.S. senator, isolationist
☆ **Borglum, Gutzon**	**1867-1941**	**240**	**400**	**550**		**American sculptor, Mt. Rushmore-$500-$900**
Borman, Frank		35	150	250	125	Gemini 7, Apollo 8
Born, Max	1882-1970	200	350	600	300	German physicist
Bose, Amar	1929-	10	20	55	15	Bose Corporation founder
Bose, Satyendranath	1894-1974	30	100	225	100	Physicist, chemist
Boskin, Michael	1942-	5	10	25	10	Economist, author
Boudin, Eugene	1824-1898	125	260	550		French painter
Boudinot, Elias	1740-1821	310		800		Pres. Cont'l Cong. Dir. of US Mint; author
Bouquet, Henry	1719-1765	345	720	1500		British general; papers in British Museum
Bourke-White, Margaret	1906-1971	100	200	250		U.S. photographer, photojournalist
Bowditch, Nathaniel	1773-1838	125	250	500		Astronomer, Mathematition
Bowen, James	1808-1886	40	75	145		Erie Railroad pres.; New Orleans provost marshal general
Bowen, John Stevens	1830-1863	150	250	600		WP; Columbus, KY, Shiloh, Vicksburg*
Bowers, Claude G.	1878-1958	30	65	120	50	Historian, diplomat, author
Bowersox, Kenneth D.		8	20	25	15	Columbia, 6/25/92, Endeavour, 12/2/93
Bowie, James	1796-1836	3000	15000			American (Texan) soldier, TWI, scarce
Bowler, Metcalf	1726-1789	75	150	300		Chief justice of RI; informer
Boyington, Gregory "Pappy"		100	200	300	165	Marine Ace WWII
Boyle, Jeremiah Tilford	1818-1871	45	100	245		Controversial; lawyer, Princeton; Shiloh
Braddock, Edward	1695-1755	420	925	1715		British general; Washington was ADC of his
Bradley, Joseph P.	1813-1892	60	125	225	160	SC: 1870-1892, NJ
Bradley, Luther P.	1822-1910	40	100	200		Bookkeeper, salesman; Murfreesboro, Chickamauga, Atlanta
Bradley, Omar Nelson	1893-1981	100	200	350	220	American general, WWI, WWII
Brady, James B. "Diamond Jim"	1856-1917	200	400	700	425	U.S. financier, philanthropist, ESPV
Brady, Matthew	c.1823-1896	300	1000	2500		U.S. photographer, Civil War, ESPV

GEN_POLIT B

NAME	DATES	SIG	DS	ALS	SP	COMMENTS
Bragg, Braxton	1817-1876	400	700	1125		WP, MW; Shiloh, Chickamauga, Chattanooga*
Bragg, Edward S.	1827-1912	55	100	200		Bragg had a distinguished political career; Hobart, lawyer, congress, diplomat; Second Manassas, AOTP*
Bram, Leon	1931-	5	10	20	10	Funk & Wagnalls Vice president
Branch, Lawrence O'Bryan	1820-1862	400	600	1200		KIA, ESPV; Princeton, editor, lawyer, USHR; New Bern, Seven Days, Sharpsburg, ESPV
Brand, Vance D.		15	45		200	ASTP, Columbia, 12/2/90
☆ **Brandeis, Louis D.**	**1856-1941**	**200**	**525**	**700**	**1300**	**SC: 1916-1939, MA, ESPV**
Brandenstein, Daniel C.		10		30	20	Challenger, 8/30/83, Discovery, 6/17/85, FA
Brandon, William Lindsay	1801-1890	70	150	250		Princeton, SL; Malvern Hill, Chickamauga, Knoxville
Brandt, Willy	1913-1992	30	150	200	75	German statesman, chancellor of W. Germ.
Brangwyn, Sir Frank	1867-1956	50	100	150		British painter, etcher and designer
Brannan, John M.	1819-1892	50	100	200		MW; Chickamauga, Chattanooga, Atlanta
Brantley, William Felix	1830-1870	500	1000			Assassinated after the war; Lawyer; Chickamauga, Chattanooga, Atlanta*
Braque, Georges	1882-1963	500	700	1300		French painter, Cubism pioneer
Brattain, Walter H.	1902-1987	35	55	165	50	Transistor inventor
Bratton, John	1831-1898	150	300	450		S.C. College, USS, USHR; Fort Sumter, Seven Pines
Braun, Eva	1910-1945	1250		3275		Mistress/Wife Adolph Hitler, scarce
Braxton, Carter	1736-1797	350	800	2125		Signer of DOI; VA; SL; rare in ALS
Brayman, Mason	1813-1895	40	100	165		Newspaper editor, lawyer, gov. Idaho Tty.; Belmont, Fort Donelson, Shiloh
Brearley, David	1745-1790	425	900			CC, UC in ALS, LS & DS, NJ, "D. Bearley"
Breathed, Berkeley	1957-	15	30		60	Cartoonist, "Bloom County"
Breckinridge, John Cabell	1821-1875	100	250	400		Confed. Sec. of War; Lawyer, VP - Buchanan, SL, USHR, USS Shiloh, Vicksburg, Chickamauga*, WD-2X
Breckinridge, Sophonisba P.	1866-1948	50	125	200	80	Social worker, educator

GEN / POLIT
B

NAME	DATES	SIG	DS	ALS	SP	COMMENTS
Brennan, William J., Jr.	1906-1997	80	125	160	85	SC: 1956-1990, NJ, served over 30 yrs., prolific
Brenner, Victor D.		225	400			Sculptor, Lincoln penny (VDB)
Brereton, Lewis Hyde	1890-1967	50	150	280	75	American air force gen., WWI, WWII
Breton, Andre	1896-1966	50	150	300		French poet, essayist, art theorist
Brevard, Theodore Washington	1835-1882	150	300	420		Last general officer appointed by Davis; Univ. of VA Lawyer; Sayler's Creek
Brewer, David J.	1837-1910	60	100	200	75	SC: 1889-1910, KS, prolific writer
Brewster, David, Sir	1781-1868	25	50	150		Physicist, kaleidoscope inventor
Breyer, Stephen	1938-	20			40	SC: 1994-, MA
Brezhnev, Leonid	1906-1982	500	1000		525	Soviet leader, 1964-1982
Bridges, Harry R.	1901-1990	50	150	220	150	Labor leader
Bridges, Roy D., Jr.		5	10		15	Challenger, 7/29/85, RS!
Briggs, Clare	1875-1930	25	50		65	Cartoonist, "Mr. & Mrs."
Briggs, Henry S.	1824-1887	50	85	160		Williams College, SL, judge, auditor; Peninsular, Seven Pines
Bright, John	1811-1889	30	65	150		Radical British statesman
Brisbin, James S.	1837-1892	60	125	200		Teacher, author; First Manassas, Peninsular, Gettysburg
Broca, Paul	1824-1880	125	260			Surgeon, anthropologist
Brogile, Louis de	1893-1987	30	60	120	300	French physicist, wave theorist
Brooke, John R.	1838-1926	50	75	200		Collegeville, military gov. Puerto Rico, Cuba; Peninsular, Fredericksburg
Brooks, Louise	1906-1985	165	350			Entertainer, ESPV
Brooks, Rupert		500	850			British poet
Brooks, Van Wyck	1886-1963	25	65	115	35	U.S. historian, author
Brooks, William T.H.	1821-1870	60	100	140		WP, MW; Peninsular, Seven Days, Sharpsburg
Broom, Jacob	1752-1810	450	1275	2250		CC, v. rare in all forms; one of rarest signers
Brougham, Henry P.	1778-1868	125	200	275		Jurist, politician
Brown, Curtis L., Jr.		10	20	25	15	Endeavour, 9/12/92, Atlantis, 11/3/94
Brown, Egbert B.	1816-1902	25	40			Whaler, grain dealer, mayor, pension agent; Springfield

William J. Bryan

Ambrose Burnside

William J. Bryan

Barbara Bush

James Buchanan

George H.W. Bush

Simon B. Buckner

George H.W. Bush

Don C. Buell

NAME	DATES	SIG	DS	ALS	SP	COMMENTS
Brown, George Scratchley	1918-1978	20	30	55	30	Amer. air force gen., KW, WWII, VW
Brown, Henry B.	1836-1913	75	150	250	175	SC: 1890-1906, MI
Brown, Jacob Jennings	1775-1828	65	140	265		American general, W1812
☆ **Brown, John**	**1800-1859**	**875**	**2150**	**4500**		**U.S. abolitionist, ALS-2X,SBC-$2800, ESPV-ALS**
Brown, John Calvin	1827-1889	100	200	400		Lawyer, Gov. of TN, railroad executive; Numerous with Army of TN
Brown, Mark N.		5	15	25	10	Columbia, 8/9/89, Discovery, 9/12/91, RS
Brown, Rachel Fuller	1898-1980	25	50	135	50	Mystatin developer
Brown, Robert	1773-1858	125	225	500		Botanist
Brown, Sir Arthur Whitten	1886-1948	265	400	550		Aviator, ESPV-SP
Brown, William W.	c.1815-1884	15	35	45		Writer, reformer
Brown, Wilson	1882-1957	12	25	55	30	American admiral, WWI, WWII
Browne, Dik	1917-1989	15			45	Cartoonist, "Hi & Lois," "Hagar the Horrible," RS
Browne, Hablot Knight	1815-1882	30	80	140		English book illustrator and painter, PU
Browne, William Montague	1823-1883	150	300	500		Personal staff of J. Davis; Editor, Univ. of GA.; Savannah
Browning, John Moses	1855-1926	225	400	600		Gunsmith, inventor
Bruce, Blanche K.	1841-1898	300	500	1175		Political leader, USS
Brummell, George B.	1778-1840	125	250	500		British fashion leader
Bruning, Heinrich	1885-1970	45	85	125		German chancellor
Bryan, Goode	1811-1885	150	300	500		WP, MW; Seven Days, Fredericksburg, Gettysburg*
Bryan, John Henry Jr.	1936-	5	10	20	10	Sara Lee chairman
Bryan, William Jennings	1860-1925	110	350	350	440	U.S. Dem. leader, SC-$125, ANS-$225
☆ **Buchanan, James**	**1791-1868**	**375**	**800**	**1250**	**1000**	**Fifteenth U.S. President; FF:500, APT-650**
Buchanan, James M.	1919-	25	50	100	50	Economist, SDS&ALS-2X
(Buchanan) Lane (Johnston), Harriet	1830-1906	125	250	350	275	Buchanan did not marry; Lane was his niece
Buchanan, Robert C.	1811-1878	50	125			MW; Seven Days, Second Manassas, Sharpsburg

NAME	DATES	SIG	DS	ALS	SP	COMMENTS
Bucher, Lloyd M.		25	75	115	80	U.S.S. Pueblo
Buchi, James F.		10	20	15	20	Discovery, 1/24/84, 3/13/89, 9/12/91, FA
Buck, Frank	1884-1950	50	100	225	100	Big-game hunter, collector
Buckingham, Catharinus P.	1808-1888	30	75	125		ESPV; WP, teacher, co. president;
Buckland, Ralph P.	1812-1892	100	175	270		Law partner with R.B. Hayes; lawyer, mayor, SL, congress; Shiloh, Vicksburg
Buckner, Simon Bolivar	1823-1914	325	650			ESPV; WP, MW, editor, Gov of KY.; Kentucky, Chickamauga, Trans-Mississippi*, ADS & ALS, WD-2-3X
Budarin, Nikolai M.		7	20	30	15	Atlantis, 6/27/95
Buell, Don C.	1818-1898	100	150	260	175	WP, MW, pension agent; AOTP, Shiloh, Corinth, Chattanooga
Buell, Marjorie	1904-1993	15	30			Cartoonist, "Little Lulu"
Buford, Abraham	1820-1884	150	300	600		Related to Union gen., SDS & SALS - 2-3X; WP, MW, SL; Vicksburg
Buford, John	1826-1863	550	1275	3850		WP; AOTP, Second Manassas, ESP-ALS, SDS-ALS-2X
Buford, Napoleon B.	1807-1883	50	130	350		Merchant, banker, railroad exec.; Belmont, Island No.10, Vicksburg
Bulfinch, Charles	1763-1844	150	400	500		American architect, ESPV-SDS&ALS-2X
Bullard, Robert Lee	1861-1947	25	55	100	75	American general, SAW, WWI
Bullitt, William C.	1891-1967	15	25	50	30	U.S. diplomat, first ambassador to USSR
Bullock, Robert	1828-1905	70	165	250		Lawyer, SL, clerk, judge; Chickamauga, Atlanta, Tennessee
Bunche, Ralph	1904-1971	60	150	250	125	Founder and diplomat of United Nations
Bundy, McGeorge	1919-	10	25	50	20	Educator, Kennedy administration
Bunsen, Robert	1811-1899	200	500	1200	1500	German chemist, Bunsen burner
Burbank, Luther	1849-1926	125	300	325	200	Plant patent program contributor
Burbridge, Stephen G.	1831-1894	35	65			Georgetown, lawyer, farmer; Shiloh, Vicksburg
Burckhalter, Joseph H.	1912-	20	40	65	35	FITC developer
Burger, Warren E.	1907-1995	50	220	250	80	SC: 1969-1986, VA, Chief Justice

NAME	DATES	SIG	DS	ALS	SP	COMMENTS
Burgoyne, John	1722-1792	1540	3130	4585		British general; buried in Westminster Abbey, ESPV-all forms
Burke, Arleigh Albert	1901-1996	25	60	120	75	American admiral, WWII, KW
Burke, Thomas	c. 1747-1783	185	350			Congressman; gov. NC
Burne-Jones, Sir Edward Coley	1833-1898	100	250			English painter, illustrator, designer
Burnham, Hiram	c.1814 - 1864	110	220			Killed in action, county commissioner, coroner; Peninsular, Fredericksburg, Overland
Burns, William W.	1825-1892	35	60	100		MW; West Virginia, Peninsular, Fredericksburg
Burnside, Ambrose E.	1824-1881	150	300	440	875	Controversial, ALS content - 2-3X; tailor, WP, MW, gov. RI, USS; First Manassas, AOTP
☆ **Burr, Aaron**	**1756-1836**	**375**	**775**	**935**		**VP; conspirator; ANS-$400; ALS-6-10X**
Burroughs, William Seward	1857-1898	150	400	825		Calculating machine developer, died young
Bursch, Daniel W.		7	15	20	15	Discovery, 9/1/93, Endeavour, 9/30/94
Burton, Harold H.	1888-1964	50	175	335	100	SC: 1945-1958, OH, SL, USS
Burton, Sir Richard (Francis)	1821-1890	175	300			Explorer, his journals were burned after his death.
Burton, William Meriam	1865-1954	45	90	200	100	Developed gasoline manufacturing
Busch, Adolphus	1839-1913	65	200	275	175	German-born businessman, brewery king
Bush, Barbara Pierce	1925-	50	160	185	95	(1945); NY; S-4; D-2
☆ **Bush, George Herbert Walker**	**1924-**	**75**	**250**	**300**	**200**	**PL, WHCC-$625, WH/EMC-550, 2X- as President; FA**
Bush, George W. Jr.		25	50		45	Governor Texas, businessman, FA, SDS-2-3X
Bush, John E. "Jeb"		15	25		25	Governor Florida, FA
Bush, Vannevar	1890-1974	50	200	300	150	U.S. elec. eng., analogue computer
Bushmiller, Ernie	1905-1982	25	50	100	150	Cartoonist, "Nancy"
Bushnell, David	c.1742-1824	300	675	1200		Inventor of submarine
Bussey, Cyrus	1833-1915	30	50			SL, merchant, New Orleans chamber of commerce; Elkhorn Tavern, western Arkansas
Busteed, Richard	1822-1898	25	60	125		Lawyer; Fort Monroe
Bute, John Stuart, 3d Earl of	1713-1792	100	150	300		British prime minister

George H.W. Bush

Pierce Butler

Guy Carleton

Pierce Butler

Thomas Carlyle

Benjamin N. Cardozo

Charles Carroll of Carrolton

NAME	DATES	SIG	DS	ALS	SP	COMMENTS
Butler, Benjamin F.	1818-1893	125	425	450		SLS/DS & SALS - 5X; Colby College, lawyer, teacher, USHR, gov. Mass.; Washington, Big Bethel
Butler, John	1725-1796	115	200	450		Loyalist leader; father of Walter
Butler, Matthew Calbraith	1836-1909	100	200	300		Son-in-law of Gov. Pickens (SC), SALS-2X; Lawyer, SL, USS, executive, historian; First Manassas, WD-2X
Butler, Nicholas Murray	1862-1947	15	40	125	45	U.S. educator, headed Columbia Univ.
Butler, Percival	1760-1821					Cont'l officer; PU
Butler, Pierce	1744-1822	100	200	300		CC, SC, "P. Butler"
Butler, Pierce	1866-1939	50	100	250	75	SC: 1922-1939, MN, ANS - $300
Butler, Richard	1743-1791	160	275			Cont'l officer; Indian commissioner
Butler, Smedley Darlington	1881-1940	25	40	80	50	Amer. marine corps gen., SAW, WWI
Butler, Thomas	1754-1805	275				Cont'l officer; mem. Washington's main army
Butler, Walter	1752?-1781	200	600	800		Tory leader
Butler, William Orlando	1791-1880	60	225	300		Amer. gen., politician, W1812, MAW
Butler, Zebulon	1731-1795	65	175			Cont'l officer
Butterfield, Daniel	1831-1901	125	300	300		"Taps" composer, SDS-2X; Union College, lawyer, diplomat; Peninsular, Second Manassas, Maryland
Byrd, Richard E.	1888-1957	100	275	425	350	Aviator, explorer
Byrnes, James F.	1879-1972	35	105	240	60	SC: 1941-1942, SC, serv. 1 yr., gov., sec. of state
Byron, John	1723-1786	200	445			British admiral; gov. Newfoundland
Cabana, Robert D.		8	15	25	12	Discovery, 10/6/90, 12/2/92, C 7/8/94, RS
Cabell, William Lewis	1827-1911	200	400	500		Helped design CSA battle flag, SALS-2-3X; WP, lawyer, Mayor of Dallas, marshall; Elkhorn
Cadmus, Paul	1904-	40	100	150		American painter
Cadwalader, George	1806-1879	40	100	140		Lawyer, MW; Advisor, Philadelphia
Cadwalder, John	1742-1786	150	300			Militia general; SL (MD)
☆ **Calder, Alexander**	**1898-1976**	**150**	**300**	**500**	**175**	**American sculptor and painter, ALS-2X**

GEN – POLIT C

NAME	DATES	SIG	DS	ALS	SP	COMMENTS
Caldwell, John C.	1833-1912	50	100	175		Amherst College, lawyer, diplomat; Peninsular, Chancellorsville, Gettysburg
Calhoun, John C.	1782-1850	150	300	450	350	U.S. political leader, states' rights advocate
Callaghan, Daniel Judson	1890-1942	50	135	245		American admiral, WWI, WWII
Callaghan, James	1912-	50	100	150	75	British statesman, Prime Minister
Calloway, Wayne		5	12		10	Pepsico Inc. CEO
Calvin, John	**1509-1564**	**8250**	**16000**			**Scarce in all forms**
Cameron, Kenneth D.		5	15	20	12	Atlantis, 4/5/91, Discovery, 4/8/93
Cameron, Robert A.	1828-1894	50	100	200		Indiana Medical College, publisher, clerk; Island No. 10, Vicksburg, Red River
Cameron, Simon	1799-1889	100	150	200	225	Political leader, USS
Campbell, Alexander William	1828-1893	70	150	250		Lawyer; Shiloh
Campbell, Archibald, (K.B.)	1739-1791	125	300	500		British officer; gov. Jamaica
Campbell, Sir Archibald	1769-1843	100	250			British general, PU
Campbell, Charles T.	1823-1895	45	100	200		MW, SL; Seven Pines, Peninsular, Fredericksburg
Campbell, Sir Colin, 1st Baron Clyde	1792-1863	25	50	100		British field marshal, PU
Campbell, John A.	1811-1889	120	225	350		SC: 1853-1861, AL, CSA
Campbell, Joseph	1904-1987	20	45	65	30	U.S. author, editor, teacher
Campbell, Lord William	?-1778	220	300			Royal gov. of SC; Nova Scotia; Parliament
Campbell, Robert H.	1937-	5	10	25	10	Sun Company Inc. executive
Campbell, William Bowen	1807-1867	50	75	100		Lawyer, congress, MW, gov. Tenn.
Camras, Marvin	1916-1995	25	45	120	50	U.S. inventor, magnetic tape pioneer
Canby, Edward R. S.	1817-1873	100	225	300		MW; New Mexico, Mobile
Candler, Asa	1851-1929	500	1400	2250	620	Founded Coca-Cola Co.
Caniff, Milton	1907-1988	30	100		175	Cartoonist, "Terry and the Pirates," "Steve Canyon"
Canning, George	1770-1827	50	100	150	100	British statesman
Cannon, Joseph G..	1836-1926	25	45	100	40	Political leader, USS
Canova, Antonio	1757-1822	100	225	300		Italian Neoclassical sculptor

NAME	DATES	SIG	DS	ALS	SP	COMMENTS
Cantey, James	1818-1874	125	250	315		Lawyer, , SL (SC), MW; Richmond, Atlanta
Capers, Ellison	1837-1908	100	200	300		SALS-2X; Episcopal minister, historian; Fort Sumter, Chickamauga, Chattanooga*
Capp, Al	1909-1979	100	200		275	Cartoonist, "Li'l Abner"
Cardigan, James Thomas B., 7th Earl of	1797-1868	100	200	300	150	British general, politician, PU
Cardozo, Benjamin N.	1870-1938	150	325	715	850	SC: 1932-1938, NY. prolific writer, dist. hand.
Carey, Henry C.	1793-1879	30	50	70		Economist
Carey, Matthew	1760-1839	25	50	65		Publisher
Carleton, Guy	1724-1808	300	600			British general; gov. of Canada
Carleton, James H.	1814-1873	50	75	150		Controversial, f. of Henry Guy Carleton; MW; "California column"
Carleton, Thomas	1736-1817	225				British officer; brother of Guy
Carlin, William P.	1829-1903	50	100	165		WP; AOTP, Second Manassas; Chickamauga, Chattanooga, Atlanta
Carlotta (Mexico)	1840-1927	350	700	1500		Mexican empress
Carlson, Chester F.	1906-1968	30	75	150	75	Electrophotography pioneer
Carlson, Evans Fordyce	1896-1947	25	50	100	50	American general, WWI, WWII
Carlyle, Thomas	1795-1881	100	200	400		Historian, critic
☆ **Carnegie, Andrew**	**1835-1919**	**240**	**675**	**1150**	**1000**	**Industrialist, philanthropist**
Carney, Frank L.		10	20	40	20	Pizza Hut Restaurant founder
Carothers, Wallace Hume	1896-1937	65	110	250	125	Synthetic fiber inventor
Carpender, Arthur S.	1884-1960	15	35	55	35	American admiral, WWI, WWII
Carpenter, M. Scott		35	100	150	125	Mercury-Atlas 7,
Carr, Eugene A.	1830-1910	55	110	225		DS&ALS content 2.5 - 3X; WP, frontiersman, Indian fighter; Texas, Elkhorn Tavern, Camden, ESPV
Carr, Gerald P.		10	25	30	20	Skylab 4, RS
Carr, Joseph B.	1828-1895	45	100	170		Sec. of state NY; Big Bethel, Peninsular, Second Manassas*
Carranza, Venustiano	1859-1920	50	225	400		Mexican statesman
Carrel, Alexis	1873-1944	80	200	325	100	French surgeon, biologist
Carrier, Willis Haviland	1876-1950	50	125	200	130	Air-conditioning systems inventor

Daniel Carroll

Jimmy Carter

Rachel Carson

Jimmy Carter

Jimmy Carter

Jimmy Carter

Jimmy Carter

Catherine II Empress of Russia

Jimmy Carter

Paul Cezanne

NAME	DATES	SIG	DS	ALS	SP	COMMENTS
Carrington, Henry B.	1824-1912	50	100	215		Abolitionist; Yale, lawyer, author, historian; Dakota Territory, western Virginia
Carroll, Charles of Carrollton	1737-1832	300	750	800		Signer of DOI (MD)-last sur.; added "of Carrollton" to sig. 1765; USS; BC-$550
Carroll, Daniel	1730-1796	175	350	750		CC, SDS/LS-2X, often confused w/nephew
Carroll, Samuel S.	1832-1893	60	100	200		WP; Cedar Mt., Fredericksburg, Gettysburg*
Carroll, William Henry	1810-1868	70	160	245		Son of Gov. Carroll (TN); Postmaster of Memphis; Fishing Creek
Carson, Rachel	1907-1964	75	225	300	250	U.S. marine biologist, "The Sea Around Us", ALS- 5X
☆ **Carter, James Earl "Jimmy"**	**1924-**	**85**	**380**	**1125**	**225**	**PL, TLS-1000, SDS&SALS-2-3X, FA.**
Carter, Jr., Manley Lanier		7	15	20	15	Discovery, 11/22/89
Carter, Rosalynn Smith	1927-	25	100	130	40	(1946); GA; S-3; D-1, First Lady
Carvel, Tom	1908-1989	30	65	80	45	Ice cream chain founder
Carver, George Washington	1864-1943	225	600	850	2950	U.S. botanist, chemist, educator, ESPV-SP
Casey, Silas	1807-1882	65	125	250		ALS - content 2X; MW, "Infantry Tactics" author; Seven Pines, Peninsular
Caspar, John H.		10	35	55	25	Atlantis, 2/28/90, Endeavour, 1/13/93, C 3/4/94
Cass, Lewis	1782-1866	45	80	140		Political leader, sec. of war (Jackson)
☆ **Cassatt, Mary**	**1844-1926**	**250**	**500**	**1000**		**American painter, printmaker, ALS-4-5X**
Cassin, Rene	1887-1976	40	80	160		Jurist, French statesman
Castelnau, Noel Marie J. E. C.	1851-1944	125	250		200	French general
Castlereagh, Robert	1769-1822	35				British foreign secretary
Castro, Fidel	1927-	575			1000	Cuban revelutionary, ESPV-all forms
Cates, Clifton Bledsoe	1893-1970	20	35	60	35	American Marine Corps general
Cathcart, Sir William Schaw	1755-1843	95	165			British officer; ambassador; distinguished car.
Catherine I	1684-1727	500	1785	4000		Tsarina of Russia
☆ **Catherine II, the Great (Russia)**	**1726-1796**	**750**	**1800**	**2650**		**LS - $1500, $1250, ESPV**

NAME	DATES	SIG	DS	ALS	SP	COMMENTS
Catlin, George	1796-1872	125	275			American painter, writer, ALS-$1000
Catron, John	1786-1865	75	150	250		SC: 1837-1865, TN
Catt, Carrie Chapman	1859-1947	75	150	275	200	U.S. suffragette
Catterson, Robert F.	1835-1914	45	80	150		Practiced medicine, mayor; Shenandoah, Carolinas, Chattanooga, Atlanta
Cavell, Edith	1865-1915	250	400	800		Nurse, executed by the Germans
Cavendish, Henry	1731-1810	275	570	1625		British chemist, discovered hydrogen, ESPV
Cavour, Camillo Benso	1810-1861	200	400			Italian statesman, PU
Cayce, Edgar		100	250		150	Philosopher
Ceausescu, Nicolae	1918-1989	75			150	Communist ldr., head of state 1967-1989
Cellini, Benvenuto	1500-1571	2000				Florentine sculptor, goldsmith, ESPV
Cenker, Robert J.		5	10	20	15	Columbia, 1/12/86
Cernan, Eugene A.		25	75	200	100	Gemini 9A, Apollo 10, Apollo 17, MW, TSS
☆ **Cezanne, Paul**	**1839-1906**	**1500**	**3000**	**4000**		**French Post-Impressionists, ALS-2X**
Chadwick, James	1891-1974	100	200	500	250	British physicist, discovered neutron
Chaffee, Adna Romanza, Jr.	1884-1941	30	75	150	100	American gen., WWI, well-respected
Chaffee, Roger	-1967	225	500		450	Apollo 1, perished in launch fire
☆ **Chagall, Marc**	**1887-1985**	**200**	**400**	**1000**		**Artist, SPC-$375, ALS-2X, ESPV, FA, ALS-scarce, FA**
Chalmers, James Ronald	1831-1898	175	350	500		Lawyer, USHR; Shiloh, Murfressboro
Chamberlain, Austen	1863-1937	50	100	150	125	British statesman
Chamberlain, Joseph	1836-1914	70	130		100	British statesman
Chamberlain, Joshua L.	1828-1914	750	1400	2000		ALS - content 1.5 - 2X; Bowdoin College, gov. Maine, author; Gettysburg, Chancellorsville, Sharpsburg*, ESPV
Chamberlain, Neville	1869-1940	75	200		200	British Con. prime minister, SDS-2X
Chamberlain, Owen	1920-	20	40	75	40	American physicist, SALS-2X
Chambers, Alexander	1832-1888	55	125	200		WP; Shiloh, Iuka, Vicksburg
Champlin, Stephen G.	1827-1864	275	550			Lawyer; Peninsular, Seven Pines, Second Manassas
Chang, Tso-lin	1873-1928	100	225		200	Chinese warlord, PU

NAME	DATES	SIG	DS	ALS	SP	COMMENTS
Chang-Diaz, Franklin R.		10	30	40	15	Columbia, 1/12/86, Atlantis, 10/18/89, 7/31/92
Channing, Edward	1856-1931	35	60	100	50	U.S. historian
Channing, William E.	1780-1842	50	100	150		Religious leader
Chapin, Darly	1906-1995	25	50	150	45	U.S. physicist, solar energy cell
Chapman, George H.	1832-1882	50	100	175		Publisher, lawyer, judge, SL; Second Manassas, Sharpsburg*
Chapman, Morris H.	1940-	5	10	15	10	Southern Baptist Convention CEO
Charcot, Jean M.	1825-1893	100	200	600		French neurologist
Charles I (England)	1600-1649	900	2000	3780		Second son of James VI of Scotland
Charles II (England)	1630-1685	900	1850	2500		DS-$2750, son of Charles I
Charles II (Spain)	1616-1700	300	425			King of Spain
Charles IV (Spain)	1748-1819	200	400	600		King of Spain
Charles X (France)	1757-1836	175	400	650		Last Bourbon king of France
Charles IX (France)	1550-1574	325	1275	1850		Second son of Henry II
Charles V (Holy Roman Emperor)	1500-1558	500	1800	4125		DS-$2300
Charles XIV (Sweden)	1763-1844	165	500	925		DS-$450
Charles, Louis John	1771-1847	160	350	900		Austrian field marshal, PU
Charles, Prince of Wales	1948-	300		1250	750	SP w/Diana- 3750, ESPV-all forms
Charlotte, Sophia	1744-1818	150	300	400		Queen of Great Britain & Ireland
Chase, Salmon P.	1808-1873	100	200	350		SC: 1864-1873, OH, Chief Justice, gov. (OH), ESPV-SP
Chase, Samuel	1741-1811	300	500	1000		SC: 1796-1811, MD, Signer DOI, ALS-2-X
Chase, William Merritt	1849-1916	100	175			American painter, PU
Chast, Roz	1954-	10	25		35	Cartoonist, New Yorker, "Bonfire of the Banalities"
Chastellux, Francois-Jean de Beauvoir	1734-1788	230	440			French officer; dignitary and writer
Chauncey, Isaac	1772-1840	15	55	100		American naval officer, W1812
Chauvel, Sir Henry George	1865-1945	30	80	125		Australian general, PU
Chavez, Cesar	1927-1993	50	125		125	U.S. labor leader, U.F.W.A., RS
Cheatham, Benjamin Franklin	1820-1886	200	400	500		MW, postmaster of Nashville, prison admin.; Shiloh, Atlanta, WD DS-2X, ESPV

Joshua L. Chamberlain

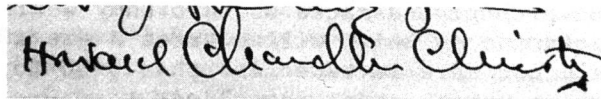

Howard Chandler Christy

Charles I of England

Walter P. Chrysler

Salmon P. Chase

Sir Winston Churchill

Samuel Chase

Winston Churchill

Claire L. Chennault

Abraham Clark

NAME	DATES	SIG	DS	ALS	SP	COMMENTS
Chennault, Claire Lee	1890-1958	385		700	600	American air force gen., WWI, WWII, ESPV-SIG.
Chesnut, Jr., James	1815-1885	215	325	450		Staff of Pres. Davis; Princeton, lawyer, SL, USS
Chetlain, Augustus L.	1824-1914	40	100	165		philanthropist; clerk, banker, pres. Chicago Stock Exchange; Shiloh, Iuka, Corinth
Chevrolet, Louis	1879-1941	825	1750			American automotive executive, ESPV
Chiang Kai-shek	1887-1975	200				Nationalist Chinese president
Chiao, Leroy		5	10	20	15	Columbia, 7/8/94
Childs, Thomas	1796-1853	25	65	100		American general, W1812
Chilton, Kevin		8	20	25	12	Endeavour, 5/7/92, 4/9/94, varied res.
Chilton, Robert Hall	1815-1879	200	500	750		Chief of staff R.E. Lee., SDS/LS & SALS-5-6X; WP, MW, Pres. of a manufacturing co.
Chirico, Giorgio de	1888-1978	165	400	700		Italian painter, metaphysical pioneer
Choiseful, Etienne Francois, Count of Stain.	1719-1785	155	325			French statesman
Chou En-lai (Zhou Enlai)	1898-1975	1100				Chinese leader, scarce
Christina (Sweden)	1626-1689	300	1500	2500		Daughter of Gustav II Adolphus
Christo (Christo Javacheff)	1935-	25				Bulgarian-born sculptor, designer
Christophe, Henry	1767-1829	1000				Haitian revelutionary
Christy, Howard Chandler		55	130	220	400	Illustrator, painter
Chrysler, Morgan H.	1822-1890	100	200			1 of 4 to go from private to m. general; military gov., farmer; Peninsular, Second Manassas, Maryland
Chrysler, Walter	1875-1940	325	600	1000	875	Automotive executive, SDS-2-3X, SALS-2X
Church, Benjamin	1734?-1777	250	575			Informer; Mass.; grandson of Indian fighter
Church, Frederick Edwin	1826-1900	200	400	800		American painter
Church, Frederick S.	1842-1924	50	100	165		American illustrator, ALS w/sketch - $500
Churchill, Clementine S.		100	200	275	175	Wife of Winston Churchill
Churchill, John	1650-1722	1250	2750			1st Duke of Marlborough
Churchill, Randolph	1849-1895	50	120	300		Father of Winston Churchill

NAME	DATES	SIG	DS	ALS	SP	COMMENTS
Churchill, Thomas James	1824-1905	100	150	300		SALS-2X; MW, Postmaster Little Rock, Gov. of Arkansas; Wilson's Creek, Red River, Jenkin's Ferry
☆ **Churchill, Winston**	**1874-1965**	**850**	**1750**	**3425**	**3500**	**British P.M., SDS-5X, ALS-2-3X, SB-2300**
Ciano, Galeazzo	1903-1944	75	225			Italian fascist foreign minister
Clanton, James Holt	1827-1871	150	275	450		MW, lawyer, SL Shiloh, Farmington, Booneville, Atlanta
Clark, Abraham	1726-1794	450	1115	4125		Signer of DOI (NJ); USHR, ESPV
Clark, Charles	1811-1877	125	250	350		SL, MW, Governor of Mississippi; Shiloh
☆ **Clark, George Rogers**	**1752-1818**	**700**	**2600**	**3500**		**Conqueror of the Old Northwest, ESPV**
Clark, Mark Wayne	1896-1985	50	175	300	125	American general, WWI, WWI, KW
Clark, Tom C.	1899-1977	35	110	125	100	SC: 1949-1967, TX, atty. gen., f. of Ramsey Clark
Clark, William	1770-1838	450	2000	2750		American army officer, explorer
Clark, William T.	1831-1905	40	100	150		Lawyer, USHR (expelled); Atlanta
Clarke, Alured	1745?-1832	220	400			British officer; Lt. gov. of Jamaica; Field Mar.
Clarke, John H.	1857-1945	100	200	350	175	SC: 1916-1922, OH
Claude, Albert	1899-1983	35	80	170	60	Founder of modern cell biology
Clay, Cassius M.	1810-1903	100	250	500		Controversial late in life; Yale, MW, diplomat
Clay, Henry	1777-1852	125	280	450		"The Great Com...," FF-$150, ALS-$7500
Clay, Lucius DuBignon	1897-1978	30	100	175	100	American general, administrator
Clayton, Henry DeLamar	1827-1889	100	200	450		SL, lawyer, circuit court judge; Murfreesboro, Chickamauga, Atlanta
Clayton, Powell	1833-1914	25	50	100		Civil engineer, gov. Ark., USS, diplomat; Missouri, Arkansas, Pine Bluff
Cleave, Mary L.		10	15	20	25	Atlantis, 11/26/85, 5/4/89
Cleburne, Patrick Ronayne	1828-1864	1200	2150	4500		Savage fighter, highly regarded, VERY RARE!; Lawyer; Shiloh, Perryville, Richmond*, ESPV-DS & ALS
Clemenceau, Georges	1841-1929	100	165		200	French statesman

NAME	DATES	SIG	DS	ALS	SP	COMMENTS
Clement IX	1600-1669		1500			Pope of Roman Catholic Church-1667
Clement X	1590-1676		1250			Pope of Roman Catholic Church-1670
Clement XI	1649-1721		1275			Pope of Roman Catholic Church-1700
Clervoy, Jean-Francois		5	15	25	15	Atlantis, 11/3/94
Cleveland, Frances Folsom	1864-1947	60	100	275	225	(1886); NY; S-2; D-3, First Lady
☆ **Cleveland, Stephen Grover**	**1837-1908**	**250**	**400**	**650**	**700**	**Only pres. to serve 2 nonconsecutive terms, APT-525, WH/EMC-340, SDS-2X, SALS-2X**
Clifford, Michael R.		7	15	25	15	Discovery, 12/2/92, Endeavour, 4/9/94
Clifford, Nathan	1803-1881	80	185	250	150	SC: 1858-1881, ME, AG (Polk)
Clingman, Thomas Lanier	1812-1897	100	250	500		Has a mountain named after him; Lawyer, SL, USHR, USS; North and South Carolina
Clinton, DeWitt	1769-1828	70	200	250		Political leader, Erie Canal advocate
Clinton, George	1739-1812	150	250	400		First gov. (NY); Cont'l gen.; V.Pres. SDS-2X
Clinton, Henry	1730-1795	500	1125	2450		British Comdr. in Chief; aristocrat
Clinton, Hillary Rodham	1947-	40	125	165	50	(1975); IL; D-1, First Lady, FA
Clinton, James	1733-1812	250	550			Cont'l gen.(NY); f. of D.Clinton; SDS-2X
☆ **Clinton, William Jefferson**	**1946-**	**135**	**500**		**400**	**TLS-1600, ALS-scarce, ESPV, FA**
Clive, Robert	1725-1774	300	600			First adm. of Bengal, helped form B.E. in India
Close, Chuck	1940-	30				American painter, ESPV
Clymer, George	1739-1813	170	600	750		Signer DOI (PA); patriot; CC
Coats, Michael L.		10	20	25	20	Discovery, 8/30/84, 3/13/89, 4/28/91, FA
Cobb, Howell	1815-1868	160	300	600		Candidate for Pres. of CSA, SDS/ALS-2-3X; Lawyer, USHR, Gov. of GA, Sec. Treasury, ESPV
Cochran, John	1730-1807	175	370			Last medical dir. Cont'l Army; s. J. Cochran(e)
Cochrane, John	1813-1898	40	100	160		ALS - content - 2X; Hamilton College, congress, atty. gen. NY; Peninsular, Fredericksburg
Cockcroft, John D.	1897-1967	75	100	275	100	British nuclear physicist

William Clark

William Clark

George Rogers Clark

Frances F. Cleveland

Frances F. Cleveland

Grover Cleveland

Grover Cleveland

Grover Cleveland

Grover Cleveland

Grover Cleveland

Grover Cleveland

Grover Cleveland handwriting sample

NAME	DATES	SIG	DS	ALS	SP	COMMENTS
Cockrell, Francis Marion	1834-1915	75	150	250		Lawyer, USS; Carthage, Wilson's Creek and Elkhorn*
Cockrell, Kenneth D.		5	15	20	10	Discovery, 4/8/93, RS
Cody, William F.	1846-1917	1000	2000	2500	5000	"Buffalo Bill," Showman
Coffee, John	?	275				American general, W1812, CW
Coffin, Issac, Sir	1759-1839	30	65	100		British admiral
Coffin, John	1756-1838	200	425			Loyalist officer; brother of Sir Issac
Coke, Sir Edward	1552-1634		2125			Jurist
Coke, Thomas	1747-1814	225	400	650		Methodist clergyman
Colfax, Schuyler	1823-1885	100	150		275	VP (1869-1873)
Colgate, William	1783-1857	25	70	125		Industrialist, philanthropist, soap maker
Collier, George	1738-1795	200				British commodore; Parliament
Collier, John	1884-1968	30	75	125	60	Reformer, educator, author
Collins, Eileen M.		5	10	20	15	Discovery, 2/3/95, RS
Collins, Joseph Lawton	1896-?	15	40	100	45	Amer. gen., WWI, WWII, "Lightning Joe"
Collins, Michael	1930-	125	300	460	275	Gemini 10, Apollo 11, book - $300
Colquitt, Alfred Holt	1824-1894	100	200	300		Princeton, USS, MW, USHR, SL, Gov. of GA; Seven Days, Sharpsburg, Fredericksburg*
Colston, Raleigh Edward	1825-1896	70	200	300		ESPV-LS/DS; VMI; Chancellorsville, Lynchburg, SDS-2X
Colton, George B.	1923-	15	40	65	25	Oral contraceptives pioneer, "pill"
Commons, John R.	1862-1945	30	75	115	40	U.S. economist, labor historian
Compton, Arthur	1892-1962	100	200	300	150	Physicist
Congreve, Sir William	1772-1828	50	150	250		British artillery officer, PU
Conner, James	1829-1883	100	200	300		USDA, attorney general (SC); First Manassas, Seven Pines, Cedar Creek
Conner, Patrick E.	1820-1891	50	120	150		Miner, newspaperman; Fort Douglas, Fort Connor
Conner, Selden	1839-1917	60	145	260		Was a full brig. general at 25; Tufts College, gov. Maine; Peninsular, Sharpsburg, Gettysburg*
Connolly, John	c. 1750-?	225	470			Loyalist conspirator
Conover, Lloyd H.	1923-	10	35	60	30	Tetracycline creator

NAME	DATES	SIG	DS	ALS	SP	COMMENTS
Conrad, Charles, Jr.	1930-	25	200	300	50	Gemini 5, Apollo 12, RS, MW, TSS
Conrad, Paul	1924-	10	25		50	Political cartoonist
Constable, John	1776-1837	300	600			English painter, gifted landscape artist
Conway, Thomas	1733-1800?	75	140	250		Cont'l general
Cook, John	1825-1910	35	90	160		Related to Mrs. A. Lincoln; real estate, mayor, sheriff, SL; Fort Donelson, District of Illinois
Cook, Lodwrick M.	1928-	5	15	20	10	Atlantic Richfield CEO
Cook, Phillip	1817-1865	125	250	375		Lawyer, USHR, SL; Seven Days, Sharpsburg
Cooke, Jay	1821-1905	150	950	1875	200	Financier, ESPV
Cooke, John Rogers	1833-1891	200	450	575		Outstanding record, highly regarded; Harvard; Numerous East Coast battles
Cooke, Philip St. George	1809-1895	55	125	200		His son is John Rogers Cooke; WP, MW, author; Washington, Peninsular
Coolidge, Grace Anna Goodhue	1879-1957	75	230	200	150	(1905); VT; S-2, First Lady
☆ **Coolidge, John Calvin**	**1872-1933**	**200**	**600**	**1200**	**600**	**TLS-800, WH/EMC-350, ALS-scarce**
Coolidge, William D.	1873-1974	50	90	175	125	Vacuum tube developer
Cooper, Douglas Hancock	1815-1879	200	450	600		SALS-2-3X; MW, U.S. agent, Indian advocate; Elkhorn, Newtonia
Cooper, James	1810-1863	165	250	500		St. Mary's College, lawyer, USHR, SL, USS; Valley, Camp Chase
Cooper, Joseph	1823-1910	40	100	200		MW, farmer, deacon; Wild Cat Mt., Murfreesboro, Atlanta*
Cooper, L. Gordon		30	75	150	65	Mercury-Atlas 9, Gemini 5, TSS
Cooper, Peter	1791-1883	80	175	280	150	Industrialist, philanthropist, inventor, Cooper U
Cooper, Roger	1953-	5	10	15	10	Doubleday Book vice president
Cooper, Samuel	1798-1876	150	300	600		WP, Ranking general officer, Adj & Insp. Gen.; No field command
Copeland, Joseph T.	1813-1893	35	90	150		Harvard, lawyer, judge, resort hotel operator; Washington, Annapolis Junction
Copley, John Singleton	1738-1815	400	750			Outstanding 18th century American painter, ESPV, ALS-scarce
Corcoran, Michael	1827-1863	575	1200	2000		ESPV; clerk; Washington, Manassas, Suffolk, ESPV

NAME	DATES	SIG	DS	ALS	SP	COMMENTS
Cornell, Ezra	1807-1874	40	150	200	100	Business, W.Union, philan., ALS-con. $1100
Cornell, Joseph	1903-1972	150				American sculptor, DS&ALS-ESPV
Corning, Erastus	1794-1872	75	160	300		U.S. financier, N.Y. Central
Cornwallis, Charles	1738-1805	225	500	1430		British general; gov. Gen. & C in C of Ireland
Corot, Jean-Baptiste-Camille	1796-1875	250	500	1000		French painter
Corrigan-Maquire, Mairead	1944-	30	60	115		"Peace People"
Corse, John M.	1835-1893	40	100	200		ESPV-LS/DS; lawyer, postmaster; Corinth, Chattanooga, Atlanta
Corse, Montgomery Dent	1816-1895	160	300	400		Blind during his final years, great soldier; MW, banker; First Manassas, Yorktown, Seven Days*
Cosby, George Blake	1830-1909	75	150	225		WP; Jackson
Cottrell, Frederick G.	1877-1948	50	100	225	70	Electrostatic precipitator
Coty, Francois	1874-1934	125	340	400		Industrialist, "Ami de People"
Couch, Darius N.	1822-1897	75	100	160		WP, MW; Peninsular, Sharpsburg, Chancellorsville*
Coué, Emile	1857-1926	150	300	400		Pharmacist, hypnotist
Coughlin, Charles E.	1891-1979	25	45	60	30	Religious leader
Coulter, John Breitling	1891-?	15	30	45	30	American general, WWI, WWII, KW
Courbet, Gustave	1819-1877	275	550	1000		French painter
Cousteau, Jacques Yves	1910-1997	65	175	250	175	Marine explorer, Aqualung, elusive signer!
Couzens, James	1872-1936	15	35	50	30	Political leader, automobile mfr.
Covey, Richard C.		5	15	20	10	Discovery, 8/27/85, Atlantis, 11/15/90, RS
Cowdin, Robert	1805-1874	200	400			Lumberman; First Manassas, Peninsular, Fair Oaks*
Cox, Jacob D.	1828-1900	30	65	120		Clerk, SL, gov. Ohio, sec. of interior, congress; Sharpsburg, Atlanta, Franklin, Nashville
Cox, William Ruffin	1832-1919	75	125	160		Among the last surviving generals; Lawyer, USHR, Sec. of the Senate; Spotsylvania Court House
Coxey, Jacob S.	1854-1951	30	50	160	45	Reformer
Craig, George		5	10	20	10	Harper Collins Publishers executive

William J. Clinton

George Clymer & James Smith

William J. Clinton

George Clymer

William J. Clinton

Howell Cobb

William J. Clinton

William F. "Buffalo Bill" Cody

William J. Clinton

William J. Clinton

William F. "Buffalo Bill" Cody

NAME	DATES	SIG	DS	ALS	SP	COMMENTS
Craig, James	1817-1888	40	60	120		MW, rrd. exec., senator; District of Nebraska
Cram, Donald	1919-	15	40		30	Chemist
Crane, Roy	1901-1977	40	75		225	Cartoonist, "Captain Easy," "Buz Sawyer"
Crane, Walter	1845-1915	50	125	250		English illustrator, designer
Crawford, Samuel W.	1829-1892	60	100	240		Univ. of Penn.; AOTP, Sharpsburg, Gettysburg, Fort Sumter*
Cray, Seymour	1925-1996	25	80	125	70	Supercomputer pioneer
Creel, George	1876-1953	25	55	90	35	Political leader, journalist
Creighton, John O.		10	20	20	25	Atlantis, 2/28/90, Discovery, 6/17/85, 91, FA
Creighton, John W. Jr.	1932-	5	10	15	10	Weyerhaeuser Company executive
Crick, Francis	1916-	30	60	110	75	Biophysicist
Crippen, Robert L.		25	75	200	80	Columbia, 4/12/81, 1st flight of reusable shut, FA
Cripps, Sir R. Stafford	1889-1952	40	100	200		British Labour statesman
Crittenden, George Bibb	1812-1880	100	225	300		Brother of Union general; WP, MW, librarian of KY
Crittenden, Thomas L.	1819-1893	95	250	390		ESPV; lawyer, MW; Shiloh, Tullahoma, Chickamauga
Croce, Benedetto	1866-1952	30	45	75	40	Italian philosopher, statesman
Crocker, Charles	1822-1888	25	50	115		U.S. railroad builder, financier
Crocker, Marcellus M.	1830-1865	350	700			WP, lawyer; Shiloh, Corinth, Vicksburg
Crockett, David	1786-1836	7250	10,000			Backwoodsman, scarce in all forms, FA, ESPV
Cromwell, Oliver	1599-1658	1650	6000			Lord Protector of England, scarce in all forms, ESPV
Crook, George	1829-1890	200	450	500		WP, western frontiersman; Western Virginia, Maryland, Chickamauga,* ESPV-ALS
Crookes, William	1832-1919	120	155	200		British physicist, chemist, inventor
Crossfield, A. Scott		10	30	60	40	National Aviation Hall of Fame
Croxton, John T.	1836-1874	175	220	315		Yale, lawyer, diplomat; Mill Springs, Tullahoma, Atlanta*
Cruft, Charles	1826-1883	65	125	200		Wabash College, clerk, lawyer; Fort Donelson, Corinth, Chickamauga*

NAME	DATES	SIG	DS	ALS	SP	COMMENTS
Cruikshank, George	1792-1878	125	200	400		English painter, illustrator, ESPV
Crumb, Robert	1943-	30	50			"Underground" cartoonist, ESPV-SP
Culbertson, Frank L., Jr.		5	10	20	15	Atlantis, 11/15/90, Discovery, 9/1/93
Culhane, Shamus	1908-1996	15	30			Animator
Cullum, George W.	1809-1892	50	100	150		WP, "Biographical Register of..."; Chief of staff Gen. Henry Halleck
Cummings, Alfred	1829-1910	100	300	400		His uncle of the same name was Gov. (UT); WP, American Military Com. to Korea; Malvern Hill, Sharpsburg, Vicksburg
Cunard, Samuel	1787-1865	100	155	240		Pioneered trans-Atlantic steam navigation
Cunningham, Sir Andrew Browne	1883-1963	40	100	220		British admiral, PU
Cunningham, "Bloody Bill"	?-1787	375				Tory partisan; notorious leader
Cunningham, R. Walter		20	30	60	30	Apollo 7, TSS
Cunningham, Robert	c.1739-1813	220	365			Tory leader
Cunningham, William	c.1717-1791	200				British provost marshall
Curie, Marie	1867-1934	1100	2000	3000		Polish/French chemist, DS content-3X, SALS-2X
Curie, Pierre	1859-1906	625	1350			French physicist, chemist, w. Marie, ESPV-all forms
Curley, James M.	1874-1958	20	40	50	30	Political leader, USHR, gov. MA
Curley, Tom	1948-	5	10	25	10	Publisher and president of USA Today
Currie, Nancy J.		5	10	15	10	STS-57, 70, 88, RS
Currier, Nathaniel (1813-88), and Ives, James M. (1824-95)		250 200	750 650			Popular lithographers
Curry, John S.	1897-1946	75	150	300		American painter
Curtis, Benjamin R.	1809-1874	50	165	265		SC: 1851-1857, MA, resigned from S. Court
Curtis, George William	1824-1892	50	100	125		Editor, reformer
Curtis, Newton M.	1835-1910	50	100	175		Teacher, postmaster, SL, congress, writer; Cold Harbor, Petersburg
Curtiss, Glenn	1878-1950	250	425	700		Aviation pioneer, inventor, ESPV-SP
Cushing, Harvey	1869-1939	170	450	700		US neurologist
Cushman, Robert Everton, Jr.	1914-1985	12	25	40	25	U.S. Marine general

	NAME	DATES	SIG	DS	ALS	SP	COMMENTS
☆	**Custer, George A.**	**1839-1876**	**4000**	**8900**	**12750**		He was a prolific writer; WP, Indian fighter; AOTP, Gettysburg, ESPV
	Cutler, Lysander	1807-1866	120	175	300		Rrd. dir., senator; Second Manassas, Fredericksburg, Gettysburg....*
	Cuvier, Georges, Baron	1769-1832	75	285	400		Anatomist, DS-ESPV
	Daimler, Gottlieb	1834-1900	450	1270	2225		German eng., inventor, automobile pion., ESPV
	Daladier, Edouard	1884-1970	35	75	150	75	French radical socialist politician
	Daley, Richard J.	1902-1976	25	55	100	45	Political leader
	Dali, Salvador	1904-1989	175	380	600		Spanish painter, sculptor, graphic artist, FA, ESPV
	Dallas, Alexander J.	1759-1817	75	165	225		American lawyer, public official
	Dallas, George Mifflin	1792-1864	70	225	350		American diplomat, politician, ESPV
	Dalling, John	?-1798	300				British general; gov. of Jamaica
	Dalrymple, William	?-1807	210				British general
	Dalton, John	1766-1844	150	500	1000		British physicist, chemist, 1st table atomic wts.
	Daly, Marcus	1841-1900	20	50	100		Irish-born copper magnate
	Damadian, Raymond V.	1936-	20	40	70	30	Cancer detection apparatus & method
	Dana, Napoleon J.T.	1822-1905	40	80	175		ESPV - DS/LS; MW, banker, rrd. exec.; Ball's Bluff, Sharpsburg
	Dana, Richard H.	1815-1882	60	175	225		Writer, lawyer, reformer
	Daniel, Peter V.	1784-1860	45	140	250		SC: 1841-1860, VA
	Daniell, Robert F.	1934-	5	15	25	10	United Technologies executive
	Daniels, Josephus	1862-1948	20	35	135	40	Political leader, sec. of the navy
	Danton, Georges	1759-1794	1250				French Revolutionist, ESPV, scarce
	Darehshori, Nader	1936-	5	10	20	10	Houghton Mifflin Company executive
	Darling (Ding), Jay N.	1876-1962	30	1550	2500	75	Political cartoonist
	Darrow, Charles	1889-1967	325	500			Monopoly inventor
☆	**Darrow, Clarence**	**1857-1938**	**400**	**1550**	**2500**	**1500**	U.S. lawyer, ANS-$650, LS-$3500
☆	**Darwin, Charles**	**1809-1882**	**675**	**2000**	**2275**		British naturalist, evolution, "Origin of ...", SALS-2-3X, ESPV
	Daubigny, Charles-Francois	1817-1878	125	250	400		French landscape painter

Schuyler Colfax

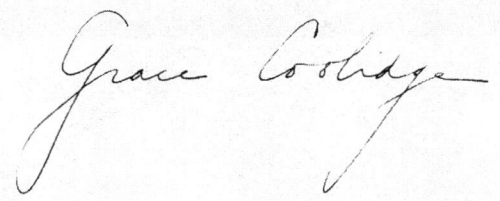

Grace Coolidge

Jay Cooke

David "Davy" Crocket

Calvin Coolidge

Marie Curie

Calvin Coolidge

Pierre Curie

Calvin Coolidge

Harvey W. Cushing

NAME	DATES	SIG	DS	ALS	SP	COMMENTS
Daugherty, Harry M.	1860-1941	20	40	90	45	Political leader
Daumier, Honore	1808-1879	275	500	1350		French painter, sculptor, caricaturist
David, Jacques-Louis	1748-1825	200	400			French Neoclassicism painter
Davidson, Henry Brevard	1831-1899	125	240	435		MW, WP, Dept. Sec. of State (NC) Island No. 10, Valley (VA)
Davidson, John W.	1824-1881	75	150	300		SALS-2X; WP; Peninsular, Missouri, Arkansas
Davie, William Richardson	1756-1820	175				Patriot officer; gov. of NC
Davies, Henry E.	1836-1894	60	100	200		Harvard, Colombia, lawyer, dist. atty.; Big Bethel, Second Manassas, Gettysburg
Davies, Thomas A.	1809-1899	45	110	165		WP, merchant writer; Corinth, Washington, First Manassas
Davis, David	1815-1886	75	250	300		SC: 1862-1877, IL, Lincoln confidant
Davis, Edmund J.	1827-1883	40	75	140		Lawyer, gov. Texas;
Davis, Jack	1926-	10				Cartoonist, "Mad" magazine
☆ **Davis, Jefferson**	**1808-1889**	**625**	**2000**	**2500**	**3000**	**LG-1350, CSA President, FA, ESPV**
Davis, Jefferson C.	1828-1879	60	125	150		Often confused with C.S.A. President; MW; Fort Sumter, Elkhorn, Corinth, Carolina
Davis, Jim	1945-	30	60		150	Cartoonist, "Garfield"
Davis, John W.	1873-1955	25	50	75	40	American lawyer, politician
Davis, Joseph Robert	1825-1896	350	750	1350		Neph. of J. Davis, ESPV, SDS/LS/ALS-2-3X; Miami Univ., lawyer; Northern Virginia, Gettysburg, Petersburg*
Davis, N. Jan		5	10	20	15	Endeavour, 9/12/92, D 2/3/94, m. Mark Lee
Davis, Varina	1864-1898	175	300	500	700	Mrs. Jefferson Davis, often signed husband's name, ESP-ALS
Davis, William George Mackey	1812-1898	70	165	300		Lawyer
Davisson, Clinton J.	1881-1958	30	80	100	65	American physicist, NP-1937, SALS-2-3X
Davy, Humphry	1778-1829	125	350	650		British chemist, ALS content-5-10X
Dawes, Charles G.	1865-1951	40	125	275	250	U.S. statesman, VP
Day, Dorothy	1897-1980	25	50	130	50	U.S. founder of Catholic Worker movement

NAME	DATES	SIG	DS	ALS	SP	COMMENTS
Day, William R.	1849-1923	45	90	135	65	SC: 1903-1922, OH, often at the ballpark!
Dayan, Moshe	1815-1981	125	250	300	275	Israeli general, politician
Dayton, Elias	1737-1807	125	250	400		Cont'l general; SL; USHR; Washington friend
Dayton, Jonathan	1760-1824	200	400	800		CC, v. rare in war dated, C after, NJ, ESPV-ALS, USHR; USS
De Forest, Lee	1873-1961	300	700	1650	1200	Audion amplifier, ALS content-5-10X, BDS-2X, ESPV-SP & ALS
☆ **De Gaulle, Charles**	**1890-1970**	**475**	**1275**	**2500**	**2725**	**French general, statesman, ESPV-ALS**
De Havilland, Sir Geoffrey	1882-1965	75	150	200	150	British aeronautical engineer, SALS-2X
de Klerk, F.W.	1936-	60	125		100	South African president, NP
de Kooning, Willem	1904-1997	150	250	500	150	American Abstract Expressionist painter
de Lagnel, Julius Adolph	1827-1912	75	150	230		Pacific steamship service; Rich Mountain
De Leon, Daniel	1852-1914	35	70	125		Reformer
De Russy, Gustavus A.	1818-1891	75	200	300		WP, MW; Peninsular, Malvern Hill, Fredericksburg
De Trobriand, Philippe R. D.	1816-1897	80	200	350		Lawyer, author, poet; Fredericksburg, Chancellorsville, Gettysburg, SDS-2X
De Valera, Eamon	1882-1975	50	130	300	100	Irish/U.S. statesman, PU
De Voto, Bernard A.	1897-1955	35	75	125	50	U.S. historian
Deane, Silas	1737-1789	275	500	1125		Con'tl Congress; first Amer. diplomat abroad
Dearborn, Henry	1751-1829	125	250	475		Cont'l officer; sec. of war; minister to Portugal, SDS-2X, ESPV
Deas, Zachariah Cantey	1819-1882	100	200	400		MW, cotton broker, stock broker; Shiloh, Kentucky, Chickamauga*
DeBeck, Billy	1890-1942	35			200	Cartoonist, "Barney Google"
Debs, Eugene V.	1855-1926	75	200	250	100	U.S. labor leader, presidential candidate
Decatur, Stephen	1779-1820	1250	3000	5275		American naval officer, W1812, ESPV-ALS
Decrane, Alfred C.	1941-	5	15	30	10	Texaco CEO
Deere, John	1804-1886	350	1000	1500		Plow developer, ESPV-DS, SDS-2X

GEN-POLIT-C

NAME	DATES	SIG	DS	ALS	SP	COMMENTS
☆ **Degas, Edgar**	**1834-1917**	**450**	**850**	**2000**		**French Impressionist painter, sight failed later**
Deitzler, George W.	1826-1884	35	65	115		Farmer, real estate dealer, mayor; Wilson's Creek
Del Valle, Pedro Augusto	1893-1978	15	30	45	40	American general, WWII
Delacorte, George T.	1893-1991	25	45	100	40	U.S. publisher
Delacroix, Eugene	1798-1863	200	400	600		French Romantic painter
Delafield, Richard	1798-1873	45	80	125		WP; Governor's Island, Sandy Hook
Delany, Martin R.	1812-1885	225	600	2350		Reformer
Delbruck, Max	1907-1981	30	50	125	50	U.S. pioneer in molecular genetics
Dell, Michael S.	1965-	5	20	35	12	Dell Computer executive
DeLucas, Lawrence J.		10		30	15	Columbia, 6/25/92, FA
Deming, W. Edwards	1900-1993	20	35	50	25	U.S. quality-control guru, influenced Japanese
Denfeld, Louis Emil	1891-1972	15	35	40	40	American admiral, WWI, WWII
Deng Xiaoping	1904-1997	975				Paramount leader of China, ESPV-all forms
Denison, Nathan	c.1740-1809	185				Militia officer, ESPV
Dennis, Elias S.	1812-1894	55	100	230		His stepson was "Jack" Slade; SL, US marshal, sheriff; Fort Donelson, Vicksburg
Dent, Frederick T.	1820-1892	50	115	245		His sister became Mrs. U.S. Grant; WP, MW, military gov.; Pres. Grant's military secretary, Ft. Trumbull
Denver, James W.	1817-1892	100	200	365		Surveyor, school teacher, MW, senator; Corinth, Shiloh
Depew, Chauncey M.	1834-1928	35	150	200	60	Lawyer, businessman, USS
Derain, Andre	1880-1954	100	200	550		French painter, sculptor, graphic artist
Deringer, Henry	1786-1868	2150	4500	7000		Arms manufacturer, ESPV
Derr, K.T.	1936-	5	10	20	10	Chevron Corporation executive
Dershowitz, Alan M.	1938-	10	25	70	25	Lawyer, writer, RS, ESPV-ALS
Desimone, L.D.	1936-	5	12	25	10	3M executive
Despard, Edward Marcus	1751-1803	240				British naval officer; gov. in S.Amer; conspirator, ESPV
Despard, John	1745-1829	255	500			British officer
Dessalines, Jean Jacques	c.1746-1806	1250	3000			Haitian general and ruler, ESPV

George A. Custer

David Davis

Salvador Dali

Jefferson Davis

Clarence S. Darrow

Jefferson Davis

Clarence S. Darrow

Jefferson Davis

Charles Darwin

Jefferson Davis

Charles Darwin

Jonathan Dayton

NAME	DATES	SIG	DS	ALS	SP	COMMENTS
Devanter, Willis Van	1859-1941	100	200	300	250	SC: 1910-1937, WY, NOT prolific
Devens, Charles, Jr.	1820-1891	50	100	200		Harvard, lawyer, SL, US atty. gen.; Seven Pines, Peninsular, Gettysburg*
Devereux, James P.	1903-	40	60	100	125	American general, WWII
Devers, Jacob Loucks	1887-1979	15	25	40	45	American general, WWII
Devin, Thomas C.	1822-1878	55	100	200		Maryland, Fredericksburg, Gettysburg*; Maryland, Fredericksburg, Gettysburg*
Dewey, George	1837-1917	95	150	225	275	U.S. Naval commander
Dewey, John	1859-1952	50	150	225	75	U.S. philosopher
Dewey, Melvil	1851-1931	50	80	125	65	Devised library book decimal system
Dewey, Thomas E.	1902-1971	45	80	150	125	New York gov., presidential candidate, SALS-2X
Diana, Princess of Wales	**1961-1997**	**1250**		**6750**	**3200**	**ALS-$10000, CC-$7500, CC w/Char. $3500, ESPV-all forms**
Diaz, Armando	1861-1928	50	125	215	125	Italian marshal
Diaz, Porfirio	1830-1915	125	200	500	250	President of Mexico
Dibrell, George Gibbs	1822-1888	150	350	430		Merchant, financier, USHR, rail pres., WD-2X
Dickinson, John	1732-1808	200	600			CC, v. rare in ALS, DS more available, DE, ESPV
Dickinson, Philemon	1739-1809	175				Militia general; USHR
Dickman, Joseph Theodore	1857-1928	75	140	250	150	Amer. gen., WWI, BR, AW, SAW
Diesel, Rudolf	**1858-1913**	**1000**	**2675**	**3500**		**German mechanical engin., diesel engine, ESPV**
Digby, Robert	1732-1814	230	475			British admiral, ESPV
Dior, Christian	1905-1957	125	450		250	Fashion designer
Dirks, Rudolph	187-1968	80		200	200	Cartoonist, "The Katzenjammer Kids"
Dirksen, Everett M.	1896-1969	25	75	135	60	Senate Republican minority leader, RS
Disney, Walt	**1901-1966**	**1425**	**3000**		**4000**	**Producer animated cartoons, Mickey Mouse, ESPV, SP-2-3X, SDS-2X**
Disraeli, Benjamin	1804-1881	175	300	500		British prime minister, SALS-2X
Ditko, Steve	1927-	15				Cartoonist, "Spider-man"
Divine, Father (George Baker)	1877-1965	150	475	600	225	American religious leader

NAME	DATES	SIG	DS	ALS	SP	COMMENTS
Dix, Dorothea	1802-1887	75	200	500		U.S. crusader for the mentally ill
Dix, John A.	1798-1879	100	250	300		Gov. NY, USS, sec. of the treasury, diplomat; Department and garrison duties
Djerassi, Carl	1923-	10	25	55	25	Oral contraceptives
Dobrynin, Anataoly F.	1919-	50	150	400	100	Soviet diplomat, statesman
Dockery, Thomas Pleasant	1833-1898	150	300	425		Civil engineeer; Wilson's Creek, Corinth, Vicksburg,* ESPV-WD material
Dodd, Francis Townsend	1899-1973	15	30	40	50	American general, WWII, KW
Dodge, Charles C.	1841-1910	50	100	200		Phelps Dodge, Corp.; Suffolk, Virginia
Dodge, Grenville M.	1831-1916	60	125	185		Military and civil engineer, USHR; Atlanta, Elkhorn
☆ Doenitz, Karl	**1891-1980**	**100**	**325**	**350**	**180**	**German admiral, TSS-$350**
Doisy, Edward	1893-1987	25	50	135	35	Biochemist
Dole, Elizabeth		15			30	Red Cross official, RS M. Robert Dole
Dole, Robert	1923-	10	25	75	40	Political leader, USS, FA, SALS-DS-2X
Dole, Sanford B.	1844-1926	50	225	400	125	Political leader, jurist
Doles, George Pierce	1830-1864	675	850	1475		Outstanding brigadier, KIA; South Mountain, Sharpsburg, Gettysburg,* ESPV- all forms
Donelson, Daniel Smith	1801-1863	355	450	750		Nephew of Andrew Jackson; SL; Murfressboro, ESPV
Doniphan, Alexander William	1808-1887	130	275	500		American general, MW
Donnelly, Ignatius	1831-1901	30	60	80		Political leader, SL, USHR
Donovan, William J. "Wild Bill"	1883-1959	100	200	300	125	Attorney, government official
Dooley, Thomas	1927-1961	100	200	400	150	"Jungle doctor"
Doolittle, Charles C.	1832-1903	50	100	200		Cashier; Peninsula, Seven Days
Doolittle, James Harold "Jimmy"	1896-1993	55	200	300	85	Amer. army air corps gen., WWI, WWII
Doppler, Christian	1803-1853	160	350	800		Austrian physicist, Doppler effect
Dore, Gustave	1832-1883	100	200			French book illustrator
Doubleday, Abner	1819-1893	500	2250	1500		Popular due to baseball association, or lack of; WP; Shenandoah, Second Manassas, Gettysburg*
Doubleday, Frank N.	1862-1943	75	150	400	165	Publisher

NAME	DATES	SIG	DS	ALS	SP	COMMENTS
Douglas, Donald	1892-1981	150	300	425	400	Aircraft designer
Douglas, Stephen A.	1813-1861	165	280	625	300	Democratic leader, opposed Lincoln, ESPV
Douglas, William O.	1898-1980	75	200		200	SC: 1939-1975, CT, served over 30 years., contro., ESPV-ALS
Douglass, Frederick ☆	**1817-1895**	**300**	**800**	**3000**		**Reformer, SDS & ALS - 2X**
Doulton, Sir Henry	1820-1897	25	50	100		Pottery manufacturer
Doumergue, Gaston	1863-1937	60	100	200		French politician
Doumer, Paul	1857-1932	75	125	165		French politician
Dow, Herbert H.	1866-1930	50	100	165	100	U.S. chemical company founder
Dow, Neal	1804-1897	50	100	175		Mayor of Portland; District of Florida, Port Hudson, SALS-2X, ESPV-ALS
Draper, Charles Stark	1901-1987	25	40	115	60	Gyroscopic equipment inventor
Drayton, Thomas Fenwick	1808-1891	125	225	285		Often labeled inefficient as a field cmdr.; WP, SL, farmer, insurance agent; Second Manassas, South Mountain,* ESPV
Drew, Ernest H.	1937-	5	10	15	10	Hoechst Celanese Corp. executive
Drexel, Anthony J.	1826-1893	40	75	150		s.Francis M., businessman
Drexel, Francis M.	1792-1863	55	125	225		American banker
Drexel, Katharine M.	1858-1955	40	100	200		Reformer
Dreyfus, Alfred	1859-1935	150	300	725		French army officer, SALS-2X
Drucker, Mort	1929-	15			25	Cartoonist, "Mad" magazine
du Barry, M. Jeanne	c.1743-1793	350	1000	1500		Louis XV mistress, ESPV
Du Bois, William Edward B.	1868-1963	40	100	150	65	Reformer, writer, historian, NAACP
du Pont, Eleuthere	1771-1834	65	145	280		French/U.S. gunpowder manufacturer, bus.
Du Pont, Pierre S.	1870-1954	80	170		200	Business leader
Duane, James	1733-1797	160	350	700		Patriot statesman; jurist; mayor (NYC)
Dubcek, Alexander	1921-1992	75	150	225	100	Czech. statesman
Dubinsky, David	1892-1982	25	60	100	75	Labor leader
DuBose, Dudley McIver	1834-1883	115	300	475		Lawyer, USHR; Gettysburg, Richmond, Sayler's Creek
Dubuffet, Jean	1901-1985	175	350			French artist
Duchamp, Marcel	1887-1968	150	300	600		French artist, art theorist

Eugene V. Debs

Benjamin Disraeli

Charles de Gaulle

Benjamin Disraeli

Princess Diana

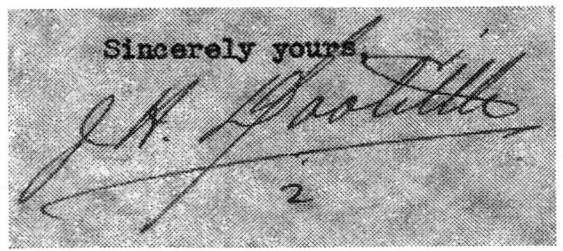

James "Jimmy" Doolittle

John Dickinson

Abner Doubleday

Walt Disney

Walt Disney

William O. Douglas

NAME	DATES	SIG	DS	ALS	SP	COMMENTS
Duer, William	1749-1799	150	345	700		Congressman; militia officer; ALS-2X
Duesenbera, Fredrick S.	1877-1932	500	1150			American manufacturer
Duffie, Alfred N.A.	1835-1880	55	115	135		ESPV; diplomat; Second Manassas, Chancellorsville,* ESPV-ALS
Duffy, Brian		5		25	10	Atlantis, 3/24/92, E 6/21/93, RS
Dufy, Raoul	1877-1953	200	325	650		French painter, graphic artist, designer
Duke, Basil Wilson	1838-1916	130	250	650		SDS/LS & SALS - 5-6X; Lawyer, legislator, author; Numerous, including escorting Davis, ESPV
Duke, Charles M., Jr.		27	125	200	60	Apollo 16, MW, TSS
Duke, James	1856-1925	125	220	375		American Tobacco founder, Duke University
Dulany, Daniel	1722-1797	110				Lawyer; political leader
Dulles, John Foster	1888-1959	35	80	140	60	U.S. sec. of state
Dumont, Ebenezer	1814-1871	50	120	200		Univ. of Ind., MW, USHR, gov. Idaho tty.; West Virginia, Cheat Mountain
Dunbar, Bonnie J.		5		25	10	Challenger, 10/30/85,Columbia, 1/9/90, 1992
Dunlap, John	1747-1812	145	350			American printer
Durand, Asher B.	1796-1886	75	150	225		American painter and engraver
Durant, Ariel & Durant, Will	1896-1981, 1885-1981	75			125	U.S. historians, RSs
Durant, Graham J.	1934-	10	25	40	20	Cimetidine (Tagamet) developer
Durant, Thomas	1820-1885	45	250	400		U.S. railroad official, financier
Durant, William C.	1861-1947	275	750	1100		U.S. industrialist, formed General Motors
Duryea, Charles E.	1861-1938	250	565			American inventor. SDS-2-3X, ALS-ESPV, scarce
Duryee, Abram	1815-1890	75	150	225		Importer, dockmaster; Big Bethel, Second Manassas, Sharpsburg
Duval, Isaac H.	1824-1902	35	75	165		Hunter, trapper, USHR, SL; West Virginia, Shenandoah Valley
Duvall, Gabriel	1752-1844	50	150	300		SC: 1811-1835, MD, unsure name SP
Dwight, Timothy	1752-1817	50	100	150		Religious leader, writer, educator
Dwight, William	1831-1888	60	125	180		WP, rrd. management; Williamsburg, Red River, Cedar Creek*

NAME	DATES	SIG	DS	ALS	SP	COMMENTS
Dyer, Alexander B.	1815-1874	100	160	285		WP, MW; Springfield armory, chief of ordnance
Eaker, Ira Clarence	1896-1987	30	75	125	150	Amer. army air corps gen., WWI, WWII
Eakins, Thomas	1844-1916	400	750			Painter, ESPV
☆ **Earhart, Amelia**	**1897-1937**	**750**	**1500**	**2000**	**1725**	**SB-$850, SDS-2X, ESPV-ALS & SP**
Early, Jubal Anderson	1816-1894	500	750	1500		ESPV, SALS-2X; WP, lawyer, SL, MW, Pres. South. Hist. Soc.; First Manassas, Salem Church, Gettysburg*
Eastlake, Charles L.	1836-1906	75	150	500		Architect, designer, SALS-2X
☆ **Eastman, George**	**1854-1932**	**200**	**850**	**1000**	**1500**	**Photography pioneer, ESPV-DS, SDS-2-10X**
Eaton, Amos B.	1806-1877	40	55	125		WP, MW; Commissary general of the U.S. Army
Eaton, Robert J.	1940-	5	10	15	10	Chrysler Corporation executive, RS
Eban, Abba	1915-	25	65	100	50	Israeli diplomat, statesman
Eccles, Sir John	1903-	25	40	50	40	Physiologist
Eccles, Marriner S.	1890-1977	30	55	80	45	Businessman, banker
Echols, John	1823-1896	175	275	450		SDS & SALS - 2-3X; Harvard, lawyer, SL, businessman; First Manassas, New Market*
Eckener, Hugo	1868-1954	250	500	700	500	Aeronautical engineer
Eckert, Jr., J. Presper	1919-1995	20	45	100	50	Co-inventor Eniac large-scale computer
Ector, Matthew Duncan	1822-1879	225	400	500		SDS & SALS - 2-3X; Lawyer, SL, judge; Richmond, Murfreesboro, Chickamauga*
Eddington, Sir Arthur	1882-1944	30	150	200		Astronomer
☆ **Eddy, Mary Baker**	**1821-1910**	**1500**	**2750**	**3750**		**Founder of Christian Science, SB-$2750, ESPV**
Eden, Sir Anthony	1897-1977	50	125		75	British foreign sec., prime minister
Edgerton, Harold E.	1903-	20	35	70	30	Stroboscope pioneer
☆ **Edison, Thomas**	**1847-1931**	**500**	**1350**	**1750**	**2250**	**U.S. inventor, held over 1,000 patents, SALS-2X-ESPV-ALS**
Edward VII (England)	1841-1910	150	250			Eldest son of Queen Victoria, SDS-2X
Edward VIII (England)	1894-1972	300	1000	750		DS-$2750, SB-$1200, SDS-2-3X

NAME	DATES	SIG	DS	ALS	SP	COMMENTS
Edwards, John	1815-1894	40	65	130		SL, newspaperman, congress; Army of the Southwest, Fort Smith, Camden
Edwards, Jonathan	1703-1758	150	300	375		U.S. preacher, theologian
Edwards, Oliver	1835-1904	50	100	150		Postmaster, businessman; Peninsular, Fredericksburg, Gettysburg
Egan, Thomas W.	1834-1887	55	120			Seven Pines, Peninsular, AOTOP*; Seven Pines, Peninsular, AOTP*
Egen, Maureen		5	10	15	10	Editor, publisher
Egleston, Joseph	1754-1811	100	220			Cont'l officer; SL; USHR
Ehrlich, Paul	1854-1915	300	1300	2000	1500	German bacteriologist, immunology pioneer
Eichelberger, Robert Lawrence	1886-1961	25	50	80	50	American general, WWI, WWII
Eiffel, Gustave	1832-1923	275	550	1000	1200	French civil engineer, ESPV-SP & ALS
Eichmann, Adolf	1906-1962	250	500	1500	825	Nazi war criminal, SALS-2-3X
Eiger, Richard	1933-	5	10	15	10	Publisher
☆ **Einstein, Albert**	**1879-1955**	**1200**	**2175**	**3125**	**3500**	**German/U.S. physicist, Theory of Relativity, SDS-2-3X, ESPV**
Eisele, Donn F.		50	100		100	Apollo 7
☆ **Eisenhower, Dwight David**	**1890-1969**	**300**	**800**	**3400**	**600**	**PL, ALS content-1.5 x-5x, TLS-$500 (DDE), TLS-625, WH/EMC-525**
Eisenhower, John S.D.		15	25	40	20	Son of President (DDE)
Eisenhower, Julie Nixon		10	20	30	25	Daughter of President (DDE)
Eisenhower, Mamie Geneva Doud	1896-1979	60	125	200	50	IA; S-1; plus a deceased infant, First Lady
Eisenhower, Milton		15	35		25	Brother of President (DDE)
Eisenstaedt, Alfred	1898-1995	30	75	150	150	German/U.S. photographer
Eisner, Will	1917-	10				Cartoonist, "The Spirit"
Elbert, Samuel	1743-1788	40	100	160		Cont'l general; gov.; PU
Elion, Gertrude B.	1918-	25	70	150	40	DNA blocking drugs inventor
Eliot, Charles W.	1834-1926	20	35	60	50	Educator
Elizabeth II (England)	1926-	350	700	850	700	
Elizabeth, (Queen Mother)	1900-	125	420	500	550	Mother of Elizabeth II
Eller, Ernest M.		25				Admiral, Pacific Commander
Ellery, William	1727-1820	180	360	700		Signer DOI; CC; ESPV-DS; DS-$185

Frederick Douglass

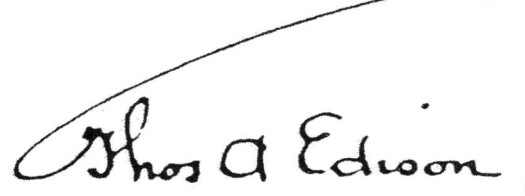
Thomas Edison

Raoul Dufy

Thomas A. Edison

Charles E. Duryea

Edward VIII, King of England

Amelia Earhart

Albert Einstein

Albert Einstein

Amelia Earhart

Albert Einstein

NAME	DATES	SIG	DS	ALS	SP	COMMENTS
Ellet, Alfred W.	1820-1895	40	75	150		Civil engineer, businessman; Dept. of Mississippi, Marine Brig., Vicksburg
Elletin, Michael		5	10	15	10	Publisher
Elliot, John	?-1808	200				British naval officer; gov. Newfoundland; Par.
Elliott, Washington L.	1825-1888	50	100	200		WP, banker; Wilson's Creek, Springfield, Corinth, Atlanta
Ellis, Havelock	1859-1939	50	135	175		Physician, ESPV-SP
Ellsworth, Oliver	1745-1807	120	315	500		SC: 1796-1800, CT, Chief Justice, hated to write!
Elphinstone, George Keith	1746-1823	200				British naval officer; first Viscount Keith
Elzey (Jones), Arnold	1816-1871	275	500	800		SALS- 2X, ESPV; WP, MW; First Manassas, Shenandoah Valley*
Emmet, John C.	1938-	10	25	40	20	Cimetidine (Tagamet) developer
Emory, William H.	1811-1887	75	150	300		Wife great-granddaughter of Ben Franklin; WP, writer; Indian Territory, Peninsular, Red River*
Enders, John F.	1897-1985	35	75	125	50	U.S. virologist, vaccine pioneer
England, Anthony W.		5	10	20	15	Challenger, 7/29/85, RS
Engle, Joe H.		10		15	20	Columbia, 11/12/81, Discovery, 8/27/85, RS
Enos, Roger	1729-1808	75	150	300		Cont'l officer; prominent VT figure
Erhard, Ludwig	1897-1977	35	100	185	75	German economist, W. German chancellor
Ericsson, John	1803-1889	100	175	500		Propeller inventor
Erikson, Erik	1902-1994	25	50	70	30	U.S. psychoanalyst, author
Ernst, Maxmillian	1891-1976	225	375	825		Painter
Erskine, William	1728-1795	160				British general
Eshkol, Levi	1895-1969	250	325	500		Israeli politician
Esnault-Pelterie, Robert	1881-1957	100	225			French aviator
Estaing, Charles Hector Theodat, Comte'd	1729-1794	200	400			French admiral, ESPV
Estey (Este), George P.	1829-1881	40	85	170		Dartmouth, lawyer; Laurel Hill, Mill Springs, Tullahoma, Atlanta
Euler, Leonhard	1707-1783	1050	6000			Swiss mathematician, calculus pioneer, ESPV

NAME	DATES	SIG	DS	ALS	SP	COMMENTS
Eustis, Henry L.	1819-1885	75	150	260		Harvard, WP, professor, author; Fredericksburg, Chancellorsville, Gettysburg
Evans, Clement Anselm	1833-1911	150	400	750		Edited "Confed, Military History," SDS-2X; Lawyer, judge, USS (?), author; Numerous with Army of North. VA
Evans, Nathan George "Shanks"	1824-1868	200	400	600		Controversial; WP, principal; First and Second Manassas, Sharpsburg
Evans, Ronald E.		35	100		70	Apollo 17, RS
Evarts, William M.	1818-1901	40	100	150	65	Lawyer, statesman
Everett, Edward	1794-1865	80	160	200		Statesman, scholar
Ewell, Richard Stoddert	1817-1872	500	700	1750		Controversial, SALS-2X; WP, MW, farmer; First & Second Manassas, Seven Days*
Ewing, Charles	1835-1883	50	100	200		Univ. of Va., lawyer; Vicksburg, Chattanooga, Atlanta
Ewing, Hugh B.	1826-1905	45	115	225		Lawyer, author, diplomat; South Mountain, Sharpsburg, Chattanooga
Ewing, Thomas Jr.	1829-1896	60	110	200		Private sec. to Z. Taylor, lawyer, first chief justice Kan., USHR; Cane Hill, Prairie Grove, Pilot Knob
Eyre, Edward J.	1815-1901	50	100	160		Explorer
Faber, Johann L.	1817-1896	200	400	600		German Manufacturer
Faber, John E.	1822-1879	200	450	700		brother of Johann
Fabian, John M.		5	15	25	10	Challenger, 6/18/83
Fagan, James Fleming	1828-1893	350	800			ESPV, LS/DS - 2X; MW, SL, U.S. Marshal; Shiloh, Prairie Grove, Missouri
Fahrenheit, Gabriel	1686-1736	3200	8000	15000		German physicist, Fahrenheit scale, ESPV
Fairchild, Lucius	1831-1896	35	80	125		Carroll College, clerk, gov. Wisc.; Falling Waters, Second Manassas*
Fall, Albert B.	1861-1944	30	75	125	45	Political leader, USS, controversial
Faraday, Michael	1791-1867	175	375	600		British physicist, chemist, electricity pioneer, ESPV-ALS
Fargo, William G.	1818-1881	365	675	1450		American Express founder, ESPV-DS
Farman, Henri	1874-1958	75	150	200	175	French aviation pioneer
Farley, James A.	1888-1976	10	30	55	20	Political leader, U.S. postmaster general

NAME	DATES	SIG	DS	ALS	SP	COMMENTS
Farnsworth, John F.	1820-1897	50	100	160		Lawyer, congress; Peninsular, Maryland, Fredericksburg
Farragut, David G.	1801-1870	200	400	800		Union admiral. SDS-3X, SALS-2X, ESPV
Featherston, Winfield Scott	1820-1891	100	200	325		ESPV; Lawyer, USHR, SL, judge; Numerous Western army
Febiger, Christian, "Old Denmark"	1746-1796	175	310			Cont'l officer; treasurer of PA; r. Va. State Lib.
Feiffer, Jules	1929-	10			70	Village Voice cartoonist
Ferguson, Samuel Wragg	1857-1917	200	400	800		Lawyer, Miss. River Com.; Shiloh, Vickburg
Fermi, Enrico	1901-1954	500	2000	3750		Italian/U.S. physicist, ESPV
Ferrari, Enzo	1898-1988	300	600		625	Racing-car designer
Ferraris, Gallileo	1847-1897	125	300	1200		Italian physicist, electrical engineer
Ferraro, Geraldine	1935-	10	20	45	15	Politician, journalist
Ferrero, Edward	1831-1899	55	130	250		SDS-2X; WP; Second Manassas, Sharpsburg,* WD-2X
Ferry, Orris S.	1823-1875	50	130	200		Yale, lawyer, judge, editor, SL, USS; Shenandoah Valley, Peninsula
Fersen, Hans Axel, Count von	1755-1810	525	1200			Swedish nobleman; controversial; ESPV
Fessenden, Francis	1839-1906	60	140	200		Bowdin, Harvard, lawyer; Red River, Shiloh, Pleasant Hill, WD-ALS-2X
Fessenden, James D.	1833-1882	40	75	100		Bowdin, lawyer, SL; Carolina coast, Atlanta, Cedar Creek
Fettman, Martin J.		5	10	20	10	Columbia, 10/18/93
Few, William	1748-1828	250	500	700		CC, ALS from GA v. rare, from NY on occasion
Feynman, Richard	1918-1988	30	40	100	35	U.S. physicist, writer
Field, Charles William	1828-1892	125	250	430		WP, varied post-bellum career; Seven Days, Cedar MT., Second Manassas
Field, Cyrus W.	1819-1892	65	250	315		Merchant, financier, ESPV-ALS
Field, Marshall	1834-1906	150	275	485		U.S. merchant, dept. store founder, ESPV-Sig. & ALS
Field, Stephen J.	1816-1899	100	150	300	250	SC: 1863-1897, CA, serv. over 30 years
Fillmore, Caroline McIntosh	1813-1881	540	800	925		(1858); NJ; No sons or daughters, First Lady

Dwight Eisenhower

Marie Geneva Doud "Mamie" Eisenhower

Dwight Eisenhower

William Ellery

Dwight Eisenhower
("DE")

Oliver Ellsworth

Dwight Eisenhower ("Ike")

Edward Everett

Edward Everett

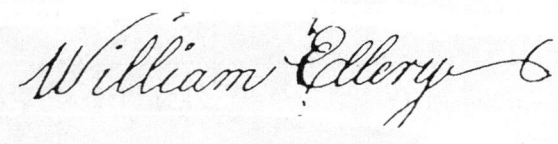

Marie Geneva Doud "Mamie" Eisenhower

William Ellery

David Farragut

NAME	DATES	SIG	DS	ALS	SP	COMMENTS
☆ **Fillmore, Millard**	**1800-1874**	**265**	**1065**	**1625**		**ALS content can vary significantly; FF:450 PD-2X**
Finegan, Joseph	1814-1885	125	200	400		SL, cotton broker; Cold Harbor, Florida
Fink, Albert	1827-1897	20	40	55		Railroad engineer
Finley, Jesse Johnson	1812-1904	100	200	300		Lawyer, SL, Mayor of Memphis, TN, USHR; Kentucky, Chickamauge, Atlanta*
Finney, Charles G.	1792-1875	40	75	125		Religious leader
Firestone, Harvey	1868-1938	150	600	1275	500	U.S. tire company founder, SDS-3X, ESPV-DS
Fish, Hamilton	1808-1893	20	75	100		U.S. sec. of state
Fisher, Anna L.		10	20	30	20	Discovery, 11/8/84
Fisher, Avery	1906-1994	25	60	115	40	U.S. industrialist, philanthropist, Fisher Elect.
Fisher, Bud	1884-1954	125	150		450	Cartoonist, "Mutt & Jeff"
Fisher, George M. C.	1940-	5	10	20	10	Eastman Kodak CEO, RS
Fisher, Ham	1900-1955	125			175	Cartoonist, "Joe Palooka"
Fisher, Irving	1867-1947	30	60	75	40	U.S. economist
Fisher, William F.		5	15	20	10	Discovery, 8/27/85
Fisk, Clinton B.	1828-1890	60	100	200		Merchant, miller, banker, Fisk Univ.; Missouri, Arkansas
Fisk, James Jr.	1834-1872	60	120	200	100	Financier
Fiske, John	1842-1901	40	80	135		U.S. historian, lecturer
Fitzsimons, Thomas	1741-1811	200	350	440		CC, sig. available in all forms, SAB-$350, PA
Flagg, James Montgomery	1877-1960	75	200	275	400	Illustrator, "Uncle Sam" recruiting poster
Flammarion, Camille	1842-1925	50	75	175	200	French astronomer
Flamsteed, John	1646-1719	1000	1250			English astronomer, ESPV
Flatley, James H.	1906-1958	45	135	300		Comm. navy air corp, "Grim Reapers"
Fleischer, Max	1883-1972	150	325		400	Cartoonist, "Betty Boop," ESPV-SIG
Fleming, Alexander	1881-1955	225	500	1000	1000	British bacteriologist, disc. penicillin, SALS-2-25X
Fleming, John A.	1849-1945	40	85	160		Electrical engineer
Fletcher, Frank Jack	1885-1973	20	45	100	50	American admiral, WWI, WWII

NAME	DATES	SIG	DS	ALS	SP	COMMENTS
Fletcher, Philip B.	1933-	5	10	15	10	ConAgra Inc. executive
Flexner, Abraham	1866-1959	40	100	150	50	Educator
Flipper, Henry Ossian	1856-1940	25	45	60	60	American army officer, controversial
Floyd, John Buchanan	1806-1863	200	400	600		Controversial, SALS-2-3X; Lawyer, SL, Gov. of VA, Sec. of War; West VA, ESPV-WD
Floyd, William	1734-1821	500	1400	2000		Signer DOI; CC; LS-$1950; ESPV
Foale, Michael		10	20	35	20	Atlantis, 3/24/92, Discovery, 4/8/93, 2/3/95
Foch, Ferdinand	1851-1929	60	120	300		French field marshal, PU
Fogel, Robert W.	1926-	10	15	20	15	Economist
Folcker, Anthony H.G.	1890-1839	180	300	500	465	Aircraft engineer
Folks, Homer	1867-1963	25	65	115	30	Reformer
Fonck, Paul Rene	1894-1953	925	1850			French officer, ESPV
Forbes, John M.	1813-1898	30	65	100		Financier, merchant
Forbes, M. Steve		10			20	Presidential candidate
Forbes, Malcolm	1919-1990	40	75	150	80	U.S. magazine publisher, RS
Force, Manning	1824-1899	50	100	175		Harvard, lawyer; Shiloh, Vicksburg, Atlanta, Carolina
Ford, Elizabeth Bloomer Warren "Betty"	1918-	30	130		50	(1948); IL; S-3; D-1, First Lady, FA
☆ **Ford, Gerald Rudolph**	**1913-**	**80**	**400**	**900**	**75**	**PL, only pres. serve w/o being elected VP & P, TLS-1500, WH/EMC-125, FA**
Ford, Henry	1863-1947	850	3000	4000	2650	U.S. auto maker, ESPV-all forms
Ford, Henry II	1917-1987	15	30	75	50	U.S. auto maker head, RS
Forney, John Horace	1829-1902	150	300	500		Brother of William Henry Forney, SALS-2X; WP, farmer, civil engineer; First Manassas, Dranesville, Vicksburg, ESPV-all forms
Forney, William Henry	1823-1894	100	150	300		SALS -2-3X; MW, lawyer,SL, USHR; Gettysburg
Forrest, Nathan Bedford	1821-1877	1000	2000	5000		Legendary cavalry commander, SALS-2-3X; Pres. Selma, Marion & Memphis Railroad; Fort Donelson, Murfreesboro, Chattanooga,* ESPV
Forrestal, James V.	1892-1949	50	100	145	40	U.S. sec. of navy, first sec. of defense
Forrester, Jay W.	1918-	15	30	55	25	Magnetic storage pioneer

NAME	DATES	SIG	DS	ALS	SP	COMMENTS
Forsyth, James W.	1835-1906	50	125	200		Commanded troops battle of Wounded Knee; WP; Peninsular, Maryland, Chickamauga
Fortas, Abe	1910-1982	30	125	180	100	SC: 1965-1969, TN, RS!
Forten, James	1766-1842	75	150	240		Reformer
Foss, Joseph Jacob	1915-	35	80	100	65	Marine Corps officer, WWII
Foster, Hal	1892-1982	125				Cartoonist, "Tarzan," "Prince Valiant"
Foster, John G.	1823-1874	50	100	200		WP, MW, construction worker; Fort Sumter, North Carolina
Foster, Robert S.	1834-1903	50	100	200		Tried A. Lincoln conspirators; US marshal; Rich Mountain, Shenandoah Valley, Suffolk
Foucho, Joseph, due d'Otrante	1763-1829	165	385	700		French statesman
Foulois, Benjamin D.	1879-1967	40	60	100	60	American general, SAW, WWI
Fourier, Jean B.J.	1768-1830	350	700	1500		French mathematician, ALS-5-10X
Fox, Charles James	1749-1806	40	100	200		British opposition politician
Fox, Fontaine	1884-1964	40	75		165	Cartoonist, "Toonerville Folks"
Francis I (France)	1494-1547	600	1250			Son of Charles, Count of Ang.
Francis II	1768-1835	150	300	460		Last Holy Roman Emperor
Franck, James	1882-1964	45	110	275	140	German physicist, quantum theorist
Franco, Francisco	1892-1975	250	700	1400	300	Spanish leader, dictator
Frank, Otto		300	600			Father of Anne Frank
Frankenthaler, Helen	1928	50			75	Abstract painter
Frankfurter, Felix	1882-1965	150	700	1200	800	SC: 1939-1962, MA, illegible hw due to old age, SDS-2X
☆ **Franklin, Benjamin**	**1706-1790**	**3575**	**8800**	**16625**		**CC, in great demand by inst., ALS-2X. SDS-3X**
Franklin, Sir John	1786-1847	150	300	650		Arctic Explorer
Franklin, William	1731-1813	175	400	775		Royal gov. NJ; Tory leader; s. of Ben. Franklin
Franklin, William	1823-1903	100	200	260		Involved in Paris Exposition of 1888; WP, MW, Colt's Firearms Mfg. Co.; First Manassas, Maryland, Fredericksburg
Fraser, Simon	1726-1782	325				Col. of Fraser Highlanders
Frazer, John Wesley	1827-1906	125	250	315	2000	WP; Kentucky, E. Tennessee
Frazer, Sir James George	1854-1941	40	100		50	British anthropologist

Ferdinand V & Isabella I

William Few

Cyrus Field

Millard Fillmore

M. Fillmore

Millard Fillmore

Millard Fillmore

Millard Fillmore

Millard Fillmore

My dear wife is no more. She died at Washington on Wednesday the 30th ult. and we left with her remains the next day for this place, and arrived here night before last, and she was buried yesterday. Her disease was inflammation on the lungs arising from a severe cold, taken about the 5th of March, which soon terminated in a dropsy of the lungs. She bore all her sufferings with uncomplaining fortitude, and at last expired without a struggle or a groan. The rest of my family are here, and as well as could be expected, but we are all saddened with grief.

Truly yours affectionate Brother
Millard Fillmore

Millard Fillmore

Harvey Firestone

Thomas Fitzsimons

NAME	DATES	SIG	DS	ALS	SP	COMMENTS
Frederick II, the Great (Prussia)	1712-1786	500	1075	2425		DS-$975, ESPV-DS
Frederick IX (Denmark)	1899-1972	60	165	330		
Frederick, William II (Prussia)	1744-1797	75	420	460		ESPV-ALS
Frederick, William III (Prussia)	1770-1840	85	375	400		ESPV-ALS
Frederick, William IV (Prussia)	1795-1861	125	450	800		ESPV-ALS
Freleng, Isadore "Fritz"	1905-1995	40			100	Animator, Porky Pig, Yosemite Sam, etc...
Fremont, John C.	1813-1890	250	750	1125		SALS-4-5X; Charleston College, USS, tty., gov. Ariz.; California
French, Samuel Gibbs	1818-1910	150	275	375		WP, MW, farmer; Numerous with Army of TN
French, William H.	1815-1881	75	150	300		WP, MW; Peninsular, Sharpsburg, Gettysburg*
☆ **Freud, Sigmund**	**1856-1939**	**1725**	**4750**	**5150**	**8000**	**Aust. fdr. of psychology, ALS-2-2.5X, ESPV-DS & ALS**
Frick, Henry C.	1849-1919	100	225	375	150	U.S. steel and coke magnate
Friedan, Betty G.	1921-	10	20	30	15	Reformer
Friedman, Jane		5	15	20	10	Publisher
Friedman, Milton	1912-	5	15	30	10	Economist, Nobel Prize winner
Frimout, Dirk D.		5	15	25	10	Atlantis, 3/24/92
Fritsch, Baron Werner von	1880-1939	65	165	225	200	German military officer, PU
Frost, Daniel Marsh	1823-1900	145	200	400		WP, MW, SL; Prairie Grove
Fuchs, Sir Vivian E.	1908-	25	65	135		Antarctic explorer
Fry, Birkett Davenport	1822-1891	175	400	500		Grad. VMI, attended WP, MW; Seven Pines, Chancellorsville, Gettysburg*
Fry, James B.	1827-1894	40	80	125		WP, writer; Washington, staff service
Fry, Speed S.	1817-1892	50	100	150		Wabash College, lawyer, judge; Fishing Creek, Shiloh, Stone's River
Fulbright, J. William	1905-1995	20	30	75	40	U.S. senator
Fuller, Alfred C.	1885-1973	100	150	200	160	Businessman, brush co. founder
Fuller, H. Laurance		5	10	20	10	Amoco Corp. executive
Fuller, John Frederick Charles	1878-1964	325	700	1400	700	British general, military theorist, PU
Fuller, John W.	1827-1891	60	125	200		Publisher, Fuller, Childs & Co.; Iuka, Corinth, Carolinas, Atlanta*

NAME	DATES	SIG	DS	ALS	SP	COMMENTS
Fuller, Melville W.	1833-1910	100	200	300	200	SC: 1888-1910, IL, Chief Justice, reclusive
Fuller, R. Buckminster	1895-1983	35	100	150	150	Inventor, designer, poet, RS, SALS-2X
Fuller, Sarah M.	1810-1850	100	200	350		Reformer, writer
Fullerton, C. Gordon		5	15	25	15	Columbia, 3/22/82, Challenger, 7/29/85
Fulton, Robert	1765-1815	400	1200			Inventor, ESPV, scarce in all forms
Funston, Frederick	1865-1917	80	175	300		American general, CI, PI
Furrer, Reinhard		20	35		70	Challenger, 10/30/85
Gadsden, James	1788-1858	125	300	550		U.S. soldier, diplomat
Gaffney, Francis A.		5	15	25	10	Columbia, 6/5/91
☆ **Gagarin, Yuri A.**	**1934-1968**	**415**	**700**		**1450**	**Vostock 1, 1st human orbital flight, ESPV**
Gage, Thomas	1719?-1787	275	900	1100		British com. in chief in America
Gaines, Edmund Pendleton	1777-1849	35	60	80		American general, W1812, SW, MW
Gaines, William	1922-1992	25	55	125	50	Mad magazine creator, ANS-$95
Gainsborough, Thomas	1727-1788	325	675	1490		Landscape, portrait painter
Galbraith, John Kenneth	1908-	20	40	75	25	Economist
Gallatin, Albert	1761-1849	80	275	400		U.S. sec. of treasury
Gallup, George	1901-1984	25	275	300	50	Pollster, ESPV-DS & ALS
Galvani, Luigi	1737-1798	2500	3625			Italian physicist, founder galvanism, ESPV-DS
Galvez, Bernardo de	1746-1786	200				Gov. LA and FL
Gamble, William	1818-1866	140	200	300		Civil engineer; Warrenton, VA, Malvern Hill, Gettysburg*
Gandhi, Indira	1917-1984	175	300	350	400	P.M. of India, assassinated, ALS-2X, RS, ESPV-SP
☆ **Gandhi, Mohandas K.**	**1869-1948**	**600**	**1150**	**1825**	**2750**	**Indian political leader, assasinated**
Gandhi, Rajiv	1944-1991	50	100	125	160	Indian prime minister, assassinated
Ganellin, C. Robin	1934-	10	25	40	20	Cimetidine (Tagamet) developer
Gannett, Frank E.	1876-1957	35	100	200	50	Newspaperman
Gano, Richard Montgomery	1830-1913	75	150	225		Doctor, SL, minister; Tullahoma, Camden
Gardner, Dale A.		10	20	20	25	Challenger, 8/30/83, Discovery, 11/8/84, FA

NAME	DATES	SIG	DS	ALS	SP	COMMENTS
Gardner, Franklin	1823-1873	250	500	750		Farmer; Shiloh, Kentucky, ALS-WD-2X, ESPV-ALS
Gardner, Guy S.		5		20	10	Atlantis, 12/2/88, Columbia, 12/2/90, RS
Gardner, John	1912-	5	10	15	10	Carnegie Corporation president
Gardner, William Montgomery	1824-1901	85	200	300		WP, MW; First Manassas, Olustee
Garfield, James Abram	**1831-1881**	**300**	**1450**	**1500**	**2000**	**DIO, scarce in all presidential material-AA, ESPV-ALS**
Garfield, Lucretia Rudolph	1832-1918	125	175	200	200	(1858); OH; S-4; D-1, First Lady
Garibaldi, Giuseppe	1807-1882	150	350	375	800	Italian patriot, soldier
Garn, Jake		12	35	50	15	Discovery, 4/12/85, US Senator, FA (USS)
Garneau, Marc		8		30	12	Challenger, 10/5/84, 1st Canadian astronaut
Garner, John N.	1868-1967	40	145	200	150	Political leader, USHR, vice president
Garnett, Richard Brooke	1817- 1863?	700				Cousin of Gen. Robert S. Garnett; WP, KIA (Gettysburg); S. Mountain, Sharpsburg, Gettysburg, ESPV-DS & ALS
Garnett, Robert Selden	1819-1861	1000				First general to fall in battle -either side; WP, MW; Northwestern Virginia, scarce in all forms
Garrard, Kenner	1827-1879	70	140	250		SDS/LS & SALS - 2X; Harvard, WP; Fredericksburg, Chancellorsville, Gettysburg*
Garrett, Pat	1850-1908	1650	2650	3175		Lawman, killed Billy the Kid, FA, scarce in sig. ESPV
Garriott, Owen K.		12		30	22	Skylab 3, Columbia, 11/28/83, RS
Garrison, William Lloyd	1805-1879	110	150	300	225	U.S. abolitionist
Garrott, Isham Warren	1816-1863	425	600	850		Lawyer, SL, KIA; Port Gibson, Baker's Creek, Vicksburg, ESPV
Gartrell, Lucius Jeremiah	1821-1891	100	300	350		Lawyer, SL, USHR; First Manassas, Coosawhatchie
Gary, Elbert H.	1846-1927	45	135	245	50	U.S Steel chairman 1903-1927
Gary, Martin Witherspoon	1831-1881	220	400	800		Harvard, lawyer, SL; First Manassas, Richmond
Gates, Bill	1955-	20	45	75	30	Microsoft founder
Gates, Horatio	1728-1806	275	500	1100		Cont'l general; Wash. 's AG; controversial

Henry Flagler

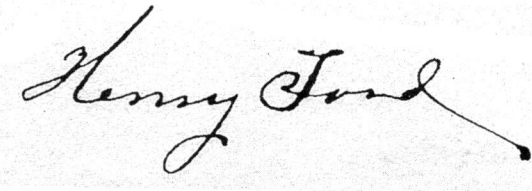

Gerald R. Ford

John Ambrose Fleming

Henry Ford

William Floyd

Nathan B. Forrest

Francis I, King of France

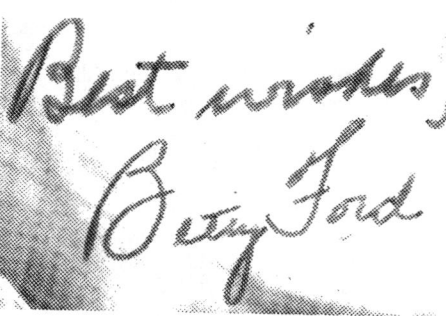

Betty Ford

Felix Frankfurter

Gerald R. Ford

Felix Frankfurter

NAME	DATES	SIG	DS	ALS	SP	COMMENTS
Gatlin, Richard Caswell	1809-1896	125	300	400		WP, MW, farmer; North Carolina coast
Gatling, Richard	1818-1903	265	600	750		Inventor, ESPV-ALS, SALS-1500
Gatty, Harold	1903-1957	100	250	500	150	Aviator and writer
Gauguin, Paul	1848-1903	600	1200	3250		Post-impressionist painter, ESPV-ALS
Gault, Stanley	1926-	5	15	20	10	Goodyear Tire & Rubber Co. executive
Gauss, Carl Friedrich	1777-1855	125	300	1150		German physicist, math., astronomer
Gay-Lussac, Joseph	1778-1850	100	300	1000		French chemist, physicist
Geary, John W.	1819-1873	75	165	340		ESPV; Jefferson College, gov. Penn., lawyer, mayor; Harper's Ferry, Lessburg, Ced. Mt., Gettysburg
Geiger, Roy Stanley	1885-1947	40	100	175	125	American marine general, WWI, WWII
Gemar, Charles D. (Sam)		8		30	12	Atlantis, 11/15/90, Discovery, 9/12/91, RS
Genet, Edmond C.	1763-1834	70	160	400		Diplomat, SALS-2X, ESPV-ALS
Gentile, Giovanni	1875-1944	50	150			Italian philosopher, educator
George I (England)	1660-1727	320	1000	3000		Son of Sophia
George II (England)	1683-1760	400	800	1250		Son of George I
George III (England)	1738-1820	250	600			DS-$250, $475, $575-SDS-2X, ESPV-ALS, King of Great Britain and Ireland
George IV (England)	1762-1830	130	400	700		Son of George III
George V (England)	1865-1936	125	500	750		Son of Edward VII
George VI (England)	1895-1952	200	400		400	DS-$375, TDS-$195, son of George V
George, Henry	1839-1897	35	125	175		Journalist, reformer
Georges, John A.		5	10	15	10	International Paper Co. executive
☆ **Geronimo**	**1829-1909**	**6000**				**American/Chiricahua Apache leader, FA, ESPV-all forms**
Gerow, Leonard Townsend	1888-1972	25	45	70	40	American general, WWI, WWII
Gerry, Elbridge	1744-1814	475	900	2750		Signer DOI and AOC;CC; gov.; VP; FF-$1000
Gerstner, Louis V.	1941-	10	15	30	20	I.B.M. CEO, unresponsive
Getty, George F. II		10	25	30	30	Oil family magnate

NAME	DATES	SIG	DS	ALS	SP	COMMENTS
Getty, George W.	1819-1901	50	100	200		SALS-3-4X; WP, MW, insp. gen. AOTP; Peninsular, South Mountain, Sharpsburg
Getty, Jean Paul	1892-1976	225	650	1750	430	U.S. oil empire head
Gholson, Samuel Jameson	1808-1883	150	300	600		Lawyer, SL, USHR, judge; Alabama, Mississippi, Louisiana
Ghormley, Robert Lee	1883-1958	30	65	80	60	American admiral, WWI, WWII
Giannini, Amadeo P.	1870-1949	125	250	400	275	Founded Bank of America
Gibbon, Edward	1737-1794	325	800	1650		British historian, ESPV-ALS
Gibbon, John	1827-1896	115	250	375		WP, MW, author; Second Manassas, Maryland, Gettysburg,* SALS-2X
Gibbons, James	1834-1921	60	150	150		Religious leader
Gibbs, Alfred	1823-1868	65	150	200		SALS-2X; Dartmouth College, WP, MW; Cook's Spring, Richmond, ESPV
Gibbs, Josiah W.	1839-1903	150	450	1000		U.S. theoretical physicist, chemist
☆ **Gibson, Charles (Dana)**	**1876-1944**	**100**	**200**	**250**	**275**	**Illustrator, cartoonist, ESPV-SP**
Gibson, Edward G.		10	30	40	20	Skylab 4
Gibson, Randall Lee	1832-1892	165	400	825		Noteworthy career, SALS-3-4X; USHR, USS, Amer. Embassy Madrid; Shiloh, Atlanta, Tennessee, ESPV-WD material
Gibson, Robert L.		10		30	15	Challenger, 2/3/84, Columbia, 1/12/86, RS
Giffen, Robert Carlisle	1886-1962	25	50	100	50	American admiral, WWI, WWII
Gilbert, Cass	1859-1934	30	75	150	50	Architect
Gilbert, Charles C.	1822-1903	40	100	150	2850	WP, MW; Wilson's Creek, Army of Kentucky, West
Gilbert, James I.	1823-1884	50	100			lumber business; Red River, Nashville, Mobile
Gillem, Alvan C.	1830-1875	50	125	230		WP, adj. gen. of Tenn.; Western North Carolina, Fourth Military Dist.
Gillette, King C.	1855-1932	50	125	275	100	Inventor of safety razor
Gillmore, Quincy A.	1825-1888	40	100	150		WP, writer; Fort Sumter, Washington
Gilman, Daniel C.	1831-1908	50	100	175		Educator
Gilman, Nicholas	1755-1814	150	350			CC, ALS extremely rare, ADS & DS-UC, NH

NAME	DATES	SIG	DS	ALS	SP	COMMENTS
Gilmer, Jeremy Francis	1818-1883	150	330	500		ESPV; WP, Pres. Savannah Gas Light Co.; Shiloh, outstanding military engineer
Gimbel, Bernard F.	1885-1966	75	150		100	Gimbel Bros.
Gingrich, Newt	1943-	10	15	40	20	Political leader
Ginsburg, Charles P.	1920-	10	30	50	25	Videotape recorder pioneer
Ginsburg, Ruth Bader	1933-	30	40	140	40	SC: 1993-, DC, RS
Girard, Stephen	1750-1831	140	300	350		French-born financier, philanthropist
Givenchy, Hubert J.M.T. de	1927-	20	65		70	Fashion designer, RS
Gladden, Adley Hogan	1810-1862	450	1575	3150		SALS-2X, ESPV; Postmaster of Columbia, SC, MW, KIA; Shiloh, ESPV
Gladstone, William E.	1809-1898	60	125	300	125	British prime minister, SALS-2X
Glass, Carter	1858-1946	20	40	50	30	Political leader
Glenn, John H., Jr.		50	200	500	100	Mercury-Atlas 6, 1st American in orbit, FA
Glover, John	1732-1797	275	575	1500		Cont'l general; r. Washington's Del. River cros.
Glubb, Sir John Bagot	1897-1986	25	50	75	35	British army officer, PU
☆ **Goddard, Robert H.**	**1882-1945**	**365**	**1600**	**1750**	**3000**	**U.S. physicist, father of modern rocketry**
Godoy, Manuel de	1767-1851	275	500			Spanish chief minister
Godwin, Linda M.		5		20	10	Atlantis, 4/5/91, Endeavour, 4/9/94, RS
Goebbels, Paul Joseph	1897-1945	400	1100	1500	1200	Nazi propagandist, ALS-2-3X
Göering, Hermann	1893-1946	500	2000	2650	1500	Nazi politico-military leader, ESPV, SDS-2-3X, SALS-2X
Goethals, George W.	1858-1928	175	650	800		U.S. army engineer, built Panama Canal, SALS-2-25X
Goggin, James Monroe	1820-1889	150	300	450		WP, TW; VA Peninsula, Cedar Creek, Sayler's Creek*
Goizueta, Robert C.	1931-	10	30	50	25	Former Coca-Cola Company CEO
Goldberg, Arthur J.	1908-1990	50	150	200	115	SC: 1962-1965, IL
Goldberg, Rube	1883-1970	65	125		160	Cartoonist, "Boob McNutt"
Goldman, Emma	1869-1940	100	250	500	130	U.S. anarchist, birth control advocate
Goldmark, Josephine	1877-1950	35	75	150	40	Reformer
Goldwater, Barry	1909-1998	15	35	65	40	Political leader, USS

Benjamin Franklin

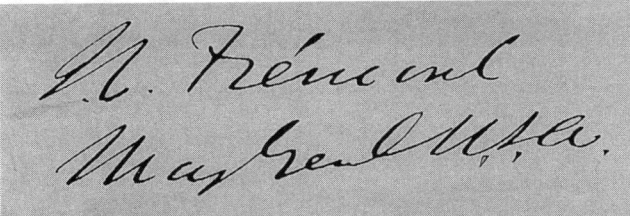

John C. Fremont

Benjamin Franklin

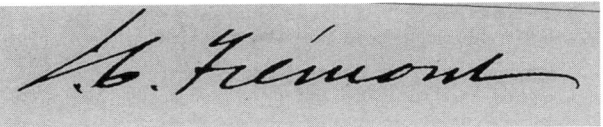

John C. Fremont

Benjamin Franklin

Sigmund Freud

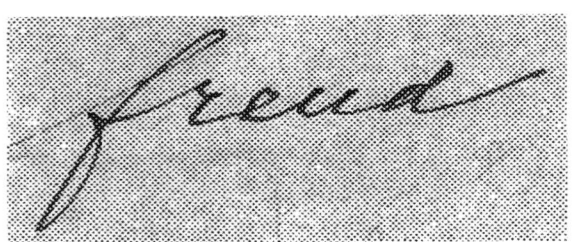

Benjamin Franklin

Sigmund Freud

"Fritz" Freleng

Robert Fulton

NAME	DATES	SIG	DS	ALS	SP	COMMENTS
Gompers, Samuel	1850-1924	125	200	300		U.S. labor leader
☆ **Goodyear, Charles**	**1800-1860**	**325**	**1125**			**Vulcanization developer, ESPV-DS & ALS, SDS-2X**
Gorbachev, Mikhail S.	1931-	275			500	Soviet statesman, ESPV-DS & ALS
Gorbatko, Viktor V.		30			65	Soyuz 7
Gore, Albert A. Jr.	1948-	30	100		75	Vice president, USS, FA
Gordon, Charles George	1833-1885	125	300			British general, PU
Gordon, George H.	1823-1886	50	100	125		WP, MW, lawyer, author, historian; Upper Potomac, Shenandoah Valley*
Gordon, George Washington	1836-1911	260	400	500		Last Confed. general to sit in the House; Lawyer, USHR; Murfressboro, Chickamauga, Chattanooga*
Gordon, John Brown	1832-1904	250	400	750		The idol of Georgia, SDS & SALS-2-5X; USS (GA), author "Reminiscenses of ... War"; Numerous with Army of Northern VA
Gordon, Richard F., Jr.		25	40	70	50	Gemini 11, TSS
Gorgas, Josiah	1818-1883	250	550	700		Key player in Confederacy, SDS-2-3X; WP, Pres. Univer. of Alabama; Chief of Ordnance of Confed. Army
Gorgas, William C.	1854-1920	140	200	350	225	U.S. sanitarian, army surgeon gen.
Gorham, Nathaniel	1738-1796	300	500	1445		Pres. Cont'l Cong.; SL; ESPV
Gorman, Willis A.	1816-1876	115	200	400		Lawyer, SL, congress, gov. Minn. Tty.; First Manassas, Ball's Bluff, Seven Pines*
Gould, Chester	1900-1985	70			150	Cartoonist, "Dick Tracy"
Gould, Gordon	1920-	20	45	80	50	Optically pumped laser amplifiers
☆ **Gould, Jay**	**1836-1892**	**200**	**775**	**1250**		**U.S. RR magnate, financier, RR pass-$425, SDS-2-3X**
Gould, John	1804-1881	125	300	650		Ornithologist, publisher
Govan, Daniel Chevilette	1829-1911	125	300	525		Indian agent state of WA; Atlanta, numerous with western army, ESPV-ALS
Goya, Francisco de	1746-1828	2650				Artist, scarce, ESPV
Grabe, Ronald J.		10		25	15	Atlantis, 10/4/85, 5/4/89, Discovery, 1/22/92
Gracie, Jr., Archibald	1832-1864	150	300			Pricing undetermined; WP, KIA; Chickamauga, Kentucky*

NAME	DATES	SIG	DS	ALS	SP	COMMENTS
Graham, Charles K.	1824-1889	125	165	300		MW, civil engineer; Peninsular, Seven Pines, Gettysburg*
Graham, Katherine		10	40	75	25	Publisher, author
Graham, Lawrence P.	1815-1905	50	100	200		WP, MW, Shakespearean scholar; Yorktown
Graham, William F. "Billy"	1918-	30	100	150	50	Religious leader
Grahame-White, Claude	1879-1959	75	135	225	125	Aviator, engineer
Grandi, Dino conte di M.	1895-1988	25	50	100	50	Italian statesman, diplomat
Granger, Gordon	1822-1876	75	150	200		WP, MW; Wilson's Creek, New Madrid, Chickamauga*
Granger, Robert S.	1816-1894	40	100	115		US atty. gen. (AJ), WP; Kentucky, Tennessee, N. Alabama, ESPV-ALS
Granit, Ragnar A.	1900-	25	50	100	50	Physiologist, SALS-2-2.5X
Grann, Phyllis E.	1937-	5	10	15	10	Publisher
Grant, Duncan	1885-1978	100	200	300		Painter
Grant, Julia Boggs Dent	1826-1902	150	400	750	500	(1848); MO; S-3; D-1; ALS content - $1500
Grant, Lewis A.	1828-1918	50	100	200		Teacher, lawyer, asst. sec. of war; Peninsular, Fredericksburg, Chancellorsville*
☆ **Grant, Ulysses Simpson**	**1822-1885**	**625**	**1500**	**1725**	**3000**	**APT-1200, WDALS-2X, SALS-2-3X, ESPV**
Graves, William Sidney	1865-1940	65	80	135	80	American general, PI, WWI
Gray, Harold	1894-1968	125			225	Cartoonist, "Little Orphan Annie"
Gray, Henry	1816-1892	100	200	300		Lawyer, SL; Red River
Gray, Horace	1828-1902	40	115	200	75	SC: 1882-1902, MA
Greatbatch, Wilson	1919-	25	40	75	40	Medical cardiac pacemaker developer
Greeley, Adolphus	1844-1935	100	200	300	175	Arctic explorer, ESPV-ALS
Greeley, Horace	1811-1872	75	250	325		Editor, politician, ESPV-ALS
Green, Hetty	1834-1916	1450				U.S. financier, "Witch of Wall Street," ESPV, scarce
Green, Martin Edward	1815-1863	365	455	800		Brother U.S.S. James S. Green; KIA; Lexington, Elkhorn, Port Gibson, Vicksburg,* ESPV
Greene, George S.	1801-1899	50	125	200		One of the oldest field commanders; Brown Univ., WP; Cedar Mountain, Sharpsburg, Chancellors...*

NAME	DATES	SIG	DS	ALS	SP	COMMENTS
Greene, Leonard M.	1918-	20	35	65	35	Airplane stall warning device inventor
☆ **Greene, Nathanael**	**1742-1786**	**1000**	**3000**	**3750**		**Cont'l general; ALS-2X, ESPV**
Greenspan, Alan	1926-	5	15	30	10	Federal Reserve chairman
Greer, Elkanah Brackin	1825-1877	135	270	375		MW, Trans-Miss. Dept.; Wilson's Creek, Elkhorn Tavern
Greer, Germaine	1939-	10			20	Feminist, writer
Gregg, David M.	1833-1916	65	135	200		SALS-2X; WP, diplomat, publisher; Maryland, Richmond, Gettysburg,* WD-2X
Gregg, John R.	1867-1948	75	110	160	100	Publisher, shorthand inventor
Gregg, Maxcy	1814-1862	500	1000	2000		SDS/LS-2-4X; Lawyer, MW, KIA; Peninsular, Second Manassas, Harpers Ferry, ESPV
Gregg, William	1800-1867	25	75	100		Launched southern textile industry
Gregory XVI	1765-1846		1200			Pope of Roman Catholic Church-1831
Gregory, Frederick D.		8		25	12	Discovery, 11/22/89, Atlantis, 11/24/91, C1985
Gregory, William G.		5	15	20	10	Endeavour, 3/2/95
Grenville, George	1712-1770	225	700			British premier; parliament; sec. of state
Gresham, Walter Q.	1832-1895	50	100	150		Sec. of state (GC), SALS-2X; lawyer, SL, postmaster gen., sec. treasury; Vicksburg, Atlanta
Grew, Joseph C.	1880-1965	10	30	50	25	Diplomat
Gridley, Charles V.	1844-1898	200	400			American naval officer
Gridley, Richard	1710-1796	200	400	750		First American chief of engineers
Grier, Robert C.	1794-1870	100	250	350		SC: 1846-1870, PA, ESPV-DS & ALS
Grierson, Benjamin H.	1826-1911	60	150	300		SDS/LS & SALS-2X; teacher; Tennessee, Mississippi, Mobile, WD-ALS
Griffin, Charles	1825-1867	100	165	300		WP, MW; First Manassas, Peninsular, Richmond,* ESPV-ALS
Griffin, Cyrus	1748-1810	375	750			Pres. Cont'l Congress; SL
Griffin, Simon G.	1824-1902	50	100	200		Teacher, lawyer, SL; First and Second Manassas, Richmond*
Griggs, S. David		35			100	Discovery, 4/12/85

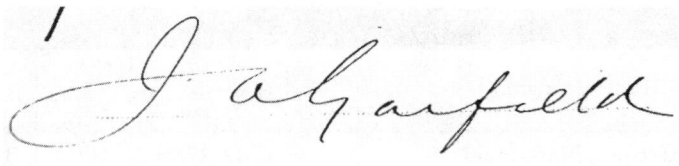

Robert Fulton

James A. Garfield

James A. Garfield

Lucretia R. Garfield

James A. Garfield

John Garner

James A. Garfield

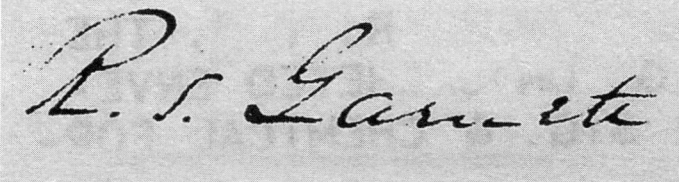

Robert S. Garnett

James A. Garfield

Pat Garrett

NAME	DATES	SIG	DS	ALS	SP	COMMENTS
Grimke, Angelina E.	1805-1879	100	150	300		Reformer, pioneer feminist
Grimke, Sarah Moore	1792-1873	75	150	300		Reformer, pioneer feminist
Grinnell, Henry	1799-1874	50	125	200		Shipping merchant, SALS-2X
Gris, Juan	1887-1927	225				Painter, scarce in all forms
☆ **Grissom, Virgil I.**	**1922-1967**	**320**	**800**		**1200**	**Mercury-Redstone 4, ESPV-DS**
Griswold, Oscar Wolverton	1886-1959	20	35	70	35	American general, WWI, WWII
Groening, Matt	1954-	30			100	Cartoonist, "The Simpsons," URS
Gromyko, Andrei A.	1909-1989	100	200	300	150	Soviet President, ESPV-DS & ALS
Gronlund, Laurence	1846-1899	25	75	150		Reformer
Gropius, Walter	1883-1969	100	200	300		Architect
Grose, William	1812-1900	40	100	175		Lawyer, judge, SL; Shiloh, Army of the Cumberland*
Grouchy, Emmanuel Marquis de	1766-1847	125	250			French Napoleon soldier, PU
Grove, Andrew S.	1936-	10	30		25	Intel executive, ESPV-DS
Grover, Cuvier	1828-1885	40	80	130		WP; Second Manassas, Peninsular, Winchester*
Gruenther, Alfred Maximilian	1899-1983	20	30	40	30	American general, WWI, WWII, RS
Grunsfeld, John M.		5	10	20	10	Endeavour, 3/2/95
Grumman, Leroy	1895-1982	50	150		100	Engineer, aircraft pioneer
Guderian, Heinz	1888-1953	75	200	300		German general, scarce SP
Guevara, Che (Ernesto)	1928-1967	500	800			Guerrilla leader, Cuban revolutionist
Guggenheim, Daniel	1856-1930	45	100	130	60	Industrialist
Guggenheim, Marguerite	1898-1979	25	40	100	40	"Peggy," art patron, collector
Guggenheim, Meyer	1828-1905	60	125	200	140	Swiss-born merchant, philanthropist, financer, ESPV
Guggenheim, Solomon	1861-1949	45	125		75	Businessman, art collector
Guillemin, Roger C.L.	1924-	25	50	125	40	Physiologist, NP, SDS-SALS-2-3X
Guiness, Sir Benjamin L.	1798-1868	50	100	165		Brewer
Guisewite, Cathy	1950-	15				Cartoonist, "Cathy," RS
Gutierrez, Sidney M.		5		20	10	Columbia, 6/5/91, Endeavour, 4/9/94, RS
Haakon VII	1872-1957	150	250			King of Norway
Habersham, Joseph	1751-1815	125	250	500		Patriot leader; U.S. Postmaster General

NAME	DATES	SIG	DS	ALS	SP	COMMENTS
Hackleman, Pleasant	1814-1862	300	445			Killed in action, ESPV; lawyer, judge, clerk; Ball's Bluff, Corinth
Haeckel, Ernest	1834-1919	65	150	300		German zoologist, evolutionist
Hagelstein, Robert	1942-	5	10		10	Greenwood Publishing Group executive
Hahn, Otto	1879-1968	150	500	2250	400	German chemist, atomic fission developer
Haig, Alexander Meigs, Jr.	1924-	15	50	65	50	American general, statesman, VW
Haig, Douglas, 1st Earl	1861-1926	30	80	150	50	British field marshal
Hailey, Edmund	1656-1742	4000				British astronomer, ESPV, scarce in all forms
Hailmann, William N.	1836-1920	150	275			Pioneer educator
Haise, Fred W.		30	120		100	Apollo 13, ESPV-DS
Haldane, J.B.S.	1892-1964	60	150	225	125	British scientist, geneticist
☆ **Hale, Nathan**	**1755-1776**	**16500**				**"Martyr Spy;" Cont'l officer; scarce in all forms**
Hall, Charles Martin	1863-1914	75	150	300		Aluminum manufacturing pioneer
Hall, Charles Philip	1886-1953	20	45	55	45	American general, WWI, WWII
Hall, Granville S.	1846-1924	60	150	250	75	Social scientist, educator
Hall, James	1761-1832	200	400			British geologist, chemist
Hall, John R.		5	10	20	10	Ashland Oil Corporation executive
Hall, Lyman	1724-1790	1875	3210	4775		Signer DOI; CC; gov. GA, ESPV
Hall, R.E.		5	10	15	10	Citgo Petroleum Corporation executive
Hall, Robert		5	10	15	10	Publisher
Hall, Robert N.	1919-	15	45	100	40	High voltage/power semiconductor pin rectifier
Halleck, Henry W.	1815-1872	150	500	1000		Controversial, SALS-4-5X; WP, asst. prof., publisher, lawyer; Department of the Mississippi, ESPV-WD material
Halsell, James D., Jr.		5	10	20	10	Columbia, 7/8/94
Halsey, William Frederick, Jr.	1882-1959	80	200	250	250	American admiral, WWI, WWII
Hamblin, Joseph E.	1828-1870	120	200			Insurance broker, Com. Fire Ins. Co.; Peninsular, Maryland, Gettysburg*
☆ **Hamilton, Alexander**	**1757-1804**	**1325**	**3650**	**3350**		**Cont'l officer; statesman; ADC GW; FF-$1500, ESPV-DS**

NAME	DATES	SIG	DS	ALS	SP	COMMENTS
Hamilton, Andrew J.	1815-1875	50	100	200		Lawyer, state atty. gen. Texas, congress; New Orleans, ESPV
Hamilton, Charles S.	1822-1891	45	100	180		WP, MW, US marshal, farmer; Iuka, Corinth, Shenandoah
Hamilton, Schuyler	1822-1903	40	80	150		WP, MW, farmer; Island No. 10, Corinth
Hamlin, Cyrus	1839-1867	150	200	300		Son of vice pres. Hannibal Hamlin; lawyer, Colby College; Cross Keys
Hamlin, Hannibal	1809-1891	100	225	325		U.S. vice president, USS
Hammarskjold, Dag	1905-1961	150	400	700		Swedish statesman, UN ec. gen. SDS-2X
Hammer, Armand	1898-1990	60	200	300	150	Occidental Petroleum, diplomat, BC-$45, SDS-2-3X, ESPV
Hammond, James H.	1807-1864	25	50	75		Political leader
Hammond, L. Baine, Jr.		5		20	10	Discovery, 4/28/91, 9/9/94, RS
Hammond, William A.	1828-1900	75	150	340		New York Univ., author; Surgeon General U.S. Army
Hampton, Wade	1818-1902	350	500	1000		SALS-4-5X, SLS/DS-3-4X; SCC, SL, Gov. SC, USS; First Manassas, Peninsular, Gettysburg
☆ **Hancock, John**	**1737-1793**	**2125**	**4910**	**7575**		**Signer DOI; gov. MA; rare in ALS; scarce sig., ESPV-ALS**
Hancock, Winfield	1824-1886	175	350	550		Nominated for pres., ESPV - SALS-2X; WP, MW; Maryland, Peninsular, Gettysburg,* WD, DS-2X
Hand, Edward	1744-1802	175	400			Cont'l general; GW AG, ESPV-ALS
Hand, Learned B.	1872-1961	75	150	300	130	Jurist
Hanford, W.E. "Butch"	1908-	25	40	75	30	Polyurethane pioneer
Hanna, Bill & Barbera, Joe	1910-, 1911-	50	275		150	Animators, "Tom & Jerry," "Flintstones"
Hanna, Marcus A.	1837-1904	30	150	215	40	Political leader, manufacturer, SDS-2X
Hansen, Alvin H.	1887-1975	20	45	70	25	Economist
Hanson, John	1721-1783	2500				Cont'l Congress President; scarce in DS/ALS
Harbaugh, Gregory J.		8		25	12	Discovery, 4/28/91, Endeavour, 1/13/93. RS
Harbord, James Guthrie	1866-1947	75	165	200	150	American general, WWI

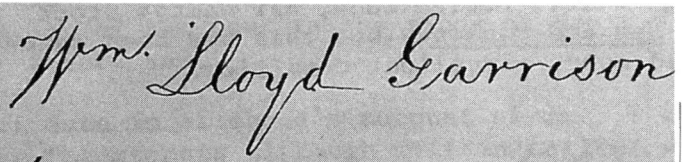

Pat Garrett

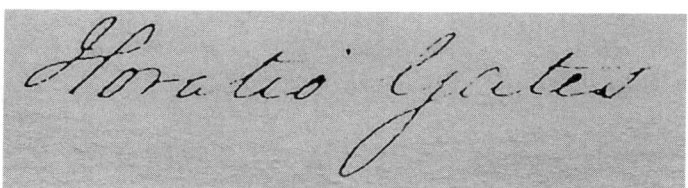

William L. Garrison

Horatio Gates

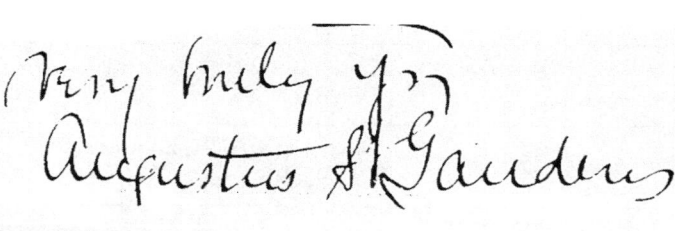

Richard J. Gatling

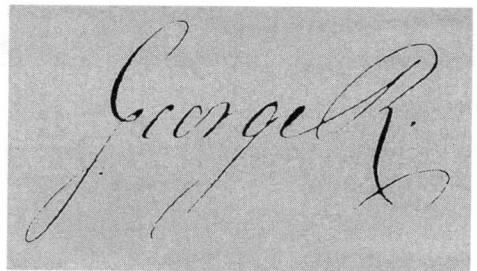

George II, King of Great Britain

George III, King of Great Britain

George III, King of Great Britain

George VI

Geronimo

Augustus Saint - Gaudens

NAME	DATES	SIG	DS	ALS	SP	COMMENTS
Hardee, William J.	1815-1873	400	925	1575		Outstanding general, one of the South's best; WP, author; Shiloh, Murfreesboro, Atlanta
Hardeman, William Polk "Gotch"	1816-1898	100	200	350		MW, planter, railroad inspector; Red River
Hardie, James A.	1823-1876	85	175	300		WP, MW, inspector gen.; Maryland, Sharpsburg
Hardin, John W.	1853-1895	1750				ESPV-scarce in all forms, outlaw, FA
Hardin, Martin D.	1837-1923	100	150	375		WP, lawyer, writer; Peninsular, Second Manassas, Gettysburg*
Harding, Abner C.	1807-1874	50	100	200		Lawyer, banker, congress; Monmouth, Fort Donelson
Harding, Florence King De Wolfe	1860-1924	75	200	325	200	(1891); OH; No sons or daughters; WHC - $85
Harding, Warren Gamaliel	**1865-1923**	**150**	**350**	**850**	**500**	**DIO, WH/EMC-600, ESPV**
Hardymon, James F.	1934-	5	10	20	10	Textron CEO
Harlan, John M.	1833-1911	55	100	175	100	SC: 1877-1911, KY, serv. over 30 years.
Harlan, John Marshall	1899-1971	60	100	175	125	SC: 1955-1971, NY, TLS-$350, AQS - $425
Harland, Edward	1832-1915	40	80	170		Yale, lawyer, SL, bank pres.; Sharpsburg, First Manassas, Fredericksburg*
Harmon, Ernest Nason	1894-1979	20	45	65	80	American general, WWI, WWII
Harney, William S.	1800-1889	75	150	300		ESPV; MW; Department of the West
Harper, James	1795-1869	30	50	75		Publisher
Harper, William R.	1856-1906	50	100	200		Educator
Harriman, Edward H.	1848-1909	45	65	125	50	U.S. railroad pioneer, Union Pacific head
Harriman, William Averell	1891-1986	30	60	125	50	Diplomat
Harrington, E. Michael	1928-1989	20	45	75	30	Exposed U.S. poverty
Harris, Bernard A., Jr.		5	15	25	15	Columbia, 4/26/93, Discovery, 2/3/95
Harris, Nathaniel H.	1834-1900	165	325	450	300	Tulane, lawyer, railroad president; Chancellorsville, Gettysburg, Petersburg
Harris, Sir Arthur Travers, 1st Baronet	1892-1984	40	100	150	130	British air marshal, PU

NAME	DATES	SIG	DS	ALS	SP	COMMENTS
Harris, Thomas M.	1817-1906	35	80	155		Tried A. Lincoln conspirators; SL, medicine; Shenandoah Valley, Washington, Cloyd's Mt.
Harris, Townsend	1804-1878	30	75	125		Diplomat, educator
Harris, William T.	1835-1909	35	125	250		Educator
Harrison, Anna Tuthill Symmes	1775-1864	700	1100	2450		(1795); NJ; S-6; D-4; FF - $975, First Lady
☆ **Harrison, Benjamin**	**1833-1901**	**245**	**450**	**950**	**2250**	**WH/EMC-500, ESPV, SDS-2X**
Harrison, Benjamin	c.1726-1791	500	875	2500		Signer DOI; CC; gov.; FF-$1250, SDS-2X
Harrison, Caroline Lavina Scott	1832-1892	175	275	1180	750	(1853); OH; S-1; D-1, First Lady
Harrison, James Edward	1815-1875	100	200	300		SL; Louisiana
Harrison, Mary Scott Lord	1858-1948	75	140	180	125	(1896); PA; D-1, First Lady
Harrison, Thomas	1823-1891	100	225	300		Brother of James E. Harrison; MW, TX SL; Chickamauga, Georgia, Carolinas
☆ **Harrison, William Henry**	**1773-1841**	**600**	**1200**	**1750**		**Shortest pres. term-31 days, DIO, SALS-2X, all material as President scarce-AA**
Harrow, William	1822-1872	100	200	300		Lawyer; Sharpsburg, Mine Run, Atlanta, Gettysburg
Hart, John	c.1711-1779	325	575	1150		Signer DOI; currency - $350
Hart, Johnny	1931-	20			50	Cartoonist, "BC," "Wizard of Id," RS
Hart, Terry		5	10	15	20	Challenger, 4/6/84, FA
Hart, Thomas Charles	1877-1971	50	75	125	65	American admiral, WWI, WWII
Hartford, George H.	1833-1917	75	265	300		Grocery store magnate
Hartranft, John F.	1830-1889	85	175	350		Tried A. Lincoln conspirators, SALS-2-3X; Union College, civil engineer, lawyer, gov. Penn.; North Carolina coast, Bull Run, Spotsylvania
Hartsfield, Henry W.		5		20	10	Columbia, 6/27/82, RS
Hartsuff, George L.	1830-1871	50	100	150		WP; West Virginia, Second Manassas, Sharpsburg
Harvey, William	1578-1657	925	3250			English physician, anatomist, ESPV-ALS
Hasbrouck, Robert Wilson	1896-1985	40	140	215	80	American general, WWI, WWII
Hascall, Milo S.	1829-1904	40	100	180		WP, teacher lawyer, real estate; Atlanta, Corinth, Murfreesboro

NAME	DATES	SIG	DS	ALS	SP	COMMENTS
Hasgood, Johnson	1829-1898	100	200	300		SCMA, Gov. SC; First Manassas, Drewry's Bluff, Cold Harbor
Haskin, Joseph A.	1818-1874	50	100	200		WP, MW; Washington, Fort Independence & Schuyler
Hassam, Childe	1859-1935	200	400	500		American painter, printmaker
Hastie, William H.	1904-1976	20	40	65	30	Jurist
Hastings, Warren	1732-1818	75	150	250		British colonial adminstrater
Hatch, Edward	1832-1889	60	125	140		Norwich Univ., lumber business; Corinth, Central Mississippi, Nashville
Hatch, John P.	1822-1901	40	100	140		ESPV-LS/DS; WP, MW; Shenandoah Valley, South Mountain
Hatio, Jimmy	1898-1963	15	60		100	Cartoonist, "Little Iodine"
Hatton, Robert Hopkins	1826-1862	150	300	400		Cumberland Univ., lawyer,SL, USHR; Cheat Mt., Seven Pines
Hauck, Frederick H.		10	20	25	20	Challenger, 6/18/83
Haupt, Herman	1817-1905	55	115	225		SALS-2X; WP, rrd. eng.; chief of construction and transportation
Hauptman, Herbert	1917-	20	40		25	Mathematical physicist
Hause, Gabriel		10	25	40	30	Banker, financier
Havemeyer, Henry O.	1847-1907	25	45	60		Manufacturer
Hawes, James Morrison	1824-1889	100	250	355		WP, MW, hardware business; Shiloh, Vicksburg
Hawkins, John P.	1830-1914	35	75	150		WP; Commissary Department
Hawley, Joseph R.	1826-1905	50	100	150		Hamilton College, lawyer, gov. Conn., USS; First Manassas, Florida
Hawley, Steven A.		5		20	10	Discovery, 8/30/84, Columbia, 1/12/86, RS
Hawthorn, Alexander T.	1825-1899	150	300	400		Mercer Univ., Yale, lawyer, Baptist minister; Shiloh, Helena
Hay, John Milton	1838-1905	65	150	200	125	U.S. sec. of state
Hayes, James B.		5	10		10	Former publisher
Hayes, Joseph	1835-1912	125	200	400		Reclusive, banking, civil engineer, real estate; Sharpsburg, Fredericksburg, Gettysburg*
Hayes, Lucy Ware Webb	1831-1889	250	300	400	675	(1852); OH; S-7; D-1, First Lady
☆ **Hayes, Rutherford Birchard**	**1822-1893**	**240**	**700**	**800**		**NC-700, WH/EMC-500**

Elbridge Gerry

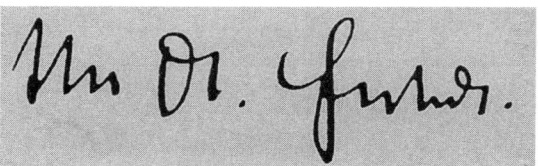

Paul Joseph Goebbels

J. Paul Getty

Charles Goodyear

J. Paul Getty

Nathaniel Gorham

Nicholas Gilman

Hermann Goering

Stephen Girard

Julia Dent Grant

NAME	DATES	SIG	DS	ALS	SP	COMMENTS
Haynie, Isham N.	1824-1868	135	200	325		Farmer, lawyer, SI, MW; Fort Henry, Fort Donelson, Shiloh
Hays, Alexander	1819-1864	300	675	1000		Killed in action; WP, MW; Peninsular, Seven Pines, Gettysburg,* ESPV
Hays, Harry Thompson	1820-1876	225	500	1000		SDS-2X; St. Mary's, lawyer, MW; First Manassas, Valley, Port Republic*
Hays, William	1819-1875	45	100	185		WP; Peninsular, Chancellorsville, Gettysburg*
Hayter, S.W.	1901-1988	25				British engraver, painter, PU
Hayward, Charles	1950-	5	10	15	10	Publishing executive
Haywood, William D.	1869-1928	35	100	165		Labor leader, controversial, reclusive
Hazen, Elizabeth Lee	1885-1975	35	50	145	45	Nystatin pioneer
Hazen, William B.	1830-1887	50	100	150		WP; Shiloh, Perryville, Atlanta, Tullahoma
Hearst, George	1820-1891	225	300	400		Political leader, businessman
Hearst, William Randolph	1863-1951	175	500	1000		Newspaper publisher
Heath, William	1737-1814	175	1100	1500		Cont'l general; SL; last surviving Maj. Gen., ESPV-ALS
Hebert, Louis	1820-1901	150	375	465		WP, SL, chief engineer, teacher; Wilson's Creek, Elkhorn, Vicksburg
Hebert, Paul Octave	1818-1880	100	200	300		very legible signature; WP, Gov. Louisiana; Vicksburg, Miliken's Bend
Hefner, Hugh M.	1926-	20	55	100	25	Pub. Playboy, elusive signer, TLS- 9X
Hegel, Georg W.F.	1770-1831	1000	2000			German idealist, philosopher
Heimbold, Charles	1933-	5	10	20	10	Bristol Myers Squibb CEO
Heintzelman, Samuel P.	1805-1880	50	100	175		WP; First Manassas, Yorktown, Seven Pines
Heinz, Henry J.	1844-1919	125	250	725		Founded U.S. food empire
Heinze, Karl G.		25			60	Challenger, 7/29/85
Heisenberg, Werner	1901-1976	50	250	800	150	German physicist, matrix mech. dev.
Held, John Jr.	1889-1958	175			300	"Jazz Age" cartoonist
Helm, Benjamin Hardin	1831-1863	200	300	400		KIA, married half sister Mrs. Abraham Lincoln; WP, SL, attorney; Chickamauga
Helmholtz, Hermann von	1821-1894	175	500	650		German physicist, anatomist, phys.
Helms, Susan J.		10	25		20	Endeavour, 1/13/93

NAME	DATES	SIG	DS	ALS	SP	COMMENTS
Hench, Philip	1896-1965	25	60	100	30	Physician
Hendriks, Thomas A.	1819-1885	50	150	200		U.S. vice president
Hennen, Thomas J.		5		20	10	Atlantis, 11/24/91, RS
Henri, Robert	1865-1929	100	200	250		American painter
Henricks, Terence T.		5	15	25	10	Atlantis, 11/24/91, Columbia, 4/26/93
Henry IV (France)	1553-1610	250	650			
Henry VI (England)	1421-1471	250	500	1100		
Henry VII (England)	1457-1509	1250				Son of Edmund Tudor, ESPV-all forms
Henry VIII (England)	1491-1547	4000	12750			Son of Henry VII, ESPV-all forms
Henry, John Joseph	1758-1811	50	100	200		Jurist; author
Henry, Joseph	1798-1878	75	150	250		Physicist
☆ **Henry, Patrick**	**1736-1799**	**1125**	**2150**	**3250**		**Patriot; orator; land grant - $2500; ESPV-ALS, SDS-2X, SALS-2-3X**
Henson, Jim	1936-1990	100	200		300	Muppets creator
Henson, Matthew A.		150	300			Explorer
Hepworth, Dame Barbara	1903-1975	100	200	300	150	English sculptor
Herkimer, Nicholas	1728-1777	2000	4000			American Revolutionary officer, ESPV-all forms
Herndon, William		200	400	750		Law partner of A. Lincoln
Herriman, George	1881-1944	75			700	Cartoonist, "Krazy Kat"
Herring, John	1795-1865	75	150	300		British sporting, animal painter
Herriot, Edouard	1872-1957	40	100	200		French radical socialist leader
Herron, Francis J.	1837-1902	50	100	200		Youngest maj. gen. on either side; Pitt Univ., lawyer, US marshal; Wilson's Creek, Elkhorn Tavern, Vicksburg
Herschel, Sir William	1738-1822	175	500	725		Astronomer, SDS & SALS-2X
Hershfield, Harry	1885-1974	25			50	Cartoonist, "Abie the Agent"
Hertz, Heinrich	1857-1894	125	260	600		German physicist
Hess, Rudolph	1894-1987	175		800	850	German politician, Nazi, SALS-2X, ESPV-DS
Hess, Victor	1883-1964	30	75		50	Physicist, NP, SDS-2X
Hess, Walter R.	1881-1973	25	65	100	40	Physicist, NP, SDS-2X
Hester, John Hutchison	1886-1976	20	35	50	35	American general, WWII

NAME	DATES	SIG	DS	ALS	SP	COMMENTS
Hewes, Joseph	1730-1779	2575	5750	11250		Signer; ESPV-ALS; one of five toughest! SDS-2X
Hewish, Antony	1924-	20	50	110	30	Radio astronomer, SDS-2X
Hewitt, Abram S.	1822-1903	35	50	60		Political leader, manufacturer
Hewitt, Henry Kent	1887-1972	25	55	80	55	American admiral, WWI, WWII
Hewlett, William R.	1913-	20	50	125	25	Hewlett Packard cofounder-founder
Heyerdahl, Thor	1914-	25	50	110	40	Anthropologist, "Kon-Tiki"
Heydrich, Reinhard	1904-1942	225		1500	725	Nazi poltician, Gestapo, ESPV-DS
Heyward, Thomas Jr.	1746-1809	525	1200	1500		Signer DOI; "Tho Heyward Jr"
Hieb, Richard J.		5		20	10	Discovery, 4/28/91, Endeavour, 5/7/92. RS
Higonnet, Rene Alphonse	1902-1983	30	60	125	50	Photo composing machine
Hilbert, David	1862-1943	150	300	550	200	German math., Euclidean formulator
Hill, Ambrose Powell	1825-1865	2500	6000	12000		"APHill"; WP, MW; Williamsburg, Peninsular, Seven Days,* ESPV-ALS
Hill, Benjamin Jefferson	1825-1880	100	200	300		SL, mercantile business, lawyer; Shiloh, Chickamauga, Chattanooga
Hill, Daniel Harvey	1821-1889	300	500	600		Won the first battle, b-i-l S. Jackson, SALS-3X; MW, educator, Washington College, NCMI; Yorktown, Williamsburg, Seven Pines,* WD-2X
Hill, James J.	1838-1916	90	200	475		Canadian-born railroad magnate, G.N. R.
Hill, Sir Rowland	1795-1879	140	310	625		Originator penny postage
Hillary, Sir Edmund	1919-	40	100	200	100	Mountaineer, explorer, RS
Hillier, James	1915-	25	45	125	30	Electron lens correction device
Hillman, Sidney	1887-1946	40	60	150	100	U.S. labor leader
Hilmers, David C.		5		20	15	Atlantis, 10/4/85, 2/28/90, D1/22/92, FA
Hilton, Conrad N.	1888-1979	75	130	205	125	U.S. hotel chain founder
Himmler, Heinrich	1900-1945	350	925	1750	800	Head of Nazi SS and Gestapo, ESPV
Hincks, Edward W.	1830-1894	100	200	300		Printer, SL; Ball's Bluff, Peninsular, Maryland
☆ **Hindenburg, Paul von**	**1847-1934**	**175**	**400**	**500**	**500**	**German field marshal WWI, pres. Weimer Re.**

Ulysses S. Grant

Ulysses S. Grant

Ulysses S. Grant

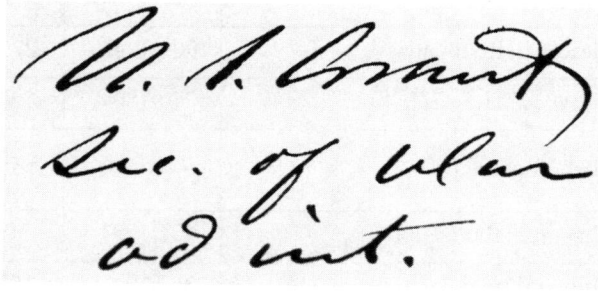

Ulysses S. Grant

Ulysses S. Grant

Ulysses S. Grant

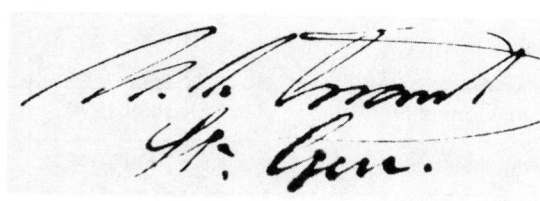

Ulysses S. Grant

Ulysses S. Grant

Ulysses S. Grant

Ulysses S. Grant

NAME	DATES	SIG	DS	ALS	SP	COMMENTS
Hindman, Thomas Carmichael	1828-1868	375	500	1000		assassinated, distinct elongated handwriting; lawyer, SL, USHR; Atlanta, Chickamauga, Chattanooga, ESPV-DS & ALS
Hines, John Leonard	1868-1968	30	75	145	70	American army officer, SAW, WWI
Hirschfeld, Al	1903-	25			125	New York Times Entertainment caricaturist
Hiss, Alger	1904-	50	75	200		Diplomat
Hitchcock, Ethan A.	1798-1870	75	200	265		WP, MW; Commissary General of prisoners
Hitler, Adolph	**1889-1945**	**1500**	**2500**		**2500**	**German dictator, LS-$3750, APPT.-$2500**
Ho Chi Minh	1890-1969	700	1500		2000	N. Vietnamese pres., Communist leader
Hoar, George Frisbie	1826-1904	15	25	25	20	Political leader, USHR, SS
Hobson, Edward H.	1825-1901	40	80	120		Steamboat operator, merchant, MW, banker; Kentucky, Buffington's Island
Hoche, Louis Lazare	1768-1797	225	500			French general
Hockney, David	1937-	50	100	150		British painter, printmaker, elusive signer! FA
Hodge, George Baird	1828-1892	100	215	275		USNA, lawyer, SL; SW Mississsippi, E. Louisiana
Hodge, John Reed	1893-1963	20	40	60	50	American general, WWI, WWII
Hodges, Courtney Hicks	1887-1966	30	125	250	125	American general, WWI, WWII, SDS-$400, ESPV-DS
Hoe, Richard	1812-1886	100	265	470		Inventor, industrialist
Hoffa, James R.	1913-1975	300	365	600	425	Union leader, ESPV, scarce in DS & ALS, SDS & ALS-2X SIG-$350
Hoffman, Jeffrey A.		10	25	30	20	Discovery, 4/12/85, Columbia, 12/2/90, A1992
Hoffmann, Roald	1937-	20	35		25	Chemist, NP
Hofstadter, Richard	1916-1970	25	50	65	30	U.S. historian
Hofstadter, Robert	1915-	20	40		30	Physicist, NP
Hogarth, Burne	1911-1996	30			100	Cartoonist, "Tarzan"
Hogarth, William	1697-1764	700	2000	3000		English painter, engraver, SIG-$995
Hogg, Joseph Lewis	1806-1862	350	450	775		Son was Texas Gov. 1892-1896; planter, MW, SL; Shiloh, ESPV

NAME	DATES	SIG	DS	ALS	SP	COMMENTS
Hoke, Robert Frederick	1837-1912	100	225	325		"R. F. Hoke"; manufacturing business; Big Bethel, Seven Days, Chancellorsville*
Hokinson, Helen	1900-1949	30			100	Cartoonist, satirized clubwomen
Holcomb, Thomas	1879-1965	40	80	150	75	American marine gen., WWI, WWII
Holland, John	1840-1914	100	175	300		Inventor
Hollander, Nicole	1939-	10				Cartoonist, "Sylvia"
Hollerith, Herman	1869-1929	65	110	265	125	Modern data processing pioneer
Holmes, Donald Fletcher	1910-1980	30	60	125	45	Polyurethane pioneer
Holmes, Oliver Wendell, Sr.	1809-1894	100	225	400		U.S. poet, novelist, ESPV-ALS
☆ **Holmes, Oliver Wendell, Jr.**	**1841-1935**	**275**	**325**	**600**	**625**	**SC, SP-$650, ALS, "OWH"-$300**
Holmes, Theophilus Hunter	1804-1880	225	300	600		SALS-2X; WP, MW; First Manassas, Seven Days, SDS-2X
Holt, John	1924-1985	25	50	75	40	U.S. educator and author
Holt, Joseph	1807-1894	80	175	350		SALS-2X; sec. of war; postmaster gen.; Judge advocate general
Holtzclaw, James Thadeus	1833-1893	145	275	400		lawyer, Alabama railroad commission; Shiloh, Chickamauga, Chattanooga
Holyoake, Sir Keith	1904-1983	50	100	150	65	New Zealand prime minister
Home, Sir Alec Douglas	1903-1995	50	100	150	150	British prime minister
Homer, Winslow	1836-1910	400	550	1000		American marine, landscape painter
Homma, Masaharu	1887-1946	80	225	350	200	Japanese general
Hood, John Bell	1831-1879	1000	1750	1800		Sig. w/rank - $1600, SALS-4-5X; WP; Peninsular, Second Manassas,* ESPV
Hood, Samuel, 1st Viscount	1724-1816	50	100	150		British admiral; Parliament; C in C Mediter.
Hooker, Joseph	1814-1879	300	500	930		Controversial, SALS-2X; WP, MW; Seven Days, Second Manassas, AOTP,* ESPV-DS & ALS
Hooper, William	1742-1790	1000	4125	6725		Signer DOI; DS-$3750; $6200
☆ **Hoover, Herbert Clark**	**1874-1964**	**150**	**325**	**675**	**400**	**PL, TLS-1100, WH/EMC-500, ESPV**
Hoover, John Edgar	1895-1972	50	175	250	150	Government official, RS
Hoover, Lou Henry	1875-1944	50	75	220	175	(1899); IA; S-2; WHC - $125, First Lady

NAME	DATES	SIG	DS	ALS	SP	COMMENTS
Hopkins, Esk	1718-1802	225	600			First C of C Cont'l Navy; ESPV - LS/DS/ALS, SDS-2X
Hopkins, Harry Lloyd	1890-1946	20	40	75	30	Reformer, political leader
Hopkins, Johns	1795-1873	200	500			American financer, SDS-2X, ESPV
Hopkins, Stephen	1707-1785	200	500	1050		Signer DOI; scarce ALS; SALS-6X
Hopkinson, Francis	1737-1791	285	665	1000		Signer DOI; writer; artist; "F. Hopkinson"
Horthy, Miklós	1868-1957	100	200	375	150	Hungarian regent
Houdry, Eugene J.	1892-1962	50	125	200	60	Catalytic cracking of petroleum, converter
Hounsfield, Sir Godfrey	1919-	20	35		25	Physicist, NP
Houssay, Bernardo A.	1887-1971	75	150	250	100	Physiologist, NP
House, Edward M.	1858-1938	30	125	250	50	U.S. diplomat, advisor
☆ **Houston, Sam**	**1793-1863**	**750**	**1925**	**3000**		**Political leader, president Texas Republic, ESPV**
Hovey, Alvin P.	1821-1891	40	90	125		MW, diplomat, congress, gov. Ind.; Vicksburg, Shiloh, Champion's Hill, Atlanta*
Hovey, Charles E.	1827-1897	40	75	140		Dartmouth, lobbyist; Arkansas Post
Howard, John Eager	1752-1827	145	315			Cont'l officer; CC;gov. MD; USS; Sec. of War
Howard, Oliver O.	1830-1909	150	300	365		Bowdin College; First Manassas, Peninsula, Seven Pines*
Howe, Albion P.	1818-1897	50	100	200		Tried A. Lincoln conspirators, SALS-2-3X; WP; Harper's Ferry, Peninsular, Chancellorsville, WD, ALS-2X
Howe, Elias	1819-1867	500				Inventor, sewing machine
Howe, Richard	1726-1799	125	400	600		British admiral; C in C; ESPV, SDS-2X
Howe, Samuel G.	1801-1876	20	40	75		U.S. social reformer
Howell, Joshua B.	1806-1864	275	500			Lawyer; Peninsula, Goldsboro, NC
Hubble, Edwin P.	1889-1953	25	85	125		U.S. astronomer, SDS & ALS-2X
Hubel, David	1926-	15	30		20	Neurophysiologist
Hudson, George	1800-1871	20	35			Financer
Huger, Benjamin	1805-1877	100	250	400		SDS-2X; WP, MW; Norfolk, Seven Days, WD-2X
Huger, Issac	1743-1797	100	200	400		Cont'l general; PU

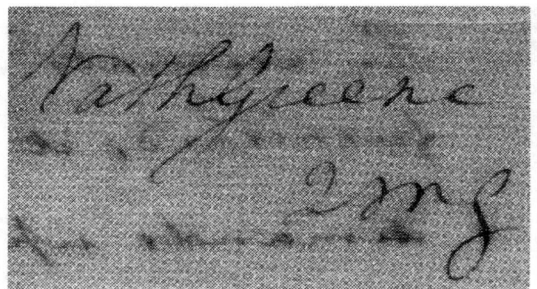

Nathanael Greene

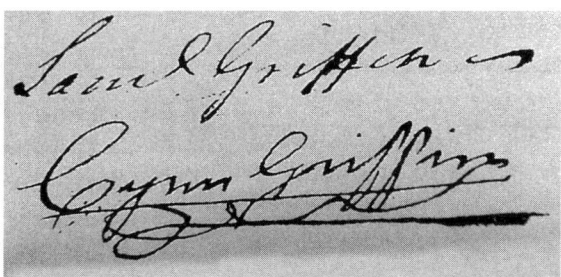

Cyrus Griffin

Nathanael Greene

David Ben - Gurion

Thomas Green

Button Gwinnett & Lyman Hall

Maxcy Gregg

William N. Hailmann

Walter Q. Gresham

Henry W. Halleck

NAME	DATES	SIG	DS	ALS	SP	COMMENTS
Huggins, Charles B.	1901-	25	45		40	Surgeon, NP
Huggins, Sir Nilliam	1824-1910	40	80	175	50	Astronomer
Hughes, Charles E.	1862-1948	50	200	400	250	SC: 1910-1916, NY, gov., sec. State, CJ
☆ **Hughes, Howard**	**1905-1976**	**1500**	**3000**	**5000**	**2500**	**U.S. industrialist, aviator, movie maker, ESPV, FA**
Hughes-Fulford, Millie		5		25	10	Columbia, 6/5/91, RS
Hughs, Mark		5	12	20	10	Herbalife International executive
Hull, Cordell	1871-1955	50	125	200	100	U.S. sec. of state
Hull, Isaac	1773-1843	200	600	650		American naval officer, W1812
Hull, William	1753-1825	175	400	750		Cont'l officer; BG in War 1812
Humboldt, Alexander von	1769-1859	75	150	300		German explorer, naturalist, earth scientist
Humes, William Young Conn	1830-1882	150	265	400		"WYCHumes"; VMI, lawyer; N. Georgia, Tennessee, N. Alabama
Humphrey, Hubert H.	1911-1978	30	150	265	50	U.S. Minnesota Democrat senator, RS
Humphreys, Andrew A.	1810-1883	100	200	250		WP, civil engineer; Maryland, Fredericksburg, Gettysburg*
Humphreys, Benjamin Grubb	1808-1882	240	440	575		WP, lawyer, SL, first elect. Gov. of Mississippi; Army of N. Virginia,* ESPV
Hunt, E. Howard		20	40	110	35	CIA, Watergate
Hunt, H.L.	1889-1974	100	320	410	200	Oil magnate
Hunt, Henry J.	1819-1889	65	120	150		Leading authority on artillery; WP, MW; First Manassas, Malvern Hill, Peninsular*
Hunt, Lewis C.	1824-1886	50	100	200		WP, MW; Peninsular, Seven Pines, Kinston, Goldsboro
Hunt, Ward	1810-1886	70	125	200		SC: 1872-1882, NY, remembered for refusal to res.
Hunt, William H.	1827-1910	100	200	300		English painter
Hunter, Charles Norton	1906-1978	25	50	75	50	American army officer, WWII
Hunter, David	1802-1886	85	175	200		Gf. signer Richard Stockton, SALS-2X; WP, real estate; First Manassas, Piedmont
Hunter, Robert M.T.	1809-1887	100	150	200		American politician
Huntington, Collis P.	1821-1900	100	350	400		U.S. railroad magnate, AQS-$175

NAME	DATES	SIG	DS	ALS	SP	COMMENTS
Huntington, Henry E.	1850-1927	75	150	265		U.S. railroad builder
Huntington, Jedediah	1743-1818	75	150	250		Cont'l general; PU
Huntington, Samuel	1731-1796	250	650	1520		Signer DOI
Hunton, Eppa	1822-1908	125	250	375		lawyer, USHR, USS; First Manassas, Army of N. Virginia*
Hurlbut, Stephen A.	1815-1882	100	200	350		SALS-5-6X; lawyer, SL, diplomat, congress; Shiloh, Corinth
Hussein (ibn Talal)	1935-1999	100	160	350	125	King of Jordan
Hutchins, Robert M.	1899-	20	45	75	25	Educator
Hutchinson, Thomas	1711-1780	200	400			Royal gov. of Mass.; historian
Huxley, Julian	1887-1975	50	150	200	75	British biologist
Huxley, Thomas	1825-1895	60	150	250		British philosopher, educator
Huxley, Thomas Henry	1825-1895	50	150	225		English scientist, humanist, evolutionist
Hyde, H.B.	1834-1899	10	20	35		Insurance executive
Iacocca, Lido (Lee) A.	1924-	10	35	65	25	Automotive executive
Ickes, Harold L.	1874-1952	25	50	90	35	Pol. leader, sec. of interior (FDR), TLS- 17X, ESPV
Imboden, John Daniel	1823-1895	175	400	500		SDS-2X, SALS - 7-9X, ESPV; SL, lawyer, businessman; Harper's Ferry, First Manassas
Immelmann, Max	1890-1916	225	400	650	500	German lt., "The Eagle of Lille, WD-2X
Indiana, Robert	1928-	50	100	200		American painter, "LOVE" repro. - $210
Ingalls, Rufus	1818-1893	60	125	250		SALS-2X; WP, MW; Fort Pickens, AOTP - quartermaster
Inge, William	1860-1954	30	75	150		British theologian
Ingersoll, Jared	1742-1822	100	250	500		CC, LS-UC, all others-C, PA, "J. Ingersoll"
Ingres, Jean-Auguste-Dominique	1780-1867	225	500	975		French painter, ESPV
Inness, George	1825-1894	100	300	750		American landscape painter, SALS-$1500
Insull, Samuel	1859-1938	60	125	200		Businessman
Irani, Ray R.	1935-	5	10	15	10	Occidental Petroleum Corp. executive
Irvine, William	1741-1804	120	350	320		Cont'l general; DS-2x, SALS-2X, ESPV

NAME	DATES	SIG	DS	ALS	SP	COMMENTS
Irwin, James B.	1930-1991	55	200		150	Apollo 15, RS, MW
Ivanchenkov, Alexander S.		50	140	250	75	Soyuz 29
Ivanov, Nicholas Yudovich	1851-1919	125	350		375	Russian general, PU
Iverson, Alfred, Jr.	1829-1911	175	350	500		Florida orange grower; Seven Days, S. Mountain, Sharpsburg
Ivins, Marsha S.		5		20	10	Columbia, 1/9/90, Atlantis, 7/31/92, RS
Jackson, Alfred Eugene	1807-1889	75	200	425		SALS-2X; farmer, quartermaster, paymaster; Greenville, TN
☆ **Jackson, Andrew**	**1767-1845**	**650**	**1685**	**3650**		**ANS- $1250; FF:1600, LG-1450, MA-2100, APT-1600**
Jackson, Helen	1830-1885	20	40	65	40	Writer, reformer
Jackson, Henry	1747-1809	70	125			Cont'l officer; PU
Jackson, Henry Rootes	1820-1898	100	200	350		Yale, dist. attorney, Min. to Mexico, GA His. So; West Virginia, Atlanta
Jackson, Howell E.	1832-1895	60	125	250	125	SC: 1893-1895, TN, serv. only 15 mos., USS
Jackson, James S.	1823-1862	300	600	1200		Killed in action; Transylvania Univ., lawyer, MW, congress; Army of Kentucky, Army of Ohio, Perrysville
Jackson, Jesse L.	1941-	15	35	75	25	Political leader, reformer, RS
Jackson, Michael	1734-1801	65	120	225		Cont'l officer
Jackson, Nathaniel J.	1818-1892	40	75	150		Machinist; Gaines' Mill, South Mountain, Sharpsburg
Jackson, Rachel Donelson Robards	1767-1828	575	2025			(1791); VA; No sons or daughters, First Lady, scarce
Jackson, Richard H.	1830-1892	35	70	135		Fort Pickens, army of the James; Fort Pickens, Army of the James
Jackson, Robert H.	1892-1954	55	200	375	125	SC: 1941-1954, NY, atty. gen., Nuremberg
☆ **Jackson, Thomas Jonathan "Stonewall"**	**1824-1863**	**4200**	**11000**	**22500**		**"T.J. Jackson," SALS - 2-3X, SDS-2X; WP, MW, VMI; First Manassas, Shen. Valley, Seven Days,* ESPV**
Jackson, William Henry	1843-1942	50	125			U.S. photographer
Jackson, William Hicks "Red"	1835-1903	100	200	250		WP, horse breeder, active in Agriculture Org.; Belmont, Vicksburg, Atlanta*

William F. Halsey

Florence Kling De Wolfe Harding

Alexander Hamilton

Florence Kling De Wolfe Harding

John Hancock

Relatives of Warren G. Harding

Edward Hand

John W. Hardin

NAME	DATES	SIG	DS	ALS	SP	COMMENTS
Jackson, William Lowther "Mudwall"	1825-1890	165	350	500		second cousin of "Stonewall"; attorney, SL, lt. gov.; Winchester, Cedar Creek, Fisher's Hill
Jacobs, Walter L.	1898-1985	30	70	100	50	Founded first car rental agency-Hertz
Jahn, Sigmund		20			40	Soyuz 31
James I (England)	1566-1625	700	1400	3650		Son of Mary, Queen of Scots
James II (England)	1633-1701	500	1350	1750		Son of Charles I
James, William	1842-1910	100	275	400	150	U.S. philosopher, SDS-2X
Jarns, Anna M.	1864-1948	75	150	300		American promoter
Jarvis, Gregory B.		150			300	Challenger, 1/28/86, killed during launch
Jawlensky, Alexi von	1864-1941	225		750		Russian painter
Jay, John	1745-1829	385	1325	2325		SC: 1789-1795, NY, Chief Justice, ALS - 2.5X
Jefferson, Thomas	**1743-1826**	**3265**	**5125**	**11500**		**ALSs of outstanding content can add 5-10x; SHIPSP:7000; FLSP:7000; FF:6200, ESPV**
Jellicoe, John Rushworth, 1st Earl	1859-1935	25	75	150	50	British admiral
Jenifer, Daniel of St. Thomas	1723-1790	150	300	600		CC, LS toughest form, all forms-C, MD, full
Jenner, Edward	1749-1823	500	1000	2000		British physician, disc. vaccination
Jenner, William	1815-1898	40	100	275		British physician, pathological anatomist
Jernigan, Tamara E.		5		20	12	Columbia, 6/5/91, Columbia, 10/22/92, 1995
Jerome, Jerome K.	1859-1927	40	80	100		Playwright, novelist
Jobs, Steven	1955-	20	30	60	25	cofounder Apple Computer, Inc.
Jodl, Alfred	1890-1946	125	400	435	225	German general, ESPV-DS & ALS
Jofre, Joseph Jacques Cesaire	1852-1931	100	175	200	200	Marshal of France
John XXIII	1881-1963	400			675	Pope of Roman Catholic Church-1958
John, Augustus	1878-1961	75	150	300		British painter
Johns, Jasper	1930-	35	125	250	60	American painter, sculptor, printmaker
Johnson, Alvin	1874-1971	10	25	50	25	Educator
Johnson, Amy	1903-1941	100	150		200	Pioneer aviator

NAME	DATES	SIG	DS	ALS	SP	COMMENTS
☆ **Johnson, Andrew**	**1808-1875**	**525**	**1450**	**7000**	**3000**	**ALS content-2x-3x, sig. pt. speech-$3000; FF:1600, ESPV-ALS & PD, FA**
Johnson, Bradley Taylor	1829-1903	150	400	500		SDS-3-4X, SALS-7-10X, ESPV; Princeton, lawyer, SL, writer; First Manassas, Valley, Seven days, WD-2-3X
Johnson, Bushrod Rust	1817-1880	125	300	540		WP, MW, teacher, Univ. of Nashville; Shiloh, Chickamauga, Murfreesboro*
Johnson, Claudia "Lady Bird" Alta Taylor	1912-	40	100	200	100	(1934); TX; D-2, First Lady
Johnson, Edward	1816-1873	140	300	525		WP, MW, farmer; Valley, Gettysburg, Wilderness*
Johnson, Eliza McCardle	1810-1876	650	1275			(1827); TN; S-3; D-2, First Lady, scarce
Johnson, Hiram	1866-1945	20	45	55	25	Political leader, USS
Johnson, Howard	1896-1972	75	150	220	100	U.S. restaurant founder
Johnson, James W.	1871-1938	40	125	250	80	Writer, reformer
Johnson, John H.	1918-	20	45	100	40	Publisher
☆ **Johnson, Lyndon Baines**	**1908-1973**	**200**	**650**	**3400**	**500**	**PL, TLS-1400, ESPV-ALS-FA**
Johnson, Richard Mentor	1780-1850	75	150	300	375	Ame. army officer, politician, W1812, VP
Johnson, Richard W.	1827-1897	50	100	175		WP, educator, author; Murfreesboro, Chickamauga, Chattanooga*
Johnson, William	1771-1834	100	300	815		SC: 1804-1834, SC, SL, 30 yrs. of service
Johnson, William Samuel	1727-1819	150	350	700		CC, ALS & LS v. rare, DS on occasion, CT, full, ESPV-all forms
Johnston, Albert Sidney	1803-1862	400	2000	2500		Controversial, SDS-4-5X; WP, MW, Texas - Sec. of war; Shiloh
Johnston, George Doherty	1832-1910	100	250	350		U.S. Civil Service Commissioner; Howard College, Mayor Marion, AL, SL; First Manassas, Army of Tennessee*
Johnston, Harriet Lane	1831-1903	225	350	550		Buchanan's niece, scarce, ESPV-DS & ALS
Johnston, Joseph Eggleston	1807-1891	300	600	1150		SDS -2X, SALS-3X, ESPV; WP, MW, USHR, U.S. Comm. railroads; Harpers Ferry, First Manassas, Army N.VA*
Johnston, Lynn	1947-	25				Cartoonist, "For Better or For Worse"

NAME	DATES	SIG	DS	ALS	SP	COMMENTS
Johnston, Robert Daniel	1837-1919	60	125	260		One of last surviving generals; UNC, UVA, lawyer, bank president; Peninsular, Seven Pines, Gettysburg*
Joliot-Curie, Frederic	1900-1958	100	400	500	275	French physicist, radioactivity theorist
Joliot-Curie, Irene	1897-1956	50	200	250		French physicist, w. Frederic
Jones, Anson	1798-1858	400	625	1250		American politician, Texas, ESPV-DS, SDS-2X
Jones, Chuck	1912-	30			100	Animator, Bugs Bunny, Porky Pig
Jones, David C.	1921-	15	35	60	40	U.S. air force general, WWII, KW, VW
Jones, John Marshall	1820-1864	375	740	1200		ESPV - ALS; WP; Gettysburg, Army of Northern Virginia*
☆ **Jones, John Paul**	**1747-1792**	**6750**		**75000**		**American naval hero; scarce; als-$45000, ESPV, AA**
Jones, John Robert	1827-1901	150	320	500		VMI, farm implement business; First Manassas, Valley, Chancellorsville*
Jones, Mary H. "Mother"	1830-1930	70	200	450	225	Labor leader
Jones, Patrick H.	1830-1900	100	200	300		lawyer, clerk, postmaster; Peninsular, Second Bull Run, Atlanta*
Jones, Samuel	1819-1887	150	460	800		MW, farmer; First Manassas, Corinth
Jones, Thomas ap Catesby	1790-1858	125	250	450		American naval officer, W1812, MW
Jones, Thomas D.		5		20	10	Endeavour, 4/9/94, 9/30/94, RS!
Jongkind, Johan Barthold	1819-1891	250	500			Dutch landscape painter, etcher
Jordan, Jerry L.	1941-	5	15	20	10	Economist
Jordan, Michael	1936 -	10	20	25	15	Westinghouse Elec. Corp. executive
Jordan, Thomas	1819-1895	110	225	465		WP roomate of W.T. Sherman, SDS/SALS-2X; WP, MW, writer, editor of Memphis Appeal; First Manassas, Shiloh*
Joseph II	1741-1790	225	400			Holy Roman Empire
Josephine de Beauharnais	1763-1814	700	1400	2250		First wife of Napoleon
Jouhaux, Leon	1879-1954	30	75	150	60	French labor leader, NP
Joule, James P.	1818-1889	65	170	250		British physicist
Juan, Carlos I	1938-	75	150	265	125	King of Spain
Juarez, Benito	1806-1872	500	1250	1625		Mexican leader, DS-$750, $1400
Judah, Henry M.	1821-1866	300	500	850		ESPV-SALS; WP, MW; Washington, Corinth

Warren Harding

Warren Harding

Warren Harding

Warren Harding

Anna Harrison

Benjamin Harrison

Benjamin Harrison

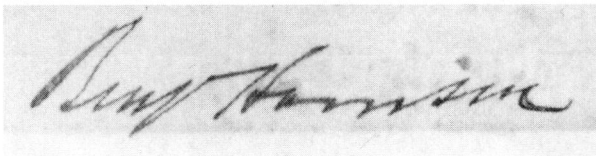

Benjamin Harrison

Benjamin Harrison

Benjamin Harrison

Benjamin Harrison

Benjamin Harrison

Benjamin Harrison

NAME	DATES	SIG	DS	ALS	SP	COMMENTS
Judge, Mike	1962-	25				"Beavis and Butt-head," "King of the Hill"
Julian, Percy F.	1899-1975	50	130	225	75	Synthesis of cortisone, other hormones
Juliana, Queen	1909-	100	200		125	Netherlands (1948-1980)
Jung, Carl	**1875-1961**	**600**	**2200**	**3750**	**2500**	**Swiss psych., analytical psychologist, ESPV-DS**
Junkers, Hugo	1859-1935	65	200	300		Aircraft designer, SDS-2X
Junkins, Jerry R.	1937-	5	12	20	10	Texas Instruments CEO
Junot, Jean Andoche, Duke of Abrantes	1771-1813	40	100	200		French general
Kadar, Janos	1912-1989	40	125	200		Hungarian premier
Kahn, Otto H.	1867-1934	20	45	100	50	Wall Street banker, broker
Kaiser, Henry J.	1882-1967	100	175	300	200	U.S. industrialist, steel aluminum czar
Kalakaua, David (Hawaii)	1836-1891	100	350	700		King of Hawaii, ESPV
Kalikow, Peter	1942-	5	10	15	10	Publisher
Kaltenbrunner, Ernst	1903-1946	175	450		250	Nazi leader, ESPV
Kamehameha IV of Hawaii	1824-1863		2500			
Kandinsky, Wasily	1866-1944	250	750			Russian-born painter, writer, ALS-2X
Kane, Bob	1916-1999	125			225	Cartoonist, "Batman"
Kane, Elisha	1820-1857	100	250	375		Physician, explorer
Kane, Thomas L.	1822-1883	100	225	360		SALS-2-3X; lawyer, businessman; Dranesville, Chancellorsville, Gettysburg,* ESPV
Kant, Immanuel	1724-1804	1250	2550			Philosopher
Karageorge	1762-1817	700	1856	16500		Serbian general, ruler, PU
Karpis, Alvin		100	200		150	Criminal
Karsavina, Tamara	1885-1978	100			275	Ballet dancer
Karsh, Yousof	1908-	25	100	100	75	Canadian photographer
Kasparov, Gary	1963-	25			40	Chess player
Kastler, Alfred	1902-1984	20	65		35	Physicist
Kautz, August V.	1828-1895	50	100	150		Tried A. Lincoln conspirators, MW, WP; Peninsular, Ream's Station
Kawakami, Soroku	1848-1899	800	1600	3000	2500	Japanese general, PU
Keane, Bill	1922-	10			30	Cartoonist, "The Family Circus"

NAME	DATES	SIG	DS	ALS	SP	COMMENTS
Kearny, Philip	1815-1862	400	650	940		Originator of "Kearny patch," KIA; Columbia Univ., lawyer; Peninsular, Second Manassas
Kearny, Stephen Watts, "The Pathfinder"	1794-1848	100	200	400		American general, W1812, MW
Keck, Donald B.	1941-	20	40	75	25	Fused silica optical waveguide inventor
Kefauver, Carey Estes	1903-1963	15	30	45	20	Political leader, USS
Keitel, Wilhelm	1882-1946	325	500	725		German general, ESPV-ALS
Keith, Minor C.	1848-1929	30	100	135	75	U.S. railroad magnate, United Fruit Co.
☆ **Keller, Helen**	**1880-1968**	**225**	**475**	**2250**	**1000**	**Crusader: handicapped rights, FA, SDS-2X**
Kellermann, Francois Etienne C., Duke of Val.	1735-1820	100				French Marshal of the Empire
Kelley, Benjamin F.	1807-1891	50	75	150		Freight agent, collector; West Virginia, Maryland
Kelley, Florence	1859-1932	55	110	225	80	Reformer
Kellogg, Frank B.	1856-1937	30	80	125	40	U.S. sec. of state, SDS & ALS - 2X
Kellogg, Will K.	1860-1951	125	200	350	200	U.S. businessman, philanthropist
Kelly, Emmett Sr.	1898-1979	75	150	300	300	American clown
Kelly, Walt	1913-1973	65	200		450	Cartoonist, "Pogo"
Kelvin, William Thomson	1824-1907	125	250	400	225	British mathematician, physicist
Kemper, James Lawson	1823-1895	200	300	400		Governor of Virginia; Washington College, MW, lawyer, VMI; First Manassas, Williamsburg*
Kendall, Amos	1789-1869	25	50	110		Political leader, journalist
Kendall, Edward	1886-1972	35	75		45	Chemist, NP
Kendall, Henry W.	1926-	15			25	Physicist, NP
Kendrew, Sir John	1917-	10			25	Biochemist, NP
Keneally, Thomas	1935-	10	30		20	Writer
Kenly, John R.	1818-1891	75	150	250		Lawyer; Shenandoah Valley, AOTP*
Kennan, George F.	1904-	10	35	50	20	Diplomat
Kennedy, Anthony M.	1936-	30	60	150	50	SC: 1988-, CA
Kennedy, Edward M.	1932-	10	30		20	USS, FA
Kennedy, Jacqueline Lee Bouvier	1929-1994	310	1200	2150	1250	(1953); NY; S-1; D-1; (padi); SB - $795, First Lady, ESPV, as FL-2X

NAME	DATES	SIG	DS	ALS	SP	COMMENTS
Kennedy, John Doby	1840-1896	130	300	430		SC College, lawyer, SL, diplomat; First Manassas, Seven Days, Harper's Ferry*
Kennedy, John Fitzgerald	**1917-1963**	**1320**	**2150**	**5125**	**3000**	**PL, DIO, doodle ("J")-$1600, TLS-4000, ESPV, FA**
Kennedy, John F., Jr.		20			50	Publisher, scarce DS & ALS
Kennedy, Joseph P.	1888-1969	100	200		175	Kennedy patriarch
Kennedy, Robert F.	1925-1968	225	700	2750	700	U.S. A.G.USS, assassinated, FA, SDS-2X, ESPV
Kennedy, Rose F.	?-1995	100	175		150	Kennedy matriarch
Kenney, George Churchill	1889-1977	30	70	125	50	Amer. army air force gen., WWI, WWII
Kenny, Sister Elizabeth	1886-1952	200	400	500	300	Australian nurse, polio treatment pioneer
Kent, Edward	1935-	50			75	British prince
Kent, James	1763-1847	70	110	200		Jurist
Kent, Rockwell	1882-1971	45	115		80	Artist
Kenton, Simon	1755-1836	450	1475			Frontiersman, ESPV
Kentridge, Sydney	1922-	20			45	Lawyer
Kerensky, Aleksandr	1881-1970	250	750	1500	500	Russian head of prov. govt. (1917), ESPV-DS & ALS
Kern, Jerome	1885-1945	275	550			Songwriter, composer, ESPV
Kershaw, Joseph Brevard	1822-1894	200	750	800		SALS-2X, ESPV - LS/DS; lawyer, MW, SL, postmaster; Manassas, Sayler's Creek*
Kerwin, Joseph P.		10	30	40	20	Skylab 2
Kesselring, Albert von	1885-1960	100	225		200	German field marshal
Ketcham, Hank	1920-	25	100		100	Cartoonist, "Dennis the Menace," RS
Ketcham, John H.	1832-1906	75	150	300		SL, USHR; Gettysburg, Resaca, Cassville, Dallas
Ketchum, William S.	1813-1871	40	90	125		WP; War and Treasury departments
Kettering, Charles Franklin	1875-1958	125	200	300	150	Engine starting/ignition devices
Kevorkian, Jack, Dr.		15			50	Assisted suicide doctor
Key, Ted	1912-	10			50	Cartoonist, "Hazel," RS
Keyes, Erasmus D.	1810-1895	75	200	350		WP, WP instructor, businessman; First Manassas, Peninsular
Keyes, Geoffrey	1886-1967	20	40	75	40	American general, WWII

Caroline Harrison

John Hart

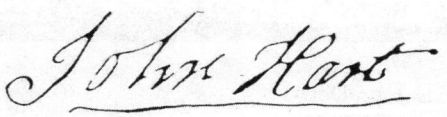

John Hart

William H. Harrison

Lucy W.W. Hayes

William H. Harrison

William H. Harrison

Rutherford B. Hayes

William H. Harrison

Rutherford B. Hayes

William H. Harrison

Rutherford B. Hayes

NAME	DATES	SIG	DS	ALS	SP	COMMENTS
Keyes, Roger John Brownlow, 1st Baron	1872-1945	25	50		40	British admiral
Keynes, John Maynard	1883-1946	100	395	700	250	Economist, TLS-4X, ESPV-DS & ALS
Keynes, John Maynard	1883-1946		800			British economist, deficit spender
Khomeini, Ruhollah	1900-1989	475				Iranian religious leader, "ayatollah," ESPV, scarce
Khrunov, Yevgeni V.		50	130		75	Soyuz 5
Khrushchev, Nikita	1894-1971	300	500	650	1125	First sec. of Communist party, USSR, ESPV
Kilby, Jack S.	1923-	25	40	75	50	Miniaturized electronic circuits
Kilpatrick, Hugh J.	1836-1881	150	300	500		SLS/DS & SALS - 2-4X, espv; WP, diplomat; Big Bethel, AOTP, Gettysburg, Atlanta
Kimball, Nathan	1822-1898	50	100	200		Teacher, MW, SL, surveyor gen. Utah Tty.; Cheat Mountain, Kernstown, Atlanta*
Kimmel, Husband Edward	1882-1968	375	600		600	American admiral, WWI, WWII, ESPV-DS
King, Corretta Scott		20	50		40	Mrs. Martin Luther King, SDS-2X
King, Edward Postell, Jr.	1884-1958	25	50	75	45	American general, WWI, WWII
King, Ernest Joseph	1878-1956	50	110	175	150	American admiral, WWI, WWII
King, Frank	1883-1969	40			100	Cartoonist, "Gasoline Alley"
King, John H.	1820-1888	60	125	200		MW; Shiloh, Corinth, Murfreesboro, Atlanta
☆ **King, Martin Luther**	**1929-1968**	**2000**	**3250**		**4000**	**Reformer, s. program - $3000, SB-$2500, ESPV-DS & ALS**
King, Richard	1825-1885	25	50	75		U.S. cattleman, rancher
King, Rufus	1755-1827	250	500	850		CC, fairly C in all forms, ALS-3X, MA
King, Rufus	1814-1876	40	80	150		WP, newspaper business;
King, W.L. Mackenzie	1874-1950	50	150			Canadian prime minister, SDS-2X
King, William R.	1786-1853	130				U.S. statesman, USS, VP, ESPV-DS & ALS
Kingsford Smith, Sir Charles E.	1897-1935	60	215		180	Pioneer aviator
Kinkaid, Thomas Cassin	1888-1972	40	80	135	100	American admiral, WWI, WWII
Kinsey, Alfred	1894-1956	125	175		250	Sexologist, zoologist

NAME	DATES	SIG	DS	ALS	SP	COMMENTS
Kirby, Jack	1917-1994	40			75	Cartoonist, "Fantastic Four," "The Incredible Hulk"
Kirby, Rollin	1875-1952	25			110	Political cartoonist
Kirk, Edward N.	1828-1863	365	550			Teacher, lawyer; Shiloh, Murfreesboro, scarce
Kirk, Russell	1918-1994	20	40	50	25	U.S. social philosopher
Kirkpatrick, Jeane	1926-	10	25		20	U.S., U.N. representative
Kissinger, Henry A.	1923-	40	185	400	75	Political leader, diplomat, FA, elusive signer
Kitchener, Horatio Herbert, 1st Earl	1850-1916	100	200	300	225	British field marshal, statesman
Kleber, Jean-Baptiste	1753-1800	150	350	600		French general
Klee, Paul	1879-1940	250	650	2000		Swiss painter, graphic artist, ESPV
Klein, Calvin	1942-	10	25	40	20	fashion designer, RS, FA
Klemperer, Otto	1885-1973	50	115		160	Conductor
Kliban, B (ernard)	1935-1991	25				Cat books
Klimt, Gustav	1862-1918	225	600	1125		Austrian painter, graphic artist, ESPV-ALS
Klimuk, Pyotr I.		50	150		75	Soyuz 13, Soyuz 18B
Kndleberger, II, Charles P.		5	10	20	10	Economist
Knight, Charles F.	1936-	5	10	20	10	Emerson Elec. Co. executive
Knight, Dame Laura	1877-1970	50	100	200		English painter
Knight, Philip H.	1938-	20	30	75	25	Nike Inc. founder
Knipe, Joseph F.	1823-1901	55	100	200		Shoemaker, postmaster, MW; Shenandoah, Cedar Mountain, Maryland
Knopf, Alfred A.	1892-1984	15	40		40	Publisher
Knott, Walter		25	75	100	135	Founder Knotts Berry Farm
Knox, Henry	1750-1806	175	300			Cont'l general; Sec. of War; ESPV, SDS-2X
Knudsen, William S.	1879-1948	25	50	100	50	Danish-born auto industry executive
Kohler, Georges	1946-1995	50	150	275	100	German immunologist
Koiso, Kuniaki	1880-1950			1600		Japanese general and statesman, PU
Kokoschka, Oskar	1886-1980	100	200	400	300	Austrian-born painter, graphic artist
Kolff, Willem J.	1911-	25	50	75	45	Artificial-kidney dialysis machine pioneer

NAME	DATES	SIG	DS	ALS	SP	COMMENTS
Kollwitz, Kathe	1867-1945	100	200	300		German sculptor, graphic artist
Komarov, Vladimir M.	1927-1967	150	250		250	Soyuz 1, 1st fatality of space program, Vos. 1, scarce, SDS-2X
Koren, Edward	1935-	10	30		80	New Yorker cartoonist
Kornberg, Arthur	1918-	15	30	50	25	Biochemist, NP
Kosciuszko, Thaddeus	1746-1817	275	500			Cont'l officer, SDS, .5-2X, ESPV
Kossuth, Lajos	1802-1894	150	400	500	125	Key figure in 1848 Hungarian revol., SDS-2X, ESPV
Kasygin, Alexey N.	1904-1980	260	425		500	Russian premier
Kresge, S.S.	1867-1966	100	200	300	150	Merchant, philanthropist
Kress, Samuel H.	1863-1955	35	75	115	75	U.S. businessman, philanthropist, "dime store"
Kroc, Ray A.	1902-1984	50	200	225	225	Founded McDonald's fast food chain, RS, ESPV-SP
Kroeber, Alfred L.	1876-1960	35	70	125	45	U.S. cultural anthropologist
Kropotkin, Pyotr	1842-1921		400	775		Russian anarchist
Kosygin, Alexey N.	1904-1980	260	425		500	Russian premier
Krueger, Walter	1881-1967	50	125	250	125	American gen., SAW, WWI, WWII
Kruger, Paul	1825-1904	100	275		200	African patriot, ESPV-all forms
Krupp, Alfred	1812-1887	125	300	400		German armaments magnate
Krzyzanowski, Wladimir	1824-1887	75	150	250		Civil engineer; treasury agent; Washington, Cross Keys, Second Manassas
Kubasov, Valery N.		50	115	225	60	Soyuz 6, Soyuz 19, TSS
Kuhn, Maggie	1905-1995	15	35	45	25	Gray Panthers founder
Kunstler, William	1919-1995	25	50	125	35	U.S. civil liberties attorney, SDS & ALS - 2-3X
Kupka, Frantisek	1871-1957	100	200	300		Czech painter, graphic artist, PU
Kuznets, Simon Smith	1901-1985	20	45	60	25	Economist
Kwolek, Stephanie	1923-	15	30	50	25	Kevlar (5X stronger than steel) developer
La Follette, Robert M.	1855-1925	25	65	100	35	U.S. Wisconsin public official
La Follette, Robert M., Jr.	1895-1953	15	25	35	25	Political leader, USS
Lacepede, Bernard de Laville	1756-1825	40	80	140		Naturalist, politician
Lachaise, Gaston	1882-1935	75	150	300		French-American sculptor

Rutherford B. Hayes

Henry IV, King of Castile

Rutherford B. Hayes

Joseph Henry

William Heath

Richard Henry Lee

William Heath

Patrick Henry

John Held Jr.

Patrick Henry

NAME	DATES	SIG	DS	ALS	SP	COMMENTS
Lacroix, Christian	1951	20			40	Fashion designer
☆ **Lafayette, Marquis de**	**1757-1834**	**575**	**1250**	**1950**		**Cont'l general; SALS-2-2.5X; ESPV-ALS, SDS-2X**
Lagrange, Joseph	1736-1813	215	435			French geometrician, astron., number theorist
LaGuardia, Fiorello H.	1882-1947	25	75	150	150	Political leader, mayor of New York City
Lahm, Frank	1877-1963	40	80	150	100	Aviator
Lake, Simon	1866-1945	75	150	250		Engineer, inventor, SALS-2X
Laker, Sir Freddie	1922-	10	25		25	Business, entrepreneur
Lamar, Joseph R.	1857-1916	50	100	200	100	SC: 1911-1916, GA
Lamar, Lucius Q.C.	1825-1893	60	125	250		SC: 1888-1893, MS, USS
Lamarck, Jean B.	1744-1829	500	1000	1250		French naturalist, evolutionary theorist
Land, Edwin Herbert	1909-1991	100	200	375	200	Polaroid camera developer, elusive signer
Lander, Frederick W.	1821-1862	200	300	500		Husband of Jean Davenport, SALS-2X; engineering, writer; Edwards Ferry, Rich Mountain
Landon, Alf	1887-1987	20	75	100	55	Political leader, governor (KS)
Landseer, Sir Edwin	1802-1873	50	120	275		English painter, sculptor
Landsteiner, Karl	1868-1943	50	100	150		Pathologist, NP
Lane, James Henry	1833-1907	120	240	360		VMI, UVA, VPI, API; Army of Northern Virginia*
Lane, Walter Paye	1817-1892	70	160	300		MW, merchant; Red River, Mansfield
Langdon, John	1741-1819	250	450	750		CC, LS most UC of all easy-to-find forms, NH
Langdon, John	1741-1819	250	425	750		Patriot merchant; USS; gov. NH; SALS-2X
Langley, Samuel P.	1834-1906	200	425	650		Astronomer, aeronautical pioneer
Langmuir, Irving	1881-1957	50	100	200	100	Incandescent electric lamp
Lansing, Robert	1864-1929	30	75	140	50	Political leader, sec. of state
Lantz, Walter	1900-1994	75	100		140	Cartoonist, "Woody Woodpecker"
Laplace, Pierre S.	1749-1827	500	1000			French astronomer, physicist
Larsen, Ralph S.	1938-	5	10	15	10	Johnson & Johnson executive
Larson, Gary	1950-	25			50	Cartoonist, "The Far Side," elusive signer

NAME	DATES	SIG	DS	ALS	SP	COMMENTS
Lasch, Christopher	1932-1994	15	25	30	20	U.S. social critic, historian
Laswell, Fred		30			65	Cartoonist
Latrobe, Benjamin	1764-1820	200	500			Architect, civil engineer, ESPV
Lauder, Estee	1910-	20	40		45	Cosmetics, elusive signer
Lauman, Jacob G.	1813-1867	100	200	300		Missouri, Belmont, Fort Donelson, Shiloh
Lauren, Ralph	1959-	10	35	50	30	Fashion designer, elusive signer
Laurens, Henry	1724-1792	1250	1740	2000		Cont'l Congress President; FF-$2000, ESPV, SALS-2X
Lavoisier, Antoine	1743-1794	600				French chemist, fdr. modern chemistry, ESPV, scarce in all forms
Law, Andrew Bonar	1858-1923	30	75	150		British conservative party politician
Law, Evander McIvor	1836-1920	100	225	300		SCMA, newspaperman, writer; First & Second Manassas, Seven Pines*
Lawler, Michael K.	1814-1882	45	100	175		SALS-2X; MW, farmer; Fort Donelson, Vicksburg
Lawrence, Amos	1786-1852	40	100	150		Merchant
Lawrence, Ernest Orlando	1901-1958	100	250	400	200	Method/apparatus for accel. of ions
Lawrence, Sir Thomas	1769-1830	175	250	265		English portrait painter
☆ **Lawrence, Thomas Edward**	**1888-1935**	**700**	**1400**	**2625**	**1500**	**"Lawrence of Arabia," ALS-2X, ESPV-SP**
Lawrence, Wendy B.		10		30	20	Endeavour, 3/2/95
Lawton, Alexander Robert	1818-1896	125	370	550		Minister of Austria, distinctive handwriting; WP, Harvard, lawyer, SL, railroad president; Seven Days, Sharpsburg,* SDS-2X, SALS-2X
Lazarus, Charles		15	25	75	20	Toys 'R' Us founder
Lazarus, Mell	1929-	10			25	Cartoonist, "Momma," "Miss Peach"
Leadbetter, Danville	1811-1866	200	475	575		engineer officer; WP
Leahy, William F.	1875-1959	55	115	160	200	Admiral, FDR Chief of Staff
Leakey, Louis & Mary	1903-1972, 1913-1996	75	200		150	British paleoanthropologists
Lear, Edward	1812-1888	125	250	460		English artist, author, traveler
Lear, William P.	1902-1978	50	125	200	100	Automobile radio developer, Learjet
Leary, Timothy, Dr.		30	75		100	Sixties icon
Lebrun, Albert	1871-1950	25	50	150	40	French statesman

NAME	DATES	SIG	DS	ALS	SP	COMMENTS
Ledley, Robert S.	1926-	15	35	70	25	Entire body CAT scanner
Ledlie, James H.	1832-1882	75	150	230		Civil engineer, rrd. engineer; Spotsylvania, AOTP
Lee, Albert L.	1834-1907	50	100	200		Union College, business; Vicksburg, Big Black River, Red River
Lee, Charles	1731-1782	300	800	1850		Cont'l general; soldier of fortune; SALS-$3500, ESPV
Lee, Charles	1758-1815	125	250	500		US atty. gen..; defense lawyer Burr; Chase
Lee, Edwin Gray	1836-1870	200	300	400		College of Wiliam & Mary; Valley, Seven Days, Second Manassas*
Lee, Fitzhugh	1835-1905	200	300	400		Nephew of Robert E. Lee; WP, farmer, Gov. of VA, diplomat; First Manassas, Peninsular, Spotsylvania, ESPV-DS
Lee, Francis Lightfoot	1734-1797	700	1250	3500		Congressman; Signer of DOI
Lee, George Washington Custis	1832-1913	225	600	625		Eldest son of Robert E. Lee, ESPV - ALS; Engineer, Washington College; On the staff of President Davis, SALS-2X
Lee, Henry "Light Horse Harry"	1756-1818	225	600	700		Cont'l cavalry leader; gov. VA; father R.E. Lee
Lee, Ivy L.	1877-1934	25	50	100		Businessman, publicist
Lee, Mark C.		6	25		15	Endeavour, 9/12/92, A89, 1st married couple
Lee, Richard Henry	1732-1794	515	2250	2875		Congressman; Signer DOI; FF-$2000, ESPV-DS & ALS
Lee, Robert Edward	**1807-1870**	**3265**	**6750**	**10250**	**7000**	**Son of Henry Lee, ESPV-ALS, WP, MW, held highest rank of any office; Army of Northern Virginia,* SALS-2X**
Lee, Stan	1922-	25			35	Marvel Comics
Lee, Stephen Dill	1833-1908	200	400	500		very capable commander, ESPV; WP, farmer, SL, Miss. State College; Mississippi, Alabama, Tennessee
Lee, William Henry Fitzhugh "Rooney"	1837-1891	200	450	600		Second son of Robert E. Lee; Harvard, farming, USHR; Army of Northern Virginia,* ESPV-DS & ALS
Lee, Willis Augustus, Jr.	1888-1945	30	75	150	85	American admiral, WWI, WWII
Leeb, Wilhelm Ritter von	1876-1956	30	65	150		German field marshal
Leech, John	1817-1864	50	100	175		English caricaturist, illustrator

☆ (next to Lee, Robert Edward row)

Joseph Hewes

Adolf Hitler

Thomas Heyward Jr.

James R. Hoffa

Heinrich Himmler

Robert F. Hoke

Oliver Wendell Holmes

Adolf Hitler

Oliver Wendell Holmes

Oliver Wendell Holmes

Adolf Hitler

Oliver Wendell Holmes

NAME	DATES	SIG	DS	ALS	SP	COMMENTS
Leestma, David C.		8	30		20	Challenger, 10/5/84, Columbia, 8/9/89
Lefebvre, Francis Joseph	1755-1820	150	300			French marshal of the Empire
Leger, Fernand	1881-1955	100	250	500		Popular French painter, teacher (Yale Univ.)
Leggett, Mortimer D.	1821-1896	45	80	115		ESPV; farmer, lawyer, businessman; Western Virginia, Atlanta, Carolinas
Leibowitz, Annie	1950-	15	40	60	30	U.S. photographer
Leighton, Frederick	1830-1896	50	100	200		Popular English painter, sculptor
Lejeune, Jerome	1927-1994	40	100	200	50	French geneticist, disc. cause Down's syn.
Lejeune, John A.	1867-1942	40	80	160	85	Marine officer
Leloir, Luis F.	1906-	20	40		30	Biochemist
LeMay, Curtis Emerson	1906-	20	55	100	60	Amer. army and air force officer, WWII
Lemnitzer, Lyman L.	1899-1988	25	50	110	35	American admiral, WWII
L'Enfant, Pierre Charles	1754-1825	375	770			Architect
Lenin, Vladimir Ilyich	1870-1924			30000		Russian rev., Soviet ldr. ALS-$30000, ESPV, scarce
Lenoir, William B.		10	20	25	20	Columbia, 11/11/82, RS
Leonov, Aleksei A.		80	125		150	Voskhod 2, made 1st "space walk", TSS, ESPV-SP
Leontief, Wassily	1906-	25	45		50	Economist, NP
Leopold I of Belgium	1790-1865	120	450			First king of Belgium
Leopold II of Belgium	1835-1909	75	400	600		Son of Leopold I
Lesseps, Ferdinand de	1805-1894	150	250	500		French dip., eng., Suez Canal, AQS-$385
Leutze, Emanuel Gottlieb	1816-1868	100	200	300		German-born American painter
Leventhorpe, Collett	1815-1889	80	150	400		very distinctive handwriting, SALS-2-3X; Army of Northern Virginia*
Lever, William	1851-1925	40	100	230	125	British philanthropist
Leverhulme, William H.	1851-1925	50	100	200		Soapmaker, philanthropist
Levine, David	1926-	10			50	"N.Y. Review of Books" caricatures
Levi - Montalcini, Rita	1909-	25	50		40	Neurophysiologist, NP
Levitt, William	1907-1994	20	50	80	30	Industrialist, "suburb maker"

NAME	DATES	SIG	DS	ALS	SP	COMMENTS
Lewis, Francis	1713-1802	425	1500	2750		Signer DOI; CC; father of Morgan Lewis
Lewis, John L.	1880-1969	50	75	215	80	U.S. labor leader, United Mine Workers
Lewis, Joseph Horace	1824-1904	75	175	300		Centre College, lawyer, SL, USHR; Shiloh, Murfressboro, Chickamauga*
☆ **Lewis, Meriwether**	**1774-1809**	**2675**	**6000**	**6000**		**American army officer, explorer, SALS-2-2.5X, ESPV**
Lewis, Morgan	1754-1844	60	110	140		Cont'l officer; gov NY
Lewis, Percy Wyndham	1884-1957	100	200	400		English painter, novelist, critic
Lewis, William Gaston	1835-1901	80	160	260		Lovejoy's Military School, UNC, teacher; Gettysburg, Petersburg, Valley
LeWitt, Sol	1928-	30	75	150		American sculptor
Ley, Willy	1906-1969	30	100	165	50	Rocket scientist
Libby, Willard	1908-1980	25	40	50	30	Chemist, NP
Lichtenberg, Byron K.		5	15	25	15	Columbia, 11/28/83, Atlantis, 3/24/92
Lichtenstein, Roy	1923-1997	50	110	150	60	American Pop artist, signed repro-$500
Liddell, St. John Richardson	1815-1870	115	270			Murdered by former C.S.A. colonel; WP; Corinth, Perryville, Chickamauga,* scarce
Liddy, G. Gordon		10	25		20	"The G Man," Watergate, FA
Lieber, Francis	1800-1872	50	125	175		Political scientist
Liebermann, Max	1847-1935	100	200	300		German painter, graphic artist
Liebig, Justus von	1803-1873	275	550	800		German chemist, est. quan. org. chem. an.,scarce, SDS & ALS-2X
Lifvendahl, Harold		5	10	15	10	Publisher
Liggett, Hunter	1857-1935	25	50	75	40	American general
Lightburn, Joseph A. J.	1824-1901	60	120	200		WP, minister; Chattanooga, Atlanta, West Virginia
Lilienthal, David E.	1899-1981	20	40	60	30	Administrator
Lilienthal, Otto	1849-1896	625	1500	2750		Aeronautical inventor, scarce in all forms
Liliuokalani (Hawaii)	1838-1917	200	400		500	Queen of the Hawaiian Islands

NAME	DATES	SIG	DS	ALS	SP	COMMENTS
Lilley, Robert Doak	1836-1886	100	200	300		Distinctive handwriting; Washington College; Western Virginia, Second Manassas*
Lin, Y.S. Maya		20	60		50	Vietnam Wall designer
☆ **Lincoln, Abraham**	**1809-1865**	**3400**	**5000**	**9750**	**50000**	**DIO, ALS content 1.5x-20x, ANS-$4500; FF:7000, MA-6250, ESPV, FA**
Lincoln, Benjamin	1733-1810	110	200	400		Cont'l general; sec. of War
Lincoln, Mary Todd	1818-1882	325	1100	9000	3000	(1842); KY; S-4; FF $4;000; ALS - $16500, ESPV
Lincoln, Robert T.	1843-1926	100	250	350		Lawyer, s. of Abraham Lincoln
Lind, Don L.		10	20	15	20	Challenger, 4/29/85, FA
Lindbergh, Anne M.		25	60	150	50	National Aviation Hall of Fame, elusive signer
☆ **Lindbergh, Charles**	**1902-1974**	**675**	**1750**	**2875**	**2100**	**ALS-2X, SB-$900, 675, VSP-$2350, ESPV, FA**
Lindsey, Benjamin B.	1869-1943	20	40	50	30	Reformer
Lineger, J.M.		5	15	25	10	Discovery, 9/9/94
Linnaeus, Carolus	1707-1778	850	1575			Botanist, scarce, ESPV
Lipchitz, Jacques	1891-1973	150	200	265		Lithuanian-born sculptor
Lippencott, Jr., Walter	1919-	5	10	20	10	Publisher
Lipscomb, William N.	1919-	20	40		35	Physical chemist
Lipton, Thomas	1850-1931	100	375	600	350	Built tea empire, merchant
Lister, Joseph	1827-1912	250	450	700		British pioneer of antiseptic surgery
Little, Lewis Henry	1817-1862	425	600			killed in action, ESPV; MW; Elkhorn, Iuka
Litvinov, Maxim	1876-1951	45	100		70	Polish/Russian revolutionary
Livermore, Mary A.	1820-1905	50	100	150		Suffragette, reformer
Liverpool, Robert Banks J.	1770-1828	100	175	225		British prime minister
Livingston, Henry B.	1757-1823	150	325	500		SC: 1806-1823, NY, SL, outstanding in content!
Livingston, Philip	1716-1778	325	1100	1250		Signer of DOI; "Phil Livingston"
Livingston, Robert R.	1746-1813	200	400	600		Statesman; adm. oath to G. Wash.; SALS-2X
Livingston, William	1723-1790	350	800	1500		CC, ALS v. rare, C in other forms, "Wil Livingston"
Livingston, William	1723-1790	350	800	1500		Congressman; gov. NY

Oliver Wendell Holmes, Jr.

Oliver Wendell Holmes, Jr.

Oliver Wendell Holmes, Jr.

Joseph Holt

John B. Hood

Joseph Hooker

William Hooper

Herbert Hoover

Herbert Hoover

Herbert Hoover

Herbert Hoover

Herbert Hoover

NAME	DATES	SIG	DS	ALS	SP	COMMENTS
Livingstone, David	1813-1873	300	675	1500		Missionary, traveller, ESPV
Lloyd George, David	1863-1945	75	200	400	250	British Liberal party prime minister
Lloyd, Henry D.	1847-1903	45	90	140		Publicist, reformer
☆ **Locke, John**	**1632-1704**	**1000**	**2000**			**English political theorist, SDS-5-6X, ESPV**
Lockwood, Belva A.	1830-1917	200	350	700		Lawyer, feminist, ESPV-all forms
Lockwood, Henry H.	1814-1899	50	100	200		Farmer, MW, professor; Maryland, Virginia, Gettysburg*
Lodge, Henry Cabot	1850-1924	45	100	225	100	U.S. Republican senator
Lodge, Henry Cabot, Jr.	1902-1985	25	50	100	30	U.N. Representative
Lodge, Sir Oliver J.	1851-1940	75	150	225	200	Physicist, SD-2X
Loewy, Raymond	1893-1987	40	80	160	50	Industrial designer
Logan, George	1753-1821	40	100	130		Political leader, USS
Logan, John A.	1826-1886	100	200	300		MW, SL, congress, USS; Belmont, Fort Donelson, Corinth, Atlanta
Logan, Thomas Muldrop	1840-1914	100	225	340		SC College, railroad mgmt., S. Railway; First Manassas, Seven Days, Sharpsburg
Lomax, Lunsford Lindsay	1835-1913	100	225	350		WP, inspector general, farmer, VPI, writer; Gettysburg, Overland, Cedar Creek*
Long, Armistead Lindsay	1825-1891	120	240	350		Was totally blind by 1870, Lee biographer; WP, Virginia canal company; Lee's military secretary
Long, Eli	1837-1903	50	100	200		Lawyer; Murfreesboro, Tullahoma, Atlanta*
Long, Elizabeth	1950-	10	25	45	20	Publisher, "People"
Long, Huey P.	1893-1924	100	160	245	140	Louisiana political czar, gov., assassin.
Longstreet, James	1821-1904	625	1150	2150	1000	Supreme battlefield tactician; WP, MW, diplomat, railroad comm.; First & Second Manassas, Peninsular,* SDS & SALS-2X, ESPV
Lorant, Stefan	1901-	20	40	80	35	Photo-journalist
Lorenz, Konrad	1904-1989	25	60		35	Austrian ethologist, animal behavior pioneer
Loring, William Wing	1818-1886	135	250	320		SL, MW, served in Egyptian army; Southwestern Virginia, Baker's Creek, SDS & SALS-2X, ESPV
Loucks, Vernon R., Jr.		5	10	20	10	Baxter International CEO

NAME	DATES	SIG	DS	ALS	SP	COMMENTS
Louis XII (France)	1462-1515	800	1625			Son of Charles, SDS-2X
Louis XIII (France)	1601-1643	650	1150			Son of Henry IV, SDS-2X
Louis XIV (France)	1638-1715	500	1000			Son of Louis XIII
Louis XV (France)	1710-1774	700	1250	5000		Son of Louis, ESPV-ALS
Louis XVI (France)	1754-1793	350	1000			DS-$900
Lounge, John M.		5		20	10	Discovery, 8/27/85, Columbia, 12/2/90
Lousma, Jack R.		10	30	40	25	Skylab 3, Columbia, 3/22/82
Lovell, James	1737-1814	100	200	300		Congressman; CC
Lovell, James A., Jr.		15			50	Gemini 7, Apollo 13, charges fee, ESPV-all forms
Lovell, Mansfield	1822-1884	125	250	300		WP, MW, engineer; Corinth, SDS & SALS-2X, WD-2X
Lovell, Sir Bernard	1913-	20	45	100	35	Astronomer
Low, G. David		5		20	10	Columbia, 1/9/90, Atlantis, 8/3/91, RS
Low, Sir David	1891-1963	20	50	125		Political cartoonist, ESPV-SP
Lowell, Abbott L.	1856-1943	20	55	120	75	Educator
Lowell, Francis C.	1775-1817	45	80	125		Industrialist, inventor
Lowell, Percival	1855-1916	25	50	100	60	U.S. astronomer, Pluto theorist
Lowrey, Mark Perrin	1828-1885	100	210	245		Baptist ministry, Blue Mt. Female Institute; Kentucky, Chickamauga, Atlanta*
Lowry, Robert	1830-1910	70	125	200		lawyer, Gov. Mississippi; Shiloh, Vicksburg, Atlanta, Tennessee
Lubke, Heinrich	1894-1972	20	45		40	President German Federal Republic
Lucas, John Porter	1890-1949	30	60	80	50	American admiral, WWI, WWII
Lucas, Thomas J.	1826-1908	50	100	200		Watchmaker, MW; Ball's Bluff, Vicksburg, Red River
Luce, Claire Booth	1903-1987	40	125	200	75	Writer, diplomat, USHR
Luce, Henry R.	1898-1967	60	125	250	100	Publisher
Lucid, Shannon W.		10		45	40	Discovery, 6/17/85, Atlantis, 10/18/89, 8/3/91, RS
Ludendorff, Erich	1865-1937	100	200	300	300	German general, SDS & SALS-2X
Ludwig II	1845-1886	50	175	400		King of Bavaria
Luks, George	1867-1933	50	100	200		American painter

NAME	DATES	SIG	DS	ALS	SP	COMMENTS
Lumiere, Louis & Auguste	1864-1984, 1862-1954	500	1200		700	French cinematograph inventor (both)
Lundy, Benjamin	1789-1839	60	120	240		Reformer, many private papers were burned!
Luria, Salvador F.	1912-1991	25	50		50	Biologist, NP
Lurton, Horace H.	1844-1914	55	180	250		SC: 1910-1914, TN, oldest jurist ever, prolific
Lyautey, Louis H.G.	1854-1934	20	45	100	45	French soldier
Lyell, Sir Charles	1797-1875	100	200	400		Geologist
Lyon, Hylan Benton	1836-1907	75	150	225		WP, farmer, commissioner of a penitentiary; Holly Springs, Vicksburg
Lyon, Mary Mason	1797-1849	70	150	300		Educator
Lytle, William H.	1826-1863	350	550			Lawyer, MW, SL, poet; Carnifex Ferry, Alabama, Perryville
MacArthur, Douglas	**1880-1964**	**250**	**500**	**850**	**675**	**American admiral, WWI, WWII**
MacArthur, John		5	10	15	10	Publisher
Macaulay, Thomas B.	1800-1859	50	100	150		British historian, statesman
Mac Cready, Paul	1925-	15	30		25	Aeronautical engineer, SSP-2X
Macdonald, Dwight	1906-1982	20	45	100	30	Critic, political activist
MacDonald, J. Ramsay	1866-1937	75	150	225	200	First Labor party P.M. of Great Britain
Macdonald, Jacques Etienne Joseph A.	1765-1840	80	150	275		French marshal of the Empire
MacDonough, Thomas	1783-1825	110	300	650		Naval officer, W1812
Machaskee, Alex		5	10	15	5	Publisher
Mackall, William Whann	1817-1891	100	265	440		SALS-2-3X; WP, farmer; Chickamauga, Atlanta, WD-2X
Mackay, John W.	1831-1902	95	200	300	150	Mining czar
Mackensen, August von	1849-1945	25	50	75	65	German field marshal, ESPV
Mackenzie, Ranald S.	1840-1889	125	250	350		WP; Second Manassas, Fredericksburg, Gettysburg...
Mackie, Bob		10	20		25	Fashion designer
MacKinnon, Catherine	1946-	10	25	45	20	Legal scholar
MacLean, Glenwood		5	15	25	10	Columbia, 10/22/92
Maclennan, Robert	1936-	15	25		20	British politician

(signature)

Lou Henry Hoover

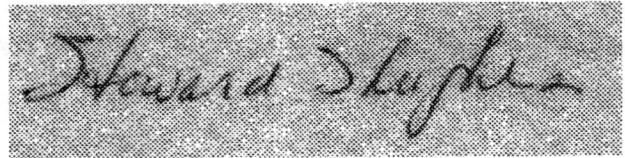

Howard Hughes

(signature)

Lou Henry Hoover

(signature)

Howard R. Hughes

(signature)

Francis Hopkinson

(signature)

Charles E. Hughes

(signature)

Francis Hopkinson

(signature)

Stephen Hopkins

(signature)

Collis P. Huntington

(signature)

Oliver O. Howard

(signature)

Collis P. Huntington

NAME	DATES	SIG	DS	ALS	SP	COMMENTS
Macmahon, Marie Edme Patrice M. de	1808-1893	50	100	200		Marshal of France
MacMillan, Harold	1895-1986	30	75	150	50	British prime minister of Great Britain
MacNelly, Jeff	1947-	15			145	Political cartoonist, "Shoe"
Madigan, John	1937-	5	15	20	10	Tribune Newspaper Co. executive
Madison, Dorothea "Dolly" Payne Todd	1768-1849	775	1850	3945		(1794); NC; No sons or daughters, First Lady, ESPV, scarce-ALS
☆ **Madison, James**	**1751-1836**	**350**	**2250**	**3500**		**Bank check-$2500, ALS content 2-3x; SHIPSP:1925; FLSP:2250; FF:1000, LG-1875, NC-2000, MA-950, ESPV-ALS**
Magritte, Rene	1898-1967	250	465	1100		Belgian Surrealist painter
Magruder, John Bankhead	1807-1871	230	475	500		ESPV; WP, MW, Mexican forces; Peninsular, Seven Days
Magsaysay, Ramon	1907-1957	25	50	125	45	Phillipino soldier and statesman
Mahan, Alfred Thayer	1840-1914	50	100	150		Naval officer U.S.
Mahone, William	1826-1895	150	275	430		VMI, teacher, railroad superintendent, USS; Army of Northern Virginia*
Mahoney, Richard J.	1934-	5	10	20	10	Monsanto Co. CEO
Maillol, Aristide	1861-1944	250	500	750		French sculptor, painter, designer
Maiman, Theodore Harold	1927-	20	40	65	30	Ruby Laser Systems
Maintenon, Francoise	1635-1719	225	400	800		Second wife of Louis XIV
Maison, Nicolas-Joseph	1771-1840	55	160	200		French soldier
Major, John	1943-	10			30	British prime minister
Makarios III, Mihail K.	1913-1977	50	100	150	65	Archbishop Orthodox church
☆ **Malcolm X (Malcolm Little)**	**1925-1965**	**1000**	**4000**	**5000**		**Reformer, TLS & ALS - 3X, ESPV-all forms**
Malenkov, Georgy M.	1902-1988	200	300		250	Soviet prime minister
Male, Emile	1862-1954	30	50			French art historian
Malik, Jacob A.	1906-1980	30			50	Soviet politician
Mallory, Stephen R.	1813-1873	100	200	265		American politician, CSA
Maltby, Jasper A.	1826-1867	125	200	300		Mayor, MW, gunsmith; Vicksburg
Malthus, Thomas R.	1766-1834	500	1000	2000		British economist, SALS-2X
Mandela, Nelson	1918-	200	400		350	South African president, scarce

GEN–POLIT L

NAME	DATES	SIG	DS	ALS	SP	COMMENTS
Mandelbrot, Benoit	1924-	15	35		25	Mathematician
☆ **Manet, Edouard**	**1832-1883**	**625**	**2000**			**French painter, graphic artist, scarce, ESPV**
Maney, George Earl	1826-1901	150	270	365		SALS-2X; Nashville Seminary, MW, Pres TN & Pacific; Cheat Mt., Army of Tennessee, Shiloh
Manigault, Arthur Middleton	1824-1886	115	250	300		MW, rice planter, inspector general SC; Shiloh, Corinth
Manley, Michael	1923-	10	20	30	20	Jamaicon prime minister
Mann, Horace	1796-1859	50	150	275		Pioneered modern public school system
Mannerheim, Carl Gustav Emil von	1867-1951	140	300	740		Russian and Finnish soldier
Mansfield, Joseph K. F.	1803-1862	200	375	600		Killed in action, SALS-4-5X; WP, MW; Washington, Sharpsburg, ESPV
Manship, Paul	1885-1966	50	200	400		American sculptor
Manson, Mahlon D.	1820-1895	50	100	150		Teacher, SL, druggist, congress, state aud.; Rich Mountain, Fishing Creek
Manstein, Erich von	1887-1973	25	75	115	60	German field marshal
Manteuffel, Baron Edwin von	1809-1885	50	150	200	100	Prussian field marshal and diplomat, SDS-2X
Mapplethorpe, Robert	1946-1989	200	500			American photographer, scarce
Marat, Jean Paul	1743-1793	820	2500	4500		French revolutionary, assassinated, scarce
March, Peyton Conway	1864-1955	35	55	80	50	American general, SAW, WWI
Marconi, Guglielmo	1874-1937	250	850	1625	750	Italian physicist, wireless telegraph dev., ESPV
Marcos, Ferdinand	1917-1989	55	120		100	Phillippines president
Marcos, Imelda	1930-	15	30		20	Wife of Ferdinand
Marcuse, Herbert	1898-1979	45	100	200	75	Philosopher, writer, educator
Marcy, Randolph B.	1812-1887	50	100	200		ESPV-ALS; WP, MW, inspector gen.; Michigan, Wisconsin, ESPV-WD-2-3X
Marey, Etienne J.	1830-1903	100	200	350		Physiologist, SDS & ALS-2X
Maria Theresa (Austria)	1717-1780	200	575	850		ESPV
Marie Antoinette (France)	1755-1793	1500	5000			Queen of Louis XVI of France, scarce, ESPV
Mariette, Doug	1949-	10				Editorial cartoonist, "Kudzu"
Marin, John Cheri	1870-1953	50	200	400		American painter

NAME	DATES	SIG	DS	ALS	SP	COMMENTS
Marion, Francis "Swamp Fox"	c.1732-1795	3450	6500	13000		Southern partisan leader; SL, ESPV
Maritain, Jacques	1882-1973	25	50	100		Neo-Thomist philosopher
Mark, Reuben	1934-	5	10	25	10	Colgate-Palmolive Co. CEO
Markowitz, Harry	1927-	10	20	25	20	Economist, RS
Marmaduke, John Sappington	1833-1887	130	300	400		ESPV - SALS - 5-6X; Yale, Harvard, WP, editor, Gov. Missouri; Shiloh, Prairie Grove, Little Rock, Red River*
Marmount, Auguste Frederic Louis Viesse de	1774-1852	50	100	200		French marshal of the Empire
Marryat, Frederick	1792-1848	50	100	200		Naval officer, author
Marsh, George P.	1801-1882	40	100	125		Diplomat, scientist, USHR
Marshall, George Catlett	1880-1959	225	360	600	375	American general, statesman
Marshall, Humphrey	1812-1872	100	225	300		SALS - 5 - 6X, ESPV; WP, MW, USHR, diplomat, lawyer; Princeton, WD-2X
☆ **Marshall, John**	**1755-1835**	**450**	**1625**	**2625**		**SC: 1801-1835, VA, Chief Justice, ADS (10 sigs)$11K, SALS-2-3X, ESPV-ALS**
Marshall, Peter	1902-1949	50	100	125	75	Presbyterian clergy, USS chaplain
Marshall, Thomas R.	1854-1925	60	130		150	U.S. vice president
☆ **Marshall, Thurgood**	**1908-1993**	**125**	**200**	**300**	**200**	**SC: 1967-1991, NY**
Marston, Gilman	1811-1890	40	80	150		Teacher, Harvard, SL, congress, USS; Peninsular, Point Lookout prison camp
Martin, Don	1931-	15				Cartoonist, "Mad" magazine, PU
Martin, Glenn	1886-1955	60	150	300	225	Aircraft manufacturer
Martin, James Green	1819-1878	150	300	400		extremely popular with his troops; MW, lawyer; Churubusco, North Carolina, SDS & SALS-2X
Martin, Kenneth	1905-1984	25				British painter, sculptor, D-$1400
Martin, Luther	1748-1826	100	200	325		American lawyer, public official
Martin, William Thompson	1823-1910	125	300	450		Centre College, SL, railroad president; Seven Days, Sharpsburg, Chickamauga
Martindale, John H.	1815-1881	50	100	180		WP, lawyer, atty. gen. NY; Peninsular, Milt. gov. (Wash., D.C.)
☆ **Marx, Karl**	**1818-1883**	**1000**	**2000**			**German pol. philosopher, communist, ESPV**

Samuel Huntington

Andrew Jackson

Jared Ingersoll

Andrew Jackson

Andrew Jackson

Alfred Iverson Jr.

Thomas "Stonewall" Jackson

Andrew Jackson

James I, King of England

NAME	DATES	SIG	DS	ALS	SP	COMMENTS
Mary I (England)	1516-1558	1000	3250	7000		Daughter of Henry VIII, ESPV-ALS
Mary II	1662-1694	550	1150			Queen of Britain
Mary of Teck	1867-1953	100	200	260	250	Queen-consort of Great Britain
Masaryk, Jan	1886-1948	100	200	300		Czech. foreign minister, died mysteriously
Masaryk, Thomas G.	1850-1937	150	300	525		Czech. statesman, 1st pres. of C. Repub.
Mason, George	1725-1792	2150	4650			Statesman; constitutionalist, ESPV-ALS
Mason, John S.	1824-1897	50	120	215		WP, MW; Fredericksburg, California, Nevada
Massena, Andre, Duke of Rivoli	1758-1817	125	280	400		French marshal of the Empire
Masson, Andre	1896-1987	35	75	125		French painter, engraver, designer, writer
Masters, W.H. & Johnson, V.E.	1915- 1925-	30	75		60	Sex researchers (both)
Mata Hari	1876-1917	525	1200			Spy, dancer, scarce
☆ **Mather, Cotton**	**1663-1728**	**850**	**2250**	**2675**		**U.S. Orthodox Puritanist, Yale, SADS-$4500**
Mathews, George	1739-1812	75	150			Cont'l officer; gov. GA; USHR
☆ **Matisse, Henri**	**1869-1954**	**750**	**1000**	**1750**		**French painter, sculptor, designer**
Matthews, Stanley	1824-1889	45	150	275		SC: 1881-1889, OH
Matthies, Charles L.	1824-1868	150	260			Liquor business, SL; Island No. 10, Corinth, Iuka, Chattanooga, ESPV
Mattingly, Thomas K. II		50	100	165	125	Apollo 16
Mauchly, John W.	1908-1980	30	100	150	50	U.S. co-inventor of Eniac lg.-scale computer
Mauldin, Bill	1921-	30			75	"GI" cartoonist of WWII
Maurer, Robert D.	1924-	20	40	55	25	Fused silica optical waveguide
Maury, Dabney Herndon	1822-1900	100	230	320		SALS-4-5X; UVA, WP, MW, diplomat, S. Hist. Soc., writer; Trans-Mississippi, Pea Ridge, Iuka, Corinth
Mawson, Sir Douglas	1882-1958	75	150	300	170	Explorer, geologist
Maxey, Samuel Bell	1825-1895	150	250	325		SALS-6-7X, ESPV; WP, MW, lawyer, USS; Vicksburg, Indian Territory, Red River, WD-2X
Maxim, Sir Hiram	1840-1916	60	145	200		Inventor, engineer, SALS-2X
Maximilian (Mexico)	1832-1867	325	550	1100		Brother of Francis Joseph

NAME	DATES	SIG	DS	ALS	SP	COMMENTS
Maxwell, James Clark	1831-1879	100	200	325		British physicist, electricity theorist
Maxwell, Robert	1923-1991	45	125		100	Publisher, politician, controversial, ESPV
Mayer, Maria Goeppert	1906-1972	40	100	175	50	German/U.S. physicist
Mayer, Peter		5	10	15	10	Publisher
Mayo, Charles H.	1865-1939	75	150		325	Surgeon, Mayo Foundation
Mayo, William J.	1861-1939	125	250		500	Surgeon, Mayo Foundation
Mazzini, Giuseppe	1805-1872	130	360	750		Italian political philosopher, ESPV, ALS-2X
McAdoo, William G.	1863-1941	30	60	115	40	Political leader, businessman
McArthur, John	1826-1906	60	150	300		Blacksmith, postmaster; Fort Henry, Shiloh, Vicksburg, Atlanta
McArthur, William S., Jr.		5	15	25	10	Columbia, 10/18/93
McAuliffe, Anthony C.	1898-1975	100	175	220	400	Amer. gen., WWII, "Nuts" he says!
McAuliffe, Christa		500			750	Challenger, 1/28/86, killed during launch
McBride, Jon A.		10	20	25	20	Challenger, 10/5/84, FA
McCain, John Sidney	1884-1945	25	50	100	45	American admiral, WWI, WWII
McCall, George A.	1802-1868	100	150	250		MW, inspector gen.; Peninsular
McCandless, Bruce		5		20	10	Challenger, 2/3/84, Discovery, 4/24/90, RS
McCarthy, Joseph R.	1908-1957	40	125	250	110	U.S. senator, Communist hunter
McCausland, John	1836-1927	75	130	175		One of the last surviving C.S.A. generals; VMI, professor, UVA; Shenandoah Valley, Petersburg
McCay, Winsor	1872-1934	65			200	Cartoonist, "Little Nemo"
McClellan, George B.	**1826-1885**	**275**	**400**	**650**		**Controversial, SALS-2-3X; WP, MW, WP instructor, gov. NJ; Rich Mountain, AOTP***
McClernand, John A.	1812-1890	60	130	200		Congress; Vicksburg, Louisiana, Texas
McClintock, Barbara	1902-1992	30	60	110	50	U.S. geneticist, mobile genetic element theor.
McComb, William	1828-1918	100	225	350		Farmer; Cedar Mt., Second Manassas, Army of N. VA
McConnell, John Paul	1908-1986	15	30	50	30	U.S. air force general, WWII
McCook, Alexander M.	1831-1903	50	100	165		WP; First Manassas, Army of the Ohio, Shiloh,* SALS & DS-2X

☆

NAME	DATES	SIG	DS	ALS	SP	COMMENTS
McCook, Edward M.	1833-1909	50	100	230		Lawyer, diplomat, tty. gov. Co.; Chickamauga, Perryville, Alabama, Georgia
McCook, Robert L.	1827-1862	365	650			Lawyer; West Virginia, Carnifix Ferry, Mill Springs, ESPV
McCormack, Mark	1930-	10	20		20	Sports agent, IMG founder
McCormick, Cyrus	1809-1884	250	850	1050		Reaper, grain not grim
McCown, John Porter	1815-1879	125	275	325		SDS-4X; WP, MW, teacher; Murfreesboro, ESPV
McCulley, Michael J.		10	20	25	20	Atlantis, 10/18/89, FA
McCulloch, Ben	1811-1862	265	500	685		killed in action; surveyor, Indian fighter, MW, U.S. marshal; Wilson's Creek, Elkhorn Tavern, scarce, ESPV
McCulloch, Henry Eustace	1816-1895	110	250			sheriff, MW, SL, U.S. marshal, farmer; Texas, ESPV
McCutcheon, John T.	1870-1949	20			45	Midwestern rural life cartoonist
McDivitt, James A.		35	75		50	Gemini-Titan 4
McDonald, Richard J.		95	250	400	190	Hamburger chain founder
McDonnell, James S.	1899-1980	20	30	100	40	Aircraft manufacturer
McDougall, Alexander	1732-1786	100	200			Cont'l general; patriot; CC; USS; USHR
McDowell, Irvin	1818-1885	100	200	300		SALS-2X; WP, WP instructor, MW; AOTP
McGill, James	1744-1813	80	175	250		University founder
McGinnis, George F.	1826-1910	50	100	220		MW, hatmaker, county auditor, postmaster; Fort Donelson, Shiloh, Vicksburg
McGovern, George	1922-	10	30		20	U.S. politician
McGowan, Samuel	1819-1897	100	200	275		SC College, SL, MW; Army of Northern Virginia*
McGowan, William C.		10	25	25	20	MCI Communications Corp. executive
McGuffey, William H.	1800-1873	125	475			U.S. public educator
McHenry, James	1753-1816	200	300	700		CC, C in all forms, ALS-4X, MD, full, ESPV-ALS
McIntosh, John B.	1829-1888	125	200			MW; Peninsular, Maryland, AOTP, Chancellorsville
Mcintosh, Lachlan	1725-1806	500	850	1250		Cont'l general; dueled Gwinnett

Thomas Jefferson

Thomas Jefferson

Thomas Jefferson

Thomas Jefferson

Thomas Jefferson

Thomas Jefferson

Thomas Jefferson

Andrew Johnson

Andrew Johnson

Andrew Johnson

Andrew Johnson

Andrew Johnson

Andrew Johnson

NAME	DATES	SIG	DS	ALS	SP	COMMENTS
McKay, Donald	1810-1880	40	75	100		Shipbuilder
McKean, Thomas	1734-1817	225	450	800		Signer DOI; Congress; gov. of PA
Mckean, Thomas J.	1810-1870	60	120	250		WP, MW, mayor, farmer; Missouri, Corinth
McKenna, Joseph	1843-1926	35	50	80	40	SC: 1898-1925, CA. USHR, prolific but reclusive
McKinley, Ida Saxton	1847-1907	400	625	975	450	(1871); OH; D-2, First Lady
McKinley, John	1780-1852	100	200	300		SC: 1837-1852, AL, later chronic health problems
McKinley, John	1721-1796	75	150			Pres. of DE
☆ **McKinley, William**	**1843-1901**	**275**	**400**	**1100**	**1250**	**DIO, MA-700, APT-600, WH/EMC-750, DS PD-2X, ALS PD-2X**
McKinstry, Justus	1814-1897	40	80	150		Controversial; WP, MW, stockbroker; Dept. of the West - chief quartermaster
McLaws, Lafayette	1821-1897	135	300	365		nephew of Zachary Taylor; WP, MW, postmaster of Savannah; Army of Northern Virginia, Knoxville
McLean, John	1785-1861	75	225	300		SC: 1829-1861, serv. over 30 yrs., postmaster
McLean, Nathaniel C.	1815-1905	75	115	200		Son of supreme court justice J. McLean; Augusta College, lawyer; Chancellorsville, Dept. of the Ohio, Atlanta
McManus, George	1884-1954	50			225	Cartoonist, "Bringing Up Father"
McMillan, James W.	1825-1903	50	100	200		MW; New Orleans, Red River, Cedar Creek*
McMonagle, Donald R.		5		25	10	Discovery, 4/28/91, Endeavour, 1/13/93, RS
McMorris, Charles Horatio	1890-1954	40	80	150	80	American admiral, WWI, WWII
McNair, Evander	1820-1902	100	200	250		MW, mercantile business; Wilson's Creek, Elkhorn, Murfreesboro*
McNair, Lesley James	1883-1944	40	100	175	90	American general, WWI, WWII, KIA
McNair, Robert E.		200	325		300	Challenger, 1/28/86, killed during launch
McNamara, Robert S.	1916-	10	40	75	20	Businessman, political leader, sec. of defense
McNeil, John	1813-1891	50	100			Hatter, SL, sheriff, commissioner, post office; Missouri

NAME	DATES	SIG	DS	ALS	SP	COMMENTS
McPherson, James B.	1828-1864	150	300	425		WP; Fort Henry, Fort Donelson, Shiloh, Corinth,* ESPV, WD-2X
McRae, Dandridge	1829-1899	100	225	275		SC College, inspector general; Wilson's Creek, Elkhorn, Red River
McReynolds, James C.	1862-1946	50	100	150	75	SC: 1914-1941, TN, atty. gen., very controversial
Mead, Margaret	1901-1978	100	150	200		U.S. cultural anthropologist, RS
Meade, Carl J.		10	25	35	20	Atlantis, 11/15/90, Columbia, 6/25/92 D1994
☆ Meade, George G.	**1815-1972**	**400**	**650**	**1500**	**500**	**SDS - 2-3X, SALS-2X; WP, civil engineering, MW; Seven Days, Second Manassas, Gettysburg,* ESPV**
Meade, James E.	1907-	15	30		25	Economist, NP
Meagher, Thomas F.	1823-1867	150	300	600		ESPV, SLS/DS-2-3X, SALS-2-2.5X; acting gov. Mont.; First Manassas, AOTP
Meany, George	1894-1980	20	35	80	100	Labor leader, AFL-CIO, RS
Medici, Cosimo I de	1519-1574	400	1150			Duke of Florence
Medicis, Catherine de	1519-1589	325	750			French, queen consort Henry II
Meigs, Montgomery C.	1816-1892	50	150	200		WP; Quartermaster general
Meigs, Return Jonathan	1740-1823	100	200	300		Cont'l officer; pioneer
Meiklejohn, Alexander	1872-1964	20	40	50	25	British-born educator
Meir, Golda	1898-1978	125	300	600		P.M. of Israel, FDC-$95, ALS-3-4X
Meitner, Lise	1878-1968	100	300	500		Austrian physicist, atomic theorist
☆ Mellon, Andrew W.	**1855-1937**	**200**	**425**	**500**	**300**	**Industrialist, financier, National Gallery of Art**
Mellon, Paul	1907-	25			50	Art collector, philanthropist, ESPV
Melnick, Bruce E.		5	15	25	10	Discovery, 10/6/90, Endeavour, 5/7/92
Mendel, Gregor J.	1822-1884	375	800	2000		Austrian botanist, genetics pioneer
Mendeleyev, Dmitri I.	1834-1907	500	1200	2000		Russian chemist, dev. Periodic Table of Elem.
Menninger, Karl	1893-1990	40	50	80	75	Founded Menninger Clinic, RS, SDS & ALS-2X
Merbold, Ulf D.		10	25	35	20	Columbia, 11/28/83, Discovery, 1/22/92, S94
Mercer, Hugh Weedon	1808-1877	100	200	260		WP, cashier; Savannah, Atlanta, Jonesboro

NAME	DATES	SIG	DS	ALS	SP	COMMENTS
Merck, George W.	1894-1957	30	60		75	Chemicals executive
Meredith, Solomon	1810-1875	175	375	500		Sheriff, SL, US marshal; Second Manassas, Gettysburg
Meredith, Sullivan A.	1816-1874	80	175	320		Wholesale drug business; First & Second Manassas
Mergenthaler, Ottmar	1854-1899	90	200	350		Linotype, printing bar machine
Merriam, Charles E.	1874-1953	10	30	75	25	Political scientist
Merrifield, Bruce	1921-	15	40		20	Organic chemist
Merrill, Aaron Stanton	1890-1961	15	25	50	30	American admiral, WWI, WWII
Merrill, Charles E.	1885-1956	35	100	150	75	U.S. financier, developed Merrill Lynch
Merrill, Frank Dow	1903-1955	250	400	400		American general, WWII, ESPV
Merritt, Wesley	1834-1910	60	125	230		WP; AOTP, Chancellorsville, Gettysburg
Merton, Robert	1910-	10	25		20	Sociologist
Meselson, Matthew	1930-	10	25		20	Molecular biologist
Mesmer, Franz	1734-1815	175	350	600		German physician, theorist: animal magnet.
Messerschmid, Ernst		10		40	20	Challenger, 10/30/85, RS
Messerschmitt, Willy	1898-1978	150	300		375	Aircraft engineer
Messick, Dale	1906-	20			55	Cartoonist, "Brenda Starr"
Metternich, Klemens W.N.L.	1773-1859	100	275	450		Austrian statesman
Meyerhof, Otto F.	1884-1951	30	50		50	Physiologist
Michelson, Albert A.	1852-1931	125	250	500	150	U.S. physicist
Middleton, Henry	1717-1784	3000	5000			2nd Pres. Cont'l Congress, ESPV
Middleton, Troy H.	1889-1976	40	115	225	125	American general, WWI, WWII
Mifflin, Thomas	1744-1800	175	400	700		CC, ALS somewhat UC; all forms available, PA
Mikoyan, Artem I.	1905-1970	40	70		75	Aircraft designer- "MIG"
Miles, Michael A.	1939-	10	20	25	15	Philip Morris CEO
Miles, Nelson A.	1839-1925	150	300	400		Writer; indian fighter, soldier, Seven Pines, Sharpsburg, Fredericksburg*
Milken, Michael	1946-	10	35	60	25	Financier
Mill, James	1773-1836	100	250	500		Philosopher, historian, economist
Mill, John Stuart	1806-1873	125	350	700		British philosopher

Andrew Johnson

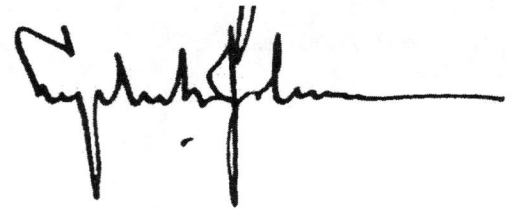

Lyndon Johnson

Joseph E. Johnston

Joseph E. Johnston

John Paul Jones

Lyndon Johnson

Thomas Jordan

Lyndon Johnson

Lyndon Johnson

Thomas M. Kean

NAME	DATES	SIG	DS	ALS	SP	COMMENTS
Mills, Wilbur	1909-1992	15	30		25	U.S. politician
Millais, Sir John Everett	1829-1896	60	125	250		English painter, graphic artist
Miller, John F.	1831-1886	40	75	115		Lawyer, SL, USS, Alaska Com. Co.; Murfreesboro, Tullahoma
Miller, Kelly	1863-1939	40	100	150	65	Educator, sociologist
Miller, Perry G.	1905-1963	20	40		30	U.S. historian
Miller, Robert L.	1949-	10	20	25	15	Time Inc. president
Miller, Samuel F.	1816-1890	100	200	300		SC: 1862-1890, IA
Miller, Stephen	1816-1881	100	200	300		Newspaper editor, gov. Minn.; Shenandoah, Seven Pines, Seven Days
Miller, William	1820-1909	70	135	200		Louisiana College, MW, SL, farmer; Kentucky, Murfreesboro
Milles, Carl	1875-1955	40	60	110		Swedish sculptor
Millet, Jean-Francois	1814-1875	250	500	1000		French painter, graphic artist, ALS-2.5X
Millikan, Robert A.	1868-1953	100	200	400	250	U.S. physicist, NP
Millman, Irving	1923-	25	60	125	40	Hepatitis B vaccine
Milroy, Robert H.	1816-1890	45	120	240		Lawyer, Indian agent; Western Virginia, Shenandoah Valley
Minton, Sherman	1890-1965	45	145	200	90	SC: 1949-1956, IN, USS
Mirabeau, H.R. Gabriel	1749-1791	100	250	450		French revolutionary
Miro, Joan	1893-1983	250	600	750	300	Spanish painter, FA, S repro $300-$350
Mitchell, Edgar D.		40	125	200	60	Apollo 14, MW, TSS
Mitchell, John	1870-1919	45	100	75		Labor leader
Mitchell, John	1913-1988	15	30			Lawyer, cabinet member
Mitchell, John G.	1838-1894	40	75	165		Lawyer, pension comm. Ohio; Tennessee, Chickamauga, Carolinas*
Mitchell, Robert B.	1823-1882	80	150	275		Lawyer, MW, mayor, Tty. gov. NM; Wilson's Creek, Perryville, Chickamauga
Mitchell, Wesley C.	1874-1948	20	35	50	60	Economist
Mitchell, William "Billy"	1879-1936	225	500	1000	1500	American officer, SAW, WWI, SDS-2X, ESPV
Mitscher, Marc Andrew	1887-1947	300	425		450	American admiral, WWI, WWII
Mitterrand, Francois	1916-1996	25	40	65	40	French president 1981-1995

NAME	DATES	SIG	DS	ALS	SP	COMMENTS
Miyake, Issey	1938-	10	25		20	Fashion designer
Modawar, Sir Peter	1915-1987	20	40		30	Zoologist, NP
Modigliani, Amedeo	1884-1920	250	600			Italian painter, sculptor, ESPV
Modigliani, Franco	1918-	15	35		30	U.S. economist
Moffatt, James	1870-1944	25	50		45	Theologian, SDS-2X
Mohri, Mamoru		15	30		30	Endeavour, 9/12/92, 1st prof. Japanese Ast.
Mollet, Guy	1905-1975	25	50	80	40	French, social politician
Moltke, Count Helmuth Johannes Ludwig von	1848-1916	20	40	75	35	German general
Moltke, Count Helmuth Karl Bernhard von	1800-1891	100	200	350	240	German field marshal
Monaghan, Thomas S.	1937-	10	25	65	25	Domino's Pizza founder
Moncey, Bon Adrien Jeannot de	1754-1842	60	125	200		French revolutionary, PU
Mondale, Walter	1928-	15	40		40	U.S. vice president
Mondrian, Piet	1872-1944	300	750	1575		Dutch abstract painter, writer
Monet, Claude ☆	**1840-1926**	**500**	**1325**	**1875**		**French Impressionist painter**
Monroe, James ☆	**1758-1831**	**400**	**1500**	**2875**		**FF:550, LG-1000, MA-1400**
Montana, Bob	1920-1975	50			200	Cartoonist, "Archie"
Montcalm, Louis-Joseph de Montcalm-Gozon	1712-1759	500	1250	2500		French general
Montefiore, Sir Moses	1784-1855	50	100	225		Philanthropist
Montessori, Maria	1870-1952	325	650	1000		Italian educator, physician
Montgomery, Alfred Eugene	1891-1961	15	25	50	30	American admiral, WWII
Montgomery, Sir Bernard Law	1887-1976	100	300		325	1st Vis...Alamein, SDS-7X, ESPV
Montgomery, William R.	1801-1871	40	100	180		WP, MW; First Manassas, Annapolis
Moody, Dwight	1837-1899	60	150	225	150	U.S. evangelist
Moody, William H.	1853-1917	50	125	175	65	SC: 1906-1910, MA, USHR, sec. Navy, atty. gen., scarce
Moore, Alfred	1755-1810	3250				SC: 1799-1804, NC, delivered only 1 opinion, very rare
Moore, George.E.	1873-1958	65	200	250	150	British philosopher, professor
Moore, Henry	1898-1986	75	200	450	125	English sculptor, graphic artist
Moore, Sir Jeremy	1928-	10	20	30	20	British soldier
Moore, Sir John	1761-1809	75	150	300		British soldier

NAME	DATES	SIG	DS	ALS	SP	COMMENTS
Moore, John Creed	1824-1910	100	200	250		Shelby College, contributor to numerous pubs; Shiloh, Corinth, Vicksburg*
Moore, John D.		5	10		10	Publisher
Moore, Patrick Theodore	1821-1883	110	200	250		Merchant, insurance agent; First Manassas
Moore, Stanford	1913-1982	25	50		40	Biochemist
Moorer, Thomas H.	1912-	25			45	US Naval officer
Moores, Dick	1909-1986	20			50	Cartoonist, "Gasoline Alley," RS
Moreau, Jean Victor Marie	1763-1813	100	250	325		French general
Morell, George W.	1815-1883	50	100	245		WP, rrd. construction, MW, farmer; Peninsular, Seven days, Sharpsburg, ESPV-ALS
Morgan Edwin D.	1811-1883	40	70	100		Gov. NY, USS, financier, philanthropist, SL; Department of New York
Morgan, Charles H.	1834-1875	50	125	250		Fort Monroe, Washington, AOTP
Morgan, George W.	1820-1893	75	150	300		ESPV, SALS-5X; MW, lawyer, diplomat, congress; Cumberland Gap
Morgan, James D.	1810-1896	50	100	175		Merchant, banker, businessman; Island No. 10, Corinth, Atlanta, Carolina
Morgan, John Hunt	1825-1864	1000	1850	2000		one of the legends of the CSA, SDS - 3-4X; Transylvania College, MW; Tennessee, Kentucky, Indiana, Ohio
☆ **Morgan, John Pierpoint**	**1837-1913**	**255**	**1000**	**1750**	**1000**	**Financier, philanthropist, M. Bond-$600**
Morgan, John Pierpont, Jr.	1867-1943	125	215	300	125	Financier
Morgan, John Tyler	1824-1907	150	245	400		ESPV, SALS-3-4X; lawyer, USS; First Manassas, Murfreesboro, Chickamauga, WD DS-2X
Morgan, Thomas Hunt	1866-1945	125	250	500	160	U.S. geneticist, embryologist
Morgenthau, Henry Jr.	1891-1967	40	80	130	50	U.S. treasury secretary
Morita, Akio	1921-	25	50		55	Manufacturer, Sony
Morrill, Justin S.	1810-1898	40	65	100		Political leader, USS
Morris, Gouverneur	1752-1816	225	600	715		CC, LS-UC, all other forms C, NY, "Gouv Morris"
Morris, Lewis	1726-1798	650	1000	1750		Signer DOI; militia general; ANS-$900, ESPV-ALS

GEN—POLIT L

With all good wishes
Helen Keller

Helen Keller

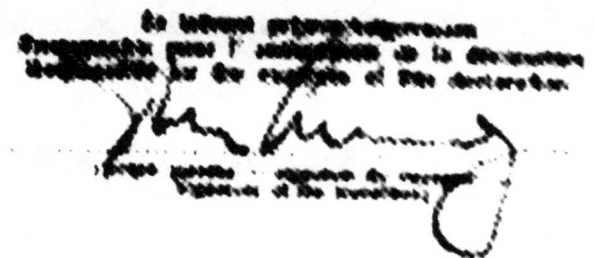

John F. Kennedy

Jacqueline Kennedy

.ncerely,

John F. Kennedy

Jacqueline Kennedy

Robert Kennedy

Jacqueline Bouvier

Jacqueline Kennedy (Bouvier)

Joseph B. Kershaw

John F. Kennedy

Husband E. Kimmel

NAME	DATES	SIG	DS	ALS	SP	COMMENTS
Morris, Robert	1734-1806	350	1200	1575		Signer; SC-$800; SDS-10-15X; ESPV-DS
Morris, William H.	1827-1900	75	150	250		WP, historian; Gettysburg, Wilderness, Spotsylvania
Morse, Samuel F. B.	1791-1872	500	1325	1575		Telegraph signals
Mortier, Edouard Adolphe Casimir Joseph	1768-1835	40	125	250		French marshal of the Empire
Morton, John	c. 1724-1777	450	1000	1275		Signer DOI; PA
Morton, Levi	1824-1920	50	100	225		Banker, U.S. vice president
Mosby, John S.	1833-1916	375	800	1950	3125	CSA general, ESPV-WD
Moses, Anna Mary Robertson	1860-1961	200	450	800		"Grandma", Amer. paint. SP-$650, ALS-2X
Moses, Robert	1888-1981	20	40	50	50	Government official
Mosley, Sir Oswald	1896-1980	25	55	150	120	Politician
Motherwell, Robert	1915-1991	75	150	300		American painter, Abstract Express., SDS-2X
Mott, Gershom	1822-1884	40	100	150		ESPV-ALS; MW, rrd. paymaster; AOTP, Seven Pines, Seven Days*
Mott, Lucretia	1793-1880	100	150	400	300	U.S. reformer, feminist pioneer
Mott, Sir Nevill	1905-	15	35		30	Physicist, NP
Moultrie, John	1729-1798	200	400	500		Loyalist; lt. gov. of E. FL.
Moultrie, William	1730-1805	150	300			Cont'l general; SL; gov. SC
☆ **Mountbatten, Louis Francis Albert V.N.**	**1900-1979**	**100**	**200**	**300**	**225**	**British admiral, statesman, SDS-3-4X**
Mower, Joseph A.	1827-1870	45	100	150		Compiled an impressive military record; carpenter, MW; Iuka, Corinth, Vicksburg, Red River*
Moyer, Andrew J.	1899-1959	40	75	100	50	Penicillin production inventor
Moynihan, Daniel P.	1927-	10	25		20	U.S. politician, FA
Moyroud, Louis Marius	1914-	15	35	45	25	Photo composing machine
Mubarak, Hosni	1928-	60	125		75	Egyptian president
Mucha, Alphonse	1860-1939	100	225	350		Czech painter, designer
Mueller, George E.	1918-	10	30		25	U.S. engineer
Mueller, Paul John	1892-1964	20	40	50	35	American general, WWII
Muhammad, Elijah	1897-1975	150	350	500	250	Religious leader

NAME	DATES	SIG	DS	ALS	SP	COMMENTS
Muhlenberg, John Peter Gabriel	1746-1807	150	350			Lutheran clergyman; Cont'l general. politician
Muir, John	1838-1914	700	1500	2000		Naturalist
Muir, Malcolm	1885-1979	40	80	150	65	Created Business Week, headed Newsweek
Mullane, Richard M.		8		25	10	Discovery, 8/30/84, Atlantis, 2/28/90, 12/2/88
Mullin, Willard	1902-1978	15			40	Sports cartoonist
Mulroney, Brian	1939-	15	30		25	Canadian prime minister
Mumford, Lewis	1895-1990	25	50	100	50	Writer, reformer, educator
Munch, Edvard	1863-1944	75	275			Norwegian painter, etcher
Munsey, Frank A.	1854-1925	25	50	70	65	Publisher, financier
Murat, Joachim, King of Naples	1767-1815	150	350	575		French marshal of the Empire, SDS-2X, ESPV
Murdoch, Rupert	1931-	10	25	50	30	News Corporation Ltd. CEO
Murphy, Frank	1890-1949	60	180	300	125	SC: 1940-1949, MI, atty. gen.
Murphy, Thomas S.		10	20	30	15	Capital Cities Communication executive
Murray, Allen E.	1929-	5	10	20	10	Retired Mobil Corp. executive
Murray, Joseph E.	1919-	20	40		25	Surgeon, NP
Murray, Philip	1886-1952	30	40	55	40	Labor leader
Musgrave, F. Story		8		30	15	Challenger, 4/4/83, Atlantis, 11/24/91, RS
Musgrave, Richard A.	1910-	10	25	50	20	"The Theory of Public Finance," economist
Muskie, Edmund S.	1914-	15	30		25	U.S. politician
Mussolini, Benito	**1883-1945**	**375**	**500**	**3000**	**1200**	**Italian fascist dictator, assassinated, ESPV-ALS**
Muybridge, Eadweard	1830-1904	250	500	750		U.S. photographer, scarce
Myers, Russell	1938-	10			30	"Broom Hilda," RS
Nadar (Gaspard-Felix Tournachon)	1820-1910	100	200	400		French photographer
Nader, Ralph	1934-	10	25	50	25	Reformer
Nagel, Steven R.		5		20	10	Discovery, 6/17/85, Challenger, 10/30/85, A91
Naglee, Henry M.	1815-1886	40	75	150		SDS-5X; MW, banking business; Washington, Peninsular

NAME	DATES	SIG	DS	ALS	SP	COMMENTS
Nagy, Imre	c.1896-1958	75	200		150	Communist premier
Naito-Mukai, Chiaki		10	20	20	10	Columbia, 7/8/94, 1st Japanese woman, RS
Nakasone, Yasuhiro	1918-	25	45		40	Japanese prime minister
Napier, Charles James	1782-1853	20	40	80		British general
Napier, Robert Cornelis	1810-1890	40	60	130		British field marshal
Napoleon I (France)	1769-1821	800	2000			LS-$1395, $2200, Emperor of the French, SDS-4X
Napoleon II	1811-1832	275	650			Son of Napoleon I
Napoleon III (France)	1808-1873	100	465	550		DS-$500, MA (DS)-$600
Nash, Sir Walter	1882-1968	25	50	75	40	New Zealand prime minister
Nasser, Gamal Abdel	1918-1970	100	200	350	250	Egypt. pres., Arab unif. advocate, SDS-2X
Nast, Thomas	1840-1902	145	375	400		Political cartoonist, created pol. party symbols
Nathans, Daniel, Dr.	1928-	15	30		30	Microbiologist, NP
Necker, Jacques	1732-1804	115	300			French statesman
Neel, Louis E.F.	1904-	15	30		25	Physicist, NP
Negley, James Scott	1826-1901	50	100	150		Pitt Univ., MW, congress; Kentucky, Murfreesboro
☆ **Nehru, Jawaharial**	**1889-1964**	**150**	**400**	**700**	**400**	**Indian prime minister**
Neill, Thomas H.	1826-1885	50	100	150		WP; Frontier, Salem Church, Mine Run
Neiman, le Roy	1927-	15	35		25	Illustrator, RS
Nelson, Allison	1822-1862	415	500			lawyer, SL, MW, mayor of Atlanta; Devall's Bluff, scarce
Nelson, George		5	15	25	15	Challenger, 4/6/84, Columbia, 1/12/86
☆ **Nelson, Horatio**	**1758-1805**	**675**	**1500**	**2900**		**British naval hero; ESPV, SDS-2X**
Nelson, Samuel	1792-1873	60	165	250		SC: 1845-1872, NY
Nelson, Thomas (Jr.)	1739-1789	550	1500	2750		Patriot; Signer DOI; militia general; gov. VA
Nelson, William	1824-1862	425	630			Only naval officer to be full-rank maj. gen.; Shiloh, Corinth, ESPV
Nevelson, Louis	1899-1988	50	100	175		Russian-born American sculptor, painter
Nevins, Allan	1890-1971	20	40		30	U.S. historian, biographer

Martin Luther King

Martin Luther King

Rufus King

Pyotr Kropotkin

Simon Lake

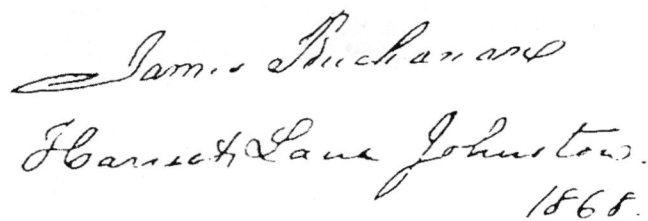

James Buchanan & Harriet Lane

John Langdon

Francis Lightfoot Lee

Robert E. Lee

Robert E. Lee

Robert E. Lee

NAME	DATES	SIG	DS	ALS	SP	COMMENTS
Newhouse, Samuel	1895-1979	25	50	75	40	U.S. publishing and broadcast magnate
Newman, James H.		5	15	25	10	Discovery, 9/1/93
Newman, John H.	1801-1890	160	340	400	400	Roman Catholic convert, cardinal
☆ **Newton, Issac**	**1642-1727**	**3500**	**4000**	**8000**		**English nat. philosopher, mathe., SLS-2-3X, SDS-2-3X**
Newton, John	1822-1895	75	150	300		Congress; Washington, Fredericksburg, Gettysburg*
Ney, Michel, Prince de la Moskova	1769-1815	150	300	525		"Le Rougeaud, Bravest of the Brave," PU
Nicholas I	1796-1855	600	1200			Tsar of Russia
Nicholas II (Russia)	1868-1918		2500			TDS-$3000, DS-$1800
Nicholls, Francis Redding T.	1834-1912	75	150	200		WP, Gov. of Louisiana; First Manassas, Valley, Chancellorsville
Nickerson, Franklin S.	1826-1917	40	75	100		Lawyer; Baton Rouge, Louisiana, Red River
Nicollier, Claude		15	30		30	Atlantis, 7/31/92, 1st Swiss astronaut, E1993
Nidetch, Jean	1923-	10	25		20	Entrepreneur
Niebuhr, Reinhold	1892-1971	45	100	150	65	Protestant theologian
Nietzsche, Friedrich	1844-1900	600	1150			German philosopher, poet, ALS-ESPV
Nightingale, Florence	1820-1910	400	800	1050		British founder of modern nursing, SB-$395
Nikolayev, Andrian G.		90	200	425	175	Vostok 3, Soyuz 9
Nimitz, Chester William	1885-1966	125	350	375	400	American admiral, WWI, WWII
Nixon, John	1733-1808	150	300	450		Patriot merchant; financier; first pu. reader DOI
☆ **Nixon, Richard Milhous**	**1913-1994**	**250**	**650**	**4000**	**400**	**PL, only pres. to resign, resig. letter-$2500; SHIPSP:5950, SDS-2X, ESPV-PD**
Nixon, Thelma Catherine Patricia Ryan	1912-1993	50	100	280	200	(1940); NV; D-2; WHC - $75 - $130, First Lady
Nobel, Alfred	1833-1896	200	400	800	400	Chemist
Nobile, Umberto	1885-1978	45	145		100	Aviator
Noel-Baker, Philip	1889-1982	15	30		30	British Labour statesman
Noguchi, Isamu	1904-1988	40	75	100		American sculptor, designer
Nordenskjold, Nils Baron	1832--1901	200	300		300	Artic navigator

NAME	DATES	SIG	DS	ALS	SP	COMMENTS
Nordenskjold, Otto	1869-1928	175	250		250	Explorer, geologist
Noriega, Manuel A.	1939-	20	35		30	Soldier, politician, RS
Norris, George W.	1861-1944	15	30	55	45	Political leader, USS
Norstad, Lauris	1907-1988	30	65	85	75	American air force general, WWII
North, Douglass C.	1920-	10	25	40	15	Economist, educator
North, Oliver	1943-	15	35	50	25	U.S. soldier, political hopeful
North, Sir Frederick "Lord"	1732-1792	100	350	500		British Prime Minister
Northrop, John H.	1891-1987	20	40		50	Biochemist
Northrop, John K.	1895-1981	30	65		75	Aircraft designer
Northrup, Lucius Bellinger	1811-1894	100	200	300		friend of Jefferson Davis; WP, practiced medicine; Commissary general of the C.S.A.
Noyce, Robert N.	1927-1990	30	75	125	50	Semiconductor device-and-lead structure
Noyes, John H.	1811-1886	35	80	135		Reformer
Nye, Gerald P.	1892-1971	10	25	30	15	Political leader, USS
Nyren, Neil S.		5	10	15	15	G.P. Putnam's Sons executive
Oakley, Annie	1860-1926	2250	5000		5000	Rodeo star, sharp-shooter
Ochoa, Ellen		5		20	10	Discovery, 4/8/93, RS!
Ochs, Adolph S.	1858-1935	50	100	200	75	Publisher
Ockels, Wubbo J.		8		25	12	Challenger, 10/30/85, RS
O'Connell, Daniel	1775-1847	100	300	700		Irish political leader, "The Liberator"
O'Conner, Bryan D.		5	15	25	10	Atlantis, 11/26/85, Columbia, 6/5/91
O'Connor, Sandra Day	1930-	35	175	250	50	SC: 1981-, AZ
Ogden, Aaron	1756-1839	50	100	200		Cont'l officer; gov. NJ; steamboat pioneer
Oglesby, Richard J.	1824-1899	50	100	130		3-time gov. Ill.; MW, SL, USS; Fort Henry, Fort Donelson, Corinth
O'Keeffe, Georgia	1887-1986	325	500	1000		American painter, ALS, DS - 2-3.5X
Oldenburg, Claes	1929-	30	75	125	40	Swedish-born sculptor
Oldendorf, Jesse Bartlett	1887-1974	50	100	160	75	American admiral, WWI, WWII
Oliphant, Sir Mark	1901-	20			40	Nuclear physicist
Oliphant, Pat	1935-	15			35	Political cartoonist

NAME	DATES	SIG	DS	ALS	SP	COMMENTS
Oliver, John M.	1828-1872	50	125	235		St. John's College, super. postal service; Shiloh, Corinth, Atlanta, Carolina
Olsen, Kenneth H.	1926-	10	20	45	20	Digital Equipment Corp. founder
Onassis, Aristotle	1906-1975	200	300	450	250	Shipping magnate, SALS-2X
O'Neal, Edward Asbury	1818-1890	70	160	250		LaGrange College, lawyer, Gov. Alabama; Peninsular, Seven Pines, Maryland*
O'Neill, Thomas P. "Tip"	1912-1994	15	35	55	40	U.S. speaker of the house, congressman
Onizuka, Ellison S.		150			200	Challenger, 1/28/86, killed during launch
Opdycke, Emerson	1830-1884	50	100			Mercantile business; Shiloh, Chickamauga, Chattanooga*
☆ **Oppenheimer, J. Robert**	**1904-1967**	**600**	**1200**		**1500**	**U.S. physicist, Los Alamos director, ESPV-all forms, SDS-2X**
Opper, Fredrick Burr	1857-1937	35			300	Cartoonist, "Happy Hooligan"
Ord, Edward O.	1818-1883	75	150	400		WP, MW; Harper's Ferry, Corinth, Vicksburg
O'Reilly, Anthony F.J.	1936-	5	10	20	10	H.J. Heinz Co. executive
O'Reilly, John B.	1844-1890	30	55	125	50	Reformer
Orpen, Sir William	1878-1931	50	150	375		Irish-born painter
Ortega, Daniel	1945-	25			50	Nicaraguan guerrilla leader
Osborn, Thomas O.	1832-1904	50	100	150		Ohio Univ., lawyer, diplomat; Drewry's Bluff, Fort Gregg
Osborne, Burl	1937-	5	10	15	10	Publisher
Osterhaus, Peter J.	1823-1917	50	100	150		Clerk, diplomat, wholesale hardware business; Wilson's Creek, Elkhorn Tavern, Vicksburg*
Ostwald, Wilhelm	1853-1932	70	140	275	150	German physical chemist
Oswald, Stephen S.		5		20	10	Discovery, 1/22/92, Discovery, 4/8/93, RS
Otis, Elisha Graves	1811-1861	150	400	550		Elevator pioneer
Otis, James	1725-1783	275	510	730		Patriot politician; publicist; orator; scarce sig., SALS-2X
Otto, Nikolaus August	1832-1891	200	400	600		Gas motor engine, SALS-2X
Oudinot, Nicolas Charles, Duke of Reggio	1767-1847	80	165			French marshal of the Empire

Stephen D. Lee

Stephen D. Lee

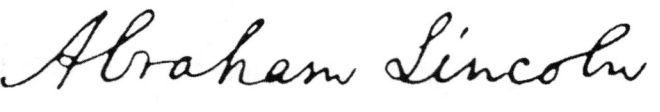

Francis Lewis

John Lewis

Abraham Lincoln

Abraham Lincoln

Abraham Lincoln

Abraham Lincoln

Abraham Lincoln

Abraham Lincoln

Abraham Lincoln

Abraham Lincoln

Abraham Lincoln

NAME	DATES	SIG	DS	ALS	SP	COMMENTS
Outcault, Richard	1863-1928	100			250	Cartoonist, "Yellow Kid," sketch 1250 "Buster Brown" sketch 800
Overmyer, Robert F.		25	50		100	Columbia, 11/11/82, FA
Owen, Joshua T.	1821-1887	50	100	165		Founded NY Daily Register; Jefferson College, teacher, lawyer, SL; AOTP*
Owen, Robert	1771-1858	75	200	300		British political philosopher, reformer
☆ **Paca, William**	**1740-1799**	**725**	**1750**	**2750**		**Signer DOI; Gov. MD; jurist; "Wm Paca"**
Pace, Arrow K.	1921-	10	20	30	15	Economist, educator
Paderewski, Ignance	1860-1941	150	400	500	400	Polish statesman, pianist, sig.-$95, ESPV
Page, Richard Lucian	1807-1901	125	210	500		first cousin of Robert E. Lee; CSN; Port Royal, Fort Morgan
Page, Robert		5	10	15	10	Publisher
Page, Robert Morris	1903-1992	25	75	150	60	U.S. physicist, radar developer
Page, Walter	1855-1918	45	90	150		Writer, diplomat
Pahlavi, Mohammed R.	1919-1980	100	200	300	225	Shah of Persia (Iran)
Pailes, William A.		5	15	25	10	Atlantis, 10/4/85
Paine, Charles J.	1833-1916	75	150	260		"America's Cup" defender, Harvard, lawyer, yachtsman; Washington, Dept. of the Gulf, Drewry's Bluff
Paine, Eleazer A.	1815-1882	60	125	200		Personal friend of A. Lincoln; WP, lawyer, dep. US marshal; Paducah, KY, Corinth, Dist. Western Kentucky
Paine, Halbert E.	1826-1905	50	100	200		Author, "A Treatise on the Law..."; teacher, Western Reserve Univ., congress; Washington, Dist. of Illinois,
☆ **Paine, Robert Treat**	**1731-1814**	**275**	**500**	**1150**		**Signer DOI & OBP; Gov. CT; CC**
Paine, Thomas	1737-1809	4000				U.S. political theorist, scarce
Palade, George E.	1912-	15	30		25	Cell biologist
Paley, William S.	1901-1990	25	45	75	40	Built CBS communication empire
Palmer, Alexander	1872-1936	15	25	40	25	Political leader, USHR, atty. general
Palmer, Innis N.	1824-1900	50	100	200		WP, MW; First Manassas, Peninsular, Williamsburg*
Palmer, John M.	1817-1900	100	150	225		Presidential candidate, Shurtleff College, lawyer, gov. Ill., USS; New Madrid, Island No.10, Corinth, Atlanta

NAME	DATES	SIG	DS	ALS	SP	COMMENTS
Palmer, John McAuley	1870-1955	45	80	150	75	American general WWI, WWII
Palmer, Joseph Benjamin	1825-1890	100	200	255		Union Univ., SL, mayor of Murfreesboro; Murfreesboro, Chickamauga, Jonesboro
Palmerston, Henry J.T.	1784-1865	40	75	150		3rd Viscount, British prime minister
Palmerston, Viscount	1784-1865	50	100	150		British Whig-liberal prime minister
Pankhurst, Emmeline	1858-1928	50	150	250		British woman suffragist
Papandreou, Andreas George	1919-1996	30	70		50	Greek leftist politician
Papandreou, Georgios	1888-1968	40			75	Greek politician, prime minister
Papen, Franz von	1879-1969	75	175	225	150	German politician
Parazynski, Scott E.		5	15	25	10	Atlantis, 11/3/94
Pareto, Vilfredo	1848-1923					Italian economist, sociologist
Parise, Ronald A.		5	15	25	15	Columbia, 12/2/90, Endeavour, 3/2/95
Parke, John G.	1827-1900	100	175	260		WP, superintendent military academy; Maryland, Fredericksburg, Knoxville, Overland
Parker, George Marshall	1889-1968	35	55	75	55	American general, WWI, WWII
Parker, Louis	1906-	10	20		15	Parker Instrument Co. executive
Parker, Louis W.	1906-	25	60	125	30	Television receiver
Parker, Robert A.R.		5	15	25	15	Columbia, 11/28/83, Columbia, 12/2/90
Parker, Theodore	1810-1860	60	110	150		Reformer
Parkinson, Roger	1942-	5	10	15	10	Globe and Mail CEO
Parkman, Francis	1823-1893	35	100	175		U.S. historian
Parrish, Maxfield	1870-1966	250	475	800		American illustrator, ALS/TLS-2X
Parson, Mosby Monroe	1822-c.1865	265	400	700		SALS - 2X; MW, lawyer, SL; Carthage, Springfield, Elkhorn, Arkansas
Parsons, John T.	1913-	15	25	40	25	Numerical control of machine tools
Parsons, Lewis	1818-1907	75	150	300		Transportation expert; Yale, Harvard, bank pres.; Dept. of the Mississippi
Parsons, Samuel Holden	1737-1789	230	375	450		Cont'l general; Indian commissioner
Pasteur, Louis	**1822-1895**	**600**	**1000**	**2000**	**3000**	**French chemist, orig. pasteurization**
Patch, Alexander McCarrell, Jr.	1889-1945	100	200	300	225	American general, WWI, WWII

NAME	DATES	SIG	DS	ALS	SP	COMMENTS
Pate, Randolph McCall	1898-1961	20	40	65	70	U.S. marine corps general, WWII, KW
Paterson, John	1744-1808	100	200	300		Cont'l general
Patrick, Marsena R.	1811-1888	50	100	150		Respected disciplinarian, canal boat driver, WP; Second Manassas, AOTP - provost marshal
Patrick, Mason Mathews	1863-1942	40	65	100	60	U.S. army officer and air corps gen., WWI
Patsayev, Viktor I.		3400				Soyuz 11, all 3 cosmonauts killed, impos. sig., ESPV
Patten, Chris	1944-	15			30	British statesman
Patten, John		5	10	20	10	Business Week Group publisher
Patterson, Clair C.	1922-1995	30	60	150	50	U.S. geochemist
Patton, George Smith	**1885-1945**	**1250**	**2600**	**4250**	**5000**	**American general, WWI, WWII, SALS-2X, ESPV-ALS**
Paul	1754-1801	250	500	1250		Tsar of Russia
Paul I (Greece)	1901-1964	60	125		115	King of the Hellenes
Paul VI	1897-1978		500		1000	Pope of Roman Catholic Church-1963
Paul, Alice	1885-1977	30	100	150	65	Reformer
Pauling, Linus	1901-1994	50	300	450	100	U.S. chemist, political activist, RS
Paxton, Elisha Franklin "Bull"	1828-1863	750	2250			Staff of Stonewall Jackson, ESPV - LS/DS; Washington Coll., Yale, UVA; First Manassas, Chancellorsville, Fredericks, scarce
Payne, William Henry Fitzhugh	1830-1904	125	250	350		ESPV - LS/DS; VMI, UVA, lawyer, Southern Railway; Army of Northern Virginia,* SALS-2X
Payton, Gary E.		5	15	25	10	Discovery, 1/24/84
Peabody, Elizabeth P.	1804-1894	125				U.S. education pioneer, fnd. 1st kindergarten
Peabody, George	1795-1869	50	115	415		U.S. financier, philanthropist
Peale, Charles Willson	1741-1827	225	450	900		American painter, inventor, ALS-2X
Peale, Norman Vincent	1898-1993	30	75	125	50	U.S. religious leader, RS
Peale, Rembrandt	1778-1860	225	450	600		American portrait painter, SALS-2X
Pearson, Lester	1897-1972	50	100	150	65	Canadian diplomat, Liberal party ldr.
Peary, Robert E.	1856-1920	200	400	425	600	Explorer

Abraham Lincoln

Abraham Lincoln

Mary T. Lincoln

Robert Todd Lincoln

Charles Lindbergh

William Livingston

Philip Livingston

James Longstreet

James Longstreet

Louis XI, King of France

Louis XIV, King of France

Louis XIV, King of France

NAME	DATES	SIG	DS	ALS	SP	COMMENTS
Peck, John James	1821-1878	100	175	350		WP, MW, banker, congress, NY State Life Ins.; Peninsular, Suffolk, North Carolina
Peck, William Raine	1818-1871	165	350			ESPV; plantation owner; Army of Northern Virginia*
Peckham, Rufus W.	1838-1909	55	125	200	125	SC: 1896-1909, NY. reclusive
Pedro II (Brazil)	1798-1834	100	200	300		Second son of John VI of Portugal
Peel, Robert	1788-1850	75	150	200		British prime minister
Pegram, John	1832-1865	700	1400			killed in action, ESPV; WP; Rich Mountain, Murfreesboro, Chickamauga, scarce
Pei, I.M.	1917-	30	60		50	Architect, RS
Pelham, Henry	1696-1754	50	125	200		British statesman
Pemberton, John Clifford	1814-1881	200	425	550		Originator of Coca-Cola; WP, MW; Vicksburg, ESPV
Pendleton, William Nelson	1809-1883	240	375	450		ESPV - Sig.; WP, teacher, rector; Army of Northern Virginia*
Penn, John	1740-1788	1750	2000	3000		Signer DOI
☆ **Penn, William**	**1644-1718**	**1750**	**4000**			**Pennsylvania founder, scarce**
Penney, James C.	1875-1971	75	275	325	255	U.S. businessman, dept. store chain
Penniman, Nicholas G.	1938-	5	10	20	10	Publisher
Pennypacker, Galusha	1844-1916	100	200	260		Youngest US gen. ever appointed; Petersburg, Fort Fisher; Petersburg, Fort Fisher
Penrose, William Henry	1832-1903	50	125	250		Dickinson College, engineer; Second Manassas, Fredericks..., Gettysburg
Penzias, Arno	1933-	10	25		25	Astrophysicist
Pepperell, Sir William	1696-1759	125	465	500		American colonial general, FIW
Perceval, Spencer	1762-1812	100	200	300		British prime minister
Perdue, Frank	1920-	10	25		20	Food executive, RS
Perkins, Frances	1880-1965	20	40	80	30	Political leader, reformer
Perkins, George W.	1862-1920	20	40	50	30	Businessman, political leader
Perkins, Maxwell	1884-1947	20	40	50	35	Editor, publisher, SDS & SALS-2X
☆ **Peron, Eva**	**1919-1952**	**500**	**600**	**700**		**"Evita," ESPV-all forms**
Peron, Juan	1895-1974	150	400	500	550	President of Argentina
Perot, Henry Ross	1930-	15	35	130	50	EDS Corp. founder, presidential candidate

NAME	DATES	SIG	DS	ALS	SP	COMMENTS
Perry, Edward Aylesworth	1831-1889	100	225	300		Yale, lawyer, Gov. of Florida; Seven Days, Chancellorsville, Wilderness
Perry, Matthew Calbraith	1794-1858	420	650	1750		American naval officer, W1812, MW, ESPV-ALS
Perry, Oliver Hazard	1785-1819	700	800	1150		American naval officer, W1812, ESPV-ALS
Perry, William Flank	1823-1901	80	175	280		lawyer, AL superintendent, professor; Second Manassas, Gettysburg, Sharpsburg*
☆ **Pershing, John Joseph**	**1860-1948**	**100**	**250**	**325**	**500**	**American general, SAW, WWI, ESPV-SP**
Perutz, Max	1914-	15	30		25	Scientist, NP
☆ **Peter I, the Great (Russia)**	**1672-1725**	**1500**	**4000**	**7250**		**ADS-$4875, scarce in sig. form**
Peters, Mike	1943-	10			25	Ed. cartoonist, "Mother Goose" & "Grimm"
Peterson, Donald H.		10	20	30	15	Challenger, 4/4/83
Pettigrew, James Johnston	1828-1863	400				often illegible handwriting, ESPV; UNC, professor, SL; Peninsular, Seven Pines, Petersburg,* scarce
Pettus, Edmund Winston	1821-1907	75	150	350		His brother was Gov. Mississippi, SDS- 8X; Clinton College, USS; Vicksburg, Chattanooga, Carolinas
Pfeiffer, Eckhard	1941-	10	20	30	10	Compaq Computer Corp CEO
Phelps, Ashton Jr.	1945-	5	10	15	10	Publisher
Phelps, John S.	1814-1886	40	100	150		Trinity College, lawyer, congress, gov. Mich.; Pea Ridge
Phelps, John W.	1813-1885	50	150	200		Prolific writer; WP, MW; Newport News, Dept. of the Gulf
Philip II (Portugal)	1527-1598	260	1375			LS-$2750
Philip, prince consort (England)	1921-	125	250	300		Duke of Edinburgh
Philipson, Morris	1926-	5	10	20	10	Publisher
Phillips, Wendell	1811-1884	50	75	150		Reformer
Phillips, William	c.1731-1781	200	400			British general; brilliant artilleryman; PU
Piaget, Jean	1896-1980	150	300			Psychologist
Piatt, Abram S.	1821-1908	50	100	200		Farmer, lawyer, editor; West Virginia, Second Manassas, Maryland*
Picard, Dennis J.	1932-	10	15	25	10	Raytheon Co. CEO

NAME	DATES	SIG	DS	ALS	SP	COMMENTS
Picard, Emile	1856-1941	75	165	360		Mathmatician
Picasso, Pablo	1881-1973	1000	2000	3000	1500	Spanish painter, FA, S. serigraph-$1100, ESPV
Piccard, Auguste	1884-1962	35	80	140	65	Physicist
Piccard, Jean	1884-1963	50	125		100	Chemist
Pick, Lewis A.	1890-1956	40	115	200	50	Amer. gen. of engineers, WWI, WWII
Pickering, Timothy	1745-1829	225	600	1400		ESPV - ALS; Sec. of War; SALS-$2800
Pickering, William	1858-1938	10	25	50	20	Astronomer
☆ **Pickett, George Edward**	**1825-1875**	**1000**	**1500**	**2650**		**ESPV; WP, insurance agent; Peninsular, Fredericksburg, Gettysburg***
Pierce, Byron R.	1829-1924	40	80	160		Dentist, hotel operator; First Manassas, Seven Pines, Gettysburg*
☆ **Pierce, Franklin**	**1804-1869**	**425**	**700**	**800**		**NC-1565, SDS-2X, SALS-2X**
Pierce, Jane Means Appleton	1806-1863	230	475	1000		(1834); NH; S-3, First Lady
Pillsbury, Charles A.	1842-1899	60	125			Flour miller, ESPV
Pike, Albert	1809-1891	75	175	250		controversial figure; teacher, poet, author, lawyer, editor, MW; Elkhorn Tavern
Pike, Zebulon Montgomery	1779-1813	250	600	1100		American general, explorer, W1812
Pile, William A.	1829-1889	50	100	150		Minister, congress, diplomat, tty. gov. NM; Benton Barracks, Mobile, Fort Blakely
Pillow, Gideon Johnson	1806-1878	130	340	425		practiced law with James K. Polk; Univ. of Nashville, MW, lawyer; Belmont, ESPV-DS
Pilsudski, Joseph	1867-1935	125	300	500	275	Polish statesman
Pinchot, Gifford	1865-1946	40	100	150	60	Political leader, governor (PA)
Pinckney, Charles	1757-1824	250	600	1250		CC, ALS-v. rare, LS-rare, SDS-2X, SC
Pinckney, Thomas	1750-1828	225	450			Cont'l officer; Gov. SC; ADC Gates
Pinkerton, Allan	1819-1884	250	575	1200	1000	Detective, ESPV-ALS
Pinkham, Lydia Estes	1819-1883	40	100	125		Businesswoman
Piper, William	1881-1970	150	300		200	Aircraft manufacturer, ESPV
Pissarro, Camille	1830-1903	300	750	1350		French painter, graphic artist

Louis

Louis XV

Henry R. Luce

Thomas Lynch Jr.

DOUGLAS MacARTHUR.

Douglas MacArthur

Douglas MacArthur

"Dolley" Madison

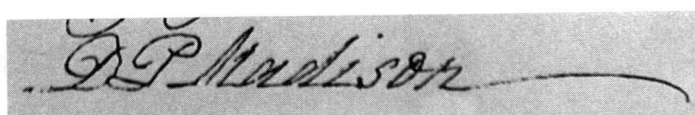

"Dolley" Madison

James Madison

James Madison

James Madison

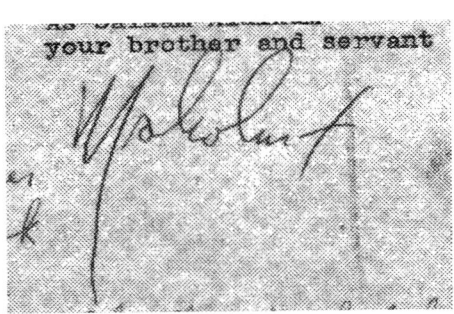
your brother and servant

Malcom X (Malcom Little)

Malcom X

NAME	DATES	SIG	DS	ALS	SP	COMMENTS
Pitcher, Thomas G.	1824-1895	50	100	150		WP, MW, WP-superintendent; Cedar Mountain, Second Manassas
Pitney, Mahlon	1858-1924	50	75	150	40	SC: 1912-1922, NJ, hard-working, controversial
Pitt, William the Elder	1708-1778	125	300			British statesman
Pitt, William the Younger	1759-1806	150	300	500		British prime minister
Pittman, H. Doyle		5	10	15	10	Publisher
Pius IX	1792-1878	70	180	230		Pope of Roman Catholic Church-1846
Pius VII	1742-1823		1750			Pope of Roman Catholic Church-1800
Pius XI	1857-1939	400	1000		1000	Pope of Roman Catholic Church-1922
Pius XII	1876-1958	350	750		700	Pope Roman Catholic Church-1939, ESPV, SDS-2X
Planck, Max	1858-1947	150	350	825	350	German physicist, quantum theory dev.
Plank, Charles J.	1915-	20	40	75	40	Gasoline and petroleum prod. pioneer
Platt, Lewis E.	1942 -	5	10	20	10	Hewlett-Packard Co. CEO
Pleasonton, Alfred	1824-1897	50	100	200		WP, MW; Washington, Peninsular, Maryland, WD-2-3X
Plunkett, Roy J.	1910-1994	30	60	150	60	U.S. chemist, created "Teflon"
Poe, Orlando M.	1832-1895	55	120	200		WP, lighthouse board, engineer; Peninsular, Second Manassas, Knoxville*
Pogue, William R.		10	30	40	20	Skylab 4
Poincare, Henri	1854-1912	75	150	275	150	French mathematician, physicist
Poincare, Raymond	1860-1934	50	100	130	100	French statesman, 9th pres. of Rep.
☆ **Polk, James Knox**	**1795-1849**	**400**	**1650**	**3450**		**ALS content $5500-$6000; FF:1000, APT-2000**
Polk, Leonidas	1806-1864	400	550			close friend of Jefferson Davis, KIA, ESPV; WP; Shiloh, Red River, Perryville, Atlanta*
Polk, Lucius Eugene	1833-1892	110	240	275		UVA, SL; Murfreesboro, Chickamauga, Chattanooga*
Polk, Sarah Childress	1803-1891	425	650	1100	1200	(1824); TN; No sons or daughters, First Lady
Pomeroy, Seth	1706-1777	200				Cont'l general; shadowy figure, ESPV

NAME	DATES	SIG	DS	ALS	SP	COMMENTS
Pompidou, Georges	1911-1974	25	50		40	French Gaulist political leader
Poniatoff, Alexander	1892-1980	40	65		55	U.S. electronics engineer
Poniatowski, Prince Jozef Antoni	1762-1813	525				Polish-French marshal of the Empire, ESPV
Poole, William	1937-	10	25	45	15	Economist, educator
Poor, Enoch	1736-1780	200	500	750		Cont'l general, ESPV-ALS
Poor, Henry W.	1812-1905	25	50	60		Business leader
Pope, John	1822-1892	100	150	300		Controversial, related to M.T. Lincoln; WP, MW; Madrid, Island No. 10, Army of Virginia, WD-2X
Pope, Norris		5	10	20	10	Publisher
Popoff, Frank P.	1935-	5	10	25	10	Dow Chemical Co. CEO
Popovich, Pavel R.		85	200	400	175	Vostok 4, Soyuz 14
Porsche, Ferdinand	1875-1951	225	500		500	Automobile designer, ESPV
Porter, Andrew	1820-1872	100	200	475		Related to M.T. Lincoln; WP, MW; First Manassas, AOTP - provost marshal gen.
Porter, David	1780-1843	60	150	275		American naval officer, W1812
Porter, Edward	1823-1889	50	100	150		Columbia, farmer; Chief of staff - Foster
Porter, Fitz J.	1822-1901	100	200	400		SALS-2X; WP, MW, WP-instructor; Peninsular, Seven Days, Gaine's Mill*
Porter, Rodney R.	1917-1985	30	75		55	Biochemist, NP
Porter, Sir George	1920-	15	40		30	Physical chemist
Posey, Carnot	1818-1863	420				ESPV; UVA, planter, MW; Army of Northern Virginia*
Post, Emily	1872-1960	50	80	125	75	Etiquette authority
Post, Marjorie M.		30	75	100	50	Philanthropist
Post, Wiley	**1999-1935**	**275**	**800**	**600**	**750**	**N.A.H.O.F., sig. w/H. Gatty-$595(FDC), ESPV**
Potter, Joseph H.	1822-1892	50	100	200		WP, MW, chief of staff of the corps; New Mexico, Chancellorsville
Potter, Robert B.	1829-1887	80	150	300		Union College, rrd. receiver; Cedar Mountain, Maryland, Vicksburg
Potts, Benjamin F.	1836-1887	75	150	260		Teacher, lawyer, tty. gov. Mont.; West Virginia, Cross Keys, Vicksburg, Atlanta*

☆

GEN
POLIT

P

NAME	DATES	SIG	DS	ALS	SP	COMMENTS
Powell, Adam Clayton, Jr.	1908-1972	40	55	75	45	Political leader
Powell, Colin Luther	1937-	40	125	350	100	American general, VW, KW
Powell, Lewis F., Jr.	1907-1998	40	125	175	75	SC: 1972-1987, VA
Powell, William H.	1825-1904	50	100	150		Ironworker, Western Nail Co.; Shenandoah, Cedar Creek
Powers, Hiram	1805-1873	75	150	375		American sculptor
Pownall, Thomas	1722-1805	175	350			Colonial Gov.
Poynter, Sir Edward	1836-1919	25	50	100		English painter, administrator
Pratt, Calvin E.	1828-1896	75	150	275		Justice of the peace, lawyer; Peninsular, Mechanicsville, Fredericksburg
Precourt, Charles J.		5	10	15	10	Columbia, 4/26/93, Atlantis, 6/27/95, RS
Prelog, Vladimir	1906-	15	30		20	Organic chemist, NP
Prentiss, Benjamin M.	1919-1901	50	100	160		MW, pension agent, postmaster; Shiloh, Dist. of Eastern Arkansas
Prescott, Oliver	1731-1804	75	150			Physician and militia general
Prescott, William	1796-1859	50	100	200		Early American historian
Preston, John Smith	1809-1881	75	150	225		Harvard, lawyer, UVA, SL; First Manassas
Preston, William	1816-1887	125	250	400		SDS-2X; Harvard, MW, SL; Murfreesboro, Chickamauga, Corinth,* SALS-2X
Price, George	1901-1995	15				New Yorker cartoonist
Price, Sterling	1809-1867	275	375	600		SALS-7-10X, ESPV; lawyer, SL, USHR, MW, Gov. Missouri; Wilson's Creek, Elkhorn, Luka, Corinth, SDS-2X
Priestley, Joseph	1733-1804	400	1125	2000		British chemist, co-discover of oxygen, ESPV
Prince, Henry	1811-1892	40	75	125		SALS-5X; MW, deputy paymaster gen.; Cedar Mountain, Rapidan
Procter, William C.	1862-1934	40	100	200	75	Headed U.S. soap company
Profumo, John	1915-	25	55		75	British statesman
Prudhomrae, Paul	1940-	10	25		25	Chef
Pryor, Roger Atkinson	1828-1919	140	275	385		SALS - 1.5 - 2X; Hampden-Sydney College, UVA, lawyer; Seven Days, Second Manassas, Sharpsburg, SDS-2X

Edouard Manet

Guglielmo Marconi

Frances Marion

John Marshall

Tomas G. Masaryk

Cotton Mather

Henri Matisse

Charles H. Mayo

William J. Mayo

George B. McClellan

Cyrus McCormick

NAME	DATES	SIG	DS	ALS	SP	COMMENTS
Puck, Wolfgang		5	10		10	Spago owner
Pulitzer, Joseph	1847-1911	150	300	465		Newspaper proprietor
Pulliam, Eugene	1914-	5	10	15	10	News America Publishing CEO
Pullman, George M.	1831-1897	250	500	600		Industrialist, inventor
Purcell, E.M.	1912-	15	30	50	30	Physicist, NP
Putnam, George P.	1814-1872	20	50	100	50	Publisher
Putnam, Isreal	1718-1790	230	500	725		Cont'l general; "Old Put;" DS w/Z.Butler-$2600, ESPV-DS & ALS, rare
Putnam, Rufus	1738-1824	200	400	600		Cont'l general; 1st Surv. Gen. of US
Pyle, Ernie	1900-1945	175	265	400	300	Journalist, KIA, ESPV
Pyle, Howard	1853-1911	200	350	500		American illustrator, teacher-N.C. Wyeth
Quarles, William Andrew	1825-1893	75	200	270		UVA, lawyer, railway president, SL; Vicksburg, Tennessee, Franklin
Quayle, J. Dan	1947-	15	40		30	U.S. vice president,USS, RS
Quinby, Issac F.	1821-1891	60	125	200		WP, professor, US marshal; First Manassas, Dist of Mississippi*
Quincy, Josiah	1772-1864	75	110	200		U.S. statesman, orator
Quinson, Bruno A.	1938-	5	10	15	10	Henry Holt & Co. CEO
Quitman, John Anthony	1798-1858	30	55	90		American general, politician
Rabi, Isidor Isaac	1899-1986	50	100	150	75	U.S. physicist, pioneered atomic exploration
Rabin, Yitzhak	**1922-1995**	**150**	**300**	**700**	**275**	**Israel pol. ldr., P.M., ESPV, assassin., SDS-2X, RS**
Rackham, Arthur	1867-1939	50	150	300		British artist, illustrator of children's book
Radford, Arthur William	1896-1973	40	55	100	50	American admiral, WWI, WWII
Raeder, Erich	1876-1960	55	100	200	150	German admiral, SDS-2X, SALS-2X
Raglan, Fitzroy James Henry Somerset	1788-1855	50	100	220		British field marshal
Rains, Gabriel James	1803-1881	100	300			ESPV - LS/DS; WP, arranged mine and torpedo defenses; Seven Pines
Rainwater, L. James	1917-	10	20		20	Physicist, NP
Rams, Dieter	1932-	15	30		25	Product designer
Ramsay, George D.	1802-1882	40	75	150		WP; Washington, Ordinance Dept.

☆ (next to Rabin, Yitzhak)

NAME	DATES	SIG	DS	ALS	SP	COMMENTS
Ramsay, Sir William	1852-1916	125	270	400		Chemist, NP, ESPV-DS & ALS
Ramsey, Norman F.	1915-	10	25		20	Physicist, NP
Randall, John	1905-1984	25	50		35	British physicist
Randolph, Edmund	1753-1813	225	450	525		U.S. statesman, ESPV-ALS
Randolph, Asa P.	1889-1979	50	125	235	100	Labor leader
Randolph, George Wythe	1818-1867	275	445	600		Thomas Jefferson's grandson; UVA, Sec. of War for CSA; Big Bethel
Randolph, John	1773-1833	125	250	450		U.S. Southern planter, advocate states' rights
Randolph, Peyton ☆	**c.1721-1775**	**450**	**1450**			**First Pres. Cont'l Con.; SDS-2X, ESPV, scarce**
Rankin, Jeannette	1880-1973	100	200	300	150	First woman member of U.S. Congress
Ransom, Jr., Robert	1828-1892	200	285	325		ESPV; WP, civil engineer; Seven Days, Maryland, Fredericksburg
Ransom, Matt Whitaker	1826-1904	100	240	300		elder brother of Robert Ransom; lawyer, UNC, SL, diplomat; Seven Pines, Seven Days, Sharpsburg*
Raos, John G.		10	15	20	15	Hanson Industries executive
Rasputin, Grigoriy	?1871-1916	2500				Peasant, mystic, ESPV-DS & ALS
Raum, Green B.	1829-1909	35	70	135		Lawyer, rrd. pres., congress; Corinth, Chattanooga, Atlanta
Rauschenberg, Robert	1925-	50	100			American artist, FA, litho. - $1400
Rawdon-Hastings, Francis	1754-1826	75	200	450		Brit. officer; ADC to King; statesman; ESPV
Rawlins, John A.	1831-1869	75	150	250		Lawyer, sec. of war; U.S. Grant staff
Ray, Man	1890-1977	275	500			American painter, photographer
Rayburn, Sam	1882-1961	45	60	115	65	U.S. Democratic leader
Raymond, Alex	1909-1956	40			80	Cartoonist, "Flash Gordon," "Jungle Jim"
Raymond, Lee	1938-	10	20	25	15	Exxon CEO
Read, George	1733-1798	300	615	1175		CC, ALS, LS, ADS-v. rare, DS-C, DE, full, Signer DOI; lawyer; USS
Readdy, William F.		5		20	10	Discovery, 1/22/92, 9/1/93, RS
Reagan, Anne Frances "Nancy" R. Davis	1921-	45	150	165	110	(1952); NY; S-1; D-1, First Lady, FA
Reagan, Ronald Wilson ☆	**1911-**	**250**	**600**	**1000**	**350**	**PL, oldest pres. leaving office, TLS-600, ESPV-ALS**

NAME	DATES	SIG	DS	ALS	SP	COMMENTS
Reard, Louis	1897-1984	30			65	French designer, bikini
Redon, Odilon	1840-1916	100	200	300		French painter, graphic artist
Reed, Joseph	1741-1785	100	200	300		GW military sec.; patriot; statesman
Reed, Stanley F.	1884-1980	45	100	175	80	SC: 1938-1957, KY
Reed, Thomas B.	1839-1902	20	40	50		Political leader, SL, USHR
☆ **Reed, Walter S.**	**1851-1902**	**445**	**100**	**2125**	**700**	**U.S. army pathologist, bacteriologist, ESPV, SALS-2X**
Rehnquist, William H.	1924-	45	130	215	100	SC: 1972-1986, AZ
Reich, Wilhelm	1897-1957	100	250	500		Psychoanalyst, SDS-2X
Reichstein, Tadensz	1897-	15	30		20	Chemist
Reid, Hugh T.	1811-1874	80	160	225		Lawyer, Des Moie Valley Rrd Co.; Shiloh, Corinth, Vicksburg
Reid, Whitelaw	1837-1912	35	70	100	50	Journalist, diplomat
Reightler, Kenneth S., Jr.		5		20	10	Discovery, 9/12/91, FA, Discovery, 2/3/94
Reik, Theodor	1888-1969	75	250	400		Psychoanalyst, SDS-2X
Reilly, James W.	1828-1905	50	100	200		Lawyer, SL, bank pres.; Knoxville, Atlanta, Franklin
☆ **Rembrandt Harmensz, van Rijn**	**1606-1669**	**2750**		**5000**		**Dutch painter, etcher, master of light/shade, ESPV, scarce**
Remington, Frederic	1861-1909	625	725	2125		American artist, FA, SALS-2X, ALS-2X, SE-$2000
Remington, Philo	1816-1889	60	125	250		Small-arms executive
Renault, Louis	1877-1944	50	150			Automobile manufacturer, SDS-2X
Renner, Karl	1870-1950	35	85		65	Austrian chancellor
Rennie, John	1761-1821	125	300			Civil engineer, SDS-2X
☆ **Renoir, Pierre-Auguste**	**1841-1919**	**275**	**750**	**2200**		**French Impressionist painter, SP-$5000**
Resnik, Judith A.		125	325		350	Discovery, 8/30/84, killed on Challenger 1/86, ESPV
Reuther, Walter	1907-1970	30	50	100	45	U.S. labor leader, headed UAW
Revere, Joseph W.	1812-1880	100	200	400		Grandson of Paul Revere, 7 Days, Fredericksburg, Chancellorsville;
☆ **Revere, Paul**	**1735-1818**	**3500**				**Patriot; silversmith; courier; ALS-$26000, DS $10,000, ESPV, scarce**
Revson, Charles	1906-1975	30	65		50	Business executive, Revlon

GEN — POLIT Q

James McHenry

James B. McPherson

John W. Mackay

George G. Meade

William M. McKinley

George G. Meade

William M. McKinley

Willy Messerschmitt

ttest:

Governor of the State of Ohio.

William M. McKinley

Arthur Middleton

William M. McKinley

Thomas Mifflin

NAME	DATES	SIG	DS	ALS	SP	COMMENTS
Rewald, John	1912-	10	25			German-born American art historian
Reynolds, Alexander Welch	1816-1876	80	175	215		WP, fought in Egypt after war; Western Virginia, Knoxville, Vicksburg
Reynolds, Daniel Harris	1832-1902	100	225	340		Ohio Wesleyan Univ., lawyer, Sl; Wilson's Creek, Chickamauga, Atlanta
Reynolds, John F.	1820-1863	425	1150			Killed in action, ESPV; WP, MW, WP-Commandant of cadets; Maryland, Fredericksburg, scarce
Reynolds, Joseph J.	1822-1899	65	150	200		WP, WP-instructor; Cheat Mountain, Chickamauga
Reynolds, Sir Joshua	1723-1792	200	350	700		English painter, writer, portraitist, ESPV
Rhee, Syngman	1875-1965	200	300	900	275	First pres. of S. Korea
Rhodes, Cecil	1853-1902	150	275	400		British imperialist, indust. magnate
Ricciardi, Lawrence R.	1941-	5	10	20	10	RJR Nabisco Inc. executive
Rice, Americus V.	1835-1904	50	100	200		Antioch College, lawyer, banker, congress; Shiloh, Chickasaw Bayou, Atlanta, Vicksburg
Rice, Elliott W.	1835-1887	100	150	275		Lawyer, Univ. of Albany; Belmont, Shiloh, Atlanta, Carolinas
Rice, James C.	1829-1864	400	600	1200		Yale Univ., teacher, lawyer; Peninsular, Second Manassas, Gettysburg,* ESPV, scarce
Richards, Dickinson	1895-1973	20	40	65	40	Physician
Richards, Richard N.		10		25	15	Discovery, 10/6/90, Columbia, 8/9/89, 6/25/92
Richards, Theodore	1868-1928	45	115			Chemist, NP
Richardson, Elliot	1920-	10	20		15	Lawyer, cabinet member
Richardson, Robert C.	1882-1954	30	55	80	40	American general, WWI, WWII
Richardson, Robert Vinkler	1820-1870	400	800			ESPV; lawyer, railroad business, assassinated; Shiloh, Corinth
Richardson, Sir John	1787-1865	125	200			Naturalist, explorer
Richelieu, Armand Jean	1585-1642	210	1125			Fr. states., C.M. to Louis XIII, SDS-$3500, SDS-2-3X
Richter, Burton	1931-	10	25	45	25	Particle physicist, NP, RS
Richter, Charles	1900-1985	30	50		75	Seismologist, SDS-2X

NAME	DATES	SIG	DS	ALS	SP	COMMENTS
Richthofen, Baron Manfred von	1892-1918	2500				German air ace, "The Red Baron," ESPV, scarce
Rickenbacker, Edward Vernon	**1890-1973**	**125**	**275**	**500**	**300**	**American officer, WWI, WWII, N.A.H.O.F., TLS-$125-$695-ESPV**
Rickert, Heinrich	1863-1936	40	100		65	Philosopher, SDS-2X
Ricketts, James B.	1817-1887	75	150	275		WP, MW; First & Second Manassas, Cedar Mountain*
Rickover, Hyman G.	1900-1986	100	225		200	Naval engineering officer, elusive signer
Ride, Sally K.	1951-	20		100	40	Challenger, 6/18/83, 1st U.S. woman in space
Ridgway, Matthew Bunker	1895-1993	75	170	200	150	American general, WWI, WWII, RS
Ridgeway, John	1938-	20			45	Oarsman, explorer
Riefenstahl, Leni	1902-	25	50	100	75	Film maker, photographer, RS
Riemann, Bernhard	1826-1866	125	325	1000		German mathematician, calculus dev.
Rifkind, Malcom	1946-	15	30		25	British statesman
Riis, Jacob A.	1849-1914	25	60	120	45	Reformer, journalist
Rines, Robert H.	1922-	20	50	75	30	High-definition radar pioneer
Ringling, John	1866-1936	130	650	850		Showman
Ripley, George	1802-1880	150	300	600		Social reformer
Ripley, James W.	1794-1870	50	175	200		WP; Ordinance Department
Ripley, Robert	1893-1949	100	200	250	250	Illustrator, cartoonist
Ripley, Roswell Sabine	1823-1887	200	250	450		SDS & SALS - 2X; MW, historian; Seven Days, Sharpsburg, Fort Moultrie
Ritts, Herb	1951-	15	40	65	30	U.S. photographer
Rivera, Diego	1886-1957	300	600	750		Mexican painter
Rivers, Larry	1923-	50	100	225		American painter, sculptor, graphic artist
Rivington, James	1724-1802	150	250			Journalist - 1st daily paper; printer; bookseller
Roane, John Seldon	1817-1867	275	500			ESPV; Cumberland College, SL, MW, Gov. of AK; Prairie Grove, Texas
Roberts, Benjamin S.	1810-1875	45	100	225		WP, MW, Yale; Second Manassas, Washington
Roberts, David	1796-1864	50	100	200		Scottish painter, PU

NAME	DATES	SIG	DS	ALS	SP	COMMENTS
Roberts, Oral	1918-	10	30	50	25	Evangelist, RS
Roberts, Owen J.	1875-1955	50	175	225	100	SC: 1930-1945, PA
Roberts, Sir Frederick Sleigh, Baron	1832-1914	50	110		120	British field marshal
Roberts, William Paul	1841-1910	100	300	500		SDS & SALS - 2-3X; SL, youngest general officer in CSA; North Carolina, Army of Northern Virginia*
Robertson, Beverly Holcombe	1827-1910	70	140	200		WP, insurance business; Jackson's Valley, Army of Northern Virginia*
Robertson, Felix Huston	1839-1928	70	140	200		son of Jerome B. Robertson; Baylor Univ., WP, lawyer; Murfreesboro, Chickamauga, Atlanta*
Robespierre, Maximillan	1758-1794	1250	4000			French Revolution leader, ESPV, scarce
Robinson, James C.	1817-1897	100	200	250		Totally blind during his final years; WP, MW, lt. gov. NY; Peninsular, Spotsylvania, Gettysburg, AOTP*
Robinson, James S.	1827-1892	75	150	260		Editor, publisher, rrd. comm., congress; Shenandoah, Second Manassas, Gettysburg
Robinson, Sir Robert	1886-1975	20	45		40	Chemist, NP
Rocard, Michel	1930-	15	30		20	French prime minister
Rochambeau, Jean Baptiste Don. de Vimeur	1725-1807	275	500	625		Commander of French army in America, ESPV
Rock, John	1825-1866	30	70	120		Lawyer, physician
☆ **Rockefeller, John D.**	**1839-1937**	**325**	**1500**	**1850**	**1500**	**Indus., philanthropist, Standard Oil, SB-$1500, ESPV**
Rockefeller, John D., Jr.	1874-1960	50	100	250	75	Industrialist, philanthro., UN, T. Deed-$2200
Rockefeller, Nelson	1908-1979	20	75	150	40	U.S. Republican governor of N.Y., VP, FA
Rockhill, William W.	1853-1914	45	115	150	50	Diplomat
Rockwell, Francis Warren	1886-1979	15	30	45	30	American admiral, WWI, WWII
☆ **Rockwell, Norman P.**	**1894-1978**	**160**	**300**	**500**		**Popular Amer. illus., SP-$400, S.Sk.-$750**
Roddey, Philip Dale	1826-1897	135	300	450		SDS - 3X, SALS - 4 - 5X; sheriff; North Alabama, Tennessee, WD-2X
Rodes, Robert Emmett	1829-1864	475	1200	1500		killed in action, SDS - 4X, SALS - 5 - 6X; VMI, civil engineer, professor; Seven Pines, Gaine's Mill, Sharpsburg,* ESPV, scarce, WD-2X

James Monroe

Gouverneur Morris

James Monroe

Lewis Morris

Bernard Law Montgomery

Samuel F.B. Morse

J. Pierpont Morgan

Samuel F.B. Morse

Robert Morris

John Morton

Robert Morris

Levi Morton

NAME	DATES	SIG	DS	ALS	SP	COMMENTS
Rodgers, John	1771-1838	100	375	165		American naval officer, W1812, ESPV-DS
Rodin, Auguste	1840-1917	215	400	500		Influential French sculptor, ESPV-SP
Rodney, Caesar	1728-1784	500	1225	1000		Signer DOI; Cont'l Congress; ALS-2X; ESPV
Roentgen, Wilhelm	1845-1923	550	1275	2720		German physicist, discovered the X ray
Rogers, Carl	1902-1987	25	50		50	U.S. psychotherapist, author
Rogers, Robert	1732-1795	350	875			Ranger hero; frontiersman, ESPV-all forms
Rogers, William P.	1913-	10	25		20	U.S. politician, sec, of state
Rohrer, Heinrich	1933-	15	30	50	20	Scanning tunneling microscope
☆ **Rommel, Erwin Johannes Eugen**	**1891-1944**	**725**	**1250**		**1625**	**German field mar., "Desert Fox," ESPV, scarce-ALS**
Romney, George	1734-1802	150	400	500		English painter, portraitist
Romney, George W.	1907-1995	10	25	45	15	Republican governor of Michigan
Roosa, Stuart A.		25			45	Apollo 14
Roosevelt, Anna Eleanor Roosevelt	1884-1962	65	200	450	225	(1905); NY; S-4; D-1; (padi); WHC - $150, First Lady
Roosevelt, Edith Kermit Carow	1861-1948	65	225	300	375	(1886); CT; S-4; D-1, First Lady
☆ **Roosevelt, Franklin Delano**	**1882-1945**	**250**	**1100**	**1500**	**1000**	**PL, only pres. to serve more than 2 terms, DIO, TLS-1100, WH/EMC-425**
Roosevelt, Theodore	1858-1919	300	1120	1600	2250	Youngest pres., MA-1450, APT-1300, TLS-1300, WH/EMC-550, SALS-2X, ESPV-ALS
Root, Elihu	1845-1937	75	130	200	150	U.S. lawyer, statesman, diplomat
Roper, Elmo	1900-1971	25	50		45	Public opinion analyst
Rops, Felicien	1833-1898	85	175	350		Neapolitan painter, poet, actor
Rosecrans, William S.	1819-1898	130	275	400		SALS-3X; WP, diplomat, congress, reg. of the treasury; Western Virginia, Murfreesboro, Chickamauga, WD-ALS-2X
Rosenbach, A.S.W.	1876-1952	30	60		60	Book dealer
Rosenberg, Alfred	1893-1946	150	325		400	German politician
Rosenquist, James	1933-	35	70	150		American Pop artist
Rosenwald, Julius	1862-1932	200	600			Business leader, philanthropist

NAME	DATES	SIG	DS	ALS	SP	COMMENTS
Rosinski, Edward J.	1921-	10	25	40	20	Gasoline and petroleum prod. pioneer
Ross, George	1730-1779	300	540	1000		Signer DOI; jurist; lawyer Lan.PA; ESPV-DS
Ross, Sir James C.	1800-1862	100	200			Polar explorer
Ross, Jerry L.		8		25	12	Atlantis, 4/5/91, 11/26/85, Colum., 4/26/93, RS
Ross, Lawrence Sullivan	1838-1898	200	550	800		Gov. of Texas, extremely popular, SALS-2X; Wesleyan Univ., Indian fighter, Texas Rangers; Corinth,* ESPV-DS
Ross, Leonard F.	1823-1901	50	100	155		Lawyer, MW, importer, livestock breeder; Corinth, Vicksburg
Ross, Sir Ronald	1857-1932	75	150	275		Physician, NP
Rosser, Thomas Lafayette	1836-1910	150	300	420		WP, chief railroad engineer; First Manassas, Mechanicsville, Overland,* ESPV-ALS
Rossetti, Dante Gabriel	1828-1882	100	200	400		English painter, poet, PU
Rostow, Walt	1916-	10	25	30	15	Economist, educator, advisor to JFK
Rothenstein, Sir William	1872-1945	30	60	75		British painter, writer, teacher, s. John, s. Mich.
Rothschild, Meyer A.	1743-1812	175	365	525		Founded international banking house
Rothschild, Nathan	1777-1836	300	700	1425		Banker
Rouault, Georges	1871-1958	250	450	800		French painter, sculptor, designer
Rous, Peyton	1879-1970	15	35		30	Pathologist
Rousseau, Jean-Jacques	**1712-1778**	**400**	**1500**	**3000**		**French social philosopher, ESPV**
Rousseau, Lovell H.	1818-1869	60	100	200		Lawyer, MW, SL, congress; Shiloh, Murfreesboro, Tullahoma*
Rousseau, Theodore	1812-1867	100	200	400		French landscape painter
Rowlandson, Thomas	1756-1827	250	500	750		English carcicaturist
Rowley, Thomas A.	1808-1892	60	125	200		Justice of the peace, MW, lawyer, US marshal; Yorktown, Williamsburg, Seven Pines*
Royce, Sir Henry	1863-1933	300	575			Engineer, Rolls-Royce
Rubbia, Carlo	1934-	10	25		20	Physicist, NP
Rubens, Sir Peter Paul	1577-1640	2210				Flemish Baroque painter, designer, ESPV-DS & ALS
Rubik, Ernö	1944-	20	50		45	Architect, "Rubik's Cube"

☆ Rousseau, Jean-Jacques

NAME	DATES	SIG	DS	ALS	SP	COMMENTS
Rubin, Benjamin A.	1917-	15	30	55	25	Bifurcated vaccination needle
Rubin, Robert	1938-	5	10	20	15	Economist, Clinton advisor
Rubin, Stephen E.	1941-	5	10	15	10	Doubleday CEO
Rubinstein, Helena	1870-1965	70	145	250	300	Cosmetics
Rucker, Daniel H.	1812-1910	30	75	100		MW; Quartermaster's Department
Rudkin, Margaret	1897-1967	65	125			Businesswoman, "Pepperidge Farm"
Ruger, Thomas H.	1833-1907	40	65	100		WP, lawyer, WP-superintendent; Maryland, Sharpsburg, Gettysburg, Carolina*
Ruggles, Daniel	1810-1897	125	300	600		SDS & SALS - 2X; WP, MW, rancher; Corinth, Shiloh, WD DS-2X
Ruml, Beardsley	1894-1960	10	20	25	20	Economist, banker, businessman
Runco, Mario, Jr.		5		20	10	Atlantis, 11/24/91, Endeavour, 1/13/93, RS
Rundstedt, Karl Rudolf Gerd von	1875-1953	200			300	German field marshal
Rupert, Anthony E.	1916-	15	30		30	Financier
Rush, Benjamin	**1746-1813**	**700**	**1350**	**2475**		**Signer DOI; physician; SDS-$6900**
Rusk, Dean	1909-1995	15	45	75	25	U.S. sec. of state, statesman
Ruska, Ernst	1906-1988	15	40		30	Physicist
Ruskin, John	1819-1900	60	150	200		English art critic, painter
Russell, Bertrand	1872-1970	100	250	500	275	British philosopher, logician, Nobel prize
Russell, John	1792-1878	40	80	150		British Liberal prime minister
Russell, Richard B.	1897-1971	12	25	50	20	Political leader, governor (GA), USS
Rust, Albert	1818-1870	75	165	245		lawyer, SL, USHR; Cheat Mt., Corinth, Arkansas
Rustin, Bayard	1910-1987	25	45	60	30	Reformer, SALS-2X
Rutherford, Ernest	1871-1937	175	400	1000	250	British physicist, disc. atomic nucleus
Rutledge, Edward (Ned)	1749-1800	275	600	1150		Signer DOI; Congress.; Gov. SC; SALS-2X
Rutledge, John	1739-1800	240	650	1350		SC: 1789-1791, SC, refused appoint. in 1795, CC, ALS-very rare, LS-rare, ADS-on occas.
Rutledge, Wiley B. Jr.	1894-1949	40	135	275	85	SC: 1943-1949, IA, died at the age of 55
Ryan, John Dale	1915-1983	20	40	65	35	U.S. Air Force general, WWII

☆ (star at left of Rush, Benjamin row)

GEN-POLIT Q

John S. Mosby

Tom Nast

Tom Nast

Mountbatton of Burma

Benito Mussolini

L. Gordon Cooper (Mercury 9)

John H. Glenn (Mercury 6)

Virgil I. Grissom (Mercury 4)

Walter M. Schirra (Mercury 8)

M. Scott Carpenter (Mercury 7)

Donald K. "Deke" Slayton

Alan B. Shepard Jr. (Mercury 3)

NASA- Original Mercury Astronauts

NAME	DATES	SIG	DS	ALS	SP	COMMENTS
Ryan, Thomas Fortune	1851-1928	30	75	165	80	U.S. financier, fdr. American Tobacco
Ryder, Samuel	1859-1936	50	110			Businessman, "Ryder Cup"
Ryle, Gilbert	1900-1976	50	150	200	50	British analytical philosopher
Saatchi, Charles	1943-	20	45		40	Advertiser
Saatchi, Maurice	1946-	20	45		40	Advertiser
Sabatier, Paul	1854-1950	60	100	120		Chemist, NP
Sabin, Albert B.	1906-1993	30	100	150	125	Russian/U.S. dev. of oral polio vaccine
Sadat, Anwar al-	1918-1981	100	200	300		Egyptian pres., assassinated, ESPV
Sagan, Carl	1934-1996	20	40	100	40	U.S. astronomer, writer
Sage, Russell	1816-1906	85	170	600	100	U.S. financier
Sagendorf, Forrest (Bud)	1915-1994	50			100	Cartoonist, "Popeye"
Saint-Cyr, Laurent Gouvion	1764-1830	60	135	200		French marshal of the Empire
Saint-Gaudens, Augustus	1848-1907	150	400	800		American sculptor, ALS-2X
Salk, Jonas	1914-1995	50	150	300	200	U.S. dev. of first successful polio vaccine
Salk, Lee	1926-1992	20			40	U.S. child psychologist, author
Saloman, Friedrich	1826-1897	40	80	150		Surveyor, surveyor gen. of Mo.; Missouri, Arkansas
Samuelson, Paul A.	1915-	10	30	50	25	Economist, educator
San Martin, Jose de	1778-1850	450	700			Latin American gen., statesman
Sanborn, John B.	1826-1904	50	100	200		Dartmouth, lawyer, SL, USHR, USS; Iuka, Vicksburg, Southwest Missouri
Sanders, Colonel Harland	1890-1980	50	125	175	125	KFC founder, RS!
Sanders, Wayne R.	1947-	5	10	20	10	Kimberly-Clark CEO
Sandwich, John Montagu, 4th Earl of	1718-1792	175	350	500		First Lord of Admirality; Sec. of State; P. Gen.
Sanford, Edward T.	1865-1930	100	175	250	150	SC: 1923-1930, TN
Sanger, Fredrick	1918-	15	30		30	Biochemist, NP
Sanger, Margaret	1883-1966	75	180	275	90	U.S. social reformer, birth control movement
Sansom, Art	1920-1991	10			35	Cartoonist, "The Born Loser"
☆ **Santa Anna, Antonio Lopez de**	**1794-1876**	**425**	**850**	**1500**		**Mexican gen., statesman, ANS-$800, ESPV**
Santayana, George	1863-1952	75	200	300	150	U.S. philosopher, poet, professor

NAME	DATES	SIG	DS	ALS	SP	COMMENTS
Sapir, Edward	1884-1939	60	125			German/U.S. anthropologist
Sarett, Lewis Hastings	1917-	20	40	65	35	Process of treating pregene compounds
Sargent, John Singer	1856-1925	125	275	400		American painter, portraitist
Sarnoff, David	1891-1971	75	150	175	100	U.S. broadcasting pioneer, NBC radio network
Sarte, Jean-Paul	1905-1980	150	300	400	200	French philosopher, ESPV
Sato, Eisaku	1901-1975	30	75	150	50	Japanese prime minister
Savile, Jimmy	1926-	20	40		35	radio personality
Saxton, Rufus	1824-1908	30	60	90		WP, WP-instructor; Harper's Ferry, McClellan's staff
Scales, Alfred Moore	1827-1892	145	265	350		Gov. of NC; Caldwell Inst., lawyer, SL, USHR; Peninsular, Seven Days, Fredericksburg*
Scalia, Antonin	1936-	45	100	200	60	SC: 1986-, VA, rarely signs autographs!
Scammell, Alexander	1747-1781	300	600	1250		Cont'l officer; ADC to GW; AG to GW
Scammon, Eliakim P.	1816-1894	45	90	175		WP, MW, teacher, professor, diplomat; Carnifix Ferry, Maryland
Scarry, Richard	1919-1994	25	50		50	Illustrator
Schacht, Hjalmar	1877-1970	100	200	300		German economist, ESPV-DS
Schally, Andrew V.	1926-	15	30		25	Biochemist, NP
Schawlow, Arthur	1921-	15	30		30	Physicist, NP
Scheer, Reinhard	1863-1928	25	50	100	50	German admiral
Scheidemann, Philipp	1865-1939	30	45		50	German Social Democratic ldr.
Schenck, Robert C.	1809-1890	35	60	100		Miami Univ., lawyer, congress, diplomat, SL; First & Second Manassas, Shenandoah...
Schiaparelli, Elsa	1896-1973	30	60		60	Fashion designer
Schiaparelli, Giovanni	1835-1910	150	400			Italian astronomer, ESPV
Schiele, Egon	1890-1918	700				Austrian painter
Schiff, Jacob H.	1847-1920	20	40	50	40	Financier
Schirra, Walter M.		25	75	175	60	Mercury 8, Gemini 6A, TSS
Schlesinger, Arthur M.	1888-1965	20	40		50	Historian
Schlesinger, Arthur M., Jr.	1917-	10	25		20	Historian

NAME	DATES	SIG	DS	ALS	SP	COMMENTS
Schmalensee, Richard L.	1944-	5	15	20	10	Economist
Schmidt, Helmut	1918-	20	40		35	W. German chancellor, FA
Schmitt, Harrison H.		25	150	200	70	Apollo 17, RS, MW
Schoepf, Albin F.	1822-1886	50	100	165		Hotel porter, patent office worker, chief exam; Fishing Creek, Perryville, Fort Delaware
Schofield, John M.	1831-1906	50	100	200		SALS-2X; sec. of war, teacher, WP, WP-superintendent; Army of the Frontier, Atlanta, Tennessee, WD-2X
Scholl, William	1882-1968	35	70		60	U.S. physician, businessman
Schopenhauer, Arthur	1788-1860	1000	3000			German philosopher, author, ESPV
Schriver, Loren J.		10	20	30	20	Discovery, 1/24/84, Atlantis, 7/31/92
Schrödinger, Erwin	1887-1961	45	80		70	Physicist
Schultz, Charles	1922-	100	200		300	Cartoonist, "Peanuts," very elusive signer
Schultz, Peter C.	1942-	15	30	50	25	Fused silica optical waveguide
Schultz, Theodore W.	1902-	10	20	25	15	Economist, educator, NP
Schumpeter, Joseph A.	1883-1950	15	30	55	25	Economist
Schurz, Carl	1829-1906	60	100	200		Lecturer, USS, editor, diplomat; Shenandoah, Second Manassas, Gettysburg
Schuschnigg, Kurt	1897-1977	50	100	200	75	Austrian chancellor
Schuyler, Phillip John	1733-1804	200	375			Cont'l general; SL; ESPV-DS
Schwab, Charles M.	1862-1939	40	80	125	100	Industrialist
Schwab, Charles R.	1937-	15	25	35	25	Charles Schwab & Co. founder
Schwarzkopf, H. Norman	1934-	45	100	200	100	Amer. gen., VW, KW, elusive signer!
Schweickart, Russell L.		20	50		40	Apollo 9
Schweitzer, Albert	**1875-1965**	**175**	**300**	**600**	**800**	**theologian, philosopher, SDS & SALS-2X, FA**
Scobee, F. Richard		85			200	Challenger, 1/28/86, killed during launch, ESPV
Scott, Charles	c.1739-1813	100	200	330		Cont'l general; SL; Gov. KY
Scott, David R.		45	100		200	Gemini 8, Apollo 9, Apollo 15, MW, ESPV, elusive signer
Scott, Emmett J.	1873-1957	25	75	100	50	Educator
Scott, Hugh Lenox	1853-1934	40	65	100	50	American general, IW, WWI

☆ (star next to Schweitzer, Albert row)

Horatio Nelson

Richard M.Nixon

Thomas Nelson, Jr.

Alfred Nobel

C.W. Nimitz

Annie Oakley

Thelma Catherine Ryan "Pat" Nixon

Richard M. Nixon

Georgia O'Keefe

Richard M.Nixon

NAME	DATES	SIG	DS	ALS	SP	COMMENTS
Scott, R.F.	1868-1912	100	200	400	200	Antartic explorer
Scott, Robert	1826-1900	65	125	160		Controversial; miner, practiced medicine, gov. SC; Vicksburg, Atlanta, South Carolina
Scott, Thomas A.	1823-1881	24	40	55	40	Businessman
Scott, Thomas Moore	1829-1876	145				ESPV; farmer; Vicksburg, Atlanta, Tennessee
Scott, Winfield "Old Fuss and Feathers"	1786-1866	185	365	600		**Presidential nominee, very distinguished; William & Mary, MW; Commander-in-chief of the army**
Scully-Power, Paul D.		5	15	25	10	Challenger, 10/5/84
Scurry, William Read	1821-1864	575				MW; Galveston, Red River, Mansfield*
Seaborg, Glenn	1912-	25	60	125	60	Nuclear chemist
Searfoss, Richard A.		5	15	25	10	Columbia, 10/18/93
Sears, Claudius Wistar	1817-1891	70	165	250		WP, teacher, St. Thomas's hall, Univ. of LA; Chicksaw Bayou, Port Gibson, Atlanta*
Sears, Richard	1863-1914	60	200	300	200	Founded U.S. mail-order company
Secchi, Angelo	1818-1878	120	300			Italian astronomer, ESPV
Seddon, Margaret Rhea		5	25		10	Discovery, 4/12/85, Columbia, 6/5/91, RS
Sedgwick, John	1813-1864	200	400	800		Killed in action; WP, MW; Sharpsburg, Chancellorsville, Rappa. Bridge, ESPV
Sega, Ronald		5	15	25	10	Discovery, 2/3/94
Segal, George	1924-	20	40	50		American sculptor, painter
Segar, Elzie C.	1894-1938	140			250	"Popeye" creator
Seiwald, Robert J.	1925-	15	30	50	25	FITC
Selassie, Haile	1891-1975	180	320	500		Ethopian emperor
Selznick, David O.	1902-1965	150	300		250	Cinema mogul
Semenov, Nikolay N.	1896-1986	50	100		75	Physical chemist, NP
Semmes, Paul Jones	1815-1863	870	1250			killed in action, ESPV; UVA, banker, planter; Yorktown, Williamsburg, Seven Pines,* scarce
Semmes, Raphael	1809-1877	340	725	1275		CSA admiral, ESPV
Semon, Waldo	1898-	20	50	75	40	PVC plastisols

NAME	DATES	SIG	DS	ALS	SP	COMMENTS
Sendak, Maurice	1928-	15	40		35	Illustrator
Serurier, Count Jean Mathieu P.	1741-1819	75	150	250		French marshal of the Empire
Sevier, John	1745-1815	650	1125	800		Pioneer; militia off.; First Gov. TN; SL; SDS-3X
Seward, William H.	1801-1872	100	140	220		U.S. sec. of state, AL assain. related-10X
Seward, William H., Jr.	1839-1920	50	100	150		Son of the sec. of state; banking, businessman; New York Heavy Artillery, Washington
Seymour, Truman	1824-1891	75	150	250		Norwich Univ., WP, MW; Fort Sumter, Sharpsburg, Ocean Pond, AOTP
Shackelford, James M.	1827-1909	50	100	200		Lawyer, judge; Fort Donelson, Cumberland Gap, E. Tennessee.
Shackleton, Sir Ernest H.	1874-1922	200	350	400		Explorer
Shaftesbury, Earl of (A.A. Cooper)	1801-1885	40	80	150		British social reformer
Shahn, Ben	1898-1969	60	150	200		American painter, graphic artist, writer
Shain, Harold		5	10	15	15	Newsweek Inc. executive
Shaler, Alexander	1827-1911	45	80	150		Pres. NYC fire dept.; Washington, AOTP, Wilderness, Chancellor...
Shamir, Yitzhak	1915-	25	50		50	Israel prime minister
Shapiro, Robert		10	25		20	Lawyer
Shapley, Harlow	1885-1972	50	100	200	75	U.S. astronomer, galaxy theorist, SDS-2-3X
Sharp, Jacob Hunter	1833-1907	160	275			Univ. of AL, lawyer, Miss. Press Assoc.; Shiloh, Murfreesboro, Chickamauga*
Shaw, Anna H.	1847-1919	40	75	150		Suffragist
Shaw, Brewster H., Jr.		10	30	40	20	Columbia, 11/28/83, 8/9/89, Atlantis, 11/26/85
Shaw, Leslie M.	1848-1932	25	40	55		U.S. politician
Sheehan, John C.	1915-1992	30	65	100	50	Semisynthetic penicillin
Shelby, Isaac	1750-1826	260	400			Militia leader; First Gov. KY; SL, ESPV
Shelby, Joseph Orville	1830-1897	350	1000	1500		very well respected, ESPV; Transylvania Univ., rope manuf., U.S. marshal; Almost every one West of Miss. river, SDS & SALS-2X

NAME	DATES	SIG	DS	ALS	SP	COMMENTS
Shelley, Charles Miller	1833-1907	70	150	215		architect, builder, sheriff, Treasury auditor; First Manassas, Vicksburg
Shepard, Alan B. , Jr.		75	150	200	160	Mercury-Redstone 3, 1st American in space
Shepard, Isaac F.	1816-1889	50	100	135		Harvard, SL, editor, diplomat; Arkansas Post, Dist. of W. Tennessee
Sheperd, Lemuel Cornick, Jr.	1896-1990	40	85	160	100	Amer. marine corps gen., WWI, WWII
Shepherd, William M.		10	20	30	20	Atlantis, 12/2/88, Discovery, 10/6/90, C1992
Shepley, George F.	1819-1878	45	90	125		Dartmouth, milt. gov. La., judge; New Orleans
Sheridan, Philip H.	1831-1888	325	950	1250	2000	SDS & SALS-2X; WP; Perryville, Murfreesboro, Five Forks, AOTP,* ESPV-ALS & WD
Sherlock, Nancy Jane		10	20	30	20	Endeavour, 6/21/93
Sherman, Forrest Percival	1896-1951	25	50	100	65	U.S. admiral, WWI, WWII
Sherman, Francis T.	1825-1905	50	100	200		Postal clerk, postmaster, SL; Murfreesboro, Atlanta, Five Forks*
Sherman, Fredrick Carl	1888-1957	20	50	85	50	U.S. admiral, WWI, WWII
Sherman, John	1823-1900	55	100	125	75	Political leader, USS, sec. of the treasury
Sherman, Roger	1721-1793	235	475	895		CC, ALS-v. rare, DS-C, DE, full
Sherman, Roger	1722-1793	235	475	895		Signer DOI; AOA; AOC & C; statesman, ESPV-DS
Sherman, Thomas W.	1813-1879	40	80	120		WP, MW; Port Hudson, New Orleans
Sherman, William T. "Cump"	**1820-1891**	**400**	**1200**	**2100**		**SB - $2750, ESPV, SALS- 2-20X; WP, MW, banker, businessman; Kentucky, Shiloh, Atlanta, Carolinas***
Shevardnadge, Eduard A.	1928-	30			60	Soviet statesman
Shields, James	1810-1879	75	120	150		Served in USS for 3 states; lawyer, SL, USS; Shenandoah Valley
Shippen, Edward	1639-1712	65	125	175		Chief justice PA, SDS-2-3X, SALS-2X
Shiras, George	1832-1924	100	250	400	200	SC: 1892-1903, PA, reclusive
Shirer, William L.	1904-1993	20	45		40	Journalist, historian
Shirley, William	1694-1771	200	400	700		Colonial Gov. of Mass; C in C
Shockley, William Bradford	1910-1989	50	125	150	100	Transistor, NP

☆ (star marking Sherman, William T. "Cump" row)

Robert J. Oppenheimer

George S. Patton Jr.

William Paca

Robert Peary

Robert Treat Paine

John Penn

Maxfield Parrish

John J. Pershing

William Paterson

Pablo Picasso

Most sincerely,

G. S. PATTON, JR.,

George S. Patton Jr.

Franklin Pierce

Franklin Pierce

NAME	DATES	SIG	DS	ALS	SP	COMMENTS
Shoemaker, Eugene	1928-1997	50	100		100	U.S. planetary geologist, comet founder
Shonin, Georgi S.		40	100	200	65	Soyuz 6
Short, Walter Campbell	1880-1949	25	40	50	30	U.S. general, WWI, WWII, controv.
Shoup, David Monroe	1904-1983	20	40	75	40	U.S. marine general, WWII
Shoup, Francis Asbury	1834-1896	100	200	325		WP, Asbury College, lawyer, Univ. Miss; Shiloh, Prairie Grove, Vicksburg*
Shriver, Loren J.		8		25	12	Discovery, 4/24/90, RS
Shrontz, Frank A.	1931-	5	15	20	10	Boeing CEO
Shultz, George P.	1920-	10	20		25	U.S. statesman
Shumway, Norman	1923-	15	40		30	Cardiac surgeon
Shuster, Joe & Siegel, Jerry	1914-1992, 1914-1996	175			1200	Cartoonist, "Superman"
Sibert, Franklin Cummings	1891-	15	25	40	25	U.S. general, WWII
Sibley, Henry H.	1811-1891	100	250	400		ESPV, Indian fighter; clerk, gov. Minn., SI, banker, writer; Gen. U.S. Volunteers
Sibley, Henry Hopkins	1816-1886	125	350	425		controversial; WP, MW, invented Sibley tent; Army of New Mexico
Sickles, Daniel E.	1819-1914	100	185	225		NYU, SL, congress, diplomat; Peninsular, Sharpsburg, Gettysburg*
Siegbahn, Kai	1918-	20	40		55	Physicist
Siegel & Shuster	1914-1996 1914-1992	200			400	Strip cartoonist
Siemens, Werner von	1816-1892	50	120	200		German industrialist, inventor
Sigel, Franz	1824-1902	80	150	200		teacher, pension agent; Carthage, Elkhorn Tavern
Signac, Paul	1863-1935	100	175	350		French Neo-Impressionist painter
Sikorsky, Igor I.	1889-1972	100	275	325	300	Helicopter controls
Silas, C.J.	1932-	10	15	15	15	Phillips Petroleum Company executive
Simms, James Phillip	1837-1887	125	225			ESPV; lawyer, SL; Seven days, Second Manassas, Sharpsburg*
Simon, Herbert	1916-	15	30		30	Economist
Simpson, William Hood	1888-1980	25	100	275	50	U.S. general, WWI, WWII
Sims, William Sowden	1858-1936	45	100	150	65	U.S. admiral, WWI

NAME	DATES	SIG	DS	ALS	SP	COMMENTS
Singer, Isaac	1811-1875	500				Inventor, ESPV-all forms
Sisler, William P.	1947-	5	10	15	10	Publisher
☆ **Sitting Bull (Tatanka Yotanka)**	c.1831-1890	6500				**American Hunkpapa Sioux chief, FA, ESPV**
Skinner, B.F.	1904-1989	30	50	75	60	U.S. psychologist, RS
Skinner, Corlandt	1728-1799	50	100	150		Tory officer
Skorzeny, Otto	1908-1975	200	350		425	German SS officer
Slack, James R.	1818-1881	75	150	200		Lawyer, county auditor, SL; Vicksburg, Dept. of the Gulf, Island No. 10
Slack, William Yarnel	1816-1862	400	500			ESPV; lawyer, MW; Elkhorn, Carthage, Springfield
Slater, Samuel	1768-1835	20	45	60		Manufacturer
Slaughter, James Edwin	1827-1901	120	200			great-nephew of pres. James Madison; VMI, MW, civil engineer, postmaster; Shiloh, Kentucky, engaged last battle of war
Slayton, Donald K.		40	100		100	ASTP, RS
Slemmer, Adam J.	1829-1868	140	215	300		WP, WP-instructor; Corinth, Kentucky, Murfreesboro
Slim, Sir William Joseph	1891-1970	25	75	150	50	British field marshal
Sloan, Alfred P.	1875-1966	50	75	125	65	Industrialist, philanthropist, General Motors
Sloan, John	1871-1951	100	200	400		American painter, graphic artist
Sloat, John Drake	1781-1867	35	70	125		U.S. admiral, W1812, MW
Slocum, Henry W.	1827-1894	100	150	200		WP, county treasurer, SL, congress, teacher; Peninsular, Second Manassas, Maryland*
Slough, John P.	1829-1867	200				SL; Military gov. of Alexandria, ESPV
Smith, Alfred E.	1873-1944	40	85	175	100	Dem. New York gov., pres. candid.
Smith, Andrew J.	1815-1897	50	125	200		WP, postmaster, city auditor; Vicksburg, Chickasaw Bluffs, Arkansas Post
Smith, Charle F.	1807-1862	250	500			WP, WP-commandant of cadets, MW; Dept. of Utah, Fort Donelson
Smith, Charles Bradford	1916-	15	30	45	20	American general, WWII

NAME	DATES	SIG	DS	ALS	SP	COMMENTS
Smith, Edmund Kirby	1824-1893	350	500	600		SALS- 2X; WP, MW, Pres. Pacific & Atlantic Telegraph; Shenandoah, First Manassas, Red River, WD-2X
Smith, Frederick	1944-	10	25	35	20	Federal Express Corp. founder, unresponsive
Smith, Giles A.	1829-1876	85	175	260		Hotel business, sec. asst. postmaster gen.; Shiloh, Corinth, Vicksburg, Atlanta*
Smith, Green C.	1826-1895	50	75	150		Transylvania Univ., MW, congress, ministry; Lebanon, TN, ter. gov. (MT)
Smith, Gustavus A.	1820-1885	200	425	875		ESPV, SLS/DS-5-6X; carriage mfr.; Fort Sumter, Elkhorn Tavern
Smith, Gustavus Woodson	1821-1896	125	300	500		SALS-2X; WP, MW, engineer, NYC street comm. writer; Army of Northern Virginia*
Smith, Hamilton	1931-	15	30		25	Molecular biologist
Smith, Holland McTyeire	1882-1967	100	200	300	200	American marine gen., WWII, WWI
Smith, James	c.1719-1806		2500	3500		Signer DOI; nearly all papers destroyed in fire
Smith, James Argyle	1831-1901	125	165	265		WP, farmer, supt. public education; Shiloh, Perryville, Murfreesboro*
Smith, John E.	1816-1897	75	150			Jeweler, goldsmith; Shiloh, Vicksburg, Atlanta, Carolinas*
Smith, Joseph	1805-1844	750	1500	9500		Religious ldr., "The Book of Mormon," ESPV, FA
Smith, Julian C.	1885-?	15	30	40	25	American marine corps gen., WWII
Smith, Margaret Chase	1897-1995	10	25	65	30	U.S. congresswoman, elected both houses
Smith, Martin Luther	1819-1866	100	150	300		WP; New Orleans, Vicksburg, Army of N. Virginia
Smith, Michael J.		250			350	Challenger, 1/28/86, killed during launch, ESPV-all forms
Smith, Morgan L.	1821-1874	100	200	260		Teacher, riverboat cpt., diplomat; Shiloh, Chattanooga, Atlanta*
Smith, Oliver Prince	1893-	25	45	65	30	Amer. marine corps gen., WWII, WWI
Smith, Persifor Frazer	1798-1858	25	40	50		American general, SW, MW
Smith, Preston	1823-1863	540				killed in action; Jackson College, lawyer; Shiloh, Kentucky, Chickamauga, ESPV, rare in all forms

Franklin Pierce

Franklin Pierce

Jane M. Appleton Pierce

Charles C. Pinckney

Charles C. Pinckney

James K. Polk

James K. Polk

James K. Polk

James K. Polk

Leonidas Polk

Sarah C. Polk

David D. Porter

Post

gator
Gatty

Wiley Post and Harold Gatty

NAME	DATES	SIG	DS	ALS	SP	COMMENTS
Smith, Ralph Corbett	1893-	20	35	50	25	American general, WWII, WWI
Smith, Steven L.		5	10	15	10	Endeavour, 9/30/94, RS!
Smith, Sydney	1887-1935	45			75	Cartoonist, "The Gumps"
Smith, Thomas Benton	1838-1923	100	150			Nashville Military Inst., worked in railroad; Mill Springs, Shiloh, Murfreesboro*
Smith, Thomas C. H.	1819-1897	35	70	120		Controversial; Harvard, lawyer; Aide-de-camp Gen. Pope
Smith, Thomas K.	1820-1887	60	115	200		Cincinnati College, US marshal, diplomat; Vicksburg, Red River
Smith, W. Eugene	1918-1978	25	60		60	Photojournalist
Smith, Walter Bedell	1895-1961	40	60	100	50	American general, WWII, WWI
Smith, William	1797-1887	125	250	320		Gov. of Virginia; First Manassas, Seven Days, Gettysburg,* DS & ALS-WD-2X
Smith, William Duncan	1825-1862	500				WP, MW; Secessionville, ESPV, scarce in all forms
Smith, William F.	1824-1903	50	100	175		WP, historian, writer, businessman; First Manassas, Maryland, Fredericksburg*
Smith, William S.	1830-1916	50	100	225		Built first all-steel bridge; WP, construction engineer; West Virginia, Shiloh, Perryville, Vicksburg*
Smuts, Jan C.	1870-1950	70	125		220	South African statesman
Smythe, Reg	1917-	10	20		35	Strip cartoonist, "Andy Capp"
Soglow, Otto	1900-1975	30			80	Cartoonist, "Little Kings," "Canyon Kiddies"
Solow, Robert M.	1924-	10	25	50	20	Economist, educator, RS!
Somervell, Brehon Burke	1892-1955	40	100	150	60	American general, WWII, WWI
Soderbloom, Nathan	1866-1931	70	140			Lutheran archbishop, NP
Sontag, Susan	1933-	10	25		20	Critic
Sopwith, Sir Thomas	1888-1989	30	100	125	100	Aircraft designer
Sorrel, Gilbert Moxley	1838-1901	200	400	500		SDS-4-5X; railroad clerk, merchant, writer; First Manassas, Wilderness, Hatcher's Run, ESPV
Soult, Nicolas Jean de Dieu	1769-1851	100	200	300		Marshal General of France
Souter, David H.	1939-	35	75	175	55	SC: 1990-, NH
Soyer, Raphael	1899-1987	50	150	250	100	Russian-born painter

NAME	DATES	SIG	DS	ALS	SP	COMMENTS
Spaak, Paul Henri	1899-1972	25	50	75	35	Belgian statesman, socialist leader
Spaatz, Carl	1891-1974	60	125		125	Aviator
Spaight, Richard Dobbs	1758-1802	275	450			CC, v. rare in all forms, however some DS, ESPV
Sparks, Jared	1789-1866	25	50	75		U.S. historian, educator
Spears, James G.	1816-1869	125	240	300		Lawyer; Wild Cat Mountain, Mill Springs, Cum. Gap
Speer, Albert	1905-1981	60	165	210	175	Architect, Nazi official
Speidel, Hans	1897-1987	40	90		75	German general
Spellman, Francis J.	1889-1967	25	50	100	60	Religious leader, prolific writer
Spencer, Herbert	1820-1903	75	150	250	125	British evolutionary philosopher
Spengler, Oswald	1880-1936		350	500		German philosopher, historian
Sperry, Elmer A.	1860-1930	200	350	500	200	Ship's gyroscopic compass, ESPV
Sperry, Roger	1913-1994	25	50	75	45	U.S. brain expert, mind theorist
Spiegelman, Art	1948-	10				Raw, Maus
Spingarn, Joel E.	1875-1939	40	100	150	60	Educator, reformer
Spinner, Francis E.		30	55	55		U.S. treasurer
Spock, Benjamin	1903-	30	100	175	60	Pediatrician and author
Sprague, Clifton Albert Furlow	1896-1955	30	55	75	35	Amer. admiral, WWII, WWI, "Ziggy"
Sprague, Frank	1857-1934	60	120	165	115	Electrical engineer
Sprague, John W.	1817-1893	50	100	175		RPI, treasurer of Erie County; New Madrid, Island No. 10, Corinth*
Sprague, Thomas Lamison	1894-1972	35	60	80	40	American admiral, WWII, WWI
Spreckels, Claus	1828-1908	100	200		150	American sugar manufacturer
Spreckels, Rudolph	1872-1958	30	45	75	50	Reformer, manufacturer, s. of Claus
Spring, Sherwood C.		10	20	30	15	Atlantis, 11/26/85
Springer, Robert C.		5	15	25	10	Discovery, 3/13/89, Atlantis, 11/15/90
Sprinkel, Beryl	1923-	10	20	40	15	Economist, educator, Reagan advisor, RS
Spruance, Raymond Ames	1886-1969	50	100	175	65	American admiral, WWII
St. Clair, Arthur	1737-1818	180	250			Cont'l general; Congress; Gov. NW Tty., SDS-2X

NAME	DATES	SIG	DS	ALS	SP	COMMENTS
St. John, Isaac Munroe	1827-1880	100	160	250		Poughkeepsie Collegiate School, Yale; captain of engineers, commissary general
St. Pius X	1835-1910	250	500			Pope of Roman Catholic Church-1903
Stafford, John R.	1937-	5	15	20	10	American Home Products Corp. CEO
Stafford, Thomas P.		25	75	140	50	Gemini 6A, Gemini 9A, RS, TSS
Stafford, Leroy Augustus	1822-1864	415				ESPV; sheriff, planter; Seven Days, Cedar MT., Second Manassas*
Stahel, Julius	1825-1912	55	100	200		Diplomat, Equitable Ins. Co., Second Manassas, Shenandoah, Piedmont
Stalin, Joseph	**1879-1953**	**2550**	**5000**			**Soviet dictator, sig/ w Pushkin-$5000, ESPV-all forms**
Standley, William Harrison	1872-1963	20	35	50	30	American admiral, WWII
Stanford, A. Leland	1824-1893	100	345	575	125	U.S. railroad official, philanthropist, ESPV
Stanley, David S.	1828-1902	40	80	125		ESPV, SALS-3-4X, WP; Missouri, Wilson's Creek, Iuka, Corinth*
Stanley, Henry M.		250	500	500	750	Journalist
Stanley, William	1858-1916	85	175	250		Electric transformer
Stannard, George J.	1820-1886	50	100	200		Teacher, USHR-doorkeeper; Fort Harrison, First Manassas, Gettysburg*
Stanton, Edwin M.	1814-1869	135	200	400	200	Political leader, war dated-2-3X, SALS & DS-2X
Stanton, Elizabeth Cady	**1815-1902**	**175**	**250**	**450**		**U.S. woman suffrage pioneer**
Stapleton, Joan		10	20	40	15	New Republic president
Stark, Harold	1880-1972	20	50	100	50	U.S. naval officer
Stark, John	1728-1822	400	650	1375		Cont'l general
Starke, Peter Burwell	1815-1888	160	250			SL, sheriff, Miss. Levee Bd.; Atlanta, Tennessee
Starkweather, John C.	1830-1890	60	150	200		Union College, lawyer; Perryville, Murfreesboro, Chattanooga*
Stassen, Harold	1907-	10	25		20	U.S. state governor
Statler, Ellsworth	1863-1928	60	125	200	125	Hotel owner
Steedman, James B.	1817-1883	80	155	275		Printer for US govmt., MW, SL; Philippi, Perrysville, Murfreesboro*

Sterling Price

George Read

George Read

Nancy Reagan

Ronald Reagan

Ronald Reagan

Ronald Reagan

Ronald Reagan

Ronald Reagan

Ronald Reagan

Ronald Reagan

Ronald Reagan

Frederic Remington

Paul Revere

NAME	DATES	SIG	DS	ALS	SP	COMMENTS
Steele, Frederick	1819-1868	100	160	240		WP, MW; Arkansas, Vicksburg, Wilson's Creek
Steele, William	1819-1885	100	200	300		WP, adjutant general of Texas; Red River, Pleasant Hill
Steere, William C., Jr.	1936-	5	10	25	10	Pfizer Inc. CEO
Stefansson, Vilhjalmur	1879-1962	50	150		300	Artic explorer, ESPV-SP
Steffens, Joseph Lincoln	1866-1936	65	125	175	100	Journalist, reformer
Steichen, Edward	1879-1973	100	225	300	450	U.S. photographer, ESPV-SP
Steig, William	1907-	25			50	New Yorker cartoonist
Stein, Herbert	1916-	5	10	20	10	Economist, s. of Ben Stein, RS
Steinem, Gloria	1934-	10	15	40	15	Reformer, RS
Steinmetz, Charles P.	1865-1923	75	150	350	125	German/U.S. electrical engineer, G.E., ESPV-DS
Steinway, William	1835-1896	75	150			Industrialist, ESPV
Stella, Frank	1936-	35	100			American painter/sculptor
Stephen, Adam	1718-1791	75	150	300		Cont'l general
Stephens, Alexander H.	1812-1883	200	345	500		Political leader, USHR, gov. (GA), VP CSA
Stephenson, George	1781-1848	225	400	700		English inventor
Stern, Otto	1888-1969	25	65		50	Physicist, NP
Stettinius, Edward R., Jr.	1900-1949	30	75	150	40	U.S. industrialists, sec. of state
Steuart, George Hume "Maryland"	1828-1903	130	260			WP, farmer; Valley, Cross Keys, Gettysburg*
☆ **Steuben, Friedrich Wilhelm Augustus von**	**1730-1794**	**1275**	**2775**			**Inspector General of the Cont'l Army, ESPV-all forms**
Stevens, Clement Hoffman	1821-1864	325	1645	2625		killed in action, SDS-2X, ESPV; cashier; First Manassas, Vicksburg, Chickamauga,* ESPV-ALS
Stevens, John Paul	1920-	30	100	160	70	SC: 1975-, IL
Stevens, Robert L.	1787-1856	50	115			Engineer, inventor
Stevens, Thaddeus	1792-1868	40	100	165		Political leader, USHR
Stevens, Walter Husted	1827-1867	300	600			WP, engineer Imperial Railroad; chief engineer Army of N. Virginia*
Stevenson, Adlai E.	1900-1965	50	75	150	100	U.S. Democratic leader, pres. candidate, SDS & SALS-2X

NAME	DATES	SIG	DS	ALS	SP	COMMENTS
Stevenson, Carter Littlepage	1817-1888	100	200	450		WP, MW, civil and mining engineer; Kentucky, Vicksburg, Army of Tennessee
Stevenson, John D.	1821-1897	75	150	200		SC College, lawyer, SL; Corinth, Vicksburg, Chickamauga, Atlanta*
Steward, Ira	1831-1883	40	100	160		Labor leader
Stewart, Alexander Peter	1821-1908	175	300	400		WP, Cumberland University, Nashville Univ.; Tennessee Army*
Stewart, Charles	1778-1869	100	250	340		American admiral, W1812
Stewart, Frederick	1904-1993	35	100	200	100	British botanist, cell biologist
Stewart, Potter	1915-1985	45	105	175	100	SC: 1958-1981, OH
Stewart, Robert		10	20	30	20	Challenger, 2/3/84, Atlantis, 10/4/85
Stibitz, George R.	1904-1995	40	125	200	75	U.S., invented first digital computer
Stickley, Gustav	1858-1942	80	175		150	Furniture designer, ESPV
☆ **Stieglitz, Alfred**	**1864-1946**	**250**	**500**	**650**		**American photographer, ESPV-SP**
Stigler, George	1911-1991	10	20	40	20	Economist, educator
Stilwell, Joseph W.	1883-1946	150	275	300	400	Amer. gen., "Vinegar Joe", WWI & II
Stimson, Henry L.	1867-1950	30	100	175	40	U.S. statesman
Stiritz, William P.	1934-	5	10	15	10	Ralston-Purina Co. executive
Stirling, Patrick	1820-1895	50	100	225		Mechanical engineer, "Stirling Single"
Stirling, Robert	1790-1878	55	120	200		Clergyman, inventor, "Stirling Cycle"
☆ **Stockton, Richard**	**1730-1781**	**525**	**975**	**2875**		**Signer DOI; lawyer, ESPV**
Stockton, Robert Field	1795-1866	100	300	400		American naval officer, W1812, MW
Stokes, James H.	1815-1890	75	150	300		WP, rrd. exec., real estate; Every fight of the western army
Stolbrand, Charles J.	1821-1894	50	100	165		State pen. superintendent; Vicksburg, Chattanooga, Atlanta, Carolinas
Stommel, Hery M.	1920-	15	30		25	Oceanographer
Stone, Charles P.	1824-1887	65	125	200		Controversial; WP, MW; First Bull Run, Port Hudson, Red River
Stone, Harlan F.	1872-1946	75	250	300	225	SC: 1941-1946, NY, Chief Justice
Stone, Lucy	1818-1893	125	250	350	340	U.S. feminist, abolitionist, SDS-2-3X
Stone, Sir Richard	1913-1991	20	45		40	Economist

GEN—POLITS

	NAME	DATES	SIG	DS	ALS	SP	COMMENTS
☆	**Stone, Thomas**	**1743-1787**	**550**	**945**	**2275**		**Signer DOI; MD; few letters have survived, ESPV**
	Stoneman, George	1822-1894	50	150	200		WP, MW, gov. Ca.; West Virginia, AOTP, Fredericksburg
	Storey, Moorfield	1845-1929	65	130	245		Lawyer, reformer
	Story, Joseph	1779-1845	100	200	300		SC: 1811-1845, MA, serv.over 30 yrs., gifted writer!
	Stovall, Marcellus Augustus	1818-1895	125	250	345		ESPV-ALS; Cotton broker, Georgia Chemical Works; Murfreesboro, Chickamauga, Atlanta
	Strand, Paul	1890-1976	50	100	250		U.S. photographer
	Stratemeyer, George Edward	1890-1969	25	40	50	40	American air force gen., WWII, KW
	Straus, Nathan	1848-1931	115	165		200	German-born merchant, headed Macy's
	Straus, Roger W.	1917-	10	20	45	15	Farrar, Starus, & Giroux, publisher
	Streicher, Julius	1885-1946	75	150	250	125	Nazi journalist, hanged, SALS-2X
	Strong, Benjamin	1872-1928	20	40	50		Banker
	Strong, Josiah	1847-1916	40	75	135	80	American religious leader, "Our Country"
	Strong, William	1808-1895	85	175	300		SC: 1870-1880, PA, ALS typically good content
	Strothman, Wendy J.	1950-	5	10	20	15	Publisher
	Strutton, Larry D.	1940-	5	10	15	10	Publisher, Rocky Mountain News CEO
	Stuart, David	1816-1868	100	175	250		Lawyer, congress, rrd. solicitor; Shiloh, Chickasaw Bluffs
	Stuart, Gilbert	1755-1828	225	500	800		American portrait painter
☆	**Stuart, James Ewell Brown "Jeb"**	**1833-1864**	**2260**	**3750**	**7240**		**legendary cavalry commander, ESPV; WP; Army of Northern Virginia,* WD-2X, most material AA.**
	Studebaker, Clement	1831-1901	50	145	250	75	U.S. wagon and carriage manufacturer
	Studdy, George E.	1878-1948	50			100	Cartoonist, "Bonzo"
	Stumbaugh, Frederick S.	1817-1897	50	100	150		Lawyer; Shiloh, Kentucky
	Sturgis, Samuel D.	1822-1889	50	100	200		WP, MW; Fort Smith, Wilson's Creek, Maryland*
	Suchet, Louis Gabriel	1770-1826	100	200	300		French marshal of the Empire
	Suharto	1921-	25			50	Indonesian soldier

Sir Joshua Reynolds

Diego Rivera

John D. Rockefeller

Norman Rockwell

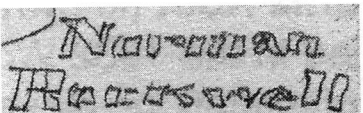

Norman Rockwell

Caesar Rodney

Erwin Rommel

Edith Kermit C. Roosevelt

Eleanor Roosevelt

Franklin D. Roosevelt

Franklin D. Roosevelt

YOURS TRULY,
NAME
ADDRESS

Franklin D. Roosevelt

Franklin D. Roosevelt

Franklin D. Roosevelt
and Eleanor R. Roosevelt

NAME	DATES	SIG	DS	ALS	SP	COMMENTS
Sukamo	1901-1970	100				First pres. of Indonesian republic
Sullivan, Anne	1866-1936	40	75		55	Educator (Helen Keller)
Sullivan, Jeremiah C.	1830-1890	40	75	150		Lawyer, clerk; Philippi, Shenandoah Valley, Iuka, Corinth*
Sullivan, John	1740-1795	165	400	600		Cont'l general; SL; Gov. NH
Sullivan, Kathryn D.		10	30	40	25	Challenger, 10/5/84, Discovery, 4/24/90, A92
Sully, Alfred	1820-1879	65	140	175		Son of artist Thomas Sully; WP, MW, Indian fighter; Peninsular, Sharpsburg, Fredericksburg*
☆ **Sully, Thomas**	**1783-1872**	**200**	**400**	**500**		**American portrait painter, ESPV-ALS**
Sultan, Daniel Isom	1885-1947	50	100	200	65	American general, WWI, WWII, 4DSM
Sulzberger, Arthur O.	1926-	10	20	40	15	New York Times CEO
Summerall, Charles Pelot	1867-1955	30	50	75	45	American general, WWI, SAW, BR
Sumner, Charles	1811-1874	100	200	250		U.S. statesman, ESPV-DS
Sumner, Edwin V. "Bull Head"	1797-1863	265	525			The oldest active Civil War commander; MW; Peninsular, Seven Pines, Sharpsburg,* ESPV
Sumner, James	1887-1955	30	50		50	Biochemist, NP
Sumter, Thomas "Carolina Gamecock"	1734-1832	400	1150	2260		Oldest surv. general; SC; USS; Congress
Sun Yat-sen	1866-1925	750	1100	1750		Chinese revolutionary
Sunday, Billy	1862-1935	100	200	300	400	U.S. evangelist, baseball player
Sutherland, George	1862-1942	75	150	300	200	SC: 1922-1938, UT, USS, well-spoken
Sutter, John A.	1803-1880	1000				California colonist, ESPV
Sutter, Joseph P.	1921-	20	35		35	Aircraft designer
Suzman, Helen	1917-	20	45		40	South African politician
Suzuki, Zenko	1911-	20	50		45	Japanese prime minister
Swayne, Noah H.	1804-1884	50	125	200		SC: 1862-1881, OH
Swayne, Wager	1834-1902	40	75	130		Yale, lawyer; Corinth, Tennessee, Kenesaw Mountain
Swedenborg, Emanuel	1688-1772	1250	3575			Swedish philos., scientist, writer, ESPV
Sweeny, Thomas W.	1820-1892	60	125	200		MW; Wilson's Creek, Fort Donelson, Shiloh*

NAME	DATES	SIG	DS	ALS	SP	COMMENTS
Swift, Gustavus	1839-1903	45	100	200		U.S. pioneer meat packer
Swift, Innis Palmer	1882-1953	20	40	55	45	American general, WWI, WWII
Swigert, John L., Jr.		40	80	125	150	Apollo 13
Swing, Joseph May	1894-1984	15	25	45	30	American general, WWI, WWII
Swinnerton, James	1875-1974	40			75	Cartoonist, "Little Jimmy"
Swops, Gerard	1872-1957	50	120	135	75	U.S. industrialist, economist, head G.E.
Sykes, George	1822-1880	75	150	220		WP, MW; First Manassas, Peninsula, Gettysburg*
Symington, Stuart	1901-1988	15	35	50	25	U.S. Senator
Szilard, Leo	1898-1964	45	150	300		Hungarian/U.S. physicist,
Tabern, Donalee L.	1900-1974	20	50	75	30	Thiobarbituric acid derivatives
Taft, Helen Herron	1861-1943	125	230	575	1000	(1886); OH; S-2; D-1, First Lady, ESPV-SP
Taft, Robert A.	1889-1953	25	45	75	35	U.S. conservative Senate leader
Taft, William Howard	**1857-1930**	**180**	**525**	**1000**	**500**	**Only pres. to serve as U.S. S. C. C.J., APT-500, PD ALS-2-2.5X, ESPV-ALS**
Takeshita, Noboru	1924-	20	50		50	Japanese prime minister
Talbot, William Henry Fox	1800-1877	350	500			British photographer
Taliaferro, William Booth	1822-1898	125	250	400		SDS-2X; William & Mary, Harvard, MW, lawyer, SL; Valley, Fredericksburg, WD DS-2X
Talleyrand, Charles de	1754-1838	200	500			French statesman, diplomat
Tallmadge, Benjamin (Jr.)	1754-1835	250	500	850		Cont'l officer; mgr. GW secret service; Cong.
Talmodge, Eugene	1884-1946	25	50		55	U.S. Governor
Taney, Roger B.	1777-1864	75	275	480		SC: 1836-1864, Chief Justice, sec. of war, atty. gen.
Tange, Kenzo	1913-	20	40		30	Architect
Tanner, Joseph R.		5		15	10	Atlantis, 11/3/94, RS!
Tappan, James Camp	1825-1906	60	110	150		Exeter Academy, Yale, SL, lawyer; Shiloh, Kentucky, Richmond, Perryville*
Tarbell, Ida M.	1857-1944	25	50	80	40	Reform journalist
Tarleton, Banastre	1754-1833	135	275	600		British officer, SALS-2X, ESPV
Tarski, Alfred	1902-1983	40	80		60	Logician, mathematician

NAME	DATES	SIG	DS	ALS	SP	COMMENTS
Tatum, Edward L.	1909-1975	40	75		65	Biochemist, NP
Taube, Henry	1915-	10	25		25	Inorganic chemist, NP
Taussig, Frank W.	1859-1940	20	50	65	50	U.S. economist, educator
Taylor, Frederick W.	1856-1915	20	40	50	35	Manufacturer, social scientist
☆ **Taylor, George**	**1716-1781**	**8000**	**17500**	**35000**		**Signer DOI; Cont'l Congress; 4th toughest, ESPV-all forms**
Taylor, Joseph P.	1796-1864	75	175	245		Brother of Z. Taylor; MW; Commissary general
Taylor, Maxwell Davenport	1901-1987	35	100	125	75	American general, WWII, KW
Taylor, Nelson	1821-1894	60	125	200		MW, Harvard, sheriff, congress, lawyer; Virginia Peninsula, Second Manassas*
Taylor, Richard	1826-1879	300	750	1175		son of Pres. Zachary Taylor, SDS-2-3X; Harvard, Yale, MW; First Manassas, Valley, Red River,* WD DS-2X, WD ALS-2X, ESPV
Taylor, Thomas Hart	1825-1901	75	140	275		Kenyon Coll., Centre Coll., MW, marshal; Peninsular, Kentucky, Vicksburg, ESPV
Taylor, William		5	10	15	10	Publisher
☆ **Taylor, Zachary**	**1784-1850**	**800**	**3000**	**4650**		**DIO, PD-2X, ESPV**
Teague, Walter	1883-1960	25			50	Designer
Theiler, Max	1899-1972	40			75	Bacteriologist
Tellep, Daniel M.	1931-	5	10	20	10	Aviation executive
Teller, Edward	1908-	20			75	Physicist, RS, ESPV
Temin, Howard	1934-1994	20	40		40	Virologist
Tenniel, Sir John	1820-1914	75	150	275		English illustrator
Tenzing, Norgay	1914-1986	35			70	Mountaineer, ESPV
☆ **Teresa, Mother, of Calcutta**	**1910-1997**	**200**	**350**	**600**	**300**	**Rom. Catholic nun, fdr. Miss. of Charity, ESPV-ALS, scarce in ALS**
Tereshkova, Valentina V.		175	315	525	300	Vostok 6, 1st woman in space, ESPV-ALS
Terkel, Studs	1912-	10	25		20	Oral and written historian
Terry, Alfred H.	1827-1890	125	300	375		SLS/DS-2X, SALS - 2X; Yale; First Manassas, Port Royal, Fort Pulaski*
Terry, Henry D.	1812-1869	55	125	175		Lawyer; Washington, Peninsular, Seven Pines, AOTP

Franklin D. Roosevelt
and Eleanor R. Roosevelt

Edward Rutledge

John Rutledge

Theodore Roosevelt

Charles M. Schultz

Theodore Roosevelt

Theodore Roosevelt

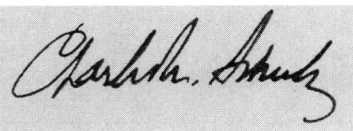

Charles M. Schultz

Theodore Roosevelt

Charles M. Schultz

George Ross

Benjamin Rush

Philip J. Schuyler

NAME	DATES	SIG	DS	ALS	SP	COMMENTS
Terry, Paul	1887-1971	65			125	Mighty Mouse animator
Terry, William H.	1824-1888	100	200	250		UVA, editor, lawyer, USNR; First & Second Manassas, Seven Days
Terry, William Richard	1827-1897	100	200	300		wounded seven times; VMI, SL, penitentiary supt.; First Manassas, Gettysburg
Tesla, Nikola	1856-1943	500	1000	1200	1000	Serb./U.S. electrical engineer
Thacher, James	1754-1844	75	300	300		Cont'l surgeon; writer; historian
Thagard, Norman E.		8		30	10	C 6/18/83, Atlantis, 5/4/89, Discovery, 1/22/92
Thant, U	1909-1974	50	150	300		UN secretary-general
Thatcher, Margaret	1925-	40	115	200	75	British prime minister, FA
Thaves, Bob	1924-	10			30	Cartoonist, "Frank and Ernest"
Thayer, John M.	1820-1906	50	100	200		Indian fighter; teacher, Brown Univ., USS, gov. Neb.; Fort Donelson, Shiloh, Vicksburg*
Theobald, Robert Alfred	1884-1957	20	40	60	40	American admiral, WWI, WWII
Thierot, Richard		5	10	20	10	Publisher
Thomas, Allen	1830-1907	70	150	265		Princeton, lawyer, planter, LSU, diplomat; Vicksburg
Thomas, Bryan Morel	1836-1905	125	280	350		WP, planter, deputy U.S. marshal; Shiloh, Kentucky, Murfreesboro
Thomas, Clarence	1948-	25	40	115	40	SC: 1991-, VA, RS
Thomas, Donald A.		5	15	25	10	Columbia, 7/8/94
Thomas, E. Donnall	1920-	15	25		30	Surgeon
Thomas, Edward Lloyd	1825-1898	115	250	330		Emory College, MW, Indian Bureau; Seven Days, Seven Pines, Army of N. Virginia
Thomas, George H.	1816-1870	125	250	500		Union general
Thomas, Henry G.	1837-1897	75	150	225		Amherst, lawyer; First Manassas, Overland
Thomas, Isaiah	1749-1831	130	275			American printer
Thomas, John	1724-1776	375	600			Cont'l general; PU
Thomas, John H. "Rock of Chickamauga"	1816-1870	125	250	400		One of the finest generals in the war!, ESPV; WP; First Manassas, Mill Springs, Perryville*
Thomas, Lorenzo	1804-1875	100	150	300		WP, MW; Adjutant general of the army

NAME	DATES	SIG	DS	ALS	SP	COMMENTS
Thomas, M. (Martha) Carey	1857-1935	60	125	250	100	Educator
Thomas, Norman M.	1884-1968	40	80	145	50	U.S. social reformer
Thomas, Seth	1785-1859	100	200	350		Clock maker
Thomas, Stephens	1809-1903	50	100	150		SL, USS, register, judge, lt. gov. Vt.; Washington, Shenandoah Valley, Cedar Crk.
Thompson, Benjamin, Count Rumford	1753-1814	250	500			Colonial administrator; physicist; Loyalist
Thompson, James Walter	1847-1928	30	75	125	50	U.S. ad executive
Thompson, John	1860-1940	100	250			U.S. soldier, ESPV
Thompson, Richard		5	10	15	10	Publisher
Thompson, Smith	1768-1843	100	165	215		SC: 1823-1843, NY, impossible from Court years!
Thomson, Eliho	1853-1937	425				Electrical engineer, ESPV
Thomson, John E.	1808-1874	30	65	110		Financier, railroad leader
Thornton, Kathryn C.		5		25	10	Discovery, 11/22/89, Endeavour, 5/7/92, RS
Thornton, Matthew	c.1714-1803	650	1500	1725		Signer DOI; NH; SL; "M. Thornton" or full
Thornton, William		5		25	10	Challenger, 8/30/83, Challenger, 4/29/85, RS
Thorvaldsen, Bertel	1770-1844	125	275			Danish sculptor
Thout, Pierre J.		5		20	10	Atlantis, 2/28/90, Endeavour, 5/7/92, RS
Thruston, Charles M.	1798-1873	50	100	135		WP, farmer, bank pres., mayor; Protected railways
Thurber, James	1894-1961	125			425	New Yorker cartoonist
Thurmond, J. Strom	1902-	10	25		20	U.S. politician
Tibbets Jr., Paul W.		20	100		75	National Aviation Hall of Fame, RS
Tibbits, William B.	1837-1880	75	150	300		Union College; Peninsular, Big Bethel, Second Manassas*
Tiffany, Charles	1812-1902	250	500			Goldsmith, jeweller, ESPV
Tiffany, Louis Comfort	1848-1933	300	600			American painter, decorator, architect, ESPV
Tikhonov, Nikolay, A.	1905-	35			55	Soviet prime minister, ESPV
Tilden, Samuel J.	1814-1886	60	125	225		Political leader

GEN—POLIT T

NAME	DATES	SIG	DS	ALS	SP	COMMENTS
Tilghman, Lloyd	1816-1863	175	350	500		Killed in action, SALS-2X; WP, railroad construction engineer, MW; Corinth, Baker's Creek
Tillich, Paul	1886-1965	50	100	150		U.S. philosopher, theologian, professor
Tillson, Davis	1830-1895	50	115	150		SL, cotton planter, businessman; Cedar Mountain, Second Manassas
Tinbergen, Jan	1903-1994	25	50		35	Dutch economist, NP
Tinbergen, Nikolaas	1907-1988	30	65		40	Ethologist
Tishler, Max	1906-	15	30	40	20	Riboflavin and sulfaquinoxaline
Tissot, James	1836-1902	100	200	265		French painter, graphic artist
Titterton, Sir Ernest	1916-1990	30	100		75	Nuclear physicist
Tito, Josip Broz	1892-1980	100	200	300	250	President of Yugoslavia
Titov, Gherman S.		50			150	Vostok 2, 1st spaceflight more than 24 hrs.
Tobin, James	1919-	10	20	30	15	Economist, educator, RS
Tocqueville, Alexis de	1805-1859	100	175	300		French political scientist, historian
Todd, John B. S.	1814-1872	50	100	200		WP, MW, lawyer, congress; Army of the Tennessee, N. Missouri Dist.
Tognini, Michael		10	25		25	Soyuz TM-15, 7/27/92, French
Togo, Heihachiro	1848-1934	125	250		200	Japanese admiral, ESPV
Tojo, Hideki	1884-1948	225	500	1250		Japanese general, Prime Minister, ESPV
Tombaugh, Clyde W.	1906-	40	75		130	Astronomer
Tompkins, Daniel	1774-1825	75	150	175		U.S. politician
Tooker, Gary L.	1939-	5	10	25	10	Motorola Inc. CEO
Toombs, Robert Augustus "Bob"	1810-1885	150	250	300		Nearly chosen President of CSA,ESPV-ALS; Union College, lawyer, SL, Congress; Second Manassas, Sharpsburg
Toon, Thomas Fentress	1840-1902	115	265	300		wounded seven times; Wake Forest College, state supt. pub. instruc.; Seven Pines, Seven Days, Fredericksburg*
Toorop, Jan T.	1858-1928	50	100	200		Dutch artist, Symbolist
Torbert, Alfred T. A.	1833-1880	110	200	300		WP, diplomat; Second Manassas, South Mt., Gettysburg*
Toscanini, Arturo	1867-1957	300	500	700	650	Italian conductor

Winfield Scott

Winfield Scott

John Sedgwick

Raphael Semmers

William H. Seward

Joseph Shelby

Philip H. Sheridan

Philip H. Sheridan

Roger Sherman

Roger Sherman

William T. Sherman

Daniel E. Sickles

Jerry Siegel

Sitting Bull

Sitting Bull

NAME	DATES	SIG	DS	ALS	SP	COMMENTS
Totten, Joseph G.	1788-1864	45	75	135		MW, WP; Chief engineer of the army, ESPV-all forms
Toulouse-Lautrec, Henri de	1864-1901	1500	3000	6000		French painter, graphic artist
Tower, John	1925-	15	30		25	U.S. politician
Tower, Zealous B.	1819-1900	30	60	80		WP, MW, engineering, WP-superintendent; Fort Pickens, Second Manassas, Nashville
Townes, Charles Hard	1915-	25	45	75	40	Masers
Townsend, Francis E.	1867-1960	50	100	175	125	U.S. pension reformist of 1933
Toynbee, Arnold	1889-1975	25	75	125	50	British historian, ESPV-DS & ALS
Tracy, Edward Dorr	1833-1863	300	600			killed in action; lawyer, politician; Shiloh, Port Gibson, First Manassas, scarce, ESPV-all forms
Trapier, James Heyward	1815-1865	150	250	300		WP, engineer; Corinth
Travis, William Barret	1809-1836	2500	5000			American adventurer, TR, the Alamo, scarce
Trevelyan, George	1838-1926	25	50	100	70	British historian, statesman
Treves, Sir Fredrick	1853-1923	175	250	360		Surgeon
Trevor-Roper, Hugh	1914-	20	50		40	Historian, SDS-2X
Trimble, Isaac Ridgeway	1802-1888	325	800	925		ESPV; WP, railroad development; Valley, Seven Days, Cedar Mt., Gettysburg,* ESPV-ALS
Trinh, Eugene H.		5	15	25	15	Columbia, 6/25/92
Trippe, Juan T.	1899-1981	50	100		75	Airline founder
Trotman, Alexander J.	1933-	5	10	30	15	Ford Motor Co. president
Trotsky, Leon	1879-1940		4500			Russian revolutionary, assassinated, ESPV-all forms
Troubridge, Sir Ernest Charles Thomas	1862-1926	100	200	250		British admiral
Trudeau, Garry	1948-	30			75	Cartoonist, "Doonesbury"
Trudeau, Pierre	1919-	30	60	100	50	Canadian prime minister
Trujilio Molina, Rafael L.	1891-1961	75	150		300	Dom. Rep. dictator, assassin., ESPV
Truly, Richard H.		25	80		50	Columbia, 11/12/81
Truman, Elizabeth Virginia "Bess"	1885-1982	75	135	240	160	(1919); MO; D-1, First Lady
☆ **Truman, Harry S.**	**1884-1972**	**165**	**400**	**1500**	**550**	**PL, pres. pardon-$2500, WH eng.-$350, TLS-1100, ESPV-all forms, PD-2X, SDS-3X**

NAME	DATES	SIG	DS	ALS	SP	COMMENTS
Trumbull, John	1756-1843	100	240	350		Amer. painter, Rev. war adc, ESPV-ALS, SALS-2X
Trumbull, John (the elder)	1710-1785	300	600	1100		Gov. CN
Trumbull, John (the poet)	1751-1831	60	150	200		Poet; jurist
Trumbull, John (the younger)	1740-1809	140	320	600		Gov. CN; Congress; USS
Trump, Donald	1946-	20	75	100	35	Businessman, RS
Trumpler, Robert	1886-1956	60			80	Astronomer
Truscott, Lucian King, Jr.	1895-1965	30	60	125	50	American general, WWI, WWII
Truxton, Thomas	1753-1822	150	300	500		U.S. Naval officer, ESPV-DS
Tryon, William	1729-1788	150	300	650		Royal Gov. of NC & NY
Tshombe, Moise K.	1919-1969	50	100		100	Congo premier (Zaire)
Tsiolkovsky, Konstantin	1857-1935	850	1750	2500		Russian physicist, scarce in all forms, ESPV
Tuchman, Barbara	1912-1989	50	150	275	75	U.S. history author
Tucker, William Feimster	1827-1881	80	175			assassinated; Emory and Henry College, SL; Perryville, Murfreesboro, Chickamauga
Tugwell, Rexford G.	1891-1979	15	25	40	20	Economist
Tully, Alice	1902-1993	25	45	75	45	Philanthropist, art patron
Tunner, William Henry	1906-1983	15	25	50	25	American air force gen., WWII, KW
Tupolev, Andrey N.	1888-1972	40	80		75	Aircraft designer
Turchin, John B. "The Russian Thunderbolt"	1822-1901	50	125	250		Ill. Central Rrd.; Huntsville, Athens, Chickamauga, Atlanta*
Turner, Frederick J.	1861-1932	55	125	250	100	U.S. historian
Turner, John N.	1929-	15	30		20	Canadian statesman
Turner, John W.	1833-1899	60	125	200		WP, street comm., business exec.; Petersburg, District of Henrico
Turner, Joseph Mallord William	1775-1851	250	600	1240		English painter, ESPV-ALS
Turner, Richmond Kelly	1885-1961	30	50	65	50	American admiral, WWI, WWII
Turner, Ted	1938-	10	60	125	30	Cable News Network founder
Tuttle, James M.	1823-1892	50	100			farmer, sheriff, SL; Fort Donelson, Shiloh, Vicksburg
Tutu, Desmond	1931-	15	50		40	Anglican clergyman, NP, RS, SALS-2X
Tweed, William M.	1823-1878	150	225	375		U.S. politician leader

NAME	DATES	SIG	DS	ALS	SP	COMMENTS
Twiggs, David E.	1790-1862	165	330	750		ESPV; MW; Dist. of LA
Twining, Nathan Farragut	1897-1982	55	125	250	75	American air force gen., WWI, WWII
Tyler, Daniel	1799-1882	50	100	150		WP, iron exec., Ala. rrd. pres.; First Manassas, Corinth, Harper's Ferry
Tyler, Erastus B.	1822-1891	40	80	150		Fur business, Granville College, postmaster; Fredericksville, Chancellorsville, Baltimore
☆ **Tyler, John**	**1790-1862**	**450**	**1000**	**1500**		**ALS content 7x-10x, pres. pardon-$1200; FF:650, SDS-2-3X, ESPV-DS & ALS**
Tyler, Julia Gardiner	1820-1889	200	500		650	(1844); NY; S-5; D-2, First Lady
Tyler, Robert O.	1831-1874	100	200	300		WP; Peninsular, Fredericksburg, Gettysburg*
Tyndale, Hector	1821-1880	50	75	100		Importer, merchant, philanthropist; Front Royal, Cedar Mt., Second Manassas*
Tyson, Laura D.	1947-	5	15	30	15	Economist, educator, Clinton advisor
Udall, Stewart	1920-	15	25		25	U.S. public official
Ueberroth, Peter		10	25		20	Businessman, Baseball Com.
Ue mura, Naomi	1942-1984	25	50		50	Explorer
Ullmann, Daniel	1810-1892	40	80	150		Yale, lawyer; Second Manassas, Cedar Mountain*
Underwood, Adin B.	1828-1888	50	75	150		Brown Univ., port surveyor; Shenandoah Valley, Chancellorsville*
Underwood, Oscar	1862-1929	35	65		55	U.S. politician
Ungaro, Emanuel	1933-	20	45		40	Fashion designer
Upham, Charles H.	1908-	15	35		30	New Zealand soldier
Upton, Emory	1839-1881	60	100	125		SDS-2-3X; WP, WP-Commander of cadets, author; Spotsylvania, Sharpsburg, Fredericksburg,* ESPV-all forms
Urbanowski, Frank	1936-	5	10	15	10	Publisher, MIT Press
Urey, Harold	1893-1981	75	150	325	100	Chemist, NP
Utrillo, Maurice	1883-1955	325	500			French painter, RSPV
Utzon, Jorn	1918-	20	50		50	Architect, ESPV-SP
Vagelos, Pindaros R.	1929-	5	10	25	10	Merck & Company, Inc. CEO, RS

Joseph Smith

Joseph Smith

Richard Dobbs Spaight

Francis E. Spinner

Francis E. Spinner

Joseph Stalin

Henry M. Stanley

Edwin M. Stanton

Alexander Stephens

George Stephenson

Walter H. Stevens

James "Jeb" Stuart

Alfred Stieglitz

Richard Stockton

NAME	DATES	SIG	DS	ALS	SP	COMMENTS
Vail, Theodore N.	1845-1920	50	160	225		Organized Bell Telephone, headed AT&T
Valenti, Carl		10	15	30	15	Publisher, The Wall Street Journal
Vallandigham, Clement L.	1820-1871	115	200	300		Political leader, USHR
Van Alen, James H.	1819-1886	60	125	200		Washington, Peninsular, Hooker's aide-de-c...; Washington, Peninsular, Hooker's aide-de-c...
Van Allen, James	1914-	30	75		70	Physicist
Van Buren, Martin	**1782-1862**	**370**	**925**	**1000**		**FLSP:1500; FF:475, SDS-2X**
Van Cleve, Horatio P.	1809-1891	50	100	165		Princeton, WP, farmer, postmaster; Fishing Creek, Corinth, Murfreesboro*
Van de Kamp, Peter	1901-	20			40	Astronomer, ESPV
Van Den Berg, Lodewijk		10	20	30	15	Challenger, 4/29/85, PU
Van Derveer, Ferdinand	1823-1892	50	90	180		Lawyer, MW, sheriff, judge; Corinth, Perryville, Atlanta*
Van Dorn, Earl	1820-1863	325				assassinated, ESPV; WP, MW; Elkhorn, Corinth, rare
Van Fleet, James Alward	1892-1990	30	75	150	60	American general, WWI, WWII
Van Hoften, James D.		10	25	35	20	Challenger, 4/6/84
Van Rensselaer, Stephen	1764-1839	50	100	160		American general, politician, W1812
Van Vliet, Stewart	1815-1901	50	100	150		WP, MW; AOTP - chief quartermaster, New York City
Van Wyck, Charles H.	1824-1895	40	75	100		Rutgers, lawyer, dist. atty., congress, USS; South Carolina
Vance, Cyrus	1917-	10	20		20	Lawyer, statesman
Vance, Robert Brank	1828-1899	75	150	260		court clerk, USHR, assist. comm. of patents; Cumberland Gap
Vandamme, Dominique Joseph Rene	1770-1830	60	135	215		French general
Vandegrift, Alexander Archer	1887-1973	55	145	250	80	American marine corps general, WWII
Vandenberg, Arthur						
Vandenberg, Arthur H.	1884-1951	15	45	65	25	U.S. senator
Vandenburg, Hoyt Sanford	1899-1954	35	150	275	100	American air force general, WWII
Vanderbilt, Cornelius	1794-1877	365	1000	1650	2650	U.S. financier, est. rrd. & steamship empire
Vanderbilt, Cornelius, Jr.	1843-1899	35	60	90	50	Financier, railroad president

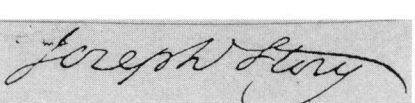

Thomas Stone

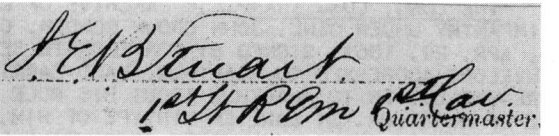

Joseph Story

James E. B. Stuart

James "Jeb" Stuart

Thomas Sully

Charles Sumner

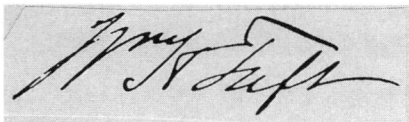

William H. Taft

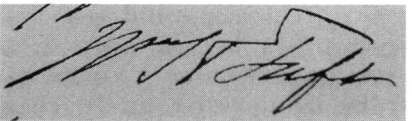

William H. Taft

William H. Taft

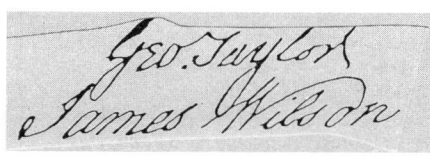

George Taylor & James Wilson

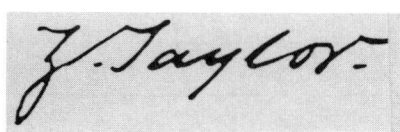

Zachary Taylor

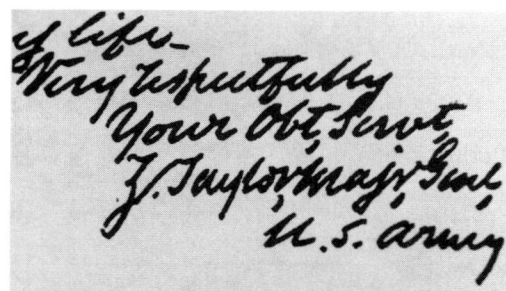

Zachary Taylor

John A. Sutter

NAME	DATES	SIG	DS	ALS	SP	COMMENTS
Vanderbilt, William H.	1821-1885	75	200	300	150	Railroad leader
Vanderlyn, John	1775-1852	200	300	410		American painter
Vandever, William	1817-1893	40	75	150		Lawyer, US Indian inspector, congress; Pea Ridge, Arkansas Post, Atlanta*
Vanzetti, Bartholomeo	1888-1927	750	1600			Political radical, scarce, ESPV
Varick, Richard	1753-1831	100	175	250		Cont'l officer; GW confidential secretary
Vasarely, Viktor	1908 -	50	125		75	Hungarian-born painter
Vaughan, Jr., Alfred Jefferson	1830-1899	115	200	300		VMI, civil engineer, farmer, court clerk; fought in every battle of the West, Atlanta
Vaughn, John Crawford	1824-1875	150	275			ESPV; MW, SL; First Manassas, Vicksburg, Shenandoah, ESPV-ALS
Veach, Charles Lacy		5		25	10	Discovery, 4/28/91, Columbia, 10/22/92, FA
Veatch, James C.	1819-1895	50	100	175		Lawyer, SL, adjutant gen. of Ind.; Fort Donelson, Shiloh, Corinth, Memphis*
Venn, John	1834-1923	85	175			Mathematician
Vera Cruz, Phillip	1905-1994	25	55	75	40	Helped found United Farm Workers Union
Verwoerd, Hendrik F.	1901-1966	100	200			S. African prime minister
Victor Emmanuel III	1869-1947	50	100		75	King of Italy
☆ **Victoria (England)**	**1819-1901**	**200**	**460**	**700**	**1000**	**DS-$750, $1500, SDS-2-3X, Queen of Great Britain, ESPV**
Viele, Egbert L.	1825-1902	35	75	100		WP, MW, chief eng. NY Central Park, congress; Washington, military governor
Villa, Pancho	1878-1923	800	1620	2275		Mexican revolutionary
Villard, Henry	1835-1900	30	65	125		U.S./German born railroad executive, financier
Villard, Oswald G.	1872-1949	45	90	135	75	Journalist, reformer
Villepigue, John Bordenave	1830-1862	300	400	600		ESPV; WP; Pensacola, Mobile, Corinth
Vinson, Carl	1883-1981	20	40		50	U.S. politician
Vinson, Fred M.	1890-1953	100	200	400	265	SC: 1946-1953, KY, Chief Justice, Congressman

Mother Teresa

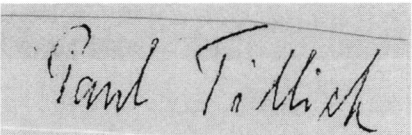

Paul Tillich

Nikola Tesla

Daniel Tompkins

George H. Thomas

Paul Tillich

George H. Thomas

George H. Thomas

Leon Trotsky

Matthew Thornton

Bess Truman

NAME	DATES	SIG	DS	ALS	SP	COMMENTS
Virchow, Rudolf	1821-1902	225	500	725		German pathologist, fdr. cellular pathology
Vlaminck, Maurice de	1876-1958	150	250	400		French painter, graphic artist, writer
Vogdes, Israel	1816-1889	50	100	150		WP, WP-instructor; Fort Pickens, Charleston, Norfolk
Volcker, Paul A.	1927-	10	25		20	Economist
Volta, Alessandro	1745-1827	500	2000	2750		Italian physicist, electricity pioneer, ESPV
Volstead, Andrew	1860-1947	60	125	160		U.S. politician
Volwiler, Ernest H.	1893-1992	25	45	125	40	Thiobarbituric acid derivatives
☆ **Von Braun, Werner**	**1912-1977**	**175**	**450**	**625**	**400**	**German/U.S. rockets developer**
von Steinwehr, Adolph W. A. F. Baron	1822-1877	75	150	230		MW, geographer, cartographer, Yale; First & Second Manassas, Gettysburg*
Voss, James S.		5		25	10	Atlantis, 11/24/91, Discovery, 12/2/92, RS
Voss, Janice E.		5		25	10	Endeavour, 6/21/93, Discovery, 2/3/95
Vuillard, Edouard	1868-1940	150	300	500		French painter, lithographer
Wade, Benjamin	1800-1878	30	65	125		Political leader, USS
Wadsworth, James S,	1807-1864	50	100	200		Harvard, lawyer; Military gov. Dist. of Columbia, Gettysburg
Wadsworth, Jeremiah	1743-1804	175	350	475		Commissary general of Cont'l Army; Congress
Wagner, Robert F.	1877-1953	25	85	150	35	Political leader, USS
Wainwright, Jonathan Mayhew IV	1883-1953	100	180	275	200	American general, WWI, WWII
Waite, Morrison R.	1816-1888	70	140		90	SC: 1874-1888, OH, Chief Justice, ALS-2X, ESPV-all forms
Waite, Terry	1939-	15	30		20	Consultant, hostage
Walcutt, Charles C.	1838-1898	40	80	130		Surveyor, mayor; Shiloh, Vicksburg, Jackson, Atlanta*
Waldheim, Kurt	1918-	20	50		40	Austrian president, RS
Walesa, Lech	1943-	20	45		50	Polish president, RS
Walgreen, Charles R.	1873-1939	50	75	150	80	Founded drugstore chain
Walker, Charles D.		5	15	25	10	Discovery, 8/30/84, RS
Walker, David M.		10	25	40	20	Discovery, 11/8/84, Discovery, 12/2/92
Walker, Frank Robinson	1899-1976	25	50	80	40	American admiral, WWII

Harry Truman

Harry Truman

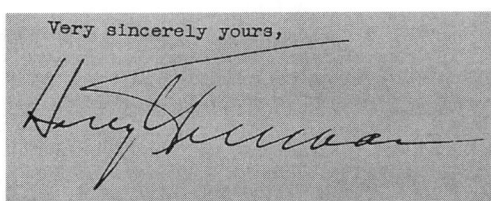

Harry Truman

Very sincerely yours,

Harry Truman

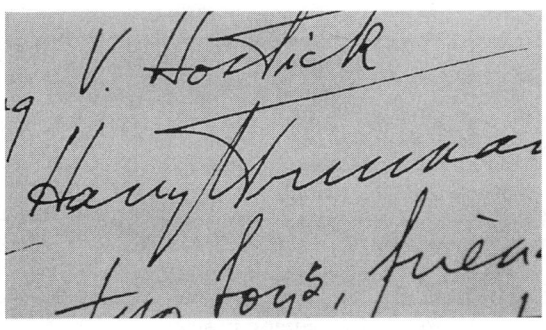

Harry Truman

Harry Truman

Tom Truxton

John Tyler

John Tyler

John Tyler

John Tyler

NAME	DATES	SIG	DS	ALS	SP	COMMENTS
Walker, James Alexander	1832-1901	140	200			Advisary of Gen. Stonewall Jackson; VMI, UVA, lawyer, USHR; Valley, Spotsylvania
Walker, John George	1822-1893	100	200	250		MW, diplomat; Army of Northern Virginia*
Walker, Leroy Pope	1817-1884	200	400	585		Sec. of War - CSA; Univ. of AL, SL, circuit court judge; no battle action
Walker, Lucius Marshall	1829-1863	400	500			nephew of Pres. James K. Polk; WP, mercantile business, killed in duel; Corinth, ESPV
Walker, Mary E.	1832-1919	250		500		Union nurse
Walker, Mort	1923-	10			40	Cartoonist, "Beetle Bailey"
Walker, Reuben Lindsay	1827-1890	115	200	300		very dedicated and active officer; VMI, civil engineer, farmer, railroad supt.; First Manassas, Seven Days
Walker, Robert J.	1801-1869	20	50	75		Political leader, USS
Walker, Walton Harris	1889-1950	45	80	100	65	American general, WWI, WWII
Walker, William Henry Talbot	1816-1864	200	450	500		killed in action, SDS & ALS - 3X; WP, MW; Vicksburg, Chickamauga, Atlanta
Walker, William Stephen	1822-1899	125	235	270		distinguished himself in Mexican War; Georgetown, MW; Petersburg, North Carolina
Wallace, Alfred Russell	1823-1913	100	175	425	225	British naturalist, evolutionist
Wallace, DeWitt & Lila	1889-1981, 1889-1984	55	175	225	150	Husband-wife cofounders of Reader's Digest (Both)
Wallace, George C.	1919-1998	10	35	75	25	Political leader, governor, RS
Wallace, Henry	1888-1965	50	125	200	100	Political leader, sec. of agriculture, VP
Wallace, Lewis "Lew"	1827-1905	175	325	500		Author of "Ben Hur: A Tale of the Christ"; MW, SL, Tty. gov. NM, diplomat; Fort Donelson, Shiloh
Wallace, William Henry	1827-1901	125	250	365		SCC, planter, newspaper pub., lawyer, SL; Second Manassas, South Mt., Sharpsburg
Walpole, Robert	1676-1745	100	200	400		First Prime Minister; 4th Earl of Orford
Walsh, Michael		5	10	20	10	Tenneco Inc. executive
Walter, Ulrich		10		30	20	Columbia, 4/26/93, German scientist, RS

John Tyler

John Tyler

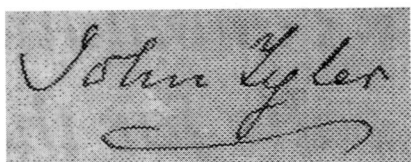

John Tyler

Martin Van Buren

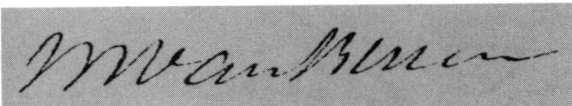

Martin Van Buren

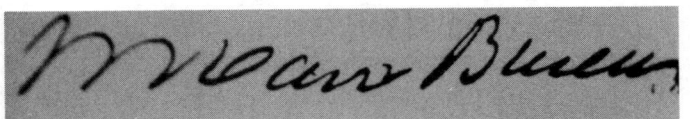

Martin Van Buren

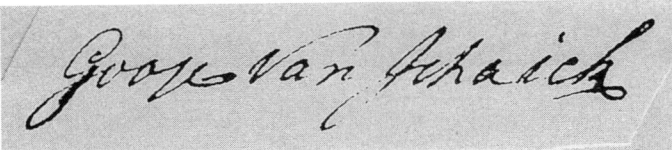

Goosen Van Schaick

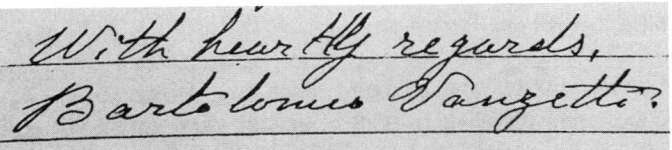

Bartholomeo Vanzetti

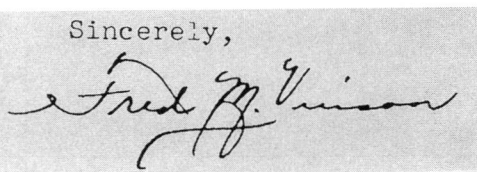

Frederick Vinson

Wernher Von Braun

Friedrich Von Steuben

Friedrich Von Steuben

NAME	DATES	SIG	DS	ALS	SP	COMMENTS
Walthall, Edward Cary	1831-1898	100	200	300		SDS & ALS - 2, ESPV; St. Thomas Hall, lawyer, USS; Corinth, Kentucky, Chickamauga, Chattanoog., WD DS & ALS-2-3X
Walton, E.T.S.	1903-1995	60	115			Nuclear physicist
Walton, George	1741-1804	375	785	1100		Signer DOI; ESPV-DS; $600-SDS-$2500
Walton, Sam	1918-1992	75	150	200	120	U.S. founder of Wall-Mart stores
Walz, Carl E.		5	15	25	10	Discovery, 9/1/93, Columbia, 7/8/94
Wanamaker, John	1838-1922	50	75	150	125	Merchant, political leader
Wanamaker, John	1838-1922	72	100	200	125	U.S. department-store merchandising pioneer
Wang, An	1920-1990	25	50	80	50	Magnetic pulse controlling device
Wang, Taylor G.		10	25	30	20	Challenger, 4/29/85
Warburg, Paul M.	1868-1932	25	40	55	45	Banker
Ward, Aaron Montgomery	1843-1913	65	150	240	125	Established first mail-order firm
Ward, Artemas	1727-1800	375	1250			American politician and general
Ward, John H. H.	1823-1903	40	75	100		MW, NY courts clerk; First & Second Manassas, Peninsular*
Ward, John Quincy Adams	1830-1910	30	75	125		American sculptor
Ward, Lillian D.	1867-1940	50	75	145		Social worker
Ward, Samuel	1725-1776	225	500	650		Gov. RI; Congress
Ward, William T.	1808-1878	50	100	175		Mary's College, MW, SL, congress, lawyer; Kentucky, Atlanta, Savannah
Warhol, Andy	1928-1987	130	225	500	260	American artist, film-maker, SB-$600, ESPV
Warner, James Meech	1836-1897	40	75	150		WP, postmaster; Washington, Spotsylvania, Fisher's Hill
Warner, Seth	1743-1784	250	500			Militia officer; VT
Warren, Earl	1891-1974	65	200		250	SC: 1953-1969, CA, Chief Justice, governor
Warren, Fitz-Henry	1816-1878	40	80	145		Sec. asst. postmaster gen., diplomat; Dept. of the Gulf, Red River
Warren, Gouverneur K.	1830-1882	125	250	400		SLS/DS & SALS - 2X; WP, WP-instructor, prolific writer; Bethel Church, Gaine's Mill, Second Man., WD & ALS-2X
Warren, James	1726-1808	125	250	500		Politician leader

Jonathon M. Wainwright

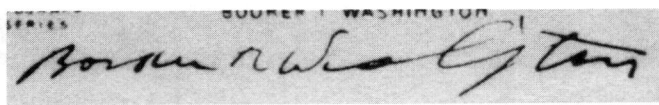

Booker T. Washington

George Washington

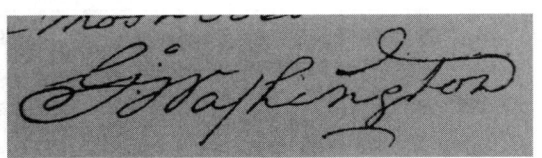

George Washington

George Washington

Lew Wallace

George Walton

George Washington

Andy Warhol

Anthony Wayne

NAME	DATES	SIG	DS	ALS	SP	COMMENTS
Warren, Joseph	1741-1775	7000				Patriot leader killed at Bunker Hill
Washburn, Cadwallader C.	1818-1882	60	100	125		Fnd. Washburn, Crosby & Co. (Gen. Mills); lawyer, congress, gov. Wisc.; Missouri, Dept. of W. Tennessee
☆ **Washington, Booker T.**	**1856-1915**	**225**	**375**	**800**	**1350**	**Educator, SALS-2-3X, ESPV**
Washington, Bushrod	1762-1829	125	350	775		SC: 1798-1829, VA, serv. over 30 years.
☆ **Washington, George**	**1732-1799**	**5000**	**12500**	**20000**		**ALS-content dependent, SALS & SDS-AA**
Washington, William	1752-1810	100	180	300		Cont'l officer; relative of C in C.
Wasserman, August von	1866-1925	75	150	300	135	German bacteriologist, ESPV
Waterhouse, Richard	1832-1876	175	300	500		MW; Red River, Arkansas, Pleasant Hill
Watson. James	1928-	20	40		30	Geneticist, NP
Watson, Thomas E.	1856-1922	20	45	55	30	Political leader, USHR
Watson, Thomas J.	1874-1956	75	150	300	150	Head of IBM 1914-1956
Watt, James E.	1736-1819	450	800	1650		British mech. eng., engine inventor, ESPV-ALS
Watterson, Bill	1958-	20			50	Cartoonist, "Calvin and Hobbes"
Watts, George Frederic	1817-1904	75	150	300		English painter, sculptor
Waul, Thomas Neville	1813-1903	115	250			SCC, lawyer, farmer; Vicksburg, Red River, Jenkin's Ferry
Wavell, Archibald Percival	1883-1950	40	140	200	75	British field marshal
Wayne, Anthony "Mad Anthony"	1745-1796	750	1750	3500		Cont'l gen.; papers in Pa. Hist. Soc.; SDA-2X, ESPV
Wayne, Henry Constantine	1815-1883	150	250	350		WP, quartermaster, lumber business, MW; Inspector General of Georgia
Wayne, James M.	1790-1867	100	225	400		SC: 1835-1867, GA, serv. over 30 yrs, SP scarce
Weaver, Robert C.	1907-	20	50	80	45	Political leader
Webb, Alexander S.	1835-1911	40	80	150		ESPV; WP, WP-instructor, pres. College of City NY; Peninsular, Fort Pickens, Gettysburg
Webb, Samuel Blatchley	1753-1807	100	375	500		Cont'l officer; ADC & Sec; to GW; SALS-2X
Webb, Sidney J. & Beatrice	1859-1947, 1858-1943	45	100	200		Fabian Society and Labor Party members

Daniel Webster

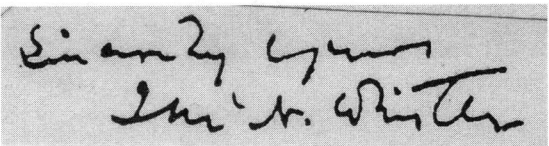

James M. Whistler

Gideon Welles

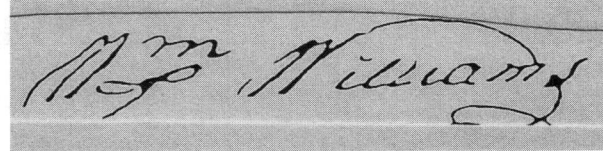

William IV of England

Benjamin West

William Williams

George Westinghouse

William Williams

William Williams

William Whipple

Hugh Williamson

William Whipple

59

Edith Bolling Wilson

- 520 -

NAME	DATES	SIG	DS	ALS	SP	COMMENTS
Weber, Max (Von Weber)	1824-1901	50	100	150		Diplomat, tax assessor; Sharpsburg, Washington, Harpers Ferry
☆ **Webster, Daniel**	**1782-1852**	**125**	**300**	**400**		**Political leader, USHR, USS, SLS-$1750, SDS-2X**
Webster, Joseph D.	1811-1876	100	200	250		Dartmouth College, civil engineer, MW; Grant's and Sherman's chief of staff
Webster, Noah	1758-1843	500	700	1250		Lexicographer, SC-$500
Wedemeyer, Albert Coady	1896-1990	35	85	175	75	American general, WWII
Weed, Thurlow	1797-1882	20	30	40		Political leader, journalist
Wegener, Alfred L.	1880-1930	65	130	220	80	German meteorologist, cont. drift theorist
Weidenbaum, Murray L.	1927-	10	20	40	15	Economist, educator, author
Weil, Andre	1906-	20	50		45	Mathematician
Weil, Louis A. III	1941-	5	10	20	10	Publisher, The Arizona Republic CEO
Weinberg, Steven	1933-	20	40		35	Nuclear physicist
Weinberger, Caspar	1917-	10	25		20	U.S. statesman
Weisiger, David Addison	1818-1899	115	250	400		SDS & ALS - 2X; MW, bank cashier, businessman; Seven Pines, Seven Days, Second Manassas
Weitz, Paul J.		8		25	10	Skylab 2, Challenger, 4/4/83, RS
Weitzel, Godfrey	1835-1884	50	100	200		WP, WP-professor, engineer; Fort Fisher, Appomattox
Weizmann, Chaim	1874-1952	625	1500	2475		Zionist leader, first Israeli pres., ESPV
Welch, John F., Jr.	1935-	15	30	85	20	General Electric Co. CEO, does not sign
Weld, Theodore D.	1803-1895	35	70	100		Reformer
Welles, Gideon	1802-1878	125	250	300	700	Political leader, LS-$295
Wells, William	1837-1892	75	150	225		Merchant, SL; Shenandoah Valley, Second Bull Run*
Wells-Barnett, Ida B.	1862-1931	120	275	575		Reformer
Wescott, Robert		5	10	25	10	Economist
Wesley, John	1703-1791	475	1000	2000		British theologian, priest
Wessells, Henry W.	1809-1889	50	100	200		WP, MW; Missouri, AOTP, Peninsular, Seven Pines
West, Benjamin	1738-1820	275	750	1500		American history & portrait painter, ESPV

James Wilson

Woodrow Wilson ("W.W.")

James Wilson

James Wilson

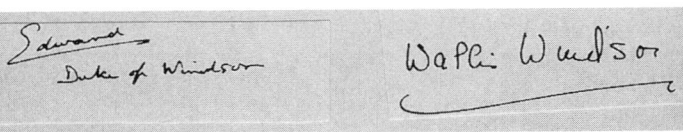

King Edward VIII of England & Wallis Warfield

Woodrow Wilson

Woodrow Wilson

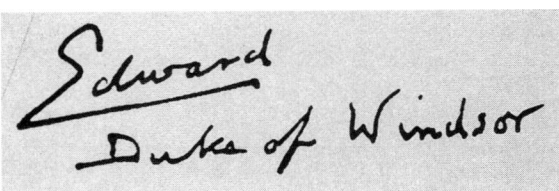

King Edward VIII of England

Woodrow Wilson

Woodrow Wilson

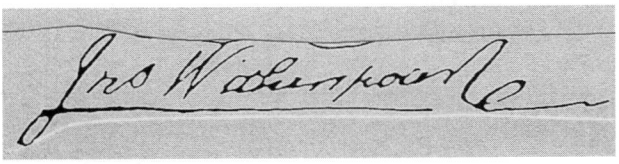

John Witherspoon

Oliver Wolcott

Woodrow Wilson

Levi Woodbury

NAME	DATES	SIG	DS	ALS	SP	COMMENTS
West, Joseph R.	1822-1898	50	100	150		Univ. of Penn., MW, Dept. US marshal, USS; Arizona, Red River
Westinghouse, George	1846-1914	150	500	750	400	Steam-powered brake devices
Westinghouse, George	1846-1914	140	650	775	300	Inventor, manufacturer, Westinghouse Elec.
Westmoreland, William Childs	1914-	25	75	125	50	American general, WWII, KW, VW
Weston, Edward	1886-1958	60	130		100	U.S. photographer, landscapes
Westover, Russ	1887-1966	25			40	Cartoonist, "Tillie the Toiler"
Wetherbee, James D.		5		25	12	Columbia, 1/9/90, Columbia, 10/22/92, RS
Weygand, Maxime	1867-1965	35	70		80	French general
Wharton, Gabriel Colvin	1824-1906	100	200	220		SDS-2X; VMI, civil engineer, SL, miner; New Market, Shenandoah, Washington
Wharton, John Austin	1828-1865	285	500	1200		ESPV; SCC, lawyer, killed during quarrel; Shiloh, Murfreesboro, Chickamauga*
Wheaton, Frank	1833-1903	65	120			First Manassas, Williamsburg, VA Peninsula*;
Wheeler, John A.	1911-	15	30		25	Physicist
Wheeler, Joseph	1836-1900	200	440	700		very distinguished cavalry officer, SDS- 5X; WP, USHR; Army of Tennessee and Mississippi, Shiloh,* WD-2X
Wheeler, William	1819-1887	75	200			U.S. politician
Whipple, Abraham	1733-1819	250	600			Cont'l naval officer; captured first British frigate
Whipple, Amiel W.	1816-1863	150	250	350		Killed in action; WP, engineer, surveyor; First Manassas, Washington, Chancellor,,,
Whipple, Fred	1906-	10	30		25	Astronomer
Whipple, William	**1730-1785**	**700**	**1500**	**1500**		**Signer DOI; NH; "Wm: Whipple;" DS-$2700, SALS-2X, ESPV-DS & ALS**
Whipple, William D.	1826-1902	40	75	100		WP, aide-de-camp W.T. Sherman; First Manassas, Chattanooga, Atlanta
Whistler, James Abbott McNeill	1834-1903	300	500	625		American-born painter, graphic artist
Whitaker, Walter C.	1823-1887	50	100	165		MW, lawyer, farmer, SL; Shiloh, Murfreesboro, Atlanta*

☆ (appears left of Whipple, William row)

Virginia Woolf

Wilbur Wright

John E. Wool

Jamie Wyeth

George Wythe

Frank W. Woolworth

Bob Younger

Frank Lloyd Wright

Florenz Ziegfeld

Orville Wright

Felix K. Zollicoffer

NAME	DATES	SIG	DS	ALS	SP	COMMENTS
White, Alfred T.	1846-1921	40	75	125		Reformer
White, Andrew D.	1832-1918	25	100	150	75	Educator, diplomat
White, Byron R.	1917-	45	120	175	60	SC: 1962-1993, CO, serv. over 30 years.
White, Edward D.	1845-1921	50	175	225	135	SC: 1894-1910, LA, first named "Chief" Justice
White, Edward H. II	? - 1967	215	400		650	Gemini-Titan 4, 1st Amer. to "space walk"
White, Julius	1816-1890	35	75	150		SL; Elkhorn Tavern, Harper's Ferry, Knoxville
White, Sir George Stuart	1835-1912	30	50	75		British field marshal
White, Thomas Dresser	1901-1965	30	60	80	50	American air force general, WWII
Whitehead, Alfred N.	1861-1947	70	200	365	125	Educator, philosopher, mathematician
Whitehead, Alfred North	1861-1947	100	250	550	250	British philosopher, author
Whitfield, John Wilkins	1818-1879	125	200			MW, Indian agent, SL; Pea Ridge, Iuka, Vicksburg
Whiting, William Henry Chase	1824-1865	300	675	1400		killed in action, distinguished academic career; WP; Shenandoah, Seven Pines, Seven Days, ESPV-all forms, scarce
Whitney, Eli	**1765-1825**	**700**	**2250**	**4000**		**Cotton gin**
Whitney, John Hay	1905-1982	20	65	140	75	U.S. publisher, sportsman, philanthropist
Whitney, William C.	1841-1904	20	30	50	30	Financier, political leader
Whittaker, Charles E.	1901-1973	50	75	170	85	SC: 1957-1962, MO
Whittle, Sir Frank	1907-	15	35		30	Aviator
Whitwan, David R.	1942-	5	10	20	10	Whirpool Corp. executive
Wickham, Williams Carter	1820-1888	100	280	400		UVA, lawyer, planter, SL, court justice; First Manassas, Maryland, Shenandoah, WD-DS & ALS-2X
Wiener, Norbert	1894-1964	35	90	185	75	U.S. mathematician, cybernetics fdr.
Wiesel, Elie		10	40		25	Educator
Wiesenthal, Simon	1908-	15	40	100	30	Nazi hunter
Wigfall, Louis Trezevant	1816-1874	115	225	325		somewhat controversial; UVA, USC, SL, USS; Member of Confederate Senate

NAME	DATES	SIG	DS	ALS	SP	COMMENTS
Wigner, Eugene	1902-1995	25	50	75	50	U.S. quantum theorist, nuclear physicist, SALS-2X
Wilberforce, William	1759-1833	60	150	275		British social reformer
Wilcox, Cadmus Marcellus	1824-1890	160	325	375		well-respected by both North & South; Univ. of Nashville, WP, MW, Land Office; Army of Northern Virginia*
Wild, Edward A.	1825-1891	100	175	250		Silver miner, Harvard; First Bull Run, Peninsular, Seven Pines*
Wiley, Harvey W.	1844-1930	100	200	300	150	Reformer, chemist
Wilkes, Charles	1798-1877	60	120	175		U.S. Naval officer
Wilkes, Maurice	1913-	10	25		20	Computer scientist
Wilkie, Sir David	1785-1841	50	100	125		Scottish painter
Wilkins, Maurice	1916-	15	35		25	Biophysicist
Wilkins, Roy	1901-1981	15	30	60	20	Reformer, NAACP, RS
Wilkinson, James	1757-1825	150	325	400		Cont'l officer; scoundrel
Wilkinson, Theodore Stark	1888-1946	50	100	125	75	Amer. admiral, WWI, WWII, MOH
Will, George	1884-1946	140	325	475	250	American Tobacco
Willard, Emma Hart	1787-1870	50	115	175		Pioneer of higher education for women
Willard, Francis E.	1839-1898	55	75	150		U.S. temperance, women's rights leader
Willard, Frank	1893-1958	45			75	Cartoonist, "Moon Mullins"
Willcox, Orlando B.	1823-1907	65	135	250		WP, MW, author; Sharpsburg, First Manassas, Overland*
Willett, Marinus	1740-1830	100	150	250		Cont'l officer
William III (England)	1650-1702	650	1600	2650		
William IV (England)	1765-1837	100	285	300		SDS-2X, third son of George III
Williams, Alpheus S.	1810-1878	100	175	330		Yale, lawyer, MW, congress, diplomat; Cedar Mountain, AOTP, Gettysburg, Atlanta*
Williams, David H.	1819-1891	40	100	165		Civil engineer, MW, prolific writer; Seven Pines, Malvern Hill, Maryland*
Williams, Donald E.		5	15	25	10	Discovery, 4/12/85, Atlantis, 10/18/89
Williams, J.R.	1888-1957	30			50	Cartoonist, "Out Our Way"

NAME	DATES	SIG	DS	ALS	SP	COMMENTS
Williams, John Stuart "Cerro Gordo"	1818-1898	75	150	275		Miami Univ., MW, SL, farmer, USS; Kentucky, SW Virginia, Army of TN
Williams, Nelson	1823-1897	40	75	120		Businessman, dept. customs collector NYC; Missouri, Shiloh
Williams, Otho Holland	1749-1794	150	300	640		Cont'l general; talented cmdr.
Williams, Robert R.	1886-1965	35	70	125	50	Isolation of Vitamin B1 (Thiamine)
Williams, Roger	c.1603-1683	4200	15750			Religious leader, founder Rhode Island
Williams, Seth	1822-1866	50	80	120		SLS/DS-2X; WP, MW; Adjutant general's department, AOTP
☆ **Williams, William**	**1731-1811**	**300**	**440**	**600**		**Signer; CT; DS - $1450 (order); ESPV-DS, SDS & SALS-2X**
Williamson, James A.	1829-1902	80	175	300		ESPV; Knox College, comm. gen. land Office; Elkhorn Tavern, Chickasaw, Vicksburg*
Willkie, Wendell L.	1892-1944	20	60	150	100	Political leader
Wilmot, David	1814-1868	70	150	200		Political leader
Wilson, Charles E.	1890-1961	25	45		40	U.S. auto industry executive
Wilson, Edith Bolling Galt	1872-1961	85	225	280	200	(1915); VA; No children; FF - $100, First Lady
Wilson, Ellen Louise Axson	1860-1914	125	375	600	400	(1885); GS; D-3, First wife of President Wilson
Wilson, Gahan	1930-	10			30	Macabre cartoonist
Wilson, Harold	1916-1995	50	125	150	75	British Labor party leader
Wilson, Henry	1812-1875	75	125	150		U.S. politician
Wilson, James (See DOI & Constitution)	1742-1798	725	1062	1600		SC: 1789-1798, PA, Signer, DS - $800, CC, DS-C, war dated tough and higher $, PA
Wilson, James H.	1837-1925	100	200	375		Prolific writer; WP, engineer, McClellan aide-de-camp; South Mt., Vicksburg, Washington*
Wilson, Kemmons	1913-	35	100	135	95	Holiday Inn chain founder, RS
☆ **Wilson, Thomas Woodrow**	**1856-1924**	**240**	**600**	**100**	**825**	**Very rare as ALS during term, NC-750, MA-1100, TLS-950, PD DS & ALS-2X**
Wilson, Tom	1931-	15			45	Cartoonist, "Ziggy"
Winchester, Oliver	1810-1880	225	500	775		Gun manufacturer

GEN-POLIT V

NAME	DATES	SIG	DS	ALS	SP	COMMENTS
Winder, John Henry	1800-1865	100	225	365		SDS-2-3X, ESPV; WP, MW, provost marshal of Richmond; Commissary general of prisoners
Winter, Alan	1937	5	10	15	10	Former publisher, Cambridge University Press
Wise, Henry Alexander	1806-1876	75	150	250		author, b-i-l of G. Meade; Wash. College, USHR, diplomat, Gov. VA; West Virginia, North Carolina
Wise, Isaac M.	1819-1900	75	150	200		Religious leader, rabbi, college pres.
Wise, Stephen S.	1874-1949	50	75	125	50	Religious leader, rabbi, editor "Opinion"
Wisoff, Peter J.K.		5	15	25	10	Endeavour, 6/21/93, Endeavour, 9/30/94
Wistar, Issac	1827-1905	40	100	140		Haverford College, lawyer, writer; Ball's Bluff, Peninsular, Sharpsburg
Withers, Jones Mitchell	1814-1890	70	165	270		WP, MW, mayor of Mobile, claim agent; Shiloh, Kentucky, Murfreesboro
Witherspoon, John	**1723-1794**	**700**	**2000**			**Signer; clergyman; Col. Pres.; scarce ALS**
Wittgenstein, Ludwig	1889-1951	50	100	200	75	Austrian philosopher, professor
Wolcott, Oliver	1726-1797	200	500	1200		Signer DOI; militia general; CT; SALS-2X
Wolcott, Oliver, Jr.	1760-1833	100	200	300		U.S. politician
Wolf, David		5	15	25	10	Columbia, 10/18/93
Wolseley, Sir Garnet Joseph	1833-1913	40	85	125	40	British field marshal
Wood, Grant	1892-1942	200	400	500		American painter, SP-$300
Wood, Leonard	1860-1927	35	75	100	160	American general, WWI, Rough Riders
Wood, Sterling Alexander	1823-1891	100	225	280		Jesuit College of St. Joseph, lawyer, SL; Shiloh, Murfreesboro, Chickamauga*
Wood, Thomas J.	1823-1906	50	100	150		ESPV-ALS; WP, MW; Shiloh, Perryville, Murfreesboro*
Woodbury, Levi	1789-1851	60	150	265		SC: 1845-1851, NH, US, sec. Navy
Woodhull, Victoria	1838-1927	130	225	500		Reformer
Woods, Charles	1827-1885	40	75	125		WP; Fort Donelson, Shiloh, Carolinas*
Woods, William B.	1824-1887	70	145	200	150	SC: 1880-1887, GA, scarce in all forms

☆ (star marker beside Witherspoon, John)

GEN POLIT V

NAME	DATES	SIG	DS	ALS	SP	COMMENTS
Woodward, Calvin M.	1837-1914	25	50	75		Educator
Wool, John E.	1784-1869	125	250	400		Oldest active cmfdr., SALS-2X; MW; Department of the East, Dept. of the Pacific
Woolard, Edgar S., Jr.	1934-	5	10		10	Du Pont chairman
Woolworth, Frank W.	1852-1919	315	800	1620		Created five and dime store, ESPV-DS
Wooster, David	1711-1777	250	740	2500		Cont'l general, scarce ALS
Worden, Alfred M.		15	40		30	Apollo 15, RS
Worth, William Jenkins	1794-1849	40	80	150		American general, W1812
Wren, Christopher	1632-1723	1650				Architect, ESPV, scarce in all forms
Wright, Frank Lloyd ☆	**1867-1959**	**1000**	**1850**	**4375**		**American architect, SP-$3150, ESPV-DS**
Wright, Horatio	1820-1899	75	150	235		Involved with completion of Washington Mon.; WP, engineer; Florida, First Manassas, Dept. of the Ohio
Wright, Marcus Joseph	1831-1922	75	130	175		lawyer, court clerk, prolific writer; Shiloh, Murfreesboro, Chickamauga*
Wright, Sewall	1889-1988	30	60	100	50	U.S. evolutionary theorist
Wright, Silas	1795-1847	15	40	75		Political leader, USHR
Wright, Orville	1871-1948	500	800	1570	2600	Aviator
Wright, Wilbur	1867-1912	750	1850		4100	Aviator
Wrigley, Philip K.	1894-1977	75	150	225	150	Cubs owner, RS!
Wrigley, William, Jr.	1861-1932	150	350	430	250	U.S. chewing gum founder
Wulcutt, Terrence W.		5		15	10	Endeavour, 9/30/94, RS!
Wyeth, Andrew ☆	**1917-**	**250**	**500**	**700**	**900**	**American painter, son of N.C. Wyeth, SB-$400**
Wyeth, Jamie	1946-	100		375	225	American painter, son of Andrew, SB-$300, -$150-signed poster
Wyeth, Newell Convers	1882-1944	175	450	900		American painter, illustrator, ALS-2X, ESPV
Wythe, George	1726-1806	500	1000			Signer DOI; VA; statesman; jurist; "G Wythe," ESPV, SDS-2-3X
Yeager, Charles E.	1923-	25	60	100	50	National Aviation Hall of Fame, RS
Yeats, Jack Butler	1871-1957	50	100	200		Irish painter, had son by the same name
Yeltsin, Boris	1931-	325			500	Russian president, ESPV

NAME	DATES	SIG	DS	ALS	SP	COMMENTS
York, Alvin	1887-1964	150	275		400	U.S. soldier, hero
Young, Andrew	1932-	10	25		25	Civil rights activist
Young, Art	1866-1943	30			55	Political cartoonist, satirist
Young, Brigham	1801-1877	520	1500	4000		U.S. Mormon ldr, SDS-5-6X, SALS-2-3X
Young, Chic	1901-1973	45			100	Cartoonist, "Blondie"
Young, Jane		5	10	15	15	Publisher, The Atlantic Monthly
Young, John W.		50	125		150	Gemini 10, Apollo 10, 1st shuttle flight C1981
Young, Pierce Manning Butler	1836-1896	75	155	285		GMI, WP, USHR; Maryland, Carolinas
Young, Whitney M.	1921-1971	15	30	55	20	Reformer
Zapata, Emiliano	c.1879-1919	625	1600	1750		Mexican revolutionary, SALS-2X
Zeppelin, Ferdinand von	1838-1917	300	550	2000	1000	German soldier, aeronaut, airship designer, SDS-2X, ESPV
Zollicoffer, Feliz Kirk	1812-1862	375	465	800		SDS-2-3X; journalist, SL, state comptroller, USHR; Camp Wildcat, Kentucky, Mill Springs, ESPV
Zumwalt, Elmo Russell	1920-	25	75	150	50	U.S. admiral, WWII, KW, VW
Zworykin, Vladimir Kosma	1889-1982	50	150	250	100	Cathode ray tube

Common Historical Documents

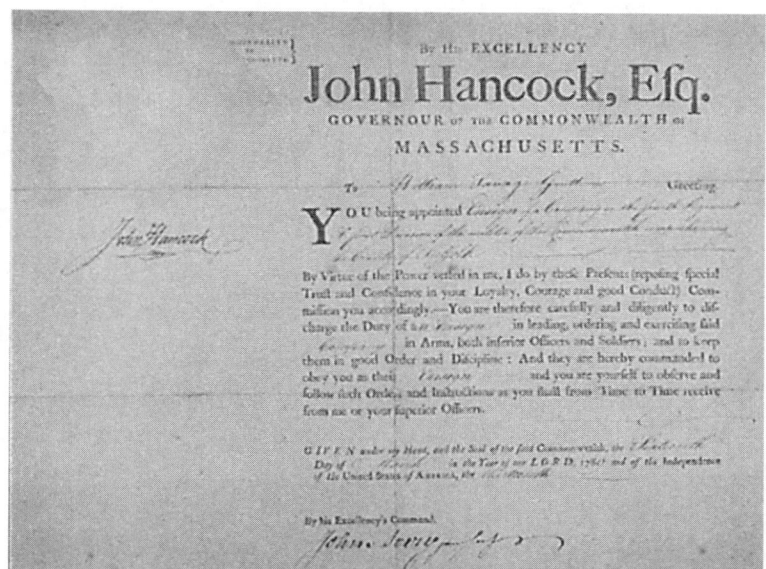

John Hancock Naval appointment

James Madison
Marine appointment

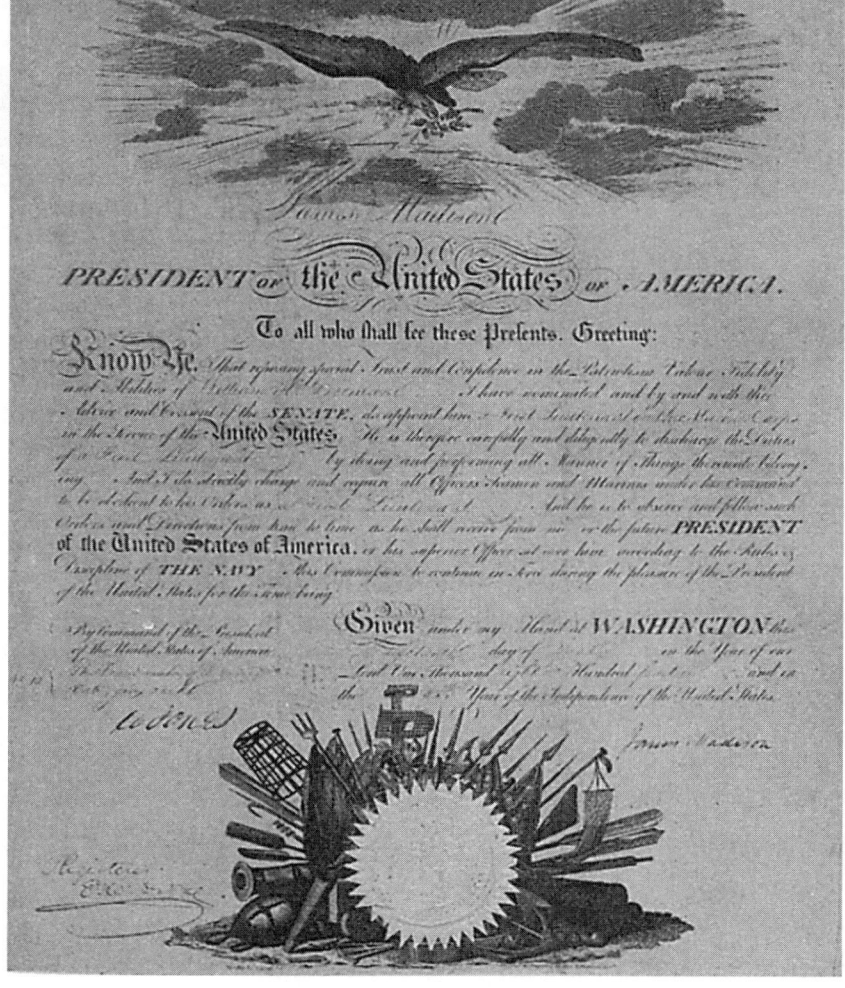

Abraham Lincoln
Naval commission

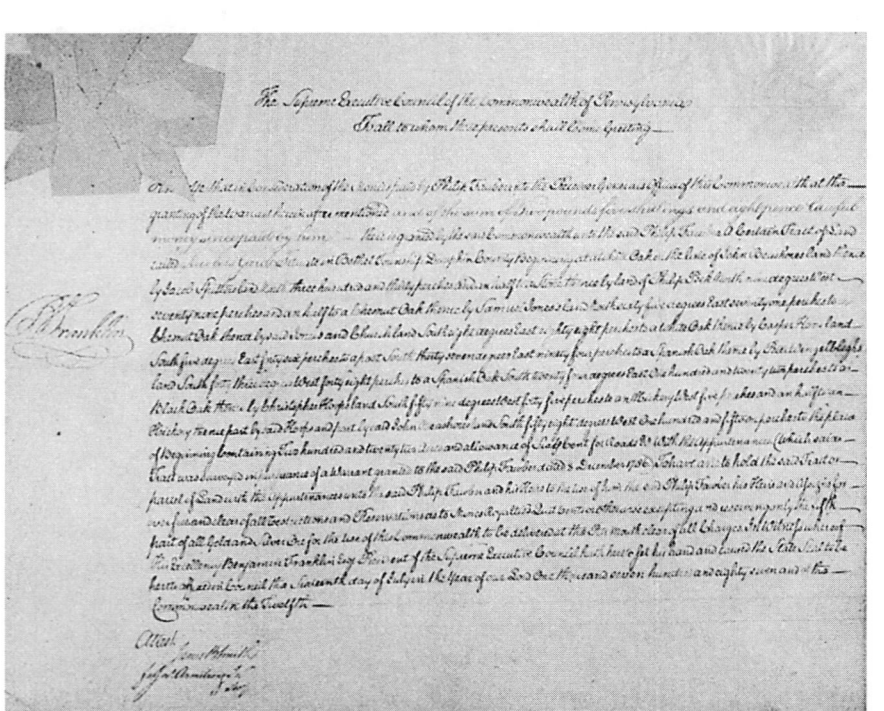

Ben Franklin
Land grant

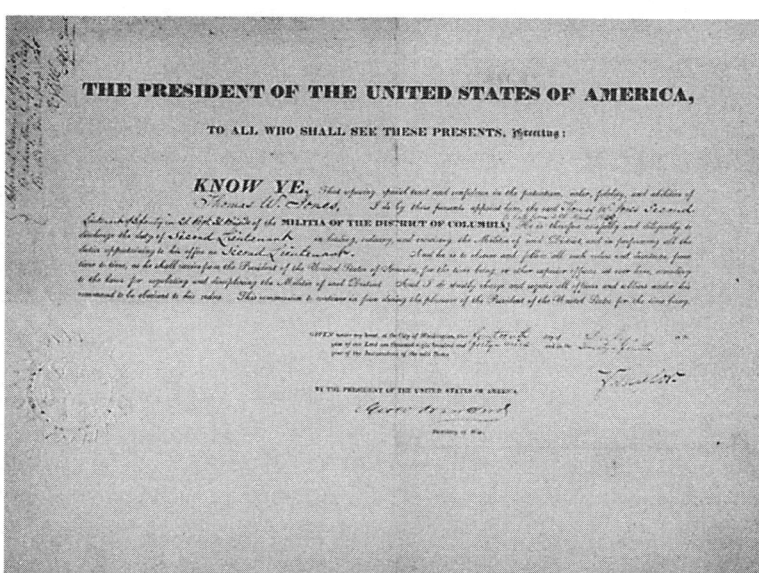

Thomas W. Jones
Military Appointment

Henry Laurens
Army Appointment

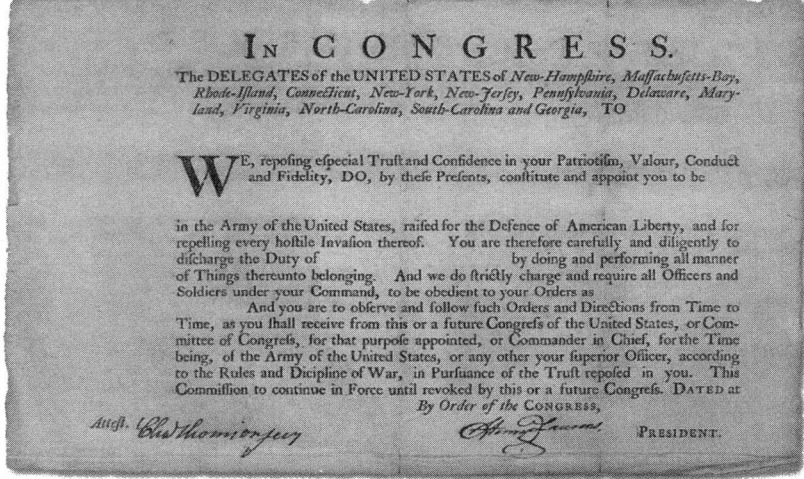

Theodore Roosevelt
Naval appointment

Index

BIBLIOGRAPHY & RECOMMENDED READING

Baker, Mark Allen, *Auto Racing Memorabilia and Price Guide* (Krause Publications, 1996).

Baker, Mark Allen, *Price Guide to Rock 'n' Roll Memorabilia* (Krause Publications, 1997).

Baker, Mark Allen, *Collector's Guide to Celebrity Autographs* (Krause Publications, 1996).

Baker, Mark Allen, *Baseball Autograph Handbook* (Krause Publications, 2nd ed 1991).

Baker, Mark Allen, *All Sports Autograph Guide* (Krause Publications, 1995).

Boatner II, Mark M., *Encyclopedia of the American Revolution* (Stackpole Books, 1974).

Chilvers, Ian, Osborne, Harold and Farr, Dennis, editors, *The Oxford Dictionary of Art* (Oxford University Press, 1988).

Cushman, Clare, editor, *The Supreme Court Justices, Illustrated Biographies, 1789-1995* (Washington, D.C., 2nd ed 1995).

Dupuy, Trevor, Johnson, Curt and Bongard, David, *The Harper Encyclopedia of Military Biography* (HarperCollins Publishers Inc., 1996).

Famighetti, Robert, ed. dir., *The World Almanac and Book of Facts 1998* (World Almanc Books, 1997).

Garraty, Jerome A. and Sternstein, Jerome L., editors, *Encyclopedia of American Biography* (HarperCollins Publishers Inc., 2nd ed 1996).

Krantz, Les and McCormick, Jim, *The Peoplepedia, The Ultimate Reference on the American People* (Henry Holt and Company Inc., 1996).

Reese, Michael II, *Autographs of the Confederacy* (Cohasco, Inc., 1981).

Warner, Ezra, *Generals In Blue, Lives of the Union Commanders* (Louisiana State University Press, 1995).

Warner, Ezra, *Generals In Gray, Lives of the Confederate Commanders* (Louisiana State University Press, 1995).

Webster's New Biographical Dictionary (Merriam-Webster Inc., Publishers, 1988).

Periodicals

Autograph Times. 1125 W. baseline Rd. #2-153, Mesa, AZ 85210.

Sports Collectors Digest. Krause Publications, 700 E. State Street, Iola, WI 54990.

The Autograph Collector's Magazine. P.O. Box 55328, Stockton, CA 95205.

The Autograph Review. 305 Carlton Rd., Syracuse, NY 13207.

Additional Source Material and Notes

Advertisements, catalogs, flyers, direct mailers, prices realized:

A. Lovell Elliott Autographs, Alexander Autographs, Inc., Batchelder, Robert F., Beverly Hills Autograph Co., Blake LeVine, Bob Colip, Butterfield & Butterfield, Celebrity Autographs of Southern California, Christie's, Colonnade of History, eac Gallery, Early American History Auctions, Inc., Elmer's Nostalgia, Inc., Executive Collectibles Gallery, Inc., Fraser's Letters & documents, Gallery of History, G&P Autographs Intd., Golden State Autographs, Herman Darvick Autograph Auctions, History Brokers, Historical Documents International, Inc., International Memorabilia Brokers Inc., Jefferson Rarities, Jim Fugate Autographs, Jim Stinson Sports Collectibles, Kohl's Celebrity Gallery, Les Perline & Co., Maine Street Fine Books & Manuscripts, Mark Vardakis, Max Rambod Autographs, Memoirs of History, Merit Adventures, Michael J. Amenta, Moments in Time, Nate's Autographs, Nelson Deedle Ent., Odyssey Group, P & P Autographs, Paul C. Richards, Autographs, Phyllis Goldman, Piece of History, Int'l, Piece of the Past, Profiles in History, R&R Enterprises, Remember When Antiquities, Richard MacCallum Fine Autographs, Rivendell Rarities Ltd., R.M. Smythe, Satrtifacts, Scott J. Winslow Associates, Inc., Stan's Sports & Celebrity Memorabilia, Seaport Autographs, Searle's Autographs, Sotheby's, Sterncastle Collectibles, Stephen Koschal, Steven S. Raab Autographs, Swann Galleries, The Kenneth W. Rendell Gallery, T. Alan Hartman, T. Vennett-Smith, Terry Patton, Theodore's, Todd Mueller, Tripper D's Autographs, University Archives, Veronica Andrew Enterprises, Vince Cutler Rarities, Visionary Memorabilia, Walk of Fame Autographs, Walter Burks Autographs, William Linehan Autographs

About the Author

Mark Allen Baker received his bachelor's degree from the State University of New York. His post graduate work has included studies and seminars at Rochester Institute of Technology, *Rochester Institute of Technology*, George Washington University and the Massachusetts Institute of Technology. His articles, artwork, and photography have appeared in more than seventy periodicals including *Computer Graphics World, Computer Pictures, CFO, Public Relations Journal, Personal Computing, Topps Magazine, Antique News, Goldmine* and *Sports Collectors Digest.*

An accomplished writer and historian, Mr. Baker is the author of ten books. He was awarded a lifetime donor membership to the National Baseball Hall of Fame for the research on his first book, the Baseball Autograph Handbook, published by Krause Publications for the first time in 1990. His work has been referenced in such prestigious media as *Sports Illustrated, ESPN* and *USA Today Baseball Weekly.* Mr. Baker also acts as a boxing historian for the International Boxing Hall of Fame in Canastota, New York. As a collector of historic autographs and manuscripts for 35 years, he has been retained in numerous court cases because of his expertise in the area.

Additional biographical information can be found in numerous professional directories, including Who's Who in the East, Who's Who in Entertainment, and Who's Who in America.

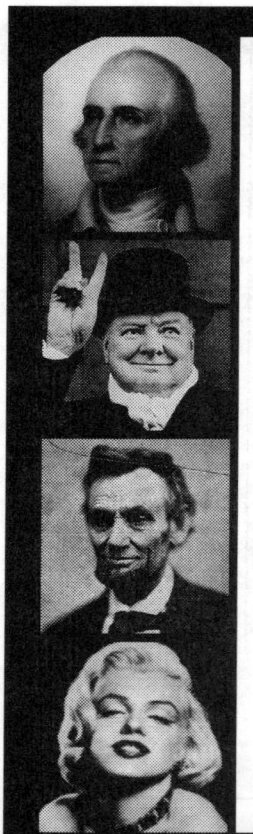

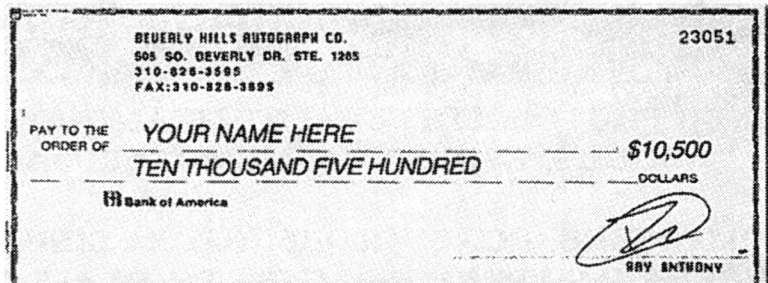

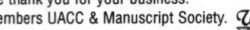